Studies in Church History

43

DISCIPLINE AND DIVERSITY

DISCIPLINE AND DIVERSITY

PAPERS READ AT
THE 2005 SUMMER MEETING AND
THE 2006 WINTER MEETING OF
THE ECCLESIASTICAL HISTORY SOCIETY

EDITED BY

KATE COOPER

AND

JEREMY GREGORY

PUBLISHED FOR
THE ECCLESIASTICAL HISTORY SOCIETY
BY
THE BOYDELL PRESS
2007

First published 2007

A publication of the Ecclesiastical History Society
in association with The Boydell Press
an imprint of Boydell & Brewer Ltd
PO Box 9, Woodbridge, Suffolk IP12 3DF, UK
and of Boydell & Brewer Inc.
668 Mt Hope Avenue, Rochester, NY 14620, USA
website: www.boydellandbrewer.com

ISBN 978–0–9546809–3–0

ISSN 0424–2084

A CiP catalogue record for this book is available
from the British Library

Details of previous volumes are available from Boydell & Brewer Ltd

This book is printed on acid-free paper

Typeset by Pru Harrison, Hacheston, Suffolk
Printed in Great Britain by
Antony Rowe Ltd, Chippenham, Wiltshire

CONTENTS

IN MEMORY OF
MICHAEL KENNEDY

PREFACE

'Discipline and Diversity', the theme chosen by Professor Dame Averil Cameron for her Presidency of the Ecclesiastical History Society in 2005–6, demonstrates the real usefulness of historical reflection at a time when Christian communities in Europe, the Americas, and Africa are engaged in painful discussion of the realities involved in pursuing an ideal of Christian unity. The present volume comprises seven main papers delivered at the Summer and Winter Meetings of the Ecclesiastical History Society, held respectively at Lancaster University in July of 2005, and at Dr Williams's Library, London, in January of 2006, along with a selection of the communications offered at the Summer Meeting.

We are grateful to the members of the Society who lent their time and expertise to the peer review of submissions, and to the authors for their cooperation in bringing the volume to publication. Thanks are also due to Lancaster University, and to Dr David Wykes and his colleagues at Dr Williams's, for providing a congenial environment in which to meet.

As the editors of this volume, we want to offer special thanks to Dr Hannah Williams, our Editorial Fellow, for her hard work and attention to detail in copy-editing this collection of essays. During the time she was working on this volume not only did Dr Williams submit her doctoral thesis, but she also dispatched the completed manuscript to the publisher two days before her viva, a compelling testimony to her gift of remaining disciplined and focussed in the face of diverse and competing obligations. Her ability to remain serene in the face of multiple commitments has been greatly appreciated, both by ourselves and by our authors. As before, we are grateful to the Society and to the University of Manchester for funding the Editorial Fellowship without which our task would have been far more laborious than it has been.

* * *

For the first time, the Society has awarded the Michael Kennedy Prize for the best contribution by a postgraduate member of the Society selected for inclusion in the volume. As many readers will know, Michael was a long time member, and secretary, of the Society. This prize has been established in his memory. Building on a central aspect of Michael's vision for the Society, it is designed to encourage the work of our postgraduate membership, colleagues whose vivid contributions are one of the acknowledged delights of the Society's meetings. The prize will be awarded annually in years when an outstanding postgraduate contribution appears in *Studies in Church History*. Congratulations to Martin Ryan on being the first holder of the Michael Kennedy Prize.

Kate Cooper
Jeremy Gregory
University of Manchester

CONTRIBUTORS

Averil CAMERON (*President*)
> Warden of Keble College, University of Oxford

David BAGCHI
> Lecturer in the History of Christian Thought, University of Hull

Philip BROADHEAD
> Senior Lecturer in History, Goldsmiths College, University of London

Frans CIAPPARA
> Senior Lecturer in History, University of Malta

Gillian CLARK
> Professor of Ancient History, University of Bristol

Alex CRAVEN
> Associate Lecturer, Department of History, Manchester Metropolitan University

Anne J. DUGGAN
> Professor Emerita of Medieval History, King's College, University of London

Ian FORREST
> Tutor in History, Oriel College, University of Oxford

Thomas GRAUMANN
> Senior Lecturer in Early Church History, University of Cambridge

Stuart George HALL
> King's College London and University of St Andrews

Melissa HOLLANDER (*EHS postgraduate bursary*)
> Research Student, University of York

E. D. HUNT
> Senior Lecturer in the Department of Classics and Ancient History, Durham University

Robert G. INGRAM
    Assistant Professor of History, Ohio University

Frances KNIGHT
  Senior Lecturer in Church History, University of Wales,
    Lampeter

G. A. LOUD
    Professor of Medieval Italian History, University of Leeds

John G. MAIDEN (*Anglo-Catholic History Society bursary*)
    Research Student, University of Stirling

Peter MARSHALL
    Professor of History, University of Warwick

Michele MOATT (*EHS postgraduate bursary*)
    Research Student, Lancaster University

Ian RANDALL
    Tutor, Spurgeon's College, London and Senior Research Fellow,
    International Baptist Theological Seminary, Prague

Catherine RIDER
    Junior Research Fellow, Christ's College, University of
    Cambridge

Christof ROLKER (*EHS postgraduate bursary*)
    Research Student, Queens' College, University of Cambridge

Miri RUBIN
    Professor of Medieval and Early Modern History, Queen Mary,
    University of London

Martin RYAN (*Michael J. Kennedy Postgraduate Prize; EHS postgraduate
bursary*)
    Teaching Fellow, Medieval History, School of Arts, Histories and
    Cultures, University of Manchester

Nigel SMITH
    Professor of English, Princeton University

M. C. STEENBERG
    Fellow, Greyfriars Hall, University of Oxford

C. W. B. STEPHENS (*EHS postgraduate bursary*)
Research Student, Christ Church, University of Oxford

Stephen SYKES
Principal of St John's College, Durham University

Christine TREVETT
Professor of Religious and Theological Studies, Cardiff University

Brett USHER
Visiting Research Fellow, University of Reading and Research Associate, Oxford Dictionary of National Biography

Emma WATSON (*EHS postgraduate bursary*)
Research Student, University of York

Martin WELLINGS
Kidlington, Oxfordshire

Hannah WILLIAMS
Editorial Fellow, EHS, University of Manchester

Diana WOOD
University of Oxford Department for Continuing Education

ABBREVIATIONS

ActaSS	*Acta Sanctorum*, ed. J. Bolland and G. Henschen (Antwerp, etc., 1643–)
AHR	*American Historical Review* (New York, 1895–)
AnBoll	*Analecta Bollandiana* (Brussels, 1882–)
BJRULM	*Bulletin of the John Rylands University Library of Manchester* (Manchester, 1903–)
BIHR	*Bulletin of the Institute of Historical Research* (London, 1923–86) [superseded by *HR*]
BL	London, British Library
CIC	*Corpus iuris canonici*, ed. E. Richter and E. Friedberg, 2 vols (Leipzig, 1879–81)
CCSL	*Corpus Christianorum, Series Latina* (Turnhout, 1953–)
CSEL	*Corpus Scriptorum Ecclesiasticorum Latinorum* (Vienna, 1866–)
CYS	Canterbury and York Society (London, etc. 1907–)
EETS	Early English Text Society, Original, Supplementary and Extra Series (London etc., 1865–)
EHD	English Historical Documents (London, 1955–)
EHR	*English Historical Review* (London, 1886–)
HMSO	Her Majesty's Stationary Office
HR	*Historical Research* (London, 1986–) [supersedes *BIHR*]
JEH	*Journal of Ecclesiastical History* (Cambridge, 1950–)
LCL	Loeb Classical Library (Cambridge, MA, etc., 1912–)
MGH	*Monumenta Germaniae Historica inde ab a. c. 500 usque ad a. 1500*, ed. G. H. Pertz et al. (Hannover, Berlin, etc., 1826–)
NF	Neue Folge
ns	new series
ODNB	*Oxford Dictionary of National Biography* (Oxford, 2004), available at: *http://www. oxforddnb.com/*
os	old series
PG	*Patrologia Graeca,* ed. J. P. Migne, 161 vols + 4 index vols (Paris, 1857–66)
PL	*Patrologia Latina*, ed. J. P. Migne, 217 vols + 4 index vols (Paris, 1841–61)

RS	*Rerum Brittanicarum medii aevi scriptores*, 99 vols (London, 1858–1911) = Rolls Series
sa	*sub anno*
SC	*Sources Chrétiennes* (Paris, 1941–)
SCH	*Studies in Church History* (London, Oxford and Woodbridge, 1964–)
SCH.S	*Studies in Church History: Subsidia* (Oxford and Woodbridge, 1978–)
Speculum	*Speculum: a Journal of Medieval Studies* (Cambridge, MA, 1925–)
TNA	The National Archive
TRHS	*Transactions of the Royal Historical Society* (London/Cambridge, 1871–)
Traditio	*Traditio: Studies in Ancient and Medieval History, Thought, and Religion* (New York, etc., 1943–)
TTH	Translated Texts for Historians (Liverpool, 1985–)
VCH	*Victoria County History* (London, 1900–)

Orthodoxy, schism and heresy are issues which have been well covered in earlier volumes of *Studies in Church History*, and these themes make their appearance again in this one. However, *Discipline and Diversity* covers a much wider range of behaviours and responses than the field of belief and doctrine alone. The subject, and the Summer and Winter Meetings of the Ecclesiastical History Society in 2005–6 at which earlier versions of many of these papers were presented, clearly appealed to many of those who are working on the history of the Church, as well as striking chords with the contemporary situation. 'Diversity' is a benign term for an often difficult and troubling phenomenon which has characterized the entire history of Christianity; it is a main theme of Euan Cameron's recent book, *Interpreting Christian History* (Oxford, 2005). There have also always been periods when diversity turned into conflict, and when discipline was used, or attempted, in the effort to control. This tension between creative and legitimate diversity and the deeply-felt desire for unity is a striking feature of Christian history and one which we see causing acute anxieties today.

The pull between diversity and control is already very apparent in the New Testament, and we can observe Christian writers from the second century onwards struggling with issues of Christian identity and issuing normative treatises which dealt with behaviour and ethics as well as belief. Judith Lieu's writings on early Christian identity, notably *Christian Identity in the Jewish and Graeco-Roman World* (Oxford, 2004), bring these issues vividly to life. A somewhat different perspective, written from the point of view of a Roman historian and historian of Judaism, can be found in Martin Goodman's recent *Rome and Jerusalem: the Clash of Ancient Civilizations* (London, 2007), which attributes the 'efflorescence' of Christian diversity in the early centuries to a lack of clarity and imprecision about the central doctrines of the faith, especially the idea of the Trinity. However, with diversity came a desire to control; Goodman refers to 'the gradual defining of Christianity . . . by the exclusion of ideas not acceptable to the mainstream' as 'the most striking innovation of all in terms of ancient religious history'.[1]

It is perhaps not surprising, then, that the volume contains many contributions from the earlier period of Church history. However, the issues first raised in the early Church often cropped up again in later centuries: for instance, the use and application of exegesis, discussed here by Matthew Steenberg, is central to the theme at all periods, as are the techniques and procedures adopted by Church councils, which, not least, provided the origin of canon law. Several papers here deal with councils and canon law, and one of the most notable of all recent publications in the field of Church history is the complete translation with commentary of all the documents from the Council of Chalcedon in AD 451 by Richard Price and Michael Gaddis, *The Acts of the Council of Chalcedon*, Translated Texts for Historians (Liverpool, 2005); the Council of Chalcedon, which led to the separation of the eastern churches, and is (regrettably) taken by many western Church historians and university syllabuses as marking the end of the patristic period, is one of the most important of all Church councils, yet the publication by Price and Gaddis has revealed just how much can still be learned from basic work on the fundamental texts.

The intervention of the state is of course one of the key issues in considering discipline and control in Church matters, and it is good to find here a set of interesting papers about the Tudor period in England. However, many other questions also arise, in relation for instance to monastic discipline, clerical orders and liturgy; Nigel Smith also points to the rich field represented by the appearance of religious themes in apparently secular literature. Discipline and control can take many forms, some of them none the less effective for being indirect, and these may co-exist with the much more obvious tactics also used in a medieval state like Byzantium. As for overall balance, Henry Mayr-Harting noted in his introduction to *The Church and Mary*, SCH 39 (Woodbridge, 2004), a concentration in that volume of Anglo- and Euro-centric contributions, and the same must be said for this one, although the two final papers in the volume address questions of authority in the Anglican communion which present a very particular combination of problems which are at once English and world-wide. Perhaps this concentration tells us something about the situation of

---

[1] Goodman, *Rome and Jerusalem*, 519.

ecclesiastical history in Britain today. Yet we can, for example, see powerful struggles about ecclesiastical control going on in the post-communist world today, and I would argue that the themes of discipline and diversity are central not only to the world-wide Church but also in some sense to the history of all religions.

Averil Cameron
Keble College, University of Oxford

ENFORCING ORTHODOXY IN BYZANTIUM*

by AVERIL CAMERON

FOLLOWING in the tradition of Montesquieu and Gibbon, Wolfgang Liebeschuetz has recently again argued that one of the two most revolutionary aspects of Christianity in its history since Constantine has proved to be religious intolerance.[1] The Byzantine state certainly made many efforts to enforce orthodoxy, and the question arises whether Byzantium was therefore a 'persecuting society', to use the now-familiar formulation of R. I. Moore.[2] In a telling aside, Paul Magdalino asked in the course of an important discussion of eleventh- and twelfth-century Byzantium whether it became 'even more of a persecuting society than before' (my italics).[3] Another strand of scholarship however has seen a contrast in this respect between western and eastern Europe, and several recent authors have argued for a comparative degree of toleration in Byzantium, or at least for a limitation on the possibilities of real repression.[4] However this desire to find a

* My thanks are due for the comments of audiences at All Souls, Oxford and The Catholic University of America. I am also grateful to the Program in Hellenic Studies at Princeton where I was a Visiting Fellow in 2005, and to discussion with colleagues and visitors there, to Joseph Streeter for bibliography on the debate on toleration, and especially to the editorial acuity of Kate Cooper.

[1] J. H. W. G. Liebeschuetz, *Continuity and Change in Roman Religion* (Oxford, 1979), 293; similarly Christianity is seen as an agent of Roman decline in his book *The Decline and Fall of the Roman City* (Oxford, 2002) and in several of his papers.

[2] R. I. Moore, *The Formation of a Persecuting Society: Power and Deviance in Western Europe, 950–1250* (Oxford, 1987); see now however John Christian Laursen and Cary J. Nederman, eds, *Beyond the Persecuting Society: Religious Toleration before the Enlightenment* (Philadelphia, PA, 1998).

[3] Paul Magdalino, *The Empire of Manuel I Komnenos, 1143–1180* (Cambridge, 1993), 383.

[4] For discussion of the idea of the East as more 'tolerant' than the West, see N. Berend, *At the Gate of Christendom: Jews, Muslims and 'Pagans' in Medieval Hungary, c.1000–c.1300* (Cambridge, 2001), 52–3; for the concept of toleration as anachronistic in medieval societies: ibid., 184, 272. Against Byzantium as 'repressive': J. Herrin, 'Toleration and Repression within the Byzantine Family', in K. Nikolaou, ed., *Toleration and Repression in the Middle Ages* (Athens, 2002), 173–88, at 174, 187–8; cf. H.-G. Beck, 'Formes de non-conformisme à Byzance', *Bibl de la classe des lettres de l'Academie Royale de Belgique* 5, ser. 65 (1979), 313–29; J.-C. Cheynet, 'Les limites de pouvoir à Byzance: une forme de tolerance?', ibid., 15–28; G. Dagron, 'La règle et l'exception: analyse de la notion d'économie', in D. Simon, ed., *Religiöse Devianz: Untersuchungen zu sozialen, rechtlichen und theologischen Reaktionen auf religiöse Abweichung im westlichen und ostlichen Mittelalter* (Frankfurt am Main, 1990), 1–18.

degree of toleration and religious freedom in earlier societies clearly derives from our own contemporary concerns, and despite recent attempts to claim the Emperor Constantine as the defender of religious toleration,[5] I agree with those who argue that it is misguided to look for an active conception of religious toleration in this period.[6] This paper starts from the position that Constantine himself, and successive emperors after him, inherited an existing assumption that religious conformity was the business of the state, and looks at some of the less obvious ways by which the Byzantine state attempted to promote and enforce orthodoxy.

The persecution of Christians themselves was something that Constantine and his contemporaries knew at first hand and by which they were deeply affected. Moreover, at the beginning of the fourth century AD, the pagan emperor Diocletian had issued a ferocious edict against the Manichaeans[7] whereby the latter became subject to all the force of late Roman law. If Manichaeans repented and wished to be received into the Church they were subject to formal processes of abjuration.[8] The model served Byzantium well, and Mani and the Manichaeans, transplanted as to time and place, were to have a long

[5] See H. A. Drake, *Constantine and the Bishops: the Politics of Intolerance* (Baltimore, MD, 2000); in this argument it is the bishops, not the emperor, who represent intolerance. See also H. A. Drake, 'Lambs into Lions: Explaining Early Christian Intolerance', *P&P* 153 (1996), 3–36; Elizabeth Depalma Digeser, 'Lactantius, Porphyry and the Debate over Religious Toleration', *Journal of Roman Studies* 88 (1998), 129–46. For a critique, see Averil Cameron, 'Apologetics in the Roman Empire: a Genre of Intolerance?', in Jean-Michel Carrié and Rita Lizzi Testa, eds, *"Humana sapit": Études d'Antiquité tardive offertes à Lellia Cracco Ruggini*, Bibliothèque de l'Antiquité Tardive 3 (Paris and Turnhout, 2002), 219–27.
[6] See J. C. Laursen and C. J. Nederman, 'Problems of Periodization in the History of Toleration', *Storia della Storiografia* 37 (2000), 55–65.
[7] 'Because everything you (i.e. the proconsul of Africa) in your prudence explained in your report about their religion demonstrates that what our laws see as their crimes are born of a wild and false imagination, we have set deserved and suitable penalties for these people. We command that the authors and leaders of these sects receive severe punishment and be burnt in the flames with their detestable books': *Lex Dei sive Mosaicarum et Romanorum legum collatio* 15.3, trans. in Roger Rees, *Diocletian and the Tetrarchy* (Edinburgh, 2004), 174.
[8] See Samuel N. C. Lieu, *Manichaeism in the Later Roman Empire and in China* (2nd rev. edn, Tübingen, 1992), 198–201; for a trial by fire recorded in the monastic literature, see 195. Public debates with Manichaeans: Richard Lim, *Public Disputation, Power and Social Order in Late Antiquity* (Berkeley and Los Angeles, CA, 1995), ch. 3, 70–108. In the context of the condemnation of Monotheletism by the Sixth Council in AD 680–1 a Monothelete was put to the test to see whether he could raise someone from the dead; he was unsuccessful and was deposed and anathematized: ed. E. Schwartz, *Acta conciliorum oecumenicorum* (Berlin, 1936) [hereafter: *ACO*], 2.2.2: 674–82.

history as the 'onlie begetters' of medieval dualist heresy.[9] The precedents set by Diocletian, and later by Justinian, in dealing with
Manichaeans made it highly convenient for later Byzantines to label
heretics as Manichaeans, and so to bring them under the weight of this
earlier practice.[10] Constantine I thus inherited the idea that it was
entirely appropriate for deviants such as (in his case) Christian schismatics and sects such as Novatians to be the target of imperial punishment. Even if he would have preferred warring groups of Christians to
come to their own consensus,[11] he did not hesitate when pushed to
apply the lesson he had learnt from his pagan predecessors,[12] and the
power of the state was used then and thereafter both to summon and
pay for Church councils and to exact the penalty of deposition and exile
on bishops who refused to assent. While Constantine did not prohibit
paganism after his victory over Licinius in AD 324, he made it crystal
clear that he would have preferred to do so if he could.[13] His sense of
personal religious duty is directly expressed by him in his policy
towards the Donatists in North Africa;[14] the same assumption lay

[9] According to Anselm of Alessandria in the thirteenth century on Cathars and
Waldensians, Mani preached 'around Dragovitsa, Bulgaria and Philadelphia' in or not long
before the period of the Latin empire in Constantinople: trans. in R. I. Moore, *The Birth of
Popular Heresy* (London, 1975), 146. On the precedent, and the development of legislation
against heresy, see Caroline Humfress, 'Roman Law, Forensic Argument and the Formation
of Christian Orthodoxy (III–VI Centuries)', in Susanna Elm, Éric Rebillard, and Antonella
Romano, eds, *Orthodoxie, christianisme, histoire* (Paris, 2000), 125–47; eadem, *Orthodoxy and the
Courts in Late Antiquity* (Oxford, 2007).
[10] Lieu, *Manichaeism*, 217: 'the majority of the laws against heretics in the
[ninth-century] *Basilica* are repetitions of Justinianic laws against Manichaeans'; an edict
issued by Justin I and Justinian in AD 527 ordered the death penalty, already prescribed by
Anastasius, and Manichaeans were persecuted and put to death (ibid., 210–15).
[11] Eusebius, *Vita Constantini*, 1.44 [hereafter: Eusebius, *VC*] (Eusebius attempts to
persuade us of the emperor's tolerance and his efforts at persuasion); 2.64–72 (Constantine's
letter to Alexander and Arius, esp. 69, 'let each of you extend pardon equally, and accept
what your fellow-servant in justice urges upon you', and 70, Christians should not engage in
such internal disputes).
[12] Compare Eusebius, ibid., 3.64–5 (Constantine's decree against sects, 'the secret
conspiracies of the heterodox . . . and the wild beasts, the captains of their sacrilege', 3.66.1).
[13] Eusebius, ibid., 2.56 (pagans may keep their temples, but need to be corrected and
brought to the right way, which is the only way of holiness).
[14] For Constantine's views, see his own words in a letter of AD 314 (Optatus, *Appendix* 3:
God's selection of Constantine as earthly ruler includes a duty to ensure correct worship); in
Appendix 7, a letter of AD 315, he threatens to come to North Africa and sort out the matter
in person; in AD 317 he ordered the property of Donatists to be turned over to Catholics
(Augustine, *Epistula* 88), and he gave up on this coercion only because he was occupied with
his war against his rival Licinius. See on the Donatists, and on the violence towards them
which followed the Council of AD 411 Michael Gaddis, *There is no Crime for Those who Have*

behind his actions against Donatists and against Christian sects,[15] and it was the assumption of every Christian emperor thereafter. Certainly great efforts were made in the direction of persuasion, but still, it was not doubted that there was indeed orthodoxy and therefore truth, and that there was therefore a duty of enforcement, even at high cost.

Byzantium is generally regarded as an Orthodox society, indeed as the Orthodox society *par excellence*, and it has often been described as a theocracy.[16] Byzantine icons, in particular, are still often mistakenly assumed to exemplify a static and monolithic view of Orthodoxy in Byzantium. This is not the way that religion in Byzantium is nowadays understood in the scholarly literature, which increasingly emphasizes difference over sameness, and change over time.[17] I want to argue here against the 'static' view of Byzantine orthodoxy that the struggle to establish what constituted Christian orthodoxy was not a feature only of the post-Constantinian period,[18] but continued throughout the entire history of Byzantium. The ideal Byzantine emperor was always presented as the guardian and defender of orthodoxy. Yet there were few emperors, from Constantine the Great in the fourth century to his namesake, the last emperor of Byzantium, in the fifteenth, who did not at times have to take action to ensure that orthodoxy was established, maintained and enforced, and many had their own view of what it was.

The centuries-long and often renewed struggle is most obviously defined in terms of doctrine: orthodoxy versus heresy. The classic Orthodox view is well expressed in Andrew Louth's recent fine book on John of Damascus:[19] 'heresies' were what enabled Christian truth to emerge over the centuries and to be recognized. However, understanding of the working of orthodoxy and heresy in Byzantium is still

Christ: Religious Violence in the Christian Roman Empire (Berkeley and Los Angeles, CA, 2005), 103–30, 131–50.

[15] Eusebius, *VC*, 3.63–5; their books are to be 'hunted out' (66.1).

[16] See for example Steven Runciman, *The Byzantine Theocracy* (Cambridge, 1973); Paul Magdalino, 'The Medieval Empire (780–1204)', in Cyril Mango, ed., *Oxford History of Byzantium* (Oxford, 2002), 169–213, at 206; see also G. Dagron, *Emperor and Priest: the Imperial Office in Byzantium*, trans. Jean Birrell (Cambridge, 2003), 282–3.

[17] See now Andrew Louth and Augustine Casiday, eds, *Byzantine Orthodoxies* (Aldershot, 2006).

[18] On which, see Averil Cameron, *Christianity and the Rhetoric of Empire: the Development of Christian Discourse* (Berkeley and Los Angeles, CA, 1991); eadem, 'Ascetic Closure and the End of Antiquity', in Vincent L. Wimbush and Richard Valantasis, eds, *Asceticism* (New York, 1995), 147–61.

[19] Andrew Louth, *St John Damascene: Tradition and Originality in Byzantine Theology* (Oxford, 2002), 155–6.

at an early stage. As noted by Nina Garsoian, Byzantine heresies have generally been understood in three ways: as manifestations of popular religion, in ethnic or regional terms, or by associating heretics in Byzantium with some form of dualism.[20] I will not go over that ground here except to observe that the debate needs to be moved in new directions. Nor do 'heresies' stand still over time, any more than the 'orthodox' core. Importantly, many of the issues which divided Christians in the Byzantine world were not about belief but about practice, raising the question of whether Byzantine Orthodoxy was constituted by a 'body of beliefs' or a 'body of believers'.[21] Byzantium was – albeit more in some periods than others – a centralized state and a successful empire. Throughout its history there was a strong rhetoric of condemnation of anyone deemed to be non-orthodox, which has led to characterizations of the Byzantine state as highly repressive.[22] In this paper therefore, I want to consider the means by which this bundle of beliefs, habits and practices labelled 'orthodoxy' was established, confirmed and promoted in Byzantium, and with what degree of success. By a concern for orthodoxy in this context I do not refer to 'eastern orthodoxy', or 'Greek Orthodoxy', or even Orthodoxy with a capital O,[23] but rather, to the rooted assumption that there must indeed be a body of belief which was true, and a body of practice which was correct, and that measures should be taken to promote it and if necessary to enforce it.

---

[20] N. Garsoian, 'Byzantine Heresy: a Reinterpretation', *Dumbarton Oaks Papers* 25 (1971), 85–113; on changing approaches to medieval heresy, see Arthur Stephen McGrade, 'The Medieval Idea of Heresy: What are We to Make of it?', in Peter Biller and Barrie Dobson, eds, *The Medieval Church: Universities, Heresy and the Religious Life; Essays in Honour of Gordon Leff*, SCH.S 11 (Woodbridge, 1999), 111–39.

[21] For the question in relation to the sixteenth century, see John Bossy, *Christianity in the West, 1400–1700* (Oxford, 1985), 170–1.

[22] For a strong statement, see A. Gurevich, 'Why I am not a Byzantinist', *Dumbarton Oaks Papers* 46 (1992), 89–96. The present paper focuses on the level of the state; it goes without saying that at ground level, and especially at certain times and in certain places, uncertainty was the norm (see e.g. G. Dagron, 'L'ombre d'un doute: l'hagiographie en question, VIᵉ–XIᵉ siècle', ibid., 59–68). Nor can I consider here the questions of mission and conversion, important though they are.

[23] For the concept of an 'essence' of Orthodoxy, see S. Averintsev, 'Some Constant Characteristics of Byzantine Orthodoxy', in Louth and Casiday, eds, *Byzantine Orthodoxies*, 215–28. In a book entitled *The Making of Orthodox Byzantium 600–1025* (London, 1996) Mark Whittow takes the early 11th century as his concluding point, while the ending of the iconoclastic controversy in AD 843 is also often seen as a turning point (though Patricia Karlin-Hayter, 'Methodios and his Synod', in Louth and Casiday, *Byzantine Orthodoxies*, 55–74, vividly brings out the extent to which our ability to understand this event is hampered by the tendentiousness of the historical record).

In considering the concept of religious orthodoxy and its role it is impossible to separate the case of Byzantium from recent work on early Christianity and late antiquity, where the subject has been transformed in recent years. The traditional view of early Christian development depended, and still depends, on the schema set out in Eusebius's *Ecclesiastical History*, where heresies are presented as the 'tares', and heretics as the 'wolves' threatening the single true faith established by Christ Himself. This conception was fundamentally challenged in Walter Bauer's *Rechtgläubigkeit und Ketzerei im ältesten Christentum*, published in 1934, which set forth a view of early Christianity as consisting of a variety of differing expressions, and of 'orthodoxy' as the imposition of a certain version over others. Following Bauer, but taking it a stage further, the current discourse of early Christian studies assumes that heretics are made, not born,[24] and that the 'genealogies of heresy' and other rhetorical tropes traced in early Christian authors such as Clement of Alexandria, writing in the early third century, are devices by which the prevailing group could contrast the supposed pedigrees of their rivals with their own.[25] Apologetic techniques in early Christian literature incorporated not only defensive explanations but also strategies of separation, whereby Jews and heretics were labelled as 'other'.[26] As for late antiquity, to quote only from a recent paper by Fergus Millar, 'It perhaps hardly needs to be stated that the characterisation, and naming, of groups within Christianity as 'heretical' represents a process of construction by others, and, as expressed by contemporaries (and indeed by moderns), can never be taken as constituting simple reports on observable realities.'[27] In a world in which scholars of early

[24] Rebecca Lyman, 'The Politics of Passing: Justin Martyr's Conversion as a Problem of "Hellenization" ', in Kenneth Miles and Anthony Grafton, eds, *Conversion in Late Antiquity and the Early Middles Ages: Seeing and Believing* (Rochester, NY, 2003), 36–60, with extensive bibliography on theoretical approaches; also Averil Cameron, 'The Violence of Orthodoxy', in Holger Zellentin and Edward Iricinschi, eds, *Heresy and Identity in Late Antiquity* (Tübingen, forthcoming).

[25] The literature is now very large; see for instance Virginia Burrus, *The Making of a Heretic: Gender, Authority, and the Priscillianist Controversy* (Berkeley and Los Angeles, CA, 1995); D. Kimber Buell, *Making Christians: Clement of Alexandria and the Rhetoric of Legitimacy* (Princeton, NJ, 1995); eadem, *Why this New Race? Ethnic Reasoning in Early Christianity* (New York, 2005).

[26] See esp. Judith Lieu, *Image and Reality: the Jews in the World of the Christians in the Second Century* (Edinburgh, 1996); eadem, *Christian Identity in the Jewish and Graeco-Roman World* (Oxford, 2004), with the papers in Martin Goodman, S. R. F. Price, C. J. Rowland and Mark Edwards, eds, *Apologetics in the Roman Empire: Pagans, Jews and Christians* (Oxford, 1999).

[27] Fergus Millar, 'Repentant Heretics in Fifth-Century Lydia: Identity and Literacy',

Christianity routinely speak no longer of 'Christianity' but of
'Christianities', the forging of identity and the processes of
self-definition have become the key topics of discussion. Thus rather
than attempting to study heresy for what it 'really was', questions of
how orthodox definitions were promoted, and the means by which
they were enforced in a broad sense become critical issues. These
approaches need to be carried forward into the study of orthodoxy in
Byzantium, not least in the later centuries.

Much of the energy which went into condemning heretics and
proclaiming orthodoxy in the early centuries had to do with the desire
to build an institutional structure for the emerging Church amid what
was in fact a plethora of differing ways of understanding Christianity.
From an early stage groups considered by others to be deviant were,
like the Jews, the targets of forceful condemnation; indeed it is no accident that condemnation of Judaism and of heresy developed in tandem.
In late antiquity and after, bishops issued synodical letters which incorporated the denigration of heretics, and when councils began to lay
down canons, they were accompanied by anathemas on 'heretics'. If
such dissenters repented and were received back into the Church they
in turn were required in a ritual of reversal to anathematize their own
former beliefs and associates.[28] The Council of Elvira in c. AD 305 laid
down canons, and a precedent had been set already for its use of anathemas, public curses on 'heretics'. Fourth-century baptismal formulae
also required anathemas on heretics, Jews, pagans and other forms of
deviation.[29] John of Damascus' great compendium on the orthodox

Scripta Classica Israelica 23 (2004), 111–30; cf. also idem, 'Christian Emperors, Christian Church and the Jews of the Diaspora in the Greek East, CE 379–450', *Journal of Jewish Studies* 55 (2004), 1–24. For late antiquity, see also for example the papers in section two of W. E. Klingshirn and M. Vessey, eds, *The Limits of Ancient Christianity: Essays on Late Antique Thought and Culture in Honour of R. A. Markus* (Ann Arbor, MI, 1999).

[28] See Rosemary Morris, 'Curses and Clauses: the Language of Exclusion in Byzantium', in Nikolaou, *Toleration and Repression*, 313–26, with attention to the Councils of Elvira (305) and Nicaea (325). Later abjuration formulae, prescribed for use in public rituals of re-reception, included lists of anathemas as an integral element: see e.g. P. Eleuteri and A. Rigo, *Eretici, dissidenti, musulmani e ebrei a Bisanzio: una racolta eresiologica del XII secolo* (Venice, 1993), 16–19.

[29] Daniel Boyarin, *Border-Lines: the Partition of Judaeo-Christianity* (Philadelphia, PA, 2004), 67–73, argues that despite references in Justin's *Dialogue with Trypho the Jew*, 16.4, 47.4 and 96.2, the introduction of Jewish liturgical cursing of heretics, that is, Jewish Christians, was a gradual process which arose in response to Christian precedents including the council which condemned Paul of Samosata in AD 260. In any case by the Council of Nicaea Christians had taken the idea on board.

faith in the eighth century known as the 'Fount of Knowledge' (*Pege gnoseos*)[30] followed earlier patterns in presenting orthodox doctrine and heresy as mirror-images of each other – by juxtaposing a statement of faith with a supporting catalogue of heresies. Imperial legislation issued by Theodosius I in AD 380 and 381 and continued by Justinian in the sixth century made heresy an actual crime;[31] but this fateful legislation had been preceded by a rhetoric of condemnation which had been in place for several centuries.

This rhetoric of condemnation was one of the ways in which the state asserted its expectations about what was orthodox. The legislation of Theodosius and Justinian laid down legal penalties for heresy, which would effectively deprive anyone labelled as heretical of their civic privileges, and went in parallel with similar laws directed at pagans and Jews. The extent to which the laws were actually enforced is an issue not easy to address, though we are told for example that some pagans were put to death in the reign of Justinian.[32] However it was not just a matter of legal enforcement, and indeed the latter seems to have been regarded as a last resort, and to have been invoked at best sporadically and for particular reasons. In the rest of this paper I want to consider instead some of the other means by which orthodoxy was enforced or promoted in Byzantium.

One such means, which we might call a 'soft' strategy, was through pedagogy. In his recent book entitled *Interpretatio Christiana*, which covers the first six centuries of Christianity, Hervé Inglebert presents this impetus in terms of the attempt to arrive at a Christian knowledge and a Christian interpretation of the world.[33] But what is less often realized is that the effort did not stop and that the same struggle continued throughout the history of Byzantium.

An important technique used in Byzantium as in other medieval societies was that of display, or public performance.[34] Both punish-

[30] This work is a trilogy, consisting of *Dialectics, On Heresies* and *On the Orthodox Faith*; for an interesting and detailed discussion of all three parts, see Louth, *St John Damascene*, chs 4–6.

[31] Humfress, 'Roman Law', 144–6; Justinian's legislation extended to pagans, Jews, Samaritans and heretics: *Codex Justinianus*, I.5.12 (AD 527); 13–16, 18, 19 (AD 529); 20 (AD 530); 21 (AD 531); *Nov.* 45 (AD 537).

[32] John Malalas, *Chronographia*, ed. L. Dindorf (Bonn, 1831), 449.

[33] H. Inglebert, *Interpretatio Christiana: les mutations des savoirs (cosmographie, géographie, ethnographie, histoire) dans l'antiquité chrétienne 30–630 après J.-C.* (Paris, 2001).

[34] For similar techniques as used to promote and enforce Islam in Umayyad Syria, see Sidney H. Griffith, 'Images, Islam and Christian Icons: a Moment in the Christian/Muslim

ments and recantations had to be visible. It was not enough to confess in private: the public confession of wrong in church or outside the church, the deposition of written statements, and the issuing of written certificates (*libelloi, semeiomata*) were always part of the reception back of those who had recanted. Measures taken against heretics, such as excommunication or anathema, or indeed abjuration, were yet another form of the display of orthodoxy, on a par with physical punishments for secular crime.[35] The process of abjuration can be seen in detail at several points, whether in the procedures applied to Manichaeans in the fifth century, or those followed in the case of repentant iconoclasts at the iconophile Council of II Nicaea in AD 787, or in surviving documents such as the *semeioma* of Eustratius of Nicaea extant from AD 1117 (see below). Whatever the current orthodoxy – Arian, Chalcedonian, or indeed Monothelete, Iconoclast or Unionist – it had to be *seen* to be receiving the support of the authorities, and conversely, 'heretics' displayed as deviant. Constantine gave the fathers of Nicaea exactly this kind of visibility. Eusebius expresses the delight and surprise of bishops at the idea that the emperor himself would sit among them at a council of bishops, and then entertain them all at a banquet.[36] Conversely, during the period of the iconoclast controversy in the eighth century, the iconophile tradition records the public humiliation of monks for all to see in the Hippodrome of Constantinople.[37] The production and subsequent regular liturgical reading of the so-called *Synodikon of Orthodoxy*, a statement of the faith with anathemas on heretics, drawn up at the ending of iconoclasm in the ninth century for a new feast commemorating the restoration of icons, was a further example of display; the feast was celebrated on the first Sunday in Lent, the 'Sunday of Orthodoxy', a custom which still survives. The text of the *Synodikon* was subsequently supplemented

Encounter in Early Islamic Times', in P. Canivet and Jean-Paul Rey-Coquais, eds, *La Syrie de Byzance à l'Islam, VIIe–VIIIe siècles* (Damascus, 1992), 121–38, at 123–31, under the headings 'The Display of Islam' and 'Religious Polemic and the Dismantling of Public Christianity'. These prohibitions on crosses and processions as visible signs of Christianity are paralleled in modern times by the banning of minarets attached to mosques in the communist Balkans.

[35] For the latter, see E. Patlagean, 'Byzance et le blason pénal du corps', in *Du châtiment dans la cité: Supplices corporels et peine de mort dans le monde antique*, Table ronde organisé par l'École française de Rome avec le concours du Centre national de la recherche scientifique, Rome, 9–11 novembre 1982 (Paris, 1984), 405–26, esp. 420–1.

[36] Eusebius, *VC*, 3.15.

[37] Theophanes, *Chronographia,* ed. C. de Boor, 2 vols (Leipzig, 1883), 1: 437–8.

under the Comneni and again in the fourteenth century in the context of the acceptance of hesychasm.

The reading of the *Synodikon* was a public ritual, and this and the depiction of such readings in visual art fed into the identification of the ending of iconoclasm by later generations as the 'triumph of orthodoxy'.[38] The message of orthodoxy was also graphically communicated in Byzantine church decoration and icons at a variety of levels, from the depiction of orthodox bishops to that of the ecumenical church councils at which orthodoxy had been laid down, with scenes of defeated heretics patterned on the treatment of conquered enemies in imperial victory representations. Accompanying this public depiction of the victory of orthodoxy was the experience of liturgical celebration, first of the Council of Nicaea in AD 312, later of all the ecumenical councils together.[39]

Legislation can equally be read as public performance. We know that state law, whether in late antiquity or later in Byzantium, could not always be enforced, especially in the provinces;[40] in such circumstances the rhetoric of imperial laws, and the public display of imperial edicts, assumed an importance in themselves.

The ritual burning or destruction of heretical books is a further example of display and performance, and again there are examples from throughout the Byzantine period. Diocletian had set an example by burning the books of Manichaeans, and by ordering the destruction of Christian books during the persecution of 303;[41] according to the edict of 303, reported by Eusebius, the Scriptures were to be sought out and burned.[42] Constantine burned the books of the pagan writer Porphyry who had attacked Christianity,[43] and extended the same

[38] J. Gouillard, ed., 'Le Synodikon d'orthodoxie', *Travaux et Mémoires* 2 (1967), 1–313; see now Dimitra Kotoula, 'The British Museum Triumph of Orthodoxy Icon', in Louth and Casiday, *Byzantine Orthodoxies*, 121–8, with bibliography.

[39] See C. Walter, *L'iconographie des conciles dans la tradition byzantine* (Paris, 1970); idem, 'Icons of the First Council of Nicaea', in his *Pictures as Language: How the Byzantines Exploited Them* (London, 2000), 166–87. Scenes of iconophile saints suffering at the hands of iconoclasts and of iconoclasts defacing images were also a feature of a well-known group of post-iconoclast illustrated manuscripts.

[40] See recently Leonora Neville, *Authority in Byzantine Provincial Society, 950–1100* (Cambridge, 2004).

[41] See W. Speyer, *Büchervernichtung und Zensur des Geistes bei Heiden, Juden und Christen* (Stuttgart, 1981), 76.

[42] Eusebius, *Historia ecclesiastica*, 8.2.4 [hereafter: Eusebius, *HE*]; *Martyrs of Palestine*, pref. 1, 2.1.

[43] Socrates, *Historia ecclesiastica*, 1.9 [hereafter: Socrates, *HE*].

threat to the writings of Christians of whom he disapproved.[44] It was not only emperors who were responsible; bishops such as Athanasius of Alexandria also argued that heterodox books were to be burnt.[45] Astrological and magical writings were burned, for instance by Zacharias Rhetor and his friends at Berytus.[46] Justinian ordered the books of Hellenes to be burned, and had done the same with the books of Severus of Antioch.[47] Later in the sixth century the Emperor Tiberius II adjudicated in a theological dispute about the resurrection body between the future Pope Gregory the Great and Eutychius, the patriarch of Constantinople, and would have had Eutychius' work burned had the latter not died meanwhile.[48] The Fifth Ecumenical Council in AD 553 and the Lateran Synod in AD 649 both anathematized the books of heretics; and the Sixth Council in the late seventh century ordered all Monothelete writings to be destroyed.[49] Books continued to be burned – or ordered to be burned – in later periods. The apocryphal Acts of John were ordered to be burnt by the iconophile Second Council of Nicaea in 787, and the same happened to the writings of the Iconoclasts.[50] Book-burning is mentioned in the *Life* of St Euthymius the Younger (d. 898)[51] and in the eleventh century, according to Michael the Syrian, a patriarchal decree of Constantine Leichoudes ordered all books of the Syrians to be burnt, certainly a tall order.[52] The idea of destroying the books of rival groups was firmly implanted: according to Matthew of Edessa, Syriac Gospels were burnt during a riot between pro- and anti-Chalcedonians at Antioch in 1053–4.[53]

[44] Eusebius, *VC*, 3.64–5, 66; Socrates, *HE*, 1.9; Gelasius, *Historia ecclesiastica*, 2.36.1–2; Sozomen, *Historia ecclesiastica*, 1.21.4; Pope Symmachus on book-burning: Lieu, *Manichaeism*, 207.

[45] *Festal Letter* 39, AD 367.

[46] Speyer, *Büchervernichtung*, 131–2.

[47] Malalas, *Chronographia* (ed. Dindorf, 449, 491); *Nov.* 42.1,2.

[48] Speyer, *Büchervernichtung*, 155, Gregory, *Moralia in Job* XIV.56, 72–4, PL 75, 1077–9.

[49] Judith Herrin, *The Formation of Christendom* (Oxford, 1987), 278–9.

[50] *Sacrorum conciliorum nova et amplissima collectio*, ed. J. D. Mansi, cont. I. B. Martin, L. Petit, 53 vols (Florence/Venice, 1759–98; Paris, 1901–27; repr. Graz, 1961) [hereafter: Mansi, *Concilia*], 13. 173–6, 200D.

[51] 'Vie et office de St Euthyme le jeune', ed. L. Petit, *Revue d'Orient Chrétien* 8 (1903), 55–205, at 200.10–12; I owe this reference to Dr Dirk Krausmüller.

[52] *Chronique de Michel le Syrien: patriarche jacobite d'Antioche (1166–1199)*, ed. J.-B. Chabot, 4 vols (Paris, 1899–1924), 3: 166.

[53] Matthew of Edessa, 'Le chronique de Matthieu d'Édesse', in E. Dulaurier, ed., *Bibliothéque historique arménienne* (Paris, 1858), 71. In the fourteenth century Nicephorus Gregoras claims that after Palamas had been shipwrecked and fell into their hands, on questioning him as to their contents the Ottomans ordered his books to be thrown into the sea (*Historiae*

Several instances date from the twelfth century; for example Eustratius of Nicaea was ordered to hand over the writings of Cyril of Alexandria to be burnt,[54] while other writings of his own were to be kept locked up in the patriarchate.[55] The books of alleged heretics were investigated by special synods, and might be ordered to be burnt, even on one famous twelfth-century occasion, posthumously.[56] It was not only the books themselves that were to be burnt: anyone who agreed with the views expressed in them was also to be anathematized. Their owners were sought out and an abbot who possessed one of them was demoted and removed to another monastery. Finally, a few years after the fall of Constantinople, the last work of George Gemistos Plethon, his 'Platonist' treatise on the *Laws*, was ordered to be burnt by no less a person than Gennadios Scholarios.[57] We do not know whether all the books ordered to be burned were in fact burned, or to what extent available copies were rounded up. It may indeed be argued that the threat or reality of book-burning in this public manner was the resort of a state which did not possess the will or the ability to search out the heretics themselves, and that its importance was largely symbolic; nevertheless the intent is very clear.

Demonstrating and displaying what was orthodox was also furthered by the practice of censoring the names of heretical bishops from the liturgical diptychs and destroying their pictures. Thus when the same Eutychius, the sixth-century patriarch of Constantinople, returned from exile he destroyed the pictures of his predecessor John

---

Byzantinae, 29.8, ed. I. Bekker, CSHB 40 [Bonn, 1855], 228), a story which recalls the similar action of the eighth-century iconoclast emperor Constantine V in relation to the relics of S. Euphemia, according to Theophanes, *Chronographia* (ed. de Boor, I, 439).

54   Nigel Wilson, *Scholars of Byzantium* (London, 1983), 14, cf. V. Grumel, *Regestes des actes du patriarcat de Constantinople* 3 (Istanbul, 1947), 1003.

55   Robert Browning, 'Enlightenment and Repression in Byzantium in the Eleventh and Twelfth Centuries', *P&P* 69 (1975), 3–23, at 18.

56   Michael Angold, *Church and Society in Byzantium under the Comneni, 1081–1261* (Cambridge, 1995), 489–90; J. Gouillard, 'Constantin Chrysomallos sous le masque de Syméon le Nouveau Théologien', *Travaux et Mémoires* 5 (1973), 313–27; J. Gouillard, 'Quatre procès de mystiques à Byzance (vers 960–1143): inspiration et autorité', *Revue des Études Byzantines* 36 (1978), 5–81; see the translated text in Janet Hamilton and Bernard Hamilton, *Christian Dualist Heresies in the Byzantine World, c.650-c.1405* (Manchester, 1998), 212–14.

57   For the disagreements between Plethon and Scholarios, in the context of the renewed debate in the last years of Byzantium on the merits and demerits of Plato and Aristotle, see the discussion of G. Karamanolis, 'Plethon and Scholarios on Aristotle', in K. Ierodiakonou, ed., *Byzantine Philosophy and its Ancient Sources* (Oxford, 2002), 253–82. For the date, see J. Monfasani, 'Pletho's Date of Death and the Burning of his Laws', *Byzantinische Zeitschrift* 98 (2005), 459–63.

Scholasticus.[58] The non-Chalcedonians were especially concerned to have correct official lists of 'orthodox' names in view of the need for valid non-Chalcedonian ordinations;[59] manipulating the liturgical diptychs was an important technique for them in establishing who was in communion with whom. This was critically important, and indeed the anti-heretical legislation of the late fourth century defined orthodoxy not only by reference to councils but also to being in or out of communion with named bishops.[60] The stance of the non-Chalcedonians often provoked the authorities – for instance the books of Severus of Antioch were not to be copied, on pain of amputation of the hand.[61] Severus himself devotes a number of letters to the issue of names appearing or not appearing in the diptychs; all names of bishops who had signed at Chalcedon were to be removed.[62] The erasure of names from diptychs could also be carried out at imperial orders in Constantinople, as it was under Justin I.[63] According to John Malalas, Justinian's 'sacred decree' of AD 527 excluding pagans from holding office, and depriving persistent heretics of civil status, was ordered to be displayed 'in all provincial cities', following the Roman practice of the public display of important decrees, and a further example of this very physical emphasis on the written word was the display of what was claimed as orthodox by pinning documents on gates or church doors; this was done in AD 638 with the decree of the patriarch Sergius known as the *Ekthesis*, proclaiming Monothelete doctrine, which was set up in the narthex of Hagia Sophia in Constantinople. More notices were placed on the doors of Hagia Sophia during the fierce arguments which followed,[64] and centuries later in a similarly fraught period the

[58] P. Van den Ven, 'L'accession de Jean Scholastique au siège patriarcale de Constantinople en 565', *Byzantion* 35 (1965), 320–52, at 345.
[59] On liturgical diptychs, see R. Taft, *A History of the Liturgy of St John Chrysostom, IV: the Diptychs* (Rome, 1991); a parallel issue in later periods was the question of whether the pope should be commemorated in Constantinople: T. Kolbaba, *The Byzantine Lists: the Errors of the Latins* (Urbana, IL, 2000), 93–4.
[60] See Humfress, 'Roman Law', 144–5.
[61] *Nov.* 42 (AD 536); J. Speigl, 'Die Synode von 536 in Konstantinopel', *Ostkirchliche Studien* 43 (1994), 105–53.
[62] Cf. Severus, *Select Letters*, 1.19; ed. E. W. Brooks, *The Sixth Book of the Select Letters of Severus, Patriarch of Antioch, in the Syriac Version of Athanasius of Nisibis*, 4 vols (London, 1902–4), I.1, 75 (text); II.1, 68 (trans.) I owe these points to the excellent discussion in the Princeton dissertation by Volker Menze, 'The Making of a Church: the Syrian Orthodox in the Shadow of Byzantium and the Papacy', unpublished Ph.D. thesis, Princeton University, 2004.
[63] *Collectio Avellana*, 167, ed. O. Günther, CSEL 35 (Vienna, 1895–8), 618–21.
[64] PL 87, 81–2, letter of Pope Theodore.

edict of Manuel I Komnenos in AD 1166 which settled a particularly difficult doctrinal issue was inscribed on marble and placed in Hagia Sophia.[65]

A combination of enforcement techniques can be seen in operation during the reign of Justinian (AD 527–65), ranging from persuasion at one extreme to force on the other.[66] The emperor summoned the Syrians to elaborately orchestrated talks in Constantinople, and later, the North African bishops who were opposed to his line on the Three Chapters. His successors held similar meetings with the Miaphysites and Armenians. If persuasion failed, harsher measures were then employed: depositions in North Africa, house arrest for Pope Vigilius, persecution of Miaphysites.[67] We can see here an alternation between toleration, severity and pragmatism, in the attempt to deal with a situation in which orthodoxy itself was contested. Justinian was trying – perhaps clumsily – not merely to enforce, but actually to define orthodoxy; to that end he composed theological treatises himself, as did the iconoclast emperor Constantine V in the eighth century. However, the reign of Justinian also demonstrates the dynamism of the process. A mass of evidence exists on the side of the non-Chalcedonians which makes clear the reluctance of bishops like Severus to be driven into schism, their struggles with issues of communion, the authenticity of priestly orders, and the lack of ordained priests of their own persuasion. Justinian and Theodora are famously accused by Procopius of deliberately playing off the opposing sides: Justinian called meetings and attempted to get them to agree, while according to non-Chalcedonian sources such as John of Ephesus, Theodora was the open patron of the

---

65 Cyril Mango, 'The Conciliar Edict of 1166', *Dumbarton Oaks Papers* 17 (1963), 317–30, at 329–30.

66 Lim, *Public Disputation*; idem, 'Christian Triumph and Controversy', in G. W. Bowersock, Peter Brown, and Oleg Grabar, eds, *Late Antiquity: a Guide to the Post-Classical World* (Cambridge, MA, 1999), 196–217; see also Michael Maas, *Exegesis and Empire in the Early Byzantine Mediterranean* (Tübingen, 2003), 72, 78–9.

67 In the 540s North African bishops were prominent in opposing the emperor's edicts condemning the Three Chapters: Maas, *Exegesis and Empire*, 49–50; when in 550 they excommunicated Pope Vigilius for accepting the emperor's position, several were summoned to Constantinople and subsequently deposed, like Reparatus of Carthage, or arrested in Constantinople (their punishments are described by Victor of Tonnuna, *Chronicon*. s.a. 550, 551, 552, 553); on the treatment of Pope Vigilius, see C. Sotinel, 'Emperors and Popes in the Sixth Century: the Western View', in Michael Maas, ed., *Companion to the Age of Justinian* (Cambridge, 2005), 267–90, at 280–4; Miaphysites: Lucas Van Rompay, 'Society and Community in the Christian East', ibid., 239–66.

non-Chalcedonians and entertained them in the palace.[68] Even if the imperial couple were not as calculating as Procopius claims, the attempt to maintain dialogue in highly complex circumstances is a very understandable strategy. One can only remark on the energy and persistence with which emperors kept up the effort to resolve disputes, given the difficulties they faced. Justinian's Fifth Ecumenical Council (also known as Constantinople II) in AD 553 was a failure; it was not accepted in the West, and it certainly did not succeed in conciliating the Miaphysites at whom it was partly aimed.[69] Nor did it work when Justinian's successor Justin II tried open persecution.[70]

Faced with this challenge, emperors also tried the tactics of issuing their own edicts or alternatively, simply ordering an end to debate.[71] Heraclius was engaged in discussions with the Armenians on the eve of the Arab conquest, but, for a considerable period during the seventh century, it was the imperial government itself that was regarded as heretical; even as the Arabs won their first victories in Syria, Chalcedonian bishops from the eastern provinces were meeting in Cyprus to oppose imperial policy, and the patriarch Sergius's Psephos of AD 633 and Ekthesis of AD 638 and the Typos of AD 647 or 648 issued by Paul in the name of the Emperor Constans II all attempted to forbid discussion of sensitive doctrinal matters altogether. Not surprisingly, this tactic was unsuccessful. It was these failed attempts to deal with dissent, as well as the action of the Lateran Synod of 649 in anathematizing Sergius, Pyrrhus, Paul and all who followed them, which drove the emperor to the unusual and very high profile step of arresting Pope Martin and Maximus Confessor and condemning them to death or exile.[72] What we see here is the spectacle of emperors out of their depth. It seems curiously modern.

[68] Procopius, Secret History, 10; Evagrius, HE, 4.10. See J. A. Evans, The Empress Theodora: Partner of Justinian (Austin, TX, 2002); Clive Foss, 'The Empress Theodora', Byzantion 72 (2002), 141–76.
[69] See Patrick Gray, 'The Legacy of Chalcedon: Christological Problems and their Significance', in Maas, Companion, 215–38.
[70] Summary in Michael Whitby, 'The Successors of Justinian', in Averil Cameron, Bryan Ward-Perkins and Michael Whitby, eds, Cambridge Ancient History 14 (Cambridge, 2000), 86–111, at 89–90.
[71] Evagrius, HE, 3.14 (Zeno); 5.4 (Justin II in 571).
[72] Several of the texts relating to these events are only now being critically edited; for some orientation, see W. Brandes, 'Juristische Krisenbewältigung im 7. Jahrhundert: die Prozessen gegen Papst Martin I und Maximos Homologetes', in L. Burgmann, ed., Fontes Minores 10 (Frankfurt am Main, 1998), 141–212; idem, 'Orthodoxy and Heresy in the

Direct methods were supplemented at all periods by attempts to manage outcomes through the manipulation of texts.[73] From late antiquity onwards, Byzantine conciliar documents have been recognized to be at times highly suspect and at best highly orchestrated, and we are in a far better position as a result of recent editorial work to appreciate the complications of such material.[74] Examples of such problematic documents include the Latin acts of the Fifth Council in 553, in two versions with differing presentations of the role played by Pope Vigilius, and the Acts of the Lateran Synod held in Rome in AD 649.[75] The fathers of the Sixth Council in AD 680–81 felt it necessary to investigate the textual record of the Fifth Council in four Greek and Latin codices; they discovered some letters contained there to be forgeries and duly anathematized the forgers.[76] Florilegia, collections of extracts designed to prove a particular case, were *de rigueur* as part of the argumentation used in Church councils,[77] though they also appear in many other contexts. But probably the most striking evidence for the fabrication and manipulation of texts comes from the Iconoclast period, when strenuous measures had to be put in place to control it.[78] After iconoclasm was over, as is well known, the iconophiles embarked on a vigorous effort to write the record in their own interest,[79] and

Seventh Century: Prosopographical Observations on Monotheletism', in Averil Cameron, ed., *Fifty Years of Prosopography: Rome, Byzantium and Beyond* (Oxford, 2003), 103–18; Andrew Louth, *Maximus the Confessor* (London, 1996), 7–18; Pauline Allen and Bronwen Neil, eds, *Maximus the Confessor and his Companions: Documents from Exile* (Oxford, 2002), 10–26.

73 For example W. Brandes, 'Apergios von Perge: ein Phantomhäretiker', *Jahrbuch der Österreichischen Byzantinistik* 48 (1998), 35–40; see also Averil Cameron, 'Texts as Weapons: Polemic in the Byzantine Dark Ages', in Alan K. Bowman and Greg Woolf, eds, *Literacy and Power in the Ancient World* (Cambridge, 1984), 198–215, at 208–10.

74 See S. Wessel, 'Literary Forgery and the Monothelete Controversy: Some Scrupulous Uses of Deception', *Greek, Roman and Byzantine Studies* 42 (2001), 201–20: Sixth Council, AD 680–1: ed. R. Riedinger, *ACO*, 2.2 (Berlin, 1990–2).

75 See Gray, 'The Legacy of Chalcedon', 214; Lateran Synod (AD 649): ed. R. Riedinger, *ACO*, 2.1 (Berlin, 1984); composition: R. Riedinger, 'Die Lateransynode von 649 und Maximus Confessor', in F. Heinzer and C. von Schönborn, eds, *Maximus Confessor: actes du Symposium sur Maxime le Confesseur, Fribourg, 2–5 septembre, 1980* (Fribourg, 1982), 111–21; Cameron, 'Texts as Weapons', 209. While this was an oppositional council, not an official one, the methodology did not differ.

76 Wessel, 'Literary Forgery', 210–15.

77 See Alexander Alexakis, *Codex Parisinus Graecus 1115 and its Archetype* (Washington, DC, 1996).

78 See Cyril Mango, 'The Availability of Books in the Byzantine Empire, AD 750–850', in *Byzantine Books and Bookmen: a Dumbarton Oaks Colloquium, 1971* (Washington, DC, 1975), 29–45.

79 See for example M.-F. Auzépy, 'Manifestations de la propagande en faveur de

destruction of iconoclast texts must have taken place. The iconoclasts were not immune from this either. For instance, if we believe the account in the Acts of II Nicaea, they actually cut out the pages of books which referred to images.[80] 'Fixing' the records of councils, falsification of evidence and manipulation of texts were, on one level, ways of enforcing orthodoxy, and this happened both at official and non-official levels.

Other types of writing were also important in formulating the idea of orthodoxy, in particular heresiology, which took off as a genre in the late antique period and became increasingly technologized thereafter.[81] Far from being the turgid and somehow irrelevant texts they often seem to modern taste,[82] these compositions, with their often repeated formulae, also helped to crystallize orthodox doctrine. Formal debates helped the process, as when the archbishop of Milan came to Constantinople in AD 1112, and on many earlier occasions.[83] Again, later Byzantine emperors and churchmen worked within late antique precedents as they continued to struggle with disunity, and the volume of heresiological literature in treatises, florilegia and compendia steadily increased. In the twelfth century Alexius I Comnenus greeted with anger the condemnation by a divided synod of Eustratius the bishop of Nicaea for alleged errors in his treatises against the Armenians; the emperor had wanted Eustratius to be accepted back, and demanded an explanation from the synod. This produced a long and detailed reply which shows that for some at least the clinching argument was that Eustratius seemed to have produced a novel heresy, in which he had come near to proving himself a Nestorian. In explaining why some of the members of the synod had refused to allow him back even after he had confessed his errors, contrary to many early precedents, their spokesman Niketas of Serres appealed to a more recent statement by

---

l'orthodoxie', in Leslie Brubaker, ed., *Byzantium in the Ninth Century: Dead or Alive?* (Aldershot, 1998), 85–100; eadem, *L'hagiographie et l'iconoclasme byzantines: le cas de la Vie d'Étienne le jeune* (Aldershot, 1999); eadem, *Vie d'Étienne le jeune par Étienne le diacre* (Aldershot, 1997).

[80] Mansi, *Concilia*, 13.189B, 192D.

[81] Averil Cameron, 'How to Read Heresiology', *Journal of Medieval and Early Modern Studies* 33: 3 (2003), 471–92.

[82] Even it seems by Margaret Mullett, *Theophylact of Ohrid: Reading the Letters of a Byzantine Bishop* (Aldershot, 1997), 73–4, of the Comnenian heresiologies.

[83] V. Grumel, 'Autour du voyage de Pierre Grossolano, archevêque de Milan à Constantinople en 1112', *Échos d'Orient* 32 (1933), 22–33; J. Darrouzès, 'Les conférences de 1112', *Revue des Études Byzantines* 23 (1965), 51–9.

the patriarch Tarasios at the Second Council of Nicaea.[84] Such cases could be decided only by precedent; strings of well-practised arguments thus needed to be marshalled by either side, for which seemingly dry heresiologies were one of several useful sources.

Alexius I himself commissioned a heresiological work known as the *Dogmatic Panoply*, from Euthymius Zigabenus or Zigadenos, as a compendium against Bogomilism.[85] The title itself, like that of the later *Sacred Arsenal* by Andronikos Kamateros,[86] expresses the metaphor of heresy or wrong belief as an attack on orthodoxy, which must be defended by the best armour, or of orthodoxy having its own arsenal of weapons; similarly one of the founding tracts in the genre, Epiphanius's *Panarion*, expressed the idea of heresy as a disease.[87] Epiphanius's work had been largely incorporated in John of Damascus work on heresies, and later works in the genre usually followed these established models. Niketas Choniates' *Treasury of Orthodoxy* reverses the title, but is in the same mode.[88] Euthymius's tract similarly built on a repertoire which had been laid down and repeated time and again in the intervening period, and did what all such texts do before getting to the matter in hand, that is, rehearsed the lists of earlier heresies and brought out an array of familiar patristic citations. This was a useful technique, no mere list of potted arguments[89] but a reassuring and confirming procedure which set the current issue of Bogomilism in the context of a long past history of orthodoxy and heresy. A counterpart to works of this sort were the liturgical hymns to which Ephrem Lash has recently drawn attention, which also denounced lists of past heretics,[90] as were

---

84 P. Ioannou, 'Le sort des évêques hérétiques réconciliés: le discours inédit de Nicétas de Serres contre Eustrate de Nicée', *Byzantion* 28 (1958), 1–30; idem, 'Trois pièces inédits de son procès', *Revue des Études Byzantines* 10 (1953), 24–34.

85 PG 130, 19–1362.

86 Kamateros was a high official of Manuel I Komnenos who in the 1170s collected in this work all the arguments used in the emperor's debates with the Roman and Armenian Churches: Magdalino, *Empire*, 290.

87 For Epiphanius, see Averil Cameron, 'How to Read Heresiology', 471–92; also eadem, 'Jews and Heretics: a Category Error?', in Adam H. Becker and Annette Yoshiko Reed, eds, *The Ways that Never Parted: Jews and Christians in Late Antiquity and the Early Middle Ages* (Tübingen, 2003), 345–60.

88 PG 139–40.

89 So Magdalino, *Empire*, 367; this and other works such as the *Sacred Arsenal* also served as a form of propaganda literature for the emperor: ibid., 369, 454–7.

90 Archimandrite Ephrem (Lash), 'Byzantine Hymns of Hate', in Louth and Casiday, *Byzantine Orthodoxies*, 151–64. These hymns are particularly connected with the commemoration of the ecumenical councils; they are impossible to date precisely but seem to have been produced over the ninth to thirteenth centuries.

the anti-Latin writings from the eleventh century on.[91] The abundant writings on heresy in the early Christian period in fact pale in comparison with the vast amount of such writing in Byzantium, whether in the context of homilies, treatises, speeches, disputations or heresiology proper. This veritable obsession with defining and condemning every form of wrong belief created a discourse of citation, polarity and tradition, in which what mattered was less a matter of whether the specific arguments were subtle or convincing in each particular compilation than the cumulative effect they had in promoting cultural norms.

Christianity in Byzantium was no longer an emerging religion making its way in a plural context, as it had been in the early Roman empire. Yet 'orthodoxy' remained contentious at all periods of Byzantine history. In early Byzantium patriarchs and independent bishops had their own power bases and were very difficult to call into line. In the period after Chalcedon (AD 451), actual violence between religious groups was not infrequently the outcome.[92] But understanding later Byzantium also presents us with a challenge. On the one hand, this was a society which placed an enormous emphasis on order (*taxis*) – in terms of precedence, hierarchy, rules, and social theory. The emperor was (in theory) at the apex of an ordered and serene establishment in which everyone including clerics was graded according to his or her precedence;[93] in the world of the Church ecclesiastical hierarchy was laid down in the liturgical diptychs; a large though very diffuse body of canon law also regulated clergy behaviour and appointments as well as many other matters.[94] The Emperor Alexius I was one who

[91] See Tia M. Kolbaba, *The Byzantine Lists: Errors of the Latins* (Urbana, IL, 2000); eadem, 'Byzantine Perceptions of Latin 'Religious Errors': Themes and Changes from 850 to 1350', in Angeliki E. Laiou and R. P. Mottahadeh, eds, *The Crusades from the Perspective of Byzantium and the Muslim World* (Washington, DC, 2001), 117–43; eadem, 'The Orthodoxy of the Latins in the Twelfth Century', in Louth and Casiday, *Byzantine Orthodoxies*, 199–214.
[92] See now Gaddis, *There is no Crime*. The voluminous Acts of the Council of Chalcedon are now available in an excellent annotated English translation by Richard Price and Michael Gaddis, *The Acts of the Council of Chalcedon*, TTH 45, 3 vols (Liverpool, 2005), and see also Fergus Millar, *A Greek Roman Empire: Power and Belief under Theodosius II (408–450)* (Berkeley and Los Angeles, CA, 2006).
[93] The extent to which this sense of hierarchy went can be seen in the tenth- and fourteenth-century books of court ceremonial and in the several surviving lists of precedence to be followed at imperial banquets and other occasions, for which see N. Oikonomides, *Les listes de préséance byzantines des IXe et Xe siècles* (Paris, 1972); the patriarch of Constantinople was included in the invitation lists and instructions for precedence.
[94] Canon law in Byzantium began with the canons issued by church councils, which were later collected, commented upon and expanded, especially from the twelfth century

sought to regulate the clergy still further.[95] Byzantium was a state in which there were essentially two kinds of law, the civil and the ecclesiastical, with different approaches. But the central relationship at the heart of Byzantine religion was itself highly unstable: emperors could and did depose patriarchs, but equally, patriarchs could and did oppose emperors and refuse to do their will.[96] It is no accident that one of the periods when Byzantium seems to have been at its most repressive, with notorious heresy trials, the Comnenian period (AD 1081–1185), was also a time when patriarchs came and went and when the emperors were aggressive towards the Church while being dependent on its cooperation.

Given its symbolic value, everyone in Byzantium claimed orthodoxy for his own, and managing such a situation was a complicated matter. In the 'repressive' Comnenian period there were again imperial edicts, and a group of heresy trials.[97] Paul Magdalino argues that under the Comnenian emperors not only the imperial authorities but also the educated elite effectively conspired to silence independent thought. This was not expressed as coercion, only as 'defending' orthodoxy, and the title Magdalino has given to his important discussion is indeed 'The guardians of orthodoxy'.[98] As we have seen, the use of force was in fact rare. It had happened in the case of Paulicians, but not without some reservations on the part of Theodore of Studios in the 820s, who disapproved of the death penalty.[99] As for Iconoclasm, the iconophiles talked

onwards; however it was characterized by diffuseness and a huge volume of material, as also by a lack of overall systematization (see Andreas Schminck, *Oxford Dictionary of Byzantium*, s.v. canon law).

95 J. Hussey, *The Orthodox Church in the Byzantine Empire* (Oxford, 1986), 310–12, 329.

96 For the shifting relationship between the emperor and the patriarch of Constantinople, and critique of the idea of 'Caesaropapism' in Byzantium, see Dagron, *Emperor and Priest*, 282–312.

97 Robert Browning, 'Enlightenment and repression', 18; see also P. Agapitos, 'Teachers, Pupils and Imperial Power in Eleventh-Century Byzantium', in Yun Lee Too and Niall Livingstone, eds, *Pedagogy and Power: Rhetorics of Classical Learning* (Cambridge, 1998), 170–91.

98 Magdalino, *Empire,* 316–412.

99 PG 99, 1481 = *Epistula* 455 (ed. G. Fatouros, *Theodori Studitae epistulae,* 2 vols [Berlin–New York, 1992], 2: 647): letter to Theophilos of Ephesus who had written in favour of putting Manichaeans, i.e. Paulicians, to death: 'What are you saying, most reverend? In the gospels the Lord forbade this, saying 'No, lest when you collect the tares you root up the wheat with them. Let them both grow together till harvest' (Migne text translated in Hamilton and Hamilton, *Christian Dualist Heresies*, 61). The representation of the Paulicians in orthodox sources is highly tendentious (another example of the manipulation of ideas): see C. Ludwig, 'The Paulicians and Ninth-Century Byzantine Thought', in Brubaker, *Byzantium in the Ninth Century,* 23–35.

up the dangers they faced, but in practice the iconoclasts were more interested in exacting conformity and bringing people to communion than in punishing them, let alone putting them to death.[100] The eighth-century *Life* of Stephen the Younger, one of the very few iconophile martyrs, presents us with a lurid picture of the saint suffering at the hands of the cruel iconoclast emperor Constantine V, but this text is of course a history written to justify opposition rather than a real record of persecution.[101] In addition, thanks to recent work, Theodore the Studite's imprisonment towards the end of the iconoclast period seems less drastic than he claimed; at least his letters show that he was able to keep in contact with a wide range of rather well-placed contacts and friends.[102]

The extent to which even the most high-profile episodes of repression tend to be surrounded by uncertainty is very striking. The trial of the intellectual and teacher John Italus, consul of the philosophers and pupil of Michael Psellus, very early in the reign of Alexius I, has been read as a show trial and a display of Alexius's desire to seem the defender of orthodoxy.[103] Yet Anna Comnena's account of her father's heroic defence of orthodoxy and learning is so distorted as to be hardly usable. It is equally hard to get a sensible account from her fanciful version of what was indeed a very unusual episode, the public burning in Constantinople of Basil, the leader of the Bogomils, around AD 1100. Such an event was only possible in the capital, where an example had to be and could be made, but even then it seems to have been a very last resort after the failure of extensive efforts by the emperor himself to produce a recantation;[104] according to Anna, Alexius also took the opportunity while on campaign in Thrace to devote long discussions to an attempt to win over local Paulicians.[105] The trial of Italus was accompanied by another sort of display – but while the addition of new clauses to the Synodikon of Orthodoxy was clearly meant to be an

---

[100] D. R. Turner, 'Parameters of Tolerance during the Second Iconoclasm, with Special Regard to the Letters of Theodore the Studite', in Nikolaou, *Toleration and Repression*, 69–85.

[101] See Auzépy, *L'Hagiographie et l'Iconoclasme Byzantin*.

[102] See I. Ševčenko, 'Was there Totalitarianism in Byzantium? Constantinople's Control over its Asiatic Hinterland in the Early Ninth Century', in Cyril Mango and Gilbert Dagron, eds, with the assistance of Geoffrey Greatrex, *Constantinople and its Hinterland* (Aldershot, 1975), 91–105.

[103] See D. Smythe, 'Alexius I and the Heretics', in M. Mullett and D. Smythe, eds, *Alexius I Komnenos, vol. 1: Papers* (Belfast, 1996), 232–59.

[104] Anna Comnena, *Alexiad*, 15.9–10.

[105] Ibid., 14.8–9.

announcement to all that orthodoxy had prevailed, it is not at all clear what the trial of Italus was really about. 'Taking seriously' the Platonic theory of Forms featured as one of the errors anathematized in the Synodikon of Orthodoxy. Yet John's teacher Michael Psellus and others had managed to avoid direct attack for Platonism, and Psellus wrote a defence of John in which he argued for the latter's orthodoxy.[106] Italus ('the Italian') was closely connected to Alexius's rivals, while Alexius himself had only recently seized the throne and was faced with severe military, political and financial problems. The surviving dossier of the trial contains several items, not in chronological order, and not all the documents that are known. Jean Gouillard comments that there was an absurd disproportion between the trial's avowed object, the mode of refutation and the punishment and concludes that 'the real nature of the affair escapes us'.[107] John disappears from view after it, but does not seem to have suffered too much, and, as one might have concluded from the mish-mash of charges recorded in the new clauses in the *Synodikon*, there is no 'heresy of Italus' in the heresiological compilations of the period.

If there was a comparison in Byzantium with the rise of a 'persecuting society' in the West, it would need to be made in the period from the twelfth century onwards, and indeed the Comnenian period was a time of change and of some tensions, though also of experimentation and novelty. Patriarchs came and went under Manuel I, but the Church was gradually gaining ground in regulation of matters such as marriage. It was also now – not accidentally – that the study of canon law revived; the evidence that we have of actual cases, for all its problems, shows the complexity of the interplay between ecclesiastical and civil law and the different considerations which applied. It was against this background that trials and punishments for heresy increased from the late eleventh century on, and were accompanied by

---

[106] On which, see A. Kaldellis, *The Argument of Psellus'* Chronographia (Leiden, 1999); Psellus and John Italus: N. G. Wilson, *Scholars of Byzantium* (London, 1983), 153–6, who argues (154) that John's punishment was 'not as drastic as it would have been in a modern society capable of exercising greater control'. Psellus's teacher, John Mauropous, himself suspected of heterodoxy, defended ancient writers against the charge of atheism (ed. P. de Lagarde, 'Quae in codice Vaticano graeco 676 supersunt', *Abhandlungen der Gött. Gesellschaft der Wissenschaften* 28 (Göttingen, 1881), no. 43).

[107] J. Gouillard, 'Le procès official de Jean l'Italien: les actes et leurs sous-entendus', *Travaux et Mémoires* 9 (1985), 133–73, at 169; cf. also L. Clucas, *The Trial of John Italus and the Crisis of Intellectual Values in Byzantium in the Eleventh Century* (Munich, 1981).

new heresiological encyclopaedias and increasingly elaborate procedures and formulae of abjuration;[108] trials became public events themselves, and the accused was required to abjure his heresy 'in a loud
voice'. Contemporaries also worried about what counted as recantation:
it was noted for instance that Bogomils could assent to the Scriptures
because they had their own meanings for the required passages, and
that they could easily take the sacraments because they did not believe
in them, tactics which Paulicians had used before them.[109] This was
certainly not a simple matter of emperor versus Church; rather, the
field on which tensions were played out was that of orthodoxy, and this
was where the display if any had to take place. Yet whatever view is
taken of the true extent, geographical spread and nature of
Bogomilism,[110] it is hard to see a major turn to popular heresy in the
heartlands of Byzantium.

In Byzantine society the habits and formulas of orthodox discourse
constituted the field within which all parties necessarily operated.
Indeed, the crucial Comnenian period – though it is not alone in this –
was notable for the interplay in individual careers between secular and
ecclesiastical or monastic posts, while the courts which heard the
famous cases included high persons of state as well as ecclesiastics. The
display or the performance of orthodoxy in Byzantium was a shared
cultural expression established through a long and often contested
process, in which all parties necessarily engaged, and within which they
all formulated their arguments.

Byzantium was neither a persecuting society nor a tolerant one.
Rather, it was taken for granted that religious orthodoxy was the
outward sign of social and political stability, and as such it was both
prized and contested. Direct means of enforcing it could certainly
include both anathemas and legal punishments for heresy, which might
on occasion include imprisonment, exile or mutilation, or the deposition of bishops from their sees. The measures attributed to the iconoclasts, such as parading monks and nuns, whitewashing images in
churches, and deposing or imprisoning bishops were all done by the

---

[108] See E. Patlagean, 'Aveux et désaveux d'hérétiques à Byzance (XIᵉ–XIIᵉ siècles)', in
L'Aveu: Antiquité et Moyen Âge, Coll. de l'École française de Rome 88 (Rome, 1986), 243–60.
[109] Ibid., 258–9.
[110] On which, see Yuri Stoyanov, *The Hidden Tradition in Europe* (London, 1994); idem,
The Other God: Dualist Religions from Antiquity to the Cathar Heresy (New Haven, CT, 2000).

iconoclasts in the name of orthodoxy.[111] Direct measures also included imperial initiatives, as well as the legal processes under which trials for heresy were brought.[112] But other measures also constituted enforcement, including writing – pamphlets, treatises, heresiologies, letters, attacking heresy and promoting 'orthodoxy', as well as symbolic and public gestures. If the state took overt action against dissent, it did so only sporadically and then not in a comprehensive way. This was not because of any active sense of toleration; rather, the quest for religious stability formed a cultural praxis and expression within which Byzantium functioned as a society; the result was a constant need for vigilance and a constant activity in the field of what I would term active promotion. The 'totalizing discourse' to which Christians had aspired in the first centuries of Christianization[113] did not succeed in establishing a settled orthodoxy, even in the last days of Byzantium. The question was how this medieval state and society, the heir to Christian late antiquity, tried to deal with the problem.

Keble College, University of Oxford

---

[111] Non-legal sources tell of physical punishments exacted on persistent iconophiles under the Emperor Theophilos, even if the number is small: Patlagean, 'Byzance et le blason pénal du corps', 415.

[112] J. Hajjar, *Le synode permanente (synodos endemousa) dans l'Église byzantine des origines au XIe siècle*, Orientalia christiana analecta 164 (Rome, 1962); Hussey, *The Orthodox Church*, 318–25.

[113] See Cameron, *Christianity and the Rhetoric of Empire*, ch. 6.

AN EXEGESIS OF CONFORMITY:
TEXTUAL SUBVERSION OF SUBVERSIVE TEXTS

by M. C. STEENBERG

'We have learned from the Scriptures . . .'

TO speak with authority in the early Church was to speak from the Scriptures. While early Christianity may not have been a 'religion of the book' in the same way it is today, it was unquestionably a religion of text, and the refrain 'we have learned from the holy Scriptures' is a chorus in the early Christian witness. Here stood the authority of divine fulfilment. To confess merely Christ might be to proclaim a man, perhaps a prophet, perhaps a deity; but to confess 'the scriptural Christ' was to proclaim the Messiah foretold in divine writ, the revealed Saviour, and to find in that revelation the character and substance of the confession newly made.[1] Nonetheless, while the text of the Old Testament might be of common heritage (though even this faced the challenge of a Marcion, who wished to do away with it[2]), the emerging textual tradition of the Christian era provided a challenge: which text? what scripture? If the Christ of the Church is the 'Christ of the scriptures', determining the content of those scriptures – or those texts accorded scriptural authority in their receipt and influence – becomes critical. More than this, subverting the potential influence of texts deemed unsuitable stands as an essential task. To approach the era authentically, scholarly reading of the rise of a New Testament canon in the early Church must be combined with an understanding of the means and methodologies of its necessary correlate, textual exclusion. I shall argue here that this was accomplished through an exegetical method of subversion more intricate and nuanced than is often perceived.

---

[1] On the concept of the 'scriptural Christ', see J. Behr, *The Formation of Christian Theology, vol. 1: The Way to Nicaea* (New York, 2001), 49–70.

[2] The common idea that Marcion wanted to eliminate the OT canon is perhaps misleading; there is widespread agreement among scholars that while the Jewish community at the turn of the millennium held to a clear view of 'scripture', it had no correlate sense of 'canon' – a fluidity of approach mirrored in the early Fathers. See S. M. Sheeley, 'From "Scripture" to "Canon": the Development of the New-Testament Canon', *Review and Expositor* 95 (1998), 513–22, at 514.

Movements of textual challenge

It is notable that among the most potent challenges to earliest Christendom, perhaps the two greatest were textual, if not directly in substance then certainly in consequence. The challenge of Marcion (d. c. 160), demanding that the radical love expressed in the message of Christ was eminently discordant with the God of the Old Testament, attempted to excise that witness from the Christian consciousness and reform nascent textual traditions along the same lines. Marcion's famous *coupage* of the Gospels and epistles of Paul evoked the indignation of nearly every source in our second-century corpus. Yet often in those same pages, challenge was levelled against the followers of Simon Magus, of Valentinus and Ptolemy, and the various other groups scholarship persists so inaccurately to call 'Gnostic', though in these groups an opposite tendency was the norm.[3] While Marcion by and large set to restrict the textual corpus embraced by Christianity, such groups as those identifying with Valentinus were willing to embrace an ever-widening pool of textual receipt. The 1945 find at Nag Hammadi provided scholarship with several new tractates, but did not surprise us in the degree of its multiplicity. The second and third centuries saw an explosion of religious literature in production, much of it purporting to be Christian, and all demanding the attention of the solidifying and expanding *ecclesia*.

These two currents – Marcion's tendency toward textual confinement and the 'Gnostic' tendency toward textual expansion – thrived simultaneously, and it is no surprise, and no new discovery, that the process of canon formation arose in the same era. One of the principal voices of the period, Irenaeus of Lyons, addressed both directly, and has for over a decade been studied for his role in the formation of a Christian scriptural canon;[4] our oldest known New Testament listing dates from roughly the same period;[5] and the widespread acceptance of a

---

[3] On difficulties with the terms 'Gnostic' and 'Gnosticism', see the already seminal work of M. A. Williams, *Rethinking 'Gnosticism': an Argument for Dismantling a Dubious Category* (Princeton, NJ, 1999), esp. 51–3 for his suggestion of alternative terminologies. While there remain challenges yet to consider, Williams's work redresses a major difficulty with modern-day usage.

[4] See the seminal work on the subject by Y.-M. Blanchard, *Aux sources du canon: le témoignage d'Irénée* (Paris, 1993).

[5] The so-called 'Muratorian Fragment', c. AD 170. See G. M. Hahneman, *The Muratorian Fragment and the Development of the Canon* (Oxford, 1992).

standardized listing emerges out of the closing pages in this early chapter in the Church's life. When Athanasius comes to refute the 'Ariomaniacs' in the mid-fourth century, he can draw on the same canonical listing in 367 as would be enshrined at the council of Carthage some three decades later.[6] A normative textual body has been established, within which all parties are content to frame their discussion.

In this sense, the project of reducing diversity in the name of Christian unity and authority is able to claim an accomplishment in the canonizing project of the second to fourth centuries, and the establishment of a normative scriptural canon was, by and large, a resounding success. Yet to this day we understand the phenomenon of its accomplishment remarkably poorly. In particular, how are we to explain the Church's success in asserting its canon over and above alternative traditions? Marcion had a strict catalogue, and so perhaps certain bodies within the so-called 'Gnostic' fray; why did these not prevail? How might one be convinced to embrace the Gospel of John, but not the Gospel of Truth? We must not assume the canonical 'obviousness' of later generations, including our own, to have been a reality in the early period. Some documents might have warranted immediate dismissal; but there was, in many texts which today seem markedly off-centred in Christian potential, a strong attraction to theoretically Christian readers – else there be little justification for the space and dedication allocated to their refutation by various patristic writers.

A canonical listing is not enough. The project of establishing canonical authority demands not only the restrictive affirmation of acceptable texts, but the subversion of potential authority proclaimed in documents outside that canon, and the proclamation of canon is in fact of little value apart from this project of discrediting texts seen as subversive to that standardizing norm. The two endeavours are necessarily correlative, though the latter has received less scholarly attention than the former. Whilst space will not allow a thorough study here (the project of subverting non-canonical texts in early Christianity is wide-ranging, inclusive of various methods and means), one aspect of such conversion warrants particular attention, precisely for its lack of notable treatment: the manner in which the refutation of subversive

---

6 So cited in Athanasius, *39th Paschal Epistle* (AD 367). Official listings of canonical books were proffered at Hippo in 393, and Carthage in 397 and 419; cf. B. Metzger, *Canon of the New Testament: its Origin, Development, and Significance* (Oxford, 1987), 237–8.

texts is made largely through subversive textual exploration and exegesis. Alternative documents must be read and explored, 'de-merited' in their own right as 'proof in the pudding' that their absence from the emerging canon is warranted. Early authors are keen to show that, above all, texts prove themselves canonical or otherwise by their own contents.

The subversion of subversive texts

It is my increasing conviction that we discover, in the project of textual conformity dominant in the second and third centuries, a methodology of subversive exegesis designed to discredit those texts seen as subversive to the solidifying orthodox norm, founded in exegetical principles of risible exposure. Mere dismissal of textual traditions, without substantive grounding for the same, holds little persuasive water, and persuasion is critical – not simply to state that a given text should not be read, but to show persuasively why not. What is required is a mode of refutation grounded in textual exposure and refutation: a means of demerit centred in subversive exegesis. Rather than stand apart from a text and declaratively devalue its worth (an approach that immediately raises defences and promotes more hard-line support by adherents), effective persuasion away from a given text, and its consequent exclusion from the normative body of Christian literature, comes more powerfully through a rhetorical 'entering in' to the theological dialogue of the document, exegeting therefrom conclusions deemed risible to speaker and hearer alike.

This method of subversive exegesis has recently been the focus of my attention in another paper, wherein I argue for its existence as a widespread and consistently-applied phenomenon throughout the second and third centuries (indeed beyond) which draws on a carefully measured employment of satire and parody in particular as chief means of exegetical subversion.[7] It is important to keep in mind this qualifier 'exegetical': what is discovered in the early witness is not merely that such tools as satire and parody are applied in refutation of pagan intellegentsia, Jewish or variously heretical documents – merely a spoofing laugh or jab at a foe deemed unreasonable – but that their use

---

[7] Unpublished paper given at the Oxford Patristics Seminar, 2005: 'How to Mock a Heretic: an Exegesis of Satire and Parody in the Early Fathers'.

forms the culminating feature of an exegetical method designed to use the texts themselves as grounding for the humour and connected discrediting of the risible. A text is met with a reading *grounded in the text*, drawing theological or historical principles from its contents in a manner designed to subvert the message by presenting its natural conclusions as patently absurd.

Space permits little more than an introduction in this paper, and for this an effective case-in-point may be offered in anticipation of three points with which I will conclude, which hold the potential to ground a better understanding of textual tradition in the early Church. This case-in-point is the Valentinian *Gospel of Truth*, and its subversive exegesis in the hands of Irenaeus. It is important to recall that the *Gospel of Truth* contained in the find at Nag Hammadi is more or less, but not exactly, identical to the text of the same name mentioned by Irenaeus in his large *Refutation and overthrow of knowledge falsely so-called*.[8] Even if it is clear that he did not have a copy of the gospel to hand when writing his tome (as seems to have been the case with the *Apocryphon of John*, and indeed, Irenaeus draws from the two as in common tradition[9]), his polemic in books I and II bears out his desire to refute its contents. It is regularly asserted that he does so in a rather uninformed, biased, and essentially unfair manner: quote very little, distort at whim, reject with blatant prejudice. While it is true that Irenaeus does wish to refute the teachings and authority of the document, claims that he does so by pure distortion of its contents in fact break down on careful reading. Irenaeus at times confuses details on the groups he attacks, but by and

---

[8] Compare *Refutation,* 3.11.9 (ed. Adelin Rousseau and Louis Doutreleau, SC 264 [Paris, 1979]), and the Nag Hammadi Codices I, 3 and XII, 2. Connection of the NHS tractate with the text mentioned by Irenaeus is longstanding and widespread; a catalogue of scholars supporting the connection is offered in T. L. Tiessen, *Irenaeus on the Salvation of the Unevangelized* (London, 1993), 44 n. 30. As to the title of Irenaeus's longer work, I am increasingly convinced that the common abbreviation 'Against heresies' is misleading, polarizing Irenaeus's focus in a way inauthentic to his own style. It additionally leaves out the emphasis on right and wrong knowledge that the proper title makes central, a contributing factor in continuing misuse of the term 'Gnostic' as applicable to the era. Throughout, I will refer to Irenaeus's main work as the *Refutation (Ref.)*. Translations herein are my own.

[9] Identification of the *Apocryphon of John* as among Irenaeus's sources goes back as far as C. Schmidt, 'Irenaeus und seine Quelle in *Adversus haereses* I 29', in P. Kleinert, ed., *Philotesia* (Berlin, 1907), 315–36 at 317. *Gospel of Truth.* has been posited at least as far back as W. C. Van Unnik, *Newly Discovered Gnostic Writings: a Preliminary Survey of the Nag Hammadi Find*, Studies in Biblical Theology 30 (London, 1960), 60, who suggests that Irenaeus may in fact have had a copy of the text at hand when writing the *Ref.*, despite the fact that he never makes direct use of it in his descriptions of Valentinian doctrine in *Ref.*, 1.

large he is markedly accurate and (perhaps surprisingly) fair. Indeed, exegeting from a document details and messages it does not contain, is precisely among the catalogue of faults he ascribes to Valentinus and his followers. It is a strange analysis to believe that Irenaeus would be willing to engage with abandon in a practice he explicitly decries as heretical.

What is in fact found in the midst of Irenaeus's often harsh words is a refutation based on exegetical exposure: he enters into the textual tradition of those he means to overthrow, exegeting from its contents – as much as he knows and understands them – conclusions he believes are demonstrably laughable. This may indeed be at times to make the text 'say what it does not say', but all exegesis, including 'proper' exegesis of canonized biblical documents, contains as integral ingredient an extrapolation of the non-explicit. In this Irenaeus would not feel himself duplicitous in his method: the whole point of exegesis is to discover not simply what a text says, but what it means, what it implies. To determine this accurately, however, one must genuinely exegete – must draw conclusions *from the text*. This is precisely Irenaeus's method when he comes to refute the traditions in question.

In the first ten chapters of *Ref.* 1, he explores the doctrines of Valentinus and his disciple Ptolemy in increasingly greater detail. His foundational belief throughout is that absurdity exposes itself: Irenaeus needs only exegete it properly. The resulting effect of this strategy is that by the time Irenaeus comes to argue against the Ptolomaean system directly in chapters nine and ten, there is little left to be said. He has exegeted the system in such a manner that the reader has already come to the conclusions on credibility that Irenaeus wishes to draw. He is then able to capstone his progressive line of argumentation with the reinforcement of outright mocking, again substantiated exegetically by material drawn from his opponents' texts. His parody of Valentinian speculation at *Ref.* 1.11.4 is one of the more amusing passages to come out of the early Christian world, and it is constructed chiefly through a recapitulation of Valentinian names for the godhead:

> Iu, Iu! Pheu, Pheu! Indeed, well may we utter these exclamations from tragedy at such a pitch of audacity shown forth in the coining of names as [Valentinus] has displayed without so much as a blush, devising a nomenclature for his system of falsehood. He declares that there is a certain 'Proarche' before all things, surpassing all thought, whom I call 'Monotes'; and then, with this 'Monotes'

there co-exists a power which I call 'Henotes'. In devising such names it is entirely obvious that he confesses them to be his own invention, and that he himself has given names to his scheme of things – [names and a system] which had never been suggested previously by any other. . . . Indeed, unless he had appeared in the world, the truth would still have been destitute of a name![10]

Irenaeus here recapitulates a point already made at *Ref.* 1.8.1 ('Theirs is a system which neither the prophets announced, nor the Lord proclaimed, nor the apostles delivered'), arguing that the novelty of such a nomenclature mitigates against its authenticity. Valentinus is directly snubbed for his brashness, and Irenaeus satirically proffers thanks to the Roman thinker without whom none would know that 'truth' ought in fact to be called 'Proarche', etc. Yet all this is merely the staging ground for Irenaeus's premiere example of textual subversion, which immediately follows the above.

If that is that case [i.e. that Valentinus can invent new nomenclature to describe reality], then nothing hinders any other person, in dealing with the same subject matter, to affix [their own] names – perhaps after such a fashion as the following: There exists a certain 'Proarche', royal, surpassing all thought, a power existing before every other substance and extended into space in every direction. Along with it there exists a power which I term a 'Gourd', and along with this Gourd there exists a power which again I call 'Utter-Emptiness'. Gourd and Emptiness, since they are one, produced – and yet did not simply produce, so as to be apart from themselves – a fruit, everywhere visible, eatable and delicious, which in fruit-language we call 'Cucumber'. Along with Cucumber exists a power of the same essence, which I call 'Melon'. These powers – Gourd, Utter-Emptiness, Cucumber, and Melon – brought forth the remaining multitude of the delirious melons of Valentinus. For if it is fitting that that language which is used respecting the universe be transformed to the primary Tetrad, and if at his pleasure any one can go about assigning names, who shall prevent us from adopting these names as being much more credible [than those which Valentinus posited], as well as being in general use and understandable to all?[11]

---

[10] *Ref.*, 1.11.4 (SC 264: 174–6).
[11] Ibid. (176).

Irenaeus is here in full form, but it is too easy to view this passage simply as a whimsical, if jeering, taunt. Even at his most humorous, Irenaeus structures his parody carefully and deliberately on an exegesis of the mythology he means to refute, a point that becomes more pronounced if we follow R. M. Grant's assertion – which seems entirely credible – that this passage may be further identified as a parody of the Naasene *Hymn to Attis*, of which we have independent evidence in Hippolytus.[12] As risible as the imagery is, it is in fact only the proper names that Irenaeus has changed; the structural elements of his parody are precise reflections of Ptolemaean speculation. Irenaeus even goes so far as to re-affirm the emanationist generative principles that underlay the whole Valentinian system, explaining the production of Cucumber by Gourd and Utter-Emptiness (they 'did not simply produce, so as to be apart from themselves'), inviting his readers to infer that his scheme is no more nor less absurd than the structure of Valentinus's pleroma. A changing of the proper names invokes laughter and makes the entirety of the system seem incredible, but this is only because the names seem so discordant with the subject matter. Yet why not such names? At least these are 'in general use and understandable to all', whereas 'Proarche', 'Monotes' and 'Henotes' are unknown and incomprehensible to most – and his overriding point is that the names, whichever one chooses, are only inconsequential glosses on a pleromatic system of no credibility. This is, in turn, only understandable in its full measure if one reads our passage from *Ref.* 1.11.4 not in isolation but as the capstone to his line of exegesis and argumentation from the prologue through to the current text. *Ref.* 1.1.1–3 and 1.2.1 have already exegeted the Valentinian system of emanations from 'Proarche' (known also as 'Propator' and 'Bythos'), with notable parallels to the Nag Hammadi *Apocryphon of John*.[13] There is in those chapters an escalating sense of satirical subversion: 1.1.3 concludes Irenaeus's exegesis of the multi-plicity of the thirty aeons of the pleroma (in 1.1.1, 2) with an implicit reference to flawed mathematics, for the pleroma is comprised of thirty members yet called 'tripartite'. Moreover, the pleroma is a composite of an Ogdoad, Decad and Deodecad, as 'proved' from what Irenaeus

---

considers desperate readings of Scripture: that Christ 'did nothing' for thirty years, or on the sums worked out from the parable of the vineyard (Matt. 20: 1–16) – for workers were sent out at the first hour, third, sixth, ninth and eleventh, the sum being the perfect pleromatic thirty. Irenaeus here employs a refined mode of satire: the Valentinian system is exposed without great flourish, simply the tone inviting the reader herself to conclude that there is no credibility to its grounding. As his argument advances, Irenaeus builds on the growing inner judgement of the reader as a resource from which to propel his satire into parody – cautiously delaying invention and flourish until a point when credibility has already been challenged by the text's own contents, refuting itself exegetically.

Subversive exegesis and a re-evaluation of early Christian textual conformity

The assertion of a tradition of subversive exegesis in the second and third centuries, of which the above case-study of Irenaeus is but a singular example, is useful not only in its potential for a more balanced understanding of what is taking place in the often aggressive attacks on texts and traditions in the early Church (though the potential here is marked, affording a means of assessing more constructively a 'method to the madness' of the great pool of polemical literature in these centuries); it also holds the potential for a refinement of our understanding of canon formation and application. Irenaeus is again an interesting reference: whilst he is the first to insist on a four-gospel canon (for symbolic reasons that to many seem rather unsatisfying[14]), and himself engages in the subversion of various texts and traditions of second-century provenance, he does not himself insist upon or suggest the formation of a permanent listing of 'canonical' Christian books – indeed, he makes authoritative use of several texts that would not appear in the fourth-century canon.[15] The interesting fact to be gleaned is that, at least for Irenaeus, exclusion of subversive texts does not necessarily warrant production of a codified and strict listing of the authoritative. Perhaps there is a measure of resistance in Irenaeus to the canonizing tendency of Marcion, which cast a negative shadow on the project of listing 'official' books and letters (as much as it may have implied a

---

[14] See *Ref.*, 3.11.8.
[15] A matter I explore in some detail in M. C. Steenberg, 'Scripture, *graphe*, and the Status of Hermas in Irenaeus', *St Vladimir's Theological Quarterly* (forthcoming, 2007).

necessity for the same); but it is equally possible that the very means Irenaeus employs to refute the authority of various texts, combined with his lack of interest in establishing a strict canon in response, reveals a more fluid understanding of the nature of textual authority. For Irenaeus, it is not a text's status as 'official' or 'accepted' that grants it authority, but its potential to provide, on authentic exegesis, witness to the deep truths of the Christian confession. Precedent to textual authority is the presence of a *regula fidei*, a 'canon of truth' (indeed, this is the only sense in which Irenaeus employs the term *kanon*), known in the Church through her apostolic heritage and which serves as the lens through which exegesis reveals a text as authoritative or subversive.[16]

Three points arise out of these observations that have potential, on further reflection and exploration, to refine our understanding of this early period. First, that the project of confronting subversive texts in the early Church was more exegetical than often assumed. As harsh as the refutations most often were, and as little empathy as there was for understanding the point-of-view of one's foe, refutations of subversive texts were not, by and large, merely judgemental in form, and they were certainly not made in reference to a canon. Rejection of authority came in the exposure of risible theology through subversive exegesis of subversive texts: reading another's document in such a way as to render discredited the teachings it contains.

Secondly, and in a connected way, this method of refutation exposes the manner in which the early Church grounded the authority of the texts it did accept: namely, in the exegetical power to witness to the confessed and experienced reality of Christ in the Church. The 'faith once delivered' (cf. Jude 1:3), the witness of the apostles, is taken as the key to the Scriptures, and the key by which to lock the door against the subversion of Scripture. Textual authority comes in the power of a text to reveal, on 'apostolic exegesis', the very truths passed down from the apostles in the Church.

Thirdly, and finally, there is in this assessment affirmation of an inherent fluidity in the early Church's approach to textual authority. It is interesting and revealing that the Christian community not only did not establish, but in fact showed little to no interest in establishing, an official listing of scriptural texts until it was two, if not three centuries of age. In refuting subversive texts by exegesis that exposes unfounded

---

16 Irenaeus's most famous expression of the *regula fidei* is at *Ref.*, 1.10.1–2.

doctrine, rather than by simple declaration of a text as 'unofficial', the early Church grounded its textual tradition in fluid terms: scriptural authority is found where apostolic exegesis reveals apostolic truth – and so Irenaeus could find it in the four gospels, in the epistles of Paul, and also in Hermas, in Ignatius, in Clement of Rome.[17] When the Church came, in the mid-fourth century, to establish a definitive listing of scriptural books for its New Testament, something of this fluidity was lost – however much the stricture may have been of value. The climate of textual authority changes permanently. If and when we come to understand more authentically the nature of that climate prior to this change, our vision of the early Christian approach to textual diversity will become clearer than it yet is.

Greyfriars Hall, University of Oxford

17 For a later example of the same fluidity apparent even after the advent of canonical lists, see V. Burrus, 'Canonical Reference to Extra-Canonical "Texts": Priscillian's Defense of the Apocrypha', in D. J. Lull, ed., *Society of Biblical Literature: 1990 Seminar Papers* (Atlanta, GA, 1990), 60–7.

HIPPOLYTUS AND THE CABBAGE QUESTION: BEYOND ACCEPTABLE DISCIPLINE AND DIVERSITY

by CHRISTINE TREVETT

USUALLY it is those of the mainstream in religion who impose upon those going against the flow discipline, doctrine and uniformity in place of flexibility. Before Christian orthodoxy and heresy had achieved clear definition, however, there were against-the-flow innovators who opposed flexibility. By requiring greater rigour and regularity in Christian practices they highlighted questions of authority and what manner of people might exercise it. The Church's own self-definition and status as an institution evolved in response to such things.

There were Montanists in the small but diverse Roman Christian community,[1] stressing spiritual gifts and continuing revelation, and well-attuned to times of uncertainty. Starting from Hippolytus's early third-century Roman *Refutation of All Heresies*,[2] I shall examine possible factors determining ('mainstream') Catholic Christians' hostile response to Montanism's discipline of fasting,[3] given that there had not been a uniform practice in Catholic congregations.

---

[1] 'Montanism', beginning in the 150s, is a fourth-century designation. 'The New Prophecy' may have been its original name. On Roman Montanism, see Christine Trevett, *Montanism: Gender, Authority and the New Prophecy* (Cambridge, 1996), esp. 55–65.

[2] Debate continues about the Hippolytan corpus: Manlio Simonetti, *Nuovo richerche su Ippolito*, Studia Ephemeridis Augustinianum 30 (Rome, 1989), 75–130; J. A. Cerrato, ' "Hippolytus" *On the Song of Songs* and the New Prophecy', *Studia Patristica* 31 (1997), 268–73; idem, *Hippolytus between East and West: the Commentaries and the Provenance of the Corpus* (Oxford, 2002) and cf. Allen Brent, *Hippolytus and the Roman Church in the Third Century: Communities in Tension before the Emergence of a Monarch Bishop* (Leiden, 1995), 204–365.

[3] Paul Wendland, ed., *Hippolytus Werke* III, *Refutatio Omnium Haeresium* (Leipzig, 1916). Sources on fasting: Rudolf Arbesmann, *Das Fasten bei den Griechen und Römern* (Giessen, 1929); idem, 'Fasting and Prophecy in Pagan and Christian Antiquity', in S. Kuttner, A. Strittmatter, and E. Quain, eds, *Traditio* 7: 1 (New York, 1949–51), 1–72; Peter Nagel, *Die Motivierung der Askese in der alten Kirche und der Ursprung des Mönchtums*, Texte und Untersuchungen zur Geschichte der altchristlichen Literatur 95 (Berlin, 1966) [hereafter: TU]; V. M. Wimbush, ed., *Ascetic Behaviour in Greco-Roman Antiquity: a Sourcebook* (Minneapolis, MN, 1990); Andrew McGowan, *Ascetic Eucharists: Food and Drink in Early Christian Ritual Meals* (Oxford, 1999); James A. Francis, *Subversive Virtue: Asceticism and Authority in the Second-Century Pagan World* (Philadelphia, PA, 1995).

Montanism had spread from Phrygia[4] and variously its followers had
seceded/were turned from Catholic congregations.[5] It was distinctive
not in terms of its doctrine of God or the Scriptures[6] but was most criticized in respect of discipline, and for acknowledging female leaders.
The *Refutation* (8.19 and 10.25) outlined Catholic complaints, citing
novelties in Montanist feasting, fasting and (perhaps) cabbage-
consumption.

Montanism and Innovation

While practice was still fluid Montanism stressed disciplined conformity rather than flexibility, prescribing for what had been optional (e.g.
Tertullian, *On Fasting* 13[7]) and extending the hours of twice-weekly
stations;[8] decrying second marriages;[9] not discouraging celibacy; being
slow to forgive and to reconcile.[10] Yet unlike Marcionites, Montanism
did not denigrate flesh or creation.

---

[4] For many of the sources for Montanism, see R. Heine, *The Montanist Oracles and Testimonia* (Macon, GA, 1989).

[5] See Eusebius, *Ecclesiastical History*, 5.16.6 (Anonymous), trans. in K. Lake, *Eusebius: the Ecclesiastical History I, Books I–V*, LCL (London, 1980) [hereafter: *EH*]; Hippolytus *Refutation*, 10.25. Origen (Frag. *On the Epistle to Titus*, PG 14, 1306) noted debate about whether Cataphrygianism (= Montanism) was heresy or schism and cf. Epiphanius's early anti-Montanist source (*Medicine Box*, 48.1.1; 48.1.3–4; 48.1.6–7; 48.12.1), in F. Williams, trans., *The Panarion of Epiphanius of Salamis*, 2 vols (Leiden, 1987–93).

[6] Later and fragmented Montanism *was* at odds with some doctrines of the Church: A. Stewart-Sykes, 'The Original Condemnation of Asian Montanism', *JEH* 50 (1999), 1–22, at 1–6; idem, 'The Asian Context of the *Epistula Apostolorum* and the New Prophecy', *Vigiliae Christianae* 51 (1997), 416–38; H. Paulsen, 'Die Bedeutung des Montanismus für die Herausbildung des Kanons', *Vigiliae Christianae* 32 (1978), 19–52; Trevett, *Montanism*, 198–232; Trevett, 'Spiritual Authority and the "Heretical" Woman: Firmilian's Word to the Church in Carthage', in J.-W. Drijvers and J. Watt, eds, *Portraits of Spiritual Authority: Religious Power in Early Christianity, Byzantium and the Christian Orient* (Leiden, 1999), 45–62 (showing common liturgical practice with Catholics).

[7] The edition of Tertullian's writings used is E. Kroymann, *Quinti Septimi Florentis Tertulliani Opera*, CSEL 47 (Vienna, 1906).

[8] *On Fasting*, 10. Among Catholic Christians there had been choice, and a station was just a few hours long. Compare Hermas, *The Shepherd: Similitudes*, 5.1.

[9] Elaine H. Pagels, 'Adam and Eve, Christ and the Church: a Survey of Second-Century Controversies Concerning Marriage', in A. B. Logan and A. J. M. Wedderburn, eds, *The New Testament and Gnosis: Essays in Honour of A. M. L. Wilson* (Edinburgh, 1983), 146–75. On Montanist compulsion versus Catholic flexibility about second marriages, see Epiphanius, *Medicine Box*, 48.9.4–8. Compare Tertullian, *Against Marcion*, 1.29.

[10] Trevett, *Montanism*, 112–20; eadem, ' "I Have Heard from Some Teachers": the Second-Century Struggle for Forgiveness and Reconciliation', in Kate Cooper and Jeremy Gregory, eds, *Retribution, Repentance and Reconciliation*, SCH 40 (Woodbridge, 2004), 5–28.

Tertullian (our only Montanist witness and perhaps atypical) opined that 'this discipline is ancient' (*On Monogamy*, 3.11 cf. 4.1). It neither avoided marriage (like heretics) nor (like Catholics) tolerated more than one (*On Monogamy*, 1.1–2.1; 15.1–3). He claimed apostolic precedents for Montanist fasts (*On Fasting*, 13 cf. *On Monogamy*, 3.11), which required no *perpetual* abstinence from foods (contrast Marcion, the Encratites and the Pythagoreans:[11] *On Fasting*, 15),[12] but occasional postponement of some.[13] If this came of false prophecy, and not of the Paraclete now active, he went on (as Catholics maintained it did), then perhaps they thought the Paraclete resided in Apicius and his culinary arts! (*On Fasting*, 12).[14] Montanism's opponents' revered guts and genitals, Tertullian observed acidly, while Montanists thought fasts should be more numerous than marriages! (*On Fasting*, 1).

As Montanists presented matters, God (and the Paraclete) revealed for a maturing Church fresh or revized discipline[15] (*On the Veiling of Virgins*, 1.5; 1.10 cf. *On Monogamy*, 2.1–3). Montanus, Prisc(ill)a and Maximilla had been Montanism's founder-prophets, their words prized by those who followed them (*Refutation*, 8.19 and 10.25 cf. Tertullian *On Fasting*, 2), and all three had imposed fasts (as Hippolytus and Apollonius reported, Eusebius *EH*, 5.18.2 [Apollonius]). In this, however, officers of Catholic congregations were side-lined and Christian writings differently interpreted by those who laid claim to the Spirit. Here was a classic dilemma about authority, charisma and tradition.

---

[11] Compare Apollonius of Tyana on his Pythagorean light, meatless diet of bread, vegetables (*lachana* – but for preference wild-grown herbs) and dried fruits (Philostratus, *Life*, 1.8; 2.37; 8.7; 18), in C. P. Jones, ed. and trans., *Philostratus: the Life of Apollonius of Tyana*, LCL, 2 vols (London, 2005).

[12] See e.g. Veronika E. Grimm, *From Feasting to Fasting: the Evolution of a Sin; Attitudes to Food in Late Antiquity* (London, 1996), 104–39 (on Tertullian) and A. Stewart-Sykes, 'Bread, Fish, Water and Wine: the Marcionite Menu and the Maintenance of Purity', in G. May and K. Greschat, eds, *Marcion und seine kirchengeschichtliche Wirkung/ Marcion and His Impact on Church History*, TU 130 (Berlin, 2002), 207–20. Compare Prisca's Saying: 'They are flesh, and they hate the flesh', in Tertullian, *On the Resurrection of the Flesh*, 11.2.

[13] Unlike some religious groups and philosophical schools, Montanists were not vegetarian and eschewed meat only during specific fasts. J. Haussleiter, *Der Vegetarismus in der Antike* (Berlin, 1935); C. Spencer, *The Heretic's Feast: a History of Vegetarianism* (Hanover, NH and London, 1995); Catherine Osborne, 'Ancient Vegetarianism', in J. Wilkins, D. Harvey, and M. Dobson, eds, *Food in Antiquity* (Exeter, 1995), 214–24.

[14] (Marcus Gavius) Apicius is the cognomen of writers of the *De re coquinaria, On the Art of Cooking*, which is the product of several centuries: J. Edwards, *The Roman Cookery of Apicius* (London, 1985).

[15] Trevett, *Montanism*, 105–19.

Having condemned Montanus, Priscilla and Maximilla for deceit, and for encouraging unacceptable diversity,[16] Hippolytus itemized fasts[17] (novel and unusual:[18] *Refutation*, 10.25.1), new feasts (probably commemorative and celebratory meals after a period of fasting[19]) and *xerophagy*.[20] This was a 'dry' diet, devoid of meat, wine or wine flavouring,[21] or succulent things such as fruits.[22] Finally came the reference to *rhaphanophagia* (cabbage/radish/'greens'–eating). Fasting was familiar to the ancient world,[23] the dry diet (*xerophagy*) was not unknown,[24] but the reference to *rhaphanophagy* has no parallel.

Hippolytus's African contemporary, Tertullian, acknowledged that there were special fasts, regular fasts kept for longer, and meatless days without succulent foods, fruit or wine (*On Fasting*, 1). Such 'dry' fasts

[16] 'Innovations', 'deviations' (Eusebius, *EH*, 4.27 [Apolinarius]), prophesying 'contrary to custom' and 'abnormally' (*EH*, 5.16.7 and 9 [Anonymous]) are early accusations preserved by Eusebius. Hippolytus decried their 'countless books' (*Refutation*, 8.19).

[17] *Nésteia*, like Latin *ieiunium*, signified complete abstention from food and drink, but the word might also encompass something less strict, involving certain *kinds* of food only. See e.g. *Acts of Thomas* 20 (bread, salt and water): trans. in G. Bornkamm, R. McL. Wilson, 'The Acts of the Holy Apostle Thomas', in E. Hennecke and W. Schneemelcher, eds, *New Testament Apocrypha* (London, 1974), 425–531, at 453.

[18] The word in the text is in fact an emendation for an evidently corrupt form.

[19] Stewart-Sykes's summary of his findings on Melito's *Peri Pascha* suggested that 'The Quartodecimans at Sardis gathered, fasting in memory of the sufferings of the Lord, before midnight of the fourteenth Nisan/Xanthikos ... and kept watch with their lamps lit. Around midnight they broke their fast and joined in a joyous table rite, with music and dancing, as they realised the presence of the risen Lord'. See A. Stewart-Sykes, *The Lamb's High Feast: Melito 'Peri Pascha' and the Quartodeciman Paschal Liturgy at Sardis, Vigiliae Christianae Suppl.* 42 (Leiden, 1998), 206, cf. 131.

[20] Tertullian contrasted it with a rich, carefully prepared diet (*On Fasting*, 15), comparing it with the 'angelic bread' which the Israelites complained of in the wilderness (*On Fasting*, 5). Canon 50 of the fourth-century Council of Laodicea described the Lent-long 'fast' as *xerophagy*: H. R. Percival, *The Seven Ecumenical Councils of the Undivided Church: Their Canons and Dogmatic Decrees* (Oxford, 1900), 123–60, esp. 155. *Xerophagy* is maintained still among Orthodox Christians: see Kallistos Ware and Mother Mary, trans., *The Lenten Triodion* (1977; rpt. London, 1994).

[21] McGowan, *Ascetic Eucharists*, 164, takes this to mean 'periods without drink'. Catholics saw no apostolic precedent for *xerophagy* (Tertullian, *On Fasting*, 9).

[22] In *On the Art of Cooking (de re coquinaria)* almost half of the recipes are for sauces. See B. Flower and E. Rosenbaum, *The Roman Cookery Book: a Critical Translation of* The Art of Cooking (London, 1958), 19. Montanist practice may show the first regularized Christian use of it. See Arbesmann, 'Fasting and Prophecy', 2 n. 9.

[23] In addition to the literature in n. 3 above, see too Wilkins, Harvey, and Dobson, *Food in Antiquity*, 218–38.

[24] This is not synonymous with the 'drying' diet especially advocated for some women, which might include taking little fluid, eating the 'dry' domesticated pigeon and no bitter greens.

occurred only two weeks a year, he observed, and then not on sabbaths and Lord's days (*On Fasting*, 15), but while 'greens' appeared like a final flourish in the *Refutation*'s list of accusations Tertullian never mentioned *rhaphanophagy*.

To Montanism's detractors, then, what might this further diversity and 'formidable culinary discipline'[25] have signified? I shall examine some possible answers which concur with other things known about Catholic (and *Roman* Catholic) views of Montanist peculiarity.

Montanist 'cabbage-eating'

The translation 'cabbage-diet'[26] may be misleading. *Rhaphanos* more usually indicates a radish but translators of *Refutation*, 8.19 have variously taken *xerophagy* to indicate dry diet, or the eating of 'roots' or 'parched food', and *rhaphanophagy* to mean vegetable food generally, or specifically cabbage or else 'repasts of radishes'.[27] Yet why should such a vegetable have figured at all, unless it carried connotations of diversity more threatening than a food-fad?

Firstly *rhaphanophagy* was not a synonym for vegetarianism, and so perhaps a pointer to heresies unspoken. Montanists probably avoided consecrated meat[28] but there is no evidence that vegetarianism was the means, just as eating 'greens' probably signified more to Hippolytus than a dietary fad or health-consciousness. Physicians knew of benefits from fasting, and from eating cabbage and radish.[29] Cabbage, its juice and especially the urine of one who had eaten it, were renowned for their health-giving and healing properties.[30] Indeed the simple bras-

---

25 McGowan, *Ascetic Eucharists*, 167.

26 G. W. H. Lampe, ed., *A Patristic Greek Lexicon* (Oxford, 1961), 1215.

27 F. Legge, *Philosophumena, or the Refutation of all Heresies* (London, 1921), 114. Cerrato similarly assumes the meaning to be vegetables and roots (*Hippolytus between East and West*, 213), while McGowan (*Ascetic Eucharists*, 167) refers to 'cabbage-eating'. Contrast J. H. Macmahon, *Hippolytus, Bishop of Rome, vol. 1: The Refutation of All Heresies* (Edinburgh, 1868), 325 n. 2.

28 More probably on the side of John the Seer of the Apocalypse than of the female prophet nicknamed 'Jezebel', who countenanced food 'sacrificed to idols' (Rev. 2: 29).

29 See Arbesmann, *Fasten*, 118–22 on the ancient schools of medicine.

30 Compare M. Porcius Cato, *On Agriculture*, 156.1 and 157.10. Cabbage types (Pliny, *Natural History*, 19.8.41) and their juice treated a huge range of ailments. The simple *brassica* and *brassica erratica* (wild cabbage) were common food and not for gourmets. Apicius mentioned only the smaller, more refined 'sprout' varieties (*De re coquinaria*, 3.9; 4.4; 5.5).

sica's greatest fan, Marcus Porcius Cato (234–149 BCE),[31] cited the wild cabbage (the *brassica erratica*) for the strongest purgative qualities *and for its use post-fasting*.[32] Radishes too (there were many varieties) were used as purgatives.[33] It seems to me unlikely, however, that Hippolytus ended with 'cabbage' his list of total fasts, feasts and dry fasts, by way of snide implication that 'they even legislate for throwing-up' (*Refutation*, 8.19).

I suspect that 'cabbage-eating' in the rhetoric of Hippolytus signals some deeper Montanist diversity. I shall consider briefly three possibilities. The first relates to quartodecimanism,[34] the second to the matter of prophesying/pseudo-prophesying, and the last to the sociology of Montanism.

Did rhaphanophagy *imply an accusation of quartodeciman practice?*

J. M. Ford wondered whether Montanism was a Jewish-Christian heresy,[35] the manifestation of an existing Jewish Christianity which was quartodeciman in practice, its fasts influenced by contemporary Judaism. *Refutation*, 8.19 sits between discussion of quartodecimanism (8.18)[36] and the Encratites (8.20) and not only were Montanists themselves quartodeciman in practice but theirs was a more rigorous, if not exceedingly rigorous, ascetic discipline. In *Refutation*, 8.19, Ford suggested, the reference would have been to dishes of radishes, as used in the Passover *seder*.[37]

Montanists were indeed accused of judaizing in abstaining from

31 W. D. Hooper, trans., *Marcus Porcius Cato On Agriculture. Marcus Terentius Varro On Agriculture*, LCL (London, 1934), esp. 156–7 (157.3 was quoted).

32 *On Agriculture*, 157.12. After Cato the humble brassica was scarcely mentioned, giving way to the gourmets' greens. It was food for the poor.

33 Neither the de-tox process nor the cabbage-soup diet (not far removed from Cato's recommendations) are new. To some the radish (associated with flatulence) was 'vulgar' but beneficial for many ailments: Pliny, *Natural History*, 20.10.12–13, trans. in W. H. S. Jones, *Pliny. Natural History*, LCL (London, 1951).

34 Quartodeciman ('fourteener') Christians celebrated Easter on the day of fourteenth Nisan, the Jewish Passover.

35 J. M. Ford, 'Was Montanism a Jewish-Christian Heresy?', *JEH* 17 (1966), 145–68.

36 B. Lohse, *Das Passafest der Quartadecimaner* (Gütersloh, 1953); Stuart G. Hall, ed., *Melito of Sardis: On Pascha and Fragments* (Oxford, 1979); idem, 'The Origins of Easter', *Studia Patristica* 15 (1984), 554–67; C. J. Talley, *The Origins of the Liturgical Year* (New York, 1986), 5–53; Paul F. Bradshaw 'The Origins of Easter', in Bradshaw and L. A. Hoffman, eds, *The Passover and Easter: Origins and History to Modern Times,* Two Liturgical Traditions, vol. 5 (Notre Dame, IN, 1999), 81–97 and (in the same volume) Israel J. Yuval, 'Easter and Passover as Early Jewish-Christian Dialogue', 98–124; Stewart-Sykes, *Lamb's High Feast*.

37 Ford, 'Jewish-Christian', 149.

certain foods and at certain times. Tertullian (*On Fasting*, 2 cf. Gal. 4: 10;
1 Tim. 4: 1–5) did not deny that Jewish practice might be justification
and precedent (*On Fasting*, 2.1; 13, cf. 14).[38] Yet the problem with Ford's
seder thesis is that details of Jewish and Christian rites[39] are un-
reconstructable for this early period,[40] with both religions developing
rapidly.[41] For Ford's suggestion to hold good, in the time of the *Refutation*, radish-eating would have had to signify immediately to Christians
the Passover ritual meal. Yet the details of the *seder* were probably not
yet fixed.

Tempting but tenuous must be the verdict on linking *rhaphanophagy*
with an accusation of quartodecimanism, though it is not improbable.
The strife sparked in the 190s between bishop Victor of Rome and the
quartodeciman Christians of the East still simmered (Eusebius, *EH*,
5.23–6).

Was rhaphanophagy *to do with prophesying?*

Dreams, revelations, visions and prophesyings run through the sources
about Montanism. *Xerophagy* attracted revelation and God's favour,
Tertullian argued (*On Fasting*, 6 and 12 and *On Patience*, 13) – as with
Daniel's consumption of pulses[42] and water (Dan. 1: 12; Tertullian, *On
Fasting*, 7 and 8 [on Dan. 16: 12] and 9).[43] Montanists *xerophagy* may
indeed point to belief in such efficacy.[44] While Catholic leaders

[38] Montanists' appeal to Scriptures and prophets, their observance of 'days' and 'months'
and abstinence from certain foods, smacked of Judaism (*On Fasting*, 2; 14; cf. Gal. 4: 10; 5: 1).
Peter J. Tomson, 'Jewish Food Laws in Early Christian Community Discourse', in A. Brenner
and J.-W. van Henten, eds, *Semeia 86: Food and Drink in the Biblical Worlds*, Society of Biblical
Literature (Atlanta, GA, 2001), 193–213.
[39] Maxwell E. Johnson, 'Preparation for Pascha? Lent in Christian Antiquity', in P. F.
Bradshaw and L. A. Hoffman, eds, *Passover and Easter: the Symbolic Structuring of Sacred Seasons*,
Two Liturgical Traditions, vol. 6 (Notre Dame, IN, 1999), 36–54.
[40] A. Stewart-Sykes and J. Newman, *Early Jewish Liturgy: a Sourcebook for Use by Students of
Early Christian Liturgy* (Cambridge, 2001), 3. So too Stewart-Sykes, *Lamb's High Feast*, 31–54.
[41] Bradshaw, 'Easter in Christian Tradition', 1–7; idem, 'The Origins of Easter', 81–97;
Hoffman 'The Passover Meal in Jewish Tradition', 8–26; Israel J. Yuval, 'Early Jewish-
Christian Dialogue', 98–124, all in Bradshaw and Hoffman, *Passover and Easter*.
[42] This was common and cook-shop fare: D. and P. Brothwell, *Food in Antiquity: a Survey
of the Diet of Early Peoples* (Baltimore, MD and London, 1998), 105–6.
[43] Daniel avoided pollution, eating 'seeds' (70 suggests pulse-eating/ospriophagy; Latin
has *legumina*). Daniel proved strong (1: 15), with knowledge of mysteries, visions and dreams
(1: 17; cf. Tertullian, *On Fasting*, 7 and 9, and *Bel and the Dragon*, 31–9).
[44] Robin Lane Fox, *Pagans and Christians in the Mediterranean World* (Harmondsworth,
1986), 374–418, at 396 assumes Montanist *xerophagy* served to elicit dreams and inspiration,
as in pagan cults and oracles.

dismissively likened Montanist practices to *superstitio*, and to the purificatory rites of a mystery cult or the *Magna Mater* (*On Fasting*, 2), the ministering Montanist was indeed promoting 'purification' according to Prisc[ill]a (Tertullian, *Exhortation to Chastity*, 10.5), for 'purification produces harmony'. Visions and auditions followed.

Montanists' fasts probably were understood to be purificatory, humbling believers and making them fitter for communing with the divine.[45] Their interest in a source such as 4 Ezra (Apocryphal II Esdr.) matched that concern (Vision 1.13.20; 3.29.2–4 cf. 6.1.1–3).[46] In 4 Ezra fasting brought understanding (cf. Vision 2.11.2). Prior to revelation only herbage ('flowers') was consumed and in texts concerning prophets such pre-revelation simple fare was a recurring theme.[47] So if Montanist *xerophagy* suggested to Hippolytus a stimulant for prophets of doubtful propriety (which is uncertain), then perhaps the reference to *rhaphanophagy* was also a barbed pointer in the same direction.

Dreams came of flatulence-inducing food (such as cabbage and radish) and gastromancy (divination from stomach sounds) was an ancient form. The art of the 'belly-speaker' too (cf. the *gynaika engastrimython* [LXX] of Endor in I Sam. 28: 7 – probably involving ventriloquism and not of the belly at all)[48] figured in prophesyings (e.g. the priestesses of Apollo and cf. Vulgate of I Sam. 28: 7; or Alexander of Abonuteichos). So was Hippolytus's last word on Montanist disciplinary diversity a slight on its prophesying? Tertullian hurled stomach-related accusations at the Catholics, who turned their cooks into priests and their own belchings into prophecy (*On Fasting*, 16). Yet it would be fanciful to conclude that Hippolytus mentioned eating 'greens' only by way of a Catholic jibe at 'flatulent' Montanist pseudo-prophesying.

---

45 See Arbesmann, 'Fasting and Prophecy', 3–25, 59.

46 Trevett, *Montanism*, 22–6 on interest in 4 Ezra.

47 Compare I Kings 19: 3–11 and Tertullian, *On Fasting*, 6 and 9; Hermas, *The Shepherd*, *Visions* 2.2.1; 3.1.2; *Ascension of Isaiah*, 2.7–11. See too Arbesmann, 'Fasting and Prophecy'.

48 See P. and M.-T. Nautin, eds, *Origene: Homélies sur Samuel*, SC 328 (Paris, 1986), on I Samuel 28. On Origen's homily concerning the woman of Endor and for the opposition of Eustathius (*De engastromytho contra Origenem*), see M. Simonetti, ed. and trans., *La maga di Endor*, Biblioteca Patristica 15 (Florence, 1989); Steven Connor, *Dumbstruck: a Cultural History of Ventriloquism* (Oxford, 2000), 75–101.

Was rhaphanophagy *about the 'common' origins of Montanists?*

In Rome as elsewhere the meatless *xerophagy* and regular eating of cabbage or radishes would have been akin to many people's basic fare. Perhaps, then, issues of 'class' lay behind the *Refutation's* portrayal of Montanism.[49]

Early detractors sneered at its origins in small places in a rural backwater (e.g. Eusebius, *EH*, 5.18.2 [Apollonius]).[50] They decried its revenue collectors, offerings, 'gifts', the making of loans and giving 'salaries' to those who promoted its teaching (Eusebius, *EH*, 5.18.2 and 4, 7, 11 [Apollonius]).[51] Its economics would have furthered democratization of authority and opportunity, opening ministry and leadership to those beyond the ranks of patrons and *episkopoi* with means to offer hospitality and gain respect in wider society (I Tim. 3: 2–7). Those empowered to travel and teach would have included women.[52]

With perhaps a hint of Roman snobbery, *Refutation*, 8.19 described Montanists as unreasoning, uncritical of their founders and writings, not deferring to those with critical skills. Catholics' promotion of the Church as *institution* would not have been served by the elevation of women, the ill-educated, or devotees of rural *proles*, whose tough discipline might be taken as a critique of societal norms and as a failure of obligation to family and state. If Hippolytus and others were concerned, it was perhaps because Montanism thrived despite its alleged 'barbarism' (Epiphanius, *Medicine Box*, 48.12.1–3).

In Hippolytus's reference to the poor man's vegetable, to 'those women' and lack of critical analysis, there may have been fear about a Christian group whose discipline was not just innovatory but also spelt identification with the un-honoured and the poor,[53] and which

49 Generally the upper classes found ascetic practices objectionable: Francis, *Subversive Virtue*, xvii, but 'to view the socially deviant aspects of asceticism as a "cry of the oppressed" is incorrect' (ibid.).
50 Trevett, *Montanism*, 15–55, on its rise in troubled times.
51 On posited conflict between rural (Montanist) and urban Christianities, W. H. C. Frend, 'Town and Countryside in Early Christianity', in Derek Baker, ed., *The Church in Town and Countryside*, SCH 16 (Oxford, 1979), 25–42; idem, 'Montanism: a Movement of Prophecy and Regional Identity in the Early Church', *BJRULM* 70 (1988), 25–34 and cf. D. H. Williams, 'The Origins of the Montanist Movement: a Sociological Analysis', *Religion* 19 (1989), 331–51; Dimitris J. Kyrtatis, *The Social Structure of the Early Christian Communities* (London, 1987), 94–5; Stewart-Sykes, 'Original Condemnation'.
52 See Trevett, 'Spiritual Authority'.
53 Fasting Montanists identified with the suffering and grieving (Tertullian, *On Fasting*, 13), and giving to the poor what was saved (cf. Hermas, *The Shepherd: Similitudes*, 5.3–5).

stemmed from disregard for the social norms of leadership. In 'the Church of the Spirit' 'bevies of bishops' might be by-passed (Tertullian, *On Modesty*, 21) and those not usually thought deserving elevated, and their injunctions obeyed.

Eating the simple brassica or radish root/leaves may have been known in Rome as a Montanist device, signalling quartodecimanism or 'prophecy'-inducing practices. Such possibilities cannot be ruled out. Yet perhaps for many Montanists (and other Christians, though probably not for Hippolytus himself) it would simply have reflected their daily existence,[54] and that may have been part of the problem, so far as Hippolytus was concerned. For notwithstanding other forms of unacceptable diversity which impacted on discipline (quartodecimanism and revelation-chasing), and which called into question existing Church officers' right to decision-making, the possibility remains that a critique of the social standing of the Montanists who harboured such things, and had even led the group, lay behind Hippolytus's jibe about 'greens'.[55]

Cardiff University

---

[54] McGowan, *Ascetic Eucharists*, 268–9: some Christians' and many Cynics' diet 'had an economic as well as a ritual aspect to it'; the early Christian ascetic meal pattern did not have 'an entirely élite social origin'. See too P. Garnsey's valuable study, *Food and Society in Classical Antiquity* (Cambridge, 1999).

[55] There is no anathematization in our source. Compare Tertullian, *On Fasting*, 1. The extant *Refutation* may be a draft, intended to become more detailed.

THE CANONS OF ANTIOCH*

by C. W. B. STEPHENS

THE death of Constantine in AD 337 brought forth a struggle between leading bishops of the eastern and western empire which proved crucially important in the development of ecclesiastical politics. Athanasius of Alexandria was one of several controversial bishops who, having been deposed during Constantine's reign, were re-instated by the new emperors after the change of regime which followed his death. As with other cases, Athanasius's restoration was fiercely contested within the Church, where many bishops felt that an imperial edict of repeal could not overrule a just and final deposition by an ecclesiastical synod. He therefore found himself quickly ejected from Alexandria by rival ecclesiastical powers. The numerous theological and polemical writings which Athanasius produced following this period became enormously influential. Historians still widely follow his version of events, seeing the struggle among bishops which his restoration sparked as centred on an 'Arian versus orthodox' theological battle, whereby western supporters of Athanasius fended off eastern attacks against the divinity of Christ. This approach is dangerous. Although the Alexandrian's writings are both detailed and prolific, they can hardly be called disinterested. Throughout his histories, bishops whom he attacks most fervently as Arians are precisely those who contested his own legitimacy as a bishop.

Our aim here is to show that, not Arian theology, but conflicting ideas about the use and structure of ecclesiastical authority, formed the basis of the struggles surrounding Athanasius. These conflicting ideas led to a rivalry between influential bishops which concerned how they would lead the Church and on what basis their authority rested. To support this view, we will seek to locate a particular list of ecclesiastical canons issued by important eastern bishops, the Canons of Antioch, to a date at the start of this struggle, between 337 and 340. Through rethinking the methodology by which historians date the conciliar

---

* This paper represents a summary of a series of detailed discussions in C. W. B Stephens, 'The Council of Antioch', forthcoming D.Phil. thesis through the University of Oxford. It aims to introduce a wider readership to the issues involved in those discussions.

sources for this period, we shall resist the claims of earlier scholars that these canons should be dated to the 320s. By bringing the canons into the later 330s, their character and content may then be used to demonstrate that, at the start of the post-Constantinian struggles, the major concern of leading eastern bishops was not an Arian desire to undermine western theology, but the concern to uphold conciliar authority over the personal ambitions of leading western bishops, particularly Athanasius and his advocates.

The canons of Antioch, twenty-five legal regulations issued by bishops at synod in that city, reflect contemporary concerns of the eastern Church.[1] Individual canons seek to resolve local disquiet (II, VII) and address wider issues, including the authority of metropolitan sees (IX) and the deposition of bishops (IV, XII, XI, XIV, XV). The canons were traditionally associated with the 'Dedication Council' of AD 341, called in Antioch by emperor Constantius to dedicate the Golden Church. However, the widely accepted dating for this collection now rests between AD 328 and 330, well before the death of Constantine, suggesting the canons cannot contribute to our understanding of the post-Constantinian struggles. However, we shall show here that there is no need to hold to this dating, and that the canons can be re-associated with the period after Constantine's death. The content of the canons can thus be used to assess eastern concerns at that time.

To understand the significance of associating the canons of Antioch with the Dedication Council, we must begin by examining that council. As author of the major sources for the period following Constantine's death, Athanasius shaped subsequent understanding of the Dedication Council as a single meeting which produced four Arian creeds.[2] Many now accept that even these creeds were not written at one synod.[3] The theological complexity and detail of the second creed would have rendered the first and fourth entirely unnecessary. Also, the uses of each, suggested internally and from wider sources,[4] indicate that

---

[1] For the canons in Greek and English, see J. Fulton, *Index Canonum* (New York, 1872).
[2] Athanasius, *De synodis*, 22–5.
[3] On the creeds, see J. N. D. Kelly, *Early Christian Creeds* (London, 1950), 263–74; R. P. C. Hanson, *The Search for the Christian Doctrine of God: the Arian Controversy, 318–381 AD* (Edinburgh, 1988; repr. 2000), 274–92; Wilhelm Schneemelcher, 'Die Kirchweihsynode von Antiochien 341', in A. Lippold and N. Himmelmann, eds, *Bonner Festgabe Johannes Straub zum 65. Geburtstag* (Bonn, 1977), 319–46; T. D. Barnes, *Athanasius and Constantius: Theology and Politics in the Constantinian Empire* (Cambridge, MA and London, 1993), 34–62.
[4] Most telling is Socrates, *Historia ecclesiastica*, 2.10 and 2.18 [hereafter: Socrates, *HE*],

Creed One originated from a smaller meeting before 341, and Creed Four from a meeting after the close of the larger council. In order to uphold Athanasian credibility, these smaller meetings have sometimes been represented as those of a subversive Arian group, determined to usurp the true faith.[5] However, the content of the creeds does not support this. The first offers little theologically and certainly does not oppose the creed of Nicaea, issued in AD 325 in order to address the Arian heresy. Creed Four openly denounced Arianism and was taken by eastern bishops to Constans, emperor of the West, as a peace offering in AD 342,[6] and again to Milan in AD 345 in the extended form of the 'Macrostich' creed.[7]

Although less famous, we cannot therefore regard these smaller meetings as any less representative of mainstream eastern thought than the meeting of 341. It is thus clear that official synodical meetings occurred frequently at this time, later becoming confused with the meeting of the dedication. The Dedication Council as it stands in the early historical sources, and even in much of modern scholarship, falsely subsumes most or all of these meetings under its name. That name should therefore be regarded as a broad concept representing a series of meetings taking place in the years from 337 to 342.

The frequency of these smaller meetings becomes evident from actions of the Antiochene bishops beyond their production of creeds. Following the death of Constantine, bishops whom he had expelled were called back to their sees by the new emperors. Athanasius, exiled to the West under Constantine in AD 335, was one such bishop. At this point, bishops collected in Antioch began to act. The council of Egypt convened by Athanasius in AD 338 described forceful attempts to ensure that he would be kept out of Alexandria, led by bishops in Antioch.[8] His opponents reiterated charges made at Athanasius's original deposition at the council of Tyre. As their pleas were ignored in the West, the Antiochenes elected Pistus as legitimate bishop of Alexandria,

which, despite presenting one unified synod, describes Creed One as an epistle sent well before the meeting which produced Creeds Two and Three.

5 On a selection of these, see C. J. Hefele, *A History of the Councils of the Church*, ed. and trans. W. R. Clark, 5 vols (Edinburgh, 1876–96), 2: 59–64.

6 Athanasius, *De Synodis*, 28; Socrates, *HE*, 2.18; Sozomen, *Historia ecclesiastica*, 3.10.3–6 [hereafter: Sozomen, *HE*].

7 Athanasius, *De Synodis*, 26.

8 Athanasius, *Apologia contra Arianos*, 3–19 [hereafter: *Apol. c. Ar.*].

with the support of Constantius.[9] When Pistus was quickly removed for his suspect ordination to the priesthood,[10] Eusebius of Emesa was chosen to replace him. When Eusebius refused the position, Gregory was elected, and accepted.[11]

In order to achieve all of this, at least four synodical meetings must have taken place in Antioch between the death of Constantine and the Dedication Council. Evidence of this appears throughout the Athanasian sources, yet his chronology in the *De Synodis* identifies at Antioch only the one Dedication Council. In following Athanasius's pattern, the early historians of the Church failed to give full credit to the various synods, associating them all with the Dedication Council.[12] This led to confusions concerning the date of Gregory's election to Alexandria, an association of that election with the creation of the Dedication Council creeds, the association of all four creeds themselves with one single meeting, and even to the forgetting of Pistus altogether.[13]

Included in this chronological uncertainty appear the canons of Antioch. Socrates states that canons were created and used at Antioch in the period following 337, placing them within the same body of synodical action as the Dedication Council, yet he provides two different points for their composition. Firstly, they emerge at the end of the Dedication Council meeting, after the creeds.[14] This identification, however, exists alongside a wrongful positioning of Gregory's election, which had taken place before that council. It is thus likely that the canons appeared before this. Indeed, the start of Socrates' discussion of the Dedication Council joins Sozomen's in describing the bishops present as citing canons they had already produced. These canons apparently justified even the election of Eusebius of Emesa. As the content of the fourth canon from our corpus of 25 is mentioned within this discussion as providing that justification, condemning Athanasius for resuming his duties without first being officially restored, the collection of Antioch is evidently that being discussed.[15]

Schwartz believed that the earliest Greek *Corpus canonum* attributed

9   *Epistula encyclica*, 6.1; *Apol. c. Ar.*, 3.5–7, 19.4–5.
10 Pistus was ordained by Secundus of Ptolemais, excommunicated at Nicaea. Julius of Rome's objection is clear in *Apol. c. Ar.*, 24.
11 Socrates, *HE*, 2.8–10.
12 Athanasius, *De Synodis*, 22–5; Socrates, *HE*, 2.8–10; Sozomen, *HE*, 3.5–6.
13 Socrates, *HE*, 2.7–10; Sozomen, *HE*, 3.5–6.
14 Socrates, *HE*, 2.10.
15 Ibid., 2.8; Sozomen, *HE*, 3.5.

the twenty-five canons to the Dedication Council itself, yet there is no direct proof of this.[16] Even later collections simply define the canons as those of a council of Antioch with no special name.[17] Likewise, Palladius's *Dialogus* concerning John Chrysostom shows that by the turn of the fifth century his sources still attributed the canons to a meeting of just forty bishops.[18] The Dedication Council association clearly came later than the council itself, just as the historical sources later subsumed other synodical actions of 337 to 342 within it.

The situation therefore stands thus: meetings of an official enough nature to produce the canons of Antioch were taking place there between the death of Constantine and AD 342, soon all wrongly considered part of the Dedication Council; canons were produced and known in Antioch, associated with the bishops who led the Dedication Council; the canons of Antioch were in fact used before the elections of Eusebius and Gregory, before the Dedication Council met; the canons appeared in collections without the Dedication Council name into the fifth century. It is therefore logical to assume the canons were the product of a subsumed synod from the period from 337 to 340, forming a part of the synodical attempts in Antioch to stop Athanasius returning to power in Alexandria after the death of Constantine. Although later collections of canons would indeed come to identify the Antiochene corpus with the Dedication Council itself,[19] recognizing the Dedication Council name as a broader body in the sources than just a single meeting easily allows us to justify this association while also holding that the canons were produced prior to AD 341.

This broader conception of the Dedication Council has been ignored in scholarship concerning the canons. Efforts have centred upon claims that the canons cannot have originated at the meeting of 341, but have neglected to ask whether they received the Dedication Council association through originating at one of the smaller synods it subsumed. Scholars have thus sought to disassociate the Dedication Council entirely from the canons of Antioch, placing the canons well before AD 337. This dating of the canons back to Constantine's lifetime resulted from works by the Ballerini brothers, Schwartz, Chadwick and

---

[16] Eduard Schwartz, *Die Kanonessammlungen der alten Reichskirche* (Berlin, 1936), 33.

[17] The Latin *Isidore*, for example. C. H. Turner, *Ecclesiae Occidentalis Monumenta Iuris Antiquissima*, 2 vols (Oxford, 1899–1939), [hereafter: Turner, *EOMIA*].

[18] *Dialogus*, 31.

[19] Turner, *EOMIA*, 2: 216–320.

others, who used signatures recorded on several Latin and Syriac manuscripts to identify the bishops present at the creation of the corpus.[20] The Ballerini showed that a group of just over thirty bishops created the canons, not the ninety or ninety-seven who attended the Dedication Council. Similarly, the appearance on the subscription lists of Eusebius of Caesarea, Jacob of Nisibis, Theodotus of Laodicea, and Anatolius of Emesa, all of whom died before the Dedication Council, made associating the two impossible.

Following Schwartz, modern scholarship located the production of the canons at a synod of Antioch, written to by Constantine,[21] which replaced Eustathius, recently deposed from that see. The problems with this suggestion are numerous. Notably, Constantine's letter addresses Aetius of Lydda, who is not actually present in the subscription lists of the canons. Chadwick suggested solving this problem by shifting the canons to the earlier synod which actually deposed Eustathius.[22] However, the reluctance of Eusebius of Caesarea to get involved in that deposition and replacement, expressed clearly in a letter correspondence he himself reports,[23] shows he cannot have been present at meetings both of and directly after the deposition, which wrongly assumed he would take up Eustathius's place in the Antiochene see. If the synod which deposed Eustathius was the synod which produced the canons, the subscription lists must be false, since Eusebius heads them all. More generally, the anti-Athanasian canons appear to have little relevance to Eustathian debates of the later 320s,[24] and there is no external evidence to suggest that canons were produced in Antioch at this point.

The broader understanding of the Dedication Council now becomes

---

[20] Pietro and Girolamo Ballerini, *Opera Sancti Leonis Magni*, 9 vols (Venice, 1753–57), 3: xxv. E. Schwartz, *Gesammelte Schriften*, 5 vols (Berlin, 1938–63), 3: 215–26. Henry Chadwick, 'The Fall of Eustathius of Antioch', *Journal of Theological Studies* 49 (1948), 27–35. Hamilton Hess, *The Canons of the Council of Sardica* (Oxford, 1958), 145–50. On the Syriac MSS, Friedrich Schulthess, 'Die syrischen Kanones der Synoden von Nicaea bis Chalcedon', *Abhandlungen der Königlichen Gesellschaft der Wissenschaften zu Göttingen. Philologisch-Historische Klasse* 10 (Berlin, 1908). On the Latin, Turner, *EOMIA*.

[21] Eusebius of Caesarea, *Vita Constantini*, 3.62[hereafter: *VC*]. G. Bardy, 'Antioche (Concile et Canons d')', in R. Naz, ed., *Dictionnaire de Droit Canonique*, 7 vols (Paris, 1935–67), 1: cols 589–98 is an important example which summarizes the scholarly debates and consensus following Schwartz but prior to the revisions of Chadwick.

[22] Chadwick, 'Fall of Eustathius', 34–5.

[23] *VC*, 3.60–3.

[24] Summaries and bibliographies of the issues surrounding the deposition of Eustathius can be found in Chadwick, 'Fall of Eustathius', and in R. P. C. Hanson, *Search for the Christian Doctrine*.

particularly significant. We have argued that one can maintain an association of the canons of Antioch with the Dedication Council even if the canons were produced before AD 341, the date of that meeting. Consequently, arguments which suggest that the group of bishops creating the canons was not identical to that which attended the Dedication Council cannot compel us to disassociate the two events completely. If the canons were produced between 337 and 340, a different group is to be expected from the dedication meeting. Up to 338, Eusebius, Jacob, and Anatolius were still in their sees. Although Theodotus of Laodicea was probably replaced by George by the time of the council of Tyre, his is one of the most questionable appearances on the lists. Schwartz's reconstruction of the oldest Syriac manuscript, from a much later copy, not the original, is the only document which mentions him.[25] None of the subscription lists are Greek originals. Schwartz's Syriac sources were late translations, dating well into the sixth century. Alongside the Latin lists, they are so conflicting that none are authoritative. They cannot oppose our stating confidently that the canons of Antioch were produced between the death of Constantine and the Dedication Council, before the attempted election of Eusebius of Emesa.

* * *

It thus remains to explain the significance of associating the canons of Antioch with the period from AD 337 to 340. By bringing them into the same body of Antiochene synodical action as the Dedication Council, they help to indicate the nature of that action more generally. The content of the canons confirms that they acted as part of a direct attack upon Athanasius after his return from exile. Canon four provides no chance of appeal for bishops who resume their duties before synodical restoration; canon eleven deposes bishops who approach the emperor without the consent of their metropolitan; canon twelve states that bishops must submit to the judgement of a greater synod if they protest against their deposition; canon fourteen states that bishops of a neighbouring province are to be brought to synod if there is a disagreement concerning a deposition; canon fifteen states that a unanimous deposition is never to be judged again. All of these represent condemnations of aspects of Athanasius's position after imperial restoration.

---

25 Schwartz, *Gesammelte Schriften*, 3: 220.

Prior to the earlier dating of the canons, scholars including Tillemont, Hefele, Hammond, Bright, Neale and Fulton recognized this, labelling them 'a new decree of deposition against Athanasius',[26] consciously using and expanding upon similar, ancient arguments made by Palladius, Innocent I, Socrates and Sozomen.[27] Crucially, this undeniable correspondence of concern was not addressed by those who led and who followed the trend of dating the canons before Athanasius's exile. Indeed, the matter is still consistently ignored, leaving a gaping hole in such work and greater evidence against such earlier dating.

Athanasius represented this attack upon himself and his acceptance in the West as one by 'Christ's foes'[28] whose Arian designs sought to undermine the council of Nicaea. The content of the canons, however, highlights clear eastern support of Nicene decisions. Canon one describes the Nicene meeting as holy and great, while canon twenty-one reiterates exactly the legislation against the translation of bishops in canon fifteen of the Nicene corpus. Eastern opposition was to Athanasius, not Nicaea. Declaring warm acceptance of the council which Athanasius accused them of subverting, and associated theologically only with creeds which condemn Arianism as defined in the Nicene anathemas, the determination of these eastern bishops to assure the continued exile of Athanasius must be understood in terms other than the Arian wickedness he himself suggests.

The canonical list makes the nature of eastern objections clear. Athanasius was regarded as having no right to re-enter Alexandria or to be protected by Rome after a legitimate and legally final deposition for serious, violent crimes. The objections are legally justified, based upon previous law and custom. By being welcomed back outside the proper synodical processes, Athanasius undermined the whole system of synodical action by which the easterns lived. The canons of Antioch continually play down the role of individual bishops against the will of synods. Athanasius, welcomed back under the protection of Rome, ignored the ruling of the council which had deposed him and the authority of the eastern bishops who upheld its decision.

---

[26] Fulton, *Index Canonum*, 63. S. Le Nain de Tillemont, *The History of the Arians and the Council of Nice*, trans. T. Deacon, 2 vols (London, 1721), 1: 102; Hefele, *History of the Councils*, 2: 75; W. A. Hammond, *The Definitions of the Faith and Canons of Discipline of the Six Ecumenical Councils* (Oxford, 1843), 153–4; W. Bright, *The Age of the Fathers*, 2 vols (London, 1903), 1: 173; J. M. Neale, *A History of the Holy Eastern Church: the Patriarchate of Antioch* (London, 1873), 108.

[27] Palladius, *Dialogus*, 30–1; Sozomen, *HE*, 3.5; 8.26; Socrates, *HE*, 2.8.

[28] *De synodis*, 20.

Much of the scholarship concerning this period continues to follow Athanasius's notion of an Arian conspiracy against him. Frend, as one example among many, described the whole period from 337 to 346 as characterized by eastern, 'anti-Nicene' attacks of the Alexandrian.[29] Yet the canons of Antioch show that objecting to Athanasius's return to Africa required no objection to Nicaea. Indeed, it illustrated no theological stance at all, unlike resistance to Marcellus of Ankyra, who was explicitly opposed during this time in the East for Sabellianism and heretical eschatology. At no point during his return from exile do eastern synods criticize, or even mention, Athanasian theology. Athanasius's presentation of this secret agenda, which shapes modern-day understandings of the whole eastern Church following Constantine's death, is not demonstrated outside his own, self-interested theorizing. It is only in Athanasius's own histories that theological differences are mentioned. The Antiochene bishops were concerned for the upholding of legal, not theological, tenets which protected the legitimate decisions of past councils over the assumed rights of individuals who chose to flout conciliar authority. Athanasius's return and subsequent refuge in Rome was symbolic of a western drive to give power to particular bishops, particularly Julius of Rome, over and above the general consensus of conciliar decisions. The Antiochene bishops were understandably affronted by Julius's refusal to submit to the will of previous synodical decisions, the basis of eastern authority, by upholding his own judicial rights.[30] This, not wicked Arianism, motivated anti-Athanasian assaults. It becomes obvious that the basis of the split concerning the privileges of individuals was Rome's high regard of itself. Western willingness to accept Julius's growing pretensions alongside the refusal of powerful eastern bishops to do so provided a dichotomy ripe for exploitation by Athanasius in order to gain strong western support against his eastern opponents.

Arguments concerning ecclesiastical authority were heightened further when the canons of the western council of Sardica, held in AD 343, upheld the right of individual bishops to appeal against deposition and the particular power of Julius of Rome in such matters. Directly opposing the eastern focus upon conciliar authority, this legislation made Rome, the defender of Athanasius after his return from exile,

[29] W. H. C. Frend, *The Early Church* (London, 2003), 152.
[30] Athanasius, *Apol. c. Ar.*, 20, 22; *Historia Arianorum*, 11.

supreme judge over all. These claims provide the foundation for the growing pretensions of that see into the Middle Ages. Significantly, the council decided not to issue a creed. The dispute the bishops identified at Sardica was not theological.

This brief summary must lead to the conclusion that canon law was of great importance to debates concerning ecclesiastical authority in the fourth century. By using canon law as an initial reaction to the matter of Athanasius's illegal restoration, the bishops at Antioch display the significance they attached to that medium. The canons of Sardica, in responding to those of Antioch, show that those in the West regarded canon law as being of equal importance within debates. It was clearly regarded by all as the means by which the divided Church could be brought to order. Canon law, therefore, should be held as providing as useful a record of the desires and intentions of the early bishops as the theological creeds they produced.

However, alongside this great reliance upon canon law, the failure of the West to submit to Antioch alongside the appearance of the Sardican canons must lead us to the conclusion that the power of canon law at this time was far from absolute. The council of Sardica simply ignored legitimate legal claims made against Rome's restoration of Athanasius. Indeed, it created further canons which legitimized such illegality, even granting Julius the right to repeat his actions.[31] The canons of Antioch represent a major stand against this move away from conciliar democracy towards western hierarchical ecclesiology. The existence of the Sardican canons shows that western refusal to accept the canons of Antioch did not display a lesser opinion of canon law as such. Even Julius of Rome, desiring every privilege for his see, clearly felt the need to have his actions backed up by canonical justification. What western rejection of the canons of Antioch does show is that powerful bishops only obeyed those canons that they wished to adhere to. Just as Sardica ignored the twenty-five Antiochene canons, the eastern bishops ignored the Sardican legislation, continuing to recognize Gregory as Athanasius's replacement after 343.

This evidence suggests that, in this early period, the effectiveness of canon law could be relied upon only where the power of its issuers was unquestioned. While the bishops of East and West, alongside their

---

[31] L. W. Barnard, *The Council of Serdica 343 AD* (Sofia, 1983), 113; H. Hess, *The Early Development of Canon Law and the Council of Sardica* (Oxford, 2002), 179–200.

emperors, questioned the legitimacy of their counterparts, the canon law each issued would not be followed outside their own spheres of control. Thus, while Athanasius maintained the favour of Rome, he and Gregory could simultaneously claim Alexandria as their own, both with canonical justification. Only when a general council met could obedience to certain laws be expected of all, since the authority of leaders from all areas was represented. This happened under Constantine at Nicaea and is clear in canon one of the council of Chalcedon in AD 451, which calls for all to respect the canonical decisions of the past councils.

Bringing the canons of Antioch into the late 330s allows us to see the following period as one in which East and West battled for fundamentally different systems of Church authority through issuing rival collections of canon law. As we have seen, the implications of this concerning a failure of canon law to bring any binding support, independent of the issuing bishops' own influence, to any cause were far-reaching. While no supreme champion of the Church existed to uphold one legal standpoint, factional struggles between rivalling bishops ensued, neither upholding the legal directives of the others. Perhaps more significant, though, are implications regarding the nature of the post-Constantinian feuds. Nicaea was not under attack, nor was Athanasius's theology. The canons show that the struggles centred on concerns regarding the authority of Rome and her powerful supporters over and against prior conciliar consensus. In countering the pretensions of these individuals, the canons also betray a sharp divide between the whole outlook of the eastern and western bishops at this point. By re-dating the canons of Antioch, we call for a vital reassessment of the whole period following Constantine's death. Athanasius's own account is undermined and can no longer provide a reliable basis for historical understanding of his treatment. The attacks upon Athanasius when he returned from his first exile cannot be interpreted as anti-Nicene.

Christ Church, University of Oxford

IMPERIAL LAW OR COUNCILS OF THE CHURCH? THEODOSIUS I AND THE IMPOSITION OF DOCTRINAL UNIFORMITY

by E. D. HUNT

O N 27 February 380, the emperor Theodosius – newly elevated the previous year to take control of the East amid the political and military turmoil unleashed by the debacle at Adrianople – addressed an edict from his current headquarters at Thessalonica to the people of Constantinople. The text famously proclaimed the religion to be followed by 'all the peoples' who fell under his rule as that handed down at Rome from the apostle Peter, now maintained by the *pontifex* Damasus and bishop Peter of Alexandria, 'that is, . . . we should believe in the single godhead of Father, Son and Holy Spirit, in equal majesty and holy trinity'. Those who subscribed to this doctrine, Theodosius ordered, were to 'embrace the name of Catholic Christians', while all the rest were branded heretics, whose places of assembly were denied the name of churches, and who would be smitten 'first by divine vengeance, and afterwards by the retribution of our own punishment, which we shall enact in accordance with the judgement of Heaven'.[1]

Traditional interpretations have been prone to exaggerate the import of this pronouncement of Theodosius. Dubbed as 'one of the most significant documents in European history',[2] it has been seen to represent the turning-point at which the Constantinian legacy of imperial deference to the Church's conciliar structures in determining the true faith finally yielded to the decisive assertion of the emperor's control of the process. Right doctrine was as the emperor determined and promulgated by law, and no longer the product of episcopal deliberation: Theodosius by imperial *fiat* made the definition of Catholic orthodoxy his own and imposed it on all his Christian subjects in the name of God's judgement.[3]

---

[1] *Theodosian Code*, 16.1.2 (ed. T. Mommsen, *Theodosiani libri XVI* [Berlin, 1905], 833); cf. Sozomen, *Historia ecclesiastica*, 7.4.5–6 (ed. J. Bidez and G. C. Hansen, Die griechischen christlichen Schriftsteller der ersten drei Jahrhunderte NF 4 [Berlin 1995], 305) [hereafter: Sozomen, *HE* and GCS].

[2] S. Williams and G. Friell, *Theodosius: the Empire at Bay* (London, 1994), 53.

[3] The view of W. Ensslin, *Die Religionspolitik des Kaisers Theodosius des Großen* (Munich,

There is much to be said by way of *caveat* here. Theodosius did not issue legal utterances in magnificent isolation. However assiduously late Roman rulers cultivated the persona of the remote and majestic potentate whose pronouncements carried a sacred authority all their own, these were in fact the outcome of court networks of petition, negotiation and debate largely hidden from view: 'although dirigiste in its language, imperial general law was in fact more often negotiated than imposed'.[4] It is substantially misleading, then, to picture Theodosius in some sort of vacuum, imposing his own view of right doctrine on subjects forced to submit to the imperial will: a properly rounded understanding of the edict would need, for example, to take account of the interests of the court assembling around Theodosius as he settled in the East, not least those among the eastern bishops who were first to gain the emperor's ear.[5]

Such limitations on the emperor's free rein were in any case evident when Theodosius finally entered Constantinople later in the year (24 November 380), and was quickly forced to descend to practical realities from the Olympian heights of vengeance and retribution scaled in his February edict. Now the issue of the rightful possession of churches, and the exclusion of those who did not conform to the western-style 'catholic' label identified by his recent edict, confronted him directly.

1953), 23–8, somewhat modified by A. M. Ritter, *Das Konzil von Konstantinopel und sein Symbol* (Göttingen, 1965), 221–8; cf. also N. Q. King, *The Emperor Theodosius and the Establishment of Christianity* (London, 1961), 28–31. For other discussions, e.g. P. Barceló and G. Gottlieb, 'Das Glaubensedikt des Kaisers Theodosius vom 27 Februar 380', in K. Dietz, D. Hennig, and H. Kaletsch, eds, *Klassisches Altertum, Spätantike und frühes Christentum* (Würzburg, 1993), 409–23; J. Gaudemet, 'L'édit de Thessalonique: police locale ou déclaration de principe?', in H. W. Pleket and A. Verhoogt, eds, *Aspects of the Fourth Century AD* (Leiden, 1997), 43–51; R. M. Errington, 'Christian Accounts of the Religious Legislation of Theodosius I', *Klio* 79 (1997), 398–443, at 411–16 (offering a more restricted interpretation aimed specifically at Constantinople), with idem 'Church and State in the First Years of Theodosius I', *Chiron* 27 (1997), 21–72, at 36–7; H. Leppin, *Theodosius der Große* (Darmstadt, 2003), 71–3.
4 J. Harries, *Law and Empire in Late Antiquity* (Cambridge, 1999), 36. For procedures, see J. Matthews, *Laying Down the Law* (New Haven, CT, and London, 2000), 171–80. Petitioners flocking to Theodosius at Thessalonica: Zosimus, *New History*, 4.25.1.
5 Principally Acholius of Thessalonica, whose influence (denied by Ensslin) has been reasserted by more recent studies, e.g. N. McLynn, *Ambrose of Milan: Church and Court in a Christian Capital* (Berkeley, CA, 1994), 107–8; Errington, 'Church and State', 37. For the nature of the court, see the classic account of J. Matthews, *Western Aristocracies and Imperial Court A.D. 364–425* (Oxford, 1975), 128–45, and further R. Lizzi Testa, 'La politica religiosa di Teodosio I', *Rendiconti dell'accademia nazionale dei Lincei (classe di Scienze morali, storiche e filologiche)*, ser. 9, vol. 7 (1996), 323–61.

How was God's punishment, of which he had proclaimed himself the agent, to be wielded against eastern Church leaders who held to a different orthodoxy formulated and agreed by past conciliar gatherings, and endorsed by Theodosius' imperial predecessors? According to Gregory of Nazianzus, a close participant in the events of Theodosius's *adventus* into Constantinople, the emperor allowed caution to temper his resolve, 'thinking it lawful to persuade, not to compel';[6] while to the Church historians Theodosius's priority was not a show of force, but the peace and harmony of the churches. Socrates (largely followed by Sozomen) has him first summoning bishop Demophilus of Constantinople and offering him the opportunity to unite the divided congregations by subscribing to the doctrine of the 'council of Nicaea'; but the bishop rejected compliance, preferring instead to lead his people outside the city walls within only three days of Theodosius's arrival.[7] Thus it was the defiant withdrawal of Demophilus which could be seen to have brought about the handover of Constantinople's churches to the Nicene congregation, and not the direct intervention of imperial force.

Although the transfer is unlikely to have been as smooth and bloodless as this Theodosian tradition implies – witness Gregory's own account of his tense installation in the presence of the emperor in the Apostles' Church, which had to be protected for the occasion from all manner of hostile crowds by a troop of soldiers, 'the picture of a town captured by force'[8] – nonetheless the fact that Theodosius should be presented as addressing Demophilus with a call to peace and unity in the Church shows a marked departure from the uncompromising rhetoric of right belief enshrined in the edict addressed to Constantinople ten months previously. It may also be significant (if the Church historians have preserved the details correctly) that the emperor now based his appeal for unity on acceptance of the doctrine ascribed to the council of Nicaea, and not – as in the edict – solely by reference to the apostolic tradition from Peter as proclaimed by the bishops of Rome and Alexandria: deferring to conciliar authority, even to so contentious

---

6 Greg. Naz. *Poems* 2.1.11 (*Autobiography*), 1293–4 (ed. André Tuilier, Guillaume Bady, and Jean Bernardi, *Saint Grégoire de Nazianze: Oeuvres Poétiques,* vol. 1.1 [Paris, 2004], 110); cf. 1304 'unwritten law of persuasion'. Gregory had been called to lead the Nicene community in Constantinople.
7 Socrates, *Historia ecclesiastica,* 5.7.3–11 [hereafter: Socrates, *HE*] (ed. G. C. Hansen, GCS NF 1 [Berlin, 1995], 278–9); cf. Sozomen, *HE,* 7.5.5–7 (GCS NF 4, 306–7).
8 *Autobiography,* 1325–41.

a legacy as had come to surround Nicaea, was more likely to strike positive chords to the ears of an eastern Church audience than legislating in
threatening tones for an orthodoxy openly derived from the claims of
the see of Rome.

A similar shift of emphasis is evident from further imperial legislation of 10 January 381, some six weeks after Theodosius' arrival in
Constantinople.[9] As in the Thessalonica edict, the emperor pronounced
upon the lawful possession of the churches. He again prescribed that
churches 'the world over' were to be handed over to the proponents of
Catholic orthodoxy, but in this case the preserved text offers considerably more detail than that of February 380: not only are named heretical groups identified ('Photinians, Arians and Eunomians'), but a
summary statement of what is approved belief forms part of the law
itself, and the penalty to be meted out to dissenters is expressly spelt out
– excluded 'from the threshold of all the churches' and banned from
assembling within the cities, they are to be banished beyond the walls.
The fate of Demophilus and his congregation at Constantinople thus
set the pattern further afield for the official outlawing of those who
disclaimed the emperor's version of the truth faith. Yet the Catholic
orthodoxy ordained by Theodosius was now no longer defined by
reference to Rome's Petrine authority as it had been in Thessalonica,
but by what had been transmitted from the council of Nicaea (the same
terms with which the emperor had challenged Demophilus): no less
than three times in the course of this law the *Nicaena fides* is invoked as
the benchmark of true religion. Moreover the 'indivisible substance' of
the Trinity included in the law's summary of the creed is here glossed
for a Greek-speaking audience by the characteristically Nicene term
ousia. Thus, although the emperor continues to use legislation to
pronounce on right belief, he has now become the mouthpiece of the
Church's collective wisdom perceived as handed down from the
bishops at Nicaea.

To see Theodosius reverting from more authoritarian models of
orthodoxy to a recognition of the contribution which the deliberation
of bishops had made to the process of defining the faith helps to
provide a setting for his summoning the council of Constantinople –
the most significant ecclesiastical occasion of his reign, and one which

[9] *Theodosian Code*, 16.5.6, with Errington, 'Church and State', 48–51 (who is concerned
to limit the scope of the law to Illyricum).

would come to be seen as second only to Nicaea in the annals of Church councils. That a ruler newly arrived in the eastern empire should issue invitations to bishops to settle pressing ecclesiastical matters directly recalled the example of Constantine and the bishops at Nicaea; and it was Constantine's successor Constantius who had repeatedly gathered bishops together around the empire to arrive at an agreed formula of belief, culminating with the last 'imperial' council at Constantinople in January 360.[10] We know of no further imperially sponsored council[11] until the bishops assembled by Theodosius gathered in Constantinople in May 381. If the emperor was looking for a pretext for this revival of Constantinian precedent, he could claim the need for ecclesiastical endorsement of his earlier installation of Gregory of Nazianzus to take charge of the church in Constantinople: as far away as Rome bishop Damasus knew that a council was being summoned to Constantinople which would have the choice of a new bishop for the eastern capital high on its agenda; and the first act of the council would indeed be the formal recognition of Gregory on his episcopal throne.[12]

With benefit of hindsight, it would be easy to portray Theodosius's summons of bishops to Constantinople as intended to be nothing more than a conciliar rubber-stamp for the orthodoxy which he had already prescribed by law, 'for the confirmation of the Nicene faith'.[13] But the bishops themselves in their final address to the emperor were careful to credit him with the renewal of their 'common mind',[14] and it does not seem unreasonable that Theodosius should have genuinely seen an imperial gathering of bishops, in the tradition of his Constantinian predecessors, as a means of settling ecclesiastical differences and bringing doctrinal harmony to the churches in his empire – to say nothing of enhancing the status of his regime at a time of political recovery from the Gothic disaster. As successful diplomacy on the Gothic front was

[10] As summarized by T. D. Barnes, *Athanasius and Constantius: Theology and Politics in the Constantinian Empire* (Cambridge, MA and London, 1993), 144–9.

[11] With the possible exception of Valens's summons of bishops to Nicomedia in 366 to force the deposition of Eleusius of Cyzicus: Socrates, *HE*, 4.6.4–5.

[12] Greg. Naz. *Autobiography*, 1525–45, with Socrates, *HE*, 5.8.1, Sozomen, *HE*, 7.7.1 'to elect a bishop for Constantinople'; cf. Damasus, *Letter* 5 (to Acholius and other bishops in Macedonia), PL 13, 365–9. On the council of Constantinople Ritter, *Konzil*, remains standard, along with *Theologische Realenzyclopädie* 19 (1990), 518–24; cf. also Errington, 'Church and State', 41–66, Leppin, *Theodosius*, 76–80.

[13] Socrates, *HE*, 5.8.1 (GCS NF 1, 279).

[14] 'homonoia': on this document, see below, 63–4.

celebrated with the defection of a once-prominent barbarian leader, Constantinople was also set to become the stage for a conspicuous display of episcopal harmony achieved under the emperor's patronage.[15] But not all those who came were willing to join in the party. Among the bishops who received the emperor's invitation were a group of thirty-six from the hinterland of the capital, the Hellespont area to the north and west of Asia Minor, led by Eleusius of Cyzicus and his colleague from Lampsacus. They had been the core of the old 'homoiousian' presence in this region which led the reaction against the *homoian* establishment in the years following Julian's amnesty permitting them to return to their sees: the fact that they had at that time sent envoys to the West and accepted letters of communion from the bishop of Rome suggested a potential willingness to embrace the Nicene formula, and their consent now at Constantinople would be a suitable advertisement for the ecclesiastical harmony generated by the council at the prompting of Theodosius. The emperor, in company with the rest of the bishops, accordingly urged them to fall into line, but to no avail, and the thirty-six left the council unreconciled to the Nicene majority.[16]

With the departure of Eleusius and his companions, an opportunity lost of welcoming dissidents into the fold of unity, the personnel of the council of Constantinople in practice left little scope for disagreement on matters of doctrine: the bishops who stayed to participate in the deliberations in the summer of 381 could fairly be described as belonging to the emperor's 'own faith', and the endorsement of Nicene orthodoxy looks like a foregone conclusion.[17] This may account for Theodosius's apparent lack of involvement in the proceedings, which is in marked contrast to the 'hands-on' role of Constantine in the debates at Nicaea, or the direct engagement of Constantius in the episcopal creed-making of the years from 359 to 360. Apart from an opening reception for the bishops in the imperial residence in Constantinople

---

[15] On hints of conciliation in dealings with the Goths at the time of Athanaric's reception in Constantinople, i.e. January 381, see R. M. Errington, 'Theodosius and the Goths', *Chiron* 26 (1996), 1–27, at 9–13 (on the basis of Themistius, *Oration* 15, 190c–191a); by then plans for the council were under way, idem 'Church and State', 42–4.

[16] Socrates, *HE*, 5.8.5–10, Sozomen, *HE*, 7.7.2–5, identifying them now as 'Macedonianists', followers of a previous bishop of Constantinople. The sticking-point was their objection to the full inclusion of the Holy Spirit in the Godhead, hence also 'Pneumatomachians': see further Ritter, *Konzil*, 68–85 (who links the episode with Greg. Naz.'s complaints about theological divisions among the bishops, *Autobiography*, 1703–44).

[17] Socrates, *HE*, 5.8.1 'bishops of his own faith'; cf. Errington, 'Church and State', 54 ('select group of guaranteed orthodox bishops').

there is no indication that Theodosius played any part in their counsels: once the formalities of welcome were concluded, unlike Constantine at Nicaea, the emperor had no further need to exercise imperial persuasiveness among bishops who were already of one doctrinal mind.[18]

By the time they dispersed in the middle of July,[19] the bishops had reaffirmed their adherence to the creed of Nicaea ('the faith of the 318 fathers who assembled at Nicaea in Bithynia is not to be rejected') and outlawed by name a kaleidoscope of heresies which had risen to challenge it in the intervening years ('Eunomians or Anomoians, Arians or Eudoxians, Semi-Arians or Pneumatomachoi, Sabellians, Marcellians, Photinians, and Apollinarians'):[20] the list is noticeably more comprehensive than that already pronounced by Theodosius in his January law. The bishops' faithfulness to the legacy of Nicaea was also reflected in their attention to ecclesiastical discipline and organization, and their extension of the principle of mirroring 'secular' arrangements in the manner enshrined by Constantine's council. Not only were the Church's structures now aligned with the secular dioceses, but the see of Constantinople, defined as 'new Rome', was assured of an ecclesiastical status in the East which was a match for its role as the second city of the Roman empire.[21]

When the council of Constantinople ended, the bishops wrote commending their work to the emperor, attaching to their letter copies of their decisions determining the boundaries of orthodoxy and heresy and of the canons on ecclesiastical order; in the name of the 'holy synod of bishops from various provinces meeting in Constantinople', they asked him to 'ratify' (*epikurōthēnai*) in writing what the council had agreed, 'so that, just as you honoured the church by your letters of invitation, so you may set your seal on its final decisions.'[22] The bishops are

---

[18] For the palace reception, see Theodoret, *Historia ecclesiastica*, 5.7.3 (ed. L. Parmentier and G. C. Hansen, GCS NF 5 [Berlin, 1998], 286–7) [hereafter: Theodoret, *HE*] (for later divergent traditions on the location of the council's sessions: R. Janin, *La géographie ecclésiastique de l'empire byzantin*, t.3: *Les églises et les monastères* [Paris, 1953], 108–9, 396). On Theodosius's (non-) involvement, see Ritter, *Konzil*, 42–3, 230–5.

[19] The council ended, according to tradition, on 9 July: J. D. Mansi, *Sacrorum conciliorum nova et amplissima collectio*, 55 vols (Florence, 1728–33) [hereafter: Mansi, *Concilia*], 3: 557.

[20] Constantinople Canon 1, cf. *logos prosphōnēetikos* (below, n. 22) and Theodoret, *HE*, 5.9.10–12 (GCS NF 5, 292–3).

[21] Canons 2 and 3, cf. my discussion in A. Cameron and P. Garnsey, eds, *The Cambridge Ancient History, vol. 13: The Late Empire, A.D. 337–425* (Cambridge, 1998), 246–8.

[22] For the bishops' *logos prosphōnētikos* (preserved with the canons), see Mansi, *Concilia*, 3: 557, and Ritter, *Konzil*, 124–5.

clear and precise in their perception of the emperor's role in relation to their proceedings. They do not accord him any part in the substance of their deliberations (confirmed, as we have seen, by other meagre evidence of the council), only at the beginning and end: as he had summoned them to meet on his authority, so now he is being asked to produce further letters to disseminate the results of their meeting. The bishops, we may assume, carried these imperial letters back to their churches as an endorsement accompanying their own conciliar documents.[23] The procedure is again analogous to what had happened at Nicaea, when Constantine had also written letters to the churches after the council giving imperial weight to its decisions. Speaking generally of Constantine, Eusebius had described him as 'putting his seal on the decrees of bishops made at synods', and the bishops at Constantinople chose precisely the same word (*episphragisēs*) in their request to Theodosius: they were seeking to add the imperial 'seal' to the results of their conciliar process.[24]

Shortly after the bishops dispersed from Constantinople, Theodosius issued further legislation requiring the transfer of all churches into the possession of bishops who professed Nicene orthodoxy, and the exclusion of all others as heretics.[25] Many scholars have seen this as the same instrument of imperial ratification which the bishops requested in their final address to Theodosius,[26] yet nothing about their letter necessarily points to legislation as the 'seal' which they were looking for from the emperor – they were expecting letters to match those with which Theodosius had summoned them to Constantinople – and the text of the law makes no direct reference to the council's conclusions: its basic demands do not differ from those of the emperor's earlier legal

[23] So Errington, 'Church and State', 62–4 (*contra* Ritter, who argued that canons and signatures were published directly by the emperor).
[24] Eusebius, *Life of Constantine*, 4.27.2 (ed. F. Winkelmann, GCS Eusebius Werke I.1 [Berlin, 1975], 130). T. D. Barnes (e.g. *Athanasius and Constantius*, 172) argues on the basis of this that Constantine gave conciliar decisions the force of law, but this may read too much into Eusebius. For Constantine's letters after Nicaea, see Barnes, *Constantine and Eusebius* (Cambridge, MA and London, 1981), 219.
[25] *Theodosian Code*, 16.1.3 (30 July 381, addressed to proconsul of Asia), cf. Sozomen, *HE*, 7.9.5–7.
[26] For example Ensslin, *Religionspolitik*, 36–7; King, *Emperor Theodosius*, 44–6; Ritter, *Konzil*, 127–30. Errington, 'Church and State', 64–6, while not denying direct connection with the council, sees the law as specifically addressing the circumstances of Asia. Sozomen, *HE*, 7.9.5 juxtaposes his report of the law with Theodosius' endorsement (*epepsēphisato*) of the council's decisions (cf. Socrates, *HE*, 5.8.20, Theodosius '*sumpsēphos*' with the bishops).

pronouncements on the rightful possession of churches which had preceded the council. Nonetheless, it seems inconceivable that imperial legislation reiterating Nicene faith as the criterion of orthodoxy within three weeks of the close of the council could have been issued without regard for the bishops' recent decisions. This may be confirmed by the fact that the law sets out detailed rules for officials to identify legitimate bishops in a manner which closely reflects the ecclesiastical hierarchy of the eastern empire as determined by the council: the test of orthodoxy is defined in terms of communion with a list of named bishops headed by Nectarius of Constantinople and Timothy of Alexandria, followed by episcopal representatives from each of the five eastern dioceses.[27] The law of 30 July is thus surely informed by the outcome of the council of Constantinople, even if not a direct response to it. While continuing to legislate for Catholic orthodoxy, Theodosius has moved even further away from the Roman and Petrine standard which he had first set at Thessalonica the previous year. In January he had already associated himself with a more conciliar principle of determining the true faith, and now the imperial perspective on ecclesiastical order is aligned to that of a council of eastern bishops which had just met in Constantinople: the bishop of Alexandria, tellingly, is named no longer as an adjunct of the see of old Rome (as he had been in the law of February 380), but now alongside the eastern 'primate' of New Rome, the bishop of Constantinople.

In the years immediately following the council of Constantinople, a spate of Theodosian legislation continued to tighten the screw of exclusion on heretical congregations, denying them the use of both public and private buildings.[28] But the emperor still kept open the route of conciliar consensus which he had followed in his dealings with the bishops of the eastern empire. Theodoret alone records that 'most' of the delegates who had been at the council of Constantinople returned again to the city the following year (382), but nothing more is known of this second session beyond the synodical letter which the bishops addressed to their counterparts in the West, in which the renewed gathering in Constantinople served as grounds for declining an invita-

---

[27] The fact that no bishop of Antioch is named reflects the continuing division of the Nicene congregation in the city after the death of Meletius.

[28] *Theodosian Code*, 16.5.11 (25 July 383), 12 (3 Dec. 383).

tion which Gratian had issued to the easterners to attend a Roman synod around the same time.[29]

Theodosius's search for ecclesiastical harmony in his domain is again evident in June 383, when he once more resorted to conciliar methods as a counterweight to the use of legislative enforcement. The Church historian Socrates relates how the emperor, reacting to the disturbances caused in the cities by the ousting of 'Arianizing' bishops in favour of Nicene replacements, summoned leaders of the churches to Constantinople, both orthodox and dissenting, in the hopes of finding the longed-for theological unity. Unable to resolve the differences in open debate, the emperor then demanded written statements of belief from the principal protagonists, which he proceeded to consider alone, calling upon God's aid in prayer: (perhaps predictably) only the Nicene *homoousios* passed the test of unity, and Theodosius tore up the rest of the statements.[30]

Socrates' account of this so-called 'conference of the sects' has rightly been described as '*einem . . . stark stilisierten Bericht*':[31] from the prominence accorded to leaders of the sect in the account of the episode, it appears to derive from Novatianist sources, and it incorporates 'patristic' criteria of orthodoxy which probably owe more to Socrates himself than to the aftermath of the council of Constantinople. Nonetheless, there is a degree of truth in the record of a Theodosian synod in the summer of 383. In a contemporary letter to the eastern praetorian prefect Postumianus (the recipient of Theodosius' laws outlawing heretical congregations) Gregory of Nazianzus commended his track-record at 'pacifying' the churches, which he expected to be of some avail at a council of bishops which Gregory had heard was then being assembled, although he was unaware of the circumstances;[32] while there is confirmation of the submission of written professions of faith in the survival of Eunomius' *Expositio Fidei*, written in response to 'imperial decrees'.[33] At the time Eunomius was attracting a following at

---

[29] Theodoret, *HE* 5.8.10–9.18. On the circumstances surrounding the invitation to Rome in 382, see e.g. McLynn, *Ambrose*, 141–5.

[30] Socrates, *HE*, 5.10, largely followed by Sozomen, *HE*, 7.12.

[31] M. Wallraff, *Der kirchenhistoriker Sokrates* (Göttingen, 1997), 78; cf. idem, 'Il "sinodo di tutti le eresie" a Costantinopoli (383)', in *Vescovi e pastori in epoca teodosiana (Atti del XXV Incontro di studiosi dell'antichità cristiana, Roma 8–11 maggio 1996)*, Studia Ephemeridis Augustinianum 58, 2 vols (Rome, 1997), 2: 271–9.

[32] Greg. Naz. *Letters*, 173.6 (ed. P. Gallay, vol. 2 [Paris, 1967], 62–3).

[33] See R. P. Vaggione, *Eunomius: Extant Works* (Oxford, 1987), 150–1, and for full discus-

his private estate across the Bosphorus at Chalcedon,[34] a fact which lends weight to the observation that the chief participants in Socrates' account of the 383 gathering (including Eunomius) are all from Constantinople itself and the surrounding region: besides Nectarius and his Novatianist counterpart in the capital, the *homoians* were represented by bishop Demophilus who had (as we have seen) withdrawn his congregation to the outskirts of the city, and the Macedonianists (erstwhile *homoiousians*) by Eleusius of Cyzicus on the Propontis, whose followers were concentrated in Constantinople's hinterland in the north-west of Asia Minor. In reverting to an attempt at a synodical solution to continuing doctrinal division, Theodosius (it seems) was focusing his efforts on the local situation around the capital.

By including Eleusius he was also restarting deliberations which had been broken off without success at the time of the council two years earlier, when Theodosius and the Nicene majority had failed to persuade Eleusius and his colleagues to join them. This previous occasion had been the emperor's only recorded participation in the theological debates, until he now resumed his direct involvement in a show of bringing the parties to unity. Realistically, it is hard to imagine that the approved Nicene orthodoxy was in any way negotiable in the summer of 383, but Theodosius might at least continue to present himself as the committed agent of episcopal consensus: whereas imperial engagement had been notably absent from most of the sessions of the council of Constantinople, it emerged openly again in the form of this 'conference of the sects', with Theodosius adopting a much more Constantinian-style role as the arbiter of true belief among the assembled bishops. The enforcer of Catholic orthodoxy gave way, at least temporarily, to the architect of doctrinal unity. Not for the first time in this sequence of events, the careful nuancing of the emperor's dealings with bishops can be seen as not dissimilar from the handling of the Gothic settlement in the Balkans at much the same time, where we find a 'rhetorical balancing act' juggling the image of the traditional military victor with the successful purveyor of diplomatic compromise.[35] In both Church

---

sion of Theodosian context, idem, *Eunomius of Cyzicus and the Nicene Revolution* (Oxford, 2000), 312–29.

[34] Sozomen, *HE*, 7.6.2, cf. Socrates, *HE*, 5.20.4 (with Sozomen, *HE*, 7.17.1).

[35] As in Themistius's sixteenth oration (January 383): P. Heather and D. Moncur, *Politics, Philosophy, and Empire in the Fourth Century: Select Orations of Themistius* (Liverpool, 2001), 259–64.

and State, it seems, persuasion and consent remained part of the imperial vocabulary. A recent treatment of the period goes too far in accusing Theodosius of 'undermining a more moderate approach' to theological dissent through the forced imposition of Nicene orthodoxy:[36] as his continued recourse to the conciliar process in the early 380s shows, bishops had not entirely lost their voice in determining the faith of the Church.

Durham University

---

[36] David S. Potter, *The Roman Empire at Bay AD 180–395* (London, 2004), 556, 560.

PATRISTIC DIVERGENCES ABOUT THE IMAGE OF
GOD IN MAN

by STUART GEORGE HALL

Epiphanius and the Audians

THE pathologically pious heresy-hunter Epiphanius, bishop of
Salamis from 365 to 403, might be reckoned a champion of
uniformity in the Church. Notoriously he promoted the
campaign against Origen in Palestine, and in his *Panarion* attacks
Origen's theology at length. Never the brightest of the Fathers, he was
confused by the question of the image of God in man.[1] He comes to it
when considering the sect of Audians, who were anthropomorphites;
that is, they held God to have a bodily form which the human body
replicates.[2] According to Genesis 1: 26-7, God made man, male and
female, in (after, according to) the image and likeness of God
(ποιήσωμεν ἄνθρωπον κατ᾽ εἰκόνα ἡμετέραν καὶ καθ᾽ ὁμοίωσιν).
When Epiphanius gets to the detail of the Audian argument, it is plain
that they argued from the use in Scripture of bodily language about
God's eyes, hand, feet, and other organs, and from the Lord's appearances to Moses and the prophets, to demonstrate his bodily shape.[3]
Epiphanius can refute this in detail, but is aware of other suggestions
about wherein what is 'in the image' consists, and regards none as
wholly coherent with orthodox faith and Scripture. He mentions the
theories that it is the soul that is in the image, or that it is virtue, or that
it is the grace received in baptism, or that it applied to Adam only
before his sin.[4]

For one so apt to pounce on heresy, his position is remarkably soft.
This is perhaps because the Audians are manifestly orthodox about the

---

[1] 'Man' in this paper refers to the species (*anthropos/homo*), not to the male sex. On the
Image-theme, see Henri Crouzel, 'Bild Gottes II. Alte Kirche', *Theologische Realenzyklopädie* 6
(Berlin, 1980), 499–502 and Antonio Orbe, *Introduccion a la teologia de los siglos II y III*, Analecta
Gregoriana 248, 2 vols (Rome, 1987), 1: 212–29.

[2] Epiphanius, *Panarion haereses*, 70 (ed. Karl Holl, Die grieschischen christlichen
Schriftsteller der ersten drei Jahrhunderte 37 [Berlin, 1931]) [hereafter: *Panarion haer.* and
GCS].

[3] Ibid., 70.6.

[4] Ibid., 70.3–4.

Trinity, and because they were monks forced out of the Church by worse men than themselves for demanding high standards of clerical conduct. That Epiphanius could waver when he found he was attacking good men would later become apparent in the case of the Tall Brothers, expelled from Alexandria for Origenism, and John of Constantinople.[5] He also had intellectual difficulties. The formula he comes up with is that we must believe that man is made in God's image because Scripture says so, but that we should not stipulate what part of man it refers to.[6]

> Those therefore who insist contentiously upon this are also them-selves departing from the tradition which accords with Church doctrine, which believes that every man is 'in the image', but does not define wherein what is in the image consists, nor clarify it in the face of those who handle these matters mythologically or even deny them.[7]

Such principled agnosticism is the nearest he comes to declaring anything heretical.[8] We shall examine some views about the Image of God among the Fathers to see whether his attitude is representative, and whether there is any good reason why severity was not applied or any view imposed as orthodox. Epiphanius is aware that views on the image of God in man were not uniform, even among Fathers he considered respectable. Perhaps this is why he was less severe, even in a context of strident disputes over Origen.[9]

---

[5] Sozomen, *Historia ecclesiastica*, 8.13–15 [hereafter: Sozomen, *HE*] (ed. Günther Christian Hansen, Fontes Christiani 73.4 [Turnhout, 2004], 996–1007), based on Socrates, *Historia ecclesiastica*, 6.7 [hereafter: Socrates, *HE*] (ed. Günther Christian Hansen, GCS NF 1 [Berlin, 1995]).

[6] *Panarion haer.*, 70.2.7–8.

[7] Ibid., 70.3.1 (GCS 37, 235), my translation.

[8] The same agnosticism appears in *Ancoratus*, 55–7 (ed. Karl Holl, GCS 25 [Leipzig, 1915], 64–7), and Riggi's attempt to interpret Epiphanius' view as positive and holistic seems to be a house of straw. See Calogero Riggi, 'Il linguaggio teologico in Epifanio da Salamina', in Alfredo Marranzini, ed., *Il linguaggio teologico oggi* (Milan, 1969), 173–204, also found in Calogero Riggi, *Epistrophe: tensione verso la divina armonia*, Biblioteca di Scienze Religiose 70 (Rome, 1985), 608–39, esp. 623–8.

[9] On this dispute, see Elizabeth A. Clark, *The Origenist Controversy* (Princeton, NJ, 1992); Winrich A. Löhr, 'Theophilus von Alexandrien', *Theologische Realenzyklopädie* 33 (Berlin, 2002), 364–8.

Irenaeus

In Epiphanius' day anthropomorphism split the monks in Egypt, and Theophilus of Alexandria, reversing his original judgement, sided with the tumultuous anthropomorphites to get rid of certain Origenists whom he had other reasons to dislike.[10] The doctrine had however some reputable precedents. In his fifth book against the heresies Irenaeus of Lyons (fl. 180) uses the ideas of the image and likeness of God in expounding the theme of unity: God is one, Christ is one, and man is one.[11] His thought is a reaction to the divisive ideas of sectarians who distinguished between the creator of physical things, including bodies, and an alleged ultimate Spirit, the origin of the elect. Soul and Spirit might be part of man, says Irenaeus, but,

> Complete man is the combination and union of a soul which receives the Spirit of God and is mingled with that flesh which is shaped according to the image of God.[12]

Later Irenaeus says,

> The Word of God became man, assimilating himself to man and man to himself, so that, by that likeness to the Son, man might become precious to God. In past times it was indeed said that man was made in the image of God, but it was not apparent (οὐκ ἐδείκνυτο), for the Word was still invisible, in whose image Man had been made; for the same reason he easily lost the likeness. But when the Word of God became flesh, he reaffirmed both: he both displayed the image truly, himself becoming that which was his image, and firmly restored the likeness, assimilating (συνεξομοιώσας) man to the invisible Father through the visible Word.[13]

Man is therefore not purely soul and spirit, imprisoned in a body of inferior origin: the body is 'in the image of God' (κατ' εἰκόνα θεοῦ).

---

[10] So Socrates, *HE*, 6.7 (GCS NF 1, 322–4) and the partly independent account of Sozomen, *HE*, 8.11–13 (Fontes Christiani 73.4, 988–9). Not yet published when this paper was written was: Dimitrij Bumazhnov, *Der Mensch als Gottes Bild in christlichen Ägypten: Studien zu Gen 1: 26 in zwei koptischen Quellen des 4.–5. Jahrhunderts*, Studien und Texte zu Antike und Christentum 34 (Tübingen, 2005).

[11] Stuart G. Hall, *Doctrine and Practice in the Early Church* (2nd edn, London, 2005), 63–6.

[12] Irenaeus, *Adversus haereses*, 5.6.1 (ed. Adelin Rousseau, Louis Doutreleau, and Charles Mercier, SC 152/153 [Paris, 1969], 72); my translation, here and hereafter.

[13] Ibid., 5.16.2 (SC 153, 216–17).

The likeness (ὁμοίωμα) is spiritual, something possessed by Adam before his disobedience and restored in Christ by the gift of the Spirit. So the image is a hidden truth which Christ reveals, while the likeness has been lost and is restored by the gift of the Spirit of God. The totality consists of body/soul/spirit. Irenaeus's idea of man's destiny is revealed in this short passage:

> If one removes the fleshly material, that is, the shape [*plasmatis*], and understands man as merely spirit, one like that is not a spiritual man, but the spirit of a man or the Spirit of God. But when this Spirit, mixed with soul, is united with this shape, because of the outpouring of the Spirit man is spiritual and complete [*perfectus*]: he it is who is made in the image and likeness of God.[14]

Origen

Celsus, Irenaeus's anti-Christian contemporary, attacks biblical anthropomorphisms, and this is dealt with by Origen in *Against Celsus*, 5.61–4:

> [Celsus] failed to understand to what characteristic of man the words 'in the image of God' apply, and that this exists in the soul which either has not possessed or no longer possesses 'the old man with his deeds', and which, as a result of not possessing this, is said to be in the image of the Creator. He says: *Nor did he make man his image; for God is not like that, nor does he resemble any other form at all.* Is it possible to suppose that the part in the image of God is located in the inferior part of the composite man, I mean the body, and that, as Celsus interpreted it, the body should be that which is in His image? If the nature that is in the image of God is in the body alone, the superior part, the soul, is deprived of being in the image, and this exists in the corruptible body. Not one of us holds this view.[15]

In view of what Irenaeus wrote, the last sentence is dubious. Origen goes on to reject the notion that the image applies both to body and

---

[14] Ibid., 5.6.1 (SC 153, 74–7).

[15] Origen, *Contra Celsum*, 6.63 (*Origen Contra Celsum, Translated with an Introduction and Notes* by Henry Chadwick [Cambridge, 1980], 378; ed. Marcel Borret, SC 147 [Paris, 1969], 336–7) [hereafter: *C. Cels.*].

soul, which is, crudely speaking, Irenaeus's view, since that would imply
that God too is composite. He concludes:

> The remaining possibility is that that which is made in the image
> of God is to be understood of the inward man, as we call it, which
> is renewed and has the power to be formed in the image of the
> Creator, where a man becomes perfect as his heavenly Father is
> perfect, and when he hears 'Be holy because I the Lord your God
> am holy', and when he learns the saying 'Become imitators of God'
> and assumes into his own virtuous soul the characteristics of God.
> Then also the body of the man who has assumed the characteristics
> of God, in that part which is made in the image of God, is a temple,
> since he possesses a soul of this character and has God in his soul,
> because of that which is in his image.[16]

This does not merely mean that the soul, as distinct from the body, is
'in the image' of God,[17] nor does it merely refer to virtue; Epiphanius,
we recall, put both of these in his list of rejected interpretations. Origen
is actually very subtle, too subtle for Epiphanius. His position, steadily
held, was that man is threefold: spirit by the grace of God, soul, and
body – the soul consisting of the mind or ruling part (*hegemonikon*) and
a lower part which tends to drag the reason downward. The mind
remains in the image of God, even when overlaid with sin, and the
image must be retrieved by grace and repentance. In the life of holiness
the lost likeness to God is gradually restored.[18]

Epiphanius wrote a long attack on Origen, to whom he was bitterly
opposed. He attacks Origen's trinitarian doctrine as in principle Arian,
and such ideas as the pre-existence of created spirits, the alleged
doctrine of metempsychosis, the spiritual interpretation of Genesis 1,
and the ultimate restoration of the devil. But Epiphanius devotes only a
few words to the image of God in man. He describes how in Origen's
doctrine Adam lost what was in the image (τὸ κατ'εἰκόνα), and was
obliged to put on a body, the 'coats of skins' of Genesis 3: 21.[19] That
Adam lost the image is yet another of the interpretations we have heard

[16] *C. Cels.*, 6.63 (Chadwick, 378–9, giving biblical references; cf. Borret, SC 147, 338–9).
[17] As implied by εἰκών II.B.1 in *A Patristic Greek Lexicon*, ed. G. W. H. Lampe (Oxford, 1961 etc.), 413.
[18] Henri Crouzel, *Origen*, trans. A. S. Worral (Edinburgh, 1989); translated from *Origène* (Paris, 1985), 87–98; more fully Henri Crouzel, *La théologie de l'Image de Dieu chez Origène*, Théologie 34 (Paris, 1956).
[19] *Panarion haer.*, 64.4.9 (GCS 31, 412).

Epiphanius reject. Why did Epiphanius not attack Origen for his doctrine of the image of God in man? It may be mere clumsiness: in *Panarion haereses*, 64 Epiphanius leans on Methodius's criticisms, which he quotes at length; lacking material from elsewhere, he was not capable of analysing Origen's arguments for himself. Origen's real teaching seems to be that the 'inner man' is potentially renewable in the image of God (καὶ ἀνακαινουμένῳ καὶ πεφυκότι γίνεσθαι κατ' εἰκόνα τοῦ κτίσαντος) by grace and virtue. As the soul becomes God-like, the body becomes a shrine or temple.[20]

Ambrose and Augustine

Origen's influence reached Ambrose (bishop of Milan, 374 to 397), and so did the doctrines of the Neoplatonists. Ambrose explained the image of God in man as the soul (*anima*), which is the man himself as distinct from the body he possesses.

> Our soul is in the image of God. In that you entirely consist, O man (*in hac totus es, homo*), for without this you are nothing, you are just earth, and to earth return.[21]

This was particularly the rational soul (*mens*), by the power of which a man can contemplate things far distant in time and space, and keep company with Christ and the saints.[22] This interpretation would become decisive for the conversion of Augustine of Hippo to Catholic Christianity. As a young student in the 370s Augustine had no answer to the Manichees when they poured scorn on the Genesis stories, and in particular ridiculed the notion that man had been made in the image of God: does God have hair and finger-nails? By the time Augustine reached Milan he was disillusioned with the Manichees, and went to listen to Ambrose. What he heard was that the Catholic Church did not interpret 'made after the image of him that created him' as implying that God has a human form.[23] As a youth he had no answer to the Manichean case, and one must suppose that naïf anthropomorphism was usual in Christian North Africa.

[20] Origen, *C. Cels.*, 6.63 (SC 147, 336–8).
[21] Ambrose, *Exameron*, 6.7.42–3 (ed. C. Schenk, CSEL 32.1 [Vienna, 1897], 233–4).
[22] Ibid., 6.8.45 (CSEL 32.1, 236).
[23] Augustine, *Confessions*, 6.3.4 (ed. Lucas Verheijen, CCSL 27 [Turnhout, 1981], 76); trans. in Albert C. Outler, *Library of Christian Classics* 7 [Philadelphia, PA, 1955], 116–17) [hereafter: *LCC*].

Augustine's considered position is that

> When he had said, 'in our image', he immediately added, 'and let
> him have authority over the fish of the sea and the flying things of
> the sky and the other animals devoid of reason', doubtless so that
> we should understand that man is made in the image of God in
> that respect by which he excels irrational animals; that means
> reason (*ratio*) itself or mind (*mens*) or intelligence (*intellegentia*) or
> whatever name it is more suitably known by. Hence the Apostle
> says, 'Be renewed in the spirit of your mind, which is renewed in
> the knowledge of God according to the image of him who created
> him,'[24] which makes it plain enough that when man is created in
> God's image, it is not in bodily lines, but by some intelligible form
> of the illuminated mind.[25]

It was precisely by entering into this part of himself that Augustine
perceived himself as having obtained his first sense, not to say vision, of
the infinite light which is the mind of God.

> Being admonished by these [Platonic/Plotinian] books to return
> into myself, I entered into my inward soul, guided by thee. This I
> could do because thou wast my helper. And I entered, and with the
> eye of my soul – such as it was – saw above the same eye of my soul
> and above my mind the Immutable Light . . . And thou didst beat
> back the weakness of my sight, shining forth upon me thy dazzling
> beams of light, and I trembled with love and fear. I realized that I
> was far away from thee in the land of unlikeness (*in regione
> dissimilitudinis*) . . .[26]

Thus Augustine saw himself grasped by the transcendent Light as he
entered into himself, into his own mind. At the sight he trembles with
love (desiring to be like his original), but recognizes that he is, in a
classic Plotinian/Platonic phrase in a place of unlikeness (ἐν τῷ τῆς
ἀνομοιότητος τόπῳ),[27] but worded with biblical overtones from the
'far country' (*regionem longinquam*; Luke 15: 13) where the Prodigal Son

[24] Augustine conflates Ephesians 4: 23–4 with Col. 3: 10.
[25] Augustine, *De Genesi ad litteram*, 3.20 (ed. Joseph Zycha, CSEL 28, 86); my translation.
See Mary R. Clark, 'Image Doctrine', in Allan D. Fitzgerald, ed., *Augustine through the Ages: an
Encyclopedia* (Grand Rapids, MI and Cambridge, UK, 1999), 440–2.
[26] Augustine, *Confessions*, 7.10.16 (CCSL 27, 103; LCC 7, 146–7).
[27] On the text and exegesis, see James J. O'Donnell, *Augustine*, Confessions II: Commentary on Books 1–7 (Oxford 1992), 443–4.

got lost. Elsewhere he freely acknowledges that the goal of being near
God and like him is a thought learnt from Plotinus.[28]

Augustine made five or six attempts to explain the early chapters of
Genesis.[29] *De Genesi ad litteram liber imperfectus* (16.57.60) shows an unex-
pected turn. Facing the question, why man should be made 'after the
likeness' as well as 'after the image', he identifies the likeness (*similitudo*)
with the Word of God, Christ himself. The likeness is the eternal form
in which everything that is like God participates. This very Platonic
thought has clear reference to those New Testament passages in which
Christ is described as the Image of God,[30] which contributed to the
general eastern conviction during the fourth-century debates that
Christ's deity is expressed in his likeness to God as Image. Origen had
held this, and against Celsus distinguished Christ the Image of God
from Man made *in* (κατά) the Image.[31] This in turn reflected a general
Platonic perspective, which saw the whole creation embedded in the
thought of God, what for Origen is the Wisdom and Word (σοφία,
λόγος), and for Plotinus Mind (νοῦς). Augustine adapts Platonism to
the Bible differently from Origen in one respect. When he wrote *De
Genesi ad litteram liber imperfectus* about 393, he saw the similitude or
likeness as the relation of all created beings to the divine ideas, participating in that Likeness to the Father which is the Word. Those made in
God's image strive to be that in whose likeness they are made. The
crucial feature is that the image of God is located in the mind, which
reflects the incorporeal and unlimited reality of God, though transcended by it:

> A rational being is both made by it (*per ipsam* [i.e. *per similitudinem
> dei*]) and is in accordance with it (*ad ipsam*), inasmuch as the human
> mind, unawares except when it is totally pure and blessed, cleaves
> to Truth itself, which is called the Image and Likeness of the
> Father, and Wisdom. Rightly therefore in accordance with that
> which is internal and predominant (*principale*) in a man, that is, in
> accordance with mind, the words are to be taken, 'Let us make
> Man in our image and likeness.' For what holds the predominant

[28] *De civitate Dei*, 9.17.1–9 (ed. B. Dombart and A. Kalb, CCSL 47 [Turnhout, 1955],
265–6).
[29] See Roland J. Teske, 'Genesis Accounts of Creation', in Fitzgerald, *Augustine through the
Ages*, 379–81.
[30] I Cor. 11: 7; II Cor. 4: 4; Col. 1: 15.
[31] Origen, *C. Cels.*, 6.63 (Chadwick, 378; Borret, 334–7).

place, what distinguishes him from the beasts, is the whole of what is to be considered human (*totus est homo aestimandus*).[32]

Augustine on the Trinity

Augustine would not however dwell here long, but immediately stated his characteristic notion, that the human mind represents, potentially or actually, the life of God as Trinity. In 393 this is a matter of demonstrating from the wording of Genesis 1: 26 that it is not possible to apply the 'our' (*nostram*), in 'our image and likeness', distinctly to Father, Son or Holy Spirit, but only to the Trinity all together. Such a move has only jejune parallels in eastern writers: their efforts are occasional and tentative and a generation later than Augustine.[33] They are also rather naïf, like Theodoret's suggestion that in the soul Mind begets Word, and Breath (πνεῦμα/spirit) comes forth with Word.[34] What Augustine achieves in *De Trinitate* is a series of parallels which involves much creditable psychological observation.

Augustine did not of course intend to demonstrate the Trinity of divine persons from human psychology. Rather it was an attempt to clarify what is known by revelation.[35] In *De Trinitate* he allows even outward analogies, like the process of perception: the thing perceived, the vision by which it is represented to us, and the deliberate looking (*intentio voluntatis*).[36] The trinitarian relationship is chiefly sketched out in the lover, the object loved and the love which unites them, which are true both in the soul and in God.[37] He goes on to three more elaborate stages: the mind, its knowledge of itself and its love of itself;[38] the mind itself (memory), its knowledge of itself which somehow replicates itself (understanding), and the will or love which makes knowledge possible;[39] this can rise above itself in the mind as remembering, knowing and loving God.[40] The last leads to the renewing of the image

[32] *De Genesi ad litteram liber imperfectus*, 16 (CSEL 28, 500–1); my translation.
[33] Lampe's entry begins with Nilus, Basil of Seleucia, and Theodoret: εἰκών III.A.1., in Lampe, *Greek Lexicon*, 413.
[34] Theodoret, *Quaestiones in Genesim*, 20 (Gen. 1: 28) (PG 80, 108).
[35] John N. D. Kelly, *Early Christian Doctrines* (2nd edn, London, 1960), 176–9, has a succinct exposition.
[36] *De Trinitate*, 11.1.1–7.12 (ed. W. J. Mountain, CCSL 50 [Turnhout, 1968], 333–49).
[37] Ibid., 8.9.12–10.2.2 (CCSL 50, 289–94).
[38] Ibid., 9.2.2–5.8 (CCSL 50, 294–301).
[39] Ibid., 10.11.17–12.19 (CCSL 50, 329–32).
[40] Ibid., 14.8.11–16.22 (ed. W. J. Mountain, CCSL 50A [Turnhout, 1968], 433–54).

in man, and a growing likeness to God, consummated in the beatific vision, when we 'see him as he is.'[41] We cannot discuss such a profound matter here, but merely note how deeply the idea of the human mind as the image of God affects the thought of the greatest theologian of the West.

Conclusions

We turn finally to the question of discipline and diversity. That there is diversity was plain to Epiphanius, and is also clear in the differences between Irenaeus's inclusion of the body in the image of God, and its exclusion in Origen and Augustine. There were other variations which we have not mentioned. At a time when the Church and empire were settling uneasily on Nicene orthodoxy, and Origenism and the conduct of John of Constantinople could cause major disruption,[42] why did the image of God in man not become a dogmatic issue, requiring a conciliar or imperial ruling? Why was this stick not used to beat Origen, when he was so controversial?

One reason might be deemed accidental: no senior figure in the Church made it an issue, or provoked another to do so. Athanasius alleging Arianism against his ecclesiastical prosecutors, Nestorius finding heresy in the cult of St Mary and Cyril finding it in the sermons of Nestorius, these all were using dogmatic differences for leverage against rivals. Theophilus of Alexandria, who turned to favour the Anthropomorphites against the Origenists, was not above that. But his enemy was John of Constantinople, and John was no heretic: he might support the Tall Brothers who were Origenists, but he could not plausibly be portrayed as one himself. Besides, John gave enough hostages to fortune by his immoderate puritanism and jurisdictional ambitions. Anthropomorphites might be placated in Egypt, but for Theophilus to promote anthropomorphism would be ridiculous in imperial politics.

For Epiphanius at least, another reason might be his theological priorities. He hated Origen chiefly because his strong Trinitarianism lay behind most eastern theology, including that of the Meletian Nicenes at Antioch. In that divided city Epiphanius preferred the unreconstructed Nicenism of Paulinus and the Eustathians. Epiphanius was

---

[41] Ibid., 14.17.23–19.26 (CCSL 50A, 454–9).
[42] See briefly Hall, *Doctrine and Practice*, 183–90; Rowan Williams, 'Origenes, Origenismus', *Theologische Realenzyklopädie* 25 (Berlin, 1995), 397–420.

therefore not so interested in Origen's views on the image of God. The anthropomorphites too had other concerns. It was the non-historical interpretation of Genesis 1 that they opposed, rather than the doctrine of the 'inner man' as the image of God. Perhaps fundamentalist enmity to intellectuals played a part, in a land where Origenists like Didymus and Evagrius Ponticus were so eminent. Epiphanius could see the weakness of the Audian position, which resembled that of the Egyptian monks. So however much he hated Origen, he could not himself adopt anthropomorphite views in order to attack him. Moreover, many churchmen, including not only the Cappadocian Fathers, but the widely respected Athanasius, held approximately Origen's view, that it is man's rational power that is made after God's image.

University of St Andrews

ROD, LINE AND NET:
AUGUSTINE ON THE LIMITS OF DIVERSITY

by GILLIAN CLARK

AUGUSTINE of Hippo is especially appropriate for the theme of this volume. He is acknowledged as a Father and Doctor of the Church, that is, as an authoritative Christian writer from the early centuries of the Church, and as a major theologian. Patristics, the study of the Fathers, used to be where it all started in terms of Church teaching: wherever possible, doctrines and practices were traced back to the Fathers. In the last half-century of early Christian studies there has been much more emphasis on ecclesiastical history, on the intellectual and political detail of a specific historical context. So patristics is where it all starts in that we can see Church leaders working out their responses to problems and tensions that recur through the history of the Church. In the case of Augustine, there is an unusual range of evidence from his own sermons and letters and theological treatises, and from records of Church councils in Roman Africa from the years when he was bishop (395 to 430). On the older model of patristics, Augustine was taken as the source for some of the most extreme forms of Church discipline. His writings were conflated to produce coherent 'Augustinian' doctrine.[1] Phrases and sentences, images and speculation, were taken out of context to be used for purposes he never envisaged. On the newer model of early Christian studies, we can trace Augustine's reflections about when and how to discipline people who appear to be rejecting the fundamental Christian principles, love of God and love of neighbour.

This paper aims to set Augustine in the specific context of Roman Africa, that is, the Mediterranean coast of Africa and its hinterland, in the late fourth and early fifth centuries. Its title uses a traditional Christian metaphor, and words with multiple meanings, because both are typical of Augustine's exegesis of Scripture. Rod and line are images of discipline and definition. In Augustine's time, the patriarchal rulers of household, city and church expected to discipline their subjects. It was a

---

[1] For example, Eugène Portalié S. J., *A Guide to the Thought of St Augustine*, trans. Vernon J. Bourke (London, 1960).

bishop's duty to intercede for criminals, but in response to a question from an imperial official, Augustine made it clear that pleas for mercy did not invalidate any of the lawful uses of physical force:

> All this does not mean that institutionalised force has no point: the might of the emperor, the judge's power of the sword, the executioner's hooks, the soldier's weapons, the correction a master gives his slave, and even the strictness of a good father.[2]

The executioner's hooks (*ungulae*) were instruments of judicial torture, used in interrogation. Latin *vis*, here translated 'force', also meant 'violence', depending on who employed it and why. As this quotation shows, force was institutionalized at all levels of late Roman culture. Children were beaten at home and at school; slaves were beaten; delinquents and criminals were beaten; serious offenders, or slave criminals, were beaten with the *flagellum*. This word is often translated 'whip', but the *flagellum* at its worst was a flail or scourge, many-stranded and weighted with leather or lead. Some laws specified its use and, like the Russian *knout* and the Turkish *kurbash*, it killed people. Augustine asked Roman officials to show mercy by imposing only the 'paternal' punishment of beating with rods; bishops could themselves order such beatings as punishment for delinquent clergy.[3] But it is the *flagellum* that provides one of his most frequent images for human suffering.[4] Augustine corrected a passage in which he had said 'Christ does nothing by force', noting that Christ used the *flagellum* to drive money-changers out of the Temple, and expelled demons by the force of his power.[5] Natural disasters, barbarian invasions and illness could all be interpreted as the *flagellum* that God the Father wields as 'tough love' to punish or to reform sinful humans. The English phrase 'to teach us a

---

[2] *Epistula* 153.16 (413/4), trans. in Margaret Atkins and Robert Dodaro, *Augustine's Political Writings* (Cambridge, 2001), 80. Where translations are unattributed, I am responsible.

[3] Gillian Clark, 'Desires of the Hangman: Augustine on Legitimized Violence', in Hal Drake, ed., *Violence in Late Antiquity: Perceptions and Practices* (Aldershot, 2006), 137–46. 'Paternal' punishment: *Ep.* 133.2. Augustine's own powers: Noel Lenski, 'Evidence for the *Audientia Episcopalis* in the New Letters of Augustine', in Ralph Mathisen, ed., *Law, Society and Authority in Late Antiquity* (Oxford, 2001), 83–97; Leslie Dossey, 'Judicial Violence and the Ecclesiastical Courts in Late Antique North Africa', ibid., 98–114.

[4] Suzanne Poque, *Le langage symbolique dans la prédication d'Augustin d'Hippone*, 2 vols (Paris, 1984), 1: 193–224.

[5] *Retractationes*, 1.13.6 [hereafter: Augustine, *Retr.*] (ed. A. Mutzenbecher, CCSL 57 [Turnhout, 1984], 39).

lesson' shows the connection between 'discipline' (Latin *disciplina*) and 'disciple' (Latin *discipulus*, 'student'): discipline should be a learning experience.

The rod stands for the use of force to discipline and punish. The line, *regula*, is a rule or standard, in Greek *kanon*. Rules determine what people should and should not do, as in rules for monastic communities and canons of Church councils. The canon of Scripture determines which texts have authority, and the rule of Christian faith, *regula fidei*, reveals deviation from the truth, in heresies and in texts that are excluded from the canon. Augustine regarded the canon of Scripture as fixed. He wrote a booklet (*libellus*) of instructions for life in community: a century later it was known as a monastic rule (*regula*), and it is still fundamental for the Order of Saint Augustine. His contemporary Tyconius wrote a Book of Rules for the interpretation of Scripture, which, according to Augustine, was useful but could not give all the answers.[6] All this sounds both controlled and controlling, but who decides the rule? In his *Confessions*, Augustine told how his mother Monnica, deeply worried because he was Manichaean, had a reassuring dream that he stood beside her on a wooden *regula*. He pointed out the difficulty: her rule or his?[7] As a bishop, Augustine followed the tradition that *regula fidei* means 'the Church's teaching', but that does not settle the question of what exactly the Church teaches.[8]

Augustine gave an example that illustrates this problem in *Christian Teaching* (*De doctrina christiana*), the handbook on expounding Scripture that he began in the mid-390s, soon after his ordination. In Book Three he dealt with the interpretation of ambiguous passages. Like all late antique teachers, Augustine knew that the first question is whether we have correctly punctuated and articulated the text. If this remains unclear, 'one must consult the rule of faith, which he has acquired from the clearer passages of the scriptures and the authority of the church. I dealt adequately with this when I was speaking of things in the first book.'[9] As often happens when one claims to have dealt with something

---

[6] Canon: Augustine, *De doctrina christiana*, 2.24–9 [hereafter: Augustine, *Doct.chr.*] (ed. J. Martin, CCSL 32 [Turnhout, 1962]). Rule: George Lawless OSA, *Augustine of Hippo and his Monastic Rule* (Oxford, 1987). Tyconius: William S. Babcock, *Tyconius: the Book of Rules* (Atlanta, GA, 1989), with Augustine's discussion, *Doctr. chr.*, 3.92–132.

[7] *Confessions*, 3.11.19 [hereafter: Augustine, *Conf.*] (ed. L. Verheijen, CCSL 27 [Turnhout, 1981]).

[8] *Regula fidei*: J. N. D. Kelly, *Early Christian Creeds* (London, 1972), 76–88.

[9] *Doctr. chr.* 3.3 (CCSL 32, 78).

in an earlier lecture, Augustine's 'speaking of things' in Book One, an exposition of the basics of Christian faith, does not in fact settle the question that follows in Book Three. This is a 'well-known heretical punctuation' of John 1.1: 'in the beginning was the word, and the word was with God, and God was'. The punctuation gives 'this word was in the beginning with God' and avoids saying 'the word was God', but it is to be refuted by the *regula fidei*, which says that the persons of the Trinity are equal.[10] But that, of course, was the question at issue in the many fourth-century debates on Trinitarian theology.

Rod and line, discipline and definition, may catch fish, but it is easier to catch them in nets. Augustine liked to use an image adapted from the gospel of Matthew:

> In these evil days . . . many reprobates are mingled with the good and both are gathered in the drag-net of the Gospel [*sagena evangelica*]. In this world, as if in the sea, both swim without distinction, held in by the meshes, until the shore is reached where the bad will be separated from the good, and God will be all in all in the good as in His own temple.[11]

This looks like an image of diversity. There is no rule for identifying those who are in the Gospel net or those among them who are good, and though the net stops the fish escaping, they have some freedom of movement within it. Augustine allowed for some diversity of interpretation, and demonstrated this in his works of exegesis, both practical and theoretical. 'Discipline' itself has diversity of meaning, for *disciplina* is a way of learning, and learning was ordered into academic disciplines.[12] Augustine's exegesis of Scripture was shaped by the *disciplina* called *grammatica*, reading and writing good Latin, in which he had been a student and a teacher. The *grammaticus* interpreted texts for his students: from a sequence of letters he established a correct text, rightly punctuated and articulated. The more extensive his learning, the wider

---

10 Ibid.

11 Matt. 13: 47–50; Augustine, *De civitate Dei*, 18.49 (ed. B. Dombart and A. Kalb, CCSL 48 [Turnhout, 1955], 647) [hereafter: Augustine, *Civ.*]. 'Reprobates' are people who are condemned.

12 Karla Pollmann and Mark Vessey, eds, *Augustine and the Disciplines* (Oxford, 2005). For Augustine's uses of *disciplina* see W. Huebner, '*Disciplina*', in C. Mayer, ed., *Augustinus-Lexikon*, vol. 2, fasc. 3–4 (Basel, 1999), 457–63.

the range of interpretation and discussion he could offer in his spoken or written notes on the text, his *commentarii*.[13]

In *Confessions* (begun, like *Christian Teaching*, in the late 390s) Augustine welcomed multiple interpretations of Scripture. Book Twelve is concerned with the opening words of the Bible, 'In the beginning God made heaven and earth.' After long reflection on what they mean or imply, Augustine summed up:

> When one person says 'Moses meant what I think' and another says 'No, he meant what I think', I myself think it would be more religious to say 'Why not both, if both are true, or a third or a fourth interpretation, or whatever other truth anyone has ever found in these words?' Why not believe that he saw all these things, I mean the person through whom the one God adapted the holy texts for the perceptions of the many who would see various truths? I say fearlessly and from my heart that if I were to write anything of the utmost authority, I would rather write it so that my words echoed whatever truth anyone could grasp on these matters, than set down one true opinion so plainly as to exclude other opinions whose falsity could not offend me.[14]

Truth itself is not diverse, and diversity has limits, but there are various truths. That was also Augustine's position in *Christian Teaching*, and he let it stand when he returned to the book after a long interval:

> So when there is not just one interpretation, but two or more interpretations, of the same words of scripture, even if it is not clear what the author meant, there is no danger, if each interpretation can be shown from other passages of the holy scriptures to be in accord with the truth. The person studying the divine pronouncements must of course try to reach the intention of the author through whom the Holy Spirit wrote that scripture: he may attain it, or he may carve out from those words another interpretation that does not conflict with right faith, using as evidence some other passage of the divine pronouncements.[15]

---

[13] Robert A. Kaster, *Guardians of Language: the Grammarian and Society in Late Antiquity* (Berkeley, CA, 1988); Gillian Clark, 'City of God(s): Augustine's Virgil', *Proceedings of the Virgil Society* 23 (2004), 83–94; Augustine as *grammaticus*: Catherine Conybeare, *The Irrational Augustine* (Oxford, 2006), 11–59.

[14] *Conf.*, 12.31.42 (CCSL 27, 240).

[15] *Doctr. chr.*, 3.38 (CCSL 32, 99–100); the interruption occurred at 3.78 (*Retr.*, 2.4.30).

This inclusive approach contrasts with the recent claim that Christians were chiefly responsible for the growth of intolerance and exclusion in pluralist Roman culture; that where philosophers aimed for right belief (*orthē doxa*), Christians insisted on orthodoxy, and where philosophers followed an option (*hairesis*) Christians saw a choice between right and wrong, orthodoxy and heresy.[16] Augustine recognized that interpretation was not so clear-cut. He rejected some interpretations as heretical, and his handbook of eighty-eight heresies was very useful to later centuries.[17] But this does not show him to be a heresy-hunter, for he wrote the handbook late in his life (428) at the request of his colleague Quodvultdeus, who wanted a checklist of heresies in chronological order, with notes on what was wrong with them, what was the orthodox response, and who counted as validly baptized. As Augustine remarked, this was quite a lot to ask, but he recognized the need to guide people 'who want to avoid teachings contrary to the Christian faith that deceive under cover of the Christian name'.[18] He wanted to show such people how to avoid heresy, known or unknown, and how to judge known heresies. But how could he define a heretic?

> Not every error is a heresy, although every heresy that counts as vice [*vitium*, literally 'defect'] cannot be a heresy without some error. But in my judgement it is extremely difficult, if not impossible, to provide a comprehensive rule for defining what makes a heretic [*regulari quadam definitione comprehendi*].[19]

'Who decides the rule of faith?' remains the central question. There were interpretations that, according to Augustine, did conflict with basic Christian principles, but according to others expressed those principles. Sometimes diversity led to physical conflict or, in Augustine's judgement, to divergence from truth and spiritual danger: then he had to think about the limits of diversity and about suitable discipline.

Two problems that Augustine faced are especially important here;

---

[16] Polymnia Athanassiadi, 'The Creation of Orthodoxy in Neoplatonism', in Gillian Clark and Tessa Rajak, eds, *Philosophy and Power in the Graeco-Roman World: Essays in Honour of Miriam Griffin* (Oxford, 2002), 271–91; see also Averil Cameron's paper 'Enforcing Orthodoxy in Byzantium', 1–24, in this volume.

[17] David Bagchi, 'Defining Heresies: Catholic Heresiologies, 1520–50', 241–51, in this volume.

[18] *De haeresibus ad Quodvultdeum,* Prol. 1. [hereafter: Augustine, *Haer.*] (ed. R. Vander Plaetse and C. Beukers, CCSL 46 [Turnhout, 1969], 286).

[19] Ibid., 7 (CCSL 46, 289).

they also prompted some of his most famous, and most misapplied, sayings. He helped to make them known to later centuries as Donatism and Pelagianism, and these names demonstrate a general problem in early Christian studies.[20] The people who were given these names did not accept them, and had a greater range of beliefs and practices than the labels suggest. Diversity lost out because the voices of those who were successfully classed as heretics rarely survive, unless through indignant and selective quotation by those who condemned them, and the voices of those who peacefully coexisted remain as the silent majority. Augustine's voice survives particularly strongly because he was a brilliant preacher and writer, as befits a former professor of rhetoric, and because he took the trouble to revise and catalogue his written work in his *Retractationes*. (He did not have time to deal with his letters and most of his sermons; some of them still turn up unexpectedly.[21]) This presents a further problem. There is much less evidence for what other people did and said, so it is easy, and perhaps misleading, to see Augustine as the instigator and leader of action against the Donatists. Recent work therefore attends to the specific historical context, trying to reconstruct the lost opposition and to imagine Augustine when nobody knew he would be Saint Augustine, Doctor of the Church, the voice of authoritative Christian teaching.[22]

The people Augustine called Donatists (after Donatus, their bishop of Carthage, 313–55) called themselves Catholic Christians and regarded themselves as members of the true, pure, disciplined Church.[23] In their view, their bishops and priests had kept the faith in the 'Great Persecution' of the early fourth century, preferring martyrdom to handing over the Scriptures. They argued that anyone who lapsed from the faith was outside the Church, so a bishop or priest who betrayed the faith could not validly baptize or ordain or consecrate. It followed that Caecilianus did not become bishop of Carthage

[20] Donatism and Pelagianism have been intensively studied: Carol Harrison, *Augustine: Christian Truth and Fractured Humanity* (Oxford, 2001) offers an excellent introduction.

[21] On the 'Divjak letters' and 'Dolbeau sermons', see Peter Brown, *Augustine of Hippo* (2nd edn, London, 2000), 441–81.

[22] The most sustained attempt to think away Augustine's later reputation is James O'Donnell, *Augustine: Sinner and Saint; a New Biography* (London, 2005).

[23] Jean-Louis Maier, *Le dossier du Donatisme*, 2 vols (Berlin, 1987 and 1989). Texts in English translation: Maureen Tilley, *Donatist Martyr Stories* (Liverpool, 1996); Mark Edwards, *Optatus: Against the Donatists* (Liverpool, 1997); Atkins and Dodaro, *Augustine's Political Writings*, 127–203. Serge Lancel, *St Augustine*, trans. Antonia M. Nevill (London, 2000), 287–305, is especially helpful on the Council of Carthage (410/11).

in 311 to 312, because one of the people who consecrated him was
accused of being a 'hander-over' (Latin *traditor*, 'traitor'), and further
that 'Caecilianist' congregations did not belong to the true Church. The
emperor Constantine recognized Caecilian as the bishop of Carthage
and provided him with funds, but that proved only that the
Caecilianists (and the bishops from Italy and Gaul who agreed with
Constantine) had sold out to the powers of this world. Eighty years after
this dispute began, when Augustine was ordained priest at Hippo
Regius, the town had two churches, near enough to each other for
Augustine's congregation to hear the Donatist church singing hymns.
Many other communities in Roman Africa also had two churches,
divided by bitter memories and outbreaks of violence. This was schism,
a split church, a rip (Greek *schisma*) in the fabric of Christian love of
neighbour; persistent schism, Augustine argued, was heresy.[24]

Augustine took Donatism very seriously. One of his first activities as
a priest was to write, in 393 to 394, a popular song against Donatists. In
it he used the image of the net, saying that the net is the Church and its
meshes have been broken by 'very proud men who say they are righ-
teous'.[25] Some Donatists preferred the image of the Church as Noah's
Ark, sealed inside and outside against the seas of the world, safely
conveying the faithful few.[26] Augustine debated with their bishops,
wrote treatises against them and preached against them. One example
of his preaching, a Good Friday sermon, shows what he saw as the
problem with Donatism. The translation, by Edmund Hill O.P., aims to
convey Augustine's conversational style:

'All the ends of the earth shall remember and be converted to the
Lord.' There you are, brothers; that's it; why look to me to answer
the Donatists? There is the psalm for you, we have read it today,
they have read it today. We should write it up on placards and
banners, and go out in procession with it, chanting 'See, Christ has
suffered, see, the merchant offers his price, see the price he paid, his
own blood shed.' He carried the price in his purse; he was pierced

[24] *Ep.* 87.4 (ed. A Goldbacher, CSEL 34.2 [1898], 400); Gerald Bonner, 'Dic Christi veritas
ubi nunc habitas: Ideas of Schism and Heresy in the Post-Nicene Age', in William Klingshirn
and Mark Vessey, eds, *The Limits of Ancient Christianity: Essays on Late Antique Thought and
Culture in Honor of R. A. Markus* (Ann Arbor, MI, 1999), 63–79.
[25] The Song against Donatists: Gerald Bonner, *St Augustine of Hippo: Life and Controversies*
(2nd edn, Norwich, 1986), 253–7.
[26] Lancel, *St Augustine*, 281.

with a lance, and the purse was spilt, and the price of the whole earth was shed. What more have you heretics got to say? Isn't it the price of the whole world? Is Africa alone redeemed? Here is it in black and white, 'All the ends of the earth shall remember and be converted to the Lord.' If he had just said 'the ends of the earth', you could have answered, 'Here they are, in Morocco.' But it's 'all the ends of the earth'; he said 'all', my dear heretic. How are you going to wriggle out of that? You have no way out left, but the way in is always open.[27]

This is one example from a very wide range of texts that Augustine used against Donatists.[28] It shows that he saw them as heretics because they did not believe that Christ had redeemed the whole world, only those whom they regarded (often on disputed evidence) as faithful members of the pure Church. It is also an example of one person finding truth in a text of Scripture that another would hear with at least a different emphasis; the Donatists had read the same psalm, but we do not know what their bishop said in his sermon.

Augustine presented the Donatists as a stubborn minority, found only in Africa. 'Throughout the world Heaven's thunder rolls, proclaiming that the house of God is being built: and the frogs sit in their marsh and croak "We're the only Christians!" '[29] To counter the impact of his rhetorical skill, scholars have argued from texts and from material culture that in North Africa, Augustine's church was the minority church that had diverged from the rigorist African tradition. This minority, they suggest, constructed 'Donatism' by imposing that name on Christians who had the same sacraments and theology and liturgy as the self-styled Catholics, and who were far more diverse than the label 'Donatist' suggests. Moreover, Augustine and his allies, lobbying to bring the Donatists under pressure from imperial laws against heretics, exaggerated the risk and the extent of violence from the militants whom they called Circumcellions. This was another name

[27] *Enarrationes in psalmos*, 21[22] [hereafter: Augustine, *En. ps.*], trans., Edmund Hill, *Nine Sermons of Saint Augustine on the Psalms* (London, 1958), 57.
[28] For other texts, see Daniel Doyle, 'Spread throughout the World: Hints on Augustine's Understanding of Petrine Ministry', *Journal of Early Christian Studies* 13: 2 (2005), 233–46.
[29] *En. ps.* 95.11 (ed. E. Dekkers and J. Fraipont, CCSL 39 [Turnhout, 1956], 1350). There was a small Donatist community in Rome (Augustine, *Haer.* 69).

that was not accepted: the militants called themselves 'soldiers of Christ' or *agonistici*, 'martyr brigades'.[30]

Augustine was right that the Donatists were a minority in relation to churches in other countries. He had spent time in Italy listening to Ambrose, and had a different perspective on African tradition: 'the world confidently judges [*securus iudicat orbis terrarum*] that those who in any part of the world separate themselves from the world are not good people.'[31] But that does not explain why he was so active against Donatists, rather than seeking peaceful coexistence, acknowledging the diversity of beliefs, and trying to discuss those that seem unacceptable. One answer is that he did all these things, but there was an immediate problem of violence. Augustine made the maximum rhetorical use of incidents of violence and intimidation against his own clergy and congregations, but we need not suppose that he invented or prompted them. Terrorist attacks, even if statistically rare, kill innocent people and create fear, and if the terrorists are inspired by what they believe to be true religion, both religious and political leaders must find a response.[32]

In 409 Augustine replied to a colleague who had written about atrocities. There were reports of barbarian attacks in places that had seemed safe: on Egyptian monks in the desert, in parts of Italy and Gaul, in Spain which had seemed untouched:

> And why look far afield? Here in Hippo, where barbarians have not yet penetrated, the ravages of Donatist clergy and Circumcellions make havoc in our churches beside which the doings of barbarians are mild. What barbarian could have devised schemes like theirs, of throwing lime and acid into the eyes of our clergy and inflicting the most dreadful injuries on every part of their bodies? They pick on houses to loot and burn, granaries to rob, and store-barrels to drain, compelling many people to be rebaptized by the threat of more of the same. Only the day before I am dictating this, news

30 'Circumcellions' probably means those who lived *circum cellas*, around the shrines [*cellae*] of Donatist martyrs; see further Brent D. Shaw, 'Bad Boys: Circumcellions and Fictive Violence', in Drake, ed., *Violence*, 177–94. On the sequence of events and the theological questions, see Bonner, *Augustine*, 237–311. On the construction of Donatism, see the classic study of W. H. C. Frend, *The Donatist Church: a Movement of Protest in Roman North Africa* (Oxford, 1952); Alan Dearn, *The Polemical Use of the Past in the Catholic/Donatist Schism* (forthcoming).
31 *Contra epistulam Parmeniani*, 3.4.24 (ed. M. Petschenig, CSEL 51 [Vienna, 1908], 131).
32 This paper was presented two weeks after the London bombings of 7 July 2005.

came in of forty-eight rebaptisms in one locality due to this kind of intimidation.[33]

Assaults on people and property fell within the remit of Roman imperial government, whose primary duty was to maintain peace and order. Augustine had no problem with the use of force as discipline, provided it was exercised by the authorized power for the purpose of maintaining peace, and provided those who exercised it were not motivated by anger or revenge and were willing to show mercy. The use of force against Donatists is the context for one of his most quoted sayings:

> Love, and do what you will. If you keep silent, do so from love. If you speak, speak from love. If you correct, do so from love. If you pardon, do so from love.[34]

'Correcting' could include physical force, as it did in the discipline of children, slaves and criminals.[35] At first Augustine argued for persuasion, but that was not because he objected in principle to force: it was because he thought that force does not change hearts and minds. He wrote to a Donatist that he had not wanted his church to be full of pretended converts, but the results in his own city made him think differently. The point is not, he said, whether somebody is made (Latin *cogitur*) to do something, but whether what he is made to do is good or bad. It is not possible to make someone be good, but if he is afraid, he will renounce falsehood and recognize truth or at least search for truth. In Hippo, Augustine heard people thanking God because their old habits had been broken and they had had to learn the truth. 'Thanks be to God who used this whip [*flagellum*] to teach us how false and empty were the lies people told about his church!'[36] Again, we need not believe that Augustine made this up, and we do not have enough information to assess the political decision to use force for maintaining peace. But it is right to force people out of believing lies? Augustine asked whether it is right not to do so:

---

[33] *Ep.* 111.1, trans. in Christopher Kirwan, *Augustine* (London, 1989), 209–18; see 210 on the problem of toleration. John Rist, *Augustine: Ancient Thought Baptized* (Cambridge, 1994), 239–45, discusses the 'theory of persecution', but overstates the penalties: see below. (The reference 240 n. 60 should be to *Codex Theodosianus*, 16.5.53 (ed. T. Mommsen, *Theodosiani libri XVI* [Berlin, 1904–5], 873), which is concerned with Jovinian not with Donatists.)
[34] *Tractatus in Iohannis epistulam ad Parthos*, 7.8 (PL 35, 2033).
[35] Frederick Russell, 'Persuading the Donatists', in Klingshirn and Vessey, *Limits of Ancient Christianity*, 115–30.
[36] *Ep.* 93.5 (ed. K.-D. Daur, CCSL 31a [Turnhout, 2005], 170).

> So what does brotherly love do? Because it fears the transitory fires
> of the furnace for a few, does it abandon all to the eternal fires of
> hell?[37]

This question, from a letter on the correction of Donatists, appears to
set a precedent for burning heretics. But 'furnace' is a metaphor:
Augustine liked it because the furnace that burns up straw also refines
gold. In a letter to Donatus, he cited Paul: 'if I give my body to be
burned, but have not love, it does not help me'.[38] Paul, like Augustine,
used this as an image of extreme self-sacrifice. Burning alive was one of
the extreme penalties of late Roman law, but it was not a penalty for
heresy. Laws against heresy typically threatened fines, confiscation of
property and, for some stubborn clergy, exile.[39] Should even those
threats be used against beliefs? As Augustine saw it, the Donatists were
in extreme spiritual danger, desperately ill and in need of treatment,
because habit and ignorance locked them into rejecting love of neighbour and love of God.[40] They appeared to be saying (as in the sermon
quoted above) that the suffering and death of Christ did not redeem all
humanity, only the Donatist churches in one part of Africa; and that, if
sacraments were not effective when the priest was a *traditor* or had been
ordained in the succession of *traditores*, God had not washed away sins
in baptism and communicants had not shared in the Eucharist, but
remained outside the pure Church. This was a refusal to accept the love
of God for themselves and for others. What was done about such
people, or rather, for such people? Augustine concluded that the answer
is *coge eos intrare*, 'make them come in.' This is a quotation from Jesus'
parable of the Great Feast. The king sent out invitations to a great feast
but was met with all kinds of excuses, until he told his servants to
search out people who were sleeping rough and 'make them come in'.
In context *coge eos intrare* means 'make them come to the party, make
them come and celebrate with others'.[41] In different contexts it was
heard differently.

Donatism, then, is a case study in the limits of diversity. It shows the
danger of categorizing people, but it also raises questions that recur
throughout the history of the Church and of politics. When some

---

37 *Ep.* 185.14 (ed. A. Goldbacher, CSEL 57 [Vienna, 1940], 13).
38 I Cor. 13: 1–3; *Ep.* 173.5–6 (Atkins and Dodaro, *Augustine's Political Writings*, 155).
39 Gillian Clark, *Christianity and Roman Society* (Cambridge, 2004), 99–100.
40 On this problem, see Richard Price, *Augustine* (London, 1996), 40–3.
41 Luke 14: 16–24; Augustine, *Ep.* 185.24–5 (CSEL 57, 22–5).

people do not tolerate others, how much physical and spiritual damage must they do, to others and to themselves, before we conclude that force is required to bring them in? In the case of Pelagianism, the questions apply differently because there was no threat to public order and no 'Pelagian' church: instead, there were theologians, not always in agreement with each other, whose teachings appeared to others to endanger the soul. Augustine's voice again dominates the evidence, but some 'Pelagian' texts have survived.[42] Augustine heard Pelagius as teaching that human beings can achieve perfection by moral effort. This, he thought, was a refusal to recognize that sin is genetic: he called it 'original sin' because it comes from human origins, inherited from Adam. Augustine's personal and pastoral experience convinced him that only the free gift of God's grace liberates us to act rightly. He was told that Pelagius was shocked when he heard a bishop quote, from Augustine's *Confessions*, the prayer 'give what you command and command what you will'.[43] This, Pelagius thought, devalued the God-given capacity of human beings to pray, think, read the Bible and follow the example of Christ. It might even suggest that God has created human nature in such a way that we are incapable of following the commands He has given us. Pelagius did not accept that sin is genetic, but argued that Adam's sin was not transmitted to his descendants.

In retrospect, Augustine and Pelagius both expressed important truths that need to be kept in balance, and the way forward was courteous debate that recognized the goodwill and the Christian commitment of all concerned. Again, that was tried, but there were also councils, forensic arguments, condemnations, and attempts to involve the emperor. One reason for this is the specific historical context. Pelagius lived for many years in Rome, among people with inherited expectations of virtuous behaviour, before (in 409) the Gothic threat displaced him to Carthage, where an imperial commissioner was chairing a major council on the Donatist problem. In the circumstances, African bishops were especially sensitive to questions of individual virtue and universal grace, and especially likely to think in terms of councils and imperial backing. The debate about Pelagianism continued long after Pelagius left Africa, and it showed that Church

---

[42] Bonner, *Augustine*, 312–93; B. R. Rees, *Pelagius: Life and Letters* (Woodbridge, 1998).
[43] *De dono perseverantiae*, 20.53 (PL 45, 1026).

councils and imperial backing did not solve the problems of discipline and diversity.

After several years of this debate, Augustine tried to argue that the case was closed and the teaching of Pelagius had been shown to conflict with fundamental Christian principles.[44] He explained why in a sermon on God's justice, preached at Carthage on 23 September 417.

> The Apostle says: if justice comes by law, Christ died for nothing. What the Apostle says of the law, we say to them about nature: if justice comes by nature, Christ died for nothing. (10) So we see in them what was said of the Jews. They have zeal for the Lord. 'I testify that they have zeal for the Lord, but not in accordance with wisdom.' What does 'not in accordance with wisdom' mean? 'They do not know God's justice and want to establish their own, so they are not subject to God's justice.' (Rom. 10: 2–3) Brothers, share my feelings: when you find such people, do not hide them, do not feel misguided pity; seriously, when you find such people, do not hide them. Argue against them, and if they resist, bring them to us. Two councils have already sent to the Apostolic See on this case, and replies [*rescripta*] have come. The case is ended [*causa finita*]; if only the error would end! We warn them so that they will take notice, we teach them so that they will learn, we pray that they will change. Turning to the Lord ...[45]

Augustine was later paraphrased as saying 'Rome has spoken: case closed' (*Roma locuta, causa finita*). He did not say that, but he did invoke the authority of Rome as the apostolic see, and affirmed it by using the word *rescripta* for the letters received from the bishop of Rome. In Roman law, a rescript was the legally binding response of the emperor (or his deputy) to a question or request on a legal matter. Augustine told Paulinus of Nola that when the two Church councils wrote to Innocent of Rome, earlier in 417, he had himself written a fuller letter, and Innocent 'replied as befits the bishop of the apostolic see'.[46] Augustine got the endorsement he wanted, and Innocent got the opportunity to say that it was appropriate to consult the apostolic see on all such matters. But as Augustine preached his sermon, there was a letter on the way

---

[44] See Bonner, *Augustine*, 343 n. 1, for other uses of 'the case is closed'.

[45] *Sermo*, 131.9–10 (PL 38, 733–4).

[46] *Ep.* 186.2 (CSEL 57, 47); Doyle, 'Spread throughout the World', offers evidence for Augustine's respect for Rome.

GILLIAN CLARK

from Innocent's successor Zosimus to say that he had examined Pelagius, and the bishop of Carthage would be delighted to know that Pelagius had not departed from the Catholic faith.[47] So the case was not closed. The African bishops did not accept the letter of Zosimus as the last word; they did not accept the general principle that the bishop of Rome had the right to say the last word. They continued to argue; the emperor Honorius was persuaded to declare Pelagius subject to the legal penalties for heresy, and eventually Zosimus also changed his view; but the debate on theology continued for centuries.

This complicated episode shows the limitations of discipline. Even when the pressure was on to distinguish orthodoxy from heresy, there were no clear and accepted procedures for deciding whether someone was heretical and what should be done about it. Appealing to the canons of Church councils did not solve the problem, for someone who was excommunicated by a council or councils could still be in communion with other groups of Christians. Recent work has focussed on the specific historical context of councils, on the people who were present or left or refused to attend, and on the pressures of imperial and ecclesiastical politics.[48] Present-day academics, whose duties include management and administration, are alert to the importance of deciding the agenda, writing the minutes, and drafting a form of words that most of those present could take back to their communities. These are not new problems: in Augustine's time, even if the authority of a given council was accepted, the record of its canons could be disputed. There was no generally accepted version even of the canons of Nicaea, the first ecumenical council (not that Nicaea was universally accepted), and the African bishops were not prepared to take on trust the version sent them by Zosimus of Rome. People argued about what the rules were, who should decide, and whether an appeal was possible, just as they argued about the specifics of the case; later ecclesiastical historians have interpreted the record in terms of their own denominational allegiance.[49] Invoking the imperial power caused further complications, for late antique Roman law, like the canons of Church councils, was usually a response to immediate protest or to a request for advice or

[47] *Collectio Avellana*, 45, ed. O. Günther, CSEL 35 (Vienna, 1895–8), 99–103, at 101.

[48] H. Hess, *The Early Development of Canon Law and the Council of Sardica* (2nd edn, Oxford, 2002); and see the papers by Thomas Graumann, David Hunt, and Christopher Stephens in this volume.

[49] Jane Merdinger, *Rome and the African Church in the Time of Augustine* (New Haven, CT, 1997).

action, and was often framed in terms of unspecific moral outrage.[50] For example, a law of 405 named Manichaeans and Donatists in threatening anyone who continued to take part in forbidden and unlawful things:

> Let him not evade the noose of the law recently promulgated by Our Mildness, and let him not doubt that, if there have been any seditious gatherings, the darts of more intense concern have been roused and will be used.[51]

The problem was getting somebody to do something, first to agree that the law applied to the particular case, then to take action. Augustine's letters may have led his readers to overestimate his political influence.[52]

Augustine emphasized that Christians cannot separate themselves out from the world, and the world as it is includes politics; but politics, secular or ecclesiastical, are not the end of the story. Historians of the early Church have moved away from the traditional model of orthodoxy transmitted through a succession of bishops and harassed at intervals by mad or arrogant heretics who have gone astray from the truth.[53] It is widely accepted that the Fathers of the Church learned their brilliant forensic rhetoric in the late antique educational system. They used the power of the spoken word against their opponents, often with ferocity that has shocked later generations, and they were quite capable of shaping diversity of practice and belief into easily identifiable heresies. Work on the 'construction' of heresies seeks to do justice to those whose voices are harder to hear. But, just as there were limits to what rhetoric and lobbying could do against heresy, so also there are limits on what rhetoric and lobbying can do as historical explanation. 'Donatism' and 'Pelagianism' raised profound theological questions about human dependence on God and about Christ as mediator between God and humanity.[54] If we do not accept that some people tried to think seriously about these questions, and to behave in accor-

[50] Jill Harries, *Law and Empire in Late Antiquity* (Cambridge, 1999), especially 88–93 on examples from Augustine's experience.

[51] *Codex Theodosianus*, 16.5.38 (ed. Mommsen, 867).

[52] Neil McLynn, 'Augustine's Roman Empire', in Mark Vessey, Karla Pollmann, and Allan D. Fitzgerald O.S.A., eds, *History, Apocalypse and the Secular Imagination* (Bowling Green, OH, 1999), 29–44, at 34–40.

[53] Clark, *Christianity*, 30–1.

[54] Robert Markus, 'Donatism', in Allan D. Fitzgerald, ed., *Augustine Through the Ages: an Encylopedia* (Grand Rapids, MI, 1999), 284–7; Eugene TeSelle, 'Pelagius', ibid., 633–40.

dance with Christian principle towards those who had different views, we risk undermining history by neglecting theology. But was it necessary to handle those questions in polemical and political mode? Why not return from the rod and line to the net, and accept that different people see different truths and that we cannot be sure who is motivated by the love of God?

Even the net is not clearly an image of diversity, fluidity and uncertainty. The citation above comes from *City of God* Book Eighteen, written probably in the early 420s, certainly after long experience of exegesis and of debates about harmful beliefs.[55] This is a good source for a concluding survey. Book Eighteen is an impressionistic survey of non-biblical history synchronized with biblical history. Its final sections contrast Christian with non-Christian texts, arguing that Jewish prophecy has greater antiquity (and therefore greater status) than Greek philosophy or Egyptian wisdom. Moreover, Christian Scripture is divinely inspired, utterly reliable, and consistent, whereas the contradictions of pagan historical and philosophical writing leave readers uncertain what to believe:

> Perish the thought that our authors, who for good reason form the fixed and final canon of holy scripture [*in quibus non frustra sacrarum litterarum figitur et terminatur canon*], should disagree in any way! That is why so many people, educated and uneducated, in town and country, have believed that God spoke to or through them when they wrote – so many, not just a few of the chattering classes engaged in litigious debates in schools and gymnasia.[56]

There is a Christian canon, but no philosophical canon. Philosophers disagree on fundamental questions of human happiness, yet no senate or people or governing power has ever regulated their disagreements. The authors of Scripture are in full agreement on everything; the authority of the Septuagint translation is shown by the divinely inspired unity of the translators; and where there are divergences between the Hebrew text and the Septuagint, that is because the Holy Spirit has worked differently in different contexts to convey the same truth. The differences are there to make us recognize hidden meanings. For

---

[55] Robert Dodaro, *Christ and the Just Society in the Thought of Augustine* (Cambridge, 2004), 72–114.

[56] *Civ.* 18.41 (CCSL 48, 636). On book 18 in context, see Gerard O'Daly, *Augustine's City of God: a Reader's Guide* (Oxford, 1999), 183–95.

example, the Hebrew text of Haggai 2: 8 says that 'the one desired by all the nations shall come.' (Augustine here follows Jerome's translation of 'the desires of all the nations shall come'.) The Septuagint has 'there will come from all nations those things that the Lord has chosen.' Both are right, for Haggai prophesies the glorious Church that Christ will build from those who have been chosen. At present the churches are full of people who will be winnowed out; and this is the context for the image of the net.[57]

So the net is a temporary holding device; Christian Scripture holds the line with a closed canon, free from disagreement; and soon Augustine turns to discipline.

> The Devil saw the temples of the demons deserted as the human race ran to the name of the Liberator and Mediator. He stirred up heretics to resist Christian teaching in the name of Christianity, as if they could be kept in the city of God indiscriminately, without any reproof, just as the city of confusion[58] indiscriminately kept philosophers who held diverse and opposed views. So when people in the Church of Christ hold some diseased and depraved view [*morbidum aliquid pravumque sapient*], and stubbornly resist when they are reproved to make them hold the healthy and correct view, refusing to correct their pestilential and lethal doctrines but continuing to defend them, they become heretics, go out [*foras*] and are counted among the enemies who give the church training.[59]

But God can make good use of evil, and even heretics have their uses.

> All enemies of the Church, whatever error has blinded them or malice corrupted them, exercise the Church's endurance if they are given the power to inflict bodily hurt. If their opposition is limited to bad opinions, they exercise the Church's wisdom. And so that even enemies may be loved, they also exercise the Church's benevolence or even beneficence, whether they are dealt with by persuasive teaching or by frightening discipline [*terribili disciplina*].[60]

Love must motivate the treatment of heretics, whatever is done to

---

57 *Civ.*, 18.48 (CCSL 48, 646–7).
58 Babylon, used to symbolize the 'earthly city', the community of those who want what they themselves want.
59 *Civ.*, 18.51 (CCSL 48, 648–9).
60 Ibid. (CCSL, 48, 649)

them. Nobody regulates philosophers, because it does not matter so much what they think. Earlier in *City of God* Augustine said that philosophers can speak freely about the fundamental principles of the universe, without fear of causing offence, but Christians must speak in accordance with a fixed rule [*ad certam regulam*] in case laxity of language begets impious opinions.[61] In *Retractationes*, he commented on things he had said that could be misinterpreted. This looks like the contrast between *hairesis* and heresy, open debate and closed doctrine, but the point made in *City of God* is that philosophers can speculate because there is much less at stake. Augustine thought that Platonism was the highest achievement of philosophy and came closest to Christianity.[62] Platonist philosophers thought that philosophy was the most important activity in the world, and debated the precise significance of everything in Plato, and its full agreement with Aristotle, with the same ingenuity that Christian theologians showed in debating the precise interpretation of everything in Scripture and the full agreement of different texts. But the difference is that Christian preachers had to explain their texts to anyone who came to church. Philosophers were sometimes accused of subversive teaching, but a Christian preacher could start a riot by stirring up emotions or by saying the wrong thing, and Augustine thought that careless phrasing, or false doctrine, could be lethal to the souls of those who listened. He did less than justice to the concern of philosophers for the souls of their students, but he had a point about the number of people they could reach.[63]

Close attention to texts and exegesis was not distinctively Christian, but three aspects of Christian texts are unusual in late antique culture: the copying that caused so many to survive at the expense of non-Christian or non-orthodox texts, the preaching that explained them to anyone who cared to come, and the official backing – sometimes, to some extent, and for a time – for agreed forms of words. This did not, and could not, amount to a discipline so rigorous and so effective that diversity was lost, and Augustine did not want to repress diversity unless it endangered peace in this world and salvation in the next. He did not expect the Spanish Inquisition. He re-read his written work and noted comments that might be misleading, but he could not predict the

[61] Ibid., 10.23 (ed. B. Dombart and A. Kalb, CCSL 47 [Turnhout, 1955], 297).
[62] Ibid., 8.9 (CCSL 47, 225–6).
[63] Gillian Clark, 'Augustine's Porphyry and the Universal Way of Salvation', in George Karamanolis and Anne Sheppard, eds, *Studies on Porphyry* (London, 2007 forthcoming).

later practice that took reflection out of context and made it doctrine. He knew the intellectual problems of interpreting an authoritative text. He knew the practical problems of maintaining peace and order in a society that authorized domestic and social violence, and among Christians who used violence against their opponents. He knew that he could invoke violence, official or unofficial, by using his status and his rhetorical skill. He had no easy answers for his fellow-bishop Paulinus of Nola, who asked him about punishment. Augustine replied that punishment is meant to help salvation, but that principle does not tell us what will work in individual cases or what limits should be set. We cannot read off answers from Scripture: there are several relevant passages, but 'we are not handling these God-given discourses, we're only fondling them, trying to find out what to think rather than giving a definite opinion.'[64] That is, we are not getting to grips with Scripture, for 'handling' a passage, *tractatio*, is the teacher's task of finding out what we need to understand and putting it in words.[65]

In his letter to Paulinus, Augustine could conclude that the problem is difficult and complex.[66] But he had to decide what to say in his sermon and what to write to imperial officials. There were no easy answers on discipline and diversity, no rules of exegesis or canons of the Church that determined who was dangerously wrong. There are only the fundamental Christian principles, love of God and love of neighbour.

University of Bristol

---

[64] *Ep.* 95.4 (CCSL 31a, 218).
[65] *Doctr. chr.* 1.1 (CCSL 32, 1).
[66] *Ep.* 95.3.

COUNCIL PROCEEDINGS AND JURIDICAL PROCESS: THE CASES OF AQUILEIA (AD 381) AND EPHESUS (AD 431)

by THOMAS GRAUMANN

I N exile in a remote and desolate place, Nestorius was still bitter about the Council of Ephesus (AD 431) some twenty years after the event. He remembered it as a travesty of a tribunal: 'I was summoned by Cyril, who had assembled the Council [. . .]. Who was judge? Cyril. Who was the accuser? Cyril. [. . .]. Cyril was everything.'[1] In view of his condemnation, and in identifying Cyril's activities on the occasion with roles usually played out in a court case, Nestorius recognized the basic pattern of proceedings of the council as that of a trial. Yet, in taking over all the major roles in such a trial simultaneously, Cyril had made a mockery of all proper judicial procedure. Minimum standards of proper procedure had been violated, and Nestorius, in his outburst against Cyril's misconduct, expects his audience to recognize the fact and share his expectations of due process. However, his frustration with the council runs deeper than a mere dispute over correct procedure. Nestorius is even more deeply angered by the apparent lack of proper examination of his theology.[2] Even if he is not explicit on the point, it seems obvious that he had expected the council to be something altogether different from a trial, something more closely resembling a philosophical dialogue or substantive doctrinal debate. In fact, the emperor's letter of invitation had expressed a similar expectation, in that it had called for an open-ended discussion of theological difficulties and admonished the participants of the council to aim for an amicable consensus.[3]

---

[1] Nestorius, *Bazaar of Heracleides*, 2.1 (ed. R. P. Bedjan and F. Nau, *Le Livre d'Héraclide de Damas* [Paris, 1910], 195; trans. in G. R. Drivers and L. Hodgson, *The Bazaar of Heracleides* [Oxford, 1925], 132). In the same context Nestorius repeats that Cyril acted as 'persecutor', 'accuser, emperor and judge', and even assumed the role of the 'bishop of Rome' (ibid.).

[2] Nestorius's lengthy exposition of the council's many failures ultimately aims to show how Cyril's doctrinal stance was wrong and how it had been imposed on the council by his underhand usurpation of all the leading roles.

[3] Theodosius II, *Sacra ad synodum*, Collectio Vaticana 31 (ed. E. Schwartz, *Acta conciliorum oecumenicorum*, Vols 1.1.1–7 [Berlin 1927–29], 1.1.1: 120) [hereafter: ACO].

Nestorius's bitter complaints conflate two distinct issues about the application of legal formats in a conciliar context. On the one hand he challenges the meeting over the application of proper court procedure, on the other hand he alerts us to the wider problem of the expediency in principle of using any juridical format when conflicting theologies vie for acceptance as 'orthodoxy'. Interestingly these issues are already intertwined in the council's activities, as we shall see, and appear to be frequently entangled in many synodal meetings in late antiquity. Here two potentially competing aims intersect. The wish to secure a binding condemnation and deposition of an opponent may conflict with the interest in examining and discussing a substantive problem, and ultimately in agreeing a common vision of 'orthodox' doctrine.

For the modern historian trying to assess the achievement of a council and the persuasiveness of its reasoning, the difficulty lies in identifying the elements in the conciliar records that address either, or both, of these concerns, and in analysing their potential interrelation. Any conciliar statement and discussion, ostensibly about 'theology', could be influenced as much by legal considerations as by the need to answer pressing theological problems of the time. Whether conciliar acts should be read primarily as a report of theological discussion, or rather as a transcript of a court-room hearing, needs careful consideration in each case. Of particular interest are those instances where our expectation of finding unequivocal characteristics of a trial on the one hand or a fair-minded heuristic discussion on the other are frustrated. Such instances witness the competing aims mentioned above, as well as the intersection of conflicting expectations about the purpose and function of a council.

To investigate specifically the potential interrelation between theological and juridical aims and modes of conciliar debates will involve a consideration of recent scholarship on the legal and forensic elements of Church councils. Here, parallels between the procedure of ecclesiastical councils and forensic practice in general have not gone unnoticed. Councils have been compared to imperial law courts and to political assemblies.[4] The main elements of an ideal Christian court procedure have been reconstructed and many parallels to the practice of law at the

---

[4] Compare J. Gaudemet, *L'Église dans l'Empire romain: IVe–Ve siècles*, Histoire du droit et des institutions de l'Église en Occident 3 (Paris, 1958; 2nd edn, 1989); K. M. Girardet, *Kaisergericht und Bischofsgericht: Studien zu den Anfängen des Donatistenstreites (313–315) und zum Prozeß des Athanasius von Alexandrien (328–346)*, Antiquitas, Reihe 1.21 (Bonn, 1975).

time have been pointed out.[5] Yet research in the area has primarily concentrated on the settling of disciplinary and organizational dispute and on the formation of early canon law.[6] How legal considerations might have impacted on doctrinal debates has attracted comparatively little attention. In a recent Cambridge Ph.D. dissertation (1999), Caroline Humfress has highlighted the importance of juridical elements to this process. In particular, she has demonstrated the creative expansion and reinterpretation of legal precedent in order to capture the new legal problems posed by the quest for a state-sponsored doctrinal orthodoxy in the post-Constantinian Empire.

'Heresy' was a new phenomenon in imperial law, and legal practitioners looked for precedent in earlier provision against dissenting groups deemed to be politically dangerous, such as the Manicheans. Churchmen struggled to make dissent identifiable as heresy and called for the application of heresy law against opponents, as the Donatist controversy exemplifies. Humfress's examination of these tendencies builds chiefly on correspondence between bishops and imperial officials and on imperial pronouncements, whereas council proceedings play only a marginal role in her analysis.[7] This is perhaps not surprising as we often know very little of the actual conduct of doctrinal debate at most of the councils of the fourth century. While reports of later historians, synodal letters and creedal declarations are extant, there are virtually no protocols or minutes of the actual deliberations and debates. A substantial portion of minuting survives only from the proceedings of the

---

5 A. Steinwenter, 'Der antike kirchliche Rechtsgang und seine Quellen', *Zeitschrift der Savigny-Stiftung für Rechtsgeschichte, Kanonistische Abteilung* 23 (1934), 1–116. The extent to which court hearings could become a predominant task of episcopal administration is also illustrated by J. C. Lamoreaux, 'Episcopal Courts in Late Antiquity', *Journal of Early Christian Studies* 3 (1995), 143–67. His examples clearly show that some familiarity with legal reasoning and procedure can be expected even with those bishops who lacked formal juridical training.

6 The exception is the trial of Eutyches before the 'synodos endemousa' of Constantinople in AD 448, which is the topic of two substantial studies: E. Schwartz, *Der Prozeß des Eutyches*, Sitzungsberichte der Bayerischen Akademie der Wissenschaften, phil.-hist. Abt., 1929, Heft 5 (Munich, 1929); G. May, 'Das Lehrverfahren gegen Eutyches im November des Jahres 448: zur Vorgeschichte des Konzils von Chalkedon', *Annuarium Historiae Conciliorum* 21 (1989), 1–61. It is important to note that the case of Eutyches was a trial of a cleric of inferior rank before a synod of bishops. The hierarchical implications of this constellation caution against an indiscriminate comparison with the cases of Nestorius and Palladius at Ephesus and Aquileia.

7 C. Humfress, 'Forensic Practice and the Development of Roman and Ecclesiastical Law in Late Antiquity, with Special Reference to the Prosecution of Heresy', unpublished Ph.D. thesis, University of Cambridge, 1999; on councils, see esp. 178–83.

Council of Aquileia (AD 381). By contrast, large bodies of acts from the fifth century have been transmitted, beginning with the Council of Ephesus (AD 431). Consideration of these two earliest examples, the *Acta* of Aquileia and Ephesus, will allow a first tentative assessment of the potential interaction between doctrinal and judicial considerations at councils.

The lack of detailed evidence from the earlier councils creates a further difficulty. As far as we know, the fourth-century meetings had not yet established a 'standard' model of synodical proceeding against which to compare what happened in Aquileia or Ephesus. Rather, the various meetings apparently worked out their own agenda and format, and it is only in retrospect from later councils that an 'ideal-type' might be described.

The comparison with court procedures of the time is equally diffi-cult. While the main components of a trial can be reconstructed from numerous documents, there is little direct evidence illustrating the procedural detail of court hearings; indeed, historians of law frequently look for analogous evidence in ecclesiastical trials. Surely, the peculiari-ties of individual cases in hand will have created much variety in the ways in which evidence might be gathered and witnesses questioned. The feature most characteristic of the typical trial of the period, called a *cognitio*, is the complete dominance of the presiding judge, who seems to have exercised great latitude in conducting the examination.[8] Respect for his prerogative may be why there is surprisingly little detailed evidence for protocol in our sources.[9]

Aquileia

The surviving minutes of the council of Aquileia confirm the princi-pally forensic character of much of the debate, which resembles nothing more than an examination as to guilt or innocence conducted by an inquiring magistrate. The place of theological argument proves to be the critical problem in this case. When the council was planned, in

---

[8] A. Berger, *Encyclopedic Dictionary of Roman Law*, American Philosophical Society, Transactions, ns 43.2 (Philadelphia, PA, 1953), svv. *cognitio* and *cognitio extra ordinem* (*extraordinaria*), 393–4. For the main features of a *cognitio* (*extra ordinem*) cf. n. 14 below.

[9] Perhaps unsurprisingly, therefore, it was the role of the 'president' Cyril which agitated Nestorius about Ephesus. And it is equally the role of Ambrose, the *de facto* president at Aquileia, which is the focus of much criticism of what happened there.

AD 379, it was envisaged as a general council of East and West. We can infer from references to Emperor Gratian's original letter of convocation that its purpose was to discuss doctrinal differences and to achieve a peaceful settlement.[10] The plan had been subverted by Theodosius's unilateral action to try to settle the affairs of the eastern Church in Constantinople. Ambrose of Milan, it seems, helped Gratian to save face by suggesting a redefined, narrower remit for a meeting on a much smaller scale. He persuaded Gratian that there was no need for a general council in order to deal with only a small number of bishops opposing the true faith.[11]

Gratian's second letter of invitation, however, does not suggest a change in the principal motivation of facilitating free discussion of doctrinal differences.[12] Nor does it technically put Ambrose in charge of a judicial inquiry into the errors of the two 'Arian' bishops, Palladius and Secundianus.[13] The structural similarities to a *cognitio*, a tribunal of inquiry,[14] are nevertheless evident and Ambrose behaves like a judge

---

[10] The imperial rescript, quoted in *Acta concilii Aquileiensis*, ed. M. Zelzer, CSEL 82.3 (Vienna, 1982) [herafter: *Acta*], 325–68, alludes to Gratian's original sentiment at 328. For the history of the council in general, and the events leading up to it, see R. Gryson, *Scholies Ariennes sur le concile d'Aquilé*, SC 267 (Paris, 1980), esp. introduction, 121–43; note however the comments by Y.-M. Duval, 'La presentation arienne du concile d'Aquilée de 381: à propos des 'Scolies ariennes sur le concile d'Aquilée', *Revue d'histoire ecclésiastique* 76 (1981), 317–31; cf. further G. Gottlieb, 'Das Konzil von Aquileia (381)', *Annuarium Historiae Conciliorum* 11 (1979), 287–306; N. B. McLynn, *Ambrose of Milan: Church and Court in a Christian Capital*, The Transformation of the Classical Heritage 22 (Berkeley, CA and London, 1994), 124–37; H. v. Campenhausen, *Ambrosius von Mailand als Kirchenpolitiker*, Arbeiten zur Kirchengeschichte 12 (Berlin, 1929), 61–80; D. H. Williams, *Ambrose of Milan and the End of the Arian-Nicene Conflicts*, Oxford Early Christian Studies (Oxford, 1995), 157–84.
[11] Gratian, *rescriptum* = *Acta*, 4 (CSEL 82.3, 328: [lines] 31–7); cf. McLynn, *Ambrose*, 125. That Gratian and Theodosius acted not so much in consonance as in competition is pointed out by Duval, *La presentation*, 326.
[12] *Acta*, 4 (CSEL 82.3, 328: 29–31): 'Neque sane nunc aliter iubemus ac iussimus on invertentes praecepti tenorem...'
[13] Palladius, bishop of Ratiaria (Arčar) and Secundianus, bishop of Singidunum (Belgrade) were the only two Homoian prelates who attended the synod and were eventually deposed. Little is known of the two apart from their involvement with the council and its preparation. For Palladius, cf. E. Hoffmann-Aleith, 'Palladios (6)', in A. Pauly, G. Wissowa et al., *Realencyclopädie der classischen Altertumswissenschaft* 36.3 (Stuttgart, 1949), cols. 207–9. My analysis concentrates on the council's dealings with Palladius; the subsequent interrogation of Secundianus (*Acta*, 65–75) commences along similar lines, but the protocol ends abruptly after only a few exchanges.
[14] For the main features of a *cognitio*, see A. Berger, B. Nicholas and A. W. Lintott, 'Law and Procedure, Roman, 3: Criminal Law and Procedure', *Oxford Classical Dictionary* (3rd edn, Oxford, 1996), 831–4, and M. Kaser, *Das römische Zivilprozeßrecht*, 2. Aufl. neu bearb. von K. Hackl, Handbuch der Altertumswissenschaft 10, Rechtsgeschichte des Altertums 3.4 (Munich, 1996).

conducting a forensic inquiry from the start of the minuting.[15] However, the records only begin after a lengthy discussion, which was not taken down by notaries.[16] The very fact that minuting commences is an indicator of a shift in the proceedings. Palladius,[17] now essentially treated as a defendant, repeatedly complains about the apparent subterfuge of Ambrose and his supporters, deviating from the Emperor's orders. He had expected and prepared for a doctrinal disputation of equals.[18] Yet Ambrose had tried to press his agenda from the earliest, unrecorded, exchanges, and to force his main opponent into a difficult position by having a letter of Arius read out.[19] With the start of note-taking the character of the meeting changes, or rather, Ambrose forcefully and unapologetically makes its intended character evident. Arius's letter is once again read, this time clause by clause, and Palladius is asked to condemn each single proposition made, or substantiate it from Scripture.[20] He repeatedly protests the illegitimate character of the meeting in general and of this procedure in particular.[21] He refuses to be pressed into the alternative of either condemning Arius, with whom he denies having any link,[22] or upholding his sentiments. Nevertheless,

---

[15] For a reconstruction of the event as an ecclesiastical *cognitio*, cf. H. J. Sieben, *Die Konzilsidee der Alten Kirche*, Konziliengeschichte, Reihe B: Untersuchungen (Paderborn, 1979), 482–9. Despite Ambrose's domineering role, formally the local bishop and metropolitan of the province, Valerian, was president of the assembly.

[16] As is evident from the very start of the minutes, *Acta*, 2 (CSEL 82.3, 327).

[17] Palladius's account of events survives, in fragments, as part of his *Apologia*, written not long after the synod and apparently still in the hope of reversing its decisions: Palladius, *Apologia* (SC 267, 264–365). See also N. B. McLynn, 'The "Apology" of Palladius: Nature and Purpose', *Journal of Theological Studies* 42 (1991), 52–76.

[18] *Acta*, 12 (CSEL 82.3, 333). He accuses Ambrose of subverting (*subripere*) the Emperor's wishes; *Acta*, 10 (331: 94).

[19] *Acta*, 2 (CSEL 82.3, 327: 9–10); 5 (329: 46–7); 43 (353: 579–81); Palladius, *Apologia*, 90; 92 (337r26–32; 338r45; SC 267, 276, 278). Several further mentions of Arius in *Apologia*, 95–6 also seem to relate to the unofficial preliminary discussions which were not minuted. The letter in question is a translated Latin version of Arius, *Epistula ad Alexandrum episcopum* in H. G. Opitz, ed., *Urkunden zur Geschichte des Arianischen Streits*, Athanasius Werke 3.1 (Berlin 1935), 12–13.

[20] *Acta*, 5 (CSEL 82.3, 329: 48–52); cf. 11 (332: 107–9); 12 (333: 135–6); see also, at a much later point, Ambrose's repeated insistence on this alternative 47 (355: 632).

[21] The debate about the legitimacy of the council (in particular *Acta*, 6–12) is never really settled, and Palladius repeatedly returns to the question, cf. for example *Acta*, 32 (CSEL 82.3, 345: 408–10); 42 (352: 558–60); 43 (353: 586). Protesting its lack of authority, Palladius time and again refuses to answer the questions put to him, *Acta*, 9 (330: 80); 14 (334: 162–3); 29 (343: 365–6); 48 (355: 637–8), and frequently, so as not to prejudice a general council: *Acta*, 11 (332: 12–13); 12 (333: 138–40); cf. 6 (329: 53–5).

[22] Palladius repeatedly asserts this point: *Acta*, 14 (CSEL 82.3, 334: 158); 31 (344: 389–90);

on occasion he also answers to the substantive points and explains his view. For a brief period he even seemingly manages to regain the status of a disputant on equal terms with Ambrose, asking probing questions about his theology.[23] Ambrose gives only rudimentary explanations and scholars have criticized him for coming up short in the exchanges.[24] He evidently wanted to avoid a broad debate at all cost, and swiftly steered the discussion back to the narrow judicial inquiry.

It is tempting to query Ambrose's ability to hold his ground in a discussion with the experienced Palladius, but this would be a failure to appreciate his objectives. Admittedly, confronting Palladius with passages from Arius is anachronistic in terms of the theological debate of the time. Equally, it fails to do justice to the finer points of Homoean theology, which Palladius was able to defend and argue coherently and forcefully. Evidently, Ambrose and his supporters deliberately used the legal framework to curtail discussion. Yet sticking closely to the patterns of a forensic inquiry in this way was not primarily an attempt to generate simplistic doctrinal alternatives for a secure and well-prepared polemic.[25] Rather it enabled the deposition of his opponent for 'heresy': suggesting an intellectual association with 'Arius' as the alleged founder of the heresy was no longer just a rhetorical device to slander an opponent, but could be used to construct a convincing legal case since 'Arians' had recently been officially banned.[26] Consequently,

cf. also, claiming a substantive disagreement, *Acta*, 25 (341: 313); *Acta*, 41–2 (351: 546–52) he again refuses to be drawn on Arius.

[23]   *Acta*, 19–25 (CSEL 82.3, 338–41). He tries again, without much success, to involve Ambrose in discussion *Acta*, 33–6 (346–8), but becomes entangled in the wording of a biblical quotation for which he is immediately censured as falsifying Scripture.

[24]   R. P. C. Hanson, *The Search for the Christian Doctrine of God: the Arian Controversy 318–381* (Edinburgh, 1988), 109–10. Compare his assessment of Ambrose's behaviour at Aquileia in general (667–9) and the scathing criticism of the theology of *De fide* (669–75), which had been composed before the council. Palladius had prepared a dossier based on this treatise and intended to refute Ambrose from it. However, he did not bring it to the meeting that turned into a trial deposing him. His motion to adjourn, giving him the chance to equip himself with it, was dismissed (*Acta*, 50 [CSEL 82.3, 356: 659–60]). Parts of his compilation of Ambrosian 'errors', with critical comments, survive in *Apologia*, 81–7 (SC 267, 264–74).

[25]   For such an assessment, see McLynn, *Ambrose*, 136–7. R. Lim, *Public Disputation, Power, and Social Order in Late Antiquity*, The Transformation of the Classical Heritage 23 (Berkeley, CA, 1995), notes the widespread misgivings against 'debate' in principle at the time (see, in particular, 195, 197–8 for restriction of debate at Aquileia). The demand of Palladius to answer 'in simplicity' (cf. *Acta*, 9 [CSEL 82.3, 331: 83–6]) is used by McLynn to illustrate the sentiment (197–8). However, this admonition is concerned with his denial to condemn unambiguously those phrases by Arius which were put to him. Primarily his refusal to answer is reprimanded here, not so much his demand for debate.

[26]   Compare *Theodosian Code*, 16.5.6.1; 16.5.8.

the recorded *sententiae* by individual bishops condemn Palladius for his refusal to anathematize Arius, and thus for being an 'Arian'.[27]

However, the precise legal background for this approach is far from unequivocal. Theodosius had issued a first explicit condemnation of 'Arians' in January 381. The council of Constantinople repeated the sentiment in canon 1. Both Ambrose and Gratian certainly knew of the council, if, at the time, not necessarily yet of its individual decisions.[28] It is therefore likely that both sides were equally aware of Theodosius's preceding anti-heretical legislation as the necessary precondition for Ambrose's strategy to be successful. Nevertheless, Theodosian laws only had legal force in Gratian's jurisdiction if he chose to endorse and promulgate them. Whether this had happened is uncertain, and, given the sense of competition between them, it is perhaps unlikely.[29] The judicial application of an anti-Arian stance could therefore be seen as an implicit appeal to sanction and enforce this legislation. Employing this legal principle had proven effective in resolving the problem of internal conflict and dissent at Aquileia and had secured a successful outcome for the council, thus commending itself to Gratian as a useful tool of religious policy-making.

Ambrose's strategy rested on shaky ground if taken solely as relating to Gratian's religious legislation. It gains plausibility and efficacy if interpreted as an effort to convince Gratian of the utility of explicit anti-Arian legislation in creating a religiously united (North-) Italy and Illyricum. As such, Ambrose's course of action in the meeting complements his literary presentation of a case for the 'Nicene' doctrine presented to Gratian in his books *De fide*.

In conclusion, the recorded part of the council of Aquileia can

---

[27] *Acta*, 54 (Valerianus): . . . qui Arrium defendit Arrianus est . . . (CSEL 82.3, 359: 712–13); 55 (Anemius): Quicumque haereses Arrianas non condemnat Arrianus sit necesse est (359: 718–19). The association with Arius is pointed out by virtually all bishops subsequently casting their vote as sufficient grounds for his condemnation (*Acta*, 55–64); only Theodorus (62) and Ianuarius (64) fail to mention it.

[28] This is clearly indicated by the lack of information evident in Ambrose, *Epistula extra collectionem* 6 (CSEL 82.3, 186–90), written in Aquileia after the meeting of 3 September 381.

[29] The council's letter, *Epistula* 2.12 (CSEL 82.3, 324: 136), is generally taken to refer to this law and seems to suggest Gratian's publicizing it; see Zelzer's apparatus, *ad locum*. However, the censuring of Photinians mentioned there, could equally refer to their exemption from Gratian's earlier edict of toleration, probably of AD 379 (Socrates, *Historia ecclesiastica*, 5.2.1). Gratian's sponsorship for the Nicene faith from the outset of his reign has long been taken for granted, but is now mostly considered with scepticism and barely suffices to presuppose explicitly anti-Arian legislation in his early years and prior to the council.

almost exclusively be interpreted as a judicial inquiry, which deliberately cut short the possibility of free doctrinal argument and expression.
Instead, one of the disputants is turned into a defendant and confronted
with the document of a known heretic; his failure to condemn it is used
in evidence against him. In this way, the theological debate might
appear to be directed quite anachronistically, but a satisfactory and
proper discussion of theology was never the intention of the council's
leadership. By forcing Palladius to decide his stance towards Arius's
words, they could not only label him rhetorically as an 'Arian'
according to heresiological conventions. More importantly, they also
demonstrated how an effective legal case against dissenting bishops
could be made if only Gratian were content to implement legislation
along the lines of Theodosius's earlier laws.

Ephesus

In the case of Ephesus the interrelation of theological and juridical
elements is even more complex. Nestorius's complaints might lead one
to expect here juridical characteristics and strategies similar to those of
Aquileia. Indeed, it is evident from the acts that legal considerations had
an important role to play. A. de Halleux has analysed the juridical
aspects of the decisive meeting of the 22 June AD 431, and highlighted
a number of features closely resembling court proceedings.[30] However,
the legitimacy of even opening the meeting, and in particular of
entering into the agenda, was contested from the start, because the
arrival of a large group of bishops from the East had been delayed and
the imperial representative Candidianus and a number of bishops allied
with Nestorius protested the need to wait for them. The claim of
Nestorius that Cyril had acted not only as both accuser and judge but
also as 'emperor'[31] in fact struck at the heart of the matter: if Cyril had
acted as emperor, accuser and judge, it was because he had persuaded

---

[30] A. de Halleux, 'La première session du concile d'Éphèse (22 Juin 431)', *Ephemerides
Theologicae Lovanienses* 69 (1993), 48–87. The legal analysis provided by de Halleux in particular hopes to avoid the speculations into the psychology of the main protagonists, the pitfalls
of taking at face value what is rhetorical self-presentation, and suspicions of secretive plotting, all rightly perceived to be problematic methodically. However, once the need to establish the legitimacy of the undertaking with the imperial court is accepted, rhetoric and
self-presentation become once again necessary considerations in the interpretation of the
acts.

[31] See n. 1 above.

his colleagues to enter on the agenda illegally and subsequently steered the proceedings according to his whim. Could a council convened on these terms be accepted as legitimate?

Indeed, the assembly was condemned by a large body of bishops from the *Oriens* diocese immediately after their arrival, and its verdict was never formally endorsed by the imperial court. This difficulty added a further layer of legal consideration, underestimated by de Halleux, which proved decisive for how the meeting proceeded and how it was presented in the edition of the acts. From a purely juridical perspective important steps in the process seem strangely redundant, others ill-placed, to serve their legal purpose in a trial aimed at convicting Nestorius of heresy. These elements need further investigation. They turn out to be of particular value for an assessment of the interplay of theological and juridical considerations. Cyril needed to make a case for the legitimacy of the tribunal with the imperial court, and demonstrating the importance of theological examination on the occasion proved the decisive difficulty.

A brief survey of the proceedings highlights the tensions between two conflicting aims. After the contested opening of the assembly, Nestorius was invited three times to attend. Because in his judgement the council was not a legitimate instrument of government, he refused to run the risk of being seen to confirm its legitimacy by his physical presence. Subsequent delegations were sent and equipped with increasingly harsh notices.[32] The last, not even delivered personally to him, as he refused to see the delegation, amounted beyond doubt to a *libellus conventionis*, an official summons.[33] As Nestorius refused to participate, Cyril could have secured a charge of contempt of court, although, again, his authority to do so was by no means beyond doubt. Yet evidently, this was perceived to be too weak a basis to secure the removal of Nestorius from office in view of the challenges and appeals that would likely be made later. Hence, the bishops decided to try him *in absentia,* and it is to justify this fact legally that Juvenal calls for further proceedings 'in accord with the ecclesiastical canons'.[34] The

---

[32] *Gesta*, 39–42 (ACO, 1.1.2: 9–12).
[33] *Gesta*, 41.3 (ACO, 1.1.2: 11).
[34] *Gesta*, 43 (ACO, 1.1.2: 12, 23). *Pace* de Halleux who believes that Juvenal tried to justify the subsequent reading of the Nicene Creed as the 'legal basis' of the inquiry, 'La première session', 73); Juvenal attempts to establish the legitimacy to begin the inquiry as such, not any specific form of, or step in it. For a trial in absence, see Steinwenter, *Rechtsgang*, 65–75.

formal inquiry into the heresy of Nestorius claims to judge his views against the Nicene Creed as the established norm of orthodoxy. However, Cyril first has his own letter to Nestorius read aloud and asks for its orthodoxy to be confirmed.[35] It is enthusiastically endorsed by the assembly as an authentic interpretation of Nicene Christology.[36] As a consequence, Nestorius's views, initially represented by a letter written in response to Cyril,[37] came to be judged not against the Creed, but against its Cyrillian interpretation. The very fact that Cyril's letter attacked Nestorius's thinking and that Nestorius's response in turn contradicted it, was sufficient to convince the assembly of the heresy of Nestorius, if indeed their previous judgement of Cyril's orthodoxy was to remain valid. It is of little surprise, therefore, that the condemnations of Nestorius proclaimed in the votes do not address any specific defects of his theology, nor give any reason for his alleged heresy. Again, a conviction of Nestorius could have been secured at this point, but the presidency presses on and enters into a new round of additional examination: the conditional condemnation by Pope Celestine, pronounced the previous year, is read out.[38] Witnesses confirm the correct delivery of the verdict and attest to the fact that Nestorius still holds the same sentiments as he did then; he had even expressed them in Ephesus only a few days earlier.[39] After this the case is bolstered by further evidence taken from extracts of his writings and sermons.

Yet, at this point, the acts present us with another detour. Before reading such examples of Nestorius's errors, quotations of orthodox Fathers are presented.[40] No reaction of the assembly either to these extracts or to those of Nestorius is noted. Only at this point is the verdict drafted and signed by virtually all present, and by further bishops over the course of the following days.[41]

This brief summary shows that at least twice in the proceedings

---

35 Cyril, *Epistula ad Nestorium 2*, Gesta, 44 (ACO, 1.1.2: 13).

36 *Gesta*, 45 (ACO, 1.1.2: 13–31), lists 126 statements.

37 Nestorius, *Epistula 2 ad Cyrillum*, read and voted upon *Gesta*, 46–7 (ACO, 1.1.2: 31–5).

38 Caelestin, *Epistula 11*: read *Gesta*, 49 (ACO, 1.1.2: 36). Lim, *Public Disputation*, 222–3, also notes that subsequent deliberations do not add anything to the decision already reached.

39 *Gesta*, 50 (ACO, 1.1.2: 37); *Gesta*, 51–3 (37–8).

40 *Gesta*, 54; excerpts from Nestorian texts follow *Gesta*, 60 (ACO, 1.1.2: 45–52). For a detailed analysis of this part of the proceedings and their presentation in the acts, cf. my *Die Kirche der Väter, Vätertheologie und Väterbeweis in den Kirchen des Ostens bis zum Konzil von Ephesus (431)*, Beiträge zur historischen Theologie 118 (Tübingen, 2002), 385–93.

41 *Gesta*, 61 (ACO, 1.1.2: 54, 16–25) notes the verdict, signed by 197 bishops: *Gesta*, 62 (55–64).

normal expectations of a judicial inquiry into the alleged heresy of Nestorius are subverted. The acclamation of Cyril's orthodoxy precedes the mirroring condemnation of Nestorius, and in a similar fashion the collection of orthodox writing precedes extracts of Nestorius's errors. Both instances juxtapose an orthodox position with Nestorius's heresy, and in both cases orthodox voices take precedence over those of the erroneous position by their placing in the acts. In the case of Cyril's letter, this sequence is essential in achieving a condemnation of Nestorius, as it effectively prejudges his opponent's claims. However, Cyril's orthodoxy is not properly a topic for discussion, if indeed the council did intend to conduct a heresy trial against Nestorius. Moreover, in a judicial inquiry the patristic quotations would have no real purpose at all.[42] They simply counterbalance the prominence given necessarily to Nestorian extracts. It is revealing that in the earliest reports of the meeting, in letters to the Emperor and to Pope Celestine, the council's dealing with patristic texts is not even mentioned.[43] Variants in the textual transmission of the passage in question[44] give further cause for suspicion that a later insertion has been made into the acts at the point of editing by the Alexandrian chancellery.

Such tensions demonstrate the apparent hybridity of the proceedings and of their subsequent representation in the acts. While some elements find a juridical explanation in a heresy tribunal, others, notably those relating to Cyril's letter and other evidence in support of 'orthodoxy', need a different explanation. The search for such an explanation brings us back to the original remit of the council set out in the imperial convocation. Theodosius II had demanded an impartial inquiry into the doctrinal differences and a fair discussion[45] – not dissimilar from Gratian's intentions in AD 379. However, this was not what Cyril intended to do and it was certainly not what happened on the day. Yet it is equally clear that the endorsement of the Emperor was decisive for the council's decisions to come into effect.

[42] Compare de Halleux, 'La première session', 78–9. This late in the process, after two rounds of evidence both of which had already established the 'heresy', a list of quotations functioning as 'accusation' is at least misplaced, if not redundant. Furthermore, the form and content of the extracts do not readily serve this purpose either. The closest we come to a direct contradiction of Nestorian terminology are some quotations that make use of the term *'theotokos'*. It is telling for the lack of real legal import that the acts do not introduce the 'reading' of patristic extracts with any sense of purpose at all.

[43] The relevant documents are discussed in my *Kirche der Väter*, 393–8.

[44] See Schwartz, ACO, 1.1.2: 45, *apparatus ad locum*.

[45] See n. 3 above.

As a result, Cyril was keen to present the court with the impression of an orderly juridical procedure. The *Acta* were produced and published by the Alexandrian episcopal offices, and thus their use of legal language and allusion to standard forensic process at important junctions of the proceeding can in some sense be assumed to reflect Cyril's own view of the course of events. At the same time, Cyril needed to suggest that despite this forensic character sound doctrinal deliberations had nevertheless prevailed, and something resembling the imperially mandated discussions had indeed taken place.

Thus, the *Acta* offer a carefully constructed simulacrum of a largely fictional theological debate. Both main opponents had been heard, it is suggested – albeit by a reading of their letters – and both had been judged. In addition, the excerpts of the Fathers had entered into a discussion with Nestorius's extracts – albeit only in the edited acts. The absence of any real discussion of doctrine – Cyril wants us to believe – was due to Nestorius's refusal to present himself and to the failure of the Antiochene bishops to arrive on time. In their stead, the reading out of documents had provided the assembly with the opportunity to come to a clear view of the alternative teachings at hand. Their judgement was as much a result of doctrinal debate, mainly by proxy of documents, as of a juridical evaluation of Nestorius's heresy. This is the main message of the *Acta* as published by the Alexandrian episcopal offices.

To sum up, the bishops meeting at Ephesus subverted the Emperor's request for doctrinal examination and settlement as much as their colleagues at Aquileia had done. Transforming the council into an ecclesiastical court of law provided the means for doing so on both occasions; and in each case the use of documents plays a decisive role. However, the use of forensic procedure and legal language served different purposes in each case. In Aquileia, the reading of Arius's letter removed any potential for a wider doctrinal investigation and offered instead a narrow inquiry into Palladius's willingness to condemn its propositions. By contrast, the acts of Ephesus demonstrate a double usage of documents, which brings about an opposite effect. For a narrow juridical purpose, the questioning of Nestorius is substituted by readings taken from his works. However, the additional consideration of Cyril's texts and the editorial bolstering of orthodoxy by the insertion of excerpts from the Fathers interrupt the strictly forensic procedure and suggest the presence of a (largely fictional) deliberative aspect to the proceedings. The implication is that the council's character as a forensic inquiry was not intended to curtail doctrinal deliberation, which could not take place in the absence of Nestorius and other Antiochene theologians anyway. Of course, the very fact that a verdict was pronounced under these circumstances could be perceived as suppressing fair doctrinal discussion. Thus the inclusion of additional documentation, which tries to counter this impression and to demonstrate legitimacy by different means, defending Cyril's contested presidency, aiming to create the illusion of unbiased doctrinal deliberations, and insinuating the Emperor's demands, had been met – albeit by proxy of documents.

* * *

The two test cases presented show a complex interrelationship between the demands and mechanisms of doctrinal discussion and definition on the one hand, and the wish to secure legally binding decisions setting in motion the execution and application of imperial religious law on the other. Legal procedure was used in both cases, chiefly in an attempt to demonstrate the legitimacy of an anti-heretical verdict. In Aquileia, only the – mostly implicit – appeal to recent imperial legal procurement elevated the strategy imposed by the presidency above previous rhetorical stereotyping in alleging 'Arianism'. It aided and justified Ambrose's unwillingness to enter into substantial argument. In Ephesus the very right to conduct a trial was contested and a double strategy employed in response. The acts aim to demonstrate the procedural correctness of the trial on the one hand, and on the other, to suggest it encompassed the deliberative elements required by imperial rescript, which it clearly did not at the time. The trial in Aquileia sought to convince Gratian that further doctrinal debate was unnecessary. The 'trial' in Ephesus was disguised by the admixture of documents suggesting an 'open-ended' discussion. Both cases prove that the juridical format was flexible enough to serve different purposes. They call for further and more detailed investigation into the interrelation of actual doctrinal debate and its prevalent legal framework throughout antiquity. Careful analysis of the application of legal procedure in cases of doctrinal difference – primarily, but not exclusively, in Church councils – and, conversely, of the role of doctrinal interest in the development and interpretation of (ecclesiastical) law allows a better understanding of both the mechanisms for settling ecclesiastical conflict and the development of officially sanctioned 'orthodox' doctrine.

University of Cambridge

'AD SEDEM EPISCOPALEM REDDANTUR': BISHOPS, MONKS, AND MONASTERIES IN THE DIOCESE OF WORCESTER IN THE EIGHTH CENTURY*

by MARTIN RYAN

Alas! brother, alas! For almost everywhere in this land the rule of regular life falls away and the secular way of life thrives.[1]

ALCUIN of York's famous lament to Abbot Æthelbald of Wearmouth-Jarrow at the end of the eighth century could serve as a neat summary of the traditional scholarly picture of eighth-century Anglo-Saxon monasticism: a movement in near-terminal decline with falling standards in religious observance and monasteries increasingly coming under secular control.[2] The bishops of Worcester have been seen by many scholars as taking a leading role in the fight-back against this creeping secularization. It was not, however,

* Numerous individuals have read and commented on various versions of the material in this paper and their input has improved it immeasurably. My thanks and gratitude go to all of them: Nick Higham; Conrad Leyser; Paul Fouracre; Barbara Yorke; Alex Rumble; Kate Cooper and the indefatigable members of the University of Manchester Centre for Late Antiquity; Hannah Williams; Julia Hillner. Last, but certainly not least, Rosa Vidal Doval: 'Dáme os teus bicos i os teus brazos ábreme'.

[1] Alcuin, *Epistolae*, ed. E. Dümmler, Epistolae Karolini Aevi II MGH, Epistolae 4 (Berlin, 1895), 18–481, no. 67: 'Heu, frater, heu, quia paene ubique regularis vite in hac terra cadit normula et secularis vitae crescit formula'. All translations are my own. J. Blair, *The Church in Anglo-Saxon Society* (Oxford, 2005), 124–5, has suggested 'by "secular" Alcuin [may] have meant the life of priests as against that of nuns and monks'. Given the lines that follow this one in the letter ('Et quod pessimum est, ipsi structores multis in locis fiunt destructores, et edificatores dissipatores. Et hoc est, quod per prophetam dictum est, "Ipsi enim pastores erraverunt." ') such an interpretation would seem to me, however, to force too negative an opinion of the life of the secular clergy onto a man who had, after all, spent his youth as part of the cathedral community at York. It is possible that Alcuin is making reference to the comfortable and luxurious way of life in the secularized monasteries through a pun on 'formula', a pattern or way of doing things but also a type of chair or bench suitable for relaxation (see, for example, Gregory of Tours, *Libri historiarum X*, bk 8, ch. 31, in B. Krusch, ed., *Gregorii Turonensis Opera*, 2 vols, MGH Scriptores Rerum Merovingicarum 1 [Hannover, 1937], 1: 398, line 1), though this usage seems to have been relatively restricted.

[2] See, for example, J. Godfrey, *The Church in Anglo-Saxon England* (Cambridge, 1962), 163–6 or N. Brooks, *The Early History of the Church of Canterbury: Christ Church from 597 to 1066* (London, 1984), 177–80. For recent discussion, see C. Cubitt, *Anglo-Saxon Church Councils c.650–c.850* (London, 1995), 110–22 and Blair, *The Church*, esp. 79–134.

that they played a key role in the drafting of conciliar legislation or that they produced texts condemning the lax standards of Anglo-Saxon monasticism. Rather, successive bishops of Worcester have been seen, since the eighteenth century at least, as challenging secularization through the property strategies they adopted.[3] In order to challenge lay lordship, secularization and declining monastic standards the bishops of Worcester in the eighth century were, in Brooks' words, 'attempting, with mixed success, to persuade lords to bequeath their family monasteries to the see of Worcester'.[4] This allowed the bishops to have greater control over the monasteries in their diocese than existing legislation would otherwise have permitted. The bishops could directly intervene in the affairs of these monasteries and impose their own abbots and staff. As Thacker argues, the bishops of Worcester were attempting to ensure 'independent proprietary monasteries were brought under their control and put in the charge of priests from the episcopal *familia*'.[5]

Such an approach is facilitated by the relative richness of the material from the diocese of Worcester. The archives of the cathedral at Worcester preserved by far the largest number of charters purporting to date from before c. AD 800. Moreover, unlike the archives of most of the other major Anglo-Saxon religious institutions from this period, the early charters preserved at Worcester contain not only direct grants to the cathedral at Worcester itself but also a large number of grants to monasteries and the subsequent re-granting of these institutions and their estates to Worcester.[6] Such re-grants sometimes occurred as a

---

[3] V. Green, *The History and Antiquities of the City of Worcester and Its Suburbs*, 2 vols (London, 1796), 1: 24–5. For more recent comment, see P. Sims-Williams, *Religion and Literature in Western England, 600–800* (Cambridge, 1990), at, for example, 140–1 and P. Wormald, 'Charters, Law and the Settlement of Disputes in Anglo-Saxon England', in W. Davies and P. Fouracre, eds, *The Settlement of Disputes in Early Medieval Europe* (Cambridge, 1986), 149–68, at 157.

[4] Brooks, *Early History*, 179.

[5] A. Thacker, 'Monks, Preaching and Pastoral Care in Early Anglo-Saxon England', in J. Blair and R. Sharpe, eds, *Pastoral Care Before the Parish* (London, 1992), 137–70, at 165.

[6] For a list of monasteries likely to have come under the control of Worcester by c.800, see Sims-Williams, *Religion and Literature*, 169. The early charters in the archive of the episcopal seat at Selsey are similarly dominated by grants to smaller religious foundations that later came under episcopal control. See S. E. Kelly, *Charters of Selsey* (Oxford, 1998), xxx–xxxi. I have used term 'monastery' in this paper rather than the term 'minster' that is sometimes preferred by Anglo-Saxon scholars as whilst 'monastery' may have misleading connotations for the Anglo-Saxon period, the term 'minster' is likely to have as many misleading connotations for non-specialist readers. For discussion of the terms, see Blair, *The Church*, 3–4 and for a recent and important reconsideration of monasteries and churches in this period, see C. Cubitt, 'The Clergy in Early Anglo-Saxon England', *HR* 78 (2005), 273–87.

MARTIN RYAN

direct grant to Worcester by the owner of the monastery, but the
majority are reversionary grants in which the monastery will only come
under Worcester's control sometime in the future either after the death
of a certain number of heirs or when some specific conditions have
been met.

It is the re-grants of these monasteries to Worcester that scholars
have seen as evidence of the bishops' 'assault on lay lordship'.[7] In the
terms of this volume, the model that has been applied to the early
charters of the Worcester archive is one of discipline: bishops were
taking monasteries under their direct control in order to raise standards
and remove excessive secular interference. Such a model, while useful,[8]
runs the risk of ignoring the very diversity that is such a feature of the
Worcester archive. By simply understanding the material in terms of
general trends across the whole of Anglo-Saxon England or by
exploring it principally from a top-down, episcopal viewpoint, scholars
have tended to ignore the motivations of the heads of the monasteries
that passed under the control of Worcester or have equated their intentions with those of their diocesan bishops.

The aim of this paper, then, is not to overturn existing studies of the
Worcester material but rather to argue that they may be supplemented
by an approach that focuses more explicitly on the owners of the
monasteries themselves. It argues that, amongst other things, the
owners of monasteries may have used the strategy of reversion to
diocesan ownership as a means of furthering their own agendas in an
environment in which the control of land was frequently contentious.
Alongside this, it stresses the need to take into full account the difficulties and complexities presented by the surviving documentary record. It
begins by briefly reviewing evidence for monastic decline in the eighth
century before moving on to consider in more detail two case studies
from the Worcester archive.

It was the Venerable Bede who first voiced concerns about the state
of the Church and monasticism in particular. In a number of his
exegetical works Bede bemoaned the sluggishness of the Northumbrian
Church of his day[9] and in his *Historia ecclesiastica* he praised the Golden

7 Brooks, *Early History*, 180.
8 Though note the important caveat about the geographical distribution of the
evidence highlighted by Blair, *The Church*, 115–16.
9 The now classic statement is A. Thacker, 'Bede's Ideal of Reform', in P. Wormald,
D. Bullough and R. Collins, eds, *Ideal and Reality in Frankish and Anglo-Saxon Society: Studies
Presented to J. M. Wallace-Hadrill* (Oxford, 1983), 130–53. For a detailed consideration of these

Age of the English Church in the 670s whilst, for the most part, remaining ominously silent about the early decades of the eighth century.[10] It is in his final surviving work, his letter to Bishop Ecgberht of York written around 734, that, despite his generally gentle and paternalistic tone, Bede's criticism is most overt.[11] He presents a picture of a Northumbria lacking in adequate provision of pastoral care and overwhelmed by monasteries that are, in his words, useless to both man and God and ruled by abbots who possess neither the necessary religious training nor love for the monastic life.[12]

Over the next few decades the state of the Church in the south-Humbrian kingdoms similarly came under attack. Around 747, the Anglo-Saxon missionary Boniface complained in a letter to the Archbishop of Canterbury that Anglo-Saxon laymen were forcibly taking control of monasteries and then ruling them as abbots.[13] The Church council held at *Clovesho* in 747 painted an equally unflattering picture of south-Humbrian Church. Amongst other things, priests were warned against drunkenness, the love of filthy lucre, and indecent speech; monasteries under lay control were condemned; and bishops were instructed to ensure the monasteries in their dioceses remain places of quiet contemplation and did not become 'shelters of theatrical [or ludicrous] arts, that is, of poets, harpists, musicians, and jokers'.[14]

It may be too simplistic to characterize the eighth century straightforwardly as a period in which churchmen, and in particular bishops, railed against the increasing secularization and declining standards of

issues in one of Bede's exegetical works, see S. DeGregorio, 'Bede's *In Ezram et Neemiam* and the Reform of the Northumbrian Church', *Speculum* 79 (2004), 1–25.

[10] W. Goffart, 'L'*Histoire ecclésiastique* et l'engagement politique de Bède', in S. Lebecq, M. Perrin and O. Szerwiniack, eds, *Bède le Vénérable entre tradition et postérité* (Lille, 2005), 149–58, esp. 150–1. The theme is discussed more generally by O. Szerwiniack, 'L'*Histoire ecclésiastique* ou le rêve d'un retour au temps de l'innocence', ibid., 159–76.

[11] On the tone of the letter, see, for example, G. Musca, *Il Venerabile Beda storico dell'alto medioevo* (Bari, 1973), 347: 'c'è il tono paterno ed affettuoso, ma anche la serietà di chi ha da dire cose gravi'.

[12] Bede, *Espitola ad Ecgbertum*, in C. Plummer, ed., *Venerabilis Baedae Opera Historica*, 2 vols (Oxford, 1896), 1: 405–23. For discussion, see Musque, *Beda*, 345–56, Sims-Williams, *Religion and Literature*, 115–29 and Blair, *The Church*, 100–8.

[13] Boniface, *Espistolae*, in M. Tangl, ed., *Die Briefen des heiligen Bonifatius und Lullus* MGH Epistolae Selectae 1 (2nd edn, Berlin,1955), no. 78.

[14] *Council of Clovesho, AD 747*, in A. W. Haddan and W. S. Stubbs, eds, *Councils and Ecclesiastical Documents Relating to Great Britain and Northern Ireland*, 3 vols (Oxford, 1869–71), 3: 362–76, canon five, for lay-controlled monasteries, canon nine for the behaviour of the clergy, and canon twenty: 'ludicrarum artium receptacula, hoc est, poetarum, citharistarum, musicorum, scurrorum'.

the Anglo-Saxon Church. Not only does it under emphasize the extent to which there could be disagreement between individual church-men,[15] but the complaints and conciliar legislation of the eighth century were arguably as much about defining what was meant by such slippery terms as 'monastic' and 'secular' as they were an attempt to return the Anglo-Saxon Church to a previous Golden Age.[16] Certainly, as Blair has highlighted, leading Anglo-Saxon churchmen in the seventh century seemed to have been prepared to tolerate attitudes to monastic property that would have been condemned by Bede or Boniface in the eighth century.[17] Moreover, some complaints voiced in eighth-century Church councils that have been taken as evidence for declining standards can be mirrored in earlier legislation. A council about the English Church held at Rome in 679 ordered, if the surviving *acta* can be trusted, 'that bishops and all who have professed the religious life of the ecclesiastical order do not bear arms, or keep harpists or other musicians[?], or permit any other jests or games in their presence'.[18]

However the complaints and conciliar legislation of the eighth century are viewed, it is clear that over the course of that century leading Anglo-Saxon churchmen were increasingly prepared to challenge what they saw as the dangers now facing the Anglo-Saxon Church and monasticism in particular. Should, then, the evidence from Worcester be read as part of these wider strategies? The first case-study concerns the record of a dispute over the control of a monastery at Withington in Gloucestershire.[19] According to this record, King

15 As is illustrated, for example, by the differing attitudes of Bede, Boniface, and the Council of *Clovesho* of 747 to what should be done about monasteries under secular control. For discussion, see Thacker, 'Monks', 165 and Cubitt, *Church Councils*, 105.

16 Stark's observations on the 'myth of past piety' are also pertinent, see R. Stark, 'Secularization, R.I.P.' *Sociology of Religion* 60 (1999), 249–73.

17 Blair, *The Church*, 90–1.

18 *Council at Rome, AD 679* in Haddan and Stubbs, *Councils*, 3: 131–5: 'ut Episcopi vel quicunque ecclesiastici ordinis religiosam vitam professi sunt, armis non utantur, nec citharoedas habeant, vel quaecunque symphoniaca, nec quoscunque jocos vel ludos ante se permittant'. The *acta* of this council survive only as part of a post-Conquest *vita* of Archbishop Theodore by Goscelin of St Bertin, see H. Vollrath, *Die Synoden Englands bis 1066* (Paderborn, 1985), 77 n. 152. For discussion of the authenticity or otherwise of the *acta*, see M. Gibbs, 'The Decrees of Agatho and the Gregorian Plan for York', *Speculum* 68 (1973), 213–46.

19 W. de G. Birch, ed., *Cartularium Saxonicum: a Collection of Charters Relating to Anglo-Saxon History*, 3 vols (London, 1885–93), 1: 156, listed as 1429 in P. Sawyer, *Anglo-Saxon Charters: an Annotated List and Bibliography* (London, 1968) with revisions by S. Kelly, at http://

Æthelred of Mercia and his subking, King Oshere of the Hwicce, granted to two nuns, Dunne and her daughter Bucge, land by the river Coln for the foundation of a monastery.[20] Shortly before her death, Dunne bequeathed the monastery and its lands to her grand-daughter, Hrothwaru. As Hrothwaru was still a child, Dunne entrusted the monastery and its foundation charter to Hrothwaru's unnamed but married mother. Subsequently, and presumably having come of age, Hrothwaru asked her mother that the charter be given back to her and her mother refused and claimed that it had been stolen.

Around 736, the matter was brought before a Church synod presided over by Archbishop Nothhelm of Canterbury that found in favour of Hrothwaru.[21] It decreed that the missing charter of donation, whether that be the original royal charter or the document recording Dunne's bequest, should be rewritten, condemned the person who had 'presumed to snatch away, either by theft or by obtaining it fraudulently by any other means, the first charter', and confirmed Hrothwaru's control of the monastery.[22] The synod also decreed that after Hrothwaru's death control of the monastery was to revert to the episcopal see of Worcester, just as her elders had originally decreed.

Sims-Williams understands this document as demonstrating that reversion of control of the monastery to the episcopal see 'had been agreed from the first precisely in order to avoid secularization of the estate by parties such as Hrothwaru's mother'.[23] Indeed, he goes so far as to argue that reversion to the episcopal see had been a condition of the original grant to Dunne and Bucge 'and when Dunne wished to bequeath the monastery to her grand-daughter she had to obtain Bishop Ecgwine's permission'.[24]

This may be to push the evidence too far. The record of the original dispute does not state that the bequest to Hrothwaru was made with the consent of Bishop Ecgwine; this detail only occurs in the record of a later lease of Withington.[25] Nevertheless, Sims-Williams is right to

www.trin.cam.ac.uk/sdk13/chartwww/eSawyer.99/eSawyer2.html [hereafter: Sawyer], accessed 4 July 2005.

[20] This initial transaction can be dated to the period 674–704, see H. P. R. Finberg, *The Early Charters of the West Midlands* (2nd edn, London, 1972), 32.

[21] For dating, see Cubitt, *Church Councils*, 265.

[22] 'cartam [. . .] primtivo vel per furta vel quolibet modo fraudulenter auferendo subripere praesumpsit'.

[23] Sims-Williams, *Religion and Literature*, 132.

[24] Ibid., 140.

[25] Sawyer, 1255 (Birch, *Cartularium Saxonicum*, 217). The list of donations to Worcester

stress that reversionary grants had the potential to place religious foundations under the protection and patronage of a larger religious institution, in this case Worcester. Importantly, and rarely commented on, reversionary grants allowed the owners of a monastery, and perhaps their heirs, to retain control of the foundation in the short term and yet still enjoy the patronage and protection of the larger institution for that foundation. Such actions are likely to have had the potential to frustrate rival claims on the foundation and its landed resources: there was a vested interest in ensuring control of the institution remained with the person who had made the reversionary grant or with their heirs.

Why, then, was such patronage needed and what rival claims might there be? In theory, lands granted by charter ('bookland'), such as the monastery at Withington and its estates, could be freely alienated by the beneficiary and their appointed heirs and, indeed, this freedom of alienation was the primary purpose of such grants.[26] In practice, however, the ability of the beneficiary to pass on the land to whomsoever they wished is likely to have been more restricted. As Reynolds notes, 'whatever the terms of charters, many alienations must have been subject to family negotiation, social values and political pressure'[27] and for all the charters' insistence on freedom of alienation when re-grants of land are recorded in the sources they are frequently said to have been made with the permission of the king or the bishop.[28]

Scholars have tended to emphasize the problems presented by the secular kin of a religious. As Yorke puts it 'Anglo-Saxon society also seems to have found it difficult to come to terms with the idea that estates granted to an individual . . . to endow a church did not give automatic rights in the land to that individual's family.'[29] Put simply, given that the grants recorded in charters were most often described as

printed by Dugdale similarly describes the bequest to Hrothwaru as made 'licentiâ Eguini episcopi', but this detail may simply be summarizing Sawyer, 1255, see W. Dugdale, *Monasticon Anglicanum . . .*, 3 vols (London, 1655–73), I: 137.

[26] See, for example, E. John, *Land Tenure in Early England: a Discussion of Some Problems* (London, 1960), 43 or P. Wormald, *Bede and the Conversion of England: the Charter Evidence* (Jarrow, 1984), 21–3.

[27] S. Reynolds, 'Bookland, Folkland and Fiefs', *Anglo-Norman Studies* 14 (1992), 211–27, at 217.

[28] See, for example, the extended series of transactions concerning land at Peppering in what is now West Sussex: Sawyer, 44 (Kelly, *Charters of Selsey*, no. 5).

[29] B. Yorke, *Kings and Kingdoms of Early Anglo-Saxon England* (London, 1990), 163–4. For similar statements, see, for example, M. M. Sheehan, *The Will in Medieval England: from the Conversion of the Anglo-Saxons to the End of the Thirteenth Century* (Toronto, 1963), 91–3.

made to a particular individual or a particular individual and religious institution,[30] there was the danger that such grants would be seen as the personal property of the named individual rather than the property of the institution. Their kindred, either unaware of or ignoring the freedom of alienation granted by charter, might then claim some stake in it on the death of the original beneficiary.[31] Such a situation clearly may have led to the secularization of a monastery or it being controlled by a person untrained in the religious life and it is presumably this type of situation that Sims-Williams was invoking in his discussion of the Withington dispute.

Yet it is also worth stressing the extent to which there could be disputes and competing claims within monasteries and between religious heirs. The mid eighth-century *Succinctus dialogus ecclesiasticae institutionis* of Archbishop Ecgberht of York offers some evidence for one of the possible causes of such factionalism.[32] In question eleven Ecgberht is asked by his unidentified interlocutor what should be done if the owner of a monastery leaves it to two people who then cannot agree on who should control it. Ecgberht answers that the monastic community should 'choose from the two the one who they desire to be in charge' and that he should be appointed abbot with the advice of the diocesan bishop.[33] Though such a source is likely to particularly emphasize episcopal power, nevertheless it hints at the potential benefits of securing the support of the diocesan bishop in disputes over the control of a monastery.

Factionalism is likely to have been an ever-present threat within monasteries,[34] and even in an institution such as Monkwearmouth-Jarrow the dangers of disunity and disputes over control of it and thus its landed resources are likely never to have been too far away. As

---

[30] A. Scharer, *Die angelsächsische Königsurkunde im 7. und 8. Jahrhundert* (Vienna, 1982), 33.

[31] The most oft-cited example is in Bede, *Historia abbatum*, in C. Plummer, ed., *Baedae Opera Historica*, 2 vols (Oxford, 1896), 1: 364–87, ch. 11. For brief discussion, see Blair, *The Church*, 90 n. 56, and Yorke, *Kings and Kingdoms*, 164.

[32] For the authenticity of this document, see A. J. Frantzen, *The Literature of Penance in Anglo-Saxon England* (Brunswick, NJ, 1983), 82 and for the manuscript tradition of the text and a discussion of dating, see D. A. Bullough, *Alcuin: Achievement and Reputation* (Leiden, 2004), 230–1

[33] Ecgberht of York, *Succinctus dialogus ecclesiasticae institutionis*, in Haddan and Stubbs, *Councils*, 3: 403–13, at 408: 'Venerabilis congregatio unum ex duobus eligat, quem praeesse desiderat, et hic cum consilio Episcopi loci constituatur abbas.'

[34] As seemed to have been understood by the *Rule* of Benedict, see J. Neufville, ed. and trans., *La Règle de Saint Benoît*, 6 vols (Paris, 1971–2), at, for example, chs 65, 69–71.

Coates has argued, though the two histories of Monkwearmouth-Jarrow produced in the early decades of the eighth century stress the unity of the twin-sited monastery, the fear of disunity and factionalism hovers menacingly in the background.[35] The absence of Abbots Ceolfrith and Sigfrith from the calendar preserved in Berlin, Phillips MS 1869, which despite a complex and much debated textual history relies in some way on a calendar compiled at Monkwearmouth-Jarrow over the course of the late seventh to mid-eighth centuries, might suggest continued hostility and factionalism into the mid-eighth century given that the other abbots from the period of the calendar's composition, Benedict Biscop, Eosterwine, and Hwætberht/Eusebius, are all included therein.[36] Episcopal protection and patronage might be invoked, then, not simply to defend against the rapacity of secular kin but also to defeat the claims of other competing factions within a monastery, factions that may, as Egberht's *Dialogus* suggests, have had equally legitimate claims. Though the record of the dispute surrounding the control of the monastery at Withington looks on first sight to set out a simple case of a synod intervening to remove lay control from a monastery it is worth remembering that in this period, at least, Anglo-Saxon charters were *Empfängerausfertigungen*.[37] As Wormald has argued, 'not only did the Church alone preserve judicial records; in this period churches alone wrote them up' and with the lack of any precisely defined forms for drawing up such records ecclesias-

[35] S. Coates, 'Ceolfrid: History, Hagiography and Memory in Seventh- and Eighth-Century Wearmouth-Jarrow', *Journal of Medieval History* 25 (1999), 69–86.

[36] The calendar is edited by A. Borst, *Die karolingische Kalenderreform*, MGH Schriften 46 (Hannover, 1998), 254–98. The Wearmouth-Jarrow connection is outlined by W. Böhne, 'Das älteste Lorscher Kalendar', in F. Knöpp, ed, *Die Reichsabtei Lorsch: Festschrift zum Gedenken an ihre Stiftung 764*, 2 vols (Darmstadt, 1977), 2: 171–220, at 174–6 who also, at 175, notes the absence of Ceolfrith and Sigfrith. For discussion of the relationship between Phillips 1869 and its Wearmouth-Jarrow exemplar, see, for example, A. Borst, *Das Buch der Naturgeschichte: Plinius und seine Leser im Zeitalter des Pergaments* (Heidelberg, 1994), 127–8 and idem, *Die karolingische Kalenderreform*, 247–52. For criticism of Borst's work, see P. Meyvaert, 'Discovering the Calendar (*Annalis Libellus*) Attached to Bede's Own Copy of De temporum ratione', *AnBoll* 120 (2002), 5–64, whose conclusions were, in the main, supported by D. A. Bullough, 'York, Bede's Calendar and a Pre-Bedan English Martyrology', *AnBoll* 121 (2003), 329–55. For Borst's response to these and other critiques of his thesis, see A. Borst, *Der Streit um den karolingischen Kalender*, MGH Studien und Texte 36 (Hannover, 2004)

[37] See, for example, Scharer, *Königsurkunde*, 17 and, with specific reference to the Withington dispute, Vollrath, *Die Synoden*, 134. Earlier views on the production of Anglo-Saxon charters are usefully summarized by R. Drögereit, 'Gab es eine angelsächsische Königskanzlei?' *Archiv für Urkundenforschung* 13 (1935), 335–436, at 335–40.

tical scribes 'had the freedom to be as biased as they liked'.[38] Such documents should not, therefore, be read as the neutral records of the
settlement of a dispute. Rather, they might present only those sides of
the case best suited to the institution that drew up the account, in this
case most probably Worcester. Charters might be seen less as adjuncts
to memory and more as a replacement for it and the records may
actually hide, deliberately so, a number of other competing claims.[39]

In the context of the Withington dispute it is worth noting that two
women, Dunne and Bucge, had originally been granted the land to
found the monastery. Bucge slips out of the record immediately and
the account of the dispute only records that when Dunne left the
monastery to her infant grand-daughter, Hrothwaru, Dunne was
presiding over it alone. It is usually assumed that Bucge had died by this
point but the record never actually states this.[40] The possibility that
Bucge has been deliberately written out of the record or role her role
underplayed is increased when the later history of the monastery at
Withington is considered. Having passed under episcopal control, in
774 Withington was leased out to an Abbess Æthelburh.[41] The document recording this lease describes the foundation of the monastery,
but Dunne is named as the sole founder and no mention is made of
Bucge.[42] It is difficult to understand why Bucge's role in the foundation
should be omitted from the record. If Bucge had died and left her share
in the monastery to Dunne, why was this not recorded? There is at least
the possibility that Bucge has been deliberately written out of the
record in order to undermine her or her heirs' claims on Withington.

The role of Hrothwaru's unnamed mother in the dispute is also
difficult to determine precisely. Though the record states that she was
unwilling to hand over the original charters to her daughter and so
claimed they had been stolen, the synod apparently accepted that the

---

[38] Wormald, 'Charters', 153.

[39] This idea of charters as a means of replacing memory and fixing one particular
version of events is explored in detail by S. Foot, 'Reading Anglo-Saxon Charters: Memory,
Record or Story?', in E. M. Tyler and R. Balzaretti, eds, *Narrative and History in the Early Medieval West* (Turnhout, 2006). I am very grateful to Professor Foot for allowing me to read a
version of this paper prior to publication; my debt to it will be immediately apparent.

[40] See, for example, M. Lapidge, 'Some Remnants of Bede's Lost *Liber epigrammatum*',
EHR 90 (1975), 798–820, at 816.

[41] Sawyer, 1255 (Birch, *Cartularium Saxonicum*, 217).

[42] Bucge is similarly absent from the description of Withington in the list of grants to
Worcester discussed above in n. 25.

charters had actually been stolen or otherwise fraudulently removed for it did not condemn the mother for the theft of the charters but instead condemned the unspecified 'qui'. Indeed, Hrothwaru's mother's position in general is difficult to understand. Unless Anglo-Saxon charters were dispositive (and remained so) rather than evidentiary,[43] she gained nothing by withholding the charters from Hrothwaru on the pretence they had been stolen as this meant acknowledging their original existence and, presumably, Hrothwaru's right to control Withington. It could be argued that the mother's actions were simply a delaying tactic enabling her to hold onto Withington for as long as possible but it is worth noting that nowhere does the record of the dispute state that the mother actually was claiming control of Withington; the only problem mentioned is the missing charters.

The document recording the Withington dispute is, then, a complex one and the issues at stake may be by no means as straightforward as previous scholars have imagined. Hrothwaru's case and her claim to the monastery at Withington may have succeeded not because it was the only legitimate claim but precisely because she was able to draw on the support and patronage of Worcester. The record is partial, one-sided, and at times evasive. The apparent writing out of Bucge and the seemingly curious reported behaviour of Hrothwaru's mother suggest much more may have been going on than simply episcopal intervention to prevent secularization.

The next case study concerns the control of a monastery at Westbury-on-Trym and centres on a document recording the will of a certain Æthelric, probably the son of Æthelmund *minister* of Uhtred the petty-king of the Hwicce.[44] According to this document at some point, possibly in 804, Æthelric had been invited to a synod at *Clovesho* to discuss the monastery at Westbury-on-Trym that previously his relatives (*propinqui*) had bequeathed and given to him.[45] Having examined

43 For dispositive, see John, *Land Tenure*, 168–77, who was expanding on the views of H. Brunner, *Zur Rechtsgeschichte der Römischen und Germanischen Urkunde* (Berlin, 1880; repr. Aalen, 1961). For evidentiary only, see, for example, D. Whitelock, ed. and trans., EHD I (2nd edn, London, 1979), 375–6.

44 Sawyer, 1187 (Birch, *Cartularium Saxonicum*, 313).

45 The charter does not specifically state that there was a monastery at Westbury-on-Trym but that the place name is given as 'West mynster' in Sawyer, 1187, and Æthelric's inheritance is later described as 'monasterium quod nominatur Westburhg' (Sawyer, 1433 [Birch, *Cartularium Saxonicum*, 379]) makes it reasonably certain this was the case. Moreover, when Westbury was originally given to Æthelric's father, Æthelmund, it was named in the charter '*Uuestburg*': that by the start of the ninth century it was named '*West mynster*' strongly

the charters relating to this land, the synod determined, in Æthelric's words, 'that I was free to give my lands and charters wherever I wished'.[46]

Æthelric then went on pilgrimage to Rome, leaving the land and charters in the care of his friends. When he returned he received back the land and paid them the price 'just as we had previously agreed and [so that] we would be at peace with each other'.[47] Some years later a synod was held at *Aclea* where Æthelric declared how he wished to bestow his inheritance, including Westbury-on-Trym which Æthelric bequeathed to his mother 'so that she has it during her life and afterwards it is handed over to the church of Worcester'.[48] This reversionary grant was made on the condition that whilst his mother is alive 'she has protection and defence against the contention of the people of Berkeley [i.e. the religious community at Berkeley]'[49] and if she did not receive this from Worcester she was able to seek it from the archbishop of Canterbury and failing that 'she is free with her charters and lands to choose protection wherever it will be pleasing to her'.[50]

The next reference to the monastery at Westbury-on-Trym occurs in the record of a Church council held at *Clovesho* in 824. There, amongst other issues, was resolved a dispute 'between Bishop Heahberht and the community at Berkeley concerning the inheritance of Æthelric son of Æthelmund, namely the monastery that is called Westbury'.[51] Bishop Heahberht of Worcester was at that time holding both the monastery and the charters as 'Æthelric had previously instructed that [the monastery] was to be handed over to the church of Worcester' and the council upheld the bishop's possession of the monastery after an oath had been sworn.[52]

---

suggests a monastery had been established there in the interim, see Sawyer, 139 (Birch, *Cartularium Saxonicum*, 274).

46 'ut liber essem terram meam atque libellas dare quocunque volui'.

47 'quasi ante pacti sumus et pacifici fuerimus ad invicem'.

48 'ut habeat suam diem et postea reddat ad Weogornensem aecclesiam'.

49 'habeat protectionem et defensionem contra Berclinga contentione'. *Contentio* also appears to have carried the sense, by the later ninth century at least, of a lawsuit and such a translation here is at least possible, see *Concilium Triburiense*, ch. 35, ed. A. Boretius, MGH Captilularia regum Francorum 2 (Hannover, 1890), 206–49, at 234, line 4.

50 'sit libera cum libris et ruris ad elegandam patrocinium ubi placitum sibi fuerit'.

51 Sawyer, 1433 (Birch, *Cartularium Saxonicum*, 379). 'inter Heabertum episcopum et illam familiam æt Berclea de hereditate Æðelrici filii Æðelmundi hoc est monasterium quod nominatur Westburhg'.

52 'Æðelricus ante praecepit ut ad Weogernensem aecclesiam redderetur'.

Though both of the records concerning the inheritance of Æthelric provide significant detail, as Wormald noted, there is much that is left unexplained or unclear.[53] There is no explanation why Æthelric was summoned to the first council at *Clovesho* to defend his right to his inheritance nor are reasons given as to why Æthelric's mother would need protection from the claims of the monastery of Berkeley. As the twelfth-century *Chronicon ex Chronicis* of John of Worcester records that a Ceolburh was the abbess of Berkeley, Wormald has suggested the evidence demonstrates that though Æthelric was 'willing to give her [his mother] a life-interest in his own house [i.e. Westbury-on-Trym], he wished to exclude the claims of her kin, even at the cost of its eventual reversion to Worcester'.[54]

Wormald's suggestion is possible, though the evidence for Ceolburh's link to Berkeley is late and may be, as Sims-Williams has argued, simply a result of 'a hazy memory of Æthelric's will' combined with the record of the death of an Abbess Ceolburh in the *Anglo-Saxon Chronicle* under the year 807.[55] It may be equally possible, therefore, that it was the community at Berkeley that had originally forced Æthelric to appear before the council at *Clovesho* to defend his rights. His reversionary grant of Westbury-on-Trym to Worcester would then have been to protect Ceolburh from Berkeley making similar claims against her or at least provide her with episcopal support should such claims again be brought before a Church council. Certainly it is difficult to understand why if Ceolburh were the abbess of Berkeley she would need to be defended against their *contentio*. Though no indication is given as to why the Berkeley community felt that they had a claim on Westbury-on-Trym that Worcester was, apparently, prepared to forge or modify documents in order to support their claims to control Westbury might suggest that the evidence was not as undeniably in Worcester's (and thus originally Æthelric's) favour as the record of the dispute would imply.[56] It is possible, though there is no evidence for this, that the eventual reversion to Worcester had been agreed even

53 Wormald, 'Charters', 155 and 157.
54 Ibid., 155 and P. Wormald, 'The Age of Offa and Alcuin', in J. Campbell, ed., *The Anglo-Saxons* (London, 1982; repr. 1991), 101–28, at 123. For Ceolburh as the abbess of Berkeley, see John of Worcester, *Chronicon ex chronicis*, in R. R. Darlington, P. McGurk and J. Bray, ed. and trans., *The Chronicle of John of Worcester, vol. 2: The Annals from 450–1066* (Oxford, 1995), sa 805.
55 Sims-Williams, *Religion and Literature*, 176.
56 Ibid., 157.

before the first council at *Clovesho* as a means for Æthelric to secure
Worcester's support in his dispute with the community at Berkeley.

Presuming it was the community at Berkeley which originally
contested Æthelric's control of Westbury-on-Trym then the decision
of the initial council at *Clovesho* would represent the archbishop of
Canterbury and the whole synod, presumably including the bishop of
Worcester, supporting the claims of a lay person to control a monastery
over the claims of another religious institution. It is impossible to
reconstruct the whole case now, the evidence leaves too many questions
unanswered and was, arguably, designed to preserve only those aspects
favourable to Worcester. Nevertheless, it is worth stressing that the
evidence might be read as indicating the support of the bishop of
Worcester for the control of a monastery in his diocese by a layperson.
That is, they were not acting to prevent lay lordship or excessive secular
interference but, rather, were facilitating the contrary.

However the surviving evidence is interpreted it does seem clear that
the bishops of Worcester were invoked as patrons and protectors of
monasteries by their owners. There are a number of possible reasons
why bishops in particular were appealing as patrons. Vollrath has
suggested that provincial Church synods may have held something
approaching exclusive jurisdiction over disputes concerning Church
property.[57] Although abbots and priests could attend such meetings, the
archbishop and his suffragans 'were formally the constituent members
of the provincial synods'.[58] As such, gaining the support of a bishop may
have gone a long way towards facilitating a favourable outcome.

Moreover, attendance at the apparently regular provincial synods
meant that bishops operated across kingdom boundaries; they played
on an international stage.[59] For the diocese of Worcester, effectively
co-terminous with the kingdom of the Hwicce, this must have been of
particular importance. The kingdom of the Hwicce seems to have been
dominated in the eighth century by successive waves of overlordship by
the kings of Mercia.[60] As the appointment of bishops was, to a certain

[57] Vollrath, *Die Synoden*, 134–41, see also Cubitt, *Church Councils*, 69–74.
[58] Cubitt, ibid., 39–44, quote at 42.
[59] For a list of the synods of the seventh and eighth centuries, ibid., 22–3.
[60] The now classic discussion is F. M. Stenton, 'The Supremacy of the Mercian Kings', *EHR* 33 (1918), 433–52 but for important caveats, see D. N. Dumville, 'The Terminology of Overkingship in Early Anglo-Saxon England', in J. Hines, ed., *The Anglo-Saxons from the Migration Period to the Eighth Century: an Ethnographic Perspective* (Woodbridge, 1997), 345–73, at 346.

127

degree, controlled or influenced by the ruler or overlord of the diocese, the bishops of Worcester are likely to have been if not appointed then at least approved by the Mercian overkings. The bishops of Worcester were part of the circle of powerful rulers such as Æthelbald or Offa and thus access to and support from the bishop of Worcester had some potential to facilitate access to these powerful overlords.

Similarly worth stressing is that, where evidence is available, there seem to have been pre-existing relationships between Worcester and those individuals who bequeathed their monasteries to the episcopal see.[61] Donation of property to Worcester may have been only one part, albeit the most visible in the surviving record, of an ongoing relationship between Worcester and the various religious institutions in its diocese. Such pre-existing relationships make it difficult to accept Thacker's argument that the bishops of Worcester were attempting in the eighth century to bring 'independent proprietary communities' under their control and place them 'in the charge of priests from the episcopal *familia*'.[62] Not only do the pre-existing relationships suggest such institutions should not be seen as wholly independent from episcopal influence but a number of monasteries that passed into Worcester's hands had originally been founded by members of the episcopal *familia*.[63]

This paper has attempted to reconsider the motivations behind the granting of monasteries and their estates to the bishops of Worcester. Instead of seeing such transactions solely from the point of view of what the bishops hoped to gain, it has argued that in some cases, at least, such grants may have been about the contested control of religious institutions and the need to find powerful patrons. This is not to suggest that all grants of monasteries to Worcester were motivated by such concerns. Some grants may have been designed to protect monasteries from the rapacity of kings,[64] whilst others may have been provoked by fear of secularization.[65] Some may have been intended to allow smaller monasteries to become part of a larger and more richly

---

[61] For details, see Sims-Williams, *Religion and Literature*, 156, 171, 227, 238–9, and also Blair, *The Church*, 116.

[62] Thacker, 'Monks', 165.

[63] See, for example, Sawyer, 1413 (Birch, *Cartularium Saxonicum*, 283).

[64] As may have been the case with Abbot Ceolfrith's grant recorded in Sawyer, 1411 (Birch, *Cartularium Saxonicum*, 220), as Worcester's control of Ceolfrith's monastery was later contested by King Offa of Mercia.

[65] See, for example, Sawyer, 1413 (Birch, *Cartularium Saxonicum*, 283).

endowed confederation of religious foundations and thus draw on a wider network of prayer and intercession,[66] and still others may have passed under the control of Worcester through episcopal avarice.[67] What this paper has tried to stress, however, is the sheer diversity of possible motivations for the granting of monasteries to Worcester and the need to recognize the complexities of the surviving records. Seeing the fear of lay lordship and declining monastic standards as the sole or primary motivation behind the property strategies of successive bishops of Worcester is to oversimplify the complex relationships between bishops and the religious institutions in their dioceses and, perhaps, to ignore the specific conditions of the diocese of Worcester in the eighth century.

University of Manchester

[66] On which see, *mutatis mutandis*, M. Innes, *State and Society in the Early Middle Ages: the Middle Rhine Valley, 400–1000* (Cambridge, 2000), 25–9.

[67] As Blair notes 'bishops were also aristocrats, and what is presented as diocesan reform could have contained elements of aristocratic encroachment', *The Church*, 117.

TAMING THE MUSE: MONASTIC DISCIPLINE AND CHRISTIAN POETRY IN HERMANN OF REICHENAU'S ON THE EIGHT PRINCIPAL VICES

by HANNAH WILLIAMS

I N 1054, the Benedictine monk Berthold of Reichenau took up the task of continuing the world *Chronicle* compiled by his friend and teacher Hermann of Reichenau.[1] The key event recorded for this year is the death of Hermann himself, with Berthold highlighting the monk's great learning, his good-natured dealings with others, but above all the particular devotion to reading and writing which he pursued despite great physical disability.[2] Even on his deathbed, we are told, Hermann's mind was focused on matters textual. Throughout the night he was caught up in a kind of vision or ecstasy, during which he was able to read – and re-read – the lost letter, much beloved by the early Fathers, of Cicero *To Hortensius*.[3] Running back and forth through the text, he displayed the same 'memory and knowledge' of the pagan author that one might expect of a Christian reader in recalling the Lord's Prayer. He was also able to set forth the remaining part of his own unfinished work, his poetic dialogue *On the Eight Principal Vices*, as if he were 'composing' and at the same time 'reading repeatedly' both

* I would like to acknowledge the support of Universities UK and the School of Arts, Histories and Cultures at the University of Manchester for funding the doctoral research on which this paper is based. My thanks must also go to Kate Cooper, Conrad Leyser, Anne Kurdock, Martin Ryan and Rosa Vidal for reading earlier versions of the paper.

   1 *Die Chroniken Bertholds von Reichenau und Bernolds von St. Blasien 1054–1100*, ed. I. S. Robinson, Ausgewählte Quellen zur deutschen Geschichte des Mittelalters 14 (Darmstadt, 2002), 163–74 for the entry on Hermann. See also Hermann, *Chronicon*, ed. G. H. Pertz, MGH SS V (Hannover, 1844), 74–133.
   2 Also known as Hermannus Contractus or Hermann the Lame, Hermann's disability was most likely caused by a motor neuron disease. See C. Brunhölzl, 'Gedänken zur Krankheit Hermanns von Reichenau (1019–1054)', *Sudhoffs Archiv zur Wissenschaftsgeschichte* 83: 2 (1999), 239–43.
   3 Cicero's letter *Ad Hortensium* was known only in fragments in the Middle Ages and was most likely known to Hermann and Berthold only by reputation. See Arno Borst, 'Der Tod Hermanns des Lahmen', *Ritte über den Bodensee: Rückblick auf mittelalterliche Bewegungen* (Bottighofen, 1992), 274–300, at 285. Hermann's vision recalls St Augustine's reading of Cicero's work, as well as St Jerome's dream in which he was accused of being a devout Ciceronian rather than a Christian. See, respectively, *Confessions*, 3.7, and *Epistula*, 22.30.

the sense and words of the text.[4] As Berthold claims, his master had always 'affected such great knowledge of both worldly and spiritual letters, that all those who came from everywhere were held stupefied and in wonder'.[5]

Since the days of C. H. Haskins, the intellectual life of the eleventh century has often been seen as the opening phase of a long twelfth-century renaissance (c. 1050–c. 1200).[6] Developments including the movement for Church reform,[7] the rise of new religious orders,[8] and the growing interest in pagan authors and the 'worldly letters' of the seven liberal arts were seen by R. W. Southern as elements of a 'secret revolution' of thought and feeling, a revolution which would establish Western Europe as a centre of 'political experiment, economic expansion, and intellectual discovery'.[9] For R. I. Moore, by contrast, they played a vital role in the formation of a new clerical elite, a powerful 'new sort' who shared the rational values of scholasticism, and who would staff the newly centralized bureaucracies that emerged following the eleventh-century social and economic revolution.[10]

It is against this background of social and intellectual upheaval that historians of educational culture have described a shift 'from *lectio divina* to the lecture room'.[11] This centred it is argued on figures like Berengar of Tours (c. 1000– c. 1088),[12] whose new interest in specula-

4 Berthold, *Chroniken*, 171.

5 'et in tam plenaria divinarum et secularium litterarum peritia magnus effectus est, ut ab omnibus ad magisterium et doctrinam eius undique confluentibus stupori et admirationi haberetur.' Ibid., 164.

6 C. H. Haskins described the eleventh century as that 'obscure period of origins which holds the secret of the new movement'. See *Renaissance of the Twelfth Century* (Cambridge, MA, 1927), 16. For a more recent analysis of the major issues and debates surrounding the idea of renaissance, see R. N. Swanson, *The Twelfth-Century Renaissance* (Manchester, 1999), esp. 12–39, on monastic versus secular schools.

7 For an overview of the eleventh-century reforms in their social contexts, see most recently Kathleen G. Cushing, *Reform and the Papacy in the Eleventh Century: Spirituality and Social Change* (Manchester, 2005).

8 On the challenge posed by these new orders to Benedictine monasticism, see esp. John van Engen, '"The Crisis of Cenobitism" Reconsidered: Benedictine Monasticism in the Years 1050–1150', *Speculum* 61: 2 (1986), 269–304. See also n. 51 below.

9 R. W. Southern, *The Making of the Middle Ages* (London, 1953), 15 and 14; and, idem, *Scholastic Humanism and the Unification of Europe, vol. 1: Foundations* (Oxford, 1995).

10 R. I. Moore, *The First European Revolution c.970–1215* (Oxford, 2000), chs 4 and 5.

11 The phrase is taken from Theresa Gross-Diaz's title, *The Psalms Commentary of Gilbert of Poitiers: from 'Lectio Divina' to the Lecture Room* (Leiden, 1996).

12 For an entry into the discussion and wider literature, see esp. Irven M. Resnick, 'Attitudes Towards Philosophy and Dialectic During the Gregorian Reform', *Journal of Religious History* 16 (1990), 115–25.

tive investigation and the liberal arts would find its expression in the
rising cathedral schools rather than the meditative reading associated
with the cloister.[13] But this view of the tension between cloister and
school does not take full account of the sophistication with which men
of the cloister approached the problem of 'worldly' learning. Far from
being viewed as a source of danger, such studies remained as a valued
part of the intellectual tradition and a source of considerable authority
for those who could master them. But how, exactly, were they to be
incorporated into the daily round of monastic study and ascetic
self-discipline?[14] For a writer such as Hermann of Reichenau, the
tension between *lectio divina* and worldly letters was a tension not
between 'old' and 'new' or cloister and school, but an age-old tension
within a living intellectual patrimony.

In the following essay I show how Hermann engaged with this
tension in the prologue to his *Eight Principal Vices*, the little-known,
unfinished work which he was remembered as trying to complete on
his death-bed. Hermann's prologue takes the form of a three-way
discussion between the character Hermannus, the pagan Muse of
poetry, Melpomene, and an audience of unidentified Sisters or nuns.[15]
A re-evaluation of this 'conversation' is long overdue. While much of
the historiography on the scholarly disciplines of this period has tended
to focus on France and England, and especially on the educational life
of the cathedral schools, C. Stephen Jaeger has recently called attention
to the schools of eleventh-century Germany, arguing that the so-called
twelfth-century renaissance was largely an attempt to codify the
achievements of a vibrant eleventh-century culture. Both the imperial
court and the episcopal schools, Jaeger suggests, served as a stage for
competitive display by charismatic masters through the medium of
pedagogy, courtly manners, and the composition of poetry.[16] What
remains to be understood, however, is the degree to which a 'tradi-

---

[13] The classic account of these tensions is found in Jean Leclercq, *Love of Learning and the
Desire for God: a Study of Monastic Culture*, trans. Catherine Misrahi (New York, 1982).

[14] On this continued presence of pagan authors in the medieval curriculum, see Susan
Reynolds, *Medieval Reading: Grammar, Rhetoric and the Classical Text*, Cambridge Studies in
Medieval Literature 27 (Cambridge, 1996), esp. 8–10.

[15] An edition of Hermann's *De octo vitiis principalibus* is available at: http://www.mgh.de/
~Poetae/Texte/Hermannus/Hermannus.pdf, accessed 8 June 2006. The text is based on
Ernst Dümmler's edition in *Zeitschrift für deutsches Alterthum* 13, NF 1 (Berlin, 1867) [here-
after: *De octo*], 385–434. I would like to thank Carole Hill for help with translations.

[16] C. Stephen Jaeger, *The Envy of Angels: Cathedral Schools and Social Ideals in Medieval
Europe 950–1200* (Philadelphia, PA, 1994), esp. Pt 1.

tional' Benedictine house such as Reichenau could revere, and offer a following to, a champion of poetry and the liberal arts such as Hermann.[17]

According to the *Rule* of St Benedict the struggle with the vices lies at the heart of monastic discipline. The activities of the daily round, including the performance of divine services, as well as acts of bodily asceticism such as vigils and fasting were all intended 'to correct vices and preserve charity'.[18] Hermann's poem in turn forms part of a long tradition of treatises on discerning the vices. It follows the order established by Gregory the Great, treating pride, vainglory, envy, anger, sadness, avarice, gluttony and lust.[19] But the discussion of these evils is in itself comparatively short.[20] Dominating the text is instead the figure of Hermann's Muse, an impulsive and rather dangerous character.[21] A strong sense of erotic tension informs the relationship between the male author and his female Muse,[22] so that Hermann's ability to command her inspiration serves ultimately to establish his own moral probity and to prove his credentials as a teacher of the spiritual life.

Hermann begins his dialogue by establishing the intimacy of his relationship with his Muse. He calls upon her as his 'beloved' and 'greatest care', while she responds to him as her 'friend' and 'beloved

[17] Hermann is best known to modern scholars as a proponent of the liberal arts and especially of the arts of the *quadrivium*, namely music, mathematics, astronomy and geometry. For an introduction to Hermann's life and work, with useful bibliography, see Walter Berschin, 'Hermann der Lahme: Leben und Werke in Übersicht', in Walter Berschin and Martin Hellmann, eds, *Hermann der Lahme: Gelehrter und Dichter (1013–1054)* (Heidelberg, 2004), 15–31.

[18] *Regula Benedicti*, Prologue (PL 66, 218).

[19] For discussion of the vice tradition in general, see Morton W. Bloomfield, *The Seven Deadly Sins: an Introduction to the History of a Religious Concept* (East Lansing, MI, 1952), and Richard Newhauser, *The Treatise on Vices and Virtues in Latin and the Vernacular*, Typologie des sources du moyen âge occidental 68 (Turnhout, 1993). For Gregory's model, see *Moralia in Iob*, 31: 45 (ed. Marc Adriaen, CCSL 143b [Turnhout, 1985], 1610–13).

[20] The text as a whole comprises 1722 lines, the discussion of the vices, 403 lines.

[21] For medieval conceptions of the Muses, see E. R. Curtius, *European Literature and the Latin Middle Ages*, trans. Willard R. Trask, Bollingen Series 36 (New York, 1953), 228–46, and more recently Jan Ziolkowski, 'Classical Influence on Medieval Latin Views of Poetic Inspiration', in Peter Godman and Oswyn Murray, eds, *Latin Poetry and the Classical Tradition: Essays in Medieval and Renaissance Literature* (Oxford, 1990), 15–38.

[22] On the ancient tradition of the erotic relationship between the author and his Muse, see, for example, Alison Sharrock, 'An A-musing Tale: Gender, Genre, and Ovid's Battles with Inspiration in the Metamorphoses', in Efrossini Spentzou and Don Fowler, eds, *Cultivating the Muse: Struggles for Power and Inspiration in Classical Literature* (Oxford, 2002), 207–27, at 209.

brother'.[23] Acting as a go-between, the Muse connects the undefined but physically separate spaces occupied by the author and the Sisters.[24] In the prologue, Hermann, his Muse, and his female disciples tease and joke with one another in turn as they try to decide on the form and content of the Muse's composition. At last, Hermann directs his Muse to 'sing harmoniously of the noxious joys of the vain world'.[25] This leads to her 'Song on Contempt of the World',[26] at the heart of which stands her account of the eight vices. At the end of the song the Sisters also receive the Muse's promise of further advice on how to fight such terrible dangers and attain eternal salvation.

It appears that despite Hermann's efforts the work remained unfinished at his death, since at this point the known version of the text comes to a close. From the evidence of the single 'complete' manuscript, as well as Berthold's witness, the poem also seems likely to have found its readership among the monks of Reichenau and also St Emmeram in Regensburg,[27] rather than among Hermann's stated audience of nuns. Exactly who the Sisters might have been remains unknown. Several historians have posited a connection between the monastery of Reichenau and the nearby women's houses of Buchau and Lindau.[28] Hermann refers to both houses in his *Chronicle*, but identifi-

[23] *De octo* [lines], 16–17; 7; 9.

[24] Thus Hermann directs 'everyone', both the Muse and the Sisters, to find another place to get the main discussion underway, urging them in clearly physical terms to 'go now by foot, if you please, and do not delay'. *De octo*, 410–11.

[25] Ibid., 393–6.

[26] For a discussion of this theme in medieval art and literature, see R. Rudolf, *Ars moriendi: von der Kunst des heilsamen Lebens und Sterbens* (Cologne, 1957), esp. 31 on Hermann.

[27] Hermann's *De octo vitiis principalibus* survives in Bayerische Staatsbibliothek Clm 14 689, fols 25–37, produced at St Emmeram in the twelfth century. Fragments also survive in the more recently discovered Gotha, Memb. II 225, saec. XII (unkown provenance). For descriptions of the manuscripts, see Karl Halm, Friedrich Keinz, Wilhelm Meyer, and Georg Thomas, eds, *Catalogus codicum latinorum Bibliothecae Regiae Monacensis secundum Andreae Schmelleri Indices: Tomi II Pars II Codices Num. 11001–15028 Complectens. Monachii A.M.D. CCC. LXXVI* (Wiesbaden, 1968), 22; and Carl Hopf, *Die abendländischen Handschriften der Forschungs- und Landesbibliothek Gotha*, Kleinformatige Pergamenthandschriften Memb. II (Gotha, 1997), 111. The monasteries shared a close liturgical relationship through the figure of the Bishop Wolfgang of Regensburg (d. 944), who had attended the monastic school at Reichenau and later supported the independence of the monastery of St Emmeram from the local bishopric. Wolfgang's canonization c. 1052 was most likely supported by Hermann's *historia*, which circulated together with a *vita* composed by Otloh of St Emmeram. See respectively, *Historia Sancti Wolfgangi Episcopi Ratisbonensis: Einführung und Edition*, ed. David Hilley, Musicological Studies 65/7, Historiae (Ottowa, 2002), and *Otloni vita s. Wolfkangi episcopi*, MGH SS IV (Hannover, 1841), 521–42.

[28] See A. Bergmann, 'Die Dichtung der Reichenau in Mittelalter,' in Konrad Beyerle, ed.,

cation of the Sisters mentioned in his text with the nuns of these communities must remain speculative.[29] The only internal evidence as to their identity lies in Hermann's tantalizing reference to a virgin named Engila, singled out in the text as being in 'first place', but otherwise unknown.[30]

A more a general context might be sought by considering the evidence for women's monasticism in the German lands. As Karl Leyser and, more recently, Katrinette Bodarwe have shown for the eastern region of Saxony, many women's houses had reached a pinnacle of cultural prestige in the years from c. 970 to c. 1050. It has been argued, however, that in the mid-eleventh century patrons began to turn their attention to canonries and monastic foundations for men. This led many women's houses to experience a significant decline of political and intellectual influence,[31] before enjoying a period of reform and renewal in the late-eleventh and early-twelfth centuries.[32] Much work remains to be done on assessing the situation in the south-German regions of Alemannia and Bavaria, where Reichenau and St Emmeram, Buchau and Lindau were located. It is tempting to suggest, however, that Hermann's poem was aimed at supporting the spiritual discipline of a community of women, as they faced a similar process of institutional uncertainty and decline.[33]

Die Kultur der Abtei Reichenau: Erinnerungsschrift zur zwölfhundertsten Wiederkehr des Gründungsjahres des Inselklosters 724–1924, 2 vols (Munich, 1925), 2: 773–802, at 750, and Arno Borst, *Mönche am Bodensee 610–1525* (Sigmaringen, 1978), 75–6.

[29] See Hermann, *Chronicon*, 120, 121, and 130 (entries for the years 1021, 1032, and 1051). On the present impossibility of identifying the Sisters, see Bernhard Theil, ed., *Das (freiweltliche) Damenstift Buchau am Federsee*, Germania Sacra, NF 32 (Berlin, 1994), 52–3.

[30] *De octo*, 61–2.

[31] See Karl J. Leyser, *Rule and Conflict in an Early Medieval Society: Ottonian Saxony* (London, 1979), 59–73, and 156–68; Katrinette Bodarwé, 'Sanctimoniales litterae': *Schriftlichkeit und Bildung in den ottenischen Frauenkommunitäten Gandersheim, Essen und Quedlinburg*, Quellen und Studien 10 (Münster, 2004), 5 on a 'krisensituation' for women's monasticism; Michael Parisse, 'Die Frauenstifte und Frauenklöster in Sachsen vom 10. bis zur Mitte des 12. Jahrhunderts', in Stefan Weinfurter, ed., *Die Salier und das Reich* (Sigmaringen, 1991), 465–50.

[32] A principal driver behind this renewal was Abbot William of Hirsau, a former monk of St Emmeram, who was responsible for establishing and reforming a number of female communities in the region of southern Germany. See esp. Julie Hotchin, 'Female Religious Life and the *Cura Monialium* in Hirsau Monasticism, 1080 to 1150', in Constant J. Mews, ed., *Listen, Daughter: the "Speculum virginum" and the Formation of Religious Women in the Middle Ages* (New York, 2001), 59–83.

[33] For an extended discussion of the possible connections between Reichenau and other women's houses in the German lands, see Hannah Williams, 'Authority and Pedagogy in Hermann of Reichenau's *De octo vitiis principalibus*', unpublished Ph.D. thesis, University of Manchester, 2006, ch. 3.

Hermann's Sisters may also have been no more nor less than a literary construct, although the lack of external evidence should not, in itself, lead us to this conclusion.[34] Hermann's work neither offers, nor indeed claims to offer, any access to the thoughts and experiences of eleventh-century women. Rather, what it presents is a series of representations and literary constructs, which can provide us with an insight into what Michael Calebrese has called the 'medieval clerical imaginings of women's language, moral capabilities, and relations to men.'[35]

Such 'imaginings' of women provided an important point of identification in the rhetorical training of medieval boys and men as readers and writers.[36] As Jodie Enders has shown, it was through the rigorous training enforced by the medieval schoolmaster, and the physical violence of the rod, that boys and men were re-formed as disciplined speakers and masters of Latin grammar.[37] Female characters were alternately sexualized or silenced, serving as the explicit objects of the rhetorical violence which facilitated this re-moulding of the male heart and mind. In Hermann's work, the Sisters are seen as loving friends and cherished spiritual companions. But the character of the Muse, initially praised and revered, is finally chastised as a 'dog, an attacker with sharp and savage teeth', whose unruly speech must be harnessed to the desires of the male author.[38]

Hermann's describes his Muse as 'untaught' or 'unteachable' (indocili) in such weighty subject matter as the vices.' He asks her to compose 'useful' songs of Christian teaching, even though she habitually devotes

[34] Scholars have often been quick to suspect the existence of highly educated female readers and authors in the Middle Ages, with the most famous example being the debate that surrounded Heloise's correspondence with Abelard. The scholarship on these letters is vast, but see esp. Michael Clanchy, *Abelard: a Medieval Life* (Oxford, 1997); Constant J. Mews, *The Lost Love Letters of Heloise and Abelard: Perceptions of Dialogue in Twelfth-Century France*, trans. Neville Chiavaroli and Constant J. Mews (New York, 1999); and idem, *Abelard and Heloise* (Oxford, 2005).

[35] Michael Calabrese, 'Ovid and the Female Voice in the *De Amore* and the Letters of Abelard and Heloise', *Modern Philology* 95: 1 (1997), 1–26, at 4.

[36] See, for example, Marjorie Curry Woods, 'Boys Will Be Women: Musings on Classroom Nostalgia and the Chaucerian Audience(s)', in Robert F. Yeager and Charlotte C. Morse, eds, *Speaking Images: Essays in Honor of V. A. Kolve* (Asheville, NC, 2001), 143–66.

[37] Jody Enders, 'Rhetoric, Coercion, and the Memory of Violence', in Rita Copeland, ed., *Criticism and Dissent in the Middle Ages* (Cambridge, 1996), 24–55.

[38] *De octo*, 296–7. For a discussion of these contrary images of women eleventh- and twelfth-century poetry, see C. Stephen Jaeger, *Ennobling Love: In Search of a Lost Sensibility*, The Middle Ages Series (Philadelphia, PA, 1999), 82–106.

herself to frivolous and playful pursuits.[39] Such images of the Muses are found in both ancient and medieval sources alike. For medieval readers, one of the best-known models was undoubtedly that found in the opening lines of Boethius's *Consolation of Philosophy*, a copy of which was held at Reichenau from the ninth century and would most likely have been available to Hermann.[40]

The *Consolation*'s famous opening scene depicts the Muses as they dictate their poetry at the bedside of Boethius who, thrown into prison, lies grieving at his misfortune. He initially draws comfort from their presence, but Lady Philosophy soon appears and demands to know who 'has allowed these hysterical sluts to approach this sick man's bedside?'[41] While she herself offers truth through the 'rich and fruitful harvest of Reason', she maintains, the Muses can offer only the 'barren thorns of Passion' and the 'sweetened poisons' of deceiving words. This prompts the Muses to flee with 'blushes of shame' and downcast eyes, thus allowing Lady Philosophy to assert her position, and her influence over Boethius, by settling herself down at the author's bedside.[42]

In Hermann's poem we find a similar depiction of the enticing and potentially dangerous Muse. Here, too, a connection is made between the work of literary composition and the space of the author's bedside.[43] Tensions arise as the Sisters demand to know what business the Muse might have with their 'beloved little Hermannlet'. They claim that they have so far remained unacquainted with her, and state that they are terrified by the attractiveness of her face. They also raise playful charges of sexual, or at least sexualized, misconduct with the author:

[39] *De octo*, 413 and 388–89.

[40] Paul Lehmann, *Mittelalterliche Bibliothekskataloge Deutschlands und der Schweiz, vol. 1: Die Bistümer Konstanz und Chur* (Munich, 1918), 259.

[41] This is a play on Propertius's *Elegy*, 4.8, in which the poet's mistress returns unexpectedly to his house and must drive away the other 'tarts' whom she finds there. See S. J. B. Barnish, 'Maximian, Cassiodorus, Boethius, Theodahad: Poetry, Philosophy and Politics in Ostrogothic Italy', *Nottingham Medieval Studies* 34 (1990), 16–32, at 22. See also Anna Crabbe, 'Literary Design in the *De Consolatione Philosophiae*' in Margaret Gibson, ed., *Boethius: His Life, Thought and Influence* (London, 1981), 237–74.

[42] Boethius, *The Consolation of Philosophy*, trans. Victor Watts (rev. edn, London, 1999), 3–5.

[43] On the importance of this connection for medieval writers, see Mary Carruthers, *The Book of Memory: a Study of Memory in Medieval Culture*, Cambridge Studies in Medieval Literature 10 (Cambridge, 1990), esp. 196 and 201. A discussion of the ancient context is found in James Ker, 'Nocturnal Writers in Imperial Rome: the Culture of *Lucubratio*', *Classical Philology* 99 (2004), 209–42.

Perhaps you are one who shares [Hermann's] bed stealthily to
snatch the dutiful embrace of a sweet kiss, to take up the silent
exploits of the night, the joys denied to us. Perhaps he whiles it
away with you, o girl, he who was thought more pure in body than
glass, more chaste and more faithful than a dove, traitor to his own
leisure (*otium*).[44]

The suggestion here is that by stealing embraces with the author,
Hermann's Muse has also been gaining undue influence when it comes
to his compositions. In contrast to the Boethian Muses, she makes no
attempt to flee the author's bedside,[45] but responds by asserting her
rightful position: 'I am one of three times three sisters,' she declares,
'Muses whom fair Fame reports to be sweet singers, born of sky-
thundering Jove, begotten of Juno, learned in playing the lute'.[46] She
stresses that her skill and learning are unchanged; they have simply
been put to good use in the service of Christian poets:

Deities falsely worshipped by the foolish crowds, and once beloved
to false-speaking poets, now already we are recognized as followers
of Christ, and, urging them to proceed on the right way, we love
chaste people, we teach holy things, always we love those who
cultivate their minds . . .[47]

The Muse also tackles the question of her supposed propensity for
deception, by stressing that as a follower of Christ she is now
committed to truthful speech. Indeed, Hermann claims that she speaks
so truthfully about the vices that the Sisters might be in danger of
learning too much about these evils, and might even turn against him
as a result. Such fears are quickly set aside, however, as the Muse reveals

[44] 'tu forsan eius conscia lectuli/ complexa dulcis munia sauii/ furare, noctis ausa
silentia/ nobis negata sumere gaudia. fors ille uitro corpore purior/ putatus, ille turture
castior/ fideliorque perfidus a sua/ tecum, o puella, conteret otia.' Ibid., 50–7.
[45] For another eleventh-century response to the Boethian text, likewise in favour of the
Muse, see Helena de Carlos, 'Poetry and Parody: Boethius, Dreams, and Gestures in the
Letters of Godfrey of Rheims', *Essays in Medieval Studies* 18 (2001), 18–30. De Carlos argues
that by using imagery drawn from the world of medieval medicine, Godfrey portrays his
Muse as assuming the role of Lady Philosophy, specifically as the healer of the 'sick man'
who needs poetry rather than rational investigation in order to cure his soul.
[46] 'sum ter ternarum una sororum,/ quas fert dulcicanas fama camenas,/ natas esse Iouis
celsitonantis,/ ex Iunone satas, psallere doctas'. *De octo*, 67–70.
[47] 'idolatrae fatui numina uulgi/ olim falsiquis grata poetis,/ nunc iam christicolae
noscimur esse/ suadentesque uiam pergere rectam,/ castos diligimus, sancta docemus,/
mentis cultores semper amantes'. Ibid., 71–6.

that in order to compose her 'truthful utterances' she must first seek out the inspiration of the Holy Spirit. This in turn serves to strengthen Hermann's own position in the process of literary composition, since it only through his prayers that the Muse can command this higher inspiration and thus aid the author of truly Christian poetry. 'By means of praying', she begs of Hermann, 'entreat the Spirit to assist my frailty, lest in a poor and good-for-nothing manner, I might rashly seek to compose what you command'.[48]

At one level, Hermann's poem may thus be read as an exercise in taming – or converting – the once-pagan Muse. Equally important in establishing his authority are the problems he must overcome in addressing his work to his 'dear little Sisters'. It is of course in the second, unfinished section of the text that the reader is promised direct instruction on how to fight the vices described in the Muse's song. Already in the prologue, however, Hermann puts forward the learned disciplines of the monastic round, such as divine reading and meditation, as weapons no less vital in the struggle against devilish attack than acts of bodily asceticism.[49] His work thus provides an important counterpoint to the rhetoric of men like Peter Damian and the so-called 'New Hermits' of the eleventh century, who claimed to reject this scholarly focus in favour of returning to the more stringent ascetic ideals of the early Desert Fathers.[50] More specifically, it shows his attempts to integrate both the reading and writing of poetry into the daily round of monastic study.

Instructing the Sisters in these learned disciplines poses a problem for Hermann at the levels both of the form and the content of his poetry. His first concern is that teaching the Sisters about the vices might easily lead them into corruption. According to his Muse, he

---

[48] 'tu modo, queso, precando pete/ pneuma sacrum fragili annuere,/ ne nimium male et lutee,/ quae reboare iubes temere/ perficiam'. Ibid., 448–52. On the Muse's truthful speech, see 287–8 and 303–5.

[49] Such technique found their origins amongst the early Desert Fathers. In the eleventh century, however, 'the desert' was associated most often with acts of extreme bodily asceticism. On the late ancient context, see M O'Laughlin, 'The Bible, the Demons and the Desert: Evaluating the *Antirrheticus* of Evagrius Ponticus', *Studia Monastica* 34 (1999), 201–15; and Conrad Leyser, '*Lectio divina, oratio pura*: Rhetoric and the Techniques of Asceticism in the *Conferences* of John Cassian', in Giulia Barone, Marina Caffiero and Francesco Scorza Barcellona, eds, *Modelli di comportamento, modelli di santità: contrasti, intersezioni, complementatità* (Rome, 1994), 79–105.

[50] On the hermits, see Henrietta Leyser, *Hermits and the New Monasticism: a Study of Religious Communities in Western Europe 1000–1150* (New York, 1984), and Phyllis G. Jestice, *Wayward Monks and the Religious Revolution of the Eleventh Century*, Brill's Studies in Intellectual History 76 (Leiden, 1997).

knows of many women who have been drawn in 'by the cruel fish hook of the demon . . . caught to be held by the line of vice'.[51]

> But since he has come to know and often perceives the feminine mind to be a wandering sort of thing, two headed, driven about by waves, an airy monster, he is suspicious and dreads and thereby grows afraid . . .[52]

To address these problems the Muse reminds Hermann that she has in no way sought to harm the 'spotless, pious', or 'modest women' with her discussion of the vices. Rather, she has sought to attack 'the good for nothings, the prostitutes, the wanton women', which neither she nor the author should expect to find amongst the Sisters.[53] She thus establishes the moral capabilities of her female audience, whose sex is otherwise aligned with formlessness of mind. More difficult for Hermann to resolve is the possibility that the very form in which his writing, the poetic form, could itself be scorned as frivolous and 'worldly' and therefore serve to distract his audience and lead their minds astray.[54]

Maintaining focus of mind was central to the discipline of monastic mediation and prayer. As Mary Carruthers has shown in her study of monastic learning, prayer itself was envisioned primarily as an exercise in memory work.[55] This relied on the individual first compiling an extensive 'mental inventory' of suitable reading matter, usually drawn from the Bible and the writings of the Fathers. The composition of prayer – and indeed of any new 'text' be it completed in the mind or written-out onto parchment – then involved drawing out the contents of one's mental inventory and piecing together new texts by finding creative connections or 'ways' between the materials at hand. But works of poetry could disrupt this process. Here we may consider the well-known example of John Cassian, whose works were recommended at

---

[51] 'et quia perplures heu mulieres,/ pro pudor, in tali crimine labi/ attractasque fero doemonis unco/ captiuas uitii fune teneri/ nouimus, ingemimus atque dolemus,/ non quimus paucis fidere uobis . . .' *De octo*, 146–51.

[52] 'nouit saepeque legit/ mentem femineam mobile quoddam,/ anceps, fluctiuagum, flabile monstrum,/ suspectus metuit perque timescit'. Ibid., 104–7.

[53] Ibid., 274–6, and 349–52.

[54] For a discussion of similar rhetoric among ancient authors, see for example Kenneth Reckford, '*Pueri ludentes*: Some Aspects of Play and Seriousness in Horace's *Epistles*', *Transactions of the American Philological Society* 132 (2002), 1–19 at 3.

[55] See Carruthers, *Book of Memory*; and idem, *The Craft of Thought: Meditation, Rhetoric, and the Making of Images 400–1200*, Cambridge Studies in Medieval Literature 34 (Cambridge, 1998).

the end of St Benedict's *Rule* and were also available at medieval Reichenau.[56] In his fourteenth *Conference*, Cassian confesses that he has often found it difficult to maintain his focus during prayer, as his mind would wander instead to the pagan poetry that he had memorized in his earliest schooling.[57] As Carruthers suggests, the problem for a writer like Cassian was that the very words of the poets, rather than simply the stories they told, tended to be so ingrained in memory that they could trigger a range of unwanted connections and verbal associations, thus leading the individual further and further away from the holy Word.[58] As a strategy to counter the *evagatio* brought on by these unwanted thoughts, Cassian offered the counter-strategy of *occupatio mentis*, engagement of the mind with meditation on edifying themes.[59]

For many medieval writers a similar rhetoric of anxiety surrounded not only pagan authors but also the form of poetry itself. Thus we find an eleventh-century monk like Otloh of St Emmeram, a near contemporary of Hermann, protesting that he had only written his first work in verse because this was the style in which he had been most practiced during his former life as a secular cleric. He also suggests, however, that works of poetry can in fact provide superior teaching tools, as they enable spiritual teachings to adhere more firmly to both inner and outer man (*utrique homini*), that is, to the mental as well as the lived habits of the reader.[60] In other words, they are ideally suited to the work of memorization, and therefore to the ongoing task of supporting a life of virtue through fruitful occupation of the mind.

Hermann, too, justifies the didactic use of verse. He suggests at the outset that his audience prefers to hear 'that which is playful, seldom that which is serious', that is, *ludicra* over *seria*.[61] The word *ludicra* also

---

[56] Listed in the modern catalogue are seven books of Cassian's *Institutiones* and also books 18–24 of the *Conlationes*. See A. Holder, *Die Handschriften der Grossherzoglich Badischen Hof- und Landesbibliothek in Karlsruhe 5: Die Reichenauer Handschriften, Bd. 1: Die Pergamenthandschriften* (Wiesebaden, 1970), and his discussion of Karlsruhe, Landesbibliothek, Bib. cod. Aug. 42.

[57] Cassian, *Conlationes*, 14.12 (ed. Michael Petschenig, CSEL 13.2 [Vienna, 1886], 413–14).

[58] Carruthers, *Craft of Thought*, 88–91 on Cassian and distraction, and esp. 11 on the concept of mental inventory.

[59] Conrad Leyser, *Asceticism and Authority from Augustine to Gregory the Great* (Oxford, 2000), 33–61 on Cassian esp. 51–5 on the use of Scripture to occupy the mind.

[60] Otloh, *De doctrina spirituali*, PL 146, 263–300, at 263–4.

[61] *De octo*, 20–1. For a discussion of jests and the concept of *ludicra* in medieval literature, see Curtius, *European Literature*, 423–8.

carries the meaning of 'verse', and Hermann clearly continues to use the form as he directs his Muse to 'cast out trifles, bring forth serious matters . . . And playing these things, dear one, delight sweet sisters'.[62] His Muse also distinguishes between the frivolous works she had once inspired in the ancient poets and the useful poetry she now inspires in Hermann. As she declares of herself and her Muse-sisters:

> . . . sometimes we are able to compose honourable jests, if we are asked; we fear to play something base, unless our faithful friend [Hermann] should ask us, who knows how to shield this decently, not subjecting the most intimate parts of the mind to a playful word, with Christ the judge looking attentively on everything from heaven.[63]

The ancient poets had written about 'base' subject matter in the form of heroes and battles and stories of love, all of which could cause distraction and a wandering of the mind. But Christian poetry, Hermann's Muse argues, will in no way disrupt 'the most intimate parts' of the mind and memory, even when sung or recited again and again.[64] This claim runs to the heart of the practical value of his poem. For the text not only provides information about discerning the vices; rather, as part of the discipline of monastic prayer and meditation the Muse's song has a performative function, serving as an instrument of *occupatio mentis*, capable of defending the mind from unwanted thoughts and thus keeping vice at bay.

A final point to consider is the value that Hermann attaches not only to the reading of Christian poetry, but also to the task of composing new poetic works. Here we must return to the role of Muse, and in particular to the charge that by stealing nocturnal embraces, she and Hermann have been indulging in pleasures denied (*negata*) to the Sisters. At one level this might suggest that the Sisters wish to claim the role of the Muse for themselves and thus become the real-life inspirers of Hermann's poetry. At the same time, by desiring the joys already afforded to Hermann, they might also want to share a similar intimacy with his Muse and thus become authors of poetry in their own right. This is supported by Hermann's suggestion that at least one of the

---

62 'ludicra respue, seria prome,/. . . His et dulces, cara, sorores/ mulce ludens'. *De octo*, 388–9; 402–3.

63 'interdumque iocos quimus honestos/ pangere, si petimur; turpe ueremur/ ludere, ni fidus poscat poscat amicus,/ hoc qui celare norit honeste,/ non ad lasciuum intima uerbum/ mentis subdendo, iudice Christo/ caelitus attente cuncta uidente'. Ibid., 77–83.

64 Ibid., 181.

Sisters, the virgin named Engila, has in fact already encountered the Muse. The Muse maintains that despite the Sisters' assertions to the contrary she is already acquainted with this particularly revered member of her audience; the implication seems to be that the Muse has inspired Engila in writing poetry.[65] Hermann does not elaborate on this point. It is significant nonetheless that Englia remains in 'first place' among the Sisters, even and especially as a potential author of poetry. For by showing that this exalted character can retain her spiritual purity and still be a companion of the Muse, Hermann is able to strengthen his own claims to authority as a fellow Christian poet.

Like Hermann's Sisters, Engila may have been a real *discipula* or merely a figure of the imagination. She is presented as an especially cherished member of Hermann's audience, and may even have been a protégée whom Hermann sought to defend against detractors. The fact that Hermann's literary heir Berthold makes no reference to her seems to support the idea that she was indeed a fictional character. But while the point cannot be pressed too far, Berthold's silence could also have its root in a certain level of competition between rival disciplines: in his *Chronicle* entry, Berthold may have wanted to present himself, rather than a rival, as Hermann's true intellectual heir.

We saw at the beginning of this essay that Hermann was praised as a master of discipline in two senses: of the diverse academic disciplines associated with pagan authors and the liberal arts, but also of that most basic monastic discipline, the daily battle against the vices. By Bethold's account, the *Eight Principal Vices* was occupying his master's thoughts even as he prepared for death, and Hermann was especially anxious to see the text completed for future readers.[66] In a period when many writers saw a growing tension between 'worldly and secular letters', Hermann's final act was to present himself as taming the once-pagan Muse. The traditional *disciplina* of the ascetic, Hermann argued, was an inheritance compatible with the life of the Christian poet, and one that could be passed on to students using poetry as a medium. The Muse, then, posed little real danger to monastic *disciplina*; indeed it was in *disciplina*'s service that her charms might find their fullest expression.

University of Manchester

---

[65] Ibid., 58–62.
[66] Berthold, *Chroniken*, 172–3.

VARIETIES OF MONASTIC DISCIPLINE IN SOUTHERN ITALY DURING THE ELEVENTH AND TWELFTH CENTURIES

by G. A. LOUD

THE conquest of southern Italy by the Normans during the eleventh century incorporated what had hitherto been a peripheral region more fully within the mainstream of Western Europe. However, notwithstanding this, in a number of respects the development of the Church in Norman Italy followed its own idiosyncratic pattern, rather different from the trends that prevailed in other parts of contemporary Latin Christendom. This distinctive evolution can be clearly observed in south Italian monasticism during the eleventh and twelfth centuries.

Scholars have, in particular, pointed to the continued dominance in the Mezzogiorno of the conventional Benedictine model of the monastic life, not least through the example of Montecassino, and the late and relatively limited impact of the so-called 'new monastic orders', at least until the thirteenth century.[1] The period from c. 1050 onwards saw a massive expansion in the monastic congregations of long-established Benedictine abbeys like Montecassino and St Sophia, Benevento, and the emergence and efflorescence of more recent foundations such as the two houses dedicated to the Holy Trinity, at Cava, near Salerno, and Venosa, on the border between Apulia and Lucania. Cava had, for example, at least 21 monastic cells and almost a hundred other dependent churches by 1169.[2] Yet this was by no means the

---

1 Thus, for example, G. Picasso, 'Il monaco', in G. Musca, ed., *Condizione umana e ruoli sociali nel Mezzogiorno normanno-svevo*, Atti delle none giornate normanno-sveve, 1989 (Bari, 1991), 279–92, at 284: 'In generale si ha l'impressione che nel Regno dei Normanni domini l'esempio cassinese della fedaltà alla Regola di san Benedetto'.

2 For the Cassinese monastic empire, see H. Dormeier, *Montecassino und die Laien im 11. und 12. Jahrhundert* (Stuttgart, 1979), 24–106; H. Bloch, *Montecassino in the Middle Ages*, 3 vols (Rome, 1986), 1: 167–464. For the development of the other abbeys, see respectively G. A. Loud, 'A Lombard Abbey in a Norman World: St. Sophia, Benevento 1050–1200', *Anglo-Norman Studies* 19, Proceedings of the Battle Conference 1996 (Woodbridge, 1997), 273–306; idem, 'The Abbey of Cava, its Property and Benefactors in the Norman Era', *Anglo-Norman Studies* 9, Proceedings of the Battle Conference 1986 (Woodbridge, 1987), 143–77, at 155 for the 1169 bull listing its dependencies; H. Houben, *Die Abtei Venosa und das Mönchtum im*

whole story; and south Italian monasticism was more varied, and more inclusive, than a superficial glance might suggest.

When the Normans first arrived in the south in the early years of the eleventh century, neither the rule of Benedict, nor conventional cenobitic monasticism, were necessarily dominant. Other models, and other rules, were also present. In part, of course, this was because southern Italy was by no means entirely Latin, and in the Greek areas in the far south there was an entirely different monastic tradition, and indeed a remarkably varied one, for south Italian Greek monasticism embodied a considerable range of practice, both cenobitic and eremitic.[3] Nor was it confined simply to those regions – Calabria, the Salento peninsula and the north-east of Sicily – where the population was overwhelmingly Greek. As Greeks had migrated north during the tenth century, Lucania had become increasingly Graecized, and with Greek settlers and Byzantine administrators had come Greek monks to settle in what had hitherto been an under-populated, and largely unexploited, region.[4] Furthermore, these Greek monks did not limit themselves to areas where their own language and people were in the majority. The case of St Nilos of Rossano, who spent some fifteen years at Valleluce on the Montecassino lands from c. 980 before moving on to Grottaferrata, is rightly famous. But there were, during the eleventh century, a number of other Greek monasteries both in the Lombard principalities of the west coast and in those parts of Apulia where, despite Byzantine rule, the subject population was overwhelmingly Lombard.[5] Some of these foundations proved far less ephemeral than did that of Nilos at Valleluce. Thus the monastery of St Peter de Foresta, near Pontecorvo in the principality of Capua, was established in 998, by a Lombard count, whose foundation charter stipulated that, 'whosoever shall wish to change this rule that is called "the Greek"

---

normannisch-staufischen Süditalien (Tübingen, 1995). In the absence of any substantial overall study of south Italian monasticism in the Central Middle Ages, the best introduction is by Houben, ibid., 11–107.

[3] G. Vitolo, 'Les monastères grecs de l'Italie méridionale', in J.-L. Lemaitre, M. Dmitriev, and P. Gonneau, eds, *Moines et Monastères dans les Sociétés de Rite Grec et Latin* (Geneva, 1996), 99–113, esp. 106–7.

[4] A. Guillou, 'La Lucanie Byzantine: Étude de géographie historique', *Byzantion* 35 (1965), 119–49.

[5] For a general survey, S. Borsari, *Il Monachesimo bizantino nella Sicilia e nell'Italia meridionale prenormanne* (Naples, 1963), 60–76; and for Nilos, ibid., 56–60, and J.-M. Sansterre, 'Saint Nil de Rossano et le monachisme Latin', *Bolletino della badia greca di Grottaferrata* 45 (1991), 339–86.

(*Attica*) into Latin shall be accursed and excommunicate'.[6] This house was still under the rule of Greek abbots in the 1060s, less than a decade before it was given to Montecassino by Geoffrey Ridel, the new Norman Duke of Gaeta.[7] Similarly the Greek monastery of St Nicholas de Gallucanta at Vietri, just to the north of Salerno, was founded, by a family of Lombard aristocrats, before 996, and remained under the direction of a Greek abbot, Theophylact, for some years after one of its proprietors gave his share of the house to the Latin abbey of Cava in 1087. Despite, or perhaps because of, this cession, in 1092 another of the founder's descendants promised that neither he nor his heirs would at any time take the monastery away 'from the order of Greek monks', nor would any abbot be installed 'without the agreement of the congregation of Greek monks who are or shall be gathered in that monastery'.[8]

As time went on, there was an increasing tendency for Greek monasteries in primarily Latin areas to be absorbed in Latin monastic congregations. But as the above example shows, we should not assume that this was always a 'hostile takeover', necessarily inimical to the interests of the Greek monks. Indeed, the latter might even be the agents of such a transfer. Thus, in 1054 a Greek abbot of a house near Lesina on the Gargano peninsula gave himself and his monastery to the Latin abbey of Tremiti.[9] Similarly in 1121 an apparently Greek inhabitant of Trani gave a church dedicated to St Basil, that he himself had built, to Tremiti.[10] But even when such a transfer was the work of one of the new Normanno-French aristocracy, we cannot presume deliberate intent towards eliminating Greek observance. For example, Hugh

---

6 E. Gattula, *Historia Abbatiae Casinensis* (Venice, 1733), 293–4.

7 In May 1065 the abbot was Arsenius, and in February-March 1067 Saba, both *de genere Graecorum*, *Abbazia di Montecassino: Regesto dell'Archivio*, ed. T. Leccisotti and F. Avagliano, 11 vols (Rome, 1964–77), 8: 181–3, nos 11–12, 14. It was given to Montecassino in February 1075, Gattula, *Historia*, 267. See also A. Nicosia, 'La Valle della Quesa e il monastero greco di S. Pietro', *Benedictina* 24 (1977), 115–38.

8 *Le Pergamene di S. Nicola di Gallucanta (secc. ix–xii)*, ed. P. Cherubini (Altavilla Silentina, 1990), 264–5, no. 104; 286–7, no. 114. Theophylact was last attested in 1100, ibid., 308–9, no. 125. G. Vitolo, 'La Latinizzazione dei monasteri italo-greci del Mezzogiorno medievale: l'esempio di S. Nicola di Gallocanta pressa Salerno', *Benedictina* 29 (1982), 437–60 [reprinted in S. Leone and G. Vitolo, eds, *Minima Cavensia: Studi in margine al IX Volume del Codex Diplomaticus Cavensis* (Salerno, 1983), 75–92].

9 *Codice diplomatico del monastero benedettino di S. Maria di Tremiti 1005–1237*, ed A. Petrucci, Fonti per la storia d'Italia, 3 vols (Rome, 1960) [hereafter: *Cod. Dipl. Tremiti*], 2: 165–7, no. 53.

10 Ibid., 269–77, no. 95. The donor was Ioannocarus son of Balsamus (Balsamon); the latter being also the name of his son.

Varieties of Monastic Discipline

of Chiaromonte (Clermont) who in 1088 gave the monastery of St Maria of Kyrozosimi, in the Val di Sinni in Lucania, to Cava was also a benefactor of the most important Greek house in the region, SS. Elias and Anastasius at Carbone.[11] His descendants continued to endow Kyrozosimi, and while this house had a Latin prior by 1112, the fact that many of its documents continued to be written in Greek suggests that any conversion to the Latin rite may have been slow and partial.[12] At least one Greek abbey, established in what was, even before the Norman conquest, a predominantly Latin area, remained in Greek hands until a remarkably late date. The abbot and at least one of the monks of St Nicholas de Morbano, near Venosa, signed a document in Greek in 1267.[13]

Modern scholarship has tended to discount any widespread influence of Greek monasticism on that of the west.[14] But it is by no means easy to estimate how much local influence such Greek monks in predominantly Latin areas may have had on their Latin counterparts in the same region. It is notable that the original version of Leo of Ostia's *Montecassino Chronicle* from the last years of the eleventh century made no mention of St Nilos, although later redactions did.[15] Montecassino's role in the translation and dissemination of Greek religious texts in the west should not be exaggerated either.[16] Nevertheless, two Cassinese

---

[11] L. Mattei-Cerasoli, 'La Badia di Cava e i monasteri greci di Calabria superiore', *Archivio storico per la Calabria e la Lucania* 8 (1938), 275–6, no. 1; G. Robinson, 'The History and Cartulary of the Greek Monastery of St. Elias and St. Anastasius of Carbone', *Orientalia Christiana* 15 (1929), 119–276, at 200–6, nos 14–15. For the Chiaromonte family, who may have originated from Clermont-de-l'Oise in the Beauvaisis, L.-R. Ménager, 'Inventaire des familles normands et franques emigrées en Italie méridionales et en Sicile (XIe–XIIe siècles), in *Roberto il Guiscardo e il suo tempo*, Relazioni e comunicazioni nelle prime giornate normanno-sveve Bari, maggio 1973 (Rome, 1975), 275–84.

[12] Thus Hugh of Chiaromonte (probably the grandson of the original donor) and his brothers made a donation in a Greek charter in 1112, in which the prior was named as William, but donors could also include a Greek judge, in 1113: F. Trinchera, *Syllabus Graecarum Membranarum* (Naples, 1865), 96–8, nos 74–5. The prior of Kyrozosimi still issued a Greek charter as late as 1200, ibid., 339–40, no. 250.

[13] Houben, *Die Abtei Venosa*, 193.

[14] For example, H. Leyser, *Hermits and the New Monasticism: a Study of Religious Communities in Western Europe* (London, 1984), 24–5; M. Dunn, 'Eastern Influence on Western Monasticism in the Eleventh and Twelfth Centuries', in J. D. Howard-Johnston, ed., *Byzantium and the West: Proceedings of the XVIII Spring Symposium of Byzantine Studies 1984* (Amsterdam 1988), 245–59.

[15] *Chronica Monasterii Casinensis*, ed. H. Hoffmann, MGH SS 34 (Hannover, 1980) [hereafter: *Chron. Cas.*], lib. II c. 17, 201. Sansterre, 'Saint Nil', 372–3.

[16] For a previous, and cautionary, discussion, G. A. Loud, 'Montecassino and Byzantium in the Tenth and Eleventh Centuries', in M. Mullet and A. Kirby, eds, *The Theotokos Evergetis*

147

manuscripts probably written during Leo's time as the abbey's librarian (from 1072 onwards) contained Latin translations of the rules of Basil and Pachomius, as well as Basil's *Admonitions*.[17] These texts had long been known in the west; but this shows that there was still an interest in them. Leo recorded the case of a monk called Liutius who on his return from a pilgrimage to Jerusalem c. 1000 had first lived as a hermit near Salerno, and then established his own monastery on Monte Albaneta about 1 km. north-west of Montecassino. 'He himself was happy to excel all others in demeaning tasks and mortification; so humbly did he conduct himself in office that as a servant would he sifted flour in the bakery to make bread, all the while never ceasing to recite the Psalms'.[18] In 'this life of humility, great abstinence and austerity', which Leo clearly thought somewhat extreme, we may well see the influence of eastern monastic ideas. The *ordines* of East and West were not seen as mutually exclusive. Hence Lombard counts could found Greek monasteries; and in 1060 a Norman lord from northern Apulia gave a church to the abbey of Tremiti with the stipulation that those who staffed it could be governed either 'by the rule of the holy father Benedict or by that of St Basil, however God shall grant'.[19]

This charter suggests that there was a degree of flexibility in eleventh-century south Italian monastic observance, an observation that is abundantly supported by other evidence. In the principality of Salerno, for example, there were mixed communities of monks and other clergy, usually headed by an *abbas* and sometimes described as *monasteria*. One might see this as simply revealing the tendency for monastic institutions to decline into communities of secular canons, as elsewhere in post-Carolingian Europe, but in some of these *monasteria* the monastic element never entirely disappeared.[20] Furthermore, there were also more conventional monastic communities within the principality in the early eleventh century, such as that of St Maria, Elce, near Conza, in existence before 1020, and in which the Benedictine rule was expressly

---

and *Eleventh-Century Monasticism* (Belfast 1994), 30–58, esp. 50–1 [reprinted in G. A. Loud, *Montecassino and Benevento: Essays in South Italian Church History* (Aldershot, 2000), no. II].

17 *Codicum Casinensium Manuscriptorum Catalogus*, ed. M. Inguanez, 3 vols (Montecassino, 1915–41), 3: 63–8.

18 *Chron. Cas.* II. 30, 221–3

19 *Cod. Dipl. Tremiti*, 2: 211–13, no. 69, at 213.

20 B. Ruggiero, *Principi, nobiltà e Chiesa nell'Mezzogiorno longobardo: l'esempio di S. Massimo di Salerno* (Naples, 1973), esp. 97–106, 121–46.

attested in 1054.[21] Meanwhile, for women, there were both communities of nuns and women, usually widows, who undertook monastic vows but remained living in their own homes. This latter practice continued into the early twelfth century.[22] Similarly, there were clergy, described as monks, ministering at local churches (*ecclesiae villanae*), but seemingly not attached to monastic houses.[23]

Montecassino was of course the *fons et origo* of Benedictine observance, even if that tradition was not as unbroken as the Cassinese monks later liked to maintain.[24] Yet within the south as a whole, even within fully constituted (and non-Greek) monastic communities, the rule of Benedict did not necessarily enjoy a monopoly. Indeed, evidence for its observance before the mid-eleventh century is curiously scanty. One presumes, for example, that it was always observed at St Benedict, Conversano, one of the few Latin monasteries known in southern Apulia before the coming of the Normans, but the first express mention in the abundant surviving documents of this abbey came only in 1092.[25] Whatever peculiarities may have marked some of its subordinate churches, Tremiti, founded c. 1005 on an island in the Adriatic off the coast of the northern Capitanata, was also probably always Benedictine.[26] But when the early eleventh-century monastic reformer Dominic of Foligno (d. 1032) established a monastery at Sora, on the

[21] R. Volpini, 'Diplomi sconosciuti dei principi longobardi di Salerno e dei re normanni di Sicilia', in *Contributi dell'Istituto di Storia medievale, 1: Raccolta di studi in memoria di Giovanni Soranzo* (Milan, 1968), 503–6, no. 2, 512–17, no. 6.

[22] Thus the nunnery of St George at Salerno was in existence by 993, and that of SS. Michael and Stephen by 1054, M. Galante, ed., *Nuove Pergamene del monastero femminile di S. Giorgio di Salerno, 1: (993–1256)* (Altavilla Silentina, 1984), 1–2, no. 1; 12–15, no. 5. For non-enclosed 'nuns', G. Vitolo, 'Prima appunti per una storia dei penitenti nel Salernitano', *Archivio storico per le provincie napoletane*, ser. 3, 17 (1978), 393–405, esp. 394–5. For the will of a nun, *monacha domi degens*, in September 1122, Cava, Archivio della badia di S. Trinità, *Arca* xxi.76.

[23] For example, *Codex Diplomaticus Cavensis*, ed. M. Morcaldi et al., 8 vols (Milan-Naples, 1873–93), 7: 33–4, no. 1077 (1047).

[24] P. Engelbert, 'Regeltext und Romverehrung: zur Frage der Verbreitung der *Regula Benedicti* im Frühmittelalter', in F. Avagliano, ed., *Montecassino dalla prima alla seconda distruzione: momenti e aspetti di storia cassinese (secc. VI–IX)*, Miscellenea Cassinese 55 (Montecassino, 1987), 133–62, esp. 153–6.

[25] *Le Pergamene di Conversano i (901–1265)*, ed. G. Coniglio, Codice diplomatico pugliese 20 (Bari, 1975), 122–4, no. 53. This house was founded shortly before 957.

[26] A church given to it in 1040 was to be ruled *secundum regulam Sancti Benedicti*, *Cod. Dipl. Tremiti* 2: 89, no. 28, and the rule was expressly mentioned in Leo IX's confirmation of the abbey's property in 1053, ibid., 2: 156–8, no. 49.

northern border of the principality of Capua, the monks were to observe the Rule of the Master.[27]

Moreover, the eremitic tradition also flourished in pre-Norman Italy, both among Greeks and Latins. The Greek monk St Sabas took up residence as a hermit in a cave on the Amalfitan peninsula in 981, and when Kyrozosimi was given to Cava in 1088 the relevant charter expressly mentioned the *metochia* attached to the main monastery.[28] Nor, of course, were hermits incompatible with the Benedictine tradition. The hagiography of Montecassino showed a continued respect for the eremitic life as the ultimate manifestation of monasticism, if only for the few. Indeed, Abbot John II of Montecassino resigned his office to become a hermit in 998.[29] Madelmus, later to be abbot of St Sophia, Benevento (1074/5–1107) had earlier lived in a solitary's cell in that city.[30] However, southern Italy saw not just solitary hermits but also eremitic communities. John of Montecassino lived in fact, not on his own but with five companions. And soon after they retired to their hermitage, two other eremitic communities that were to have a long-lasting influence were established in different parts of southern Italy. By 1010 there was a community of hermits on Monte Majella in the Abruzzi, headed by John, 'prior, priest and anchorite'.[31] A few years later, c. 1020, Alferius, a courtier of Prince Guaimar III of Salerno retired to the same 'huge and terrifying cave' that Liutius had earlier inhabited near Salerno, before founding the monastery at Albaneta. This was the origin of what was to become the great Benedictine monastery of Cava. Yet when Cava formally adopted a cenobitic form, and the Benedictine rule, is a good question. Its founder was determined that the monastery should remain small, with no more than twelve brothers, and the early monks seem to have lived in individual

---

27 A. Lentini, 'La *Vita S. Dominici* di Alberico Cassinese', *Benedictina* 5 (1951), 57–77, at 76.

28 Borsari, *Monachesimo bizantino*, 49, and above n. 11.

29 *Chron. Cas.* II. 20, 203–4. More generally, J.-M. Sansterre, 'Recherches sur les ermites de Mont-Cassin et l'eremetisme dans l'hagiographie cassinienne', *Hagiographica* 2 (1995), 57–92.

30 *Die Briefe des Petrus Damiani*, ed. K. Reindel, MGH *Die Briefe der Deutschen Kaiserzeit* 4, 4 vols (Munich, 1983–90), 2: 184–5, no. 57.

31 'Dissertatio de antiquitate, ditione, viribus varieque fortuna abbatiae S. Salvatoris ad Montem Magellae', in *Collectio Bullarum SS. Basilicae Vaticanae*, 3 vols (Rome, 1747–52), 1: vi.

cells rather than in a dormitory. The full Benedictine regime was probably only adopted under the second abbot Leo (1050–79).[32]

After 1050 this monastic diversity diminished. New foundations, of
which there were many, tended to be expressly Benedictine *ab initio*,[33]
and the smaller independent foundations were increasingly absorbed in
the congregations of the major Benedictine monasteries. Several of the
foundations of Dominic of Sora, for example, ended up as part of the
Cassinese monastic empire, as their major lay patrons, the Counts of
Marsia and Sangro switched their pious generosity towards the abbey of
St Benedict, during its 'golden age' under Abbot Desiderius (1058–87).[34]
Gregorian reform ideas of the sinfulness of lay possession of churches
exerted at least some influence: in 1094 Count Robert of Caiazzo gave
the nunnery of St Maria, Cingla, to Montecassino, stating that it had
been held by his predecessors *male et seculariter*, and in 1101 a donor
offered his share of a church near Monte Sant'Angelo to the Cassinese
pilgrim hospice on the Gargano peninsula 'because I have heard from
wise men that no layman should have what is from God under his
power'.[35] As we have seen, Greek monasteries too became part of these
congregations. Cava was not the only Benedictine mother house to
profit. Montecassino, for example, was given the former imperial
monastery of St Peter at Taranto by Robert Guiscard in 1080.[36] Nor was

---

[32] *Vitae Quatuor Priorum Abbatum Cavensium*, ed. L. Mattei-Cerasoli, Rerum Italicarum
Scriptores, ns: vol. 6, pt 5.1 (Bologna, 1941) [hereafter: *VQPA*], 7 (twelve monks only), 8
(Alferius retires to his cell to die), 12 (Leo's cell). The Rule of St Benedict was, however,
observed at the subordinate monastery of St Nicholas de Palma, that Leo founded, S. Leone
and G. Vitolo, eds, *Codex Diplomaticus Cavensis*, ix (Cava, 1984), 328–32, no. 103 (1071), and
presumably therefore by the mother house as well by this date, and perhaps before St Nicholas was founded in 1062. Cava itself was founded between 1016 and 1025, S. Leone, 'La
Data di fondazione della badia di Cava', *Benedictina* 22 (1975), 335–46 [reprinted in Leone
and Vitolo, *Minima Cavensia*, 45–59].

[33] For example, the foundation charters of the monastery of St Andrew of Brindisi in
1059: *Faciatis exinde secundum testum regule Sancti Benedicti docet, Codice Diplomatico Brindisiano* i
(492–1299), ed. G. M. Monti (Trani, 1940), 7–9, no. 4; Holy Trinity, Mileto, in 1080, L.-R.
Ménager, 'L'Abbaye bénédictine de la Trinité de Mileto en Calabre à l'époque normande',
Bullettino del archivio paleografico italiano, ns 4–5 (1958/9), 41–3, no. 13; and in a donation by
the founder to the nunnery of St John the Evangelist at Lecce in 1133, M. Pastore, ed., *Le
Pergamene di San Giovanni Evangelista in Lecce*, (Lecce, 1970), 1–3, no. 1.

[34] J. Howe, *Church Reform and Social Change in Eleventh-Century Italy: Dominic of Sora and
his Patrons* (Philadephia, PA, 1997), 123–48.

[35] E. Gattula, *Accessiones ad Historiam Abbatiae Casinensis* (Venice, 1734), 713–14. *Le
Colonie Cassinesi in Capitanata ii: Gargano*, ed. T. Leccisotti, Miscellanea Cassinese 15 (1938),
42–3, no. 6.

[36] *Recueil des Actes des ducs normands d'Italie (1046–1127)*, i : *Les Premiers Ducs (1046–1087)*, ed.
L.-R. Ménager (Bari, 1981), 101–4, no. 31.

Cava's progression from eremitic to cenobitic house in any way unique. Thus the hermitage founded by a Spanish monk of Montecassino on Monte Castellone, about 4 km. north of the abbey, under Abbot Richer (1038–55), had developed by 1082 into a fully fledged monastery, St Matthew *Servorum Dei*, that was important enough to attract the patronage of the Norman Prince of Capua.[37]

A similar process was followed by one of the most significant twelfth-century foundations on the southern mainland, Montevergine. Its founder, William of Vercelli, settled as a hermit with one companion on a mountain near Avellino.[38] After some two to three years, according to his biographer, a number of disciples had joined him, and they asked by what rule (*norma*) they should live. He replied that they should work with their own hands, be charitable to the poor, and celebrate the holy office at the customary hours.[39] By 1125, the date of its first charter, the community was described as a monastery, although it was still relatively informal, with William designated as the *custos et rector* rather than abbot.[40] Even this was more than the founder really wanted, for fairly soon afterwards he retired to become a hermit once again.[41] In his absence the community developed into a more conventional monastic form; by 1131 it had an abbot and prior, and at least one dependant church, but the Benedictine rule was only finally adopted about a generation later, between 1161 and 1172.[42]

The situation is less clear with regard to Pulsano, founded on the southern slope of the Gargano massif by William's friend and mentor, John of Matera. Pulsano, founded about 1129, was in some respects very similar to Montevergine. Like William, John had lived as a hermit for

[37] *Petri Diaconi: Ortus et Vita Iustorum Cenobii Casinensis*, ed. R. H. Rodgers (Berkeley, CA, 1972), 75. *Regesto della antica badia di S. Matteo de Castello o Servorum Dei*, ed. M. Inguanez (Montecassino, 1914), 2–5, nos 2–3. Sansterre, 'Recherches sur les ermites du Mont-Cassin', 68.

[38] *Vita*, cc. 12–13, ActaSS Iun. 7 (Paris, 1867), 101–2. The *Life* has also been edited by G. Mongelli, 'Legenda de Vita et Obitu S. Guilielmi Confessoris et Heremite', *Samnium* 24 (1961), 144–72; 25 (1962), 48–73.

[39] Ibid., c. 16, at 103.

[40] *Codice diplomatico verginiano*, ed. P. M. Tropeano, 13 vols (Montevergine, 1977–2000), 2: 199–203, no. 148.

[41] *Vita* c. 24; ActaSS Iun. 7, 105–6.

[42] *Codice diplomatico verginiano*, 2: 382–4, no. 191. Houben, *Die Abtei Venosa*, 70–1. G. Vitolo, 'Vecchio e nuovo monachesimo nel regno svevo di Sicilia', in A. Esch and N. Kamp, eds, *Friedrich II: Tagung des Deutschen Historischen Institut in Rom im Gedenkjahr 1994* (Tübingen, 1996), 182–200, at 190.

some years before founding a community.[43] His biography, probably written within about fifteen years of his death in 1139, and certainly by someone who knew him personally, also stressed the importance of manual labour, and of poverty. One of his miracles took place when he had gone out with the brothers to cut wood to build houses. When John's prayers cured the only son of a family with whom he was lodging, he refused their attempts to endow his monastery with their property, and avoided staying with them in the future. He also expelled a monk who had brought stolen treasure to the monastery, despite the latter's penitence.[44] Both John and William were strict in enforcing an austere diet, forbidding the consumption of cheese and wine.[45] But John was unequivocally described as 'abbot', and in a vision attributed to a seriously injured monk John was seen appealing to St Benedict in Heaven to justify the practice of discarding the *scapula* while undertaking manual labour.[46] By 1177 Pulsano was observing the rule of St Benedict,[47] but when it was formally adopted is unclear: unlike Montevergine almost no charters survive from the Gargano abbey. However, a third monastic foundation by a former hermit, the monastery of St Maria in Gualdo, near Benevento, founded in 1156 by John of Tufara (d. 1170), followed the rule of Benedict from the first, albeit with considerable stress on the importance of manual labour, and with an exemption from the tithe of the monks' own labour, following the Cistercian model.[48] The tendency in reformed monasticism in southern Italy during the twelfth century was therefore overwhelmingly to bring eremitic foundations into the Benedictine mainstream.[49] The one significant exception was the Holy Saviour on Monte Majella, still

[43] *Vita Iohannis*, cc. 5–6, ActaSS Iun. 5 (Paris, 1867), 37–8.
[44] Ibid., cc. 26–7, ActaSS Iun. 5, 43. Manual labour, ibid., cc. 35, 37, at 44–5. For the date and models of composition, F. Panarelli, *Dal Gargano alla Toscana: il Monachesimo riformato latino dei Pulsanesi (secoli XII–XIV)* (Rome, 1997), 279–86.
[45] *Vita Iohannis*, c. 102, at 50. *Vita Guilielmi*, c. 39, at 109, giving his regulations for his foundation at Goleto: 'there was no one who, even in sickness, had acquaintance with wine. They considered meat, cheese and an egg a sin even to name'. See Panarelli, *Dal Gargano*, 90. For north European comparisons, cf. Leyser, *Hermits and the New Monasticism*, 53, 66–7.
[46] *Vita Iohannis*, cc. 49–50; ActaSS Iun. 5, 49–50.
[47] Stated in the first surviving papal bull for Pulsano, Panarelli, *Dal Gargano*, 291–3.
[48] *Italia Pontificia*, ed. P. F. Kehr, 10 vols (Berlin, 1905–75), ix; *Samnium-Apulia-Lucania*, ed. W. Holtzmann (Berlin, 1962), 109, no. 1.
[49] Leyser, *Hermits and the New Monasticism*, 86–96, points to a general tendency of eremitic monks towards adoption of a conventual lifestyle: in southern Italy, however, the model was specifically Benedictine.

unequivocally a community of 'hermits' even in the later twelfth century; but this was an isolated house in the mountains of the Abruzzi – a region that was only politically incorporated with the rest of the south in 1140.[50]

The Norman conquest might have been expected to have opened out south Italian monasticism to external influence, and to an extent this was true. Monks from Normandy, for example, colonized the foundations of the ruling Hauteville dynasty at Venosa, at S. Euphemia and Mileto in Calabria, and Catania in Sicily.[51] Peter, the third abbot of Cava, who had spent some years as a monk of Cluny, attempted to introduce Cluniac customs to the Salernitan monastery, although this proved extremely unpopular with the monks, and led to him abandoning Cava, perhaps for several years, before peace was restored.[52] However, while the author of the 'Lives of the First Four Abbots' (which dates from the 1130s) seems to have felt some pride in his abbey's connection with Cluny, modern scholars see little or no Cluniac influence on monastic observance at Cava.[53] Montecassino was indeed openly hostile to the spread of Cluniac customs – Abbot Desiderius went so far as to denounce these as an infringement of the rule in a letter to the Abbot of Hersfeld in 1072/3, even if he was prepared to welcome Abbot Hugh of Cluny to Montecassino in 1083.[54] There was during the twelfth century one single Cluniac priory on the island of Sicily, probably founded before 1135, but that was the only one in the kingdom.[55]

[50] 'The prior of the hermits of Majella' received a grant from the Bishop-elect of Chieti in 1141, and the community was still described as one of hermits in a bull of Alexander III in 1175, although at some point between 1164 and 1175 its head had become an abbot, *Collectio Bullarum Vaticanae*, 1: xxi, 62–4.

[51] *The Ecclesiastical History of Orderic Vitalis*, ed. and trans. M. Chibnall, 6 vols (Oxford, 1969–81), 2: 98–103. L.-R. Ménager, 'Les foundations monastiques de Robert Guiscard, duc de Pouille et de Calabre', *Quellen und Forschungen aus italienischen Archiven und Bibliotheken* 39 (1959), 1–116; Houben, *Die Abtei Venosa*, 138–47.

[52] *VQPA*, 17–18. These events took place in the late 1060s, during the lifetime of his predecessor Leo, while Peter was acting as the latter's deputy. They did not prevent him succeeding Leo as abbot in 1079.

[53] G. Vitolo, 'Cava e Cluny', in Leone and Vitolo, *Minima Cavensia*, 19–44. The death of Abbot Peter in 1123 was presaged by a vision of three of the holy abbots of Cluny, *VQPA*, 26.

[54] *Die Ältere Wormser Briefsammlungen*, ed. W. Bulst, MGH *Die Briefe der Deutschen Kaiserzeit* 3 (Weimar, 1949), 13–16, no. 1. *Chron. Cas.* III.51, 433–4.

[55] L. T. White, *Latin Monasticism in Norman Sicily* (Cambridge, MA, 1938), 149–51. H. Houben, 'Il monachesimo cluniacense e i monasteri normanni dell'Italia meridionale', *Benedictina* 39 (1992), 341–61, at 354–7 [reprinted in idem, *Mezzogiorno normanno-svevo:*

The influence of the Augustinian canons was slightly greater, but still relatively minor. Count Roger I established a house of canons at Bagnara in southern Calabria about 1085.[56] According to their first papal bull in 1113, the Hospitallers, at this stage still simply Augustinians, had houses at Bari, Otranto, Taranto and Messina, but whether these actually existed has been doubted.[57] A priory near Siponto, in northern Apulia, probably Benedictine at first, was converted to the Augustinian observance between 1137 and 1146, and flourished modestly thereafter, although it was to fall on hard times in the thirteenth century, and finally was transferred to the Teutonic Knights in 1260.[58] The church of St Peter *ad Aram* in Naples was transferred to Augustinian canons by the Neapolitan-born cardinal John of S. Anastasia c. 1170.[59] There may also have been an Augustinian house at Foiano, near Benevento, subject to the monks of St Maria in Gualdo, but if so its existence was brief, being mentioned only once in the foundation bull of John of Tufara's abbey.[60] Most notably, King Roger of Sicily entrusted his intended burial church at Cefalù to Augustinians from Bagnara in 1131, and this was eventually confirmed as a bishopric and one of the major patrimonial landowners on the island.[61] Yet compared with the number and significance of canonical houses in northern Europe, their impact in the kingdom of Sicily was meagre.

The one province of the Mezzogiorno where there was some noticeable degree of external influence was Calabria. Here, in addition to the

monasteri e castelli, ebrei e musulmani (Naples, 1996), 7–22, at 17–20], suggests tentatively that the impetus for this foundation may have come from Roger II of Sicily's Spanish wife Elvira, whose father Alfonso VI of Castile was one of Cluny's greatest patrons.

56 White, *Latin Monasticism*, 184.

57 *Cartulaire general de l'ordre des Hospitaliers de St. Jean de Jérusalem (1100–1310)*, ed. J. Delaville Le Roulx, 4 vols (Paris, 1894–1906), 1: 29–30, no. 30. A. Luttrell, 'Gli Ospedalieri nel Mezzogiorno', in G. Musca ed., *Il Mezzogiorno normanno-svevo e le Crociate*, Atti delle quattordicesime giornate normanno-sveve, 2000 (Bari, 2002), 290–1.

58 *Regesto di San Leonardo di Siponto*, ed. F. Camobreco, Regesta Chartarum Italiae 10 (Rome, 1913), esp. 8–9, no. 10, 15–16, no. 23 (the first reference to canons). A bull of Alexander III in 1167, ibid., 45, no. 70, listed 9 dependant churches. For the takeover by the Teutonic Order, ibid., 129–33, nos 194–7. See also, H. Houben, '*Iuxta stratam perigrinorum*: la canonica di S. Leonardo di Siponto', *Rivista di storia della chiesa in Italia* 56 (2002), 323–45, esp. 328–31.

59 M. Fuiano, *Napoli nel Medioevo* (Naples, 1972), 120.

60 See n. 48 above.

61 White, *Latin Monasticism*, 189–204. According to the papal taxation lists of the early fourteenth century Cefalù had an annual income of 350 *unciae*, compared with 600 for the archbishopric of Palermo, but only 150 for the nearby see of Patti, *Rationes Decimarum Italiae–Sicilia*, ed. P. Sella, Studi e Testi 112 (Vatican City, 1944), 15, 30, 37.

canons of Bagnara, the late eleventh century saw the establishment by
St Bruno of the Carthusian house of St Maria della Torre, in the diocese
of Squillace, about 22 km. east of Roger I's Calabrian capital, Mileto, in
or about 1090.[62] This in turn spawned two further abbeys in the early
twelfth century, St James in Montauro and St Stephen *de Nemore* [S.
Stefano del Bosco]. Interestingly, the Greek Bishop of Squillace assisted
in the foundation of St Maria, and took part in its consecration in 1094:
the eremitic lifestyle of the Carthusians was after all closer to Greek
ideas of monasticism than that of the Benedictines who staffed most of
the ducal and comital foundations in the region.[63] But, as with the
indigenous foundations of Montevergine and Pulsano, as time went on
there was a tendency to evolve from an eremitic to a conventual model.
When the abbey of Montauro was founded about 1114, it was specifically for 'the brothers who are unable to bear the austerity of the
hermitage', and they were to observe the rule of St Benedict. And eventually, in 1192, S. Stefano del Bosco was affiliated to the Cistercian
order.[64]

Half a century earlier the first Cistercian monastery in the kingdom
of Sicily had been established in Calabria: St Maria Requisita, later
known as Sambucina, in the Val di Crati, near Cosenza.[65] This was
probably the Cistercian foundation to which St Bernard referred in two
letters to King Roger written soon after the conclusion of the papal
schism in 1139.[66] But, after this initial foundation the Cistercians had
little further impact on southern Italy for almost half a century.

[62] For the date, L-R. Ménager, 'Lanfranco, notaio pontificio (1091–3), la diplomatica
ducale Italo-normanna e la certosa di S. Stefano del Bosco', *Studi storici meridionali* 3 (1983),
1–37. There is no satisfactory study of the Calabrian Carthusians, and the documentation has
been seriously corrupted by early modern forgeries.
[63] Trinchera, *Syllabus*, 69–71, no. 53. F. Ughelli, *Italia Sacra,* 2nd edn by N. Colletti, 10
vols (Venice, 1717–21), 9: 425.
[64] PL 163, 395, no. 452, also found in *Italia Pontificia, vol. 10: Calabria-Insulae*, ed. D.
Girgensohn (Berlin, 1975), 72, no. 14. H. Houben, 'Le Istituzioni monastiche dell'Italia
meridionale all'epoca di S. Bernardo di Clairvaux', in H. Houben and B. Vetere, eds, *I
Cistercensi nel Mezzogiorno medioevale* (Lecce, 1994), 73–89, at 80.
[65] Its first charter dates from 1145, *Carte latine di abbazie calabresi provenienti dall'Archivio
Aldobrandini*, ed. A. Pratesi, Studi e Testi 197 (Vatican City, 1958), 41–2, no. 14. For its subsequent history, and the identity between the original foundation and the later Sambucina, P.
De Leo, 'L'insediamento dei Cistercensi nel "Regnum Siciliae": I Primi monasteri Cistercensi
calabresi', in Houben and Vetere, *I Cistercensi nel Mezzogiorno medioevale*, 317–37.
[66] *Sancti Bernardi Opera*, ed. J. Leclerq and H. M. Rochais, 8 vols (Rome, 1977), 8: 67–9,
nos 208–9. [English trans. in B. Scott James, *The Letters of St. Bernard of Clairvaux* (London,
1953), 349–50, nos 277–8].

Another abbey was established at Prizzi in Sicily c. 1155, but since its founder, Matthew Bonellus, was the ringleader of the Sicilian conspiracies against King William I in 1160/1 this was hardly a recommendation for the order's future progress within the kingdom. A generation later this house was converted into a nunnery for refugees fleeing from the collapsing Crusader states.[67] The next Cistercian house on the mainland, St Maria di Ferraria, was consecrated in 1179, but it was not until the very last years of the twelfth century that the Cistercians had any widespread impact. Ferraria remained for another generation the only Cistercian house in the Campania; there were none in Apulia until the 1190s, and the first Cistercian foundation in the Abruzzi came only in 1197. Even in 1200 there were in total no more than 12 or possibly 13 Cistercian abbeys in the kingdom of Sicily, more than half of which had either been founded or converted to the Cistercian *ordo* within the previous decade.[68] And it was only with the election of Abbot Lucas of Sambucina as Archbishop of Cosenza in 1203 that there began the recruitment of Cistercians for the kingdom's episcopate.[69] The Cistercians only made a significant impact on southern Italy in the first half of the thirteenth century.

Indeed, a generation before 1200 the extraneous 'new monastic orders' had made less of an impression in the south than the reformed monasteries of indigenous origin. By 1177 Pulsano, for example, had at least fourteen dependencies within the *regno*, albeit most of them in northern Apulia.[70] In addition, within little more than a decade after the founder's death, the Pulsanese observance had spread to the Abruzzi (St Peter of Vallebona 1148), to Lombardy (the Holy Saviour, near Piacenza 1144), and to Dalmatia (St Maria, Meleta, 1151). By the 1170s Pulsano had also gained dependencies in Tuscany and at Rome.[71] The heyday of the Pulsano observance was brief, and already by the pontificate of Honorius III the mother house was suffering grave internal problems, both economic and disciplinary.[72] But for a generation it had

---

67 White, *Latin Monasticism*, 166.

68 Houben and Vetere, *I Cistercensi nel Mezzogiorno medioevale*, 189–90, 194–5, 206–10, 270–1, 293, 339, 346. White, *Latin Monasticism*, 168–79.

69 N. Kamp, 'The Bishops of Southern Italy in the Norman and Staufen Periods', in G. A. Loud and A. Metcalfe, eds, *The Society of Norman Italy* (Leiden, 2002), 185–209, at 205.

70 Panarelli, *Dal Gargano*, 93.

71 Ibid., 137–236. For one of its Tuscan dependencies, D. Osheim, *A Tuscan Monastery and its Social World: San Michele of Guamo (1156–1348)* (Rome, 1989).

72 Panarelli, *Dal Gargano*, 240–4.

spread a monastic discipline from the *regno* to the north, and that discipline was a reformed, but essentially Benedictine one.

The religious impulses propelling south Italian monasticism during the eleventh and twelfth centuries were similar to those elsewhere in Christendom – certainly in the growing influence of eremitic ideas. But the situation before 1050 was rather different and more diffuse than in other regions, and different influences were present – not least the presence of Greek monasticism, even in areas where the majority of the population were Latins. And the Benedictine efflorescence that accompanied, and was to some extent caused by the Norman arrival, proved remarkably tenacious. South Italian monasticism was still overwhelmingly Benedictine at the overthrow of the 'Norman' dynasty in 1194, and the ascetic instincts of south Italian monastic reformers had been domesticated within the Benedictine ideal.

University of Leeds

KINGS, BISHOPS AND INCEST:
EXTENSION AND SUBVERSION OF
THE ECCLESIASTICAL MARRIAGE JURISDICTION
AROUND 1100

by CHRISTOF ROLKER

IF we set out to explore 'discipline and diversity' in the medieval Church, canon law presents itself as a possible starting point: canon law was first of all disciplinary law. Its history can be, and has been, told as an interplay of moral decline and reform, as a conflict between discipline and diverse customs, as a struggle between one eternal order and a multitude of transgressions.[1] However, the imposition of norms is never a unilateral process; the success of a given set of norms is often shaped by an interplay between enforcement and subversion. In the present article, I want to explore this theme for a crucial phase in the history of medieval incest legislation and the ecclesiastical jurisdiction over marriage.

Medieval incest legislation has attracted very divergent interpretations.[2] It was not static, but from the ninth to the early thirteenth century, the essentials remained largely unchanged.[3] The key concept was the idea that consanguinity extended to the seventh degree;

---

[1] Paul Fournier and Gabriel Le Bras, *Histoire des collections canoniques en Occident: depuis les Fausses Décretales jusqu'au Décret de Gratien*, 2 vols (Paris, 1931/2); Gabriel Le Bras, Charles Lefebvre and Jacqueline Rambaud, *L'âge classique, 1140–1378: sources et théorie du droit*, Histoire du droit et des institutions de l'Eglise en occident 7 (Paris, 1965).

[2] See Jack Goody, *The Development of the Family and Marriage in Europe* (Cambridge and New York, 1983) (stressing that exogamy prevents property concentration); David Herlihy, 'Making Sense of Incest: Women and the Marriage Rules of the Early Middle Ages', in Bernard S. Bachrach and David Nicholas, eds, *Law, Custom, and the Social Fabric in Medieval Europe: Essays in Honor of Bryce Lyon*, Studies in Medieval Culture 28 (Kalamazoo, MI, 1990), 1–16 (domestic peace and 'circulation of women'); David L. d'Avray, 'Lay Kinship Solidarity and Papal Law', in Pauline Stafford et al., eds, *Law, Laity and Solidarities: Essays in Honour of Susan Reynolds* (Manchester, 2001), 188–99 (social cohesion).

[3] See Joseph Freisen, *Geschichte des canonischen Eherechts bis zum Verfall der Glossenlitteratur* (Paderborn, 1893), 387–405; Pierre Daudet, *L'établissement de la compétence de l'Église en matière de divorce et de consanguinité, France, Xème-XIIème siècles: études sur l'histoire de la juridiction matrimoniale* (Paris, 1941); Patrick Corbet, *Autour de Burchard de Worms: l'Église allemande et les interdits de parenté (IXème-XIIème siècle)*, Ius commune, Sonderhefte 142 (Frankfurt, 2001), 8–49; and most recently David L. d'Avray, *Medieval Marriage: Symbolism and Society* (Oxford, 2005).

marriages within these degrees were prohibited and, where they were contracted, canon law could demand their dissolution. However, canon law could be a two-edged sword – from Louis VII to Henry VIII there are many well-known examples of how incest legislation could be turned to the advantage of those 'subjected' to it. This is commonly seen as a later form of abuse of the ecclesiastical jurisdiction.[4] However, as I want to argue, the knowledge, use and abuse of incest legislation by the nobility was also an important element in preparing the extension of this very jurisdiction from an early stage.

The decades around 1100 are generally seen as the crucial phase for the extension of ecclesiastical marriage jurisdiction. Consanguinity as a pretext for repudiation was nothing new in the eleventh century, but there are two reasons why it became more important. First, the causes for canonical divorce were gradually reduced, preparing the classical doctrine according to which there was no divorce proper. Annulment on grounds of consanguinity remained as one of very few options to terminate a marriage. At the same time, the emphasis of the Church on incest prohibitions made it in fact easier to have a marriage annuled. So, the Church certainly extended its jurisdiction; but how did this jurisdiction win acceptance? Duby famously argued for a conflict between an 'ecclesiastical model' and a 'lay model' of marriage, suggesting that the Church around 1100 imposed her 'model' on an unwilling nobility.[5] In particular, he saw the second marriage of Philip I of France as 'the major turning point' in the conflict between the 'two models of marriage'.[6] Bouchard, in contrast, stressed that already in the ninth and tenth centuries, the nobility avoided cousin marriages.[7] According to

4 Constance Brittain Bouchard, *Those of My Blood: Constructing Noble Families in Medieval Francia* (Philadelphia, PA, 2001), 39, holds that tenth- and eleventh-century nobility did not abuse the ecclesiastical incest prohibitions in the same way as did later generations. Accordingly, her account of the divorce of king Henry's daughters (ibid., 44) and the second marriage of Constance (ibid., 49) is very different from mine.

5 Georges Duby, *Medieval Marriage: Two Models from Twelfth-Century France* (Baltimore, MD, 1978), and idem, *The Knight, the Lady and the Priest: the Making of Modern Marriage in Medieval France* (London, 1984). For important criticism, see Bouchard, 'Consanguinity and Noble Marriages in the Tenth and Eleventh Centuries', *Speculum* 56 (1981), 268–87; Carolyn Janet Moule, 'Entry into Marriage in the Late Eleventh and Twelfth Centuries, c. 1090–1181', unpublished Ph.D. thesis, University of Cambridge, 1983; and Amy Livingstone, 'Kith and Kin: Kinship and Family Structure of the Nobility of Eleventh- and Twelfth-Century Blois-Chartres', *French Historical Studies* 20 (1997), 419–58.

6 Duby, *Medieval Marriage*, 45.

7 Bouchard, 'Consanguinity and Noble Marriages', esp. 278–9.

her, these became common only in the eleventh and twelfth centuries.[8] As I will argue below, the marriage affair of Philip I needs a re-evaluation; at the same time, I want to compare it to a number of contemporary cases from England and France to see it in a broader context.

England

As St Anselm complained in one of his letters, the nobility in England commonly married within the prohibited degrees.[9] This clearly troubled Anselm, but his extant letters, and the cases touched upon there, do not suggest that Anselm had any means to prevent such marriages. Sometimes, however, certain noblemen themselves discovered that their marriages were uncanonical. Nigel of Aubigny may serve as an example here. Under royal patronage, Nigel rose from a landless knight to a powerful baron. Most of his Norman lands came to him by his marriage to Matilda of Laigle in 1107.[10] Matilda had been married to Robert of Mowbray in 1095 – a few months before his rebellion against the king. Robert was imprisoned for life, and Matilda could not remarry. However, a distant blood-relationship offered an escape. The case was made known to the pope 'by men of the court', as Orderic Vitalis relates, and in 1107 Anselm, with papal backing, dissolved the marriage.[11]

As it seems, the king was behind the 'men of the court' who sought to annul the marriage. Anselm complied with their wishes to arrange a new marriage for Matilda, by which Henry I could elegantly reward his protegé from the estates of one of his enemies. This is not to say that canon law played no role in Anselm's decision to act as he did. But it is

---

8 Eadem, 'Eleanor's Divorce from Louis VII: the Uses of Consanguinity', in Bonnie Wheeler and John Carmi Parsons, eds, *Eleanor of Aquitaine: Lord and Lady* (New York, 2002), 223–35, at 225.

9 Anselm, *Epistula* 365, in Franciscus Salesius Schmitt, ed., *S. Anselmi Cantuariensis archiepiscopi opera omnia*, 6 vols (Edinburgh, 1946–61) [hereafter: Schmitt], 5: 308.

10 Diana E. Greenway, *Charters of the Honour of Mowbray, 1107–1191*, Records of Social and Economic History, ns 1 (London, 1972), xvii–xxiv.

11 Orderic Vitalis, *Historia ecclesiastica* 8.23, in Marjorie Chibnall, ed. and trans., *The Ecclesiastical History of Orderic Vitalis*, Oxford Medieval Texts, 6 vols (Oxford, 1969–80) [hereafter: Chibnall], 4: 284; Anselm, *Epistula* 423 (Schmitt, 5: 369); *Regesta pontificum romanorum ab condita ecclesia ad annum post Christum natum MCXCVIII*, ed. P. Jaffé, rev. edn by S. Löwenfeld, F. Kaltenbrunner and P. Ewald, 2 vols (Leipzig, 1885–8) [hereafter: Jaffé, *Regesta*], Paschal II, 6178 (PL 163, 232).

evident that he could not have intervened, had the king not wished
Nigel to marry Matilda. However, the story does not end here. As it
turned out, Nigel had gained less than he had hoped for. While the
marriage established him in Normandy, it remained childless. Within
ten years, the marriage which Anselm had helped to arrange had
become undesireable for Nigel. In 1118, he repudiated his wife and
quickly remarried, pretending that his first marriage was invalid
because he was related to Robert of Mowbray.[12]

Nigel's marriages were clearly determined by royal patronage,
transfer of landed property and inheritance concerns. He certainly was
not the only noble rather selectively to remember canon law. For
example, early in his reign, King Henry had promised one of his daughters to William of Warenne, a decision he regretted later. Again it was
Anselm who wrote a timely letter on the blood-relation between
William and the king.[13] Taken at face value, this letter would suggest
that the initiative was with Anselm, but the circumstances suggest that
Henry learned from this letter only what he wanted to hear in any case.
However, it was not always the king who won. In the case of another
daughter of Henry, Ivo of Chartres dissolved the marriage arrangement
because the groom, Hugh FitzGervais of Châteauneuf-en-Thimerais,
was related to her in the sixth degree of canonical computation; from
Ivo's letter, it seems clear that he acted at the request of Hugh's kin.[14]
Presumably this part of his family was happier with the marriage Hugh
contracted some years later – in 1121, he married a sister of the rebel-
lious Waleran II Beaumont.[15]

The cases quoted so far have in common that the incestous
marriages or marriage arrangements in question were dissolved by the
Church, but only at the request of powerful laymen. Frequently, the
ecclesiastical sentence was little more than a legitimisation of de facto
divorce. Such cases are hardly to be taken as evidence for the Church's
power to enforce her marriage legislation; they only suggest that, in
certain cases, ecclesiastical jurisdiction was welcomed to terminate

12 Greenway, *Honour of Mowbray*, xix.
13 Anselm, *Epistula* 424 (Schmitt, 5: 369–70).
14 Ivo, *Epistula* 261 (PL 162, 265–6); see C. Warren Hollister, *Henry I* (New Haven, CT, 2001), 263.
15 David Crouch, *The Beaumont Twins: the Roots and Branches of Power in the Twelfth Century*, Cambridge Studies in Medieval Life and Thought, ser. 4.1 (Cambridge, 1986), 15–17.

unwanted marriages. The question remains whether the case was different in France.

France

If we now turn to France, we have to begin with one of the most prominent contemporary cases: King Philip's marriage affair. The story has been told many times.[16] In 1092, the king, after twenty years of marriage, repudiated his wife, Berta of Holland, and began his famous affair with Bertrada of Montfort. While most French bishops seem silently to have agreed, there were prominent opponents, namely the famous canonist Ivo of Chartres and Pope Urban II. Before considering the course of events, let us briefly turn to the canon law background of the case. From a legal point of view, there were two main objections to the king's second marriage. First, the king was legitimately married to Berta, and Betrada was married to Fulk of Anjou, though the validity of this latter union was itself doubtful. Second, Philip was distantly related to Fulk; if the latter was legitimately married to Bertrada, this would create a bond of affinity lasting even after Fulk had died. There are other potential canon law objections to the marriage, in particular that Philip and Bertrada were distantly related.[17] This, however, was unknown to the contemporaries. Ivo, Urban, Hugh of Lyon and Fulk of Anjou, who all objected to the marriage, would have mentioned the relationship, had it been known to them.

The important point is that the most prominent ecclesiastics involved held different views in this matter. Ivo opposed the marriage for only one reason, namely that the king had remarried in Berta's lifetime.[18] Unless his first marriage was ended by death or a canonical

---

[16] See e.g. Augustin Fliche, *Le règne de Philippe Ier, roi de France, 1060–1108* (Paris, 1912), 36–77, Rolf Sprandel, *Ivo von Chartres und seine Stellung in der Kirchengeschichte*, Pariser Historische Studien 1 (Stuttgart, 1962), 102–12, and Alfons Becker, *Papst Urban II. (1088–1099): Herkunft und kirchliche Laufbahn*, MGH Schriften 19.1 (Stuttgart, 1964), 192–205. The most influential account is still that of Duby, *Medieval Marriage*, 29–45; for a more balanced view, and corrections to Duby's model, see e.g. Moule, 'Entry into Marriage', 32–45, and Christopher Nugent Lawrence Brooke, *The Medieval Idea of Marriage* (Oxford, 1989), 119–26.

[17] Marie-Bernadette Bruguière, 'Canon Law and Royal Weddings, Theory and Practice: the French Example, 987–1215', in Stanley Chodorow, ed., *Proceedings of the Eighth International Congress of Medieval Canon Law*, Monumenta iuris canonici, Subsidia 9 (Vatican City, 1992), 473–96, at 482.

[18] Ivo knew that at Clermont Philip was excommunicated for 'incestuous adultery', but never mentioned this in the king's lifetime (against Duby, *Medieval Marriage*, 41). Neither Ivo

divorce, the king's second marriage could not possibly be valid.[19] As for
Bertrada, he did not regard her liaison with Fulk as a marriage impediment because Fulk himself was married when taking Bertrada as wife.
Indeed, Fulk was notorious for his polygamy.[20] Ivo referred to Bertrada
as the 'so-called wife of Fulk' only, and never argued that her first
marriage played any role.[21] For this reason, the supposed legal affinity
between Bertrada and Philip to Ivo was non-existent.[22] Pope Urban, in
contrast, assumed that Bertrada was married to Fulk. Therefore, he
opposed the royal marriage because, in his opinion, both Philip and
Bertrada were married. Neither could remarry in the lifetime of their
respective spouse, and, even after the death of the latter, Philip would
still be prohibited from marrying his late relative's widow. Consequently, Urban from the beginning accused Philip not only of adultery
but incestous adultery, that is, adultery with his cousin's wife.[23]

In the two years immediately following the repudiation of Berta,
these differences played no role. Ivo famously chose openly to resist the
king, and although negotiations continued, their initially good relations
detoriated rapidly.[24] At the same time, the papacy was remarkably
silent; Urban tried to avoid a public condemnation of the French king
for as long as possible, fearing to lose him as an ally.[25] With Berta's
death in 1094, however, the situation changed completely, and much in
favour of King Philip. Now the different legal interpretations came into
play. From Ivo's point of view, any marriage of Philip and Bertrada was
still illicit after Berta's death, but was no longer necessarily invalid.
From this time, their union was a concubinage which, under certain
conditions, Ivo thought could be legitimized.[26] However, there was
little need for the king to comply with Ivo's conditions. After Berta's

nor Urban claimed that Bertrada and Philip were related (against Brooke, *Idea of Marriage*,
122–3).
  [19] Ivo, *Epistula* 15 (PL 162, 27).
  [20] See e.g. Hugh of Lyon (PL 157, 518) and Orderic Vitalis, *Historia ecclesiastica*, 8.10
(Chibnall, 4: 186). On Fulk's marital affairs cf. Louis Halphen, *Le comté d'Anjou au XIe siècle*
(Paris, 1906), 169–70.
  [21] Ivo, *Epistula* 13 (PL 162, 26). Bertrada married Fulk before 24 April 1090 as can be
seen from an unpublished charter, no. C363 in Olivier Guillot, *Le comte d'Anjou et son entou-
rage au XIe siècle*, 2 vols (Paris, 1972), 2: 226–7.
  [22] Against Duby, *Medieval Marriage*, 41.
  [23] Urban II, Jaffé, *Regesta*, 5469 (PL 151, 354), written 27 October 1092.
  [24] Sprandel, *Ivo von Chartres*, 103–6.
  [25] Becker, *Urban II.*, 195.
  [26] An instructing parallel case is Ivo, *Epistula* 18 (PL 162, 31–2). See also *Epistulae* 16, 148,
155, 161.

death there was less opposition from the French episcopate than ever, and the papacy was apparently unable to pursue a rigorous policy. Indeed Urban continued his former policy. While in principle he still demanded that the king part with Bertrada, he refrained from excommunicating the king and gave him time until Pentecost 1095 to repudiate Bertrada. The situation was a paradox: while Ivo, for the first time, would have been willing to absolve the king, the pope, after years of silence, began to take action against Philip. Yet if there had been an opportunity to settle the affair in the time following Berta's death, it had passed by late 1095: at the Council of Clermont, more than three years after Berta's repudiation, Urban eventually excommunicated the king. However, Philip reacted promptly, threatening to withdraw his obedience if the pope failed to absolve him before too long.[27] Much against Ivo's will, the pope gave in and absolved the king under the nominal condition that he renounce Bertrada. Once more, the king failed to deliver his promise, and Hugh of Lyon imposed an interdict in spring 1097; Urban, however, lifted the ban again in April 1098, and did not repeat it before he died in July 1099. His successor continued Urban's policy. In 1100 a legatine council in Poitiers repeated the excommunication, but Paschal II himself avoided condemning the king. However, in 1104, after long negotiations, a solution was reached that is often seen as a victory of the Church.[28] In December 1104, Philip and Bertrada were absolved after swearing an oath not to see each other henceforth.

Was this a victory of 'discipline' and canon law? The idea that in 1104 the Church had achieved some sort of victory is mainly based on the silence of our main sources after this date, and on the good relations between Paschal and Philip. Admittedly, neither Ivo nor the pope mention that Philip continued to live with Bertrada after 1104. But was this because, this time, the Church was able to enforce the separation of

---

[27] Ivo, *Epistula* 46 (PL 162, 58–9). Both Sprandel, *Ivo von Chartres*, 187 and Becker, *Urban II.*, 198–200, dated the letter 1096 or 1098 but thought 1098 most likely. However, the letter mentions that the king was supported by the archbishops of Reims and Sens, i.e. Rainaud of Reims (†21 February 1096) and Richer of Sens (†27 December 1096). From Richer's death to March or April 1098 the see was vacant. *Epistula* 46 cannot have been written in this time, and it is extremely unlikely that Daimbert of Sens (consecrated in spring 1098 by the pope) participated in the planned schism. Fliche, *Philippe I*, 56–7 argued that *Epitula* 46 was written in 1095 and that it explained why Urban refrained from confirming Hugh's excommunication until the Council of Clermont. However, it seems more likely to me that Philip reacted against the papal excommunication rather than the legatine.

[28] Duby, *Medieval Marriage*, 54.

the royal couple? It seems not. Both narrative sources and charter evidence confirm that Bertrada continued to act as queen in Philip's last years. In 1106, she was received as queen in the Anjou; contemporary sources refer to her as queen, and crucially, she continued to issue royal charters together with Philip.[29] The Church, and this time including Ivo, remained silent, not because they had achieved their goals, but rather out of resignation. When King Philip died in 1108, he had spent most of the last sixteen years with his second wife; he had to suffer from ecclesiastical sanctions,[30] and more than once the couple had to accept public humiliation, but, on the whole, the Church had failed to end a union that according to the most benevolent interpretation was illicit and according to the pope was incestuous. The whole affair is therefore not a good example of the victory of one 'model' of marriage over another; but if this is taken away, what others remain? There are in fact a number of other cases which show that there was considerable co-operation between the Capetians and the Church on questions of marriage. If we turn from Philip's marriage to those he arranged for his children, a rather familiar picture emerges. Ironically, it is another second marriage where the co-operation between crown and Church can be seen best. Philip's daughter Constance had been married to Hugh of Troyes some time before 1097; however, the king sought to arrange a more advantageous marriage for her. In 1104, the opportunity had come when Bohemund of Antiochia returned to France to seek a wife.[31] As mentioned above, around 1104 Ivo and Philip had settled their conflict at least temporarily. Ivo declared Constance's marriage null and void, acting specifically at the request of King Philip and his son Louis.[32] Two years later her second marriage with Bohemund was solemnly celebrated at Chartres. So for his daughter's second marriage, the king turned to the very bishop who had caused him so much

[29] Bertrada appears as queen in at least two royal charters after 1104: nos 157–8, in Maurice Prou, *Recueil des actes de Philippe Ier, roi de France (1059–1108)* (Paris, 1908), 395–6; an Angevin chronicle reports that she was received as queen in the Anjou in 1106, where these charters were issued (Léopold Delisle, ed., *Recueil des historiens des Gaules et de la France* 12 [Paris, 1877], 486). Compare also Prou's charter no. 168 and the document C441, in Guillot, *Comte d'Anjou*, 2: 273 (dated between 1106 and 1109).

[30] While stories like those related by Orderic Vitalis, *Historia ecclesiastica* 8.20 (Chibnall, 4: 262) are presumably fictitious, charter evidence suggests that Philip's scope of political action was seriously limited by the ecclesiastical sanctions (Fliche, *Philippe I*, 62).

[31] Suger, *Vie de Louis VI le Gros*, ed. Henri Waquet, Classiques de l'histoire de France au Moyen Age 11 (Paris, 1964), 46–8. In a clearly apologetic stance, Suger glosses over Constance's first marriage.

[32] Ivo, *Epistula* 158 (PL 162, 164).

trouble. This contradicts the common picture of Philip and Ivo as the 'champions' of two conflicting models of marriage; there was conflict but also co-operation between them. In a sense, Ivo successfully implemented ecclesiastical incest laws; but it would be more apt to say that he dissolved a marriage at the request of the parties involved. The case of Philip's son Louis fits the same pattern. In 1107, he was able to escape an undesirable marriage by claiming that he was related to his fiancée. Ivo himself was unable to attend the council but sent his deputies, and the assembly duly dissolved the king designate's marriage.[33]

* * *

We have surveyed only the most prominent English and French cases of the time under study. It would of course be beyond the scope of this essay to consider a quantity of examples great enough to draw definitive conclusions, but both the other marriage cases Anselm and Ivo were involved in and other contemporary cases suggest that the trends identified in the material discussed above are not anomalous.[34] How much evidence is there for the Church imposing her discipline on an unwilliging nobility? There are some examples of the Church intervening against the wishes of the parties, though normally unsuccessfully. Where, in contrast, we see marriages dissolved on grounds of consanguinity, there is often good reason to believe that the initiative was with the parties, not the Church.[35] The cases studied, including the marriages of the Capetians, suggest that already around 1100 the nobility was used to successfully employing ecclesiastical incest legislation as a means of legitimizing their marriage arrangements. This is not to deny that there was conflict, especially between Philip I and Ivo of Chartres. But even this conflict may have taught Philip to employ canon law arguments for arranging the second marriage of his daugther Constance. In any case, Philip I and Ivo of Chartres were not the 'champions' of two incompatible models of marriage; and if they go, it is hard to see who remains.

The point is not that kings could find some compliant bishop. One

---

[33] Ivo, *Epistula* 175 (PL 162, 178).

[34] Both Anselm's and Ivo's letter collection contain numerous letters dealing with marriage, e.g. Anselm, *Epistulae* 238, 297, 365, 419, 427, 435 or Ivo, *Epistulae* 16, 18, 45, 99, 129–30, 148, 155, 161, 170, 188, 211, 225, 229, 232, 246, 261.

[35] In the case of Ivo, for example, there are only two cases (*Epistulae* 158 and 261) where he successfully dissolved an existing marriage on grounds of consanguinity, and clearly he did so at the request of the parties in both cases.

may say this, for example, of the bishop of Senlis, who blessed Philip's second marriage, but certainly not of Anselm or Ivo. It would also be misguided to see these abuses of the law as obstacles to the success of canon law. Rather, the imposition of discipline and subversive uses of the law were closely interrelated. If the Church was able to extend her jurisdiction in the eleventh and twelfth centuries, it was due to co-operation in which both sides gained something. The Church was able to have her marriage legislation applied in more and more cases and was increasingly accepted as court of appeal for contested marriages; the noble families who invited ecclesiastical jurisdiction in the first place achieved often favourable judgements and had their marriage arrangements confirmed by the Church. However, both sides also bound themselves: lay parties had in the long run to accept ecclesiastical jurisdiction even where it was not welcome, and the Church all too often had to accept abusive appeals to incest legislation, a burden that was only partly removed with the dramatic legal changes of the Fourth Lateran Council.

Queen's College, University of Cambridge

DISCIPLINE AND THE *RULE OF BASIL* IN WALTER DANIEL'S *LIFE OF AILRED OF RIEVAULX**

by MICHELE MOATT

He made his little body free of everything that is pleasant in this present life. He sacrificed himself on the altar of unfailing suffering: hardly any flesh clung to his bones; his lips alone remained a frame to his teeth. The excessive emaciation of his body and the thinness of his face gave an angelic expression to his countenance. Eating scarcely anything and drinking less, by his unbelievable fasting, he lost altogether, and no wonder, the desire for food.[1]

SO wrote Walter Daniel of his erstwhile friend and mentor, Ailred, in his *Life of Ailred of Rievaulx,* some time after Ailred's death in 1167. This was written in an attempt to demonstrate his abbot's sanctity with the clear hope that as a result he might eventually be canonized. It is hard, therefore, to understand why this image of the abbot who, if we are to believe Walter, governed 'over one hundred monks and five hundred laymen',[2] is so at odds with the instructions to abbots contained within the generally moderate *Rule of Benedict,* which governed the lives of all Cistercian monks. The Cistercians interpreted the *Rule* more rigidly than the Benedictines, but even for them there should be no ostentatious exhibitions of pious self-starvation since a monk must exhibit *mediocritas* or moderation in all he did.[3] Moreover,

* I would like to thank the AHRC for sponsoring this research.

[1] *The Life of Ailred of Rievaulx by Walter Daniel,* ed. and trans. F. M. Powicke (London, 1950), XLI, 49. Throughout this paper roman numerals refer to the chapter number in the primary text, followed by arabic numerals to denote page numbers in the modern edition.

[2] 'Letter to Maurice', in Powicke, *Life of Ailred,* 49–65, at 79.

[3] Tom License, 'The Gift of Seeing Demons in Early Cistercian Spirituality', *Cistercian Studies Quarterly* 39: 1 (2004), 49–65, at 50; citing a more developed study of the Cistercian preoccupation with *mediocritas* by Giles Constable, 'Moderation and Restraint in Ascetic Practices in the Middle Ages', in Haijo Jan Westra, ed., *From Athens to Chartres: Neoplatonism and Medieval Thought; Studies in Honour of Edouard Jeauneau,* Studien und Texte zur Geschichte des Mittelalters 35 (Leiden, 1992), 315–27; reprinted in idem, *Culture and Spirituality in medieval Europe* (Aldershot, 1996), no. X.

regulation of eating must not be at the expense of life itself.[4] In order to resolve Walter's anomalous portrait of his abbot I will first seek the source of the textual representation of the ascetic Ailred and then, very briefly, consider its relationship to what we can surmise about Ailred's actual practices in order to hypothesise about what kind of influences helped to form them. In the process, I will suggest that the extreme form of monastic *disciplina*, exemplified by the literary model of Ailred, causes us to question Foucault's notion that: 'Discipline produces practiced bodies, docile bodies. Discipline increases the forces of the body (in economic terms of utility) and diminishes these same forces (in political terms of obedience).'[5]

Historians such as Brian Patrick McGuire and Aelred Squire have made links between Walter's descriptions of Ailred's austerities and Celtic practices.[6] Squire sees Ailred's behaviour as possibly inspired by his family's role as guardians of the ancient Northumbrian saints' shrines at both Durham and Hexham, which Ailred himself explored in his work *On the Saints of Hexham*,[7] as well as perhaps the works of Cassian, Palladius, Jerome and Gregory the Great.

Maurice Powicke noted that Walter borrowed from the *Rule of Benedict* to illustrate Cistercian life,[8] and, as Figure 1 reveals, such borrowings were also applied to Ailred as 'ideal abbot' – probably because Walter needed to demonstrate Ailred's credentials in response to criticisms that he had been lax.[9] Moreover, in Ailred's *Mirror of Charity*, he had placed an emphasis on the importance of disciplined observance to the exact detail of the *Rule* to the extent that Squire accuses him of 'monastic pharisaism',[10] all of which makes it unlikely that Walter would consciously disregard the *Rule* in any aspect of the biography of his abbot.

[4] William of St. Thierry, *The Golden Epistle: a Letter to the Brethren of Mont Dieu*, trans. T. Berkeley, intro. J. M. Dechanet (Kalamazoo, MI, 1980), XXXII, 53.
[5] Michel Foucault, *Discipline and Punish: the Birth of the Prison*, trans. Alan Sheridan (Harmondsworth, 1977), 138.
[6] B. P. McGuire, *Brother and Lover: Aelred of Rievaulx* (New York, 1994), 60; Aelred Squire, *Aelred of Rievaulx: a Study* (London, 1981), 12, 24, 127.
[7] Aelred of Rievaulx, *De sanctis ecclesiae haugustaldensis*, in James Raine, ed., *The Priory of Hexham*, vol. 1: *Its Chroniclers, Endowments and Annals*, Surtees Society 44 (Durham, 1863–4), 173–203.
[8] *Life of Ailred*, V, 12 n. 1.
[9] Ibid., XXVI, 34.
[10] Squire, *Aelred of Rievaulx*, 28.

Theme	Charactaristics	Place in Narrative	Rule
Withdrawal	*Impassivity* →	* at court	Basil: Int. 2
		* in novice house	Basil: Int. 2
	Suffering and Tomb	* as abbot	Basil: Int. 2
			9
			Ben: ch. 36
		* last four years	Basil: Int. 9
			57
			89
			126
Love: Of God	*Contemplation Obedience* →	* at court	Basil: Int. 2
		* in novice house	Ben: chs 4, 5
			7, 48
	Spiritual Gifts of Prophecy and Healing	* as abbot	58
		*last four years	Basil: Int. 3
Of Neighbour	*Acceptance of criticism Wisdom Peacemaking*	* at court	Basil: Int. 2
			Ben: ch. 2
		* in novice house	Ben: ch. 3
	Miracles of Healing and Love	* as abbot	Ben: ch. 2
			27
			Basil: Int. 2
		* last four years	Basil: Int. 4

Figure 1

The *Rule of Benedict* appears to offer balanced instructions for the conduct of monks. In its practical presentation of the rules, which promote expectations of obedience on the part of a monk to the abbot and to the rule itself, its application in the course of ordinary monastic observance closely resembles Foucault's maxim. Yet Benedict (c. 480– c. 550) makes clear that he has offered certain compromises in order to accommodate the actual situation found by most abbots: that their brethren are likely to include men of varying degrees of spiritual strength.[11] Despite his very practical acceptance of reality, and the resultant projection of his ideas onto a kind of 'lowest common denominator', he nevertheless hints at what the spiritually gifted should aim for.[12] He reveals a concern with issues surrounding food and perceptions of the body which can be identified as being drawn from the writers who had informed his rule, and to whom he directs his hearers and readers for more advanced guidance. In his last chapter, Benedict makes clear that, among other things, he intended his Rule to be read along side the more detailed and developed *Rule of Basil*.[13]

A version of the *Rule of Basil* was available to Walter Daniel in the library at Rievaulx, where it was catalogued as *Regula Sanctae Basilii*,[14] and, by comparing Walter's intimate portrait of Ailred with this text, it becomes apparent that it informed his illustration of Ailred as 'spiritual man'. There are two dominant themes which Walter endeavours to convey throughout his work: Ailred's ever-deepening withdrawal from the world; and Ailred's perfect love, or *caritas*, for both God and his 'neighbours'. Walter examines each of these themes in relation to four periods of his life: his adolescence, spent at the court of King David of Scotland; his time in the novitiate; the period when he became an abbot at Lindsey and later Rievaulx; and finally, during the last four years of his life. In each period, the *Rule of Basil* helps him to demonstrate the extent to which Ailred went beyond 'the rule for beginners', becoming perfected in holiness. Exactly *which* version of this multifarious text has informed his narrative I will consider below, but for now I will cite

---

[11] *The Rule of Saint Benedict: in Latin and English*, ed. and trans. Justin McCann, (London, 1952), II, 17–23.

[12] Ibid., Prologue, 13; XL, 97; LXXIII, 161.

[13] Ibid., LXXIII, 161.

[14] There are two surviving library catalogues for the abbey compiled between 1190 and 1200: Cambridge, Jesus College, MS 34, fols 1–5r and 5v–6. They have been edited by David N. Bell, *The Libraries of the Cistercians, Gilbertines, and Premonstratensians*, Corpus of British Library Catalogues 3 (London, 1992) [hereafter: Bell, *Libraries*], 87–137.

examples from Rufinus's Latin translation of the *Little Asceticon*,[15] since there is no evidence that the library at Rievaulx contained the Greek text.

Walter uses the *Rule of Basil* first when he describes Ailred's internal withdrawal. As he takes his readers through the stages of Ailred's novitiate, abbacy and approaching death, his withdrawal becomes associated with both fasting and 'entering the tomb'. As a novice, he built a little chamber under the floor of the novice house which was full of cold running water, where he would secretly hide from the others and 'quench the heat of every vice'.[16] By the time he became abbot of Rievaulx, his further withdrawal is exemplified by his increased fasting, which led his brethren to wonder whether he was a man or a spirit. He suffered a malady, the stone, 'which grievously tormented him every month . . . The agony was intense for very often his urine contained fragments of stone as big as a bean, the passage of which was . . . unbearable'.[17]

Four years before his death Ailred's suffering and fasting reached the climax described in my opening citation. Walter explains that Ailred is now severely emaciated, *corporis maciem et faciei extenuacionem*. He is more interested in the health of his soul than in the cure of his body, and his periods of prayer, vigil and contemplation are so lengthy that he forgets about the regular hours and meals. He neglects the present and only dwells on the thought of things to come. About six years previously he had built a little 'mausoleum' next to the infirmary, in which he lives, and now he constructs a small oratory in one corner of the mausoleum in which there is 'a little kind of grave'. Here he sits and weeps 'remembering how he was but dust' and asking God, how long must this wretchedness continue.[18]

This journey of Ailred's, into what seems like absolute withdrawal and extreme suffering, accurately echoes the trajectory of an ideal monk in the *Rule of Basil* who progresses from being an *inferior* to being

---

[15] *Regula Sancti Basilii Episcopi Cappadociae ad Monachos* (PL 103, 487–554); and *Basili Regula a Rufino Latine Versa*, ed. Klaus Zelzer, CSEL 86 (Vienna, 1986).

[16] *Life of Ailred*, XXX, 25. Although both McGuire and Squire use this scene to illustrate Ailred's use of Celtic practices it also resembles a scene in the *Lausiac History* concerning Evagrius of Pontus: *Palladius: Lausiac History*, ed. and trans. Robert T. Meyer, Ancient Christian Writers 34 (Westminster, MD, 1965), XI, 38, 113. There was a copy of this text in the Rievaulx library during the twelfth century: MSS no. Z19, 136a, in Bell, *Libraries*, 110.

[17] *Life of Ailred*, XXX, 34.

[18] Ibid.

a *senior*, 'those with the spirit, the perfect'.[19] In Basil's *Rule*, even for the most expert ascetic, the discipline for pleasing God is not practiced by withdrawal to a solitary life in the desert, but by detaching oneself from the cares of the world and by complete withdrawal from its distractions *whilst living in a community*.[20] Those aiming to separate from the world should only eat enough to preserve bodily life, but not more than that. Even though the desire for food is natural, burdening the body with food is harmful, therefore a monk should never eat all the way to satiety. This would be to make the stomach one's God. Furthermore, it is absurd to take food because of the substance of the body, and yet cause harm to the body by that food. In fact, abstinence gives a man the opportunity to pursue more precious and more difficult things,[21] so a man who fasts to extremes is deemed to have been granted the power by God to do so.[22] Finally, Basil states quite clearly that the condition of his soul is attested by the condition of his body which shows that he does not eat carelessly, but as if God is watching him.[23] Implying that, as he more clearly states in the Greek version of his *Long Rules*: 'the Christian is betokened by emaciation of body and paleness which is the bloom of continence, showing that he is truly the athlete of Christ's commandments'.[24] Thus extreme fasting is not a form of self flagellation, but a sign of internal spiritual perfection.

In Basil, then, we have an explanation for Ailred's extreme fasting which resulted in emaciation. But what of his intense suffering, due to the stone and, later, as Walter tells us, severe arthritis? How can we explain his desire to sleep and pray in a 'mausoleum' and then in a grave? Entering an isolated tomb to fight demons for a long period of time is a theme in the lives of the desert fathers such as Antony, and also in the *Life of Guthlac*, which was bound together at Rievaulx with the *Vitae Patrum*.[25] But Ailred is not fighting demons in his tomb,

19 *The Ascetic Works of Saint Basil*, ed. and trans. W. K. L. Clarke (London, 1925), Introduction, 45.

20 *Basili regula*, III, 1–39, 25–32.

21 Ibid., IX, 7–22, 46–9.

22 Ibid., LXXXVIIII, 3, 123.

23 Ibid., LVII, 1–3, 96.

24 'The Longer Rules', in Clarke, *Ascetic Works*, 145–228, XVII, 181. See also: Peter Brown, *The Body and Society: Men, Women and Sexual Renunciation in Early Christianity* (New York, 1988), 101–2, for a discussion of sexual continence as a way back to 'the full humanity of Adam and Eve'.

25 Bell, *Libraries*, Z19: 129, 109.

although he does in his miracles which take place out in the world,[26] and his tomb is not isolated but in the centre of the monastic enclosure. Moreover, Antony emerges from his tomb, whereas Ailred's life is increasingly centred on the tomb; whilst Anthony's body is miraculously strong and healthy when he emerges, Ailred's is ever more emaciated.

Most obviously these descriptions emulate the bodily suffering of Christ on the cross and during his three days in the tomb before the resurrection. For this reason I believe Walter wants to show that Ailred took Benedict's injunction to share in Christ's sufferings to an extreme not envisaged by Benedict himself.[27] Once again, Basil provides a model for emulating Christ: 'For to be ready for death on behalf of Christ, and to mortify one's members which are on the earth, and on behalf of the name of Christ willingly to bear all danger, this is to take up his cross.'[28] As W. K. L. Clarke wrote in 1925, a Basilian senior must live a 'dying life, ever mortifying his will by obedience to God's command'.[29] It seems to me that Walter's portrait of Ailred, suffering and so obviously preparing for death in his little grave, is the concrete embodiment of this Basilian ideal. This extreme of monastic *disciplina*, moreover, has transcended any notion of Foucauldian discipline, which could be acknowledged as present in the ordinary temporal existence of a monastery. By the process of giving precedence to the concept of a man having a direct relationship with God, without the intermediary of rule or abbot,[30] it has reversed it, so that the forces of Ailred's docile body seem to have decreased '(in economic terms of utility)'. Yet through absolute obedience to God's will '(in political terms of obedience)'[31] he is presented as gaining power by matching the ideal, to the extent that in Walter's text he is presented as a saint, capable of miracles and imbued with the authority of perfect *caritas*.

There remains the question to which version of the *Rule of Basil* Walter Daniel is likely to have had access. Of the surviving manu-

---

[26] For example, the story of the boy who swallowed a demon in the shape of a frog: *Life of Ailred*, XXXIX, 46–8.

[27] *Rule of Benedict*, Prologue, 13.

[28] *Basili regula*, 11, 101–4, 22.

[29] Clarke, *Ascetic Works*, 45.

[30] For an examination of the significance of this contrast see: Giles Constable, 'From Cluny to Citeaux', in Claudie Duhamel-Amado and Guy Lobrichon, eds, *Georges Duby: l'ecriture d'histoire* (Brussels, 1996), 317–22, at 320 [reprinted in idem, *Cluny from the Tenth to the Twelfth Centuries* (Aldershot, 2000), no. VI].

[31] See n. 5 above.

scripts, the most common version found under the heading *Regula Basilii* is the *Admonitio ad filium spiritualem*,[32] which is probably drawn from the *Little Asceticon*, not by Basil but, according to Adalbert de Vogue, possibly by Abbot Porcarius of Lerins.[33] A twelfth-/thirteenth-century manuscript of this text survives with a fifteenth-century *ex libris* and pressmark for Fountains Abbey: BL Add. Fountains Abbey (Vyner), MSS 62129, Vol.1. It is possible that Rievaulx also had a copy of this text, perhaps this manuscript, since it is unclear where it was before the fifteenth century. However, it is unlikely to have been this text which influenced Walter Daniel's work. The *Admonitio* is not directed at monks specifically, nor does it offer the ultimate, idealistic vision of the perfect man which is projected by Basil from his *Little* and *Great Asceticons*. In fact it consists of largely practical directions to the reader, who is assumed to be a relative beginner at ascetic practice.

There is a slim chance that the *Regula Basilii* listed in the twelfth century Rievaulx catalogue was Rufinus's Latin translation of the *Little Asceticon*.[34] If the whole text was not available, then perhaps it was a collection of florilegia taken from Rufinus's version. In which case, judging by its echoes in Walter's text, such a collection is likely to have included the whole of *Interrogatio II*. It is conceivable that the monks who arrived from Clairvaux to found the daughter house at Rievaulx brought a copy of the text or florilegia with them.[35]

We cannot know exactly which version of the *Rule of Basil* informed Walter's literary construction of Ailred, nor can we be certain to what extent it was related to the living man. Nevertheless, it seems reasonable to speculate that Basil's ideas were somehow linked in Walter's mind to Ailred himself, as Brian Patrick McGuire suggests: 'there were too many witnesses, too many varying opinions about the abbot, and so he had to stick to the facts.' Furthermore, Ailred did regard ascetic discipline as important, especially in his own battles against sexual impulses.[36] He wrote of it in several of his spiritual works, including

---

32 Bell, *Libraries*, 97: 104. The text is found in PL 103, 487–554; and is translated into English in Robert Rivers and Harry Hagen, 'The *Admonitio Ad Filium Spiritualem*: Introduction and Translation', *American Benedictine Review* 53 (2002), 121–46.
33 Cited in ibid., 123.
34 Bell, *Libraries*, 97, 104.
35 A well-used, grubby, twelfth-century manuscript of the *Regula sancti Basilii episcopi Cappadociae ad monachos*, translated by Rufinus, survives from Clairvaux with simple marginal annotations: Troyes, BM, 1422, fols 1r–79v.
36 McGuire, *Brother and Lover*, 61.

Institutione Inclusarum, of which Squire writes that no work better explains Aelred's asceticism.[37] In a longer piece, this must be further explored in the light of my conclusions above. For now, however, let us assume, along with Powick, Squire and McGuire, that Walter's description does resemble the man and consider from where such eastern monastic influence might have come.

Transmission of rules and practices by imitation rather than by text had a place in the western monastic tradition.[38] Bernard Hamilton has offered a way by which eastern ascetic practices could have influenced western monasticism during the tenth and eleventh centuries through contacts with eastern monks in southern Italy, Rome, or via monks who travelled between East and West.[39] He writes: 'The most important contribution which eastern monks made to the western Church is imponderable, for it consisted in their great personal sanctity of life. The high degree of spirituality which certain Basilian ascetics attained made them universally respected in their lifetime, and venerated as saints after their death.'[40]

Those who have cast doubt on this idea are inclined to focus on Egyptian monastic practices, suggesting that their emphasis on solitude is at odds with the sense of community and culture of nobility valued by western monks such as the Cistercians.[41] It has also been suggested that, while monks of both eastern and western traditions quarried the same sources during the eleventh and twelfth centuries, they used them in two different ways.[42] The *Rule of Basil*, however, was formed not in Egypt, but in Asia Minor, and the culture in which it developed was very different from that which informed Egyptian practice. Basil of Caesarea (AD 330–70), a founder of coenobitic monasteries, was

---

[37] Squire, *Aelred of Rievaulx*, 127.

[38] In the anonymous *Life of Ceolfrith*, written after 716, the writer says that Benedict Biscop brought back his rule from Gaul 'as if hidden in the coffers of his breast and delivered them to us to follow': D. Whitlock, ed., 'The Anonymous Life of Ceolfrith, Abbott of Jarrow', *EHD* 1 (1979), 758–70.

[39] Patricia M. McNulty and Bernard Hamilton, 'Orientale lumen et magistra latinitas: Greek Influences on Western Monasticism (900–1100)', in *Le Millénaire du Mont Athos, 963–1963: Etudes et mélanges*, 2 vols (Chevetogne, 1963–4), 2: 181–216 [reprinted in idem, *Monastic Reform, Catharism and the Crusades (900–1300)* (Aldershot, 1985), no. V.

[40] Ibid., 215.

[41] Benedicta Ward, 'The Desert Myth: Reflections on the Desert Ideal in Early Cistercian Monasticism', in M. Basil Pennington, ed., *One Yet Two: Monastic Tradition East and West* (Kalamazoo, MI, 1976), 183–98, at 187.

[42] Marilyn Dunn, 'Eastern Influence on Western Monasticism in the Eleventh and Twelfth Centuries', *Byzantinische Forschungen* 13 (1988), 245–59.

fiercely polemical against solitary monks,[43] and his own background was as a member of the landowning elite in Cappadocia.[44]

Most significantly in the case of Ailred, during the eleventh and twelfth centuries, Greek Orthodox monks familiar with Basil's rule were among the international communities of hermits dwelling in rock hewn tombs of the Valley of Jehosaphat, at the western end of the Kidron Valley in the Judean desert.[45] It was here that a friend of Ailred's, Godric of Finchale (d. 1170),[46] spent some time during his second pilgrimage to the Holy Land, after 1106.[47] On his visits to the hermits, Godric is likely to have observed Basilian practices, and possibly imitated them himself.[48] Reginald of Durham implies that his sparse diet at least was influenced by eastern practice when he describes Godric living off 'Grass and wild honey'.[49] This has always been interpreted as a reference to John the Baptist's diet of 'locusts and wild honey',[50] but in several Greek texts there is mention of a category of hermit called 'boschoi' or 'grass eaters', who ate a diet of edible plants.[51] Godric could not have read the texts because he had no Greek, but it seems that he may have imitated the practice of boschoi, whom he witnessed in Palestine, and may also have continued his eastern practices whilst living in Finchale.

If that is the case, Ailred will have also witnessed eastern ascetic practices, via Godric, when he visited him at Finchale. Reginald records

43 *Regula S.Basilii*, Interrogatione III (PL 103, 494).

44 William Harmless, *Desert Christians: an Introduction to the Literature of Early Monasticism* (New York, 2004), 428.

45 Andrew Jotischky, *The Perfection of Solitude: Hermits and Monks in the Crusader States* (Pennsylvania, PA, 1995), 71–2; J. Patrich, *a Comparative Study in Eastern Monasticism, Fourth to Seventh Centuries* (Washington, DC, 1995), 28–31.

46 Anslem Hoste, *A Survey of the Unedited Work of Laurence of Durham With an Edition of His Letter to Ailred of Rievaulx* (Brugge and s-Gravenhage, 1960), 261.

47 Andrew Jotischky, *Perfection of Solitude*, 72.

48 Ibid.

49 J. Stevenson, ed., *Libellus de vita et miraculis S. Godrici, heremitae de Finchale, Auctore Reginaldo monacho Dunhelmensi*, Surtees Society 20 (London and Edinburgh, 1847), 10, 42–3.

50 Andrew Jotischky, *Perfection of Solitude*, 72–3, argues that in the Palestinian monastic tradition John the Baptist was believed to have eaten the locust bean plant rather than locusts.

51 I would like to thank Andrew Jotischky for drawing my attention to references to this practice in John Moschos' seventh-century text, *The Spiritual Meadow*, in PG 87, 2851–3112; the practice is also mentioned in the sixth-century text, *Cyril of Scythopolis: Lives of the Monks of Palestine*, trans. R. M. Price (Kalamazoo, MI, 1991); and in the fifth-century Byzantine historian Sozomen's *Ecclesiastical History*, ed. and trans. Philip Schaff and Henry Wace, The Nicene and Post Nicene Fathers Series, 2nd ser. (Grand Rapids, MI, 1957), 2: 236–427.

just such an occasion, which is relevant to our discussion: one day Godric showed Ailred the tomb which he had carved for himself from 'hard rock' as a constant reminder during life of his own death,[52] and, perhaps, as an imitation of the hermits in the rock tombs of Jehosaphat. Since Ailred also built himself a mausoleum and a grave it would not be unreasonable to pursue further the idea that Godric might have practised certain eastern ideals and transmitted them to Ailred. A closer examination of Reginald's descriptions of Godric's practices as well as of Ailred's own writings might further this hypothesis in the future.

Lancaster University

---

[52] *Libellus de vita et miraculis S. Godrici*, LXXVII, 126.

'TEMPERING THE WIND . . .':
MODERATION AND DISCRETION IN
LATE TWELFTH-CENTURY PAPAL DECRETALS

by ANNE J. DUGGAN

EDIEVAL canon law has generally had a bad press. Its professionalization in the period c. 1140 to 1234 can easily be caricatured as the emergence of a rigid, centralized, and authoritarian system which paid small heed to the needs of the people it was supposed to serve. This conclusion is readily sustained by perusal of the *Liber Extra*, the Gregorian *Decretales* of 1234, which enshrined the legal developments of the period, from about 1140, which followed the establishment of Gratian's *Decretum* as the principal authority for the teaching and practice of canon law. The genesis of the *Liber Extra* is well known. Pope Gregory IX commissioned Raymond of Peñafort to compile an authoritative collection of papal decretals and conciliar legislation to supplement Gratian's *Decretum*, and it drew, principally but not exclusively, on the so-called *Quinque compilationes antique* which had been compiled for teaching purposes in Bologna between c. 1189–91 and 1226.[1] And when the work was completed, it was authorized by the bull *Rex pacificus*, which ordered that 'everyone should use *only* this compilation in judgements and in the schools (*ut hac* tantum *compilatione universi utantur in iudiciis et in scholis*);[2] and a copy was duly dispatched to the canon law school in Bologna. The image of centralized, authoritarian lawmaking could not be clearer; and that perception is reinforced by an examination of its structure, where the individual extracts are organized systematically under Titles, which define the subject matter.[3] Such a compilation, like the *Quinque compilationes* themselves, was the result of an analytical method, which totally obscured the processes of consultation which had preceded many of the

---

[1] *Quinque compilationes antiquae necnon collectio canonum Lipsiensis*, ed. E. Friedberg (Leipzig, 1882; repr. 1956), for *Compilatio prima* and *Compilatio secunda* [hereafter: 1 *Comp.* and 2 *Comp.*].

[2] *Decretales Gregorii IX* [hereafter: *Decretales*] (CIC 2: 3).

[3] For example, *De officio et potestate iudicis delegati* (*Decretales*, 1.29); *De appellationibus, recusationibus, et relationibus* (*Decretales*, 2.28); *De matrimonio contracto contra interdictum ecclesiae* (*Decretales*, 4.16); *Qui filii sint legitimi* (*Decretales*, 4.17), etc.

decisions, as well as depriving them, in many cases, of their historical context in terms of the identity of the pope, the recipient, the litigants, and the local circumstances.[4] What emerged was a disembodied code, shorn of the nuances and hesitations which had characterized the decisions which it enshrined.

But a very different picture emerges when one examines the original letters from which the *canones* were extracted or constructed. In the overwhelming majority of cases, the decisions or directives had emerged either from specific litigation or from episcopal requests (consultations) for advice or judgement on matters which had arisen in their dioceses. If it had not been for the willingness of numerous bishops, lesser ecclesiastics, and lay people to seek clarification or judgement from the papal *Curia*, the creation of this decretal law could not have taken place; and the problems arose both from the more searching analysis to which Gratian's compilation was subjected in the schools and from the ambiguities revealed in application. The *Curia* thus found itself inundated with appeals and queries which demanded clarifications of and often adjustments to the written law. An early example of this process was Adrian IV's highly important declaration on the right of serfs to marry without their master's consent. The decretal *Dignum est*, which responded to a lost letter from Archbishop Eberhard of Salzburg, silently corrected Gratian's C.29 q.2 c.8. This had declared that 'the marriages of serfs may not be dissolved, even if they have different lords . . .', but the rider, 'This is to be observed in those instances where there was a lawful marriage, and with the lords' approval',[5] added a significant limitation, which implied that the absence of prior consent on the part of the lord of the estate constituted an impediment to the lawful matrimony of the unfree. Without reference to the *Decretum*, Adrian directed that 'marriages between serfs (*inter seruos . . . matrimonia*) should not be forbidden on any account, and if they are contracted against the prohibition and against the wishes of lords they should not for this reason be dissolved by ecclesiastical law,

---

[4] Note that Raymond's compilation, the *Liber Extra (Decretales)*, contained only the excerpts printed in Roman font in Friedberg's edition; it was the latter who inserted, in italics, the often extensive passages which Raymond had omitted: *Decretales*, xlv, 'Ut vero quae inserui a Gregoriano textu discerni possent, illa italicis quos vocant typis exprimenda curavi'.

[5] *Decretum Gratiani* [hereafter: Gratian], C.29 q.2 c.8 (CIC 1: 1095). 'Coniugia servorum non dirimantur, etiam si diversos dominos habeant . . . Et hoc in illis observandum est, ubi legalis coniunctio fuit, et per voluntatem dominorum.'

although the service due to their lords should not be reduced on this account'.[6] Here was an example of the pope taking the opportunity of a specific question from a German archbishop to define a universal right to Christian marriage, and the two key sentences which expressed the principle found their way into Gregory's *Decretales*, and thus into the very fabric of the marriage law of the West.[7]

Numerous similar instances could be drawn from the 'avalanche of decretal legislation' of Adrian's successor, Alexander III (1159–81),[8] but two particularly striking examples may be cited from answers to questions raised by Bishop Bartholomew of Exeter. In the first, *Sicut dignum est* (1172), the pope made important modifications to Canon 15 (*Si quis suadente*) of the Second Lateran Council (1139). This had decreed that anyone who laid violent hands on a cleric or religious should be automatically excommunicated and compelled to seek absolution in person from the Holy See.[9] The canon was so widely drawn, however, that it embraced everything from minor scuffles to serious assault, and Alexander allowed a series of exceptions: for students; for monks and canons regular who strike one another within the cloister; for secular doorkeepers and other laymen who strike clerks found in questionable circumstances with a wife or close female relative or in self defence. In all these instances, suitable penance could be imposed by the relevant ecclesiastical authority, without recourse to the Apostolic See.[10] Even

---

[6] *Regesta pontificum romanorum: ab condita ecclesia ad annum post Christum natum MCXCVII*, ed., P. Jaffé, rev. edn by S. Löwenfeld, F. Kaltenbrunner, and P. Ewald (Leipzig, 1885–88) [hereafter: Jaffé, *Regesta*], 10445; *Decretales*, 4.9.1. A. J. Duggan, *'Servus servorum Dei'*, in B. Bolton and A. J. Duggan, eds, *Adrian IV, the English Pope (1154–1159): Studies and Texts* (Aldershot, 2003), 181–210, at 189–90, 204, no. 2.

[7] C. N. L. Brooke, *The Medieval Idea of Marriage* (Oxford, 1989), 51–2, 264–5; Peter Landau, 'Hadrians IV. Dekretale 'Dignum est' (*Decretales*, 4.9.1) und die Eheschliessung Unfreier in der Diskussion von Kanonisten und Theologen des 12. und 13. Jahrhunderts', in Giuseppe Forchielli und Alphons M. Stickler, eds, *Collectanea S. Kuttner 2, Studia Gratiana* 12 (Bologna, 1967), 511–53; idem, 'Frei und Unfrei in der Kanonistik des 12. und 13. Jahrhunderts am Beispiel der Ordination der Unfreien', in J. Fried, ed., *Die abendländische Freiheit vom 10. zum 14. Jahrhundert* (Sigmaringen, 1991), 177–96, at 178; A. Sahaydachny Bocarius, 'The Marriage of Unfree Persons: Twelfth-Century Decretals and Letters', in Peter Landau, ed., *De iure canonico medii aevi: Festschrift für Rudolf Weigand, Studia Gratiana* 27 (Rome, 1996), 481–506, at 485, 489–95.

[8] A. J. Duggan, 'Making the Old Law 'New', II: Canon Law in New Environments; Norway and the Latin Kingdom of Jerusalem', in S. A. Szuromi, ed., *Medieval Canon Law Collections and European 'Ius commune': (Középkori kánonjogi gyűjtemények és az európai 'ius commune')* (Budapest, 2006), 236–62, at 243.

[9] For the implications of excommunication *latae sententiae* in this context, see E. Vodola, *Excommunication in the Middle Ages* (Berkeley, CA, 1986), 28–31.

[10] Jaffé, *Regesta*, 12180; *Decretales*, 5.12.6(a), 5.39.1(b)–2(c)–3(d); cf. C. Duggan, 'St Thomas

more important was the declaration, in *Meminimus nos* (1162–81), of what became known as the principle of *legitimatio per subsequens matrimonium*. 'So great is the power of matrimony (*tanta est vis matrimonii*)', Alexander wrote, that children born before marriage are legitimized by their parents' subsequent matrimony.[11]

In these cases Adrian and Alexander modified the application of the canonical norms for marriage and violence against clerks and religious, not in the manner of ecclesiastical autocrats but in response to queries presented to them by local bishops who had experienced the problems of the written law first hand.

Not all issues were as easy of solution as these; not all environments were as relatively settled as the Austria of Eberhard of Salzburg or the England of Bartholomew of Exeter. In more remote regions like Norway and the disintegrating Latin Kingdom of Jerusalem, for example, the Church and its leaders often found themselves confronted by complex and difficult situations which defied the easy application of the *ius commune*. For conscientious churchmen, the tension between the law of the canons and the social, political, or personal predicaments of the time raised questions of conscience as much as law; and in their responses the popes again and again held back from imposing global solutions.

The twelve decretals which Alexander III addressed to Archbishop Øystein of Trondheim between 1163 and 1173,[12] for example, reveal a pope who was particularly sensitive to the predicament of Christian communities on the periphery of the Latin world. On the problem of

---

of Canterbury and Aspects of the Becket Dispute in the Decretal Collections', in C. E. Viola, ed., *Mediaevalia christiana XIᵉ–XIIIᵉ siècles: hommage à Raymonde Foreville* (Paris, 1989), 87–135, at 110–11, no. 23; repr. with the same pagination in idem, *Decretals and the Creation of 'New Law in the Twelfth Century: Judges, Judgements, Equity and Law* (Aldershot, 1998), no. II.

[11] Jaffé, *Regesta*, 13917; *Decretales*, 4.17.6: 'Tanta est vis matrimonii, ut qui antea sunt geniti post contractum matrimonium legitimi habeantur.' Compare C. Duggan, 'Equity and Compassion in Papal Marriage Decretals to England', in W. Van Hoecke and A. Welkenhuysen, eds, *Love and Marriage in the Twelfth Century* (Leuven, 1981), 59–87, at 77; repr. with the same pagination in idem, *Decretals and the Creation of 'New Law'*, no. IX.

[12] For this revised dating, see A. J. Duggan, 'The English Exile of Archbishop Øystein of Nidaros (1180–83)', in L. Napran and E. van Houts, eds, *Exile in the Middle Ages: Selected Proceedings from the International Medieval Congress, University of Leeds 8–11 July 2002* (Brussels, 2004), 109–30, Appendix. These important texts are treated more fully in A. J. Duggan, 'The Decretals of Archbishop Øystein of Trondheim (Nidaros)', in Kenneth Pennington and Uta-Renate Blumenthal, eds, *Proceedings of the Twelfth International Congress of Medieval Canon Law, Washington, DC, 2004* (Vatican City, 2007); cf. W. Holtzmann, 'Krone und Kirche in Norwegen im 12. Jahrhundert', *Deutsches Archiv* 2 (1938), 341–400, at 383–95, nos 1–11.

the inhabitants of an island more than twelve days' sailing from the mainland,[13] who found it difficult to observe the canonical rule which forbade marriage up to the seventh degree of consanguinity, Alexander declined to lay down a general principle, *quoniam scripta nostra super talibus legem facere non consueuerunt* – 'because our letters do not usually make law on such matters'; but he allowed Øystein and his suffragans to permit marriages within the fifth, sixth, and seventh degrees, until such time as the Almighty removed the pressing need – *donec omnipotens dominus tantam ab eis aufert necessitatem*.[14] In the same way, when Øystein asked him to determine the penance for homicide, he reiterated the general rule of seven years' penance, but declared that he could not give a definitive ruling – *nullam tibi certitudinem possumus respondere* – since individual circumstances are matters of judgement – *quoniam arbitraria sunt*. The archbishop was told that he could increase or decrease the penance, according to the facts of the case and the 'quality' of the person.[15] Similarly, on the appropriate penance for causing the death of young children under the age of seven, killed in fire or water, Alexander held back from giving specific instructions, because individual cases must be judged according to circumstances (*secundum qualitas casuum et personarum*).[16]

Local conditions also had a bearing on general ecclesiastical disci-

---

[13] This estimate of distance strongly suggests Greenland: see A. Forte, R. Oram, and F. Pedersen, *Viking Empires* (Cambridge, 2005), 330, quoting the *Landnámabók*: 'Learned men state that from Stad [north of Bergen] in Norway it is seven days' sail west to Horn in the east of Iceland; and from Snæfellsnes, where the distance is shortest, it is four days' sea west to Greenland.'

[14] *Ex diligenti: Decretales Ineditae Saeculi XII*, ed. S. Chodorow and C. Duggan, Monumenta Iuris Canonici, ser. B: Corpus Collectionum 4 (Vatican City, 1982), 149–51, at 149, no. 86; cf. Holtzmann, 'Krone und Kirche', 383–4, no. 1. A similar dispensation was made on the grounds of the *duritiam populi* to Archbishop Gerard of Split/Spalato (Dalmatia, then in Hungary) in 1168–70: C. Duggan, 'Decretal Letters to Hungary', *Folia Theologica (Budapest)* 3 (1992), 5–31, at 23–4, no. 10; repr. with the same pagination in idem, *Decretals and the Creation of 'New Law'*, no. V: 'Verum super eo quod quarto vel quinto gradu consanguinitatis in provincia tua dicuntur esse coniuncti, propter duritiam populi talia matrimonia, licet sint contra sacrorum canonum institutionem contracta, sub silentio et dissimulatione poteris preterire (But on the point that people in your province are said to be married within the fourth or fifth degree of consanguinity, because of the obduracy of the people, you may pass over such marriages in silent dissimulation, even though they are contracted contrary to the institution of the sacred canons).'

[15] Holtzmann, 'Krone und Kirche', 388–90, no. 6 (*Quoniam in parte*, now dated 1163–73), at 389, § 2.

[16] Ibid., 391–2, no. 8 (*Audiuimus quod*, 10 Dec. 1169), at 392, § 2.

pline. Where the absence of bread made fasting on bread and water almost impossible (Norway had to import much of its corn from England), penitents might eat fish or other alternatives, so long as they avoided rich fare and consumed only what was necessary to sustain life (*non ad delicias, sed ad necessariam solummodo sustentationem*).[17] Similarly, strict observance of the prohibition of 'servile work' on Sundays and feast days caused hardship where living conditions were severe, and where people lived from the fruit of the sea: so, 'except for the major festivals of the year, at times of need your parishoners may catch fish (perhaps herring) if they turn towards the land on Sundays and other feast days'.[18] Equally, the timing of festivals, which should run from evening to evening (*de uespera ad uesperam*), caused problems of interpretation in the land of the midnight sun: so Øystein was instructed to consider the custom of the region and the length of the days.[19] Even on matters relating to liturgical celebration, Alexander held back from 'making law'. He refused to issue instructions for the observance of the feast of the Holy Trinity, for example, since it was celebrated at different times in different places, *secundum diuersarum consuetudinem regionum*, and the Roman Church itself did not have such a feast: so, he could not give a definitive answer (*certum nequaquam potuimus dare responsum*).[20] Nor could he speak authoritatively on the lections on the *Inventio S. Stephani martyris*[21] used in Norway, since he had not seen them, but he confirmed that those on Lucian of Antioch were read in the Roman Church.[22] This pope was certainly not afraid to make changes in the law—as we have seen in the case of the punishment of violence against clerks—but while he responded with sympathy to difficult situations, he was anxious to ensure that temporary concessions relating to unusual circumstances should not be used to change the

---

[17] *Decretales*, 2.9.3 (CIC 2: 271–2), here wrongly addressed 'Triburiensi Archiepiscopo'; cf. Holtzmann, 'Krone und Kirche', 388, no. 5, without text (*Licet tam ueteris*, 1164–81).

[18] Ibid.: 'liceat parochianis vestris diebus dominicis et aliis festis, praeterquam in maioribus anni solennitatibus, si alecia terrae se inclinaverint, eorum captioni ingruente necessitate intendere'; cf. Holtzmann, ibid.

[19] Ibid., 388–90, no. 6 (*Quoniam in parte*, now dated 1163–73), at 388–9, § 1.

[20] Ibid., 389, § 4.

[21] *Bibliotheca hagiographica latina antiquae et media aetatis*, ed. Société des Bollandistes (Brussels, 1898–1902; repr. in 2 vols, 1949), nos 7850–6.

[22] Holtzmann, 'Krone und Kirche', 384–6, no. 2 (*Uestre discretionis*, now dated 1163–73), at 386, § 6. But Alexander pointed out (ibid., § 5), relying on the current legend, that it was [Pope] Sylvester, not Eusebius, who had baptized the emperor Constantine!

general law. His declaration that his letters 'did not usually make law on such matters' implied a recognition that they could.[23]

A similar discretion characterized the decretals of Pope Celestine III (1191–98), the former Cardinal Hyacinth who was elected pope at the age of eighty-five or so. In his case, one example addressed to the Holy Land must suffice. In *Laudabilem pontificalis officii*, Celestine responded in 1192–3 to a series of questions posed by Bishop Theobald of Acre on various legal matters, including the validity of marriages contracted in bizarre circumstances between Christians and converted Saracens.[24] Bishop Theobald had asked what should be done about Saracen captives who killed their captors, with the connivance of their captors' wives, and then, having been converted to Christianity by the same women, married them or wished to do so. Relying on Gratian's *Decretum*, Celestine's answer cited the 'council of Tribur' (a mistake for Meaux, 845),[25] to the effect that women who compassed their husbands' deaths could not marry the agents. To the question of what should happen where Saracens or Christians married the wives of those whom they had killed in battle and where the wives, subsequently learning of the manner of their husbands' deaths, sought to have the marriage dissolved, Celestine replied that since there had been no conspiracy to kill the husbands, the marriage contracts were lawful.

In another very difficult case, Bishop Theobald sought advice in the same letter on the appropriate action where a Christian husband had abandoned his wife and married a pagan, and the abandoned wife, with the approval of her archdeacon had married another husband. What was to be done if the first husband returned to Catholic unity, with his now converted wife and children? This was not a theoretical case

[23] Decisions addressed to one recipient in one context could enter the tradition of written law and be circulated as authoritative definitions through the schools and courts of Europe. For the rapid transmission of some of Adrian IV's decretals, see Duggan, 'Servus servorum Dei', 185–90, 202–7, esp. nos 1, 2, 6, 7, 8, and 9.

[24] Fulcher of Chartres, *Historia Hierosolymitana*, ed. H. Hagenmeyer (Heidelberg, 1913), 748–9 (iii, 37, cc. 3–4) recorded that Latin men married converted Syrian, Armenian, and Saracen women. For conditions in Acre following the Christian defeat at Hattin (1187) and the loss of the greater part of the Latin kingdom to Saladin, see B. Hamilton, *The Latin Church in the Crusader States: the Secular Church* (London, 1980), 243–4, 301. Theobald, the recipient of this letter, former prior of the cathedral of Nazareth and a canon in Nazareth from 1174, was elected bishop of Acre on 17 Aug. 1191; he died c. 1200.

[25] Gratian, C.31 q.1 c.4 (CIC I: 1109). 'Tribur' was a mistake. The council was held at Meaux in 845. See *Sacrorum conciliorum nova et amplissima collectio*, ed. J. D. Mansi, cont. I. B. Martin and L. Petit, 53 vols (Florence/Venice, 1759–98; Paris, 1901–27; repr. Graz, 1960–61), 14: 835, c. 69.

presented in a law school but an extraordinary human predicament which involved two families. Celestine was being asked to make a judgement of Solomon: not, indeed, to decide which mother should have the baby they both claimed, but which man should be declared the lawful husband of the Christian woman. Celestine's reply was that the Christian woman's second marriage was lawful, because she had been abandoned in contempt of Christ and had remarried with ecclesiastical permission; that the returned husband could, if he wished, enter a monastery; or he could, when his first wife died, lawfully marry the second: in both cases, *tanta est uis matrimonii*[26] – here citing the words of *bone memorie Alexandri* (Alexander III) – the children were legitimate.[27]

Underlying this complicated decision was the commitment to defend the bond of Christian marriage while permitting a humane solution to an intractable problem. The last thing Celestine wanted, was to create a precedent which enabled disgruntled Christian husbands (or wives) to use the device of temporary abandonment of Christianity to marry a non-Christian and, after returning to the faith, enter into lawful Christian marriage while the first spouse still lived. It is highly significant, nevertheless, that this judgement was not included in the *Liber Extra*. Although Raymond of Peñafort put most of the decretal, which he received from *Compilatio secunda*, into the *Decretales*, he excluded the two segments relating to this unusual case.[28] The reason for its omission is not far to seek. The circumstances were too unusual and, despite Celestine's careful language, the legal experts who shaped the law at Bologna considered that the risk of providing an opportunity for collusive action to circumvent the marriage law was too great. Indeed, Bishop Hugh of Ferrara, better known as the great canonist Huguccio of Pisa, raised this very question with his former pupil Innocent III[29] in 1199, and the new pope took the opportunity to rescind the decision of *quidam predecessor noster*, and declared that a lawful Christian

[26] Jaffé, *Regesta*, 13904; *1 Comp.* 4.18.6, *Decretales*, 4.17.6 (CIC 2: 712).
[27] *Decretales*, 3.33.1, *ad fin.* (CIC 2: 588), supplied by Friedberg from earlier collections, including *2 Comp.* 3.20.2.
[28] *2 Comp.* 2.9.2 = *Decretales*, 2.16.2 (Clem. III); *2 Comp.* 4.12.3 = *Decretales*, 4.18.4; *2 Comp.* 4.4.2 = *Decretales*, 4.6.6 (Celest. III); *2 Comp.* 3.20.2 = *Decretales*, 3.33.1 (omitting the passages cited here, which were supplied by Friedberg); *2 Comp.* 2.12.4 = *Decretales*, 2.20.27; *2 Comp.* 4.9.3 = *Decretales*, 4.15.5; *2 Comp.* 2.11.un = *Decretales*, 2.25.1.
[29] The assumption that Innocent had been a pupil of Huguccio was challenged by K. Pennington, 'The Legal Education of Pope Innocent III', *Bulletin of Medieval Canon Law* 4 (1974), 70–7; but compare J. C. Moore, 'Lotario dei Conti di Segni (Pope Innocent III) in the 1180s', *Archivum Historiae Pontificiae* 29 (1991), 255–8.

ANNE J. DUGGAN

marriage could not be dissolved when one spouse lapsed into heresy or
the error of paganism (*vel labatur in heresim, uel transeat ad gentilitatis
errorem*), partly on the ground of the binding character of the Christian
sacrament, and partly to avoid the trickery of those who might feign
heresy in order to escape from their marriage commitments.[30]

Another issue treated in Celestine's advice to the bishop of Acre
related to a marriage whose validity was challenged by the couple
themselves after twenty years of matrimony, on the ground of spiritual
relationship, in that the father of the wife was the god-father of the
husband. They claimed that their consciences had troubled them for
five years before the matter was brought before an ecclesiastical court,
which duly annulled the marriage. In this case, Celestine declared that
since there was no ambiguity about the spiritual relationship, the
couple must separate, but he added humane conditions. Not only were
they to be mutually responsible for one another's welfare thereafter, but
he 'judged' that the children should be regarded as legitimate, 'if
nothing stands in the way'. This highly significant rider acknowledged
that practical obstacles might impede his compassionate judgement.
The verb *censemus* expressed a pastoral opinion rather than a directive;
and his *si aliud non obsistit* allowed the demands of compassion to be
weighed against familial circumstances.

Running through these letters is a profound sense of the pastoral
responsibility of bishops and of the pope as chief bishop. Where one
might have expected an automatic application of the general law (*ius
commune*), irrespective of circumstance, one finds popes struggling to
find workable solutions to sometimes intractable problems. Unusual
and difficult circumstances required delicate handling; at the same
time, Alexander and Celestine were reluctant to allow changes to ecclesiastical law and practice on the basis of 'hard' or unusual cases; but
ameliorations and dispensations could be allowed, *moderata discretione*,
in the light of necessity (*necessitas*). These were not new ideas. They
grew from the philosophy of pastoral care which had been circulated

---

[30] *Die Register Innocenz III., 2: Pontifikatsjahr, 1199/1200; Texte*, ed. O. Hageneder, W.
Maleczek, and A. A. Strnad, Publikationen der Abteilung für historische Studien des
Österreichischen Kulturinstituts in Rom, 2. Abt., 1st ser., 2 vols (Rome/Vienna, 1979), 2:
88–9, no. 48 (50), *Quoniam te novimus*, to Hugh, bishop of Ferrara, 'Per hanc autem
responsionem quorundam malitie obviatur, qui in odium coniugum, vel quando sibi
invicem displicerent, si eas possent in tali casu dimittere, simularent heresim, ut ab ipsa
nubentibus coniugibus resilirent.' It was this correction which entered the legal tradition as
Decretales, 4.19.7 (CIC 2: 722–3, at 723).

through the writings of canonist-bishops from Burchard of Worms (1000–1025) onwards,[31] and was summed up in the Prologue with which Bishop Ivo of Chartres (d. 1116) had prefaced his *Decretum* and *Panormia*.[32] One passage in particular, a quotation from a letter of Pope Leo I (440–61) to Rusticus of Narbonne (427/430–61), contains the essence of his concept of dispensation:[33]

> Just as there are certain things which cannot be overturned for any reason, there are many things which may be tempered either because of the necessity of the moment [*pro necessitate temporum*] or in consideration of the times [*pro consideratione etatum*], always bearing in mind that we should recognize that in those things which may be doubtful or obscure we must follow what is not contrary to the Gospel precepts or found to be against the decrees of the Holy Fathers.

But such dispensation should be limited to the circumstances which gave rise to it, and 'should cease when the necessity ceases [*cessante necessitate*], nor should something be considered as law which either utility has urged or necessity imposed'.[34]

These principles were widely disseminated, not only in Ivo's works, which continued to be copied and read throughout the twelfth century, but through their absorption into Gratian's *Decretum*, which trans-

---

31 His great work was the *Decretum* (1008–1012; 1023): PL 140, 537–1065 (from Jean Foucher's 1549 edition); cf. E. van Balberghe, 'Les éditions du Décret de Burchard de Worms', *Recherches de Théologie ancienne et médiévale* 37 (1970), 5–22; G. Fransen, 'Le Décret de Burchard de Worms: valeur du texte de l'édition; essai de classement des manuscrits', *Zeitschrift der Savigny-Stiftung für Rechtsgeschichte, Kanonistishe Abteilung* 63 (1977), 1–19, at 3; H. Fuhrmann, *Einfluss und Verbreitung der Pseudoisidorischen Fälschungen*, Schriften der Monumenta Germaniae Historica 24, 3 vols (Stuttgart, 1972–74), 2: 442–85, 576–82.
32 See now B. C. Brasington's edition and commentary, *Ways of Mercy: the Prologue of Ivo of Chartres*, Vita Regularis: Ordnungen und Deutungen religiosen Lebens im Mittelalter, Editionen, 2 (Münster, 2004).
33 Ibid., 58–9, 126: 'Sicut quedam sunt que aut pro necessitate temporum aut pro consideracione etatum oportet temperari illa semper consideracione seruata ut in his que dubia fuerint aut obscura id nouerimus sequendum quod nec preceptis euangelicis contrarium nec decretis sanctorum patrum inueniatur aduersum.' There is an unresolved debate about whether Ivo composed the *Prologus* for the *Panormia* or for the *Decretum*: see the summary in ibid., 9–10.
34 Ibid., 90, 140: 'cessante necessitate, debent et ipse cessare, nec est pro lege habendum quod aut utilitas suasit aut necessitas imperauit.' On an analogous principle, see A. Gouron, 'Cessante causa cessat effectus: à la naissance de l'adage', *Académie des Inscriptions & Belles-Lettres* (1999), 299–309. Compare Innocent I (PL 63, 259–60): 'cessante necessitate, cessat pariter quod urgebat.'

mitted a summary of the limit of dispensation[35] as well as the Leo letter,[36] and thus exercised a profound influence on the evolving canonical jurisprudence. From this perspective, canon law could be seen as an instrument of discipline tempered with mercy. The law was not abandoned when particular historical circumstances made it difficult or impossible to apply, but it could be temporarily disregarded. As Alexander III had written to Thomas Becket in August 1165, 'Because the days are evil, and many things should be tolerated because of the temper of the times [*Quoniam dies mali sunt, et multa sunt pro qualitate temporis toleranda*].'[37] At the same time, with charitable understanding of the weakness of the human condition – *considerata fragilitate uasis*,[38] room could be found for adjustment to new and difficult circumstances, subject, of course, to the fundamental principle that nothing was done contrary to the Gospel or to the teaching of the Apostles – *nichil contra euangelium nichil contra apostolos usurpauerit*.[39]

King's College, University of London

[35] Compare Gratian, C.1 q.1 c.41 (CIC 1: 374): 'Quod pro necessitate temporis statutum est, cessante necessitate debet utique cessare quod urgebat: quia alia est ordo legitimus, alia usurpatio, quam ad presens fieri tempus impellit.'

[36] Gratian, D.14 c.2 (CIC 1: 33)

[37] *The Correspondence of Thomas Becket, Archbishop of Canterbury 1162–1170*, ed. and trans. A. J. Duggan, Oxford Medieval Texts, 2 vols (Oxford, 2000), 1: 224–5, no. 54 (Melgueil, c.22 August 1165).

[38] Brasington, *Ways of Mercy*, 117, 116.

[39] Ibid., 141–2. Compare J. Van Engen, 'From Practical Theology to Divine Law', in Peter Landau and Joers Müller, eds, *Proceedings of the Ninth International Congress of Medieval Canon Law: Munich, 13–18 July 1992*, Monumenta Iuris Canonici, ser. C: Subsidia 10 (Vatican City, 1997), 873–96.

'DANGER, STUPIDITY, AND INFIDELITY': MAGIC AND DISCIPLINE IN JOHN BROMYARD'S *SUMMA FOR PREACHERS*

by CATHERINE RIDER

O NE of the places in which medieval churchmen tackled questions of discipline and diversity was in their writing on magic. Magic appeared in many different kinds of ecclesiastical writing, including canon law, theology, and the records and manuals of the inquisition. Some of these sources have been well studied; in particular, historians have often attempted to trace the medieval origins of the early modern witch-hunts in theology and inquisition records.[1] However, many other texts have received little attention, among them the pastoral manuals written from the thirteenth century onwards, which instructed priests on how to preach and hear confessions. In contrast to academic theology and inquisitors' manuals, which catered for specialist readers, pastoral manuals were aimed at any Latin-literate cleric, perhaps especially at students in England's secular and religious schools.[2] Because they reflect what this wider audience might be expected to encounter, they offer a broader perspective than do the specialist texts on why medieval people employed diverse ritual practices, and why churchmen labelled some of these practices as 'magic' and sought to discipline them.

The theme of discipline and diversity also links the pastoral manuals' discussions of magic with recent developments in the study of late medieval heresy. From the twelfth century onwards, religious movements run by laypeople were on the rise, and some devout laypeople were becoming interested in mystical forms of devotion which encouraged the individual to seek his or her own experience of God. Recent historians have argued that these developments worried educated

[1] The historiography on this is vast. For bibliography, see Michael Bailey, 'From Sorcery to Witchcraft: Clerical Conceptions of Magic in the Later Middle Ages', *Speculum* 76 (2001), 960–90, and nn. 30–1 below.
[2] Leonard Boyle, 'The Fourth Lateran Council and Manuals of Popular Theology', in Thomas J. Heffernan, ed., *The Popular Literature of Medieval England* (Knoxville, TN, 1985), 30–43, at 31; Joseph Goering, *William de Montibus (c.1140–1213): the Schools and the Literature of Pastoral Care* (Toronto, 1992), 59–65.

clerics, who were concerned that mysticism might lead the uneducated into heresy.[3] This anxiety about heresy may also reflect a more general hardening of clerical attitudes to religious diversity in the later Middle Ages. In particular, R. I. Moore argues that from the twelfth century onwards, churchmen were defining Christian society ever more closely, and encouraging the persecution of those who did not conform, such as Jews and heretics.[4] Much of this recent historiography on heresy does not discuss magic in detail,[5] but in this paper I will argue that the same concerns about religious diversity can be seen in medieval pastoral writing on magic.

This paper will focus on one pastoral manual, the *Summa for Preachers* of John Bromyard (d. 1352), a Dominican friar based in Hereford. The *Summa* is an encyclopaedia of sermon material, which survives in five manuscripts and several sixteenth-century printed editions.[6] It is organized alphabetically by subject, with chapters on the virtues and vices, the sacraments, and many other topics, including 'War', 'Drunkenness', 'Death', 'Truth', and 'Magic' (*Sortilegium*). Much of John's material comes from earlier pastoral manuals, but he also includes some information that seems to come from his own observation. The *Summa*'s organization makes it a good source of anecdotes about a wide range of subjects, for modern historians as well as medieval preachers,[7] but John's discussion of magic has attracted little attention, although G. R. Owst published quotations from it in 1957.[8] Nor has it been analysed

    3 Malcolm Lambert, *Medieval Heresy* (2nd edn, Oxford, 1992), 174, and n. 29 below.
    4 R. I. Moore, *The Formation of a Persecuting Society* (Oxford, 1987). For a different view see David Nirenberg, *Communities of Violence: Persecution of Minorities in the Middle Ages* (Princeton, NJ, 1996).
    5 But see for the fifteenth century Michael Bailey, *Battling Demons: Witchcraft, Heresy, and Reform in the Late Middle Ages* (University Park, PA, 2003).
    6 John Bromyard, *Summa Praedicantium* (Nuremburg, 1518) [hereafter: Bromyard, *Summa*]. Subsequent references to the *Summa* will be to the article number within the chapter and the folio number from the 1518 edition. For discussion, see Peter Binkley, 'John Bromyard and the Hereford Dominicans', in Jan Willem Drijvers and Alasdair A. MacDonald, eds, *Centres of Learning: Learning and Location in Pre-Modern Europe and the Near East* (Leiden, 1995), 255–64; Leonard Boyle, 'The Date of the *Summa Praedicantium* of John Bromyard', *Speculum* 48 (1973), 553–7, repr. in idem *Pastoral Care, Clerical Education and Canon Law 1200–1400* (Aldershot, 1981), no. X; Richard Sharpe, *A Handlist of the Latin Writers of Great Britain and Ireland before 1540* (Turnhout, 1997), 221.
    7 See G. R. Owst, *Preaching in Medieval England* (Cambridge, 1926) and idem *Literature and Pulpit in Medieval England* (Cambridge, 1933); Ruth Mazo Karras, 'Gendered Sin and Misogyny in John Bromyard's "Summa Predicantium"', *Traditio* 47 (1992), 233–57.
    8 G. R. Owst, '*Sortilegium* in English Homiletic Literature of the Fourteenth Century', in J. Conway Davies, ed., *Studies Presented to Sir Hilary Jenkinson* (London, 1957), 289–96.

in the light of the recent historiography mentioned above on medieval religious unorthodoxy.

Many different beliefs and practices appear in John's chapter on magic, including necromancy (the invocation of demons), divination, and beliefs about omens. However, this paper will focus on three subjects in particular: a group of magical practitioners whom John calls *carminatrices*, 'women who use charms'; the belief that dreams can fore-tell the future; and the belief that certain women can fly around at night with the goddess Diana. In each of these cases, John suggests that some people believe that these beliefs or practices are legitimate forms of religious diversity, ways of interacting with the sacred. In doing so he shows us that many different factors encouraged medieval people to engage in so-called 'magical' practices. Then he shows us why church-men felt the need to discipline them, denouncing these practices as 'danger, stupidity and infidelity'.[9]

Women who use charms

John offers a detailed description of *carminatrices*:

> they teach that certain objects or unknown words should be worn round the neck or carried in a purse or tied or sewn into the hat or clothes; or perhaps that certain things should be noted and other observations made when going to a certain place, or when walking round it so many times. Or they teach that something of this kind should only be given or done through which [their client] will regain a lost object or love or health, or will continue to have it, or will obtain what he wants in all things.[10]

He also gives an example of a charm (*carminatio*): ' "St Mary sung a charm to her son against the bite of elves [*alphorum*] and the bite of men, and she joined bone to bone, and blood to blood, and joint to joint, and so the boy was healed." What Christian,' he continued, 'would not say that these words were lies and contrary to the Catholic faith, because such unfaithfulness would never occur to the mother of God? Therefore how do they have the power to save a man or animal?'[11]

9 Bromyard, *Summa*, 'Sortilegium', Prologue, 356r.
10 Ibid., 2, 356v.
11 Ibid., 7, 357v.

These passages suggest that one reason why medieval people employed unorthodox ritual practices was in order to solve everyday problems, such as illness in people or animals, or the loss of property. In the Mary charm, we can see how elements of Christian prayer were adapted in order to provide solutions to these problems. Moreover, John also says that many people saw these actions as legitimate. He mentions

> both the doers and the believers who say 'What [the magician] predicted, happened. I have found truth in his words, for I have found the thing that I lost, or I have regained my health, or that of my children or animals. So why is it a sin to believe in this or to do it? Or [they ask]: how can [a magician] speak the truth in an evil spirit, and why is it a sin to believe in dreams, for I have found dreams to be very true?'

John's hypothetical believers go on to argue that when they speak charms, 'they say holy words about God and St Mary and the other saints, and many prayers [orationes]', and that 'God has given power to these words.'[12]

The attitude of John's imagined audience is not surprising, because these 'prayers' shared many characteristics with orthodox piety. It was perfectly acceptable to appeal to the saints for healing or to find lost objects, for example. This is perhaps an obvious point, since historians from Keith Thomas to Eamon Duffy have discussed (with varying emphases) the ways in which so-called 'magical' practices overlapped with religion in the Middle Ages.[13] Duffy in particular emphasizes that charms were part of the 'devotional mainstream', and were copied by clerics as well as by laypeople, by the devotionally sophisticated as well as the less well-educated. They also appear in some Latin medical texts.[14] However, if the overlap between charms and orthodox religion was so great, then it becomes interesting to ask why John and other pastoral writers diverged from what seems to have been the norm, and condemned charms. What was it that pushed charms beyond the bounds of acceptable religious diversity?

[12] Ibid., 6–7, 357v.
[13] Keith Thomas, *Religion and the Decline of Magic* (London, 1971), 25–50; Eamon Duffy, *The Stripping of the Altars: Traditional Religion in England 1400–1580* (New Haven, CT, 1992), 266–98.
[14] Duffy, ibid., 275–8; Lea Olsan, 'Charms and Prayers in Medieval Medical Theory and Practice', *Social History of Medicine* 16 (2003), 343–66.

One factor was John's estimation of the *carminatrices* themselves. He ignores the fact (or was perhaps unaware) that educated writers might copy charms, and instead presents *carminatrices* as poor and female. He never mentions a male *carminator*, although he does mention men engaging in other magical practices, such as necromancy.[15] Moreover, he says that 'all of those who use the art are poor, as everyone agrees; hence it is presumed that they practise the art for money, or in the hope of receiving money.'[16] Religious diversity was probably particularly difficult to accept when coming from this doubly marginalized group of poor women, and John acknowledges this when he marvels at how people believe

> one old woman who hardly knows the rudiments of faith or the Lord's Prayer, or a trifling teller of lying and stupid tales, rather than the best master of theology who has always studied how he can speak the truth, and more than all the clerics in the world, or the doctrine of the church.[17]

This same reluctance to believe women over educated clerics can also be found in ecclesiastical writing on women visionaries from the late thirteenth century onwards.[18] However, the *carminatrices'* poverty may also have an additional significance, because earlier pastoral writers often argued that if money changed hands, an otherwise acceptable religious practice automatically became illicit. Thus the influential thirteenth-century *Summa* of Raymond of Peñafort stated, quoting St Jerome, that prophets who charged for their services became diviners: 'because they accepted money, their prophecies became divination'.[19]

But the fact that *carminatrices* were poor women was not the only problem. John also argued that all magical practitioners, male necromancers and female *carminatrices* alike, shared certain moral failings, which he illustrates by contrasting them with the saints. The saints

> despite all their other virtues and abstinences and pure life, also had such humility that they fled the places where they performed

---

15 A point also made by Karras, 'Gendered Sin', 256.

16 Bromyard, *Summa*, 'Sortilegium', 2, 356r.

17 Ibid., 8, 358r.

18 Barbara Newman, 'Possessed by the Spirit: Devout Women, Demoniacs, and the Apostolic Life in the Thirteenth Century', *Speculum* 73 (1998), 733–70, at 769.

19 Raymond of Peñafort, *Summa de penitentia*, ed. Xavierus Ochoa and Aloisius Diez (Rome, 1976), col. 387.

miracles, so that the people's praise would not make them vain-glorious. But [magicians] gather and stay most willingly where they have more praise from the people, and profit. This means that even if they were saints at first, they would lose that sanctity because they did not keep their humility.[20]

This idea that to a casual observer a saint's miracles might look similar to magic is striking, but again John's concerns were shared by other late medieval churchmen, especially in relation to women saints. Richard Kieckhefer has discussed the cases of several women whose contemporaries seem to have been unsure whether the wonders they performed were due to sanctity or magic.[21]

The objections to *carminatrices* discussed so far could be described as 'authoritarian': John believes that the women are not qualified by gender, status or holiness to initiate diverse religious practices. However, he also objects to the charms themselves, and here he provides a different definition of the limits of religious diversity. Quoting Thomas Aquinas, he argues that any procedure that cannot work by natural means must rely on demons to bring about its effects.[22] Then he gives some examples. Following the fourth-century theologian John Chrysostom, Bromyard singles out the use of words whose meanings were not known (because the unknown words might be the names of demons), and the belief that holy words or the sign of the cross would only be effective if they were written down at particular times.[23]

Certain characteristics thus automatically turned ritual practices into 'magic', because they were signs that demons were involved in them. These characteristics could even render otherwise acceptable prayers illicit, because by combining orthodox prayers with unknown words, the demons attempted to deceive the unwary: 'they join lying words to good words, just like honey tainted with gall, just as a person who wants to poison someone does not give him poison alone, but mixes it with good food or drink.'[24] John's discussion of charms thus suggests that many medieval people might extend the boundaries of

---

[20] Bromyard, *Summa*, 'Sortilegium', 7, 358r.
[21] Richard Kieckhefer, 'The Holy and the Unholy: Sainthood, Witchcraft and Magic in Late Medieval Europe', in Scott L. Waugh and Peter D. Diehl, eds, *Christendom and its Discontents* (Cambridge, 1996), 314–24.
[22] Bromyard, *Summa*, 'Sortilegium', 2, 356r.
[23] Ibid., 3, 356v.
[24] Ibid., 7, 357v.

religious diversity in order to provide concrete solutions to everyday problems, but also several reasons why this made pastoral writers uneasy.

Dreams

John's discussion of prophetic dreams offers a different view of why people might adopt diverse beliefs. Here, the problem arises from the Bible itself. On the one hand, John quotes several biblical passages that forbid attempts to predict the future by interpreting dreams.[25] He also argues that the devil sends prophetic dreams to lull his victims into a false sense of security before deceiving them. To illustrate this, he tells a story about a man who,

> dreamt that if he killed a certain hermit, he would become the king of Sicily. He had faith in this, just as he was accustomed to have faith in his other dreams and divinations. He sometimes found by chance that there was truth in his divination, and so in the end he was deceived. For when he killed [the hermit] he was captured and hung.[26]

On the other hand, John also recognized that the Bible contained examples of prophetic dreams sent by God, such as the Pharaoh's dreams interpreted by Joseph, and Nebuchadnezzar's dreams interpreted by Daniel. These examples could encourage a more tolerant attitude to dream interpretation, because in theory anyone might assume that their dreams had been sent by God. John is therefore quick to discourage this. Just because some dreams are divine revelations, he says, this does not mean that our own dreams are. Even if our dreams were divine revelations, we would not know it because we have no Joseph or Daniel to interpret them for us. Moreover, John argued, if God sent the dreams to predict something good, we would expect that the event predicted would happen in any case. However, if the dreamer showed bad faith by believing the dream, God might then punish the dreamer by withdrawing his blessing. Conversely, if God sent the dreams to predict something bad, and the dreamer showed his faith by ignoring the dream, God might reward him by sparing him the bad event. All dreams should therefore be ignored.[27]

---

[25] Ibid., 4, 356v.
[26] Ibid., 4, 356v.
[27] Ibid., 4, 357r.

This tortuous reasoning suggests that in the case of prophetic dreams, the pressure towards diversity originated in the ambiguity of the Bible itself. Nor was John the only writer to struggle with this problem: many patristic and medieval writers cautioned against believing in dreams too readily. However, these writers did not go as far as John did because, unlike him, they did not deny that some dreams might really be divinely inspired.[28] John's hard line on this subject may be linked to his authoritarian view of diversity which we have already seen in the case of charms. Just as John refused to believe the poor women who he thought used charms over the educated theologians who condemned them, he was equally unwilling to believe that divine revelations could be made to any individual. In this, he is probably also reflecting the anxieties of other late medieval churchmen, who (as mentioned above) were worried about mystical forms of devotion, and about people, especially women, who claimed to be in direct contact with God.[29]

Women who fly at night

After talking about the general deceptiveness of dreams, John goes on to quote a famous piece of canon law. This is the canon 'Episcopi', dating from the early tenth century, which states that certain women believe that they can leave their beds at night and fly around with the goddess Diana. The canon's anonymous author argues that these women do not really fly, and that the whole experience is an illusion created by demons. Who, he asks, does not see things in dreams that he never saw in waking life?[30] This text has received a great deal of attention from historians of witchcraft. 'Witchcraft' here denotes a special kind of belief about magic. In the early fifteenth century, the idea emerged that there existed a secret sect of magical practitioners, who had made a pact with the devil, whereby they received magic powers in exchange for renouncing God and worshipping Satan. These witches

28 Steven F. Kruger, *Dreaming in the Middle Ages* (Cambridge, 1992), 84–9.
29 See Rosalynn Voaden, *God's Words, Women's Voices* (York, 1999); Dyan Elliott, 'Seeing Double: Jean Gerson, the Discernment of Spirits, and Joan of Arc', *AHR* 107.1 (2002), 26–54; Nancy Caciola, *Discerning Spirits* (Ithaca, NY, and London, 2003).
30 C.26 q.5 c.12 (CIC 1: 1030–1). See Valerie Flint, *The Rise of Magic in Early Medieval Europe* (Oxford, 1991), 122–5, and Werner Tschacher, 'Der Flug durch die Luft zwischen Illusionstheorie und Realitätsbeweis: Studien zum sog. Kanon *Episcopi* und zum Hexenflug', *Zeitschrift der Savigny-Stiftung für Rechtsgeschichte*, Kan. Abt. 85 (1999), 225–76.

were believed to fly at night to meetings called sabbaths. There is no evidence that a devil-worshipping sect ever existed, but historians have long recognized that the night-flying women of the canon 'Episcopi' are one of the ingredients that later made up the image of the witch.[31]

Writing before the image of the witch came together in the fifteenth century, John Bromyard agrees with the canon's anonymous author that night flights are merely dreams: 'these illusions which they believe happen to them while they are awake, [in fact] happen while they are asleep.'[32] However, he goes on to say that if his listeners insist that these experiences really happen, then the beings that the women meet must be demons. This concession suggests that some churchmen were beginning to admit that night flights might be real. But he also implies that popular belief provided yet another explanation:

> in the other world it should be believed that there is nobody who is not good or bad. The good are those in Heaven or Purgatory; the bad are demons and the damned. But the first group cannot deceive in this way, because as the women themselves affirm, [the spirits] beat them or make them ill from time to time when they speak to them. But the good do not do evil after death. Nor can [the women] say that they are the souls of the damned, because those are in Hell, and cannot leave at will. Therefore it should be conceded that they are demons.[33]

It seems that here, John is confronting beliefs about spiritual beings that were not part of orthodox Christian doctrine. These beings might be the souls of the dead, since the idea that some dead souls rode around at night is recorded from the twelfth century onwards,[34] but they might be a different kind of being altogether. Another fourteenth-century English preaching manual calls them 'elves' [*elves*],[35] and John himself, in his contents list for the chapter on magic, calls them the 'beautiful people' [*populo pulchro*].[36] Thus, as when he quotes John Chrysostom's

---

[31] Norman Cohn, *Europe's Inner Demons: the Demonization of Christians in Medieval Christendom* (3rd edn, London, 1993), 144–61. The earliest witchcraft texts are edited in Martine Ostorero, Agostino Paravicini Bagliani, and Kathrin Utz Tremp, *L'Imaginaire du Sabbat* (Lausanne, 1999).

[32] Bromyard, *Summa*, 'Sortilegium', 5, 357r.

[33] Ibid.

[34] Jean-Claude Schmitt, *Ghosts in the Middle Ages*, trans. Teresa Lavender Fagan (Chicago, IL, 1998), 100–1.

[35] *Fasciculus Morum*, ed. and trans. Siegfried Wenzel (University Park, PA, 1989), 579.

[36] Bromyard, *Summa*, 'Sortilegium', Prologue, 355v.

condemnation of charms that use unknown words, John uses an old, authoritative text to oppose a range of contemporary beliefs.

Conclusion

The discussion of magic in John Bromyard's *Summa for Preachers* shows how slippery religious diversity can be. It suggests that many people did not distinguish as clearly as he did between orthodox religious practices and so-called 'magical' ones. Thus John's imaginary audience asks why it is wrong to use healing charms, or to believe one's dreams. In trying to discipline these practices, it is John who seems to be out of step with the 'devotional mainstream', rather than the *carminatrices* he criticizes. He also shows us how different forms of religious diversity might arise for very different reasons. Charms provided solutions to everyday problems; dream divination appeared as legitimate in the Bible; and beliefs about night-flying women reflected unorthodox beliefs about the dead or elves. John calls them all 'magic', but as forms of religious diversity, they vary considerably.

On the other hand, the factors that encouraged John to discipline these practices are remarkably consistent. In each case, authority was important. One aspect of authority was the use of existing legal texts to cover a multitude of individual practices and beliefs. Charms fell foul of a blanket prohibition of the use of unknown words, and the canon 'Episcopi' was used to prohibit a range of beliefs about otherworldly beings. The way in which John perceived these diverse beliefs was thus linked to a legal system that was designed to discipline unorthodox ritual practices, and so labelled them all as 'magic', and all magic as demonic. Another important aspect of authority was the question of who should be allowed to initiate diverse practices. John says most about this in the context of charms, where he describes how *carminatrices* are suspect because of their gender, their poverty and their morality, and women are again singled out in his discussion of night flights; but his discussion of dreams emphasizes that ordinary people of either sex do not receive revelations from God. In this respect, John's concerns reflect wider anxieties in the Church about unorthodox or heretical beliefs, especially those springing from the laity and from women.

So widespread were the 'magical' practices that John describes, and so persuasive the pressures that led to them, that John's attempts at discipline were probably doomed. Certainly charms and dream divination could still be found in England centuries later.[37] In the case of night flights, a compromise seems to have been reached: witchcraft writers from the fifteenth century onwards accepted that these experiences were real, but reinterpreted them as the witches' flight to the sabbath. However, even if he could not convince his listeners, John still tells us much about the way in which late medieval writing on magic was influenced by wider concerns about religious diversity, at a time when this issue was becoming ever more pressing in the Church as a whole.

Christ's College, University of Cambridge

---

[37] Thomas, *Religion*, 128–30, 179–84.

DISCIPLINE AND DIVERSITY IN THE MEDIEVAL ENGLISH SUNDAY*

by DIANA WOOD

THE medieval Church had strict disciplinary rules about how Sunday should be observed, but in England there was considerable diversity in interpreting and honouring them. The medieval English Sunday is a vast and challenging subject, yet despite this, and the controversy excited by the Sunday Trading Act of 1994 which allowed shops to open, it has excited little recent attention.[1]

The discipline of Sunday was laid down in the Third Commandment (Exod. 20: 8–11), where Christians were ordered to keep holy the Sabbath day and told 'In it thou shalt not do any work.' This was reinforced in canon law, in episcopal mandates, in commentaries, in theological treatises, in sermons, in *pastoralia*, and in popular literature. The Sunday Christ, the image of Christ surrounded by craftsmen's tools, which enshrined the idea that Sunday working with such implements crucified him anew, adorned the walls of many late medieval English parish churches.[2] Secular rulers, starting with Wihtred of Kent (695), included Sabbath-keeping in their legislation.[3] Diversity occurred in the varying interpretations of the law on Sunday observance, and in the patchiness of its enforcement. The questions to be addressed here are, firstly, what actually constituted Sunday? Secondly, what were people supposed to do on Sundays, and did they do it?

---

* My thanks are due to Robert Swanson for his helpful suggestions.

[1] Most useful is Kenneth Parker, *The English Sabbath: a Study of Doctrine and Discipline from the Reformation to the Civil War* (Cambridge, 1988), ch. 1. In general see Max Levy, *Der Sabbath in England: Wesen und Entwicklung des englischen Sonntags* (Leipzig, 1933); H. Thurston, 'The Medieval Sunday', *The Nineteenth Century* 46 (1899), 36–50; Edith Cooperrider Rodgers, *Discussion of Holidays in the Later Middle Ages* (New York, 1940; repr. 1967); C. R. Cheney, 'Rules for the Observance of Feast Days in Medieval England', *BIHR* 34 (1961), 117–24; Barbara Harvey, 'Work and *festa ferianda* in Medieval England', *JEH* 23 (1972), 289–308; Susanne Jenks, 'Bill Litigation and the Observance of Sundays and Major Festivals in the Court of King's Bench in the Fifteenth Century', *Law and History Review* 22 (2004), 619–43.

[2] See Athene Reiss, *The Sunday Christ: Sabbatarianism in English Medieval Wall Painting*, British Archaeological Report, British series, 292 (Oxford, 2000).

[3] The Laws of Wihtred, King of Kent (695), EHD 1, 363, no. 31, cl. 9–11. For further Anglo-Saxon examples see Levy, *Der Sabbath*, ch. 4.

Finally, how well observed was the work prohibition as applied to Sunday trading?

The original Old Testament Sabbath was Saturday, the seventh day: 'In six days the Lord made heaven and earth, the sea, and all that in them is, and rested the seventh day; wherefore the Lord blessed the sabbath day, and hallowed it' [Exod. 20: 11]. But the Christian Holy Day is Sunday. Pauper, in the fifteenth-century prose dialogue *Dives and Pauper*, provides a comprehensive summary of earlier discussion on the change. Augustine had recognized that God hadn't actually *laboured* in creating the world, 'but only he bade that it should be done and it was done anon what he would.'[4] The real travail had been that of his son in the recreation and redemption of the world, when he 'sweated blood for anguish and died for travail and shed his heart's blood and ceased not of travail till in the morrow of the Sunday when he rose from death to life . . . therefore the Sunday is called the lord's day, *dies dominicus*'.[5]

But could a commandment be altered? Basing his argument partly on Aquinas, Pauper explained that in the Old Law God had given three types of precept, ceremonial, judicial, and moral. The ceremonials symbolized future events, but when these had happened the ceremonials vanished.[6] The Third Commandment was part-moral and part-ceremonial. Morally it taught Christians to worship God, and to cease from vice on the Sabbath, and this was unalterable. The ceremonial aspect, the time it was observed, had been changed to Sunday for the better. What it had symbolized, the rest of Christ in the sepulchre after his labour in redeeming mankind, had been fulfilled, and so was no longer binding.[7]

What constituted Sunday? According to canon law, it lasted from Saturday evening to Sunday evening, in order to distance Christians from the Jews' observance of their Sabbath.[8] Yet many people seem to have stopped work at midday on the Saturday. The thirteenth-century commentator Thomas of Chobham expressed wonder that priests ordered that the day be kept from the ninth hour on the Saturday, by which he meant Nones, or noon,[9] until the following evening, and that

---

[4] *Dives and Pauper*, ed. Priscilla Heath Barnum, EETS 275 (Oxford, 1976), Commandment III, iii, 270, lines 47–9.

[5] Ibid., lines 49–57.

[6] Ibid., III, ii, 265, lines 4–8.

[7] Ibid., 266, lines 12–22.

[8] Gratian, *Decretum*, D.3 c.1. (CIC 1: 1353).

[9] Thurston, 'Medieval Sunday', 39.

they harassed simple folk if they worked during that time. Anyway, Sunday has no vigil, and so should be celebrated only from the previous evening.[10] Early the following century Robert Mannyng of Brunne referred to the peculiarly English custom of keeping Saturday holy to honour the Virgin.[11] The fifteenth-century English canonist William Lyndwood pointed out that the beginning and end of feasts must be fixed by the custom of local areas, where they might begin sooner and end later.[12] Pauper echoes this, but warns that when the bells start ringing from Saturday midday, this does not mark the beginning of Sunday, but a warning to people to arrange their work so that they can celebrate Sunday properly when it does come.[13] Such diversity is reflected in secular legislation. The ordinances of the lorimers of London (1260), for example, state that 'no one of the trade shall work upon Saturday after noon sounded and rung out at his parish church.'[14] In 1401 Parliament ordered that 'no labourers shall take any Hire for the Holy-days nor for the Evens of Feasts [which would have included Saturdays] but till the Hour of Noon, but only for the half Day' on pain of a twenty-shilling fine.[15] In 1490 the journeymen shoemakers of Norwich were forbidden to exercise their craft after 4 o'clock on Saturdays.[16] Whatever canon law decreed, it was variously interpreted.

What were people supposed to do on Sundays? The day was to be spent in 'hymn, psalm, and spiritual song' according to Gratian's *Decretum*.[17] As William Langland observed, Christians were supposed to hear matins, mass, and, in the afternoon, evensong.[18] But did they?

From the late thirteenth century, bishops were concerned that they did not. Statutes of Peter Quivel of Exeter in 1287 ordered punishment for non-attendance.[19] In 1291 Archbishop Pecham commanded his

[10] Thomas of Chobham, *Summa confessorum*, D.3, q.1a, ed. F. Broomfield, *Analecta mediaevalia Namurcensia* 25 (Louvain and Paris, 1968), 267.
[11] Robert Mannyng of Brunne, *Handlyng Synne*, ed. F. J. Furnivall, EETS os 119 (London, 1901), 31-2, lines 846-76.
[12] William Lyndwood, *Provinciale* (Oxford, 1679), 102, *s.v.* 'vespertina'.
[13] *Dives and Pauper*, III, xiv, 287, lines 7-12.
[14] H. T. Riley, ed., *Liber custumarum*, RS 12, 3 vols in 4 (1859-62), 2.1: 78.
[15] 4 Henry IV, cl. 14, ed. A. Luders et al., *Statutes of the Realm*, 11 vols (London, 1810-28), 2: 137.
[16] R. H. Tawney and Eileen Power, eds, *Tudor Economic Documents* 1 (London, 1924), 97.
[17] D.3 c.16. (CIC 1: 1356-7).
[18] William Langland, *The Vision of William concerning Piers the Plowman*, ed. Walter W. Skeat, 2 vols (Oxford, 1924; repr. 1969), C10, 240, lines 227-9.
[19] F. M. Powicke and C. R. Cheney, eds, *Councils and Synods, AD 1205-1313*, 2 vols in 4 (Oxford, 1964), 2.1: 1021, cl. 22.

archdeacon to use every possible censure to persuade rebel diocesan parishioners to return to the solemn observances of Sunday, even the threat of refusing them Christian burial.[20] At Chichester the following year Bishop Gilbert directed parishioners to be in church 'silently and devotedly' at least during the singing of mass on Sundays.[21] The 'at least' implies that attendance at matins or evensong would have been unlikely. In 1359 Archbishop Simon Islip threatened Sabbath-breakers who had reached years of discretion with canonical censures.[22]

From the late fourteenth century the records of the church courts, and of visitations in the archdeaconries and other jurisdictions, become more abundant. Amongst their riches are presentations and accusations for non-attendance at church on Sundays. They are never more than a small proportion of the total cases, but in general they increase in the late fifteenth and early sixteenth century, except for those in London church courts, which declined.[23] By 1511–12 the parishioners of the deanery of Lyminge, Kent, had to be ordered devoutly to attend high mass, matins, and vespers in their parish churches, under threat of being reported to Archbishop Warham if they defaulted.[24] The penalties imposed on those presented simply for not keeping the Sabbath varied, if they were recorded at all. In the diocese of Canterbury some people were told to attend in future; others were threatened with excommunication.[25] Most cases in the Buckingham archdeaconry courts were dismissed.[26] The unfortunate Isabella Bovyngton of Penn, however, was whipped three times round the church.[27]

If people did attend mass on Sunday, the church was a noisy place. The fourteenth-century Dominican John Bromyard deplored people hurrying from church to attend feasts, adding, 'If they can't get away, and do spend a fleeting hour in church, they pass that brief time in idle

---

[20] Ibid., 1097.

[21] Ibid., 1117, cl. 4.

[22] D. Wilkins, *Concilia Magnae Britanniae et Hiberniae*, 4 vols (London, 1737), 2: 43.

[23] Richard M. Wunderli, *London Church Courts and Society on the Eve of the Reformation* (Cambridge, MA, 1981), 123.

[24] K. L. Wood-Legh, ed., *Kentish Visitations of Archbishop Warham and his Deputies, 1511–12*, Archaeologia Cantiana 24 (1984), 143–4.

[25] Ibid., nos 18b, 52d, 108c, 174n, 1740, 204d. For those threatened, see nos 68a, 138a.

[26] E. Elvey, ed., *The Courts of the Archdeaconry of Buckingham, 1483–1523*, Buckinghamshire Record Society 19 (1975), 76, no. 103, 107, no. 153, 175, no. 247.

[27] Ibid., 124, no. 178. On ritual penance see Dave Postles, 'Penance and the Market Place: a Reformation Dialogue with the Medieval Church (c.1250–c.1600)', *JEH* 54 (2003), 441–68.

gossip and useless chattering . . .'.[28] Pauper echoed this: 'When men come to church, they leave bedes-bidding and spend their time in sinful jangling.'[29] They did not exaggerate. Archbishop Stephen Langton in the early thirteenth century ordered priests to remind their parishioners forcibly to devote themselves to prayer in church, rather than shouting or vain story-telling.[30] Some noisy and unpleasant Sabbath-breakers were presented in the church courts. Of Henry Merekote of Minsterworth in the diocese of Hereford, for example, it was reported that when he does go to church, 'he disturbs divine service. He sits in the chancel without the curate's consent and against his will . . . and is a common defamer of his neighbours and a fomenter of disputes.'[31] From the diocese of Lincoln in 1530, John Hill of Eynsham, Oxfordshire, 'is a common swearer and does not hear divine service nor does he go to church'.[32] Several of those presented for non-attendance in the deanery of Wisbech disturbed divine service by chattering, story-telling, and swearing when they did attend.[33] About 1460 John Freeman defamed Margareta Dygby during vespers on the second Sunday in Advent as a 'strong whore', 'and this caused great tumult in the church', adds the record.[34] At Whittelsey in the deanery of Wisbech, the Sabbath-breaker Alicia Kelsall, publicly declared a common scold, and a defamer and detractor of her neighbours, was threatened by the lord official with three whippings round the church in penitential guise.[35] Some of the regular church-goers were little better: Henry, servant of John Lawrence of Walpole St Andrew 'plays and disturbs divine service in church on Sundays and feast days, and warned by the vicar does not wish to desist'.[36] In Tenterden, Kent, in 1511–12 Johan Frank and 'other eville disposid persones' were in the

28 John Bromyard, *Summa Praedicantium* (Venice, 1586), cap. 3, *s.v.* 'feriarum', fol. 279v, §11.
29 *Dives and Pauper*, III, vi, 275, lines 33–5.
30 Powicke and Cheney, *Councils and Synods*, 2.1: 31, cl. 35.
31 A. T. Bannister, ed., 'Visitation Returns of the Diocese of Hereford in 1397, II', *EHR* 44 (1929), 444–64, at 452.
32 A. Hamilton Thompson, ed., *Visitations in the Diocese of Lincoln, 1517–1531*, Lincoln Record Society 35 (1944), 56; 33 (1940), 24.
33 L. R. Poos, ed., *Lower Ecclesiastical Jurisdiction in Late Medieval England: the Courts of the Dean and Chapter of Lincoln, 1336–1349, and the Deanery of Wisbech, 1458–1484* (Oxford, 2001): Thomas Bluwyk of Wisbech, 282; John Sawer of Wisbech, 304; Simon Lambhard and John Raynold of Emneth, 405, John Reynold of Birdes [sic] of Leverington, 551.
34 Ibid., 316.
35 Ibid., 541.
36 Ibid., 536.

churchyard gossiping during divine service, and other people would sit still in the church at procession times rather than participating.[37] A general warning had to be issued to the people of the deanery of Ospringe, Kent, to abstain from all gossiping or conversation about secular matters in church both during divine services and the time between them.[38]

The Ospringe charge continued with an order to abstain from fairs and other places of buying and selling on Sundays. Buying and selling constituted forbidden 'servile' work. As Pauper defined it, 'servile' meant 'every bodily work done principally for temporal lucre and worldly winning', and buying and selling topped his list.[39] The moral aspect of the Third Commandment also proscribed vice. 'As a nail sticketh fast between the joining of the stones; so doth sin stick close between buying and selling', according to Ecclesiasticus (27: 2). Simon Islip's impassioned diatribe against Sunday markets in the province of Canterbury provided resounding confirmation. Diabolical power grew at such places. Not just victuals were traded, but other diverse business took place which usually could not be conducted without fraud and deception. Possibly he meant usury, banking, and exchange. Among other evils, illicit conventicles and associations were formed, feasting was joined to drunkenness, and many hideous crimes were committed. These led to brawling, violence, threats, blows, and even murder. Deserting their churches, the whole population often flocked to market – a grave danger to souls, in contempt of the Christian religion, and a manifest scandal.[40] Archbishop Arundel made similar observations in 1401 when suppressing Sunday fairs at Harrow-on-the-Hill.[41] Small wonder that Pauper warned 'in the Sunday reigneth more lechery, gluttony, manslaughter, robbery, back-biting, perjury and other sins, more than reigneth in all the week before.'[42]

Sunday trading had been a problem since the ninth century, when Alfred and Guthrum had imposed heavy penalties.[43] In 1201 Eustace, abbot of Flay, a fire-and-brimstone preacher, made his second visit to

---

[37] Wood-Legh, *Kentish Visitations*, no. 174m.
[38] Ibid., 222 (5).
[39] *Dives and Pauper*, III, vii, 277, lines 35–7.
[40] Wilkins, *Concilia*, 2: 43.
[41] Ibid., 3: 266.
[42] *Dives and Pauper*, III, vi, 275, lines 31–3.
[43] F. L. Attenborough, ed., *The Laws of the Earliest English Kings* (Cambridge, 1922), 107, cl. 7.

England exhorting observance of the Lord's Day, and especially the abolition of Sunday markets. He based his preaching on the spurious 'heavenly' letter, which called down Christ's curses on Sabbath-breakers:

> Faithless people you have not kept the day of my resurrection. I swear to you by my right hand, unless you keep the Lord's day ... I will send pagan races to slaughter you . . . and worse beasts to devour the breasts of your women. I shall curse those who do any forbidden work on the Lord's day.[44]

Many Sunday markets were shifted to weekdays, but then, Roger of Wendover lamented, 'Alas, like a dog to vomit, there was a return to holding markets on Sundays.'[45] As James Cate showed, there was another drive, unconnected with Eustace, towards changing market days beginning in 1218.[46] Before that Stephen Langton had ordered priests to forbid their parishioners to frequent markets on Sunday when they should be in church.[47] During the rest of the century at least eight other episcopal statutes either prohibited visits to Sunday markets or banned them altogether.[48] In 1230 canon law also condemned them.[49] The website *Gazetteer of Fairs and Markets to 1516* lists some eighty-six markets which had been held at some point on Sundays.[50] With seven additional ones found by Cate, the total is ninety-three. Some sixty of these were changed to different days, but probably there were Sunday markets which left no records, or places where the change was temporary. By the mid-fourteenth century Bromyard complained that few

[44] Roger of Hovedon, *Chronica*, ed. W. Stubbs, RS 51, pt 4 (London, 1871), 168–9. On Eustace's mission see J. L. Cate, 'The English Mission of Eustace of Flay (1200–1201)', in *Études d'histoire dédiées à la mémoire de Henri Pirenne* (Brussels, 1937), 67–89, and on the letter, W. R. Jones, 'The Heavenly Letter in Medieval England', *Medievalia et Humanistica*, ns 6 (1975), 163–75.

[45] Roger of Hovedon, *Chronica*, 172.

[46] James Lea Cate, 'The Church and Market Reform in England during the Reign of Henry III', in James Lea Cate and E. N. Anderson, eds, *Medieval and Historiographical Essays in Honor of James Westfall Thompson* (Chicago, IL, 1938), 27–65.

[47] Powicke and Cheney, *Councils and Synods*, 2.1: 35, cl. 58.

[48] Ibid., 2.1: William of Blois of Worcester, 174, cl. 22; an unknown bishop, 194, cl. 83; Walter Cantilupe of Worcester, 297, cl. 83; William Raleigh of Winchester, 410, cl. 46; Richard de Wich of Chichester, 461, cl. 5; Fulk Basset of London, 647, cl. 64; Nicholas of Farnham of Durham, 432, cl. 42; 2. Ibid., 2.2: Peter Quivel of Exeter, 1021, cl. 22.

[49] X 2.9.1. (CIC 2: 270)

[50] Centre for Metropolitan History, *Gazetteer of Markets and Fairs in England and Wales to 1516* (available at: www.history.ac.uk/cmh/gazweb2.html, accessed 2003).

people could be found who did not go to Sunday fairs and markets or send their servants with loaded pack animals. He added that in many places markets were held on Sundays throughout the year.[51] Official condemnations recalled Simon Islip's attitude. John Thoresby of York, after biblical warnings about turning the house of God into a den of thieves, forbade markets to be held in churches on Sundays.[52] Simon Langham of Canterbury denounced Sunday markets on the Isle of Sheppey held near the church; the tumult impeded divine service.[53] Edward II had issued a proclamation against Sunday markets in 1321,[54] and in 1448 Henry VI's Parliament legislated against fairs and markets on 'high and principal feasts . . . as in Trinity Sunday, with other Sundays', warning buyers and sellers of 'the horrible Defiling of their souls in buying and selling, with many deceitful Lyes and false Perjury, with Drunkenness and Strifes and . . . specially withdrawing themselves and their Servants from divine Service'.[55] The Church's disciplinary records reflect this concern. There are presentations for attending or holding markets in the dioceses of Durham and Hereford and in the archdeaconries of Buckingham and Wisbech.[56] In Kent there are general charges in 1511–12 in the deaneries of Lyminge, Canterbury, Ospringe, Sittingborne, and Sutton against Sunday trading at fairs, markets, and shops. At Lydd, during divine service, 'many goo in the churcheyards . . . and there [are] many buyers and sellers', while 'barbours and bochers sett theire shoppis opene on Sonedayes'.[57] Those most often prosecuted here as elsewhere were the butchers. At Canterbury 'bochers kepe their shopis opene on Sonedayes and other holy daies when they shuld be atte divine service'. The same was true at Temple Ewell and Milton.[58] In the deanery of Wisbech in 1468 no less than seventeen butchers, mainly from Leverington, were presented

---

[51] Bromyard, *Summa*, fol. 279v, § 10.

[52] Wilkins, *Concilia*, 2: 68.

[53] Ibid., 73.

[54] *Registrum Hamonis Hethe, diocesis Roffensis, AD 1319–52*, ed. C. Johnson, CYS 49 (1948), 117.

[55] 27 Henry VI, cl. 5, *Statutes of the Realm* 2: 351–2.

[56] J. Raine, ed., *Depositions and Other Ecclesiastical Proceedings from the Courts of Durham*, Surtees Society 21 (1845), 35; Bannister, 'Visitation Returns of the Diocese of Hereford, III', *EHR* 45 (1930), 92–101, at 92; 'Visitation Returns of the Diocese of Hereford, IV', ibid., 444–63, at 452; Elvey, *Buckingham*, 30, no. 32; Poos, *Lower Ecclesiastical Jurisdiction*, 327, 331, 333, 339, 411, 417.

[57] Wood-Legh, *Kentish Visitations*, nos 102b, 102c.

[58] Ibid., nos 18a, 64a, 323h.

simultaneously.[59]A few bakers also feature.[60] Amongst non-victuallers, shoemakers were frequent offenders: in 1391 seven from Berkshire were presented for skipping church on Sundays and 'selling shoes elsewhere',[61] and one Sutton of Whitchurch, who sold shoes at Wodesdon, Buckinghamshire.[62]

There was plenty of discipline, but where was the diversity? The discipline admitted exceptions. Much of the legislation allowed the selling of 'necessary victuals'. This was so for the dioceses of Chichester and London in the mid-thirteenth century, and for Exeter in 1287.[63] Simon Langham repeated this in 1368, and Archbishop Arundel in 1401 added that it was lawful to buy and sell on Sundays during the autumn harvest, according to the custom of the country, because of the need to gather in the crops during the week.[64] Edward II allowed the sale of necessary victuals on Sundays, as did Henry VI, who also exempted the four weeks of harvest. Yet despite all this, parishioners continued to be presented for selling victuals on Sundays. The seventeen butchers of Leverington are a case in point, to say nothing of the numerous open butchers' shops in Kent and the bakers who were prosecuted. A certain Sledmer of Southwell Minster was presented in 1490 for shirking prime and buying, amongst other things, barley, grain, cheese, and pears on Sundays[65] – admittedly items which might appear less 'necessary' than meat or bread.

Over the course of time exceptions to strict discipline developed. Several were detailed by Pauper. Merchants travelling a great distance by land or water might carry their goods on Sundays if they could not do so at any other time.[66] He also qualified his stern resistance to Sunday trading, admitting that it was lawful for victuallers to sell from their own premises, provided that they did so for the comfort of their fellow Christians.[67] When Dives inquired how people knew what was

59 Poos, *Lower Ecclesiastical Jurisdiction*, 394.

60 Hamilton-Thompson, *Diocese of Lincoln*, 1, 81; Poos, *Lower Ecclesiastical Jurisdiction*, 270, 333.

61 T. C. B. Timmins, ed., *The Register of John Waltham, Bishop of Salisbury, 1388–95*, CYS 80 (1994), nos 926, 927, 930 942.

62 Elvey, *Buckingham*, 3P, 7.

63 Powicke and Cheney, *Councils and Synods*, 2.1: 461, cl. 5 (Chichester); 647, cl. 64 (London); 2.2: 1021, ch. 22 (Exeter).

64 Wilkins, *Concilia*, 3: 266–7.

65 A. Francis, ed., *Visitations and Memorials of Southwell Minster*, Camden Society, ns 48 (1891), 53.

66 *Dives and Pauper*, III, xv, 289–90, lines 14–16.

67 Ibid., xvi, 291, lines 24–34.

allowed on Sundays, and what degree of need qualified them for exemption from the work prohibition, Pauper based his advice on the work of John of Freiburg, OP (d. 1304) – in effect, that necessity knows no law:

> If they are able readily to approach their bishop they should ask his counsel, or else their curate, or some other good wise man of holy church, or else some other wise man. And if the need be great and open their own conscience ought to excuse them for working rather than the authority of the law.[68]

There was clearly a gulf between the discipline of Sunday as originally laid down by the Church, and its practice. Not only did Christians break the rules, in some cases with impunity, but exceptions to them were beginning to appear, however unevenly they were implemented. They may well have been occasioned by the increasing commercialization of society and the more favourable attitude to trade and merchants which was developing throughout Europe by the late medieval period.[69] Ultimately the Church had to tolerate a diversity of practice, especially about Sunday trading amongst a future nation of shop-keepers, which it was seemingly unable to control.

University of Oxford

---

[68] Ibid., 292, lines 41–51.
[69] Diana Wood, *Medieval Economic Thought* (Cambridge, 2002), 115–20.

MARY AND THE MIDDLE AGES:
FROM DIVERSITY TO DISCIPLINE

by MIRI RUBIN

FOR just over a thousand years the Virgin Mary was central to any attempt to defend or explain Christian Orthodoxy. From the formulations at Ephesos and Chalcedon Mary formed part of the understanding of a God made Flesh and of a picture of redemption which was all-embracing in its promise and tantalizing in its accessibility. This essay shows just how wide and diverse were the medieval ways of thinking about Mary and the ways of exploring the possibilities inherent in the figure of the Mother of God. In liturgy and prayer, in homilies and devotional poetry, in a vast array of material forms Mary was made familiar, above all as mother, as intercessor and companion. Unlike the sacraments, among them the all-important Eucharist, Mary was rarely a subject of discipline or of scrutiny; she entered people's lives early and seemingly effectively. She stood, however, as a boundary-marker of Christian identity, the quintessential barrier between Christians and Others. Mary did become a subject of discipline to people in the lands of conquest and disease outside Europe.

* * *

Of Mary the gospels speak little, but in the world that saw the birth of a belief in a God made Flesh – the world which Peter Brown has described as 'rustling with the presence of many divine beings'[1] – stories were told about the birth of a Messiah. Those Jews in Galilee and Judaea who believed that Jesus was indeed the Messiah lived alongside Jews who did not. The gospel of Mary's life is but a generation or two younger than the gospels of Matthew and Luke. Its stories tell of a Jewish girl of good birth and careful upbringing, of unsurpassed purity, who was chosen to fulfil a divine mission. Everything about Mary was cast in narrative, and continued to be. And the narrative thrust led to the possibility of believing that a young Jewish woman – *una mulier hebrea* – might bear a Redeemer. From the early second century stories

---

[1] Peter Brown, *Authority and the Sacred: Aspects of the Christianisation of the Roman World* (Cambridge, 1995), 3.

survive which were told with the aim of bolstering the belief in a God
made Man, made human in almost every embarrassing and familiar
way. Averil Cameron has described this as 'filling in the gaps in the
Gospel stories, working out their logical consequences'.[2] The *Protogospel
of James* provided Mary with a family and childhood. She was a Jewish
maiden of good and strict upbringing; she was precocious – walked,
talked and danced – and was unparalleled in her purity.[3]

Yet elsewhere during the first centuries of co-emergence, which saw
Mediterranean religions meet and collide, Mary was discussed very
little. Such a figure was of no interest to philosophers who pondered
the new religion in technical and abstract terms; yet it benefited from
proximity to the Jewish figure of *Shekhinah*, of a feminine divine presence, approached through poetry and praise.[4] Hence in Syriac
Christianities, which grew out of and were destined to coexist with the
Jewish communities of the eastern Roman Empire and the Persian
Empire, the mother of the Christian God was reverenced in poetry and
prayer. When the politics of empire determined Christianity as a state
religion, with an officially formulated creed, the Incarnation was at its
heart, hence Mary was not far from mind:

> We believe in one God the Father all powerful, maker of all things
> both seen and unseen. And in one Lord Jesus Christ, the Son of
> God, the only-begotten begotten from the Father, that is from the
> substance of the Father, God from God, light from light, true God
> from true God, begotten not made, cosubstantial with the Father
> through whom all things came to be, both those in heaven and
> those in earth; for us humans and for our salvation he came down
> and became incarnate, became human, suffered and rose up on the
> third day, went up into the heavens, is coming to judge the living
> and the dead. And in the Holy Spirit.[5]

[2] Averil Cameron, *Christianity and the Rhetoric of Empire: the Development of Christian Discourse* (Berkeley, CA, 1991), 104.

[3] Mary F. Foskett, *A Virgin Conceived: Mary and Classical Representations of Virginity* (Bloomington, IN, 2002), 141–64.

[4] Arthur Green, 'Shekhinah, the Virgin Mary, and the Song of Songs: Reflections on a Kabbalistic Symbol in its Historical Context', *American Jewish Studies Review* 26 (2002), 1–52; Peter Schäfer, 'Daughter, Sister, Bride, and Mother: Images of the Femininity of God in the Early Kabbala', *Journal of the American Academy of Religion* 68 (2000), 221–42.

[5] Norman P. Tanner, ed., *Decrees of the Ecumenical Councils*, 2 vols (London, 1990), 1: 5–5*.

By the Council of Constantinople of 381 Mary's place is more explicit:

> for us humans and for our salvation he came down from the
> heavens and became incarnate from the holy Spirit and the virgin
> Mary, became human and was crucified on our behalf under
> Pontius Pilate.[6]

In the fertile and creative cities and monasteries of Egypt a comfortable
confluence of existing attachments to another mother-goddess – Isis –
made possible a transformation of the material culture – temples,
sculpture, inscriptions – into the artefacts and signs of worship of
Mary.[7] It was Egyptian thinkers and writers who contributed greatly to
the figure of Mary as mother of God. This converged with the devotions and aspirations of female members of the imperial family. They
enjoyed the power to enhance and promote the dual nature of Christ –
the crux of the Christian message – through emphasis on the role of his
mother as dignified, majestic, adorned. By 431 politics and devotion
combined to formulate beyond doubt the powerful statement of imperial will in the word *theotokos* – Mary as human bearer of God. This
was a simple formulation, and it was not amenable to philosophical
parsing. It could either be accepted sympathetically, or rejected with
abhorrence. And so it was. For Nestorius of Constantinople and several
Syrian bishops and monks, the implicit emphasis on Christ's humanity
was distasteful, and so a break was created in the imperial Church, one
accompanied by high political persecution and enduring polemic.[8]
Large parts of eastern Christianity remained apart for centuries and
even unto this day. A will of iron aligned *theotokos* with the choices and
dignities of imperial religion, the result of circumstance but also of
deep logic; henceforward Mary's appellations, and her visual representation, were the stuff of official example and scrutiny.

More than any figure of the Christian imagination Mary has the
power to penetrate the innermost places of privacy, the tightly guarded
domains of fantasy and desire. For Mary inhabits the meeting point of

---

[6] Ibid., 24–24*.

[7] Jan den Boeft, 'Propaganda in the Cult of Isis', in Pieter W. van der Horst, Maarten J. J.
Menken, Joop F. M. Smit and Geert van Oyen, eds, *Persuasion and Dissuasion in Early Christianity, Ancient Judaism, and Hellenism* (Leuven, 2003), 9–23.

[8] Kate Cooper, 'Empress and *Theotokos*: Gender and Patronage in the Christological
Controversy', in R. N. Swanson, ed., *The Church and Mary*, SCH 39 (Woodbridge, 2004),
39–51; eadem, 'Contesting the Nativity: Wives, Virgins, and Pulcheria's *imitatio Mariae*', *Scottish Journal of Religious Studies* 19 (1998), 31–43.

body and mind, of mundane reality and imagination. Like the mother, both within and without the person, Mary belongs to the emotions, to that which is ineffable and yet powerfully possessed. Mary was fittingly celebrated in song and in image – arts which are highly participatory, which delight and inspire hope in ways that are private and highly personal. Mary was not experienced through sacraments and catechisms, although these indeed mention her and assume her central importance. Unlike the sacraments she was available to all, requiring no test for entry. Nor was she an exciting subject for theology; rather, she was appreciated in the rhythms of biblical exegesis, and in the cadences of preaching.

Mary was mentioned in the creeds formulated by the imperial Church from the fourth century, and in the fifth century became a powerful representation of the Christian empire, through her own dynastic power as *theotokos*, bearer of God. But in most of Europe in the first Christian millennium Mary was much less known and cherished only in specific niches, at particular times. Mary was offered as a model for virgins in Ambrose's Milan, was discussed in debates with adoptionists in Charlemagne's court; the Assumption was interpreted by Ottonian artists as a reflection of the transcendence of the imperial court; Mary's life inspired Anglo-Saxon homilists' themes for instructing the laity.[9]

Mary remained a marginal figure for the people of first-millennium Europe, who drew inspiration above all from the relics and legends of martyrs whose sacrifice and example dramatized the process by which Christianity had taken root. The prodigious sixth-century poet Venantius Fortunatus, who was born in Italy but became a bishop in Gaul, mentions Mary in only two of his poems. A hymn to Mary ends with an invocation to a celestial lady, one who restores that which sad Eve had removed, and offers a window unto heaven:

O gloriosa domina,	O glorious Lady
Excelsa super sidera,	Elevated above the stars
Qui te creavit provide,	He who created you wisely,
Lactasti sacro ubere.	You suckled at the sacred breast.
Quod Eva tristis abstulit	What sad Eve has removed

[9] Kate Cooper, *The Virgin and the Bride: Idealized Womanhood in Late Antiquity* (Cambridge, MA, 1996); Celia M. Chazelle, *The Crucified God in the Carolingian Era: Theology and Art of Christ's Passion* (Cambridge, 2001), 56–9, 242–58, 268–9; Henry Mayr-Harting, *Ottonian Book Illumination: an Historical Study* (2nd edn, London, 1999), 139–56; Mary Clayton, *The Cult of the Virgin Mary in Anglo-Saxon England* (Cambridge, 1990).

Tu reddis almo gremine;	You have restored with a nourishing bosom.
Intrent ut astra flebiles,	May the wretched enter like stars,
Coeli fenestra facta est (21–8).[10]	A window to the heavens has been created.

For all that Venantius magnified Mary so ably, and created strings of images that were to resound in Christian poetry for centuries, Mary inspired only a fraction of his poetical and devotional oeuvre. She featured little even in his poem on virginity. This was a roll call of martyrs, heroes who gave their lives in torment and abuse, but who might inspire the chaste virgins of his day to offer their own lives in the present.[11] Venantius Fortunatus saw virgin martyrs as being like gems; they were as fragrant lilies like Agatha, Justina, Agnes, Paulina, and others. Mary trailed lower down the list.

Close to the end of the millennium Hrotswitha of Gandersheim (c. 930–c. 1002) experimented with the story of Mary's life. This was an intellectual exercise in the chaste and lofty life of a high-born canoness. She used every bit of narrative about Mary's childhood, setting them to strict poetic metre.[12] A little later Fulbert of Chartres (born between 952 and 962, d. 1028/9) found in Mary a fitting inspiration for the liturgical routines of his cathedral and benefited from a generous offering of Mary's healing milk.[13]

Early medieval Latin Europe lived the transcendent through the heroic legacy of martyrs. But this was about to change. Mary was realized in the lives of articulate monks and priests like Fulbert in the first decades of the second millennium.[14] Just as fifth-century Greek thinkers had formulated the bridging concept of the *theotokos* – the human bearing the divine – eleventh-century thinkers created a Latin bridge. The theology of Incarnation and the penitential rule of life were formulated by ambitious and powerful monks like Anselm of Canterbury (1033–1109), as a vision of a Christian society. Always close to the

---

[10] *De sancta Maria*, PL 88, 265.

[11] *De virginitate*, PL 88, 266–76.

[12] *The Non-Dramatic Works of Hrosvitha: Text, Translation, and Commentary,* ed. Gonsalva Wiegand (Saint Louis, MI, 1936).

[13] For a discussion of Fulbert's work, see Margot Fassler, 'Mary's Nativity, Fulbert of Chartres, and the Stirps Jesse: Liturgical Innovation circa 1000 and its Afterlife', *Speculum* 75 (2000), 389–434, at 402–22.

[14] On monastic and clerical sensibilities around the year 1000, see Rachel Fulton, *From Judgement to Passion: Devotion to Christ and the Virgin Mary, 800–1200* (New York, 2003).

core of the vision was Mary, who bore the God made flesh, the God who alone can save. Monks worked hard at self-examination, at penitential prayer, and summoned to their side the author, the maker of that God, she who could intercede and beg him to forgive. Prayers to Mary were painful offerings, created out of deep self-knowledge and abject regret. We see this in the prayer of Maurilius of Rouen (d. 1067):

> Sed quid ago, obscenitates meas referens auribus illibatis? Horresco, Domina, horresco, et arguente me conscientia, male nudus coram te erubesco.[15]

> But what am I doing, pouring my obscenities into your purest ears? I am appalled, lady, appalled, and my conscience argues against me, naked in front of you I blush terribly.

Mary's purity was a stark backdrop against which a vivid picture of sin as ugly and deforming was painted. This sense was conveyed in this very popular prayer, known in its earliest version from a Psalter of Moissac abbey, of 1075:

> O beatissima et sanctissima Virgo semper Maria, ecce asto maerens ante faciem pietatis tuae, et confundor nimis pro abominationibus peccatorum meorum quibus deformis factus sum et horribilis angelis et omnibus sanctis.[16]

> O blessed and most saintly Mary, always Virgin, I am thus afflicted in face of your goodness, I am greatly confused by the abominations of my sins which have made me deformed and horrible in the eyes of angels and all saints.

The supplicant turns to Mary, and recounts her glories; she was, after all, born to bear a Redeemer:

> Tu enim nosti, misericordissima Regina, quia ad hoc nata es ut per te nasceretur idem Deus et homo, Dominus noster Ihesus Christus, uerus Deus et uerus homo, in quem ueracissime credo.[17]

> You know, most merciful queen, that you were born so that of you

---

[15] *Anima mea: prières privées et textes de dévotion du Moyen Âge latin; Autour des Prières ou Méditations attribuées à saint Anselme de Cantorbéry (XIe–XIIe siècle)*, ed. and French trans. Jean-François Cottier (Turnhout, 2001), 114, lines 7–9. English translations are my own.

[16] Ibid., 230, lines 1–3.

[17] Ibid., lines 12–14.

would be born he who is God and Man, Our Lord Jesus Christ, true God and true Man, in whom I most truly believe.

* * *

The eleventh and twelfth centuries saw the making of many of the frames of discipline and scrutiny, legislation and correction associated with medieval Christianity. The period saw the construction of a clear bureaucratic structure that reached each and every person through the provision of sacraments that were administered by priests alone, and which marked progression through the life cycle. To the sacraments were attached moments of discipline around which instruction was provided and penance required. Here was a domain of mediation, by priests, by men, by those who knew Latin (even to a small degree). Mary features little in the efforts and formulations of this structure, and yet she is taken as a given, as omnipresent. The *Ave Maria* was taught and used as a token in spiritual exchange; images of Mary adorned churches, and many features of monastic and cathedral practice – liturgy, miracles, chant, processions – were absorbed into larger churches, and even in rural ones. So while councils and synods, bishops and archdeacons, composers of penitentials and canon lawyers constructed the *societas Christiana*, they actually dealt little with Mary, but could assume her presence in civil society as well as in the hearth and home.

Mary did not tax the minds of theologians greatly, but she challenged the gifts of devotional writers. She was not taught in detail in catechism, but was approached through prayer. The stories of her life strained credulity, so they inspired much suggestion but little discourse. Mary's realm was that of narrative – miracle or history – sometimes violent, always familiar and always offering resolution. By 1140 a powerful collection emerged, in Bury St Edmunds, of well-established miracles of Mary. Few Christians were ever tried, tortured or burnt on account of comments about Mary; this was more likely to happen to converted Jews. Certain discussions raised sensibilities and could occasionally generate localized violence, but above all Marian discourse was cast in a multitude of niches of habitual practice, repetitive prayer. Mary was part of the *habitus* of Christian life, more regularly than she was of Church ideology. Here is the conundrum: why was the Marian sphere left alone by the architects of medieval Christian doctrine? Was it too private to penetrate? Or was it too trivial? In the absence of rifts calling for discipline, but in the presence of ubiquity and variety, let us turn to a few instances of unusually dense comment upon ideas and practices touching Mary.

Immaculate Conception

The closest we get to a theological debate about Mary is the discussion of the Immaculate Conception in the later centuries of the Middle Ages. Mary's intimacy with Christ required, according to some, and even as early as the fifth century, a unique order of purity. Thus it followed logically that Mary was born free of Original Sin, without concupiscence, the vehicle of sin. An English monk and disciple of Anselm, Eadmer (?1064–?1124) elaborated this view in his *De conceptione sanctae Mariae*. The occasion for reflection was liturgical: the re-introduction of the Anglo-Saxon feast of the Conception of Mary. Eadmer's argument was simple: God had chosen to honour Mary, and what he wished to do, he did.

> Voluit enim te fieri matrem suam, et quia voluit, fecit esse.[18]

> He wanted you indeed to be his mother, and because he wanted it, he made it happen

Among the opponents of the Immaculate Conception was the great poet of Mary's praise, Bernard of Clairvaux (1091–1153). He objected to the practice of celebrating the feast of Mary's Conception by the canons of Laon Cathedral. In a famous letter of 1139 he argued that he did not doubt that she had never sinned, but he could not accept that her generation in a natural way failed to transmit original sin through the sexual act. At issue were tradition and authority:

> The royal Virgin has in more than abundant measure titles to honor, true marks of dignity. What need, then, for false claims? Honor her for the integrity of her flesh, the holiness of her life. Marvel at her virginal fecundity . . . Proclaim her as reverenced by angels, desired by nations, foretold by patriarchs and prophets, chosen from among all, preferred to all. Aught else I should scruple to admit . . .[19]

---

[18] *Tractatus de conceptione sanctae Mariae*, ed. Herbert Thurston and Thomas Slater (Freiburg-in-Breisgau, 1904), 11.

[19] *The Letters of St Bernard of Clairvaux*, trans. Bruno Scott James (London, 1953), letter no. 215, 289–93, at 289; for the Latin, see *Sancti Bernardi opera* VII, ed. Jean Leclercq and H. Rochais (Rome, 1974), 388–92.

According to Bernard Mary received a special dose of grace at her conception to erase the Original Sin, and this in itself was a mark of distinction, of sanctification.

Bernard's homilies on Mary extol the purity of her life, but this reflection is carefully balanced within a larger frame of reflection on the Incarnation and the promise of redemption. As a mystical thinker, he was attracted by the possibilities offered by the Song of Songs, [20] but he did not explore the book through the Marian route marked by Rupert of Deutz a little earlier in the century.[21] Bernard's Song of Songs was, as it had been for Origen eight hundred years earlier, a discourse in which the bride is the human soul, seeking her lover – God. His choice, as developed in eighty-six sermons written in the last eighteen years of his life, affected generations of Cistercian writers. The Bible was a treasure-trove of gems, fitting illuminations of Mary's place in salvation history. Mary's praises were elaborated as part of the quest for union with God, through penance, contemplation and the working of grace.

Mary and Trinity

Elaboration of Mary's purity and uniqueness was expressed in a whole series of related images and ideas: Mary's special death-dormition, her coronation in heaven. Mary's imperial makers explored those qualities that would be appreciated a millennium later by the Christian emperors of the fifteenth century, and which aligned Mary and sacred governance. The Teutonic Order named its castles in Prussia and Livonia after Mary: Marienwerder, Frauenberg, Marienburg.[22] The churches they founded in conquered and newly Christianized lands often sported triumphant statues of Mary within which were enfolded Father, Son and Holy Ghost. This was an elaboration of the idea of the all-encompassing Mary, like the *vierge ouvrante*, which was also used as a Eucharistic vessel. When opened, these figures revealed God the Father

---

[20] *On the Song of Songs*, trans. Kilian Walsh and Irene M. Edwards, Cistercian Fathers Series 31 (Kalamazoo, 1979); for the Latin, see *Sancti Bernardi opera* I–II, ed. J. Leclercq, C. H. Talbot, and H. M. Rochais (Rome, 1957).

[21] *Commentaria in Canticum canticorum*, ed. and trans. Helmut Deutz and Ilse Deutz, Fontes Christiani 70, 2 vols (Turnhout, 2005).

[22] Eric Christiansen, *The Northern Crusades* (2nd edn, Harmondsworth, 1997), 221.

holding the crucifix, while either side showed exalted people painted against a gold background, as if under Mary's wings.[23]

This absorption of the Trinity into Mary, or the creation of something new – a quaternity? – delighted the creative minds of poets too, again mostly in the German language. Mary could be a fourth part, like the fourth light imagined by the fourteenth-century poet Konard of Würzburg.[24] More commonly the dialectic of three-one is preserved. The poet Frauenlob (d.1318) in his poetic commentary on the Song of Songs imagined the Trinity as three lovers sleeping with Mary, or Mary as the throne of the Godhead.[25] These attempts express a fascination with the problem of Mary's relevance to the all-important symbols of Christian faith. They also reflect a sheer desire to see her everywhere.

The alignment of the Trinity within Mary's body was a rich late medieval symbolic possibility, yet its very overabundance was troubling. Jean Gerson ((1363–1429) d. 1429) found images with the Trinity in Mary's womb to be troubling. He expostulates against them in a Christmas sermon, which celebrates Mary's virginity:

> Je le dy en partie pour une ymaige qui est aux Carmes et semblables qui ont dedans leur ventre une Trinité comme se toute la Trinité eus prins cher humainne en la Vierge Marie. Et qui plus merveille est, il y a enfer dedans paint. Et ne vois pas pour quelle chose on le mire ainsy, car a mon petit jugement il n'y a beauté ne devocion en telle ouverture, et puet estre cause d'erreur et d'indevocion.[26]

> I say it in part about an image in the Carmelite church and about others which have a Trinity in the womb, as if the whole Trinity had taken flesh in the Virgin Mary . . . And I do not see why it should be put that way, because in my humble opinion there is

---

[23] For an example from late fourteenth-century Paris, see *Musée national du Moyen Age* (Paris, 2003), 58, plate 71.

[24] *Die Sammlung von Meisterliedern in der Heidelberger Handschrift cpg 680: Edition und Kommentar*, ed. Elisabeth Wunderle (Göppingen, 1993), no. 22.

[25] For Frauenlob, see Barbara Newman, *Frauenlob's Song of Songs: a Medieval German Poet and His Masterpiece* (University Park, PA, 2006), 23, 25, 188–97.

[26] Jean Gerson, *Oeuvre complètes* VII, ed. Palémon Glorieux (Paris, 1968), no. 385, 948–67, at 963. On the critique of Trintarian image making, see Robert Mills, 'Jesus as Monster', in Bettina Bildhauer and Robert Mills, eds, *The Monstrous Middle Ages* (Cardiff, 2003), 28–54, at 45–6.

neither beauty nor devotion in such an opening, and it can be cause of error and impiety.

Mary's pure body continued to be used as receptacle for precious things, as reliquary, especially in northern Europe. A silver gilt statue of Mary enthroned, with the Child in her lap, is a sumptuous gem-encrusted work, made for Osnabrück Cathedral in 1483.[27] Less sumptuous but equally elegant is a gilt silver statuette of Mary and Child, where the child holds the transparent (now reproduction) container of a relic of the umbilical cord that had fed him in his mother's womb.[28] Erect Mary and Child statues served as reliquaries, equally sumptuous, like the gilt silver statuette of the Church of St Martin, in Emmerich (Lower Rhine) of c. 1480.[29] Even when a reliquary contained remains from several saints – each separately packed and labelled – the image of Mary and Child offered focus and cohesion, as in the reliquary at Krakow Cathedral dated c. 1450–60.[30] Reliquary or Eucharistic vessel, by the later Middle Ages many believed that the whole Christian story could be enfolded in material representations of Mary's pure body.

The emergence of the alternative spheres in which Mary was queen, majestic, dominant, bejewelled, surrounded by angels – Mary away from home and hearth – turned her into an object *de luxe*. Within these spaces some of the most challenging images of Mary occurred; Mary removed from the propriety of home, village, and parish church. An extreme case is offered by the right wing of a diptych, the Virgin and Child Surrounded by Angels, by Jean Fouquet (c. 1420–c. 1480) of Tours; the second wing shows Etienne Chevalier with St Peter Martyr.[31] This is a most fashionable Mary, with a high (shaven) forehead, smooth skin, dainty veil, sumptuous crown, tight bodice, and bulging bare left breast. Although her eye is downcast the whole effect is courtly, celestial, otherworldly. What devotional message could this have elicited from viewers?

---

[27] Henk van Os, *The Way to Heaven: Relic Veneration in the Middle Ages* (Amsterdam, 2000), 123–4 and colour image on 125.

[28] *Musée national du moyen age*, 106–7; also van Os, *Way to Heaven*, 40 and image on 39.

[29] Van Os, *Way to Heaven*, 129, figure 156.

[30] *The Treasures of the Cracow Monasteries*, ed. Janusz Tadeusz Nowak and Witold Turdza (Cracow, 2000), 29.

[31] Antwerp Koninklijk Museum voor Schone Kunsten c. 1450; and second wing in Berlin Staatliche Museen.

Rosary

At the same time as Mary was being depicted with jewels and crowns, the most popular and enduring eruption of Mary into devotional life was under way. Men and women in urban churches, those who flocked to confraternities and purchased mass-produced cheap devotional prints and alabaster carvings, were offered something new: the rosary, the quintessential aid for Marian prayer. Like so many of the practices around Mary this too resulted from a creative cultural translation from the world of the monastery to that of the layperson's home. The mediators were engaged groups of religious – Carthusians and Dominicans. Sequences of Ave Marias were a well-established routine for personal prayer, favoured by many and open even to the least literate. Marian psalters were formulated for the use of religious. They often adhered to the number 150 (like the number of psalms) in stanzas of Marian meditation, each opening with Ave Maria.[32] The collective chanting of the *Salve regina* was adopted by some Italian confraternities. Yet the new type of prayer – the Rosary – was patterned in an exciting way: it linked the Ave Maria prayer with the Pater Noster, and both to meditations on the Passion.

The Rosary was a discipline of prayer made out of familiar materials and themes central to late medieval Christian life. It spawned a whole series of artefacts: woodcuts, beads, prayer books, narrative booklets. One early proto-rosary, of around 1300, was a life of Christ cum rosary for the use of Cistercian nuns of St Thomas of Kyll, in the diocese of Trier. Over the next one hundred years several versions of vernacular 'rosaries' were written, psalters of Mary's names, strings of praise. One example is titled 'rôsenkrenzlein' – a little garland of roses. The Latin salutation has been dropped in favour of the German 'a. ma'ya roze ane dorn' or 'Ave. du sunne clar'.[33]

A devotion designed for religious women, in German speaking areas, formed the basis for the late medieval rosary conceived by a Carthusian monk, Dominic of Prussia (1384–1460), of the Charterhouse of Trier. While he claimed to be the inventor of the rosary, he confessed having been influenced by a vision of the mystic Mechthild of Hackeborn

[32] Anne Winston, 'Tracing the Origins of the Rosary: German Vernacular Texts', *Speculum* 68 (1993), 619–36, at 624–5.
[33] Joseph Klapper, 'Mitteldeutsche Texte aus Breslauer Handschriften', *Zeitschrift für deutsche Philologie* 48 (1918), 83–98, esp. 83–7; cited 83, 85.

223

(1241–99).[34] The power of the rosary was in combining Marian prayer with the contemplation of the Passion. The crucifixion had become the most dramatic moment of Mary's life and a great deal of effort had been invested in these centuries in its vernacular representation in image and poetry. By the early fourteenth century a rhymed Marian psalter dedicated the last fifty invocations to the life of Christ.[35] While Mary was invading the space of the Passion, Marian psalters, often made for the use of women, introduced Jesus into prayerful meditations on Mary's life. In Dominic of Prussia's rosary Mary and Jesus's lives are intertwined.[36] This monastic devotion, which spread very quickly to other Charterhouses throughout Europe, marked the shape of things to come, for laypeople too.

It took a Dominican, Alan of Rupa (1428–75), to mediate the new devotion to large groups of lay people. He introduced it by founding a confraternity in the city of Douai around 1468. Members were required to recite the rosary/psalter daily. He provided instruction in prayer as well as edifying *exampla*, short instructive tales about the power of the rosary. Other Dominicans followed his lead and in 1474/5 Jakob Sprenger founded a rosary confraternity in the city that epitomized Dominican learning: Cologne. The fraternity grew quickly, as it only required the weekly recitation of the rosary; it benefitted from the pleasing approval of the Dominicans, later of popes, and a series of useful indulgences. In 1485 confraternities were founded in Antwerp and Colmar, three years later in Lyons. The Colmar confraternity revised Alan of Rupa's model. The obligation was for a sole weekly recitation of the rosary: each ten Ave Marias were followed by a Paternoster and linked to a mediation of the Passion:

> Und dar noch X ave maria zů lob unser lieben frowen als sy von dem engel Gabriel den grůss enpfieng. Dar noch sprich das erste Pater noster dem liden Christi das er enpfieng an dem olberg do er schwitzet blůtigen sweiss.[37]

---

[34] Winston, 'Tracing the Origins of the Rosary', 622.

[35] Ibid., 625–7. For more details about precedents to the rosary, see Anne Winston-Allen, *Stories of the Rose: the Making of the Rosary in the Middle Ages* (University Park, PA, 1997), ch. 1.

[36] Winston, 'Tracing the Origins of the Rosary', 627–31.

[37] Jean-Claude Schmitt, 'La confrérie du rosaire de Colmar (1485): textes de fondation, "exempla" en allemande d'Alain de la Roche, listes des prêcheurs et des sœurs dominicaines', *Archivum fratrum praedicatorum* 40 (1970), 97–124, at 106.

And then two more Ave Marias in praise of our beloved lady as she received the greeting from the angel Gabriel. Then again recite the first Pater Noster of Christ's suffering, which he received on the Mount of Olives where he sweated bloody sweat.

The rosary resulted from a strategic combination of the simplest Marian prayer with mind-images of Christ's life, above all the crucifixion. Those who worried about the Marianization of devotional life found balance in it; those who wished to acknowledge Mary's place at the crucifixion as co-sufferer, even co-redeemer, were similarly satisfied. Jakob Sprenger, founder of the Cologne fraternity, was, after all, a true expert on ortho-doxy; he was associated with the publication of the *Hammer of Witches* (*Malleus maleficarum*), the handbook for inquisitors in the identification of error. The rosary similarly disciplined the 'feminine' Mary worship with the contours of meditation on Christ's suffering.

The rosary spread through the foundation of confraternities and through the circulation of prints. Rosary woodcuts travelled with the promise of salvation, indulgences were related to their use as aids in rosary prayer. Erhard Schön (c. 1491–1542) of Nuremberg created in 1515 a woodcut which was subsequently hand-painted – the Great Rosary. At the centre was Christ on the Cross, surrounded by a garland (chaplet) of fifty roses, a third of the whole rosary; between each group of ten roses there was a medallion marked by a cross, a prompt for contemplation of the crucifixion. The circle was full of figures of saints and martyrs and angels of every type. Below the chaplet, on earth, stood hopeful humans led by pope and emperor, and under them, below the crust of the earth, the suffering dwellers of hell. Over this busy, hectic Christian story the serene circle of roses was laid.[38] At the very bottom of the image the details of the indulgence for those who prayed the Crown of Roses were spelled out.

The plenitude and multitude that was the rosary tested existing conventions of representation. A house belonging to a branch of the Observant Franciscans, devoted to the legacy of Bernardino of Siena (1380–1444) – the Bernardines – commissioned a fascinating visual display. Around 1500 a panel entitled *The Crown of the Most Blessed Virgin* (*Corona beatissimae virginis*) was made for the Bernardine church of Wroclaw (it now hangs in the National Museum in Warsaw). At the foot of the image Mary and Child stand surrounded by the familiar rays

---

[38] For a colour reproduction, see James Clifton, ed., *The Body of Christ in the Art of Europe and New Spain 1150–1800* (Munich and New York, 1997), no. 65, 142–3.

of chastity and virtue, flanked by friars in prayers and obeisance. Two angels hold on to an enormous crown – some ten times the appropriate size of a crown. But this was no ordinary queenly ornament: it was an all-embracing crown adorned with seven layers of seven scenes, producing forty-nine medallions in all, representing:

Mary's seven joys
Mary's seven sorrows
The seven heavenly choirs (angels, apostles, martyrs, bishops, widows, virgins and saints)
The seven deadly sins
The seven virtues
The seven gifts of the Holy Spirit
The seven human groups protected by Mary: parents, clergy, laity, friars, the needy, sinners and the dead.

The elaborate scheme was a visual rendering of some of the numerical patterns of a rosary tract by brother Wladislaw of Gielniow.[39] At 5 x 3.4 m² it could serve as an enticing object for the friars' prayers, but also as a pastoral tool: for the illustrated rows of vices and virtues were the stuff of pastoral care and catechism, just as the joys and sorrows of Mary told the whole Christian story from Incarnation, through Passion and Resurrection.

* * *

The rosary reflects a desire to associate all areas of Christian experience with Mary, but it also exposes anxiety about the prominence of Mary in contemporary devotional practices. For it had become all but impossible to tell the Passion fully and movingly, without addressing Mary's pain; some could even tell the Passion through reference to Mary's pain alone.[40] Following the reform of the Cistercian nunnery at Weinhausen in Saxony in 1469, a devotional tract on the Crown of Thorns, *Dornenkron*, became the preferred devotional text, recommended to the nuns. Here was the telling of Christ's Passion, in its final, painful, bloody stages. Yet as this booklet was copied by nun-scribes it was

---

[39] On the image and this tract, see Katarzyna Zalewska, '*Corona beatissimae Virginis Mariae*: Das mittelalteriche gemalte Marientraktat aus der Bernhardinerkirche in Breslau', *Zeitschrift für Kunstgeschichte* 55 (1992), 57–65.

[40] James H. Marrow, *Passion Iconography in Northern European Art of the Late Middle Ages and Early Renaissance: a Study of the Transformation of Sacred Metaphor into Descriptive Narrative* (Courtrai, 1979).

moulded into a Marian experience too: its parts were punctuated by recitations of the *Ave Maria*; in another, convent nuns were instructed to recite the *Dornenkron* before an image of Mary.[41] Mary's relatives were invoked too; one author addressed Mary's own teacher, her mother Anne, in prayer. The pristine, reformed and impeccable meditation on the Crown of Thorns, on Christ's suffering on the Cross, was bedecked and elaborated with Marian prayers and salutations. Female copiers and users turned the meditation on Christ's bleeding head into a passionate encounter with his suffering mother. Perhaps the two were inseparable. The crucifixion seemed incomplete without Mary, and Mary was sufficiently compelling to make the crucifixion real.

It was this Marianization, this feminization of the culture, with Mary's stories, new feasts, the profusion of images, and repeated devotions that inspired the desire to reach a better balance. In the sixteenth century one of the meanings and imports of *sola scriptura* may have been the banishment of apocryphal stories that told Mary's life from the life of Christians, where they were so securely fixed.

* * *

If we ask why so little discipline surrounded Mary, why so little institutional effort was invested in patrolling the boundaries of beliefs about Mary, we may consider the opinion of the thirteenth-century Cistercian theologian Guy de l'Aumône. When writing about quodlibetal questions posed at the University of Paris this master claimed that theological questions of this type arose from perplexity – *perplexitas conscientiae* – when someone out there simply did not know what to do or how to act in securing the cure of souls.[42] Mary features in no such questions, for Mary did not perplex. The issues raised in quodlibets covered all areas of life – the just price, the duty of charity, marital relations, sex in its many forms. Above all, these were questions that expressed doubt, lack of clarity as to how best to lead a good life.[43] Mary

[41] June L. Mecham, 'Reading between the Lines: Compilation, Variation, and the Recovery of an Authentic Female Voice in the *Dornenkron* Prayer Books from Wienhausen', *Journal of Medieval History* 29 (2003), 109–28. I am grateful to Professor Mecham for enlightening conversations and exchanges on this most interesting text.

[42] Ian P. Wei, 'Guy de l'Aumône's *Summa de diversis questionibus theologie*', *Traditio* 46 (1988), 275–323, esp. 281. I am extremely grateful to Ian Wei for sharing with me so generously his erudition on quodlibetal questions and Paris theology in general, and for pointing me to the relevant bibliography.

[43] Leonard E. Boyle, 'The Quodlibets of St. Thomas and Pastoral Care', *The Thomist* 38 (1974), 232–56; Palémon Glorieux, *La littérature quodlibétique de 1 260 à 1 320*, 2 vols (Paris, 1925

seems to have raised no such doubt; knowing her was an experience made of liturgy and song, image and resounding miracle tale.

Yet if theological consideration displays a paucity of Marian *perplexitas*, in other spheres Mary is marked by superabundance, by plenitude that truly stunned. Gautier de Coinci (c. 1177–1236), who familiarized Mary to French knights and ladies, saw Mary as inexhaustible. While the poet's knowledge may be finite, Mary is not:

Ma povre sc̈ience espuisier	My poor knowledge I can very soon
Et essorber assez tost puis	Exhaust and extinguish
Se j'en son parfont puis ne puis	If I do not dip in her deep well,
Qu'espuisier ne puet nus puisieres,	that no well-digger can exhaust no matter how well the well-
Tant soit espuisans espuisieres:	digger draws:
C'est mers c'onques nus n'espuisa.	It is a sea that no one ever exhausted.
Veez son nom: M et puis A,	See her name: M and then A,
R et puis I, puis A et puis	R and then I, then A, and then
Mers troverés, ne mie puis:	a sea you will find, not a well at
Marie es mers que nus n'espuise;	all; Mary is the sea that no one exhausts;
Plus i treuve eui plus i puise (I Pr 1, lines 40–50).	The more one draws from it the more he finds.[44]

The ever-eloquent Dante expressed this in his canto 31 of the *Divine Comedy*:

E s'io avessi in dir tanta divizia	And if I had as much wealth in words
Quanta ad immaginar, non ardirei	As in imagining, I would not dare,
Lo minimo tentar di sua delizia[45] (136–8).	to attempt even the least of her delights.

From earliest times a mode of addressing Mary was through strings of appellations full of praise, in strings of associations, not dialectical

and 1935); Palémon Glorieux, 'L'enseignement au moyen âge: techniques et méthodes en usage à la faculté de théologie de Paris au xiiie siècle', *Archives d'histoire doctrinale et littéraire du moyen âge* 35 (1968), 65–186, at 128–34

44 Translation, together with instructive comments, is offered in Michelle Belduc, 'The Poetics of Authorship and Vernacular Religious Devotion', in Susan Karrant Nunn, ed., *Varieties of Devotion in the Middle Ages and the Renaissance* (Turnhout, 2003), 125–43, at 131–5; citation from 133–4.

45 Dante Alighieri, *La divina commedia*, ed. Tommaso di Salvo, 3 vols (Bologna, 1987), 3: 594; English translation Dante Alighieri, *The Divine Comedy*, trans. C. H. Sisson (Oxford, 1993), 490.

parsing. The words of the Byzantine *Akathistos* hymn, a hymn of praise for Mary, saviour of Constantinople, was to be chanted by erect monks, diligently.[46] This continued to be a preferred mode, used by late medieval poets such as Guillaume de Deguileville (fl. 1330) and Geoffrey Chaucer (c. 1343–1400).

It was this abundant late medieval Mary, rejected by Erasmus and Luther alike, that was about to break loose upon the world: she led the crusade against the Turks, and headed the introduction of Christianity to the Americas and Africa. In the Congo as in Mexico and Peru the figure of Mary was creatively received by new Christians, whose Christianity revolved around Mary. It was here that we observe the seeds of discipline: friars in Mexico worried about the presence of figures of Mary in far-flung parishes served by indigenous Christian priests: they had not been reared at the mother's knee, their minds had not been habituated to the Mary of story and miracle, by a profusion of images in churches at street corners.[47] Fears of mis-possession and error – the like of which were rarely voiced by pastoral carers in old Europe – were more evident in the world where social life did not provide the local, vernacular, maternal context for a Mary of tale and song. Without that context Mary could seem alien, open to error and abuse, just as Jewish use of her had been imagined in old Europe. The comfort zone of ineluctable absorption did not so readily exist in the lands of conquest and disease, and here a more disciplining attitude to the possession and nurture of Marian images developed. A mirror is raised by this encounter to 1500 years of solace and ineffable possession of and through Mary, the Mother of God. And it portends another loss of comfort, a new zone of pain and disruption in Old Europe, as Mary became an issue for confrontation between her devotees and her vocal detractors. Mary's comfortable diversity was about to cede to violence and discipline among early modern Christians.

Queen Mary, University of London

---

[46] Leena Mari Peltomaa, *The Image of the Virgin Mary in the Akathistos Hymn* (Leiden, 2001), 21.

[47] David Brading, *Mexican Phoenix: Our Lady of Guadalupe; Image and Tradition 1531–2000* (Cambridge, 2001). A summary of Brading's argument is offered in 'Divine Idea and "Our Mother": Elite and Popular Understanding in the Cult of Our Lady of Guadalupe of Mexico', in K. Cooper and J. Gregory, eds, *Elite and Popular Religion*, SCH 42 (Woodbridge, 2006), 240–60.

THE DANGERS OF DIVERSITY:
HERESY AND AUTHORITY IN
THE 1405 CASE OF JOHN EDWARD

by IAN FORREST

W HEN John Edward of Brington in Northamptonshire
abjured heresy in the 'Greneyerd' of Norwich cathedral
close on Palm Sunday 1405, he was presented to the gathered crowds as a living example of the dangers of diversity in the Christian faith.[1] Because heresy was feared as a fundamental challenge to
doctrine, authority, and social harmony, the agents of Church and
crown went to great lengths in the period between 1382 and the Reformation to advertise its depravity and illegality. The anti-heresy message
was not, however, a simple one, and the judicial performances that
constitute the Church's propaganda campaign on this issue sometimes
used highly equivocal rhetoric and images.[2] In these performances
heresy was capable of being represented as a minority sectarian
problem, or one diffused throughout society. In truth it was both, and
so the anti-heresy message had to encompass much more nuance than
one might imagine. This essay focuses on the campaign against the
lollards in late medieval England, in particular John Edward's staged
abjuration, which is recorded in a letter sent by the presiding bishop,
Henry Despenser, to his archbishop, Thomas Arundel.[3] This certification presents a compelling *tableau vivant* encompassing the penitent, the
crowds, and the authorities of Church, crown, and city. In their efforts
to stage-manage the abjuration of heresy, however, these authorities
had not only to navigate the complexity of anti-heretical rhetoric and

---

[1] Edward is mentioned in A. Hudson, 'Lollardy: the English Heresy?', in idem, *Lollards and their Books* (London, 1985), 141–63, at 156; A. Hudson, *The premature Reformation: Wycliffite Texts and Lollard History* (Oxford, 1988), 291, 326.

[2] For studies of anti-heresy and inquisition, see A. Hudson, 'The Examination of Lollards', in idem, *Lollards and their Books*, 125–40; M. Aston, 'Bishops and Heresy: the Defence of the Faith', in idem, *Faith and Fire: Popular and Unpopular Religion, 1350–1600* (London, 1993), 73–94. My recent book *The Detection of Heresy in Late Medieval England* (Oxford, 2005), discusses anti-lollard rhetoric and legal practice, without going into the detail of the Edward case.

[3] London, Lambeth Palace Library, Register of Thomas Arundel, vol. i, fols 390r–v. To avoid repeating identical references, this MS will not be cited again in the notes.

present it to a large audience, but, perhaps more importantly, had to overcome considerable rancour and division within their own ranks, to present a unified front against the threat of heresy. For they had to show that there was a unity from which heretics were deviating. Edward's abjuration, therefore, offered an important opportunity to demonstrate repentance, and to invite the clergy and people of Norwich to consider the dangers posed by their own tendencies towards disunity.

The defeat of heresy was vital to the Church's perception of its own unity, and to society's sense of its own cohesion. It is unsurprising then that when a convicted heretic abjured, much would be made of his schism with the Church, his symbolic reconciliation, and the unity of his prosecutors as representatives of orthodoxy.[4] Leading the group of local potentates present at the abjuration were Despenser, who had been bishop of Norwich since 1370, and Thomas Erpingham, the most powerful layman in East Anglia in the early fifteenth century.[5] Joining them in the 'Greneyerd' were the cathedral prior Alexander Tottington, the archdeacon of Norwich John of Derlyngton, the mayor William Appleyard, two sheriffs, 'and other chief magnates'.[6] Also in attendance were four notaries, one of whom, John Fermer, was involved in the judicial proceedings, while the others, William Friseby, John Wade, and Hugh Bridham, acted as witnesses to the events.

The wider audience for Edward's abjuration consisted of a crowd gathered in the cathedral close composed of 'clergy and people assembled in no small number', and we must not forget that a report of the proceedings was also sent to Archbishop Arundel, who wanted to be kept abreast of what happened. The crowd, we are told, had gathered 'to hear the word of God there and then being proffered, expounded, or preached by that venerable and circumspect man, Master John of Derlyngton', but the implied popular appeal of his sermons is some-

---

[4] R. I. Moore, *The Formation of a Persecuting Society: Power and Deviance in Western Europe, 950–1250* (Oxford, 1987), famously argues that the prosecution of heresy had as much to do with the Church's perception of its own unity as it did with its perception of heretics as deviants. On publicity in the punishment of heretics, see B. H. Hamilton, *The Medieval Inquisition* (London, 1981), 55; F. Bethencourt, *L'Inquisition à l'époque moderne: Espagne, Italie, Portugal Xᵛᵉ–XIXᵉ siècle* (Paris, 1995), 249.

[5] There are good articles by Richard Davies (Despenser) and Simon Walker (Erpingham) in the *ODNB*.

[6] For Tottington, see J. Greatrex, *Biographical Register of the English Cathedral Priories of the Province of Canterbury c.1066–1540* (Oxford, 1997), 566; for Derlyngton, see A. B. Emden, *A Biographical Register of the University of Cambridge to 1500* (Cambridge, 1963), 185–6.

what undermined by the remark that Edward's abjuration 'had previously been announced' and that he appeared 'with the expectation of the assembled clergy and people'. There was clearly some fanfare and preparation for this public show of anti-heretical zeal, and the people of Norwich had had their appetites whetted in advance.

Edward had already been convicted when he appeared before the crowd, and his appearance for ceremonial judgement and abjuration was pure theatre. He had, it was said, preached and taught 'various heresies, errors, conclusions, and opinions repugnant and contrary to holy writ and the sacraments and determinations of the Church...in various parts of the diocese, without any proper authority'. He was made to stand in the open on a sort of stage erected for this purpose 'and listen to his heresies . . . read out in succession by Master John Fermer clearly and publicly in a loud voice . . . first in Latin and then in the mother tongue'. Edward had then to revoke his errors, responding likewise 'in a loud and intelligible voice' after each one was read out:

> I sey þat this article is fals and erronee and by fals informacion y held it; the wheche y, being beter enformed at this tyme by clerkes þat cunnyn more the lawe and the holy doctrine of god thanne y, renounce and aske foryeuenesse ther of and swere to these holi euangelies by me bodily touched þat fro þis tyme forward y shal it never prechin, techin, ne holdyn priueliche ne in apert.

This formulaic revocation was drafted in advance and Edward would either have read from it directly, or repeated after the notary. The cumulative force of these denunciations was meant to reinforce the depravity of his beliefs, and prevent anyone from confusing heresy with orthodoxy, thus drawing a line around correct belief and excising incorrect belief.

There were nine opinions that Edward had to revoke. They were: that laymen are able to preach without licence; that giving charity to the mendicant orders is a sin; that offerings should not be made for prayers for the dead; that confession to a priest is unnecessary; that any good man, even if illiterate, is a priest; that un-baptized infants may still be saved; that popes, prelates, and bishops cannot force anyone to swear on the Gospels; that bishops, priests, and laymen are equal in spiritual power if they live well; that no one is bound to respect an alien prelate. Many of these were opinions common to other lollards or Wycliffites, but hostility towards mendicants, debate about the validity of customary offerings, and concern for the souls of un-baptized infants were not confined to the heretical fringe. So while some of his opinions, particularly those on preaching, were well known to be signs of heresy, Edward's revocations may have drawn the boundaries of Christianity more starkly than the audience was used to.[7]

The extent of his deviance from the Church was reiterated in the formal abjuration that followed the revocation. In it he acknowledged sowing 'weeds' that were 'repugnant to the determinations and institutions of the Holy Church and condemned by law ... to the subversion of the catholic faith and the estate of the Church, in manifest danger to my soul and those of others, causing a pernicious example and scandal to many other people.' He then swore on the Gospels never to hold or preach heresy again, and expressed his desire to return to the bosom of the Church. By controlling his words throughout the performance, the Church was able to stamp its authority on the day's events. It is surely no accident that the penitent should be made to look so ridiculous as to assert the inability of prelates to force a man to swear on the Gospels, while he was doing exactly that. In moments of such self-mockery and humiliation, all penitent heretics became personifications of error and pride.[8]

If Edward epitomized the dangers of diversity, then what should we make of the show of unity put on by Despenser, Erpingham et al.? Is the community of the faithful from which Edward had deviated capable of definition in terms of the absence of diversity and its attendant dangers? The short answer is no. So great were the fissures separating Despenser from Erpingham, Despenser from the priory, and the citizens of Norwich from each other and almost everyone else, that little unity is in evidence anywhere. We would do well to see this document as an attempt by Despenser to *present* a united front in order to help *create* a united front. That all was not well in Norwich is indicated by the fact that our document is a certification sent by Despenser to Arundel at the latter's request, suggesting that the archbishop felt it necessary to supervise the activities of a suffragan ten years his senior.

There had been difficulties between Arundel and Despenser in the

---

[7] For legislation on preaching prior to 1405, see *Decretales Gregorii IX*, 5.7.13 (CIC 2: 787–8; Cambridge University Library, Ely Diocesan Registry, MS G/1/2, fols 41v–42r; London, Lambeth Palace Library, Register of William Courtenay, fol. 26r. For discussion, see H. L. Spencer, *English Preaching in the Late Middle Ages* (Oxford, 1993); Forrest, *Detection of Heresy*, 60–8.

[8] This theme is important in P. Strohm, *England's Empty Throne: Usurpation and the Language of Legitimation, 1399–1422* (New Haven, CT, 1998), 32–62.

past, but on the whole their relationship was pragmatic. Arundel wanted to keep an eye on someone he thought a loose cannon, but he recognized the older man's strengths too. The first occasion on which their paths crossed was in 1381, when rebels destroyed rolls from Arundel's Ely estates and disrupted the consistory court in Cambridge. Arundel was powerless and order was only restored when Despenser led an armed force into the diocese, beheading two ringleaders and hanging a third.[9] At this point Arundel was a supporter of Richard II, but by the time of the Edward trial he was loyal to the Lancastrian regime of Henry IV, and keen to encourage the new king's interest in defeating heresy. Despenser's attitude towards the Lancastrians was much less enthusiastic, a personal history whose importance leapt into the foreground during the staged unanimity of the 1405 trial. In 1383 his plan for a crusade against the Flemish supporters of Urban VI had been in competition before Parliament with the expedition to Spain proposed by Henry IV's father, John of Gaunt. Despenser's campaign attracted Parliament's support, but it did not go well, and on his return a possibly jealous Gaunt initiated impeachment proceedings, accusing him of squandering his finances and acting recklessly. The animosity between the two was not helped when in 1392 the bishop was impli-cated in the murder of one of Gaunt's leading East Anglian supporters, Edmund Clippesby. When Gaunt's son Henry made his bid for the throne in 1399 the bishop declared openly for Richard II and spent some time in prison, while his nephew, Thomas Despenser, was deprived of his earldom of Gloucester.[10]

Under the new regime, the bishop of Norwich had to deal with the Lancastrians whether he liked it or not, and, in particular, with their local representative, Thomas Erpingham, who was prominent in the tableau of the great and the good at the Edward trial. Both Despensers, Henry and Thomas, were involved in the 'Epiphany plot' in 1401, after which Erpingham, who was fast attracting royal patronage and displacing the bishop as the most powerful man in the region, began a second impeachment process against him.[11] Despenser was saved from

[9] M. Aston, *Thomas Arundel: a Study of Church Life in the Reign of Richard II* (Oxford, 1967), 139–40; Thomas Walsingham, *Historia Anglicana*, ed. H. T. Riley, RS, 2 vols (London, 1863–4), 2: 7–8.

[10] M. Aston, 'The Impeachment of Bishop Despenser', *BIHR* 38 (1965), 128–37, at 147; R. Allington-Smith, 'Not a Yorkist but Anti-Lancastrian: Henry Despenser, Bishop of Norwich, 1370–1406', *The Ricardian* 10: 124 (1994), 16–18.

[11] T. John, 'Sir Thomas Erpingham, East Anglian Society and the Dynastic Revolution of

disaster by the good sense of Arundel, who stepped in and orchestrated
a ritual kiss of peace between the bishop and Erpingham in Parliament.[12] This symbolic reconciliation has led some to argue that after
this date the two became firm friends, but it may indicate little more
than resignation to the new political landscape.[13] In 1403, for example,
Erpingham was one of the arbitrators in a long-running dispute
between Despenser and the burgesses of Lynn, who were complaining
about his neglect of the waterfront in their town.[14] Even if this
encounter were amicable, the seniority of the commoner Erpingham
over the noble Despenser must have been a dent to the latter's pride.

But Despenser was not simply an enemy to be crushed by Henry
IV,[15] since his attitude to disorder and dissent was wholly in tune with
that of the new king. Despenser had attracted a lot of Wycliffite criticism for his 1383 crusade, and he reciprocated in his prosecution of
William Sawtry in 1399, a trial that provided Arundel with the information on whose basis Sawtry would later be executed.[16] The chroni-
cler Walsingham, indeed, went so far as to say that Despenser was the
only bishop to have taken active steps against lollardy at the time.[17]
While an exaggeration, this assessment seems to have been shared at
court, since Despenser and Erpingham were commissioned to act
together against seditious preaching in the region in 1402.[18] In the years
after his reconciliation with Erpingham, Despenser clearly saw the
political value in being seen to work with the regime, and it is important for our analysis of the Edward trial that he found the suppression
of dissent a convenient outlet for this.[19]

1399', *Norfolk Archaeology* 35 (1970), 96–108, at 100; H. Castor, *The King, the Crown, and the Duchy of Lancaster: Public Authority and Private Power, 1399–1461* (Oxford, 2000), 64; *Calendar of the Patent Rolls Preserved in the Public Record Office* (HMSO, 1891–) [hereafter: *Patent Rolls*] *1399–1401*, 274; *Patent Rolls 1401–5*, 47.

12 *Rotuli Parliamentorum*, ed. J. Strachey, 6 vols (London, 1767–7), 3: 456–7.

13 K. Mourin, 'Norwich, Norfolk and Sir Thomas Erpingham', in A. Curry ed., *Agincourt 1415: Henry V, Sir Thomas Erpingham and the Triumph of the English Archers* (Stroud, 2000), 78–90, at 82.

14 *Patent Rolls 1401–5*, 67, 274; A. Goodman, *Margery Kempe and her World* (Edinburgh, 2002), 29.

15 John, 'Erpingham', 99.

16 *Concilia Magnae Britanniae et Hiberniae*, ed. D. Wilkins, 4 vols (London, 1737), 3: 256; Strohm, *England's Empty Throne*, 40–5.

17 Walsingham, *Historia Anglicana*, 2: 188–9

18 *Patent Rolls 1401–5*, 128; S. Walker, 'Rumour, Sedition and Popular Protest in the Reign of Henry IV', *P&P* 166 (2000), 59–62.

19 P. McNiven, *Heresy and Politics in the Reign of Henry IV: the Burning of John Badby* (Woodbridge, 1987), 81–6.

As a political bishop, and a heresy-hunting bishop, Despenser may have been content to work with the Lancastrian regime, but, having got him out of trouble four years earlier, Archbishop Arundel still wanted to keep an eye on him. But there were other fissures in the body politic of East Anglian society that concerned the archbishop as well. Despenser found it much less easy to reach an accommodation with the priory of his cathedral church, with whom relations had been blighted for years by disputed rights of visitation. In 1393 Despenser had visited the priory, but the monks believed he had exceeded his rights in the area of monastic discipline.[20] Throughout the 1390s and early 1400s all the obedientiaries contributed funds to the ensuing litigation.[21] Boniface IX favoured the priory's claims and wrote to William Courtenay and John Trefnant in April 1395, reserving the case to the papal Curia. He also confirmed the judgement of Celestine III, inhibiting Despenser from dispossessing the monks, sending them away, restricting their movements, or promulgating sentences of excommunication, suspension, or interdict against them or their servants and clerks 'without manifest and reasonable cause'.[22] Despite papal involvement, the prior and chapter were forced to appear before king and council in 1396, where Richard II and Courtenay imposed a compromise settlement acknowledging that Despenser had some rights of visitation, but that he had overstepped these in 1393. Boniface was furious that his reservation of the case had been ignored and wrote to remind the archbishop (now Arundel) that any further action in England was unlawful.[23] However, when the papal settlement finally arrived in 1402 it confirmed everything in the royal compromise, although it rejected the crown's right to determine the case.[24] Disappointment on both sides caused the dispute to rumble on until 1411, when former prior Alexander Tottington's accession to the see made it easier for Arundel to enforce his judgement.[25]

[20] N. P. Tanner, *The Church in Late Medieval Norwich 1370–1532* (Toronto, 1984), 160; C. Harper-Bill, 'The Medieval Church and the Wider World', in I. Atherton, E. Fernie, C. Harper-Bill, and H. Smith, eds, *Norwich Cathedral: Church, City and Diocese* (London, 1996), 281–313, at 297–8.
[21] Greatrex, *Biographical Register*, 470.
[22] *Calendar of Entries in the Papal Registers Relating to Great Britain and Ireland: Papal Letters* (HMSO, 1893–) [hereafter: *Papal Letters*] *1362–1404*, 518, 525.
[23] *Papal Letters 1396–1404*, 11–12, 273–4, 318–19.
[24] Ibid., 526–7, 586–7.
[25] Greatrex, *Biographical Register*, 470.

Continuing disharmony in Norwich was another reason why Arundel should be so keen to monitor co-operation between bishop and priory, and reassure himself that the danger of a heretical preacher was met with a united front. But the enthusiasm of this united front, in particular from the people of Norwich, cannot be taken for granted. Given the presence of the mayor and sheriffs of the city, it may be that some coercion was involved in the crowd's mobilization. In addition, there was such disunity in the civic body that their presence as the symbolic 'community of the faithful' must be seen both as an attempt to set the archbishop's mind at rest, and to forge some sort of civic unity from the allegorical fires of heresy.

Civic politics in early fifteenth-century Norwich revolved around the city's elevation to county status by charter in 1404. This meant the replacement of four bailiffs with two sheriffs and a mayor, but the election of William Appleyard as the first mayor alienated a body of citizens calling themselves 'the twenty-four' or the 'prudeshommes', who had had the office of bailiff to themselves since about 1380. Appleyard had been elected by the wider urban community, but the strong-arm tactics of 'la bachelry' (muscle hired by the twenty-four) eventually ensured that their man, Walter Daniel, was installed in his place in 1406. Appleyard may have been a popular choice, but his election had split the citizens.[26] Tellingly, Despenser was not among the five bishops and six lords who had witnessed the charter, whereas Erpingham had been instrumental in securing it from the king.[27] The citizens had been further disappointed by the ambiguity with which the word 'comunaltee' was deployed in the charter, suggesting that 'every person of the smallest reputation in the city has as much authority and power in all elections and other business as the city's more sufficient persons.'[28] They were also aggrieved about another blunder, which appeared to give them extended suburban jurisdiction, rights which were quickly denied.[29]

There was, then, considerable ill-will in Norwich around the time of

[26] *The Records of the City of Norwich*, ed. W. Hudson and J. C. Tingey, 2 vols (Norwich, 1906), 2: 31–3; B. R. McRee, 'Peacemaking and its Limits in Late Medieval Norwich', *EHR* 109 (1994), 831–66, at 847–50.

[27] *Records of the City of Norwich*, 1: 66, 2: 54; *Calendar of the Close Rolls Preserved in the Public Record Office: Henry IV*, 5 vols (HMSO, 1927–38), 2: 245; John, 'Erpingham', 101.

[28] *Records of the City of Norwich*, 1: 81–2.

[29] McRee, 'Peacemaking', 851; L. Attreed, 'Urban Identity in Medieval English Towns', *Journal of Interdisciplinary History* 32 (2002), 571–93, at 582.

Edward's abjuration, perhaps even the potential for violence between rival factions. All interested parties were at odds with one another. Despenser very likely resented the patronage of Erpingham being preferred to his own, while Erpingham was not popular with the twenty-four. The priory had been the main victim of the jurisdictional encroachment into the suburbs, while royal pastures and meadows had actually been annexed by acquisitive citizens in 1403. The citizens meanwhile objected to the priory's annual fair and court, which was held on city rather than cathedral land.[30] Clearly some unity was much needed in 1405, even if this could only be achieved under Arundel's watchful eye. If the Palm Sunday message preached by Derlyngton was to be that heresy represented dangerous diversity, then it was perhaps equally intended to highlight the dangers of political diversity amongst the supposedly faithful community.

There was in addition a deeper message in the abjuration of a heretic, which made it more immediate for every person present. Edward's rejection of heresy was merely the prelude to his return to the Church. After he had abjured all heresy and sworn that 'I wish to stand, I do stand, and I will stand by the catholic determinations of the Holy Church', he pleaded 'because the bosom of the Church never closes to the penitent wishing to return to it, but rather opens wide, thereby I implore your most reverend paternity to receive me thus penitent to grace and mercy.' The threatening display of judicial coercion is here the vehicle for a more universal message of sin, repentance, grace, and mercy.

The salient reason for communicating mercy and reconciliation in circumstances normally associated with persecution was that heresy was a nebulous crime and difficult to pin down to an individual or group. Although we habitually see heretics as a 'sect' or a community, medieval canonists and theologians saw it as an expression of original sin, and a problem that the whole Church had to face together.[31] In this judicial drama as in many others that took place in the late Middle Ages, the greatest fear was not that the penitent would return to his or her heresy, but that it would spread and, like a disease, infect others.[32]

30 Patent Rolls 1401–5, 273; Tanner, Late Medieval Norwich, 144–5.
31 M. Aston, 'Were the Lollards a Sect?', in P. Biller and B. Dobson, eds, The Medieval Church: Universities, Heresy, and the Religious Life; Essays in Honour of Gordon Leff, SCH.S 11 (Woodbridge, 1999), 163–91; S. McSheffrey, 'Heresy, Orthodoxy and English Vernacular Religion 1480–1525', P&P 186 (2005), 47–80.
32 Forrest, Detection of Heresy, 143–58.

This is suggested in Edward's admission that he sowed weeds amongst the faithful that posed a danger to the souls of others. The hint of contagion here is no accident, since heresy was closely analogous with disease in the Middle Ages.[33] One component of contagion theory particularly relevant to heresy is the notion of susceptibility to certain diseases, a necessary precondition to their contraction.[34] In the same way, heresy was thought to be a result of outside infection (preaching or a text) activating the susceptibility that was concupiscence. Because it was an expression of lust and the will, heresy manifested itself in disobedience.[35] As the citizens of Norwich and the gathered authorities were told in 1405, it appeared from the heart like 'a rasping and ravenous wolf... fickle in the faith', igniting spiritual pride and leading to presumptuous opinions, for example on the equality of laymen with prelates.

Familiarity with the meaning of Palm Sunday would have helped reinforce the message, as the usual course of processions and liturgy could easily be augmented to remind people that triumphal entries (or prosecutions of heresy) can quickly turn to evil and the betrayal of Christ. It is surely significant that although on a scaffold, Edward stood 'in the midst of the clergy and people there gathered' as if to emphasize that his place might easily be theirs if they were not vigilant over themselves and one another. So in terms of anti-heresy activity at least, the commonalty's claim that 'every person of the smallest reputation' had a part to play in civic affairs, was vindicated. This participation, however, demanded repentance and humility on the part of all who wished to be considered part of the unity of the Church, whether mere citizen or one burdened with authority.

Diversity was not only to be found amongst convicted heretics, and discipline involved self-control as well as coercion. This essay has endeavoured to show just how nuanced these messages could be in a

---

[33] R. I. Moore, 'Heresy as Disease', in D. W. Lourdaux and D. Verhelst, eds, *The Concept of Heresy in the Middle Ages* (Louvain, 1976), 1–11; P. Ormerod and A. P. Roach, 'The Medieval Inquisition: Scale-Free Networks and the Suppression of Heresy', *Physica A* 339 (2004), 645–52.

[34] V. Nutton, 'The Seeds of Disease: an Explanation of Contagion and Infection from the Greeks to the Renaissance', *Medical History* 27 (1983), 1–34; *The Middle English Translation of Guy de Chauliac's Treatise on 'Apostemes'*, ed. B. Wallner (Lund, 1988), 152.

[35] C.24 q.3 c.27 (CIC I: 997–8); *Glossa ordinaria* to *Decretales Gregorii IX*, 5.7.9; Johannes Balbus, *Catholicon* (Lyon, 1492), v. *Heresis*; William of Pagula, *Summa summarum*, V. X. q.41 (Oxford, Bodleian Library, MS Bodley 293, fol. 178v).

situation where the heresy of an individual became the focus for much more generalized warnings about sin and Christian unity. Heresy was not primarily a danger because of the numbers of its adherents, but because it had the potential to arise anywhere, and because it was a mirror to disunity in the self and in the state. Arundel was worried about heresy when he demanded a report on the prosecution of John Edward in 1405, but he also worried about disunity in Church and state brought about by more secular concerns. We can also say that he was less interested in the fate of one man than in the possibility that heresy could spring up anywhere if not stamped out, and if occasions of it were not turned to the proclamation of Christian unity.

Oriel College, University of Oxford

DEFINING HERESIES:
CATHOLIC HERESIOLOGIES, 1520–50

by DAVID BAGCHI

F EW historians nowadays would endorse a simple causal connection between the Reformation and the rise of toleration. Indeed,
reformations Protestant and Catholic have become almost synonymous with 'confessionalization' and 'social disciplining'. Nonetheless,
the transition from the persecuting society of the Middle Ages to something approaching a pluralist society was an early modern phenomenon
which has attracted renewed attention in recent years.[1] This transition
was facilitated by the breakdown of the traditional understanding of
heresy. The role of Protestantism in de-stabilizing the heresy discourse
of mid-seventeenth century England has been expertly delineated by
Ann Hughes in her study of Thomas Edwards's *Gangraena* and the
responses to it.[2] But it would be a mistake to suppose that the Catholic
understanding of heresy was entirely stable during this period. As I
hope to show in this survey of Catholic heresiologies from the period
1520 to 1550, controversialists encountered difficulties when they tried
to conscript patristic and medieval heresy discourses into the
sixteenth-century conflict. An instability at the heart of the traditional
definition of heresy – over whether heresy is primarily a doctrinal error
or a moral failing – seemed at first to provide a solution to these

---

[1] Notable among recent studies, in addition to those mentioned elsewhere in these
notes, are John Christian Laursen, ed., *Histories of Heresy in Early Modern Europe: for, Against,
and Beyond Persecution and Toleration* (New York and Basingstoke, 2002), and Ian Hunter, J. C.
Laursen, and Cary J. Nederman, eds, *Heresy in Transition: Transforming Ideas of Heresy in Medieval and Early Modern Europe* (Aldershot, 2005). The essays in Nederman and Laursen, eds,
Difference and Dissent: Theories of Toleration in Medieval and Early Modern Europe (Lanham, MD,
1996) include examples of the way in which the 'history of heresy' genre was developed to
promote toleration of religious diversity, while Alexandra Walsham, *Charitable Hatred: Tolerance and Intolerance in England 1500–1700* (Manchester, 2006) amply refutes any notion that
persecution and toleration were binary opposites in the early-modern period. Francisca
Loetz's *Mit Gott handeln: von den Zürcher Gotteslästeren der frühen Neuzeit zu einer Kultur-
geschichte des Religiösen*, Veröffentlichungen des Max-Planck-Instituts für Geschichte 177
(Göttingen, 2002) sheds important light on the Reformed construction of heresy at official
and popular levels.
[2] Ann Hughes, *Gangraena and the Struggle for the English Revolution* (Oxford, 2004).

difficulties. Ultimately and ironically, however, it made their case vulnerable to a Protestant charge of subjectivism.

The controversialists' difficulties began in June 1520, when the bull *Exsurge Domine* was published. This condemned forty-one statements drawn from the writings of Martin Luther, but the validity of the condemnation was widely questioned, not only by Lutheran sympathizers but also by Roman loyalists – including members of the Roman *Curia* itself.[3] A treatise published by Cardinal Cajetan almost a year after the bull was designed to allay 'the alarm of certain outstanding persons' over the condemnation of five specific articles.[4] This alarm was evidently based on the fact that some of the condemned statements were supported variously by Scripture (article 28), the Fathers (article 7), papal teaching (article 17), or by the common understanding of the faith (articles 10 and 15). We do not know how wide or deep sympathy with this view was in the *Curia*, but it was clearly significant enough for the pope himself to have commissioned this defence from Cajetan. Outside Rome, opposition to *Exsurge Domine* was widespread even in traditionalist strongholds: Catholic polemicists reported disaffection from Paris, Louvain, Antwerp, and Bavaria; the staunchly anti-Lutheran Duke Georg of Saxony refused to publish the bull in his territories; and the university of Vienna issued a formal protest against it on legal grounds. The objections varied: some, it was reported, believed that the question of Luther's heresy could be decided only by a council; others were thought likely to harbour doubts unless clear reasons for the condemnation were forthcoming.[5]

Concerns about the validity of *Exsurge Domine* were therefore widespread. One answer, indicated by Catholic controversialists, was to publish a point-by-point defence of the bull. But, as Johann Eck pointed out even as he suggested this solution to the *Curia*, such a course carried the risk of inviting popular discussion and weakening

[3] H. Denzinger and A. Schönmetzer, eds, *Enchiridion Symbolorum Definitionum et Declarationum de Rebus Fidei et Morum* (36th edn, Barcelona, Freiburg im Breisgau, and Rome, 1976), 1451–92. Full text in G. Tomassetti et al., eds, *Bullarum, Diplomatum et Privilegiorum Romanum Pontificum Taurinensis editio*, 25 vols (Turin, 1857–72), 5: 750a.

[4] See Cajetan, *Opuscula omnia* (Turin, 1582), fols 184a–186a. English trans., 'The Five Articles of Luther: Justification for their Condemnation', in Jared Wicks, ed., *Cajetan Responds: a Reader in Reformation Controversy* (Washington, DC, 1978), 145–52.

[5] On the contested reception of *Exsurge Domine* and other formal condemnations of Luther, see David V. N. Bagchi, *Luther's Earliest Opponents: Catholic Controversialists, 1518–1525* (Minneapolis, MN, 1991), 179, 201–4, 252, and the sources cited there.

the authority of the original condemnation. There was however another solution that soon commended itself to Eck and to the Louvain theologian Jacques Masson ('Latomus'). If it could be demonstrated that Luther's teachings were identical with teachings that had already been condemned as heresy in the past, by properly constituted councils, his guilt could be proved without reference to the disputed bull. Indeed, as Latomus noted, Canon Law specifically provided that one who imitates old errors is already condemned.[6] Catholic writers thereupon set about demonstrating the identity of Lutheran teachings with old errors, and the heresy discourse of the Reformation period explicitly appropriated the heresy discourse of the patristic and medieval periods.

Two traditional genres were available for this purpose. The first was the *summa de haeresibus*, deriving ultimately from Augustine, which set out in an ordered way to answer questions about the nature and treatment of heresy: What is heresy? What are its origins and causes? What counts as evidence of heresy? Should heresy be punished, and how? The second available genre was the *catalogus haereticorum*, deriving ultimately from Hippolytus in the third century, which typically listed the names of all the heretics from the foundation of the Church, together with a note of the date at which they flourished and of their principal beliefs. There was, however, a good deal of overlap between the two genres: even Augustine's original *Summa de haeresibus ad Quodvultdeum* had listed past heretics and heresies, while writers of catalogues attempted to add value to their compilations by deducing generalizations about the nature of heresy.

The extent of overlap between the two genres is evident from the very first anti-heresy treatise systematically to relate Luther's teaching to that of the heresiarchs of old. The *Catalogus haereticorum* of the Dominican Bernard of Luxembourg was published in four books in Cologne in 1522.[7] The first book, however, is taken up with questions appropriate to a *summa*: what are the causes of heresy, why heretics should be avoided, why they should be punished, why those who support heretics – even if orthodox themselves – deserve to be put to death, and so on. Not until Books 2 and 3 does the advertised catalogue

---

[6] Latomus, *De quaestionum generibus* (1525) in idem, *Opera omnia* (Louvain, 1579), 88v–89r. The reference is to *Decretum Gratiani*, pars II, C.24 q.1 (CIC 1: 966).

[7] Bernard of Luxembourg, O. P., *Catalogus haereticorum omnium pene, qui a scriptoribus passim literis proditi sunt, nomina, errores, & tempora quibus vixerunt ostendens, a F. Bernardo Lutzenburgo sacrarum literarum professore quatuor libris conscriptus. Quorum quartus Lutheri negotium nonnihil attingit* [Cologne, 1522].

of heretics appear. The final book consists of a treatment of Luther, which places him firmly within the tradition of heresy just described. At the beginning of this last book, Bernard describes Luther as resurrecting the impure doctrines of the heretics of old, and towards the end cites Canon Law in relation to his support for the Hussite teaching: no new condemnation is needed, only the revival of old ones.[8] But Bernard has surprisingly little to say about the *papal* condemnation of Luther as a heretic. Catholic scholars who had written against him are individually named, the actions of Charles V are described in detail, and the edict of Worms is quoted at length. Where papal action is mentioned, in relation to the burning of Luther's books, it is however only as an adjunct to imperial actions. We can assume that Bernard's *Catalogus* was written to demonstrate the fact of Luther's heresy for the benefit of those Catholics who harboured doubts about the validity of *Exsurge Domine*.

A subtler way of associating new heretics with old was to reprint classic heresiological texts. So, in the 1520s, the list of heretics from Book 8 of Isidore of Seville's *Etymologiae* was published by the Strasbourg schoolmaster Hieronymus Gebweiler, and the anti-Cathar summarist Gui de Terrena de Perpignan was resurrected by the Parisian presses.[9] But these exercises had limited appeal. Gebweiler's intention seems to have been as much to provide his pupils with wholesome reading matter as to contribute to the defence of the faith, and Gui's work made such a small impact that it did not trouble the typesetters again until 1631.[10] In an age when the editing of ancient texts was big business, there seems to have been little call for out-of-date heresiologies, and perhaps no more than half-a-dozen appeared between the outbreak of the Reformation and the opening of Trent.[11]

---

[8] Ibid., l3r, m2r.

[9] Hieronymus Gebweiler, ed., *Contenta in hoc libello. Ysidorus de sectis et nominibus haereticorum. Divi augustini libellus aureus de fide & operibus. S. Hieronymi liber de perpetua gloriosae Virginis Mariae virginitate. Epistola eiusdem contra Vigilantium de venerandis sanctorum reliquiis* (Strasbourg, 1523); Gui [Terreni] de Perpignan, *Summa de haeresibus et earum confutationibus* (Paris, 1528).

[10] '[A]liqua ex diversis auctoribus lectu non iniucunda congessimus . . . sperantes & senibus & pueris horum lectione nonnihil profectus accessurum'. (Gebweiler, *Ysidorus*, Aiiii[r–v]). The second reprinting of Gui's work (optimistically described as 'diu desideratum, & nunc primum in Germania editum' in the publisher's title-page puff) was Cologne, 1631.

[11] The two already mentioned were the only 'Catholic' editions. A Lutheran, Janus Cornarius, edited Epiphanius's *Panarium* (Basel, 1542). Joannes Sichardus, a humanist associate of Philipp Melanchthon, compiled the patristic miscellany *Antidotum contra diversas*

The point they made was perhaps too subtle, their bearing on current affairs too indirect.

Although earlier catalogues such as Bernard's could hardly be described as slim volumes, the late 1520s and early 1530s saw the appearance of very substantial catalogues from the pens of the assorted Casaubons who had been labouring on them for a decade or more. Konrad Koch 'Wimpina' (the professor from Frankfurt-on-Oder last heard of defending the indulgence-seller Tetzel in early 1518) went to press in 1528 with his *Anacephalaeosis* 'of the sects, errors, wanderings, and schisms, from almost the beginning of the Christian Church until our own day, together with the confutations of some heresies of the Pickarts, Wycliffites, and Lutherans'.[12] Book 7 of volume one includes a detailed but by now very dated defence of *Exsurge Domine*: Wimpina clearly still felt that the pope's condemnation needed bolstering. In the early 1530s there appeared arguably the most important anti-heresy treatise of the Reformation era before Trent, Alfonso de Castro's fourteen books *Adversus omnes haereses*.[13] The Spanish Franciscan's work differed from earlier catalogues in many respects, most obviously in that it provided a list of themes rather than of heretics. If a priest found his parishioners exhibiting worrying tendencies regarding shoes, for example (in Book 4), or nudity (in Book 11), he could quickly locate the corresponding heresies, as he could for more obvious theological topics. Castro's immensely popular work was continuously in print throughout Western Europe for thirty years, until the closure of the Council of Trent.

The *catalogus* format continued to be used for many more years, either by Catholics in different contexts (as with Gabriel du Préau's *Elenchus alphabeticus* of 1569), or else subverted to a different end by Protestants (as with Flacius Illyricus's *Catalogus testium veritatis* of 1556).[14] But it was during the 1530s that the dangers inherent in the

---

haereses (Basel, 1528). Desiderius Erasmus edited Irenaeus's *Opus eruditissimum in quinque libros* (Basel, 1526, 1528, 1534, and Paris, 1545); but his preface, containing only the briefest allusion to current affairs, clearly flagged his edition as a work of scholarship, not Catholic polemic.

[12] Konrad Koch ('Wimpina'), *Sectarum, errorum, hallutinationum, & schismatum, ab origine ferme Christianae ecclesiae, ad haec usque nostra tempora, consisioris Anacephalaeoseos, Una cum aliquantis Pigardicarum, Vuiglefticarum, & Lutheranarum haeresum: confutationibus, librorum partes tres* (Frankfurt on Oder, 1528).

[13] Alfonso de Castro, OFM, *Adversus omnes haereses libri XIIII* (Paris, 1534). The references in this paper are to the Paris, 1541 edition.

[14] Gabriel du Préau, *De vitis, sectis, et dogmatibus omnium haereticorum, qui ab orbe condito, ad*

genre first became evident. Castro himself was particularly alert to these dangers, and unsparing of what he saw as the shortcomings of his predecessors. In the first place, he insisted, a catalogue needed to provide sufficient information. Bernard of Luxembourg was singled out as the duffer in this respect: 'I ask you, what use is it to know who the heretics of the past were, but not the grounds on which they were condemned?' The rest of the class hardly escaped Castro's scorn: 'It seems to me (and I say this without hatred or insult) that they would have acted more wisely had they expended their labours on exposing heresies rather than merely listing the names of heretics.'[15] Castro himself makes a point of providing arguments against each heresy, and of citing the council which condemned it.

In addition, the information such a catalogue contained needed to be accurate. This was especially important if the catalogue were to serve the quasi-judicial function of listing positions that had been declared heretical for all time. According to Castro, Gui de Perpignan was responsible for the worst howlers on this respect. He left out of his catalogue heretics he should have known about, living when and where he did: Peter Abelard, Amalric, and others. He also got his heresies mixed up, matching them to the wrong heretics and sometimes attributing to an heresiarch the exact opposite of his actual beliefs. '[Gui] often drifted from the point,' Castro tells us, 'listing many who should have been judged more favourably, such as Papias.'[16] He also included Muslims in his list of Christian heretics, much to Castro's annoyance.[17]

A third requirement of the catalogue approach was the need to establish some connection between past heresies and the contemporary position one intended to refute. Luther had already made this connection himself, when he had openly defended some of the condemned positions of Wycliffe and Huss. But, as Castro pointed out, older catalogues such as Gui's did not include these more recent heresies.[18] Even the more comprehensive catalogues were not ideal. For historical

---

nostra usque tempora, proditi sunt, elenchus alphabeticus (Cologne, 1569); Matthias Flacius Illyricus, Catalogus testium veritatis qui ante nostram aetatem reclamarunt papae (Basel, 1556). On the Protestant subversion of the genre, see esp. Euan Cameron, 'Medieval Heretics as Protestant Martyrs', in Diana Wood, ed., Martyrs and Martyrologies, SCH 30 (Oxford, 1993), 185–207.

15 Castro, Adversus haereses, 3r.
16 Ibid., 2v.
17 Ibid.
18 Ibid., 3r.

reasons, Arianism and Pelagianism almost always stood out as the defining heresies, but it was no straightforward matter to equate them with Lutheran teaching. One way of compensating for this weakness of the catalogue method was to stress the essential unity of all heresies. Each heresy tends to attack one aspect of the Christian faith, and be completely orthodox in other respects – the better to ensnare the unwary. But between them the Devil attempts to overthrow the faith as a whole. The fact that individual heresies are concerned with more or less important doctrines is therefore irrelevant – every heresy is as satanic in origin as any other. The point was made repeatedly by heresiologists,[19] but as an argument it begged the question: of itself, it did not prove that Protestants were heretics. Some other way of linking the new heretics and the old had to be found, one that was open to public verification.

In 1537, Georg Witzel published at Leipzig a pamphlet entitled *De moribus veterum haereticorum et quibus cum illi hac aetate affinitatem habeant.* Witzel had at first thrown in his lot with the evangelical cause, had become a Lutheran pastor, had married and had children. But then he converted back to Catholicism, disillusioned by the failure of the Reformation to produce the moral improvement it had promised. If anything, he believed, the lives of Protestants were worse than those of Catholics, and this is the theme of much of his polemic. The 1537 pamphlet was therefore in one sense simply a continuation of his polemical programme. But for him it also offered a solution to the failings of the *catalogus* approach. In his preface, he acknowledges that the traditional tactics have failed to hit home because Lutherans do not accept that they are heretics. They are not Arians, they say, because they do not deny the Trinity; nor are they Manichaeans, because they do not reject the Old Testament; nor are they Nestorians, because they do not deny that Mary is *theotokos.*[20] But if Protestants could be shown to *behave* in the same way as past heretics, there was no need to establish a doctrinal identity between them for 'similitude of spirit and of morals everywhere carries great force'.[21] Freed from the necessity of making a doctrinal case, Witzel was able to associate Protestants with the most

---

[19]   On the essential (diabolical) unity which the summarists saw as underlying the many disagreements between heretics, see D. V. N. Bagchi, 'Tyndale, More, and the Anatomy of Heresy', *Reformation* 2 (1997), 261–81, esp. 274–5.

[20]   *De moribus haereticorum*, Av^{r-v}.

[21]   'Similitudo ingenij ac morum magnam ubique vim habet' (ibid., Avi^v).

infamous heresies, spending twenty-two pages on a comparison with Arianism, twenty-three on Manichaeism, and nine on Islam (seen here, as often in medieval heresiology, as a Christian heresy).[22] Like the Arians, Lutherans promote their doctrines through song;[23] like the opponents of the homoousion, they reject anything they cannot find in Scripture;[24] like the Donatists, they claim the title of martyr for those justly put to death;[25] like the Novatianists they lack charity, the mark of the true Christian;[26] and like Paul of Samosata they deliberately court public opinion.[27]

It must be admitted that many of Witzel's parallels are surprisingly weak, given his inside knowledge of Lutheran practice. One of his more desperate efforts is the connection he sees between Arius and Martin Luther at the level of their names (Ares and Mars), which he gives up in embarrassment.[28] But despite these weaknesses in execution, Witzel in fact had a strong case for regarding heresy as moral depravation rather than intellectual deprivation. St Augustine had famously defined the heretic as one who 'for the sake of worldly gain, and especially for glory and dominion, either creates or follows false and new opinions'.[29] For Augustine, heresy was a moral crime before it was an intellectual one, arising from inordinate love of self, and more specifically was a species of the sin of pride.[30] During the Middle Ages, Augustine's moral definition came to eclipse Jerome's more strictly intellectual definition, so that it was the presence of a moral failing, obstinacy, that turned common error into heretical pravity. All the summarists attempted to identify the cause or causes of heresy, which were moral rather than intellectual: self-love, vainglory, and arrogance; avarice, gluttony, and lust; contentiousness, misplaced zeal, and disobedience towards higher clergy – or all of these in varying proportions.[31]

---

[22] Ibid., Avii^r–Ci^v (on Arianism), Cviii^r–Eiii^r (on Mani, Faustus, and other Manichees), Giv^v–Gviii^v (on Islam).

[23] Ibid., Biv^v, Civ^v.

[24] Ibid., Bvi^v.

[25] Ibid., Biv^v.

[26] Ibid., Giii^r.

[27] Ibid., Ciii^r.

[28] Ibid., Aviii^v.

[29] Augustine, *De utilitate credendi*, ch. 1 (PL 42, 65–92, at 65).

[30] 'Sed una mater superbia omnes [haereticos] genuit; sicut una mater nostra Catholica omnes Christianos fideles toto orbe diffusos' (Augustine, *Sermo* 46, ch. 8 [PL 38, 270–95, at 280]); 'Superbia, mater omnium haereticorum' (idem, *Contra epistolam Manichaei*, ch. 6 [PL 42, 173–206, at 177]).

[31] Especially comprehensive lists of the intrinsic and extrinsic causes of heresy are given

Witzel's moral understanding of heresy was therefore simply the development of an already strong tendency in the heresiological tradition. But his *De moribus haereticorum* marked the beginning of a new stage in that tradition. From the 1540s, the moral depravity of heretics became a dominant theme of the anti-heresy treatise. It is evident in Ambrosius Catharinus's *Speculum haereticorum* of 1540, a long meditation on the text 'By their fruits shall you know them'. The fifth chapter, or *consideratio*, in particular, is a sort of compendium of all the moral causes and effects of heresy alleged by the heresiological tradition: lust, malice, strife, self-love, arrogance, contumely, inconstancy.[32] It is evident also in the great works of Konrad Brunus that appeared in Germany at the end of the decade.[33] Book 1 of his *Libri sex de haereticis in genere* is essentially a re-working of Book 1 of Castro, but with interpolated chapters whose titles echo Witzel's themes: 'de vita et moribus haereticorum' (chapter 7) and 'de moribus haereticorum, ad doctrinam spectantibus' (chapter 8). At the very end of our period comes the similarly themed *Fructus quibus dignoscuntur Haeretici* of Johann Fabri of Heilbronn.[34] Here Fabri attempts to hold the line on the definition of heresy as primarily an intellectual crime. But, with Witzel, Catharinus, and Brunus, he ascribes heresy ultimately not to an intellectual motive but to hatred and contempt of prelates.[35]

The transformation of Catholic heresy discourse in the sixteenth century from a doctrinal to a moral discourse, as represented by Witzel's *De moribus haereticorum* and similar titles of mid-century, was, I believe, a fateful one. How fateful can be seen from the reception of some major continental *catalogi* in England in the 1560s. In 1565, the English Catholic Richard Shacklock translated Stanislaus Hosius's account of the origin of the Reformation heresies as *The Hatchet of*

by Castro (*Adversus haereses*, 21v–29r) and Brunus (Johann Cochlaeus, ed., *D. Conradi Bruni iureconsulti libri sex de haereticis in genere* [Mainz, 1549], 15–28).

32 *Speculum haereticorum* (Cracow, 1540), sigs Cviiiʳ–Dviiʳ.

33 Johann Cochlaeus, ed., *Breve D. Conradi Bruni jureconsulti Introductorium de haereticis. E sex libris eius excerptum, Hoc tempore summopere consyderandum et tam scitu necessarium quam lectu iucundum. Tribus capitulis compraehensum* (Mainz, 1548); idem, ed., *D. Conradi Bruni jureconsulti libri sex, De haereticis in genere* (Mainz, 1549); and idem, ed., *De seditionibus libri sex, rationibus et exemplis ex omni doctrinarum et authorum genere locupletati, authore clariss. et doctiss. viro D. Conrado Bruno jureconsulto. Joannis Cochlaei theologi De seditiosis appendix triplex, contra quosdam rebelles huius temporis* (Mainz, 1550).

34 Johann Fabri, *Fructus quibus dignoscuntur Haeretici, Eorum quoque Nomina, Ex Philastro, Epiphanio, Augustino, Eusebio, &c. Et quibus armis devincendi* (Ingolstadt, 1551).

35 Ibid., Biiʳ–Biiᵛ.

Heresies.[36] In the same year, the Welsh Catholic Lewis Evans translated part of a series of elaborate heresiological catalogues and tables of correspondences drawn up by Willem van der Lindt, bishop of Roermond in the Low Countries.[37] Both Shacklock and Evans went beyond mere translation to supply extensive prefatory matter of their own. When the Church of England minister John Barthlet replied to the translations the following year, he exploited what he saw as a discrepancy between the arguments of the original writers and the intentions of their translators.[38] Hosius had made the root of Luther's heresy to be covetousness, but Shacklock made it contentiousness, 'a thing clean contrary'; van der Lindt's tables had emphasized Luther's deceitfulness, but Evans ascribed Luther's fall to his 'filthy lust'.[39] This diversity allowed Barthlet to accuse all four writers of subjectivity: '[e]very one of them labouring to set out their peculiar devise, of their braynesicke mindes, bewrayeth his cause, to be onely private and personall: and not religion common to us al.'[40] In serio-comic style, Barthlet literally turns the tables on van der Lindt and the rest with his 'Pedigree of Popish Heretiques', tracing all characteristic Roman doctrines back to Judas Iscariot and Simon Magus.

The medieval *catalogus haereticorum*, for all its faults, had at least some claim to being objective: it could prove that a particular teaching had been condemned by a particular council. The transition in the mid-sixteenth century to a primarily moral definition of heresy, and to

[36] Stanislaus Hosius, *A Treatise of the Beginning of Heresies of Our Time, translated by Richard Schacklock and intituled by him 'The Hatchet of Heresies'* (Antwerp, 1565). Hosius's original was book one ('*De haeresibus nostri temporis*') of his *Verae, christianae, catholicaeque doctrinae solida propugnatio, una cum illustri confutatione prolegomenorum, quae primum Ioannes Brentius adversus Petrum a Soto Theologum scripsit, deinde vero Petrus Paulus Vergerius apud Polonos temere defendenda suscepit* (Cologne, 1558).

[37] Willem van der Lindt (Wilhelmus Lindanus), *Certaine Tables sett furth by the right Reverend father in God, William Bushopp of Rurimunde, in Ghelderland: wherein is detected and made manifeste the doting dangerous doctrine, and haynous heresyes, of the rashe rablement of heretikes, translated by Lewis Evans, and by hym intituled, 'The betraing of the beastlines of heretykes'* (Antwerp, 1565). Van der Lindt's original was *In hoc libello contenta tabulae grassantium passim haereseon anasceuasticae, atque analyticae authore D. Wilhelmo Lindano Dordraceno, Doct. Theologo atque Palatij Haghen. Decano. Quibus subtexitur Sectae Lutheranae Trimembris Epitome, per Fridericum Staphylum Regis Rom. consiliarum* (Antwerp, 1562).

[38] On Barthlet, see Brett Usher, 'Bartlett, John (fl. 1562–1567)', *ODNB*.

[39] John Barthlet, *The Pedegrewe of heretiques. Wherein is truely and plainely set out, the first roote of Heretiques begon in the Church, since the time and paßage of the Gospell, together with an example of the ofspring of the same* (London, 1566). Facsimile reprint as *The English Experience* 76 (Amsterdam and New York, 1969), 2v.

[40] Ibid., 2v–3r.

catalogues of heretical immorality, deprived Catholic apologists of that objectivity. Their accusations of heresy could now be dismissed by their opponents – to an extent that had not been possible before – as expressions of their own prejudices. It could be argued that when Protestants such as Flacius Illyricus and Barthlet turned the *catalogus* on its head, as a catalogue of 'witnesses to the truth' or as a catalogue of Roman Catholic heresy, they were but bringing to completion a subversion of the genre begun by Catholic heresiologists.

University of Hull

IN DEFENCE OF MAGISTERIAL REFORMATION: MARTIN BUCER'S WRITINGS AGAINST THE SPIRITUALISTS, 1535

by PHILIP BROADHEAD

T HE Protestant Reformation was the largest and most sustained challenge to authority ever experienced within the western Church. It involved a repudiation of existing teachings and forms of worship, along with a rejection, even a demonization, of the clergy and ecclesiastical hierarchy. From the 1520s a number of evangelical Churches developed which were often as hostile to each other as they were to the Catholic Church, and, as a result of polemical public discussions over competing teachings and beliefs, it was no longer clear to many people what constituted the Church or who should exercise authority over religious life. Some were led to question whether there was any need for a Church which imposed dogma and religious discipline on all people within a community or country. It is the discussion on the role and powers of the visible Church which will be examined here, by focusing on the city of Augsburg, but doing so through two significant writings by Martin Bucer, the leading theologian of the Protestant Church in Strasbourg. Recent research has added to our awareness of Bucer's understanding of the relationship between Church and community, and this contribution will provide insight into how the views of Bucer impacted upon the debate on religious separatism which was taking place in Strasbourg, Augsburg and elsewhere in Germany.[1] They show that even after Bucer had persuaded the government of his own city to expel religious radicals, he continued to believe that support for separatist and spiritualist ideas constituted a

---

[1] Some of the most important recent work on Bucer's views on the Christian community includes: Martin Greschat, *Martin Bucer: Ein Reformator und seine Zeit* (Munich, 1990), English trans., Stephen E. Buckwalter, *Martin Bucer: a Reformer and his Times* (Louisville, KY and London, 2004); D. F. Wright, ed., *Martin Bucer: Reforming Church and Community* (Cambridge, 1994); Andreas Gäumann, *Reich Christi und Obrigkeit: Eine Studie zum Reformatorischen Denken und Handeln Martin Bucers* (Bern, 2001); Christian Krieger and Marc Lienhard, eds, *Martin Bucer and Sixteenth-Century Europe*, Actes du colloque de Strasbourg (28–31 août 1991), 2 vols (Leiden, 1993); Christoph Strohm, ed., *Martin Bucer und das Recht: Beiträge zum internationalen Symposium vom 1. bis 3. März 2001* (Geneva, 2002).

substantial challenge to the establishment of disciplined Protestant Churches.

The two publications are *Vom Ampt der Oberkait* (*Of the Office of Government*) and *Dialogi oder Gesprech* (*Dialogues or Discussion*), both of which were published in Augsburg in 1535.[2] These are not Bucer's only publications on these topics, but they are particularly significant as they represent his first attempts to bring together his ideas on the role of the visible Church and its relationship with secular authority. They also demonstrate the extent to which Bucer relied upon the example of Augustine in formulating and carrying out his campaigns against religious radicalism. These two works are directed against those who challenged the need for a visible organized Church and who opposed any involvement of the secular authorities in spiritual life. It is clear that Bucer had particular opponents in mind, as Sebastian Franck is mentioned by name and, although he is not specifically identified, the arguments he used are directed against the views of Caspar Schwenckfeld von Ossig. Both Franck and Schwenckfeld had been resident in Strasbourg and were placed under pressure to leave as a result of the constant attacks from Bucer.[3]

Schwenckfeld had been an early supporter of Luther in Liegnitz in Silesia, but by 1527 had rejected Lutheran teaching on free will and the role of the spirit in redemption.[4] Forced to leave Liegnitz in 1529, he had sought refuge in Strasbourg, where he had developed his spiritualist ideas. He rejected the notion that ecclesiastical institutions could mediate between God and an individual, seeing churches and sacramental practices as a barrier to finding true faith, rather than a means to it.[5] More important for Schwenckfeld was the belief in a living faith, which could come only directly from God and was made evident by the

---

[2] Martin Bucer, 'Vom Ampt der oberkait in sachen der religion und Gotsdienst. Ain bericht auß götlicher schrifft des hailigen alten lerers und Bischoffs Augustini an Bonifacium, den Kayserlichen Kriegsgrauen in Aphrica. Ins Teütsch gezogen durch Wolfgangen Meüßlin, Prediger beym Creütz zu Augspurg' [hereafter: *Of the Office*] in Robert Stupperich, ed., *Martin Bucers deutsche Schriften*, 17 vols (Gütersloh, 1960–99), 6.2: 17–38; 'Dialogi oder Gesprech Von der gemainsame vnnd den Kirchen übungen der Christen Vnd was yeder Oberkait von ampts wegen auß Göttlichem befelch an den selbigen zuuersehen vnd zu besseren gebüre' [hereafter: *Dialogues*], in idem, 6.2: 39–188.

[3] Gäumann, *Reich Christi*, 431.

[4] R. Emmet McLaughlin, *Caspar Schwenckfeld Reluctant Radical: His Life to 1540* (New Haven, CT and London, 1986), 104–5.

[5] Ibid., 106; André Séguenny, 'Caspar von Schwenckfeld', in Carter Lindberg, ed., *The Reformation Theologians* (Oxford, 2002), 351–62, at 353–4.

performance of works of love. Faith as a spiritual gift could not there-fore be the product of external measures, and where, for example, Luther saw Scripture as essential in creating faith, for Schwenckfeld it served only to inform and guide the outer man, and had no part in justification, which was solely a matter of the spirit.[6] Sebastian Franck was a prolific writer, who absorbed many of Schwenckfeld's spiritualist ideas within his own views on religion.[7] Franck believed that the true Church existed only in heaven, and not on earth. The word for him was essentially a spiritual force which was not tied to the pages of Scripture; 'In short God's word remains for ever and can actually not be heard, written or spoken from outside. Whatever is preached therefore is merely a testimony, a remembrance, pointer and directive, a shadow of this treasure and light in us'.[8] Schwenckfeld found supporters who, while not numerous, were concentrated within the elite families in south German cities, such as Strasbourg, Esslingen, Ulm and Augsburg, and exercised considerable local political and social influence.[9] It was probably the fear that, if Schwenckfeld's influence amongst the ruling elites was allowed to flourish unchecked, the introduction of urban religious reformations and the creation of godly communities would be impeded, which prompted Bucer to devote so much time in the 1530s to campaigning against him. Bucer's efforts to silence radicals and dissi-dents were a clear indication that he believed they represented a signifi-cant challenge to him.[10]

Bucer saw clear parallels between the spiritualists and the earlier heresy of the Donatists, and he was keen to enlist the authority of Augustine to undermine his opponents. Like the spiritualists of the 1530s, the Donatists of the fourth and fifth centuries saw themselves as representing the pure Church, which was uncorrupted by compromises with secular government or subordination to it.[11] Augustine had considered this separatist group to be the main challenge to the north

---

[6] McLaughlin, *Caspar Schwenckfeld*, 96–9.

[7] R. Emmet McLaughlin, 'Sebastian Franck and Caspar Schwenckfeld: Two Spiritualist *Viae*', in J.-D. Müller, ed., *Sebastian Franck, 1499–1542* (Wiesbaden, 1993), 71–86, at 71.

[8] Sebastian Franck, *280 Paradoxes or Wondrous Sayings,* ed. E. J. Furcha (Lewiston, NY, 1986), 487.

[9] For a more detailed account of these groups see, McLaughlin, *Caspar Schwenckfeld*, 160–72.

[10] R. Emmet McLaughlin, 'The Politics of Dissent: Martin Bucer, Caspar Schwenckfeld, and the Schwenckfelders of Strasbourg', *Mennonite Quarterly Review* 68 (1994), 59–78, at 60.

[11] Carol Harrison, *Augustine: Christian Truth and Fractured Humanity* (Oxford, 2000), 147.

African Catholic Church, and had devoted great energy into preaching and writing against Donatism. The main component of Augustine's assault was that Donatists were schismatics and their refusal to be reconciled to the Church, despite undisputable proof of the falseness of their objections, amounted to a serious form of heresy.[12] This was substantially the position adopted by Bucer, as he sought to reassure the spiritualists that there was no need to separate themselves from the Protestant Church. Unable to achieve reconciliation, both Augustine and Bucer held public disputations, which were designed to identify to their governments the dangerous heresy contained in the views of their opponents. Augustine had grown to accept the necessity for government intervention in the work of the Church, viewing it as a form of benevolent discipline, which helped sinners break free from sin through fear of punishment.[13] These arguments were also prominent in Bucer's justification for state involvement in the Church, which while it could not create faith, could produce the circumstances in which faith developed.

In Augsburg the introduction of religious reform had been a protracted process. Support for evangelical ideas was evident from the time of Luther's visit to the imperial diet held in the city in 1518, but from the middle of the 1520s this appeared to have moved in favour of sacramental teachings and religious practices more closely related to Zwinglian reforms.[14] The ruling magistrates, although divided over religion, were not hostile to reform, but hesitated over taking a lead. They feared that religious division would exacerbate political and economic tensions in the city, and that religious changes would damage the close links of Augsburg with the Habsburgs.[15] For these reasons, from the late 1520s, the city adopted a policy of following the 'middle way' in religion, which involved avoiding legislation on religion and thereby offered a considerable degree of religious toleration.[16] As a result of lobbying from pastors and agitation from Protestant

---

[12] Ibid., 150–1.

[13] Ibid., 153.

[14] For a detailed account of these events see Friedrich Roth, *Augsburgs Reformations-geschichte*, 4 vols (Munich, 1901–11).

[15] P. Broadhead, 'Politics and Expediency in the Augsburg Reformation', in P. N. Brooks, ed., *Reformation Principle and Practice: Essays in Honour of A.G. Dickens* (London, 1980), 55–70, at 56.

[16] The most recent analysis of these 'middle way' policies is found in, Andreas Gößner, *Weltliche Kirchenhoheit und reichsstädtische Reformation: Die Augsburger Ratspolitik des 'milten und mitleren weges', 1520–1534* (Berlin, 1999), 46–52.

supporters within the population, some reforming measures were introduced in 1534, allowing only preaching by the Protestant preachers appointed by the Council, and limiting the celebration of the Mass to specified churches.

Bucer had been invited by the Council to help with organizing the religious affairs of Augsburg in 1530, and he undoubtedly found the reforms of 1534 to be unsatisfactory.[17] There had been little attempt formally to turn Augsburg into a Protestant city, for the Mass was still celebrated, and there were no efforts to impose religious discipline upon the community. He had been requested to advise the Council and the pastors of Augsburg on the basis of the religious leadership he had demonstrated in Strasbourg, and his reputation was subsequently increased by his success in negotiating compromises between Luther and south German cities, facilitating their admission to the Schmalkaldic League.[18] Bucer was nevertheless disappointed by the failure of the ruling authorities in Strasbourg to introduce what he considered to be effective religious discipline when they had legislated in favour of religious reform, for he felt that the government had been more interested in enforcing order than in sanctification.[19] He was therefore keen to use his influence in other cities to encourage the establishment of disciplinary structures which were focused on the creation of godliness, rather than obedience.[20] Bucer was aware that Schwenckfeld had influential sympathizers within the Council and the ruling elite of Augsburg, even amongst certain of the preachers.[21] He was also concerned that this support for Schwenckfeld was becoming apparent in attempts to discourage the secular authorities from becoming involved in religious life and imposing acceptance of a Protestant civic Church on all citizens. One of the clearest examples of this was the circulation of an anonymous text in the early 1530s, based on Franck's writings and condemning the involvement of government

[17] Augsburg, Stadtarchiv, *Literalien* 2, 1530, fol. 241.

[18] Greschat, *Martin Bucer*, 99.

[19] Thomas A. Brady Jnr, ' "The Earth is the Lord's and Our Homeland as Well": Martin Bucer and the Politics of Strasbourg', in Krieger and Lienhard, *Bucer and Sixteenth-Century Europe*, 1: 129–43, at 134–5; Gäumann, *Reich Christi*, 111.

[20] Eike Wolgast, 'Bucers Vorstellungen über die Einführung der Reformation', in Krieger and Lienhard, ibid., 1: 159–72, at 152–3.

[21] McLaughlin, *Caspar Schwenckfeld*, 164–7. When Schwenckfeld arrived in the city he stayed with the preacher Bonifacius Wolfhart. McLaughlin, 'The Politics of Dissent', 67, suggests that members of the Augsburg elite gave a warmer greeting to Schwenckfeld than to Bucer when both men were in the city in 1534.

and the use of secular force in matters of religion.[22] Bucer clearly feared that further progress towards religious reform in Augsburg would be impeded if Schwenkfeldian teachings were not challenged.

Bucer had also been concerned by the tolerant attitudes of the Strasbourg government towards Anabaptists and other religious dissidents, that had made the city a haven for those with radical and unorthodox views and which he believed were a barrier to the creation of a godly community. This situation came to a head with a synod held over three sessions in 1533, during which Bucer confronted his radical opponents, including Melchior Hoffman, Clemens Ziegler, and Schwenckfeld.[23] The rulers of Strasbourg took action only in 1534, when they became aware of the connections between the teachings of Hoffman and the events in Münster. Even though Anabaptists were expelled, Schwenckfeld, who was absent on a visit to Augsburg, was only informally advised by the Council not to return to Strasbourg.[24] Eager to associate the excesses of Anabaptists in Münster with incorrect teaching on the Church and sacraments, Bucer published in March 1534 his *Bericht auß der heyligen geschrift* (*Report from Holy Scripture*).[25] His disappointment at the slowness and limitations on the reform process in Strasbourg, especially in relation to dealing with heresy, made him keen to ensure that the same mistakes were not repeated elsewhere.

This is the background to the two main texts by Bucer under consideration. *Of the Office* comprised a translation by Wolfgang Musculus, of an attack by Augustine on the heresies of the Donatists.[26]

[22] Augsburg, Stadtarchiv, *Literalien* Nachtrag I, 1534, Nr 16. There has been speculation that the author was the patrician, Christoph Ehem, W. Hans, *Gutachten und Streitschriften über das ius reformandi des Rates vor und während der Einführung der offiziellen Kirchenreform in Augsburg, 1534–7* (Augsburg, 1901), 38. This claim has been called into question by J. T. Ford, 'Wolfgang Musculus on the Office of the Christian Magistrate', *Archiv für Reformationsgeschichte* 91 (2000), 149–67, at 154–5. A repudiation of the views in this document was also circulating in the city, 'Confutacion und Ablainung etlicher vermainten Argumenten so neulich von ainem nachdichter aufgetzaichnet seinnd, darinne angetzogen wirdet, das kainen daruor dess Evangelions in der Religion und glaubens sachen die weltlichen Oberkait zu erwecken, noch viel weniger weltlichen Oberkaiten, darein zu greiffen gezymen wölle'. Hans suggests several possible authors, amongst whom Musculus was the most likely, Hans, *Gutachten*, 40.

[23] Greschat, *Martin Bucer*, 121–2.

[24] Ibid., 123; McLaughlin, *Caspar Schwenckfeld*, 175.

[25] 'Bericht auß der heyligen geschrift von der recht gottseligen anstellung und haußhaltung Christlicher gemeyn, Eynsatzung der diener des worts, Haltung und brauch der heyligen Sacramenten', in Stupperich, *Martin Bucers deutsche Schiften*, 5: 109–258. The work was dedicated to the mayors of Augsburg.

[26] Wolfgang Musculus was an Augsburg preacher and a close associate of Bucer, and was

An introduction and endnote written by Bucer were also included.[27] The purpose of the translation was partly to refute a claim by Franck that the early Fathers had not called on the support of secular power, but it also allowed Bucer to use the authority of Augustine to advance his own views on the proper organization of the Church and its relationship with secular authority.[28] The *Dialogues* are a much longer and more detailed exposition of these views.[29] They are written in the form of a discussion between three men: Hartmut, a convinced supporter of the need for magisterial Reformation; Sinnprecht, a spiritualist sympathizer; and Friedlieb, who in general supports the aims of Hartmut but also wishes to win over Sinnprecht. The discussion is dominated by Friedlieb, whose statements are given the greatest prominence, who speaks at the greatest length and who, unsurprisingly, represents the views of Bucer. The tone of the document is striking, for Bucer describes the participants as agreeing that all will be conducted in an amicable manner and this is reflected in the text, which includes no polemics or insults.[30] Clearly this is an attempt by Bucer to use persuasion to win over his opponents and their sympathizers.

In both of these works three themes are apparent: the necessity for a visible Church; the importance of unity of belief and worship; and the need for government to play a role in controlling the religious life of the community. Challenging the attitudes of the separatists, Bucer produces many justifications for there being a unified Church to which all belong. The arguments which he employs are not original, but the need for him to make them indicates that he faced a significant challenge to these basic principles. In *Of the Office* Bucer, cites biblical evidence that faith is strengthened when Christians join together to

regularly consulted by the Council on religious matters. For an account of his hostility to Schwenckfeld see, Horst Weigelt, 'Wolfgang Musculus und die radikale Reformation: Die Auseinandersetzung zwischen Musculus und Kaspar Schwenckfeld', in Rudolf Dellsperger, Rudolf Freudenberger and Wolfgang Weber, eds, *Wolfgang Musculus und die oberdeutsche Reformation* (Berlin, 1997), 159–72, at 160–8.

[27] *Of the Office*, as published in 1984, does not include the translation of Augustine by Musculus, for which the copy in the Staats- und Stadtbibliothek in Augsburg was consulted. Augustine's, *De correctione Donatistarum* is published in Alois Goldbacher, ed., *CSEL* 57 (Vienna, 1911), 1–44.

[28] *Of the Office*, 30. The desire to challenge Franck's misunderstanding of Augustine is also made explicit in, 'Dialogues', 133.

[29] André Séguenny, 'Why Bucer Detested the Spiritualists: Some Reflections on Reading of Bucer's *Dialogues* of 1535', *Mennonite Quarterly Review* 68 (1994), 51–8, at 55.

[30] *Dialogues*, 57.

pray, to hear the Word expounded, and to share the sacraments.[31] In the *Dialogues* he further insists that unified preaching and worship encourage piety, and hence can strengthen faith.[32] Sinnprecht claims not to be impressed by ceremonies, saying that in this respect little had changed from the past, but is reminded by Friedlieb of the instruction by Christ that his followers should re-enact the Lord's Supper together.[33] The most significant objection raised by Sinnprecht is that a single visible Church, which is supported by secular authority, will try and use external means to force people to profess faith, even if they feel they do not have it, which is spiritually pointless and creates only hypocrisy.[34] Faced with this Friedlieb accepts that such a situation would be undesirable, but he also voices Bucer's view, that governments have a duty to provide proper public worship for their subjects, as it is a means through which they can know that those for whom they have responsibility are aware of what pleases and what offends God.[35] He also insists that people can be led to true piety through external measures, by hearing the Word, and by avoiding ungodliness through the fear of punishment by the authorities. Additionally, the enforcement of godly conduct is justified by saying that those brought up in the Christian Church and following Christian customs are given the best possible opportunity to find God and lead a life pleasing to him.[36]

Speaking through Friedlieb, Bucer defines the true Church as that which teaches only according to God's word, and all the participants in the discussion accept that this definition excludes the Roman Catholic Church, even though Sinnprecht believes that this does not justify encouraging secular authorities to enforce religious reforms.[37] In *Of the Office*, Bucer writes that only those things in the Church which are contrary to the Word of God should be changed, but explicitly includes the Mass, confession and the papacy amongst them.[38] This is then used as the basis for arguing that if the teaching and organization of the Church comply with Scripture, everyone can and should join in its worship without fear of damaging their conscience. Friedlieb's descrip-

---

[31] *Of the Office*, 29.
[32] *Dialogues*, 50, 65.
[33] Ibid., 74.
[34] Ibid., 147–8.
[35] Ibid., *Of the Office*, 28.
[36] *Dialogues*, 148.
[37] Séguenny, 'Why Bucer Detested Spiritualists', 53.
[38] *Of the Office*, 33.

tion of the marks of the true Church come in his explanation of the responsibilities of government towards religion and justify his view that government should support the work of the Church which exhibits those qualities. The marks are: that the Gospel is correctly preached; the sacraments correctly performed; and discipline upheld. This implied that all should hear the word and none should deviate from it in their life or conduct.[39]

Bucer was alert to the fact that Protestants were criticized by their Catholic opponents for being sectarians and might therefore themselves be said to warrant punishment by the secular authorities.[40] This was an argument he counters by saying that it is not the Protestants who have separated from the Church, for they represent its true identity, rather it is the Catholics who have deviated from it. In *Of the Office* he says that the Catholic clergy, from the pope down to the lowest sacristan, are rooted in greed, envy, hate, immorality and drunkenness and, because of this, they had through their own unworthiness deprived themselves of their offices, from which they should now be driven.[41] Hartmut urges vigorous action to punish the spiritual tyranny of the papacy, while Friedlieb mocks the clergy who are experts on war, carousing, hunting and womanizing, but are unable to explain a single verse from a Psalm.[42] He sees real pastors as serving the people, but claims that the Catholic clergy serve the Devil, which justifies their expulsion and punishment by secular government.[43]

A key part of the texts concerns what role, if any, secular government should play in the Church and in enforcing religious orthodoxy and obedience. In *Of the Office*, Bucer insists that one of the most important duties of a godly magistrate is to protect his subjects, and in no area of life was this more important than in matters pertaining to religion.[44] Sinnprecht challenges this assertion in the *Dialogues* by pointing out that in the New Testament Christ and his followers never called on the secular powers for support. Although this objection is countered by Friedlieb with a string of examples which seek to establish

[39] *Dialogues*, 153. 'Derohalb werden sy [die obren] verschaffen, das yederman doch höre das Evangelium und im niemand widerspreche oder davon abziehe, weder mit falscher leer noch üppigem leben, alle unzucht und unerbarkait werden syzum ernstlichen anziehen'.
[40] *Of the Office*, 32.
[41] Ibid., 33.
[42] *Dialogues*, 98.
[43] Ibid., 100.
[44] *Of the Office*, 29.

precedents through the intervention of the Old Testament kings of Israel in matters of religion, he produces no evidence from the New Testament to support his views.[45] Friedlieb shifts his ground by justifying intervention on the basis that false religion was the most serious threat to the well-being of any community. Since governments were ordered by Scripture to deal with wickedness in order to protect their communities, heresy should be punished as it posed a threat to all subjects.[46] He also frequently returns to the assertion that governments should deal with secular matters, but because external actions can have an influence on the soul by affecting the heart, governments have a proper role to play in enforcing religious observance and discipline.[47]

At the Strasbourg synod, Bucer had attempted to create a situation which would lead to Schwenckfeld and other instigators of heresy being silenced and expelled from the cities of south Germany, although he may have also held out some hope that through debate he could persuade them of their errors. The two publications under consideration were part of a different aim and directed at winning over the supporters of the radical leaders, in this case especially the followers of Schwenckfeld and Franck. In *Of the Office* Bucer makes a plea that true Christians should be united and have a true community in the Lord.[48] The aim of the *Dialogues* was to show those who sympathized with Schwenckfeld, that this unity in Christ would be achieved by the establishment of a Protestant Church. Bucer warned that religious differences were harmful in two ways. Firstly, he believed that God abhors false teaching, so that when this is identified it should be eradicated. As the new Church was based on Scripture, unlike the Catholic Church, its teachings were true and threatened the salvation of none. Secondly, Bucer said that religious division damaged civic unity, fractured society, impaired the common good and impeded public piety.[49] For these reasons he believed it was essential that governments used their authority to restore correct teaching and establish Christian unity.

Despite the pressure from Bucer, the ruling Council of Augsburg

---

[45] *Dialogues*, 130.

[46] Ibid., 167–8.

[47] Ibid., 148. 'So mag das mitt der warhait nit widersprochen werden, die gutthaten und straffen, durch die oberkaiten recht gemässiget und in namen Gottes wol außgespendet, vermügen vil, die leüt vom gotlosen wesen zu warer und selbwilliger gotsaligkait zu füren und auch entlich zu bringen'.

[48] *Of the Office*, 33.

[49] *Dialogues*, 178.

proved to be reluctant to expel Schwenckfeld, who eventually left the city of his own accord. A complete Protestant reform of religious life in Augsburg occurred only in 1537, when the Council forbad the celebration of the Mass and expelled all the Catholic clergy. By the 1530s most Protestant clergy were convinced of the need for magisterial Reformations, in which they would co-operate with the secular authorities to create an ordered Protestant Church, with unified teaching and effective religious discipline. This was the pattern that prevailed in the cities and territories in Germany which accepted the Protestant Reformation. The influence of Schwenckfeld in Strasbourg and the impact he had in Augsburg should, however, alert historians to the misgivings of many within ruling elites concerning the problems posed by magisterial Reformations. These carefully crafted works by Bucer are useful because they encapsulate his arguments against Schwenckfeld and other religious separatists. At another level they also show how Bucer used his extensive knowledge of urban politics and society to identify and address the doubts that most concerned magistrates over the introduction and enforcement of the Protestant Reformation.

Goldsmiths College, University of London

RELIGIOUS EXILES AND THE TUDOR STATE

by PETER MARSHALL

UCH of the best recent scholarship on the implementation of the Tudor Reformations has chosen as its leitmotif the themes of obedience, conformity and acquiescence, collaboration even.[1] The revisionism of the 1980s and 1990s overthrew convincingly the notion of widespread popular enthusiasm for religious change. But given that change *was* successfully imposed, part of revisionism's legacy has been a somewhat optimistic assessment of the capabilities of the Tudor state. Whether allied to the cause of religious reform, or that of religious reaction, Tudor governments were apparently remarkably effective at enforcing their will, largely because of their ability to co-opt the energies and loyalties of locally-based elites and sub-elites. In terms of this volume's twin themes, it appears to be a case of discipline successfully exerted; diversity effectively curtailed.

This essay represents a case-study in the ability of the Tudor state to control dissent, focused around the theme of religious exile. In a society obsessed with conformity and order, exiles were among the most flamboyant and flagrant of dissenters. In choosing to forsake the realm, exiles exposed the limitations of the regime's ability to exercise physical and ideological control over its subjects. Moreover, by their defining action of taking up residence on foreign soil, they represented a complication in international relations, and sometimes, a direct threat to national security. All Tudor monarchs were acutely conscious they had an 'exile problem'. Nonetheless, exile is an under-developed theme in the historiographies of Tudor governance and the English Reformation. The search for 'exiles' in the indexes to standard works on the Tudor period leads almost exclusively to the Marian exiles, the Protestants who fled England for Germany between 1553 and 1558.[2] Yet despite their evident importance, the Marian exiles were, in both

---

[1] Christopher Marsh, *Popular Religion in Sixteenth-Century England* (Basingstoke, 1998); Eamon Duffy, *The Voices of Morebath: Reformation and Rebellion in an English Village* (New Haven, CT, and London, 2001); and for the concept of collaboration, E. H. Shagan, *Popular Politics and the English Reformation* (Cambridge, 2003).

[2] Penry Williams, *The Later Tudors: England 1547–1603* (Oxford, 1995); A. G. Dickens, *The English Reformation* (2nd edn, London, 1989).

numerical and chronological terms, only a fraction of the total
phenomenon. Before and after the Marian interlude, religious exiles
were much more likely to be Catholics – more precisely, *Roman* Catholics who rejected the royal supremacy. For the Elizabethan period at
least, the activities of individual Catholic exiles have attracted a number
of specialist studies (there is much less on the Henricians and
Edwardians).[3] Yet to date, there has been no comparative overview of
the different forms of religious exile, and the often remarkably similar
tactics employed against it by successive regimes.

Yet what actually is 'religious exile', and how was it represented in
the period itself? Tudor governments invariably denied that anyone
was driven abroad for the sake of religion, and in a sense they were
right. Departures were small-scale, and in a technical sense, voluntary.
There were no large expulsions or migrations, as in parts of continental
Europe. Nor did the Tudor state make much use of banishment as a
punishment for religious opponents. One result was that by the later
sixteenth century, England was clearly a net importer of religious
refugees, a place of safety for thousands of French and Dutch Protestants.[4] Another was that persons fleeing from England or Ireland were
taking an overtly political step. They were in the regime's eyes not
exiles or refugees at all, but fugitives, rebels, and traitors – phrases
endlessly recycled in official propaganda. Attempts are sometimes made
to assign exiles to clear-cut categories, by claiming for example that the
English refugees in German and Swiss territories during Mary's reign
were religious exiles, while those who plotted against the Queen in
France or the Venetian Republic were political.[5] But in truth this
distinction is difficult to uphold with much conviction. In an increasingly confessional age, oppositional politics conducted from abroad
almost inevitably involved resistance to the regime's religious policies,

[3] The lineaments of Henrician Catholic exile are sketched in ch. 11 of Peter Marshall, *Religious Identities in Henry VIII's England* (Aldershot, 2006). There is no equivalent for the Edwardian years. Relatively little has been published on the Elizabethan Catholic exiles *qua* exiles, though see Peter Guilday, *The English Catholic Refugees on the Continent 1558–1795* (London, 1914); A. J. Loomie, *The Spanish Elizabethans: the English Exiles at the Court of Philip II* (New York, 1963).

[4] On the 'Stranger Churches' established in Tudor England, see A. D. M. Pettegree, *Foreign Protestant Communities in Sixteenth-Century London* (Oxford, 1986); O. P. Grell, *Calvinist Exiles in Tudor and Stuart England* (Aldershot, 1996).

[5] K. R. Bartlett, 'The English Exile Community in Italy and the Political Opposition to Queen Mary I', *Albion* 13 (1981), 223–44, at 223–4; David Loades, *Two Tudor Conspiracies* (2nd edn, Bangor, 1992).

just as any withdrawal overseas from state-sanctioned religion represented a provocative challenge to political authority.

A broad overview of religious exile in the Tudor period shows some
recurring patterns and some significant developments. The first exiles
were evangelical converts of the mid-1520s, men like William Tyndale
and John Frith. Their numbers were small, but their activities under-
lined the insidious potential of exile in a couple of key ways. Firstly,
they exploited established networks of trade and travel on the continent, usually to the English merchant community of Antwerp.
Secondly, they produced subversive pamphlets and books to be smug-
gled back into England through these same networks – the most explo-
sive of these was the English Bible itself. Unlike later exiles, the
evangelicals could not always establish themselves in religiously sympa-
thetic centres, and important sites of book production, such as Antwerp
and Cologne, remained Catholic territories. The risks were graphically
displayed by Tyndale's arrest and execution by the imperial authorities
in 1536. Henry's break with the papacy reduced the pressure on evangelicals at home, but did not end the phenomenon of evangelical exile.
The more reactionary policies prevailing from the end of the 1530s led
to a second wave of departures, with at least 37 mainly sacramentarian
believers seeking more comfortable berths in places like Strasbourg and
Zurich. Again, some of these exiles set impassioned pen to paper,
though Alec Ryrie has concluded that they were little more than 'a
sideshow' in the development of the Reformation.[6]

It would be difficult to come to this judgement about the Catholic
opponents of the royal supremacy who left England or Wales between
1533 and the end of 1546. It has been possible to identify 127, though
this figure is certainly an under-estimate, and does not include what
may have been a significant number of Irish exiles.[7] The pacesetters
were the Franciscan Observants, William Peto and Henry Elston, who
had removed themselves to the house of their order at Antwerp by the
summer of 1533. By 1538, around thirty Observants were reported to
have fled abroad, either to Scotland or to the Low Countries, making
Henry's decision to suppress the order in England in 1534 seem something of an own goal. A trickle of friars and other religious followed
suit, though the tally was not much increased by the closure of the reli-

---

[6] Alec Ryrie, *The Gospel and Henry VIII: Evangelicals in the Early English Reformation*
(Cambridge, 2003), 266–70, 112.

[7] For the following paragraphs, see Marshall, *Religious Identities*, 230–5.

gious houses in the late 1530s. Only one community of religious, the Bridgettine nuns of Syon in Middlesex, attempted to re-establish themselves on the continent during Henry's lifetime.

Without doubt the most significant English exile of the reign was Reginald Cardinal Pole. As both a kinsman of the king, and a papal legate, he combined in his person a source of alternate ideological legitimation and an implicit dynastic challenge. Refusing to return to England from Italy after the executions of John Fisher and Thomas More, he spent the autumn and winter of 1535 to 1536 composing a blistering attack on Henry in his *De unitate ecclesiae*. Pole's emergence in 1536 as the regime's principal opponent coincided with a development which was to become a recurring pattern, the association of the exile threat with the aftermath of failed rebellion. After the Pilgrimage of Grace, dozens of rebel leaders fled across the border into Scotland, to brood and to plot.

Henry's opponents were spoiled for choice when it came to suitable destinations. His territories were ringed with potential bolt-holes. Scotland lay overland to the north, though after the outbreak of war with England in 1542, it became less favoured as a haven. France and the Low Countries beckoned from the south-east, with Antwerp, the university town of Louvain and the semi-independent bishopric of Liège all exerting a pull. Exiles, moreover, did not always remain in the place of first resort. Many moved from Scotland or Louvain to join the orbit of Cardinal Pole in Italy, particularly after the pope created him superintendent of the hospice which served English pilgrims in Rome, later to become the Venerable English College. Another characteristic of the Henrician exiles was that they did not leave in one co-ordinated wave after the break with Rome. Individuals chose their moment, for a variety of personal and political reasons. One of the most spectacular defections came in early 1541, when Henry's ambassador to the emperor, Richard Pate, fled to Rome, where the pope provocatively appointed him bishop of Worcester.

Henry's death brought no respite for the Catholic exiles, and their tally was added to in the reign of Edward VI. Some conservative ecclesiastics who had toughed it out under Henry now followed the well-trodden routes to St Andrews and Louvain – for example, Richard Smyth and John Christopherson. The Louvain community was boosted in 1549 by a mixed band of lay and clerical refugees, linked by ties of kinship and association to Thomas More – those who, Roger Ascham remarked coldly in 1551, 'to see a mass freely in Flanders, are content to forsake, like slaves, their country'.[8] In fact, the Edwardian exiles at Louvain did more than satisfy their yearning for the mass. Smyth rapidly produced three polemical attacks on the reformer Peter Martyr Vermigli; John Story organized the smuggling of works of Catholic piety and propaganda into England, and William Rastell prepared an edition of More's complete works. Small wonder that the Edwardian Privy Council resolved in April 1552 that there must be 'some order for the fugitives of the realm'.[9]

Unlike the Pilgrimage of Grace, the Catholic rebellions of 1549 did not produce a backwash of exiles. Neither, directly, did the coup d'etat which brought Mary to the throne in the summer of 1553. Nonetheless, Mary's reign witnessed an escalation of scale in the pattern of religious exile. The martyrologist John Foxe claimed in 1563 that the number who had gone to Zurich, Basel, Frankfurt and other places 'almost rises to a thousand', though in 1570 he revised the figure downwards to 'well neare to the number of 800'.[10] Christina Garrett's researches in continental archives in the 1930s corroborated the latter estimate, though more recently, Andrew Pettegree's work on archives which Garrett neglected, such as that of the English church at Emden, has suggested that Foxe may have been closer to the mark first time around.[11] The Marian Protestant exile resembled the Henrician Catholic one in a couple of key respects. Neither was straightforwardly a response to persecution. The great bulk of the clergy exiles had made their way to the centres of Swiss and German Protestantism in 1553, before the revival of the heresy laws. As in 1537, a second and more emphatically lay exodus was produced by the failure of rebellion, in this case Thomas Wyatt's Rising and associated plots of January 1554. The leaders of the abortive midland and western insurrections of 1554 made their way to France, where their anti-imperial zeal allowed Henry II to turn a blind eye to their heretical leanings. The exile of the Marians was

8 Quoted in S. Brigden, *London and the Reformation* (Oxford, 1989), 453.
9 A. Löwe, *Richard Smyth and the Language of Orthodoxy: Re-imagining Tudor Catholic Polemicism* (Leiden, 2003), 44–5; H. de Vocht, *History of the Foundation and the Rise of the Collegium Trilingue Lovaniense, 1517–1550*, 3 vols (Louvain, 1951–5), 3: 424–5; Brigden, *London*, 453–4; C. S. Knighton, ed., *Calendar of State Papers, Domestic Series of the Reign of Edward VI, 1547–1553* (London, 1992) [hereafter: *CSPD Edward VI*], 239.
10 John Foxe, *Acts and Monumentes* (London, 1563), 1691; (1570), 1587.
11 C. H. Garrett, *The Marian Exiles: a Study in the Origins of Elizabethan Puritanism* (Cambridge, 1938), 40–2; A. D. M. Pettegree, *Marian Protestantism: Six Studies* (Ashgate, 1996), 4–5, 87.

remarkably short-lived, and virtually all of the exiles returned after the accession of Elizabeth in November 1558. For all its vigour, the Marian exile lacked a clear leader or figurehead, something its Henrician and Edwardian precursors had possessed in the person of Reginald Pole.

The third chapter of Catholic exile was initiated by the religious settlement of 1559, and followed precedent in unfolding as a staged process. The opening years of the reign saw a mainly clerical movement to established centres at Antwerp and Louvain. There was a drainage from the universities, particularly Oxford, with over a hundred scholars departing within the first year or two of Elizabeth's accession. In contrast to the first dissolution of 1536 to 1540, inmates of most of the handful of re-established religious houses departed to continue communal life on the continent. Once again, the character of exile was transformed by rebellion at home. The defeat of the Rising of the Northern earls in 1569 produced an influx of Northern Catholic notables into the towns of the Low Countries, under the feckless leadership of Charles Neville, earl of Westmoreland. The volume of exile from Ireland was also dramatically increased at the end of the reign after the 1601 defeat of the rebels at Kinsale.

The Elizabethan exile distinguished itself from earlier manifestations, not only in its duration, but in the way it institutionalized itself through the establishment of colleges for the education of exiled youth and training of clergy: the English foundations at Douai-Rheims, St Omer, Valladolid and Seville; the Irish colleges at Paris, Douai, Bordeaux and Antwerp.[12] No one, so far as I know, has attempted to calculate the total number of Catholics who went into exile in Elizabeth's reign, though there is no doubt it represented a step change in scale. Some sense of numbers can be gleaned from the reports commissioned by the authorities in England. In April 1580, a list of English papists currently residing in Paris identified no fewer than 348 individuals, not including wives and dependants. There were also believed to be at least a hundred more, English and Irish, 'who living secretly and disguised as they do, cannot so readily be known', as well as many others at Rheims, Orleans and other places.[13] In the mid-1590s, a listing of Catholics 'beyond seas' identified over 530 persons, 'with many other

---

[12] P. O'Connell, 'The Early Modern Irish College Network in Iberia 1590–1800', in Thomas O'Connor, ed., *Irish in Europe, 1580–1815* (Dublin, 2001), 49–64, at 51–2.

[13] Joseph Stevenson et al., eds, *Calendar of State Papers Foreign Series of the Reign of Elizabeth*, 23 vols in 26 (London, 1863–1950) [hereafter: *CSPF*], 4: 250–2.

eyther unknown or unworthy the naming'. An early twentieth-century historian thought there were probably never more than 3,000 English exiles at any one time during Elizabeth's reign, though it is unclear on what basis he made the estimate.[14] The numbers certainly pall compared to the tens of thousands of Flemish and French Protestant artisans entering England during the same period, but they significantly outstripped the Marian exodus at its height.

Unlike the incomers, both Marian and Elizabethan exiles were generally persons of 'quality' – clergy, gentry, and their dependents. This endowed them with significance out of proportion to their numbers, though the numbers themselves were sometimes inflated by rumour and anxiety, and the authorities probably never knew the real size of exile groups. In 1537 the government was hearing wild reports of upwards of 15,000 Englishmen gathered in Edinburgh, swearing to be the 'voweward' of a Scots invasion. By the following year, rumour had it that no fewer than 60,000 'of good Inglysshe men and fytynge men' were in the service of the king of Scots.[15] Less dramatically, but slightly more plausibly, Richard Morrison was alarmed to hear in Augsburg in 1551 that a host of English gentlemen, 'some say 100, others 400' had fled the realm to enter the emperor's service. 'There are many bad Englishmen at Paris', an anxious Sir Amias Paulet warned Francis Walsingham in April 1577.[16]

What, however, was the exact nature of the threat the exiles represented? Here we can identify some commonalities across the period, as well as some disparities. Understandably, it is the literary activities of the exiles which have commanded most attention among modern historians, particularly the output of the Marians who are conventionally adjudged to have won 'the battle of the books' against the Catholic authorities at home.[17] Some foundational texts of the English Reformation were certainly published abroad by the first evangelical exiles: William Tyndale's *Obedience of a Christian Man*, John Frith's *Disputation of Purgatory*, though such heretical and anticlerical works were not directed at the regime in England per se. Pole's *De unitate* aside, the

[14]   Guilday, *English Catholic Refugees*, 14–18, xix–xx.

[15]   London, *The National Archive* [hereafter: London, *TNA*], SP 1/121, fol. 6r; SP 1/138, fol. 148r.

[16]   *CSPD Edward VI*, 179; *CSPF*, 11: 567.

[17]   J. W. Martin, 'The Marian Regime's Failure to Understand the Importance of Printing', in his *Religious Radicals in Tudor England* (London, 1989), 107–23; Dickens, *English Reformation*, 311–12; David Loades, *The Reign of Mary Tudor* (2nd edn, London, 1991), 280–8.

Henrician Catholic exiles produced a very meagre tally of polemical works, despite their access to centres of printing, and the presence in their midst of some formidable scholars such as the Dominicans Robert Buckenham and William Peryn, and the secular priest John Helyar. Some may have wished to avoid the bridge-burning that the act of publishing against the regime represented. William Peryn, for example, was able to return to England in the more conservative conditions of 1543, one of the few Henrician exiles to do so. When Richard Smyth, however, made overtures to the Edwardian authorities about coming home in 1550, Privy Councillors responded that they knew Smyth 'too well to be deceived by him', and would not forgive him his recent 'slanderous book against the Bishop of Canterbury'.[18]

The greater polemical output of the Edwardian exiles in Louvain reflects the clarifying and hardening of confessional positions in the middle decades of the century. They were outgunned by the Marians, who produced around 120 vernacular tracts, as well as 40 works of Latin polemic. The great bulk of this was religious satire and controversial theology, though as the persecution at home intensified a number of works attacked the Queen's regime directly. John Ponet's *Short Treatise of Politic Power* and Christopher Goodman's *How Superior Powers Ought to be Obeyed* have been hailed retrospectively as milestones of resistance theory, though their impact at the time is less clear, with most of the exiles themselves repudiating their arguments. A third resistance tract, John Knox's *First Blast of the Trumpet Against the Monstrous Regiment of Women* is notable chiefly for its memorably misogynistic title and for the spectacular mistiming of its 1558 publication, as a Protestant Queen was preparing to replace a Catholic one on the English throne. The two most important literary undertakings of the Marian exiles only bore fruit after the exile was over. William Whittingham and others prepared the groundwork for the 'Geneva Bible' which was to imprint itself on the religious culture of Elizabethan England. Meanwhile, John Foxe was collating the materials for his famous martyrology, which would shape perceptions of the period for centuries to come.[19]

Historians are divided about the authorities' response to the textual onslaughts of the Marian exiles, with some suggesting a serious derelic-

18 *CSPD Edward VI*, 52, 65, 67, 108.
19 Williams, *Later Tudors*, 114–15; Pettegree, *Marian Protestantism*, 118–19.

tion of duty, and others arguing that they could afford to ignore such off-stage jeering.[20] Either way, it is a credit to the first wave of Elizabethan exiles that the Protestant authorities took their writings so seriously. The 'Louvainists' published nearly fifty English books between 1564 and 1568, and were answered by John Jewel, Edward Dering, Alexander Nowell and others. In William Allen's words, 'fiftene heades or rectors of colledges in Oxford and Cambridge ... and above twentie doctors of diverse faculties for conscience sake fled the realme' at the start of Elizabeth's reign. They represented a phalanx of theological heavyweights, whose distinctions the Marian exiles would struggle to match.[21] In the 1560s, the Louvain exiles generally confined themselves to doctrinal questions, and avoided direct assaults on the government.[22] But in the changed circumstances of the 1570s, with Mary Stuart a prisoner in England, and Elizabeth formally deposed by the pope, radicalization set in, and many exile publications of the next decades were overtly political in nature.

For Mary's reign and Elizabeth's, historical attention has focused on the works of propaganda directed towards sympathizers at home. But it was the ability of exiles to inflame opinion abroad that may have been of greater concern to the authorities in England. Andrew Pettegree is surely right to insist that the Latin polemics of the Marian exiles, aimed at an international audience, are at least as important as the better-known English works.[23]

Under Elizabeth, official paranoia about the ability of exiles to poison the minds of foreigners ratcheted up several notches. A 1580 proclamation complained of the exiles' wandering 'from one prince's court to another' with the intention 'to irritate all estates against her Majesty and the realm'.[24] In June 1585 Sir Francis Walsingham heard

---

[20] Compare the works cited in note 17 with Jennifer Loach, 'The Marian Establishment and the Printing Press', *EHR* 101 (1986), 135–48; Christopher Haigh, *English Reformations: Religion, Politics, and Society under the Tudors* (Oxford, 1993), 216–17; Eamon Duffy, *The Stripping of the Altars: Traditional Religion in England, 1400–1580* (New Haven, CT, and London, 1992), 529–30.

[21] Quoted in T. H. Clancy, *Papist Pamphleteers: the Allen-Persons Party and the Political Thought of the Counter-Reformation in England, 1572–1615* (Chicago, IL, 1964), 37; Haigh, *English Reformations*, 253–4; Peter Milward, *Religious Controversies of the Elizabethan Age: a Survey of Printed Sources* (Lincoln, NE, 1977), 1–24.

[22] P. J. Holmes, *Resistance and Compromise: the Political Thought of Elizabethan Catholics* (Cambridge, 1982), 11–22.

[23] Pettegree, *Marian Protestantism*, 119.

[24] P. L. Hughes and J. F. Larkin, eds, *Tudor Royal Proclamations*, 3 vols (New Haven, CT,

that the slanders of the popish rebels at Paris had provoked a friar to
preach 'abusive things' about the Queen's chastity, 'calling her Jezebel'.
Two years later, not fewer than 5000 Parisians a day were reportedly
coming to see Richard Verstegan's prints illustrating the torture and
execution of priests in England, on public display in the cloister of St
Severin. Sir Edward Stafford reported that 'some Inglish knave priestes
that be there ... pointe with a rodde and shewe every thinge'. When the
same engravings were copied for the frescoes of the English College in
Rome, citizens were promised a plenary indulgence for visiting the
chapel and praying for the conversion of England.[25] Books by the
Jesuits John Gibbons and Joseph Cresswell, itemizing the sufferings of
English Catholics, were European hits, particularly at the Spanish court.
At the same time, the Queen herself was complaining to the Grand
Duke of Tuscany about a history of the Reformation in England by the
Dominican Friar, Girolamo Pollini, who had no doubt 'heard his lies
from English traitors in Italy'.[26]

All of this was embarrassing, but the real fear was that it might
flower into action against the realm. Alarmingly, Catholic exiles played
their part in reinforcing what Geoffrey Parker has called the 'messianic
vision' of Philip II of Spain. In March 1572, for example, Thomas
Stukely urged him towards intervention in Ireland, telling him 'I do not
know how Your majesty will be able to excuse yourself before God' if
he failed to assist potential rebels there.[27] In fact, religious exiles posed a
really serious threat to the security of the Tudor state on only two occasions: in the late 1530s, when Reginald Pole attempted to co-ordinate
Franco-Imperial military action against Henry VIII, and in the late
1580s, when William Allen and Robert Persons were urging Catholics
to rise up against the 'wicked Jezebel' in support of a projected Spanish
invasion. In between, there were periodic, if insubstantial, scares. In

and London, 1964-9), 2: 469. For the part English exiles played in getting Elizabeth's ambassador banished from the Spanish court in 1568, see Geoffrey Parker, *The Grand Strategy of
Philip II* (New Haven, CT, and London, 1998), 154-5.

[25] *CSPF*, 15: 584; *CSPF*, 19: 524-5; Richard Williams, ' "Libels and Payntinges": Elizabethan Catholics and the International Campaign of Visual Propaganda', in Christopher
Highley and J. N. King, eds, *John Foxe and His World* (Aldershot, 2002), 198-215, at 205-8.

[26] Quoted in Guilday, *English Catholic Refugees*, 25 (where Gibbons's work is erroneously
attributed to John Bridgewater); Loomie, *Spanish Elizabethans*, 205-6; R. B. Wernham, ed.,
List and Analysis of State Papers Foreign Series Elizabeth I, 7 vols (London, 1964-2000) [hereafter:
LASPF], 3: 454-5.

[27] Quoted in Geoffrey Parker, 'The Place of Tudor England in the Messianic Vision of
Philip II of Spain', *TRHS* ser. 6, 12 (2002), 167-221, at 210.

April 1551 the Council learned that Cormac O'Connor had arrived in
Paris offering the service of Irish rebels to the French king if he would
send troops there. In the following reign, there were fears that Henry II
might back military action by the Protestant exiles in France, though it
seems unlikely that he sanctioned the one piece of real militancy on the
part of the Marian exiles, Thomas Stafford's seizure of Scarborough
Castle in April 1557.[28] This act nonetheless supplied the *causus belli* for
war with France in June 1557, just as the presence of English exiles in
Scotland had been a major factor in Henry VIII's decision to attack
James V in 1542.[29]

It was after the outbreak of war with Spain in 1585, however, that
the exile threat reached its height. The year 1587 witnessed the most
notorious episode of defection since Reginald Pole's half a century
before: Sir William Stanley's surrender to the Spanish of the Dutch
town of Deventer, and the transfer of his regiment to Spanish service.
Viewed at home as an unspeakable act of treachery, William Allen
defended it as the correct course for any Catholic caught up in a war
pitting true religion against heresy. The military contribution of
Stanley's 'English Regiment' (largely Irish in composition) is questionable. But it stood ready to be shipped across the Channel during the
Armada campaign, and placed a question mark over the loyalty of
thousands of Irish soldiers in Elizabeth's forces. While clerical leaders
like Allen and Persons propagandized for the Spanish cause, Catholic
exiles could help the war effort in practical ways: vessels scouting out
the defences of the English coast in 1590, and again in 1595, carried
English exiles to interrogate captured fishermen.[30]

So far not much has been said about how the authorities in England
sought to neutralize the activities of the exiles. A prerequisite, of course,
was to keep tabs on who and where they were: throughout the period,
there was a flow of information from ambassadors, spies, and ad hoc
informants. Whether there was any such thing as an efficient Tudor
'spy network' is open to question. Individual ministers employed their
own agents and tended to receive the messages they wanted or expected

---

[28] *CSPD Edward VI*, 89, 92; Williams, *Later Tudors*, 109.

[29] Loades, *Reign of Mary Tudor*, 304–11; Claire Kellar, *Scotland, England, and the Reformation, 1534–1561* (Oxford, 2003), 24–8, 36–45, 71–6.

[30] On Stanley, see Loomie, *Spanish Elizabethans*, 129–81. *LASPF*, 1: 369; Robert Lemon et
al., eds, *Calendar of State Papers Domestic Series of the Reigns of Edward VI, Mary, Elizabeth and
James I*, 12 vols (London, 1856–1950) [hereafter: *CSPD*], 4: 59.

to hear. There were also doubts over the reliability of information gleaned from within or close to the exiles' own counsels. In April 1551, the government's Venetian agent Peter Vannes employed a friend going to Rome on business 'to bring himself by some feigned occasions in acquaintance with such fugitives and wandering Englishmen as be there, allowing in some part their sayings, to the intent that the more boldly they may enlarge their communication.'[31] But could the government be sure that such 'feigning' and 'allowing' was genuinely ungenuine? Thomas Cromwell thought he had secured a coup in June 1536 by subverting Pole's factotum Michael Throckmorton. But Throckmorton's loyalties remained firm, and he fed Cromwell a drip of low-grade information.[32] The extensive use of double agents among the Elizabethan Catholic exiles by Walsingham and Burghley was even more problematic. Even now, it is hard for historians to decide whose side some of them were really on.[33]

The unreliability of the regime's agents on the ground may help to explain the relative scarcity of 'direct action' against the exiles abroad. No Tudor regime was above contemplating the kidnapping, even assassination of its enemies abroad. But successful instances were remarkably few. There were at least three officially-inspired attempts to kidnap or murder Reginald Pole in the late 1530s, though in each case failure seemed to involve a suspicious degree of prevarication and ineptitude by the senior agents involved.[34] Mary's government was rather more successful, arranging for the seizure of Sir John Cheke and Sir Peter Carew near Antwerp in May 1556. Carew was probably complicit, securing his pardon in return. Cheke abjured his Protestantism, providing the Marian authorities with an unparalleled propaganda coup.[35] There was no such outcome in the other notorious political kidnapping of the period. In 1571, William Cecil, working at

31 CSPD Edward VI, 81–2.
32 T. F. Mayer, 'A Diet for Henry VIII: the Failure of Reginald Pole's 1537 Legation', Journal of British Studies 26 (1987), 305–31, at 313–14; Thomas Cromwell on Church and Commonwealth: Selected Letters, 1523–1540, ed. A. J. Slavin (New York, 1969), 78–82.
33 On the shadowy world of counter-Catholic espionage, see Leo Hicks, An Elizabethan Problem: Some Aspects of the Careers of Two Exile-Adventurers (London, 1964); Alan Haynes, Invisible Power: the Elizabethan Secret Services, 1570–1603 (Stroud, 1992); C. C. Breight, Surveillance, Militarism, and Drama in the Elizabethan Era (Basingstoke, 1996); P. E. Hammer, 'An Elizabethan Spy Who Came in from the Cold: the Return of Anthony Standen to England in 1593', HR 65 (1992), 277–95.
34 Marshall, Religious Identities, 243–4.
35 J. P. D. Cooper, 'Carew, Sir Peter (1514?–1575) and Alan Bryson 'Cheke, Sir John (1514–1557), ODNB. Garrett, Marian Exiles, 36; Anne Overell, 'A Nicodemite in England

second and third hand with a team of agents in the Netherlands, secured the seizure of Dr John Story, a civil lawyer and leading figure in the Marian persecution, who had escaped to the continent in 1563. Defiant to the last, Storey was executed for treason. Subsequently, there were a couple of abortive attempts to arrange the capture of the earl of Westmoreland, but Elizabeth and her ministers, like their predecessors, used the strategy extremely sparingly. The diplomatic price was certainly high. Over ten years after the incident, the Spanish ambassador was urging Philip to remind Elizabeth to her shame of how 'she had ordered an Englishman to be kidnapped in the Netherlands'.[36]

Diplomacy was the first line of defence against the exiles' machinations. All Tudor governments expended considerable efforts to get foreign governments to disavow the 'traitors', and ideally to hand them over. International treaties almost invariably specified mutual assurances not to favour or entertain each other's rebels.[37] Henry VIII's envoys bombarded James V with demands over the issue in the 1530s, just as Mary's emissaries to France did in the 1550s. Elizabeth's ambassadors likewise repeatedly raised the question of 'rebels and fugitives' with their hosts.[38] There were periodic and patchy successes: the mayor of Louvain was prevailed upon to detain an English fugitive in 1540, as was the governor of Milan in 1543. The Lutheran city of Wesel nervously expelled some of the English congregation there in 1556, and Catholic exiles were temporarily sent out of the Spanish Netherlands due to a 1575 commercial treaty.[39]

Yet there was a persistent sense of banging one's head against a wall. Both James V and Philip II saw their patronage of English exiles as part of their duty as Catholic princes.[40] Henry II of France reacted badly in 1554 to hectoring about Protestant rebels from Mary's ambassador,

---

and Italy: Edward Courtenay, 1548–56', in David Loades, ed., *John Foxe at Home and Abroad* (Aldershot, 2004), 117–35, at 130.

[36] Quoted in R. Pollitt, 'The Abduction of Dr John Story and the Evolution of Elizabethan Intelligence Operations', *Sixteenth Century Journal* 14 (1983), 131–56, at 140.

[37] Mayer, 'A Diet for Henry VIII', 318–19; Hughes and Larkin, *Tudor Royal Proclamations*, 2: 413.

[38] Marshall, *Religious Identities*, 239–41; E. H. Harbison, *Rival Ambassadors at the Court of Queen Mary* (Princeton, 1940), 162–4; *CSPF*, 18: 82–3, no. 180; 11: 4; *LASPF*, 5: 421–2, 432–7.

[39] Muriel St Clare Byrne, ed., *The Lisle Letters*, 6 vols (Chicago, 1981), 6: 112–13; J. S. Brewer et al., eds, *Letters and Papers, Foreign and Domestic, of the Reign of Henry VIII*, 21 vols in 33 (London, 1862–1910) [hereafter: *Letter and Papers*], 18 (1): nos. 505, 739; Garrett, *Marian Exiles*, 50; Guilday, *English Catholic Refugees*, 72.

[40] R. K. Hannay, ed., *The Letters of James V* (Edinburgh, 1952), 271; Loomie, *Spanish Elizabethans*, 3–13.

saying that he had no intention to be her *boia*, 'which word spoken in Italian signifieth a hangman'. Mary herself remarked huffily to the French ambassador in England, that regarding the fugitives, 'she would not have used a semblable part towards the French King for the gain of three realms'.[41] Elizabeth similarly assumed a posture of hurt innocence. Her ambassador to France in 1596 was instructed to assure Henry IV that she would never suffer any disobedient subject of his to live in her country. A propaganda tract composed by Burghley piously protested that Elizabeth had never 'at any time given any pension or maintenance within her realm to any rebel or person condemned by the king of Spaine'.[42]

Such exchanges highlight the ambiguous legal status of religious exiles. One monarch's fugitive and traitor was another's émigré of conscience. When the French ambassador described Henry Dudley and company as 'refugees' in 1556, Mary asked him sharply to call them 'abominable heretics and traitors, and worse still, if possible'.[43] There was no recognized right of asylum for political refugees. Exiles depended on the goodwill of sometimes nervous host communities, and had a vested interest in portraying themselves as simple martyrs of conscience. The imperial cities in Germany were particularly reluctant to accept political fugitives. Arriving in Strasbourg in 1555, Sir Anthony Cooke, Sir Richard Morison and Edwin Sandys assured the magistrates they had been 'banished by Queen Mary because they could not accept the religion of the Papacy'. John Hales was equally vehement in protestations at Frankfurt that he for 'concyens sake were commed thyther to flye persecucion'. Garrett's judgement that the Marian exiles propagated 'a legend of persecution and banishment' is perhaps unduly harsh.[44] But it is one of the ironies of the exile phenomenon that exiles had an interest in 'confessionalizing' their situation, while the state, supposedly the prime instrument of confessionalization in this period, sought to do precisely the opposite.

Even Bloody Mary's government hesitated to proceed against the fugitives as if they were principally heretics, despatching an agent to

---

[41] W. B. Turnbull, ed., *Calendar of State Papers Foreign Series of the Reign of Mary* (London, 1861), 73, 87, and 221.
[42] *LASPF*, 7: 197; William Cecil, *A True Report of Sundry Horrible Conspiracies* (London, 1594), 15–17, 23–4.
[43] Quoted in Harbison, *Rival Ambassadors*, 293.
[44] Garrett, *Marian Exiles*, 12–15.

Germany in 1556 with formal warrants commanding the return of eleven leading lay exiles.[45] Burghley's memoranda for projected talks with the Duke of Parma in 1588 aimed to let the Duke understand 'what untruths the rebels of this land that are with him shall deliver', there being none in England who suffered death for professing the Catholic religion, but only for stirring the people to rebellion. Instructions for an abortive 1594 mission to the governor of the Netherlands complained of attempts against the Queen's life, devised by subjects 'fled thither for rebellion, though coloured with cloak of religion'.[46] In his 1584 apologia for the regime's policy towards Catholics, Burghley lamented that traitors had falsely informed foreign rulers 'that the cause of their fleeing from their countries was for the religion of Rome'. In fact, they were a rag-bag of paupers, frustrated clerics and bankrupt merchants – none of them genuine religious refugees.[47] The counter-case was put starkly by John Story at his trial. Reciting God's injunction to Abraham 'to go fourth from the lande and countrey where he was borne', Story asserted that he 'for conscience sake did forsake his countrye'. He now claimed to be 'not the Queens subiect ... but was the subiect of the most catholicke and mightty prynce Kyng Philip'.[48]

Such assertions were anathema to every precept of political order, and it was almost certainly with the Story trial in mind that the 1571 act 'against fugitives over the sea' condemned those departing the realm 'as thoughe they were soveraigne rulers themselves', placing themselves under the dominion of foreign princes and becoming their subjects.[49] Across the Tudor period, governments used the law against exiles, both as a practical means of control, and as a symbolic declaration that they were still subjects of the Crown. Fugitives were invariably exempted from parliamentary general pardons.[50] They were also made the subjects of acts of attainder, though this was a strategy used more

[45] Ibid., 36; Sarah Covington, 'Heretic Hunting beyond the Seas: John Brett and his Encounter with the Marian Exiles', *Albion* 36 (2004), 407–29.

[46] *CSPF*, 21: 543; *LASPF*, 5: 421–2, 432–7.

[47] Quoted in William Cecil, *The Execution of Justice in England*, ed. R. M. Kingdom (Ithaca, NY, 1965), 4–6.

[48] *A Declaration of the Lyfe and Death of Iohn Story, Late a Romish Canonicall Doctor* (London, 1571), B3v–4v.

[49] 13 Eliz. I, c. 3 (A. Luders et al., eds, *Statutes of the Realm*, 11 vols [London, 1810–28], 4: 531).

[50] 35 Hen. VIII, c. 18; 1 Edw. VI, c. 15 (*Statues*, 4: 35); 5 Eliz. I, c. 30 (*Statues*, 4: 463–4); 8 Eliz. I, c. 19 (*Statues*, 4: 520–1); 18 Eliz. I, c. 24 (*Statues*, 4: 653–4); 23 Eliz. I, c. 16 (*Statues*, 4: 699–700); 39 Eliz. I, c. 28 (*Statues*, 4: 953–5); 43 Eliz. I, c. 19 (*Statues*, 4: 1011–14).

heavily by Henry than by his successors. In Elizabeth's reign, attainder was largely confined to the rebels who fled abroad after the 1569 rising.[51] The treason law itself was progressively finessed to take account of the exile phenomenon. The act of 1534 made treasons committed abroad triable within the realm, while that of 1552 contained provisions for overseas treasons to be tried *in absentia* by royal commissioners in any English county. The act of 1571 explicitly made it treason to 'move or to sturre any forreyners or straungers with force to invade this realme'.[52]

A more immediate way to strike at the exiles overseas was to threaten their property within England. Under a statute of Richard II's reign, the government could confiscate the goods of individuals who fled the realm, but short of a conviction for treason, or the political sledgehammer of an act of attainder, there was no way to make permanent seizures of landed wealth.[53] In 1555, a bill for this purpose produced a famous defeat for Queen Mary's government, with members blockading the door of the Commons to prevent government reinforcements being brought in. Rather than dislike for the government's policy in general, parliamentary opposition probably reflected that hypersensitivity about gentry property rights, and rights to former monastic lands in particular, which is so marked a feature of the period.[54] Nonetheless, what looks an almost identical measure was pushed through in 1571, this time aimed at Catholic exiles. It stipulated that persons going abroad without a license and failing to return when summoned were to forfeit all their goods, and the profits of lands for life. It also outlawed the setting up of trusts, whereby the income from lands could be secretly channelled to exiles abroad. But this too seems to have been contentious. An act of the following year reported doubts arising over whether the Queen could make grants of confiscated land, and over whether it had to be proved that those setting up conveyances or trusts did so with the intention not to return. Both questions were settled in the Crown's favour. Yet the conveyance of land by exiles remained difficult to police, and in 1593 a separate statute was required to nullify arrangements made by the longstanding fugitive, Francis Englefield.[55]

51 Marshall, *Religious Identities*, 238–9; 13 Eliz. I, c. 16 (*Statutes*, 4: 549–52).
52 Ibid., 237; 5 & 6 Edw. VI, c. 11 (*Statutes*, 4: 145); 13 Eliz. I, c. 1 (*Statues*, 4: 526).
53 Covington, 'Heretic Hunting', 411.
54 Jennifer Loach, *Parliament and the Crown in the Reign of Mary I* (Oxford, 1986), 138–41.
55 13 Eliz. I, c. 3 (*Statutes*, 4: 531–4); 14 Eliz. I, c. 6 (*Statutes*, 4: 598–9); 35 Eliz. I, c. (*Statutes*, 4: 549–52).

The evident difficulties encountered by successive governments in the implementation of diplomatic, legal and extra-legal efforts against exiles suggests the need to exercise caution about the enforcement abilities of the Tudor state. Indeed, it may require us, rather late in the day, to start deconstructing that term itself. It is hard to identify at any point in the century a monolithic state apparatus in action against the exiles, operating a coherent policy to which all members of the regime were fully signed up. There was persistent ambivalence, for example, about the importance of preventing departure in the first place. In the 1530s, Thomas Cromwell was an advocate of watching the ports to forestall flight, but after the Pilgrimage of Grace, the duke of Norfolk simply sent back to Scotland exiled Observant friars who had re-entered the country.[56] Under Mary, the bishop of Chichester, William Barlow, was twice arrested attempting to flee, but other Protestants were simply allowed, even encouraged to leave: Mary's chancellor Stephen Gardiner clearly believed this the best policy with clerical trouble-makers. At the start of Elizabeth's reign, some would-be exiles were seized at the ports, but others with connections were quietly allowed to go. Elizabeth later had reason to regret permitting Sir Francis Englefield to depart for the Low Countries in 1559, or issuing a license for the controversialist Thomas Stapleton to reside outside the realm.[57]

Uncertainties about whether malcontents were better out than in suggest that it was not so much the exiles' absence, as their potential immanence, that made them so unsettling. One thing uniting virtually all the religious exiles of the Tudor period is their retention of ties with kinsfolk, allies and supporters at home. A proclamation of 1570 complained of the 'seditious messages' being sent into the realm by 'fugitives and rebels'. In 1595 the former exile Lewis Lewknor condemned the 'ambodexter felowes, who upon fained colours and pretended passes' shuttled between the fugitives and 'credulous Catholikes' at home.[58] Again, most attention to collusion between exiles and home-based dissidents has been paid in the Marian context. We are rightly alerted to the importance of 'sustainers', London merchants providing

---

56 Marshall, *Religious Identities*, 236–7.

57 Covington, 'Heretic Hunting', 414, 425, 428; Garrett, *Marian Exiles*, 4, 6–7, 11; Loach, *Parliament and the Crown*, 141; Wright, 'Marian Exiles', 234; Guilday, *English Catholic Refugees*, 3; Loomie, *Spanish Elizabethans*, 17; Marvin R. O'Connell, 'Stapleton, Thomas (1535–1598)', *ODNB*.

58 *Tudor Royal Proclamations*, 2: 347; Lewis Lewknor, *The Estate of English Fugitives under the King of Spain and his Ministers* (London, 1595), A2r.

the exiles with funds, and to the activity of parliamentary sympathizers like William Cecil.[59] But, at both ends of the period, Catholic exiles were more likely to have dangerous friends in high places. There is much evidence of continuing bonds of sympathy in the 1530s and 1540s between 'papalist' Catholics abroad, and conformist 'Henricians' at home. As reconstructed by Thomas Mayer, Pole's circle of well-wishers among the aristocracy and gentry was alarmingly extensive.[60] Elizabethan Catholic exiles, too, were suspected of having supporters within the ramparts of the regime. Writing from Rouen in 1585, Walsingham's agent Thomas Rogers claimed that 'the papists here have some friends very near her majesty'. He named them as the earls of Cumberland and Rutland, Lord Herbert and Sir Edward Herbert. In December 1590, John Sparrowhawk reported to Burghley from Bergen-op-Zoom that members of the Privy Council were granting passports to women 'to go to their husbands who were with the enemy'.[61]

While it might look to us an unambiguous statement of identity and intention, the insidiousness of exile seemed to some contemporaries a defining characteristic. Both then and since, it has been difficult to determine exactly who the exiles were. Garrett has been criticized for including on her list some who were simply continuing the tradition of attending university in Italy.[62] Yet the English authorities were recurrently troubled by the converse possibility: that studying abroad was a cover for religious and political disaffection. In 1539, Thomas Wriothesley told Cromwell that he considered enrolment at Louvain to be 'but a cloke for the rayne'.[63] Peter Vannes warned in 1551 of Englishmen coming to Italy 'under the protest of studying languages and seeing countries'.[64] A generation later, this was still the cover story routinely employed by itinerant papists. In his exposé of the English College in Rome, the renegade seminarian Anthony Munday protested implausibly that he had travelled to the continent in 1578 solely because of a 'desire to see straunge countreies, as also affection to learne

59 Garrett, *Marian Exiles*, 7; Pettegree, *Marian Protestantism*, 103–5.
60 Marshall, *Religious Identities*, 247–54; Mayer, 'Diet for Henry VIII', 325–7.
61 *CSPF*, 19: 716; 20: 707; *LASPF*, 2: 363.
62 K. Bartlett, 'The Role of the Marian Exiles', in P. W. Hasler, ed., *The House of Commons, 1558–1603*, 3 vols (London, 1981), 1: 102–10.
63 London, *TNA*, SP 1/143, fols 56r–v.
64 *CSPD Edward VI*, 82.

the languages'.[65] Exiles abroad were dangerous: secretly returning exiles arguably more so. Anxieties about their transgression of boundaries, physical and political, are neatly illustrated in the criss-crossing triple injunction of a 1585 statute: children were not to be sent abroad for education, unordained seminarians were ordered to return, and Jesuits and seminary priests within England were to leave within forty days.[66]

There is a danger of giving the impression that exiles regularly shook the foundations of the Tudor polity. Most of the time, of course, they were hardly in a position to do so; their literary outpourings, however eloquent, were the cries of the dispossessed. It is worth noting the persistent phenomenon of factionalism within exile communities, if only because this was something of which the authorities in England themselves often gleefully took note. The Marian exiles were divided over the wisdom of political activism, and even more so by questions of liturgy and ceremonial. The 'Troubles at Frankfurt' over the use of the 1552 Prayer Book cast a long shadow over the Elizabethan Church. Elizabethan Catholics were even more fractious, rebels arriving in the Low Countries after 1569 considering the established Louvainists to be 'too sever and scrupulous'.[67] The exiles later split into 'French' and 'Spanish' factions, English and Welsh groupings, Appellants and Jesuits. Lewis Lewknor imagined none could be 'ignorant of the diuisions, partialities, and factions that are betweene them . . . I think scarcely in the world is to be found such a diuided sorcerie of men'.[68] The phenomenon of exile was itself fragile and permeable. The state papers contain a steady stream of pathetic letters from impoverished or disillusioned exiles, exuding heartfelt repentance and begging permission to come safely home. Some of these approaches were rebuffed, but others had been solicited by the regime's agents and ambassadors abroad.[69]

Homesickness and poverty were the common lot of Protestant and Catholic exile. But some further generic differences between the two phenomena are worth considering. Garrett's sketch of the Protestant

65 Anthony Munday, *The English Romayne Life*, ed. G. B. Harrison (Edinburgh, 1966), 2.
66 H. Gee and W. J. Hardy, eds, *Documents Illustrative of English Church History* (London, 1896), 485–92.
67 Loomie, *Spanish Elizabethans*, 20.
68 Lewknor, *Estate of English Fugitives*, G3r.
69 Henrician examples: *Letters and Papers*, 13 (1): 710; 13 (2): 597; London, TNA: PRO, SP 1/143, fol. 34v. Edwardian: *CSPD Edward VI*, 52, 65, 67, 108; T. F. Mayer, 'Pole, Sir Geoffrey (d. 1558)', *ODNB*. Marian: *CSPF Mary*, 109, 278. Elizabethan: *CSPF*, 23: 397; Loomie, *Spanish Elizabethans*, 11; *CSPD*, 4: 221, 380; 7: 342; 3: 484.

exiles in Germany is certainly overdrawn: 'if they had been surrounded by a wilderness of nature instead of a wilderness of foreign tongues they could hardly have been more isolated from their fellows'. We have become more aware in recent years of mid-sixteenth-century Protestantism as a truly international movement, and, in Geneva at least, the exiles gloried in the possibilities for association with the like-minded of all nationalities.[70] Nonetheless, for a variety of reasons – language, liturgy, congregational organization – Protestant exiles were generally more insular, less integrated into host communities than many of their Catholic counterparts – despite Edmund Grindal's valiant efforts to teach himself German. Henrician exiles who were members of religious orders slotted naturally into the structures of those orders, whether in St Andrews or Antwerp, while high-ranking secular churchmen like Pole or Pate moved easily in curial circles, and made their mark on the deliberations at Trent.[71] In the succeeding generation, membership of the Society of Jesus supplied many expatriate Englishmen with a genuinely cosmopolitan perspective on their predicament as exiles.[72] Lay refugees lacked the ready-made institutional networks of their clerical brethren, though for many, service in the Spanish military provided an enduring point of contact with non-English Catholic society. The ability to move freely through, and to some extent influence, the ambient world of European Catholicism undoubtedly gave Catholic exile a political potency and self-renewing power its Protestant counter-part might well have been seen to lack, had it been called upon to sustain itself beyond the five years of Mary's reign. But the flip side was the possibility of dilution, the tendency to be drawn into the life of the host community at the expense of the restoration of the faith at home. In Henry's reign, the Newcastle Dominican Richard Marshall turned his back on English affairs and threw himself wholeheartedly into the life of the Scottish Kirk. Later in the century, a number of Catholic exiles made respectable careers for themselves in the local church. George Chamberlain, for example, became dean of Ghent cathedral, and later Bishop of Ypres; Robert Chambers was chaplain to the Benedictine nuns of Brussels. From the 1570s, clerical exile leaders became increasingly concerned about the number of students at Rome,

---

[70] Garrett, *Marian Exiles*, 19; Kellar, *Scotland, England, and the Reformation*, 167–8.

[71] Marshall, *Religious Identities*, 272.

[72] T. M. McCoog, *The Society of Jesus in Ireland, Scotland and England, 1541–1588: 'Our Way of Proceeding?'* (Leiden, 1996).

Douai, Valladolid and Seville entering religious orders, and thus dis-qualifying themselves from availability for the English mission.[73]

Perhaps in the end, exiles of all confessional hues did not achieve much. It was, after all, the vagaries of the Tudor gene pool, rather than the plotting of exiles, that decided the major questions of the English Reformation. The contribution of returning Marian exiles to the nature of the Elizabethan Church has, of course, been endlessly debated. Recent research is inclined to roll back earlier lavish assessments, downplaying the role of a probably fictitious 'puritan choir' of exiles in Elizabeth's first parliament, and stressing the importance of 'Nicodemites' – like William Cecil, Archbishop Mathew Parker, and indeed Elizabeth herself – who had remained in England through the dark days of persecution.[74] By contrast, the significance of an earlier cohort of homecoming exiles – Catholics returning after the accession of Mary – deserves more attention.[75] Elizabethan Catholic exiles did not get the opportunity to return, at least not legally and corporately, though their importance for maintaining recusancy in Britain and Ireland, and for helping to transform residual medieval Christianity into Counter-Reformation Catholicism, is beyond question.

In sum, what does the study of religious exile have to tell us, beyond the observation that discipline had its limits, and that diversity had geographical as well as theological aspects? It is a reminder that the Reformation in these islands possesses not just a 'European context' in which it can helpfully be viewed, but a European *dimension* from which it cannot meaningfully be separated. All the major confessions were to some extent shaped and defined by the experience of exile. At the same time, many of the anxieties and tensions bedevilling what we can in shorthand call 'the state', are thrown into sharp relief by the nature of its responses to the defiance of distance. Instead of seeing exile as evidence of the government's ability to isolate and divide the opposi-tion,[76] we should note its capacity to expose fractures within the regime itself, and to reveal its relative weakness vis-à-vis neighbouring powers.

---

[73] Marshall, *Religious Identities*, 257; Patrick McGrath and Joy Rowe, 'Anstruther Analysed: the Elizabethan Seminary Priests', *Recusant History* 18 (1986–7), 1–13, at 3; Guilday, *English Catholic Refugees*, 218.

[74] N. L. Jones, *Faith by Statute: Parliament and the Settlement of Religion, 1559* (London, 1982). Pettegree, *Marian Protestantism*, 86–117, 129–50; Bartlett, 'Role of the Marian Exiles', 102–10.

[75] Some preliminary comments in Marshall, *Religious Identities*, 258–60.

[76] This, implicitly at least, is part of the case for the effectiveness of early and mid-Tudor

It is a commonplace of sociologists and anthropologists that communities are defined by their boundaries. There are lessons to learn about the Tudor religious polity from a study of its porous and leaky edges.

University of Warwick

rule in Shagan, *Popular Politics*, which argues that the existence of religious exiles points to a 'division among Catholics, as important as the nascent division between Catholics and evangelicals'. Ibid., 127.

THOMAS WALBOT: THE LAST 'FREEWILLER' IN ELIZABETHAN ENGLAND?

by BRETT USHER

THE special character of discipline and diversity in the London of the 1560s has never lacked commentators. Following Elizabeth I's settlement of religion in the parliament of 1559 the new government had many factors to consider. Although convinced Roman Catholic clergy were no longer to be tolerated Elizabeth was anxious not to alienate leading Catholic laymen. Convinced Protestant clerics or potential ordinands, many of them returning from exile or else emerging from prudent seclusion in the British Isles, would either accept her Settlement and shoulder the burden of governing her Church or else, wanting more than it had offered them, move into increasingly militant revolt.[1] These things have been intensively studied and altogether the government's agenda, like that of many a government swept suddenly to power, can be described as 'the imposition of discipline and the quashing of diversity'.[2]

Within this scenario, Thomas Walbot, briefly (1561–6) rector of St Mary Magdalen Milk Street, London, falls into a category all of his own. His career has never previously been elucidated, even though his one significant contribution to the religious debate, a letter he wrote in early 1563, was printed as long ago as 1709 by John Strype. Unfortunately – and unusually – Strype misread the name at the bottom of this document, transcribing it as 'Thomas Talbot'.[3] Thus historians have remained baffled.

Prima facie evidence suggests that he was the Thomas 'Walbet' ordained deacon and priest by John Scory, bishop of Hereford, at the instance of Matthew Parker, archbishop of Canterbury, on 22 December

---

[1] For a full bibliography of the Vestiarian Controversy, which wrecked any future possibility of blanket conformity to the 1559 Settlement, see Brett Usher, 'The Deanery of Bocking and the Demise of the Vestiarian Controversy', *JEH* 52 (2001), 434–55.

[2] The most comprehensive bibliography of the Elizabethan Settlement is now that appended to Felicity Heal, *Reformation in Britain and Ireland* (Oxford, 2003); see also Brett Usher, *William Cecil and Episcopacy* (Aldershot, 2003).

[3] John Strype, *Annals of the Reformation*, 3 vols (2nd edn, Oxford, 1824), I, pt 2: 494–8.

1559.[4] Thus he was one of the first men ordained under the revived protestant ordinal.[5] In the record Walbot is described simply as *Norviciensis* – that is, born in the diocese of Norwich. It seems likely, therefore, that he was the son of John Walbot 'Senior' of Terrington, Norfolk, yeoman.[6]

He is not heard of again until his arrival at St Mary Magdalen Milk Street, a tiny but populous parish, scarcely three acres in area, at the heart of the City of London. It shared its longest boundary, to the north and east, with that of St Lawrence Jewry, where stood the Guildhall, seat of city government.[7] Although technically a peculiar of the Dean and Chapter of St Paul's, who had rights of presentation, institution and induction, its incumbents were in practice subject to the bishop of London's officials for disciplinary purposes.

Parish registers survive from 1558 and churchwarden's accounts from 1519.[8] Thus, the actual date of his institution apart (none survive for the Dean and Chapter for this period), it is possible to reconstruct the circumstances of Walbot's incumbency with some precision. His predecessor was still in possession in late 1560 but, as 'Mr Thomas Walbowte, curate' he was present at the primary visitation of his diocese by Edmund Grindal, Elizabeth's first bishop of London, on 22 April 1561.[9] He had compounded for the living on 20 March, bringing in sureties to the Exchequer to guarantee the payment of his first fruits.[10] These were Richard Hill, mercer, and William Kynge, grocer,

[4] *Registrum Matthei Parker diocesis Cantuarensis, AD 1559–1575*, ed. W. H. Frere, CYS 39, 3 vols (London, 1928–33), 1: 338.

[5] Parker was consecrated on 17 December and Scory (consecrated under Edward VI) confirmed to Hereford on 20 December 1559.

[6] This Thomas Walbot stood surety with John Woode of Terrington, *generosus*, for the first fruits of Marmaduke Wood as rector of 'Terrington' – but St Clement or St John? – on 14 November 1559: TNA, E334/7, fol. 31r.

[7] It was further bounded to the east by All Hallows Honey Lane; to the west by St Michael Wood Street and St Peter Westcheap; and to the south, where it briefly straddled Cheapside, by All Hallows Bread Street. No memory of the parish, razed in the Great Fire of 1666, survives. Today Milk Street is merely a corridor of modern concrete buildings connecting Cheapside and Lombard Street. No plaque commemorates the site of the church or churchyard.

[8] *The Registers of St. Mary Magdalen Milk Street 1558–1666 and St. Michael Bassishaw London 1538–1625*, ed. A. W. Hughes Clarke, Harleian Society 72 (London, 1942) [hereafter: *Registers*]; Churchwardens' Accounts 1518/9–1605/6: London, G[uildhall] L[ibrary], MS 2596/1 [hereafter: 'Accounts'].

[9] Cambridge, C[orpus] C[hristi] C[ollege], MS 122, [page] 28; London, GL, MS 9537/2, fol. 28r.

[10] TNA, E334/7, fol. 111v. They were set at £15 11s 8d in 1535, but from the church-

both of St Mary Magdalen and – since both are further described as *alias mercatores* – established entrepreneurs rather than humble members of their livery companies.

In 1560 and again in late 1561 Archbishop Parker demanded full-scale surveys of the incumbent clergy of his province from his diocesans and their subordinates. Walbot is accordingly described in detail in a report drawn up by John Mullins, archdeacon of London, in the latter year. A widower and a non-graduate, yet learned in Latin and the Scriptures, Walbot preached only within his own parish and held no other benefice. Technically 'non-resident' he nevertheless lived in Lime Street – that is, less than a ten-minute walk away via Cheapside and Lombard Street.[11]

Behind this ostensibly favourable portrait of a conscientious parish priest there lurks a multiplicity of problems. On 11 November 1561, only weeks before Mullins's report was finalized, Walbot had been summoned into Grindal's consistory court and ordered, on pain of suspension, not to exercise any ecclesiastical function or to preach.[12] Although the records fall silent for several months he certainly remained in place for on 14 April 1562, as 'Thomas Walbott, person', he was married in his own church to Johan Eliot. On the following 17 November it was presumably he himself who officiated at the marriage of Leonard Pilkington, brother of the bishop of Durham, to Ewart Holiwel.[13]

In early 1563, evidently still under pressure, he took what may have been a unique step for an Elizabethan incumbent, personally petitioning Convocation.[14] From this it finally emerges what lay at the root of Walbot's troubles. The only beneficed minister who, surviving one of the fiercest struggles within the emergent English Protestant

wardens' calculations it appears that in 1566–7 the 'p[ar]sons dewtie' now amounted to £24 5s 4d: the *Valor Ecclesiasticus*, ed. J. Caley and J. Hunter, 6 vols (London, 1810–34), 1: 372; 'Accounts', fol. 137r.

11 CCCC, MS 122, [page] 80.

12 L[ondon] M[etropolitan] A[rchives], DL/C/332, fol. 45r.

13 *Registers*, 1. The Pilkington family's connection with the parish remained strong throughout Walbot's tenure. John Chapman, merchant tailor, had stood surety for James Pilkington, future bishop of Durham, as prebendary of Mapesbury in St Paul's (12 February 1560). One of Walbot's own sureties, Richard Hill, also guaranteed John Pilkington's first fruits as archdeacon of Durham later that year. The latter was married in the parish on 6 November 1564: ibid.; TNA, E334/7, fols 47v, 182v.

14 Elizabeth's second parliament met on 12 January and was prorogued on 10 April: J. E. Neale, *Elizabeth I and Her Parliaments 1559–1581* (London, 1953), 93, 125.

tradition, was prepared to stand up and be counted, Walbot was that
rapidly-disappearing phenomenon, a Freewiller – one who did not
subscribe to Calvinist doctrines of predestination in all points.

The story of this struggle was first fully mapped out by Andrew
Penny and has more recently been the subject of a detailed survey of
the surviving evidence by Thomas Freeman.[15] Both studies chart the
course of what proved a surprisingly virulent ideological battle between
England's emergent Protestants – on the one hand the Edwardian
coterie which, largely university trained, came to reject Luther and
espouse Genevan doctrines of salvation; and, on the other, an initially
influential band of roving evangelists who had imbibed their notions of
reformed religion for themselves, setting up 'popular' congregations
whenever they had the opportunity. The former, not unnaturally,
tended to lay emphasis on their own theological training and disparage
their opponents for their lack of it.

Thomas Walbot's letter may well be the last attempt to state the
Freewillers' case in formal, 'educated' terms.[16] If not a trained lawyer
himself, he evidently took the trouble to employ one to draft his careful
submission. It begins with a time-honoured legal word:

> Where as there be many both of the clergye and laytie of this
> Realme of England, that doo feare god and hate and abhorre all
> papistry and forreyne power which the Pope in times paste
> usurped within this Realm, under the pretence of gods worde, and
> have for the same in the raigne of the Quenes Maiesties noble
> Sister, Quene Mary, suffered exile, emprisonment and great
> penurye w^t other losse of frends and goods as other protestaunts
> have done, and nowe looke and hope to enioye toguether w^t the
> rest of the Quenes Maiesties obedient Subiects, The good and
> merciful benefits of god geven unto this Realme, under the Quenes
> Maiesties most noble and prosperous Raigne (that is to saye)
> quietnes of conscience not being compelled to any Idolotry or false

---

[15] D. Andrew Penny, *Freewill or Predestination: the Battle over Saving Grace in Mid-Tudor England* (Woodbridge, 1990); Thomas S. Freeman, 'Dissenters from a Dissenting Church: the Challenge of the Freewillers, 1550–1558', in Peter Marshall and Alec Ryrie, eds, *The Beginnings of English Protestantism* (Cambridge, 2002), 129–56.

[16] What follows, with interpolated comments, is a full transcript from the original manuscript preserved in London, Inner Temple Library, MS Petyt 538, vol. 38, fols 59r–60r. Surviving evidence from the Convocation of 1563 is preserved in the same collection, vol. 47, fols 575r–588r.

serving of god, and a quiet time by gods grace to frame their life according to their profession.

Walbot here aligns himself firmly with all those who did not, in the contemporary phrase, 'bow the knee to Baal' under Mary, even implying that he himself was a member of one of the clandestine Protestant congregations. He does not present himself as the leader of any sect or spokesman for any organized group, simply asking that in future there will be liberty of conscience for all.

> Yet notwithstanding contrary to their expectac[i]on to their great grief and sorowe, bicause they do holde contrary to a great nomber of their brethren the protestants, that gods holy predestinac[i]on is no maner of occasion, or cause at all in any wise of the wickedness, iniquytye or sinne, that euer was or euer shalbe wrought commytted or done in the worlde, wherby any parte of mankinde should be predestinate of an unavoydable necessyte to com[m]ytte and perpetrate the sin and wickednesse that mankinde, from the beginning hath or shall co[m]mytt or perpetrate and so to be ordeyned before all worldes by force of gods holy predestinac[i]on, of an unavoydable necessyte to be damned eternally.

A significant number of true Protestants, Walbot suggests, cannot accept that God's *holy* predestination – he is throughout careful never to belittle it – implies that God predestined any evil, wickedness, iniquity or sin. He proceeds to explain his reasons:

> It[e]m that if god shoulde predestinate from euerlasting any of the afore said euil, wickednesse and sinne, to be com[m]yted done and perpetrated of an inevytable necessyte, that then god through his predestinac[i]on were the chief author and occasion therof, and also an example therof unto all the whole world, which by his comaundment is bounde to folowe his example, and to be holly as he is holly.

> It[e]m that god doth foreknowe and predestinate all good and goodnesse but doth only foreknowe and <not> predestinate any euill wickedness or sinne, in any behalfe which thinge all the learned fathers unto this or age haue alwayes most firmely holden and maynteyned, and a great many of the learned of this or age yet do firmely holde and maynteyne.

These propositions, Walbot suggests, are both logical and reasonable. But he and others have been violently abused for maintaining them:

> For this cause they be esteemed and taken of their brethren the protestants, for fautors of false religion, and are constrayned hitherto to susteyne at their hands daily, the shameful reproche and infamye of freewill men, Pelagians, Papists, Epicures, anabaptistes, and enemyes unto gods holly predestinac[i]on and prouidence, with other such like opprobrious words and threatenings of such like, or as great ponishments and correcc[i]ons, as upon any of the aforesaid errours and sects is meet and due to be executed, what time discipline which of all things is most meete and necessary to be hadd in a christian congregac[i]on, shalbe fully com[m]ytted into thands of the clergye: wheras neverthelesse they holde no such thing as they be burthened withall, but doo only holde concerning predestinac[i]on as above briefly is declared/ [fol. 59v] which thinge they be readye at all times, and haue many times offred unto diverse of their foresaid brethren the protestants and learned, for avoyding of contentions, brawlings, ambiguyte, misplacing, and misunderstanding of wordes, which may fall in so highe and weighty a matter to maynteyne and proue by disputac[i]on in writing that they iustly and according to gods worde do holde and may holde the same, without any preiudice or suspic[i]on to be hadd towards them of the opprobrious infamye of such hereticall names, above named, and do nothing doupte at all but by such kinde of conference and disputac[i]on in writing (by the grace of god) to make this so highe and waightye a matter (which is not well possible by argumentac[i]on with tonge and wordes directly to be expressed most cleare and euident to be judged, discerned, and understanded of all men.

It is difficult to resist the conclusion that the phrase 'great punishments and corrections' refers directly to Walbot's own experiences in Grindal's consistory court and the hostility he evidently encountered. And,

> Please it yo[r] gracious fatherhodes therfore that it may be promysed and enacted, that none of those corrections, ponishments and execuc[i]ons which the clergy hath in their authoryte allreadie and herafter by aucthoryte of this present parliament from hensforth shall haue in their aucthoryte to execute upon any of the aforesaid

errours and sects, or any other shall in no wise extend to be executed upon any maner of person or persons, that doo holde of predestinac[i]on as is above declared, excepte it be only proued that the same person or persons doo by their expresse wordes or writings, affirme and maynteine that man of his own naturall power is abell to thinke, will or worke of him selfe any thinge that shoulde in any case helpe or serve, towards his own salvac[i]on or any parte therof, or else some other manifest articles, or poynte of errour, which any of the aforesaid sects, or any other do holde.

It[e]m that all other their brethren and learned the protestants which doo not holde of predestinac[i]on as is abovesaid, shall from hensforth cease, desist and leave of[f] from calling any man by the name of free will man, Pelagian, papist, epicure, anabaptist, as other hereticall name contrary to thorder of charytie, except the partye whom they so doo call be conuicted of the same by order of a lawe.

It[e]m that all disputac[i]on concerning gods holy predestinac[i]on shalbe from hensforth hadd and made <onely> by writing and not by worde of mouthe for the avoydiung of all unreuerent speaking of gods holy predestinac[i]on and to avoyde all contenc[i]on and brawling, and other uncharitable behavio[r] which of such unreuerent speaking must needes procede and come.

It[e]m that from hensforth it shalbe lawfull for bothe part[i]es, aswell them that holde of predestinac[i]on (as is abouesaid) as thother freely to write and put in print whatsoeuer they be able to alleadge and bringe in for the maintenaunce and proving of the truthe of their opinyon, wherby all men may be able to iudge and discerne the truthe/ [fol. 60r] betwixte both parties, and brotherly charyte be obserued, and kepte amonge suche, as doo professe gods worde, hate all papistry, and be true and obedient subiects unto the Quenes Maiestye, to the god ensample [sic] of all the rest of the people, bothe within this Realme and without.

God save the Quene. Amen[17]

There never was to be a decorous, dispassionate debate on the subject of

---

[17] On fol. 60v, in a different hand, is an endorsement: 'Touching y[e] quarrell of p[re]destination'; and a pasted slip (fol. 60x): 'Exhibited by Thomas Walbot person of mary magdaleens in milk strete'.

predestination in Elizabeth's Protestant, strictly Erastian, England. Calvin's doctrines were increasingly adopted as the norm and his opponents' swept aside, as John Bradford had urged that they should be. Bradford had opined of Freewillers in 1555 that 'more hurt will come of them than ever came by the papists'.[18] His disciples took this warning seriously and, quite remarkably, they had all but disappeared by the end of 1558. Once Elizabeth's Settlement had got under way, Thomas Freeman asserts, 'predestinarian divines who attacked the Freewillers were wrestling with ghosts'.[19] Yet both Jean Veron (in 1561) and Robert Crowley (as late as 1566) felt it necessary to lambast their views in militant terms[20] and thus Freeman's claim that the Freewillers were discredited and eliminated only 'through persuasion, without coercion or state sanctions'[21] may not be the whole truth. Indeed, when it came to Thomas Walbot's reasoned and respectful objections to his treatment at the hands of his opponents 'coercion' seems to have been their preferred method of retaliation. On 15 June 1563, only weeks after the dissolution of Parliament and Convocation, Walbot was pronounced contumacious for failing to answer a further summons into consistory and ordered to appear on 24 June.[22] His petition had evidently cut little ice with their 'gracious fatherhoods'.

At this point hostilities may have been suspended. London was now struck by the first of those epidemics of bubonic plague which would assail it intermittently until the final and Great Plague of 1665. From late August until mid-December 1563 St Mary Magdalen's register records 37 burials – roughly one every three days over a period of nearly four months.[23] The Walbots themselves survived: on 24 July 1564 their first child, Matthew, was baptized in the parish.[24] Thomas is then recorded as appearing in consistory on 4 October, this time before Grindal himself at Fulham Palace. The bishop ordered him to 'conform'.[25]

'Conform' to what? And did he do so? Presumably not: at some point between 15 April 1565 and 3 May 1566 he resigned the benefice,

[18] Freeman, 'Dissenters', 136.
[19] Ibid., 145.
[20] Penny, *Freewill or Predestination*, 194–204.
[21] Freeman, 'Dissenters', 147.
[22] LMA, DL/C/332, fol. 75r.
[23] *Registers*, 38–9.
[24] *Registers*, 18.
[25] LMA, DL/C/332, fol. 95r.

292

the churchwardens recording that 'p[ar]son Walbott' was paid £4 'at hys dep[ar]tyng at yᵉ agrement of the mastars of the p[ar]yshe'. During this same accounting period they also paid a curate, 'Mr Martens', £20 for serving the cure for eleven months, 20s to one 'Mr Dowse, mynester of colchester, for his chardgys when he dyd sew to be our p[ar]son' and finally lent £10 to 'Mr Bullingam, our new parson'.²⁶

Was it Bishop Grindal who had put Walbot under pressure to resign or rather 'the masters of the parish'? Although Grindal was famously anxious to satisfy 'tender consciences' with regard to the strict provisions of the 1559 prayer book, he proved in other respects a harsh disciplinarian, falling on occasion like a ton of bricks on deviants from a Protestant/Calvinist norm.²⁷ Walbot may have been caught in the cross-fire, since within his parish there dwelt an impressive phalanx of the wealthy merchants of early Elizabethan London. In 1582, a spectacular 90% of all householders were to be assessed for a Higher Subsidy, which placed St Mary Magdalen at the pinnacle of that particular exercise.²⁸

At the first vestry meeting recorded during Walbot's tenure (22 February 1562) a stunning roll-call of names confirms the parish's reputation as a particular haunt of the good and the godly. It is headed by Clement Newce, mercer, whose son-in-law Francis Goldsmith had been a member of Queen Katherine Parr's household and an MP in 1559;²⁹ two future Lord Mayors (Lionel Duckett and William Rowe); the goldsmith Robert Brandon (father-in-law of the painter Nicholas Hilliard); and by Walbot's sureties at the Exchequer, William Kynge and Richard Hill. Indeed, of the twenty-one signatories, at least nine (two names are now illegible) can be traced as sureties at the Exchequer for the first fruits of leading Protestant divines.³⁰ These men were

²⁶ 'Accounts', fol. 135v. John Bullingham, later bishop of Gloucester (1581–98), evidently had the full backing of the 'masters' of the parish. When he compounded for the living (20 December 1566) his sureties were two parishioners, John Whitebroke, cloth-worker, and William Jennyns, mercer. Two others, Richard Seintman, grocer, and Richard Procter, merchant tailor, stood surety for his prebend of Wenlakebarn in St Paul's (10 January 1567) and a fifth, John Hunt, clothworker, for his bishopric in May 1582: TNA, E334/8, fols 96v, 98r; /10, fol. 12v.
²⁷ For examples of Grindal's methods as a disciplinarian, see Patrick Collinson, *Archbishop Grindal: the Struggle for a Reformed Church* (London, 1979), 113–26.
²⁸ R. G. Lang, ed., *Two Tudor Subsidy Assessment Rolls for the City of London: 1541 and 1582*, London Record Society 29 (London, 1993), xli, lxxii.
²⁹ P. W. Hasler, *The House of Commons 1558–1603*, HMSO, 3 vols (London, 1981), 2: 201–2.
³⁰ In order of signing the minutes they are Clement NEWCE, mercer (for Robert Wisdom, archdeacon of Ely, 30 December 1559; for John Aylmer, archdeacon of Lincoln, 15

undoubtedly in a position to hound Walbot from their parish had they chosen collectively to do so.

In fact they appear to have taken pity on him in some limited sense. How else to interpret the payment of £4 – mere pence for these 'masters of the parish' – at his 'departure'? Compensation, perhaps, for the one year's income he would have enjoyed by renting out the parsonage house while his family continued living in Lime Street? Certainly the Walbots remained in the vicinity. Little Matthew was buried in the churchyard, at 22 months old, on 3 June 1566, weeks after his father's resignation. Margaret Walbot was baptized on 27 March 1569.[31] Since nothing else is heard of Thomas himself, inside the parish or without, he and Joan perhaps lived out their days in Lime Street, muzzled but provided for.

Such a compromise would not have been out of place in Grindal's London: in 1562 the Italian Jacobus Acontius noted that ecclesiastical policies of 'extreme narrowness' coexisted with 'excessive latitude', a state of affairs which Patrick Collinson has characterized as 'Calvinism with a human face'.[32] It is one, perhaps, which Thomas Walbot's brief career accurately reflects. And did outspoken Edmund Grindal – who, suspended from his metropolitical functions as archbishop of Canterbury in 1577, thereafter languished in a species of ecclesiastical limbo – ever pause to consider that the queen had meted out to him precisely the same form of rough justice as, fifteen years earlier, had been meted out to an equally outspoken city pastor?

London

December 1562): TNA E334/7, fols 40v, 182v. Robert OFFLEY, haberdasher (for John Pullan, prebendary of Wenlakebarn in St Paul's, 25 October 1561): ibid., fol. 163v. Christopher RINGSTEAD, goldsmith (for Gregory Garth, vicar of Hemel Hempstead, Herts, 13 February 1566): E334/8, fol. 72v. Richard HILL, mercer: see n. 13, above. William KYNGE: see 286–7, above. John WHITEBROKE, clothworker (for Thomas Cole, rector of High Ongar, Essex, 10 November 1559; for John Bullingham, rector of St Mary Magdalen Milk St): E334/7, fol. 30r; and see n. 26, above. Nicholas CAREW, clothier (for Thomas Jenkinson, rector of St Mary Woolchurch, London, 22 February 1560): E334/7, fol. 50r. John LACYE, clothworker (for Bishop Gilbert Berkeley as chancellor of Wells Cathedral, 16 Oct 1560; for Thomas Edmunds, rector of St Mary Magdalen Milk St, 16 October 1571): E334/7, fol. 79r, /8, fol. 266r. Richard PROCTER, merchant tailor (for John Bullingham, prebendary of Wenlakebarn; for William Sage, rector of St Andrew by the Wardrobe, 29 April 1570; for Thomas Edmunds, rector of St Mary Magdalen Milk St, 16 October 1571): E334/8, fols 203v, 266r; and see n. 26, above.

31 *Registers*, 19, 39.
32 Collinson, *Archbishop Grindal*, 152.

DISCIPLINED DISOBEDIENCE? WOMEN AND THE SURVIVAL OF CATHOLICISM IN THE NORTH YORK MOORS IN THE REIGN OF ELIZABETH I

by EMMA WATSON

THE history of post-Reformation Catholicism in Yorkshire can be divided into two distinct periods: pre- and post-1570. Only in the aftermath of the 1569 Northern Rebellion did the Elizabethan government begin to implement fully the 1559 religious settlement in the north, and to take firm action against those who persistently flouted religious laws by continuing to practise the traditional religion of their forefathers. In the Northern Province, serious efforts to enforce conformity and to evangelize did not begin until the arrival of Edmund Grindal as Archbishop of York in 1571. He was joined a year later by the Puritan sympathizer Henry Hastings, Earl of Huntingdon, as President of the Council of the North and together they spear-headed the region's first real evangelical challenge to traditional religion. 1571 also saw the enactment of the first real penal law against Catholics, although only in 1581 was the term 'recusant' coined. Grindal and Huntingdon formed a powerful team committed to Protestant evangelization and the eradication of Catholicism in the North, however, in Yorkshire, their mission was not entirely successful. The North Riding consistently returned high numbers of recusants in the Elizabethan period, and was home to some well-established Catholic communities. In the West and East Ridings recusancy was not so widespread, although religious conservatism persisted, and Catholicism remained a much more significant force across Yorkshire than elsewhere.[1]

The rest of this essay will concentrate on the deanery of Cleveland. Situated in the far north-east of the North Riding, and covering an area roughly equivalent to the North York Moors, Cleveland was a notori-

---

[1] Hugh Aveling, *Northern Catholics* (London, 1966); idem, 'Post Reformation Catholicism in East Yorkshire 1558–1790', *East Yorkshire Local History Society* 11 (1960), 5–31; idem, 'The Catholic Recusants of the West Riding of Yorkshire 1558–1790', *Proceedings of the Leeds Philosophical and Literary Society: Literary and Historical Section*, vol. 10, pt 6 (Leeds, 1963), 191–229.

ous stronghold of traditional religion in the late sixteenth century and, significantly, over half those convicted for recusancy in this region were women, mostly of below gentry status. Previous scholars have suggested the gentry, missionary priests, and the isolation of Cleveland from the ecclesiastical authorities at York as key factors behind the continuing strength of Catholicism in the region.[2] Christopher Haigh has claimed for southern England that an over-concentration by missionaries on gentry households led to an increasingly seigneurial faith with little appeal to those of lower social status,[3] but my own research has demonstrated that in the North York Moors the religious disobedience of the non-gentry Catholic laity, and especially the women, was as vital in the preservation of traditional religion as that of the gentry.[4] The numbers of female recusants revealed during the course of this research by the archbishop's visitation returns for Cleveland suggested that the recusant women of the area should now be studied in their own right. Other scholars have already demonstrated the importance of early modern women in religion, but the role of recusant women in general, and in North Yorkshire in particular, has not yet received the attention it deserves.[5] Sarah Bastow's article on the Catholic Recusant women of Yorkshire establishes the importance of female Catholics in Elizabethan Yorkshire. However the brevity of this article, and Bastow's concentration almost wholly upon the women of the City of York and upon gentry women has left many unanswered questions about the role of female Catholic recusants in the county as a whole during this period.[6] This neglect has led to an incomplete understanding of the techniques of religious discipline and resistance amongst historians of post-reformation Catholicism, which needs to be addressed. There are as yet no other regional studies of recusant women against which this account of the North York Moors can be compared, but the invisibility of female recusants in modern historiography conceals their contem-

---

[2] Ibid; and also B. W. Beckinsale, 'The Characteristics of the Tudor North', *Northern History* 4 (1969), 71–8; J. T. Cliffe, *Yorkshire Gentry from the Reformation to the Civil War*, University of London Historical Studies 25 (London, 1969), 169.

[3] C. Haigh, *English Reformations* (Oxford, 1993), 266.

[4] Emma Watson, ' "A stiff-necked, wilful and obstinate people": the Catholic Laity in the North York Moors c.1559–1603', *Yorkshire Archaeological Journal* 77 (2005), 181–204.

[5] See, for example, Patricia Crawford, *Women and Religion in England 1500–1700* (London, 1993); Marie Rowlands, 'Recusant Women 1560–1640', in Mary Prior, ed., *Women in English Society 1500–1800* (London, 1985), 149–75.

[6] Sarah Bastow, ' "Worth Nothing but Very Wilful": Catholic Recusant Women of Yorkshire 1536–1642', *Recusant History* 25 (2001), 591–603.

porary importance. Documentary evidence for women in Cleveland is scarce, but their disciplined role in maintaining Catholicism in the area, as revealed in the archbishop's visitation returns, and the willingness with which they flouted government attempts to impose religious uniformity, are too important to ignore, perhaps especially because it seems certain that the Elizabethan government was aware that women were often the main, if surreptitious, force behind the maintenance of Catholic households.

The visitation returns provide the most extensive record of lay Catholic non-conformity, although, being designed for administrative use by diocesan authorities, they are not a comprehensive testimony of religious belief. However, they offer a valuable glimpse into religious practice in Cleveland, and of the lengths to which parishioners would go to avoid participating in official services; they are also one of few records that name women independently of men. Individuals presented were called before the ecclesiastical courts, but Aveling has demonstrated that few of those charged with recusancy in Cleveland ever appeared,[7] and across Yorkshire conservative parochial officials would have been reluctant to impose strict compliance when dealing with non-conformity. Social harmony was important and many local authorities were reluctant to jeopardize this, especially where Catholics lived amicably alongside their conformist neighbours. Surviving presentments are probably only a small percentage of actual cases, with only the most persistent offenders presented, and churchwardens may have exercised a selective blindness towards recusants to ensure that leading members of communities were not presented whilst they still had an important secular role to play. This may account for the preponderance of women presented: churchwardens had to demonstrate to central authority that they were acting against Catholics, but at the same time wanted to preserve the stability of their communities.[8] Nevertheless, the very fact that there were so many female recusants must indicate the importance of their role in resisting the Established Church.

Churchwardens may also have deliberately presented the poorest recusants in their parishes. Poverty was an accepted reason for non-

---

7 Aveling, *Northern Catholics*, 147.

8 W. J. Sheils, 'Household, Age and Gender among Jacobean Yorkshire Recusants', in Marie B. Rowlands, ed., *English Catholics of Parish and Town 1558–1788*, Catholic Record Society Publications, Monograph 5 (London, 1999) [hereafter: *CRSP*], 131–52, suggested this for the early seventeenth century, but the same can be argued for the later sixteenth.

attendance at church, and poor recusants largely went unpunished, given their inability to pay the required fines. Again this may explain the predominance of women. Cleveland was a poor region, and women were often amongst the poorest of the poor. It is also vital to consider the importance of community solidarity, which may account for the way in which parishioners can be seen dropping in and out of the visitation returns, suggesting that the returns themselves reveal more about the system of presentment for religious misdemeanours than they do about the pattern of Catholic non-conformity. Differences in religious belief and practice probably mattered little to people in the small moorland communities, which might explain why the Catholic communities here, although always a numerical minority, were allowed to thrive. Indeed the fluidity of categorization and a lack of any real concept of 'the Other' before the late 1580s may have meant Catholic householders in this region were not regarded as different by their conformist neighbours, and any presentments were as likely to have been for an obdurate failure to perform public duty as for religious beliefs.

Prior to the reign of Elizabeth the effect of Tudor religious change in Cleveland was slight. The impoverished benefices were unattractive to educated Protestant ministers, and the flooding of the clerical market by the dissolution of the monasteries ensured a constant stream of conservative priests into vacant livings into the 1560s and beyond. Parishioners in Cleveland rarely presented their clergy for failing to preach or use prescribed service books. Perhaps non-compliance with the requirements of the Elizabethan prayer book was of little importance to them, or, as shown by Duffy for the parish of Morebath in Devon, it could simply indicate acquiescence with the religious settlement.[9] However, the numbers accused of recusancy, non-communication and non-attendance at church grew continuously throughout Elizabeth's reign, prompting Cecil's principal informant to call the area a 'Bishopric of Papists'.[10] Perhaps this growth was the result of changing government policies and more determined efforts against Catholics, but the numbers nonetheless reflect the presence of substantial Catholic communities.

---

[9] Eamon Duffy, *Voices of Morebath: Reformation and Rebellion in an English Village*, (New Haven, CT, 2001), 170–1.

[10] Jack Binns, 'Sir Hugh Cholmley of Whitby 1600–1657: His Life and Works', unpublished Ph.D. thesis, University of Leeds, 1990, 50.

The 1582 presentment of Jane Burton, wife of Robert Burton of Egton, was the first for actual recusancy in the Cleveland returns,[11] and subsequently the numbers of female recusants in the visitations are consistently higher than those of men. Parishes with significant recusant communities invariably had a higher proportion of women, and often only women were named in parishes where numbers presented were small. In addition the recusant rolls of the 1590s and Edward Peacock's 1604 list of recusants both name more women than men in all social classes.[12] Even missionary priests recognized that recusancy was more common amongst women than men. John Mush, best known for his biography of Margaret Clitherow, told colleagues in London that the gentlemen in Yorkshire had 'fallen off from the priests, but the gentlewomen stood steadfastly to them',[13] and Thomas Clarke, a frequent visitor to the household of George Tocketts of Guisborough, admitted that Tockett's wife and household had not attended the parish church, although George himself appears to have done so.[14]

Although it is possible that Catholicism was deliberately overlooked amongst certain members of the community, it is also probable that in Cleveland as elsewhere many male heads of household conformed to the Established Church sufficiently to avoid prosecution, whilst their wives maintained a Catholic household. Some, such as Roger Radcliffe of Lythe, were particularly successful in keeping their Catholicism hidden from the authorities. In 1572 Thomas Gargrave, then vice-president of the Council of the North, drew up a list of the religion of all Yorkshire gentlemen.[15] Amongst others, Gargrave listed Radcliffe as Protestant, yet his household was one of the most notorious centres of Catholicism in the area. Several members of the Radcliffe family, and many of their neighbours, appeared repeatedly in the visitation returns for Lythe, and their manor at Ugthorpe became an important mass

---

[11] York, Borthwick Institute [hereafter: Borthwick], V1 582, fol. 234r. Jane Burton is not named in 1582, only listed as Robert's wife, but she appears repeatedly under her own name in subsequent visitation returns.

[12] *Recusant Roll 1 (1592–1593)*, ed. M. M. C. Calthrop, *CRSP* 18 (1916), 84–102; *Recusant Roll 2 (1593–1594)*, ed. Hugh Bowler, *CRSP* 57 (1965), 199–222; *Recusant Roll 3 (1594–1595) and Recusant Roll 4 (1595–1596)*, ed. Hugh Bowler, *CRSP* 61 (1970), 113–27, 245–55; Edward Peacock, *A List of the Roman Catholics in the County of York in 1604* (London, 1872), 89–110.

[13] Aveling, *Northern Catholics*, 95–6.

[14] M. A. E. Green, *Calendar of State Papers Domestic, Elizabeth 1591–1594* (London, 1867), 305. George Tocketts does not appear in any visitation returns.

[15] See J. J. Cartwright, *Chapters in the History of Yorkshire* (Wakefield, 1872), 66–72 for Gargrave's list.

centre.[16] However, Roger was a substantial figure in the local community and held considerable social power. He may thus have been exempted from prosecution in order to maintain his public role, despite the evidence that his wife and household were actively encouraging and facilitating the survival of Catholicism. Had there been a strong Protestant presence in Lythe it is unlikely that Radcliffe would have escaped prosecution, but his social standing meant the authorities relied on him to keep order in the area. Had he been indicted for recusancy, an important source of local social control would have been lost. There were no such qualms about prosecuting female recusants. Women could not exercise social control and their presentments would enable local authorities to demonstrate that they were acting against recusancy; hence Katherine Radcliffe frequently appeared in the visitation returns, although her husband did not.

Mary Harding, a relative of Radcliffe's living at Hunt House in Goathland, was also a known Catholic, and her home became a refuge for Catholics in the area. Mary employed several poor villagers, some of whom, in particular Dorothy and James Crosby, were persistent recusants,[17] and this may be significant in explaining why Mary herself appears to have escaped prosecution. Goathland was a poor, sparsely populated parish and, had Mary been unable to employ poorer residents, the burden of providing relief would have probably fallen upon the other parishioners. This tacit permission to continue practising her faith enabled Mary to establish Hunt House as an important calling point on the North York Moors mass circuit, but also allowed her to offer a measure of protection to other Catholics in the area, and to use her connections to build a role in a disciplined network of religious disobedience.

Several other mass centres existed in the region, notably at the former Grosmont priory, which was leased by the Hodgesons from the Cholmleys of Whitby. It is impossible to tell whether John Hodgeson or his wife Jane took the commanding role in inviting priests to the priory; their whole family appears repeatedly in the visitations.[18] Hodgeson's nearest neighbours, the Salvins of Newbiggin Manor in

[16] Aveling, *Northern Catholics*, 160; W. J. Sheils, 'Catholics and their Neighbours in a Rural Community: Egton Chapelry 1590–1780', *Northern History* 34 (1998), 109–33, at 111.

[17] Alice Hollings, *Goathland: the Story of a Moorland Village* (Whitby, 1971), 16; York, Borthwick, V1595–6 (CB3), fol. 145v; V1600 (CB.1B), fol. 231v.

[18] York, Borthwick, V1586, fol. 116r; V1590–1/CB1, fol. 199r; V1594, fol. 133r; V1595–6/CB3, fol. 148r; V1600/CB.1B, fol. 233v.

Egton, another Mass House, and the Smiths of nearby Bridge House were also habitual recusants, and it was the women of both families who appeared most frequently in the visitations. The number of mass centres in the relatively small geographic area of the North York Moors indicates both the establishment of a structured network of resistance, and largely harmonious relations between Catholics and their conformist neighbours. In Egton, the Catholic community grew to become the largest in the area, and work by Bill Sheils has demonstrated that Catholics and conformists here lived together and intermarried with little sign of conflict.[19] These safe houses were vital not only for the provision of Catholic priests in the local communities, but also for the dispersal of these priests across the north of England. It is probably no accident that the long, isolated Cleveland coastline became a favoured landing point for the Catholic Mission, as did West Sussex, which was similarly isolated from the centres of ecclesiastical control.

Traditionally the household was the woman's domain, and as Catholicism became more and more a household religion the importance of women in maintaining the old faith steadily increased, albeit with the collusion of their husbands. Women's responsibility for household routines meant that they arranged for the attendance and concealment of priests and mass equipment, often when their husbands were away. Thomas Clarke stated that Margaret Cholmley received him at Whitby 'during her husband's absence';[20] such practice must have been common amongst Catholic families, and it is likely that the men knew of it and deliberately absented themselves when the priests were due to attend. Women also organized their household's religious education. This was particularly important in gentry households, and the pattern of the Puritan godly household revealed in Lady Margaret Hoby's diary was mirrored in many Catholic homes.[21] Devotional tracts were printed for both faiths, and women of the same social status followed similar patterns of piety whatever their beliefs.[22] Although access to Catholic priests was relatively easy in Cleveland, most women were unable to rely upon a regular clerical presence in their households. Many therefore had little choice but to provide religious education

[19] Sheils, 'Catholics and their Neighbours', 115, 119.
[20] Green, *CSPD 1591–1594*, 305.
[21] Joanna Moody, *The Private Life of an Elizabethan Lady: the Diary of Lady Margaret Hoby 1599–1605* (Stroud, 2001).
[22] Crawford, *Women and Religion*, 75–80.

themselves, using printed devotional works such as Robert Persons's *The First Booke of the Christian Exercise* (1582). In doing so they demonstrated further conscious disobedience to state injunctions. Although it became increasingly common for the children of recusants to be educated abroad, in reality few could afford this, and the high risks meant eldest sons were rarely sent.[23] Evidence that Catholic women were a key factor in the education of their children can be found amongst reports that almost a quarter of students at the English college at Rome said directly that their mothers had influenced their vocation, and perhaps more importantly that this was often against the wishes of their Protestant fathers.[24]

Women were ideally placed to instil Catholic beliefs into their households, and it may have been the recognition of this which led to the 1591 laws permitting the punishment of married recusant women in their own right. Despite this, many wives, such as Lady Babthorpe of Osgodby, continued to practise Catholicism. Lady Babthorpe regularly sheltered priests, had seven of her eight children baptized in the Catholic faith, and successfully prevented all of them from attending church, despite her husband being under a bond of £4,000 to ensure their presence.[25] Several Cleveland families had children baptized as Catholics, once more exercising active resistance to the state that required considerable organization and relied heavily upon the discretion of friends and neighbours. A number of presentments occur in the visitations for failure to baptize children into the Established Church, and some parents, such as Elizabeth and Robert Simpson of Egton, and Jane and William Philips of Danby, reappear repeatedly, suggesting that few presentments resulted in any serious punishment.[26] The Simpsons and the Philips were prominent members of their communities, which may explain why little action was taken against them, but both must have relied upon strong social bonds with conformist neighbours.

[23] Foreign education became illegal from 1585 and there was a danger that heirs might renounce their rights for the priesthood. However some Catholics, such as the Meynells of North Kilvington, still ensured that their children received a Catholic education. Hugh Aveling, ed., 'Recusancy Papers of the Meynell Family', *CRSP* 56 (London, 1964), xv, xvii. There is only one visitation presentment for the employment of a Catholic schoolmaster: York, Borthwick, VI595–6/CB3, fols 148v–149r.

[24] Crawford, *Women and Religion*, 61.

[25] Christine Newman, 'The Role of Women in Early Yorkshire Recusancy: a Reappraisal', *Northern Catholic History* 30 (1989), 6–16, at 10.

[26] York, Borthwick, VI594, fols 133r, 136v; VI586, fol. 120r; VI590–1/CB1, fol. 199v; VI595–6/CB3, fols 148r, 150r; VI600/CB.1B, fols 233v, 234r, 237r, 242r, 248v.

Elizabeth Chapman of Fylingdales also appears to have exerted a strong
religious influence over her family, and was not put off by increased
government persecution. Elizabeth was presented for recusancy in each
visitation from 1586 to 1600, but by 1600 her husband, son and daughters also appear. It seems that Elizabeth took a leading role in the religious education of her children, and either persuaded her husband to
stop conforming, or converted him from a genuine Protestant belief,
although it is also possible that his role in the Fylingdales community
was such that existing Catholic beliefs had previously been ignored.[27]

By 1560 Fylingdales, along with much of the rest of the Liberty of
Whitby Strand, was held by Richard Cholmley. Contemporaries recognized Richard as a Catholic, and largely through the efforts of his
second wife Katherine Clifford, Lady Scrope, and his daughter-in-law
Margaret Babthorpe, the Cholmley home became a sanctuary for Catholic priests and Whitby developed a substantial recusant community.
Katherine and Margaret were notorious recusants, and although Lady
Katherine was too elderly and too well connected to be severely
punished, Margaret was jailed for several months in 1593, along with
her sister-in-law Katherine Dutton, Katherine Radcliffe of Ugthorpe
and the wives of several other Yorkshire gentlemen.[28] Only a year
earlier, in 1592, Katherine Dutton, a daughter of Henry Cholmley,
married her husband Richard in a secret Roman ceremony in the
private chapel of the Ingleby family at Ripley in the West Riding.[29] The
Ingleby home was also used as a dispersal point for priests, and was
some distance inland from Whitby. The Duttons were not alone, other
Catholics were also prepared to travel to be married according to
Roman tradition, emphasizing the strength of their belief, and the
extent of their communication with other Catholics. Such communication was vital to ensure the survival of post-reformation Catholicism
throughout England, but networks did not just exist between gentry
families. Groups of travelling players such as that based at Egton in the
1590s played a crucial role in transmitting information and messages
amongst Catholics of all social levels. Even Lord Sheffield, a member of
the Council of the North and a notorious prosecutor of recusants, who
had inherited the Mulgrave estate from the Radcliffes, was married by a

[27] York, Borthwick, VI586, fol. 108v; VI590–1/CBI, fols 164r, 184r; VI594, fol. 139r;
VI595-6/CB3, fol. 153v; VI600/CB.IB, fol. 235v.
[28] Binns, *Cholmley*, 42, 44, 48; Rowlands, 'Recusant Women', 154.
[29] Aveling, *Northern Catholics*, 149.

priest to his Catholic wife in 1581. Despite his activities against Catholics, Sheffield was still suspected of papistry as late as 1598.[30] That year also saw the death of Katherine Clifford, after which Henry and Margaret Cholmley conformed to the Established Religion. Continued persecution and mounting financial difficulties doubtless contributed to this, but committed Protestant preachers were emerging in the area by this time, and perhaps their conformity would have occurred earlier without Lady Scrope's obstinate recusancy. Margaret disappears from ecclesiastical court records after this, but Henry seems to have become a zealous Protestant. In 1604, as JP for Whitby, he personally presented twenty-three recusants, a 'retainer of recusants', a private baptism and three cases of secret marriage before the Council.[31] The Elizabethan government hoped to eliminate Catholicism by removing the influence of families such as the Cholmleys, and like their European counterparts they worked to mobilize noble and gentry landowners as both agents and enforcers of religious change.[32] In areas where gentry support was vital for the maintenance of traditional religion they were reasonably successful. In the North York Moors, however, recusant communities were able to exist without the direct support of the gentry. The spread of recusancy in Whitby Strand was not halted by the conformity of the previously Catholic Cholmleys after 1598. Nor did the arrival of anti-Catholic government agents Sir Thomas Hoby at Hackness and Lord Sheffield at Mulgrave in the mid-1590s encourage their neighbours to conform. The importance of gentlemen and their wives in the preservation of Catholicism must not be underestimated, but scholars ought now to pay more attention to their socially subordinate neighbours and their womenfolk.

Though visitation returns are the most revealing source for lay religion in Cleveland, further valuable insights into the diverse religious beliefs of women can also be provided by wills. Few survive for Cleveland women and the majority of those are neutral, but a few are more revealing. As late as 1596, Agnes Whitby of Lythe bequeathed her soul

---

[30] Ibid., 130; John Bossy, *The English Catholic Community* (London, 1975), 136; Crawford, *Women and Religion*, 61.

[31] A. G. Dickens, 'The Extent and Character of Recusancy in Yorkshire, 1604', *Yorkshire Archaeological Journal* 37 (1948–51), 24–49, at 25.

[32] Joseph Patrouch, *A Negotiated Settlement: the Counter-Reformation in Upper Austria under the Habsburgs* (Boston, 2000) is a good illustration of the way in which local landowners could be used to aid authorities in implementing religious change, and of the resistance they could offer.

to God, Jesus Christ, and 'all the blessed company of heaven'.[33] Following a traditional belief that the prayers of widows and the poor were especially efficacious for the soul, Agnes also bequeathed money to the poor widows of Lythe. The legal requirements of the late sixteenth-century dictated that prayer was not explicitly mentioned, but Agnes demonstrated considerable obstinacy in setting forth her divergent beliefs so clearly. Women, particularly widows and the elderly, were an important part of the Catholic network, and Agnes probably believed them most likely to remember her after her death. Later still, in 1602, Margaret Robson of Robin Hood's Bay in Fylingdales also bequeathed her soul to God, Christ and 'all the Holy Company of Heaven' though her bequests were entirely secular.[34] Whoever was responsible for composing these preambles, no Protestant would have agreed to the inclusion of Catholic saints in their will, and other evidence shows that Agnes was presented as a recusant in the visitations of 1590 to 1591, and that Lythe and Fylingdales had thriving Catholic communities with numerous female recusants.[35]

Similar sentiments can be found in other women's wills across the period, all in parishes which returned high numbers of recusants during Elizabeth's reign.[36] It must be noted that there are also a very small number of women's wills from Elizabethan Cleveland which have overtly Protestant preambles, but few of these are particularly explicit, and all are from parishes with few or no recusants.[37] The small numbers of extant women's wills from Elizabethan Cleveland are insufficient to build a definitive pattern of women's religious beliefs in the area, and the neutral form of the majority gives little or no indication of personal faith, whilst confirming that will preambles alone are insufficient guides to religious belief. However, the proportion of women continuing to use Catholic language, particularly in parishes with high numbers of known recusants, can only serve to emphasize the traditional nature of religious beliefs in the North York Moors, and to demonstrate the importance of women's willingness to defy the state in order to maintain those beliefs.

[33] York, Borthwick, Prob. Reg. 26, fol. 321v.

[34] York, Borthwick, Prob. Reg. 28, fols 590v–591r.

[35] York, Borthwick, V1590–1/CB1 fol. 190r; Fylingdales and Lythe each returned 40 female recusants in the Elizabethan visitations.

[36] York, Borthwick, Prob. Reg. 18, fols 101v and 183r; PR 19, fol. 351v; PR 21, fol. 316r.

[37] York, Borthwick, Prob. Reg. 27, fols 460v–461r.

Catholicism in Cleveland remained a statistical minority, but it successfully resisted all attempts by the Elizabethan government to crush it, and by 1603 it could be suggested that there were scarcely more convinced Protestants than Catholics in the area. The people of the North York Moors were particularly well positioned to gain maximum benefit from the English Catholic mission, and made the most of the resources available to them. Many made a conscious decision to reject the Established Church, and the growing number of names occurring in the visitation returns suggests that new converts were continually being made, in some cases building up religious communities that remain today. Undoubtedly the arrival of the missionary priests from the 1580s was critical to the survival of Catholicism, but without the determination of the Catholic laity, and particularly the women, the priests would have had little to work with. Sarah Bastow argued that it was women who made Catholicism a 'living religion in an age where it was in danger of dying a quiet death',[38] and the unobtrusive and disciplined work of the women of Cleveland in support of the Catholic faith suggests that here at least this was true. The women of the moorland communities worked together to resist the state; the coherent and disciplined nature of that resistance, coupled with the relative religious toleration exercised by individual communities which gave these women the space and time within which to create and build up the vital cross-class networks, made it all the more effective and enabled the establishment of a continuing recusant tradition in the area which survived into the eighteenth century and beyond. Although the role of women seems to have become less significant in later years, without the disciplined resistance of recusant women under Elizabeth it seems unlikely that such a strong foundation of Catholicism could have been established in the North York Moors.

University of York

[38] Bastow, ' "Worth Nothing but Very Wilful" ', 599.

DISCIPLINE AND DOMESTIC VIOLENCE
IN EDINBURGH, 1560–1625

by MELISSA HOLLANDER

As no Citie, Towne, howse, or familie can maynteine their estate
and prospere without policie and governaunce, so the Churche of
God, which more purely to be governed than any citie or familie,
can not without spirituall Policie and ecclesiasticall Discipline
continewe, encrease and florishe. [sic]

*The form of prayers and ministration of the sacraments, &c., used in the
English congregation at Geneva, 1556.*[1]

IN June 1620 George Johnsoun was 'scharplie rebukit for his hynous
sin of disobediens to his parents in stryking of his mother' and
imprisoned for one week whilst the Session of St Cuthbert's parish,
Edinburgh, decided how to deal with him.[2] The following week the
Session ordained 'george Johnsoun to ga to his parents everie mornyng
and evening upoun his kneis and promeis with his grace never to do ye
lyk in tymes cumyng'. The Session elders seem to have been aware both
of the menace that George represented to his parents, his mother in
particular, and of the extent to which he had become a disorderly trou-
blemaker. They therefore required him to '[promise] to tak ane office
man [with] him quher he so gets yair blissin'. The Session could thus
monitor George's behaviour and the fervency of his repentance, and
guarantee that discipline was properly enacted. With this punishment
the Kirk sent a clear message to the parishioners of St Cuthbert's, and
the whole Edinburgh Presbytery, that disobedience and disorder in the
domestic sphere were entirely unacceptable. Perhaps more significantly, in this case the parish authorities publicly and explicitly declared
and demonstrated that violence against domestic authority, particularly
against one's mother, was insupportable.

The Scottish Kirk had no explicit policy with regard to domestic

---

[1] David Laing, ed., *The Works of John Knox*, 6 vols (Edinburgh, 1855) [hereafter: Knox,
Works], 4: 203.
[2] Edinburgh, National Archives of Scotland [hereafter: Edinburgh, NAS], CH2/718/4, f.
50. The minute books of the St Cutherbert session comprise four volumes.

violence. There were no specific guidelines upon which to call in such cases except for the Confession of Faith's assertion that

> murtheraris, oppressouris, cruell persecutaris, adulteraris, whore-mongaris, filthy personis, idolateris, drounkardis, theavis, and all workaris of iniquitie, have neather trew faith, neather any portioun of the spreat of Sanctificatioun, whiche proceadeth frome the Lord Jesus, so long as thei obstinatelie continew in thair wickednes.[3]

In the late sixteenth and early seventeenth centuries the synods, general assemblies, and Sessions were more concerned with reinvigorating the unwieldy Church infrastructure in Scotland,[4] and addressing the ever-pressing problems of adultery, irregular marriage, and fornication.[5] Each Presbytery and Session, made up of lay elders and Kirk representatives, was left to devise its public response to, and appropriate punishment for, a sinful disruption which did not quite fall into any of the categories listed in the Books of Discipline,[6] but which incorporated aspects of many of the vices the Kirk most abhorred.

This essay examines cases of domestic violence in Edinburgh that became public knowledge by being subjected to ecclesiastical discipline, and untangles the cultural and physical responses that the Reformed Kirk demanded and imposed upon those who transgressed their moral boundaries. These cases, in which violence was perceived to disrupt good household order and governance, are a means to examine further how the ideology of discipline functioned and was used within the Reformed Scottish Church. These cases illustrate how the Kirk's notion of good social order and the moral community was tied to the harmonious and orderly functioning of domestic spaces and relationships. When these relationships were perceived to be in disorder they became dangerous, potentially damaging the aims and intentions of the Kirk. Reformed discipline thus drew upon a patristic interpretation of authority, one conceived primarily as a means to promote and reinforce

---

3 Knox, *Works*, 2: 104.
4 James Kirk, ed., *The Second Book of Discipline* (Edinburgh, 1980), 159–244.
5 Michael Graham, 'Social Discipline in Scotland, 1560 to 1610', in Raymond Mentzer, ed., *Sin and the Calvinists: Morals, Control and the Consistory in the Reformed Tradition* (Kirksville, MO, 1994), 129–58, at 137.
6 John Knox, *The History of the Reformation in Scotland*, ed. Cuthbert Lennox (London, 1905) [hereafter: Knox, *History*], 396. Kirk, *Second Book of Discipline* and James K. Cameron, ed., *The First Book of Discipline* (Edinburgh, 1972).

household/communal order and hierarchies. This was a social and behavioural as well as religious reformation.

As we have already glimpsed in the Johnsoun case, this analysis allows me to question whether the Scottish Kirk generated an atmosphere that condoned or condemned violence within the household, and in particular to question the idea that domestic violence was in some way acceptable during this period.[7] But most significantly this paper examines the powerful conceptual link in the Calvinist theology adopted by the Scots reformers, as highlighted by the opening quotation, between domestic and social order and the godly community. Within this model the punishment of household violence was a means by which to generate good, obedient, and socially aware parishioners, making the household an intrinsic element of the good communal order and governance that so dominated both Calvinist[8] and Scots Presbyterian thinking.[9] Within this configuration of Kirk discipline the purpose of punishment was not to harm or humiliate, but to encourage repentance, redemption, and reintegration.

The violent acts committed by George Johnsoun do not stand alone in the records of St Cuthbert's parish for the late sixteenth and early seventeenth centuries. Five additional cases concerned violence either against parents or spouses; significantly more addressed the common problem of brawling and 'flyting' in the street.[10] The records of South Leith, another Edinburgh parish, during this period present four more

---

[7] Fay Bound, 'An "Uncivil" Culture: Marital Violence and Domestic Politics in York, c.1660–c.1760', in Mark Hallett and Jane Rendall, eds, *Eighteenth-Century York: Culture Space and Society*, Borthwick Texts and Calendars 30 (York, 2003), 50–8. This perspective on the material is not always accepted as unproblematic: Susan Dwyer Amussen, ' "Being Stirred to Much Unquietness": Violence and Domestic Violence in Early Modern England', *Journal of Women's History* 6: 2 (1994), 70–89, at 71–2, and J. A. Sharpe, 'Domestic Homicide in Early Modern England', *The Historical Journal* 24: 1 (1981), 29–48.

[8] Heinz Schilling, 'Reform and Supervision of Family Life in Germany and the Netherlands', in Mentzer, *Sin and the Calvinists*, 15–63, is a good survey of the family in the policies of reformed consistories.

[9] Margo Todd, *The Culture of Protestantism in Early Modern Scotland* (Yale, 2004), 183–5. Graham, 'Social Discipline', 137–8. This is in line with reformed thought in England, see, Amussen, ' "Being Stirred to Much Unquietness" ', 75. Scots Calvinism also gave the Scots 'a sense of their own distinctive place in the world', as leaders of the reformation, David Allen 'Protestantism, Presbyterianism and National Identity in Eighteenth-Century Scottish History', in T. Claydon and I. McBride, eds, *Protestantism and National Identity: Britain and Ireland, c.1650 to c.1850* (Cambridge, 1998), 182–205, at 185, and Kirk, *Second Book of Discipline*, 241.

[10] Edinburgh, NAS, CH2/718/1–4, 2: 146, 2: 328, 3: 60, 4: 165, 4: 170.

instances of what would today be considered domestic violence.[11] Such cases pepper the minutes of both the Kirk and Burgh authorities, periodically refocusing their attention on the potential brutality of domestic life. Yet the understanding and acceptance of that brutality was complicated by ideas of life cycle, status, and order. Husbands, wives and parents were figures of authority and power within the early modern household, with the right to impose their own corrective punishments on disorderly or idle children and servants. As Knox asserted, '[i]f thou be a subject, sonne, or daughter, be obedient to thy superior'.[12]

The English and Scottish ecclesiastical and civic legal systems differed considerably. In English towns the civic courts and justices of the peace monitored and cautioned overtly aggressive and excessively violent behaviour both within the household and on the street. However, cases of domestic violence only appeared in the ecclesiastical jurisdiction when a marital separation was being sought, or in the most extreme and public cases of violence.[13] This not only impacted on the content of the records – the English consistory inviting deponents to construct brutal narratives of physical and bodily torment – but has also had a profound impact on their interpretation and use by historians.[14] By contrast, the Edinburgh Sessions worked in conjunction with the civic authorities, sharing resources in the correction of deviant and socially disruptive behaviour.[15] The terms by which Scottish discipline operated produced different, less extreme, narratives of violent behaviour which were then reflected in attitudes to, and the recording of, that behaviour. Therefore, the Kirk's response to domestic violence drew on its attitudes to disobedience, brawling, excess, and in many cases drunkenness.

The *Book of Discipline* noted a relationship between excess, particularly in the consumption of alcohol, and violent or disruptive behaviour,[16] and this was made explicit in the Kirk minutes. Luke Lennox, in February 1611, was warned 'under ye pane of making his publick

11 D. Robertson, ed., *South Leith Records: Compiled from the Parish Registers for the Years 1588 to 1700; and from Other Original Sources* (Edinburgh, 1911), 3, 9, 10, and 11.

12 Knox, *Works*, 3: 539.

13 Bound, 'An "Uncivil" Culture', 52. Elizabeth Foyster, 'Male Honour, Social Control and Wife Beating in Late Stuart England', *TRHS* ser. 6, 6 (1996), 215–24, at 216–17.

14 Sharpe, 'Domestic Homicide in Early Modern England', 31.

15 Knox, *Works*, 6: 468–9.

16 Cameron, *First Book of Discipline*, 168.

repentance before ye congregatioun yt he sall never be fand strykand his wyf nor prophaning the sabboth nor be drunkan in tymis cummyng'.[17] Similarly in 1602 David Wilson, 'confest that upon the Sabboth day afternone in tyme of preiching he was drunkin and struik his wyfe publiclie in the streit'.[18] For this first offence St Cuthbert's Session ordered that Wilson 'sit doune wpon his kneis and confes the secunde faulth, and that he sall stand wpon the Piller on the Sabboth nixtocum and thair in the presens of the peopill to confes his vyces'. In both cases wife-beating was not the sole matter at issue: both men had publicly profaned the Sabbath with their disorderly behaviour. Yet the connection between drunkenness, irreverence to the Kirk, and domestic violence was made clear. David Wilson's 'secunde faulth' of striking his wife in public precipitated a most degrading public punishment, apology, and repentance. Both men were disciplined for their failings as respectable householders, for, as Knox wrote, 'if a man make no thought of his owne, and specially of his household or familie, hee hath denyed the faith, and is worse than an infidele'.[19]

The imposition of Kirk discipline in these disorderly households was a means of re-establishing and reasserting domestic order and authority. The interventions of the Session in cases of domestic violence demonstrate not only how the 'power' of the household head was reinforced by the Kirk, [20] but also how that power was monitored and on occasion restricted. The policy of the Session was to intervene in cases of domestic disorder only after the head of the household had failed to resolve the problem at hand.[21] The language of the Kirk presented the household as a microcosm of the godly community.[22] Within the household the marital partnership was considered to be the lynchpin guaranteeing domestic harmony and authority; wives were subject to their husbands, just as children were subject to parental authority, and the congregation was subject to the Kirk.[23] Knox clearly articulated this reciprocity in his advice to wives, 'as the church is subject to Christ,

---

[17] Edinburgh, NAS, CH2/718/52, 165.
[18] Edinburgh, NAS, CH2/718/2, 146.
[19] Knox, *Works*, 3: 536.
[20] Amussen, ' "Being Stirred to Much Unquietness" ', 70–1.
[21] Knox, *Works*, 3: 540–1.
[22] Ibid., 3: 535–9. Todd, *Culture of Protestantism*, ch. 6. Amussen, ' "Being Stirred to Much Unquietness" ', 73.
[23] Knox, Works, 3: 535–7. Todd, *Culture of Protestantism*, 299. Bound, 'An "Uncivil" Culture', 53.

even so be thou subject to thy husband in all lawfull things';[24] to children, 'obey your parents with great humilitie; love, feare, and honour them'; and to servants, 'obey your carnall lords and maisters, with feare and trembling, with simplenesse of hart, as it were unto Christ'.[25] Within these relationships the need for humility, love, and honour were considered paramount. The Kirk therefore built its authority by fostering the patriarchal hierarchies of family and household. Acts of violence undermined the orderly and respectful communities that the Sessions and Presbyteries sought to perpetuate, up heaving the hard work that ministers and elders engaged in amongst their parishes.

Private admonition and arbitration were used as a means to resolve social and domestic disorder 'if the offence be secret or known to few men'.[26] If arbitration was unsuccessful, or, '[i]f the crime be publick, and such as is heinous, as fornication, drunkenesse, fighting, common swearing or execration',[27] then the offender ought to be called to perform public acts of punishment and repentance.[28] These public displays of disciplinary power tied together the judicial structures and methods of the Kirk and Burgh authorities, both systems sharing the use of officers of the town, means of restraining, parading, labelling, and humiliating those undergoing punishment.[29] These displays also made the congregation part of the process of discipline, both through the election of elders, and through participation in punishments, through prayers for God's 'mercy' and by receiving the penitent back into the community.[30] Crucially, it was never the intention of discipline to ostracize or isolate offenders, but rather to '[b]ring the rude and ignorant to knowledge, [and] inflame the learned to greater fervency'.[31] Discipline was specifically constructed to keep the subject within the community of the Kirk, and to encourage repentance through a combination of humiliation, education and awareness, 'so that his conscience

24 Knox, *Works*, 3: 536.
25 Ibid., 3: 540–1.
26 Cameron, *First Book of Discipline*, 167–8. Todd, *Culture of Protestantism*, 243.
27 Ibid., 168.
28 Ibid., 62–7 and 165–7. Knox, *Works*, 3: 107–19.
29 John G. Harrison, 'Women and the Branks in Stirling, c.1600 to c.1730', *Scottish Economic and Social History* 18: 2 (1998), 114–31, at 116–17.
30 Cameron, *First Book of Discipline*, 168. Harrison, 'Women and the Branks in Stirling', 127–8.
31 Knox, *History*, 404.

may feel how farre he hath offended God and what slander he hath raised in the Kirk'.[32]

It is within this context of penitential punishment that we can evaluate more fully the seriousness of George Johnsoune's sin and subsequent discipline. Having been ordered to go, morning and evening, to the house of his parents, and there to promise 'with [all] his grace never to do ye lyk in tyme cumyng', under the watchful eye of an officer of the court, George was made acutely aware of his subordinate position within both his domestic and religious contexts. He was made into a symbol of household disorder and disruption to be employed by the Kirk. George had undermined and violently rejected the authority of his parents within their own domain. This offence against the familial order was at the same time an outrage against the religious and social order as it rejected the hierarchy and morality that the Kirk promoted. The journey that George was to undertake twice daily 'upoun his kneis', and the promise that he made at each of these visits to his parents' house, was a ritual display to the neighbours of the Johnsoune family that George was aware of the significance of his actions. When used as a forum for discipline the early modern street became a transitional, performative, and redemptive space. The public declaration of his sins and the insistence that George beg his parents' forgiveness on his knees were symbolic of his removal from their ordered domestic space, as well as a demonstration of his – imposed – desire to be re-included in that space. This public performance functioned in the same way as discipline within the body of the Kirk. Men and women performed their apologetic repentance from subordinate positions within the congregation, and were made to stand outside the door, on the threshold of the godly community, whilst the congregation arrived.[33] These performances were constructed to subordinate the person being punished and to invite an audience to the repentance of that person.

After three weeks 'Johne Johnsoune and his wyf' petitioned their Session, asking that George's punishment be concluded. They 'confest yt thaire sone hes humblit him self upoun his kneis sundrie and diverse tymes'. The Session then ordered George onto his knees one last time to ask the forgiveness of the Session and Parish. Having shown his family

---

32 Cameron, *First Book of Discipline*, 168.
33 Knox, *Works*, 6: 468–9: 'The order of excommunication and public repentance, 1569'.

their due respect, he was now to demonstrate his respect for the institution and values of the Kirk, values which his actions had undermined. George was ordered to appear the following week to complete his repentance within the church itself, having 'actit him self willinglie vnder ye pane of baneshement yt he sall nether trubill or molest his parents or any vyer nytbouris in tymes cumyng wt gud his grace'. With these words George Johnsoune, who had beaten his mother and others within his parish, was received back into the community of God, once again made a part of the Kirk's godly community.

Strikingly, the Edinburgh Presbytery did not consider violent behaviour to be a purely masculine trait. The minutes of the Burgh's Sessions reveal a clear understanding of the danger that women could present to other women, to children, and to husbands. The infanticidal mother and murderous wife were female stereotypes that abounded in popular English and Scottish pamphlets and ballads particularly during the seventeenth century.[34] Yet, only two cases in which women initiated domestic violence have survived in the records of the Edinburgh Presbytery during this period. In December 1612, Jonet Proveane, spouse to John McDull, 'confest yt scho struik him with ane knyfe in ye thrut'.[35] For this Jonet was made to 'stand thrie sabboth dayis in saccloth vpon the piller and lykwyis to stand at the Kirk Dur qll the preitching begin'. Jonet confessed her sin in the case, offering herself to the discipline of the Session. Notably, she was not threatened with banishment as Johnsoun, Lennox, and Wilson had been. Given contemporary anxieties about cuckoldry and female rebellion, one would expect Jonet to have received a more severe punishment than her male counterparts.[36] Yet, this is one of the very few cases in which a public apology was not made explicit in the Session minutes.[37] This might indicate that the Session was being relatively lenient, perhaps taking into account the unre-

[34] Yvonne Galloway Brown and Rona Ferguson, eds, *Twisted Sisters: Women, Crime and Deviance in Scotland Since 1400* (East Linton, 2002), esp. chapters 9 and 10. Deborah A. Symonds, *Weep Not for Me: Women, Ballads, and Infanticide in Early Modern Scotland* (University Park, PA, 1997). Mark Jackson, ed., *Infanticide: Historical Perspectives on Child Murder and Concealment, 1550–2000* (Aldershot, 2002). Frances Dolan, *Dangerous Familiars: Representations of Domestic Crime in England 1550–1700* (Ithica, NY, 1994). Amussen, ' "Being Stirred to Much Unquietness"', 75.
[35] Edinburgh, NAS, CH2/718/3, 60.
[36] Foyster, 'Male Honour, Social Control and Wife Beating', 216.
[37] In cases of violence initiated by women in other presbyteries, parading and processions of a similar kind to those imposed on George Johnsoune were used, see Todd, *Culture of Protestantism*, 153.

corded context of the violence, although Jonet's time 'in saccloth vpon the piller', and 'at the Kirk Dur', still subjected her to the humiliating and public rituals of display characteristic of Kirk discipline.

In some cases the interests of the victims needed to be put before the redemption of the perpetrator or the discretion of the Session. In the Royal Burgh of the Canongate, alongside the eastern wall of Edinburgh, just such a case arose in 1564, when the Session gave John Roger an admonition 'that he in no way commit . . . [his] barn to the care of his wif because scho afoir in drukinnes smorit twa former bernis'.[38] His wife's drunkenness and violence had become incontrollable and she had stepped beyond the discipline of either the ecclesiastical or Burgh courts. The Session elders clearly felt a responsibility to reinforce and oversee John's fatherly duty to protect his child. It was declared that, 'gif he be negligent in keeping of this said barn, that thay [the Session] will persew him as ane common mortherar of children'. John's wife's crime was to become his if he failed to protect his child. In this case, Kirk discipline became an explicit form of surveillance, an attempt to ensure the safety of a family in extreme disorder. The deaths of John Roger's 'twa former bernis' almost certainly occurred prior to the establishment of an effective Session within the parish, and there is clearly an intent within this case to demonstrate the social significance and role of Reformed Kirk discipline within the Burgh. This is in many respects an inversion of the Johnsoun scenario. John Roger did not receive a public, humiliating punishment, and apparently his wife managed to evade the usual indictment that followed cases of child murder. In this case discipline became a moral and emotional duty that was imposed on John Roger to ensure the safety of his child and to bear the responsibility for any harm inflicted upon that child. The Session often needed to re-establish the hierarchical duties that bound even the most senior members of the domestic space.

The Session in Edinburgh did not impose humiliating or violent punishments wilfully. Parading, carting, kneeling and public apologies were part of a process of maintaining the compliance of the parish in a reciprocally reinforcing regime of domestic, civic, and ecclesiastical discipline, all of which were undermined by household disorder and violence. The punishments imposed can be interpreted as both a means

---

[38] Alma B. Calderwood, ed., *Buik of the Kirk of the Canagait 1564–1567* (Edinburgh, 1961), 78.

of scourging that disorderly behaviour from the community, and of pulling the godly community together through focused group events: punishments. Even those who were punished became part of this process, offering themselves up to the Session for correction, and making the choice to participate in these acts of discipline. Their reward was inclusion in the godly, social, and economic society of the town, and all the moral and financial privileges that inclusion afforded. Discipline was carried out with the genuine intention of redeeming and reintegrating those whose violent behaviour was perceived as damaging to themselves, their household, and to the larger parochial and Burgh communities. The Kirk was clear in its message that domestic violence, just like any other form of violent or aggressive behaviour that usurped household and social hierarchies, was incompatible with the needs and aspirations of the Reformed community. Discipline was constructed, not as a means of repression, but rather as a means to educate and inte-grate those individuals whose behaviour transgressed the moral bounds of the Kirk. The final act of all Kirk punishment, sitting on the early modern naughty step, the stool of repentance, was thus a public display of the complicity of the men and women of Edinburgh in the almost domesticated discipline of the Kirk.

University of York

LITERATURE AND CHURCH DISCIPLINE IN EARLY MODERN ENGLAND

by NIGEL SMITH

THAT English literature is suffused with religion is news to no
one; the English language is throughout history part of the
structure of the Church or churches. But there is a way in
which Church history and English literature have been missing each
other for a good many years. This is in part because, until recently, religion in literature has been the preserve of relatively small groups of
enthusiasts with partisan views. Their work has appeared unattractive
or irrelevant to a largely secular mainstream that has been preoccupied
with the 'political' (as opposed to the religious) in early modern literary
studies (this is especially so with regard to the drama).[1] But we now
have an account of Church history that is more sophisticated and varie-
gated, more attuned to confessional variety and its politics, local and
national. This is crying out for engagement with literary studies in ways
that literary scholars would find compelling, not least in offering many
solutions to the kinds of questions they have come to ask. To some
extent the dialogue has already begun, and indeed several exemplary
studies are cited in what follows. Nonetheless, we are at the beginning
of what may well be a long and extremely fruitful interdisciplinary
encounter.

English drama was originally an aspect of popular religious culture
in mysteries and moralities. The drama articulated the scenario of
medieval Christendom, and this was not forgotten when the Elizabethan theatre companies made drama an expression of joint stock
venture capital. While we may not wish to go as far as Jeffrey Knapp in
arguing that the Elizabethan theatre was a Church, and a Church of
vagabonds (since actors were often legally defined as vagabonds) at that,
there is no doubt that the business of worship and the matter of
soul-saving is deeply embedded in the imaginative life of our most

---

[1] For two benchmark publications of this kind, see Jonathan Dollimore and Alan
Sinfield, eds, *Political Shakespeare: New Essays in Cultural Materialism* (London and Ithaca, NY,
1985; 2nd edn, 1994); John Drakakis, ed., *Alternative Shakespeares* (London and New York,
1985).

famous plays.[2] Part of the story is told with renewed interest in respect of the transformation of medieval drama into Renaissance theatre.[3] From a doctrinal perspective, the stony heart was one of the most familiar bodily corollaries for a state of reprobation, as with Marlowe's Faustus: 'My heart's so hardened I cannot repent' (2.3.18–32). Calvinist divines such as William Perkins counselled that only God could work on the heart: 'Pray God so to soften thy stony heart, that thou maist turne to him'.[4] We can therefore read treatments of the work of grace, and of the failure of the work of grace, as in Shakespeare's Othello's temptation and his final murder of Desdemona, as the embodiment of an inherently theological as well as aesthetic theatre. When Othello tells Iago of his intent, it is because he believes Desdemona is unfaithful: 'She shall not live. No, my heart is turned to stone: I strike it, and it hurts my hand' (4.1.179–80). That is to say, Othello loses religious faith at the point at which he believes (mistakenly) that Desdemona has manifested lack of conjugal faith. Elsewhere a further, typically Shakespearean fusing of Jesus with Ovid (for instance, Othello imagines Desdemona's gracefulness as an Orphic ability to make animals sing) is an element of educated eclecticism. But this does nothing to weaken Jennifer Waldron's strong contention that the English Renaissance theatre was offering an intelligent theology of the 'living image', a counterblast, she claims, to those Puritan divines who had suggested in a number of pamphlets in the late sixteenth century that watching plays was an act of idolatry.[5] There were even Puritan ladies who stood with the sixteenth-century equivalent of sandwich boards outside the public theatres threatening damnation to all who stepped within.[6] It does not really matter whether you think Shakespeare was a Catholic or not.[7] Irrespective of authorial intention, the plays themselves reveal a

[2] Jeffrey Knapp, *Shakespeare's Tribe: Church, Nation, and Theater in Renaissance England* (Chicago, IL 2002).

[3] See, e.g., John Parker, *The Aesthetics of Antichrist: from Christian Drama to Christopher Marlowe* (Ithaca, 2007 forthcoming).

[4] William Perkins, *A declaration of the true maner of knowing Christ crucified* (London, 1596), 33. See also his *Two Treatises: of the nature and practise of Repentance: of the combat of flesh and spirit* (London, 1597).

[5] See Jennifer Waldron, 'Eloquence of the Body: Aesthetics, Theology, and English Renaissance Theater', unpublished Ph.D. thesis, Princeton University, 2004.

[6] Allan Pritchard, 'Puritans and the Blackfriars Theater: the Cases of Mistresses Duck and Drake', *Shakespeare Quarterly*, 45: 1 (1994), 92–5.

[7] Another topic that has returned with much interest: see most recently Clare Asquith, *Shadowplay: the Hidden Beliefs and Coded Politics of William Shakespeare* (New York, 2005).

complex structuring order in which the whole business of how we sinners have access to God and how we might come to be saved is presented in sophisticatedly complex and aesthetically pleasing ways.

Thus in *The Winter's Tale*, the Ovidian and Christian strains that Waldron detects in *Othello* reappear to converge in Paulina's dual role as playwright and prophet in the final scene of the play. As Pauline prophet, she tells the audience, 'It is required/ You do awake your faith' (5.3.94–5); as Orphic playwright, she then uses music to awaken the stony Hermione: 'Music; awake her; strike!' (5.3.98). Repetition of 'awake' suggests the play's synthesis of 'the Orphic capacity to make stones move with the Protestant objective of piercing marble hearts.'[8] Shakespeare liked to play with doubles, be it in plotting, in naming, or in imagery. The way Leontes is moved to wake up his lost wife raises, it has been argued, the whole question of how it was that people were properly converted into Christians in the early modern period and how they were sustained in that faith. Was it through hearing the preached word and making perfect sense of it? And what was the role of services of worship and the parts thereof, from the sacraments to the singing of music?

In another moment that brings religious issues together with theatrical ones, Othello demands that Desdemona confess her adultery:

Othello:	For to deny each article with oath
	Cannot remove nor choke the strong conception
	That I do groan withal. Thou art to die.
Desdemona:	Then Lord have mercy on me
Othello:	I say amen.
Desdemona:	And you have mercy too . . .
Othello:	By heaven, I saw my handkerchief in's hand!
	O perjured woman, thou dost stone my heart
	And makest me call what I intend to do
	A murder, which I thought a sacrifice! (4.3.51–65)

Othello's conviction that Desdemona must die, together with his apparent assumption that it is possible to make a legal human 'sacrifice,' invokes contemporary religious debates about idolatrous forms of worship.[9] How should Church ordinances (or theatrical ones) be so

---

8 Waldron, 'Eloquence of the Body', 5.
9 Ibid., 6.

organized to avoid the charge of idolatry? You might be able to read a play profitably, claimed Stephen Gosson, the anti-theatrical pamphleteer, but you certainly could not watch it.[10] Yet the dramatists, Shakespeare foremost among them, seem to be suggesting that the theatre offered an experience that was at once verbal and visual and in this way avoided the charge of idolatry, while acknowledging the vital interconnectedness of word and image. This would be in much the same way that we now understand that 'sacramentalism', the celebration of the Lord's supper, was seen as an accompaniment to the preaching of the word for most Protestants, Puritan or not, even if Puritans might stress sacrament as assurance of grace, rather than as a reminder of the need for repentance (which, it has been argued, is a Laudian emphasis).[11]

In this respect, Shakespeare's theatre has what we might term an incarnational logic, reinvested from the medieval cycles in a post-Reformation theological, aesthetic and political context. To some degree, he found some of his inspiration in Marlowe's outrageous drama of heresy and overkill, and there are resonances of a more shallow kind in the comedies of Ben Jonson, the sometime genuine recusant who truly ridicules the Puritan take on ordinances in 'The Alchemist' and 'Bartholomew Fair.' And when in Shakespeare's 'Measure for Measure', Lucio says over the dinner table in the city brothel 'Grace is grace, despite of all controversy' (1.2. 24–5), he is not just referring to disputes surrounding solafideism and predestination, but also referring to the 'grace' received by receiving the sacrament and whether it was still considered efficacious.[12] More daring still, Peter Lake would now see the history plays and some of the tragedies as embodying a coming together of these issues with the issue of religious allegiance in the context of the succession crisis. Hamlet's dilemma is that he must take revenge in such a way as is faithful to his own sense of

10 Stephen Gosson, *Playes confuted in fiue actions: prouing that they are not to be suffred in a Christian common weale, by the waye both the cauils of Thomas Lodge, and the play of playes, written in their defence, and other obiections of players frendes, are truely set downe and directlye aunsweared* (London, 1582); also available in two modern editions, ed. Arthur Freeman (New York, 1972), ed. Peter Davison (New York, 1972).

11 Arnold Hunt, 'The Lord's Supper in Early Modern England', *P&P* 161 (1998), 39–83.

12 For the religious politics of *Measure for Measure* and its context, see now Julia Lupton, *Citizen-Saints: Shakespeare and Political Theology* (Chicago, IL, 2005), ch. 5; Debra Shuger, *Political Theologies in Shakespeare's England: the Sacred and the State in 'Measure for Measure'* (Basingstoke and New York, 2001); Nigel Smith, 'The Two Economies of Shakespeare's *Measure for Measure*', *English* 36 (1987), 197–232.

justice without, as an agent of revenge, becoming the cause of his own damnation.[13]

Now it has been attested that in the absence of a national Church with an agreed and accepted order of governance and worship during the middle years of the seventeenth century some unusual things happened. The Independents or Congregationalists kept the regular celebration of the Lord's Supper alive, and it has been argued that in some areas language was just about the only element that kept the Episcopal Church going.[14] Hence the significance of poetry collections like Herbert's *The Temple* (1633) and Vaughan's *Silex Scintillans* (1650).[15] While the latter arguably involved a transference of liturgy into a poetry of praise of nature, it might also be said therefore that Vaughan made sacraments of nature even as he railed against the Puritan and in particular the Committee for the Propagation of the Gospel. With the former, we have now to understand the meaning of the fact that *The Temple* was appropriated in a variety of different ways, across the Protestant diaspora, by Puritans as well as Anglicans, and high ones at that; even by Antinomian divines protesting against their displacement by Protectorate intruders.[16] One of the great discoveries in literary studies of the last fifteen years has been the vast quantity of literature, much of it poetry, by women; some of it in print, more of it in manuscript. There is evidence here of devotional poetry, such as that of Ann Collins, embodying major catechetical works once considered to be at the heart of the English Church, such as those of William Perkins.

Catechisms raise the issue of private devotional reading and the greater role it might be said to have played during a period when regular services were either disrupted or absent. This is so in a broader context where continental texts of all kinds were being drawn into the vernacular market either to be translated or to be used as a com-

13 Peter Lake with Michael Questier, *The Anti-Christ's Lewd Hat: Protestants, Papists and Players in Post-Reformation England* (New Haven, CT, 2002). Forthcoming work on the history plays and *Hamlet*.

14 Hunt, 'Lord's Supper', 54–6.

15 One interpretation among very many here in this tradition would be John N. Wall, *Transformations of the Word: Spenser, Herbert, Vaughan* (Athens, GA, 1988). The point in respect of studies of the seventeenth-century religious lyric in particular is that literary scholarship and the new Church history referred to in this essay have yet to connect.

16 Helen Wilcox, 'Something Understood: the Reputation and Influence of George Herbert to 1715', unpublished D.Phil. thesis, University of Oxford, 1984; Nigel Smith, 'George Herbert in Defence of Antinomianism', *Notes and Queries*, ns 31 (1984), 334–5; Sharon Achinstein, *Literature and Dissent in Milton's England* (Cambridge, 2003), 200–8.

positional model for English texts. There are cases here not merely of lay reading of the Bible or other devotional texts causing very unorthodox kinds of worship and theology (such as is the case with the origins of the Quakers) but also texts meant for contemplation and meditation playing a far more significant role.[17] The poetry circulating among the Grindletonian sect of Antinomians in early seventeenth-century far west Yorkshire and east Lancashire was gnomic, curative and medicinal as well as soteriological in its function.[18] It certainly worried the Archbishop of York. Lamenting the death of Roger Brierley, the chief Grindletonian, William Algin wrote:

> that mighteye man is dead and so the dole
> is done, alas, both in the parte and whole,
> how many came to thee a fountaine faire
> to drinke thy wine, how many did repaire
> unto thy courtes to feed upon thy bread
> hungrye and thirsty yea and ill bestead
> but went away with wonderfull content
> blessing the lord that ever he was sent
> to be their feeder, and they home returne
> to their owne countrye wherein they weare borne
> in strengh of that same pot of water they
> inabled have beene long and many a day
> to walke and goe not feeling any wante
> nor that their morcell waxing less or scant
> for as is said he that doth drinke the wine
> or water of the Christall streame devine
> shall never thirst againe, but now we goe
> from streame to streame, but they are mudded soe
> that we cannot abide to drinke thereon
> its souered soe, yea and the taste is gone.[19]

[17] The classic general case is made by Keszek Kolakowski, *Chrétiens sans église: la conscience religeuse et le lien confessionnel au XVIIe siècle* (Paris, 1969), and elaborated variously in different particular areas: see for instance Barbara K. Lewalski, *Protestant Poetics and the Seventeenth-Century Religious Lyric* (Princeton, NJ, 1979), Pt I.

[18] See Nigel Smith, 'Elegy for a Grindletonian: Poetry and Heresy in Northern England, 1615–1640', *Journal of Medieval and Early Modern Studies* 33: 2 (2003), 335–51, and more generally David Como, *Blown by the Spirit: Puritanism and the Emergence of an Antinomian Underground in Pre-Civil-War England* (Stanford, CA, 2004).

[19] William Aglin, 'Heare followeth certaine vearses made upon the death of this aforesaid Author Roger Breierley: by William Aglin: minister', in London, Lambeth Palace Library, MS 3461, 230.

Brierley's alleged powers of physical cure and his further recommendations for poetry as a kind of therapy are met with a description of Grindletonian (i.e. Antinomian) life as an earthly paradise, either literally or symbolically imagined:

> our garments that weare white
> of trimmed silke to give our mindes delite
> are turned now to hayrecloath rough and torne
> tattered and all to ragged peeces worne,
> not able for to save our naked skinne
> from shamefull sight, this plight we now are in
> for loss of thee our beds that weare of downe
> with linnen sheetes soe pleasantly bestrowne
> soft pillowes whereupon to rest our heads
> into thy pallace faire thou didst us lead
> where musicke sweet was tuned every day
> where seecretly we did rejoyce and play.[20]

Much has been made of print culture's facilitation of reformed agendas.[21] Printed catechisms embody confessions of faith and therefore reflect Church ordinances. It was these forms of reform propagated by print culture that facilitated such variety, in a context in which sacramental religion, howsoever much intended as a means of fostering unity, fell prey to the pressure of confessional diversity. This arose during the absence of a national Church (and where works of state-sponsored Church government, such as the Presbyterian-influenced *Directory* of 1646, were notably imprecise and vague). The competition for a national catechism in the early 1650s, in which Richard Baxter and John Owen opposed each other, was accompanied by the appearance of an anti-trinitarian work by John Biddle, seizing an opportunity to spread Socinianism. The force of Faustus Socinus's (1539–1604) teachings lay precisely in his denial that Christianity was a sacrificial religion, that Adam's Fall applied to all men, and that Christ's atonement was necessary in anyone's redemption.[22] Socinus argued that

---

[20] Ibid., 238.
[21] Ian Green, *The Christian's ABC: Catechism and Catechizing in England c.1530–1740* (Oxford, 1996); idem, *Print and Protestantism in Early Modern England* (Oxford, 2000).
[22] I have benefited greatly from consulting Sarah Mortimer's impressive 'Refuting Satan: Owen, Socinianism and the Interpretation of Scripture', unpublished M.Phil. thesis, University of Oxford, 2003. I have discussed these issues further in Nigel Smith, ' "And if God was one of us": John Biddle and Socinianism in Seventeenth-Century England', in David

Christ's life and death were to be taken as an inspiring example. As Biddle later said:

> **Qu.** *Forasmuch as Christ, in that he died; died unto sin once; but in that he liveth, liveth unto God: what reckoning should we make with our selves hereupon?*
> **A.** Likewise reckon ye also yourselves to be dead indeed unto sin: but alive unto God through Jesus Christ our Lord. *Rom.6: 11*.[23]

Justification by faith alone was thus attacked, as was the notion that God could predestine anyone to damnation or salvation. It was agreed by the Racovian Socinians that salvation depended upon God renouncing his right to punish a person, while the exemplary Christ, although divine, was not God. The Socinians thus refused to make the traditional distinction between person and essence upon which the definition of the Holy Trinity was founded (distinct in person, united in the essence of the Godhead). This refusal was rightly seen across Protestant Europe as a dangerous challenge to Reformation principles. The challenge was even more evident when the Socinians argued their case from the primacy of Scripture and from reason, the two fundamental instruments of Protestantism. Indeed, *The Racovian Catechism* claimed that it was possible to attain eternal life through the exercise of reason in the understanding of the Bible.[24]

Literature plays an important role here. The two men regarded as the first English Socinians, Paul Best and John Biddle, were both poets, and used rhetorical and philological methods to establish their anti-Trinitarian arguments (in contradistinction to the poetry of Herbert and Vaughan).[25] Paul Best's *Mysteries Discovered* (1647) argues that the Holy Trinity is a fiction by showing that its key biblical sources are not literal descriptions but instances of figurative language. Christ is the Word only through metaphor and metonymy (3); he only appears to be co-equal with the Father; there are further instances of figural solecism (5), enallage (7), prosopopeia (9), hysteron proteron (10), tautology (11).

Loewenstein and John Marshall, eds, *Heresy, Literature and Politics in Early Modern English Culture* (Cambridge, 2007), 160–84.

[23] John Biddle, *A Brief Scripture-Catechism for Children* (London, 1654), 19.

[24] See further, George Hunston Williams, ed., *The Polish Brethren: Documentation of the History and Thought of Unitarianism in the Polish-Lithuanian Commonwealth and in the Diaspora 1601–1685* (Missoula, MO, 1980).

[25] For the lives of Best and Biddle, see Stephen D. Snobelen, 'Best, Paul (1590–1657)', *ODNB* [http://www.oxforddnb.com/view/article/2291], and idem, 'Biddle, John (1615/16–1662)' [http://www.oxforddnb.com/view/article/2361 [accessed 24 Jan 2007].

All this means that Trinitarianism is 'a verball kinde of Divinity' that has ensured the survival of polytheism and apotheosis (the making of Jesus Christ as a man-God) in a religion that was meant to abandon these notions.

The opening paragraph of Biddle's *XII arguments drawn out of the Scripture, wherein the commonly received opinion touching the deity of the Holy Spirit, is clearly and fully refuted* (1647) is an exercise in logical analysis. By the analysis of logical compartments, Trinitarian concepts make no sense:

> He that is distinguished from God, is not God; the holy Spirit is distinguished from God. *Ergo.* The *major* is evident, for if he should both b[e] God, & be distinguished from God, he would be distinguished from himselfe, which implyeth a contradiction. The *minor* premise is confirmed by the whole currant of the Scripture, which calleth him the *Spirit of God*, and saith that *he is sent by God, and searcheth the depths of God* &c. Neither let any man he think to fly to that ignorant refuge of making a distinction between the Essence and Person of God, saying that the Holy Spirit is distinguished from God, taken personally not Essentially. For this wretched distinction (to omit the mention of the Primitive Fathers) is not only unheard of [in] the Scripture, and so to be rejected, it being presumption to affirme any thing of the unsearchable nature of God, which he hath not first affirmed to himselfe in the Scripture: but is also disclaimd by Reason. For first, it is impossible for any man, if he would but endeavour to conceive the thing, and not delude both himselfe and others with empty terms and words without understanding, to distinguish the person from the Essence of God, and not to frame two Beings or Things in his mind, and consequently two Gods. Secondly, if the person be distinct from the Essence of God, then it is either something or nothing; if nothing, how can it be distinguished, since nothing hath no accidents? If something, then either some finite or infinite thing; if finite, then there will be something finite in God; and consequently since by the confession of the adversaries themselves, every thing in God is God himselfe, God will be finite, which the adversaryes themselves will likewise confesse to be absurd. (7)

By 1653, Biddle claimed that his position was consistent with both Aristotle's definition of universals and with 'common understanding.'[26] But

---

26 John Biddle, Preface to second edition of *A Confession of Faith touching the Holy Trinity*

unlike Best, Biddle is at first unwilling to use rhetorical categories in order to demystify biblical figures. Logic might expose contradictions in the interpretation of theological categories, but God can only be understood as a person since that is how He always appears in the Bible (6–7). Logic keeps the two categories of God and not God apart: 'to say that one is dependent, and yet God, is in effect to say he is God and not God, which implyeth a contradiction.' (8) A description of the Holy Spirit in Acts 5: 3–4, taken by some as a metonymy for God, turns out to be impossible when the logic of the grammar is properly construed. In this respect, Biddle aligns himself with the critical philology of Erasmus, Calvin and Aretius, as the early historians of Socinianism were quick to show,[27] but he is in fact presenting a far more sharply focused and uncompromising version of this approach (in the 1653 edition, 21–2).

In all of this, and arising from this critical philology, the significance of Christ's passion is played down. Remarkably, says Biddle, Christ's atonement did not happen during his crucifixion, but afterwards, in an encounter with God, following his resurrection and ascension to Heaven.[28] Until 1654, Biddle's publications were consistent with Socinian teaching. But in that year he went beyond them in arguing that the Scriptures must be understood literally, and that the God they presented must be understood as a person, with the attributes natural to persons both in physical and psychological terms:

> **Qu.** *What saith the Apostle John?*
> **A.** Now are we the sons of God, and it doth not yet appear what we shall be: but we know that, when he shall appear, we shall be like him: *for we shall see him as he is.* 1 John 3: 2.[29]

Thus he ascribed to God a body that existed in a specific place and which had a specific shape. This view was supported from the Scripture, with particular reference to the anthropomorphic language of the Old Testament. According to Biddle, God had right and left hands. God also had emotions, or, as the Committee for the Propagation of the Gospel called them, passions, like anger or sorrow. This made God effectively a superior kind of person, nothing more than an agent

in *The Apostolical and True Opinion concerning the Holy Trinity* (1653), BL, Thomason Tracts E1479 (1), sig. [D5r].
[27] See Stephen Nye, *A brief history of the Unitarians, called also Socinians in four letters, written to a friend* (London, 1687), 31, where Erasmus is cited defending the Arians.
[28] Biddle, *A Confession of Faith* (2nd edn, London, 1653), 38.
[29] Biddle, *Scripture-Catechism*, 5.

subject to circumstances, and thus an intelligence with limited knowledge. Biddle's catechisms were ordered to be burned and only by Oliver Cromwell's personal intervention was his own execution prevented. His incarceration effectively prevented him from growing a church, although he left behind a vigorous group of followers, and his writings were widely influential. Even if his perceptions were not adopted wholesale, his writings were widely read, annotated and assimilated into other systems, such as those of John Locke.

At the same time, he was coupling this use of reason with a strict recourse to the language of Scripture. It was the final triumph of the grammar school, to the detriment of ancient formulations that had survived the Protestant Reformation. To the hostile, Biddle's writings looked like the sad mangling of the esteemed English translations by a demented schoolmaster. Another schoolmaster of sorts was John Milton, a poet with strong but distinctive anti-Trinitarian interests. In the mature Milton's view ordinances and sacraments in particular are redefined ideally as an edification that should come by reading:

> Therefore what he gives
> (Whose praise be ever sung) to man in part   [405]
> Spiritual, may of purest Spirits be found
> No ingrateful food: and food alike those pure
> Intelligential substances require
> As doth your Rational; and both contain
> Within them every lower facultie   [410]
> Of sense, whereby they hear, see, smell, touch, taste,
> Tasting concoct, digest, assimilate,
> And corporeal to incorporeal turn. (*Paradise Lost*, V.404–14)

And again:

> So down they sat,
> And to thir viands fell, nor seemingly
> The Angel, nor in mist, the common gloss   [435]
> Of Theologians, but with keen dispatch
> Of real hunger, and concoctive heate
> To transubstantiate; what redounds, transpires
> Through Spirits with ease. (*Paradise Lost*, V.433–9)

The reinvention of the meaning of worship is equally problematic when Milton presents the Son as priest. This is because in doing so he severely relegates the significance of the crucifixion. Milton has to reinvent the atonement, especially since he downplays the crucifixion. In Books III and X–XI, the atonement occurs as a conversation between God and the Son, in which the Son offers to undergo death in order to pay the ransom for mankind's sins. And in Book X, it is not God, or accurately speaking, 'the voice of the Lord God' (Gen. 3: 8) that confronts Adam and Eve after their temptation but the Son. Adam and Eve hear the voice of God, but it is the Son who makes contact possible by being physically present (10.85–102). As the Son facilitates the voice of God in Eden, promising that the seed of the woman will bruise the serpent's head, so he is able to see the future when Jesus will defeat Satan: a passage (10.182–92) that resembles the closing movement of *Paradise Regained*.

A more extensive episode of intercession occurs early in Book XI when the Son is moved by the penitent prayers of Adam and Eve. Milton bases his text, it has been argued, on Heb. 9: 24, where Christ is imagined 'to appear in the presence of God for us.' This refers to Christ's ascension after his resurrection, and some of the Socinians imagined this to mean that Christ interceded on behalf of mankind after his crucifixion. Since they also believed that the Son was created for the first time when he was born of a woman, the episode as Milton describes it, coming shortly after the Fall but a long time before most of the events recounted in the Old Testament, cannot in their view have taken place. It has been conjectured that the Son's intercession in this way is in fact an adaptation by Milton of the Socinian position, and that it is a crucial part of Milton's downgrading of the crucifixion in his explanation of the atonement.[30] After all, the Son hears the prayers of Adam and Eve, which are then 'engrafted' onto his own payment and offered up to God, who receives them and grants immortal life to those who follow his ways. Adam and Eve, we are told, have been moved to prayer by the 'prevenient grace' that has wafted down from heaven and that presumably has been in existence since the Son first offered himself as a redemptive sacrifice for mankind in Book III. The Passion of Christ is squashed into eight lines Book XII, ll. 412–19, and seemingly replaced in significance with an immediately postlapsarian intercession. One can see in Milton's text the kinds of objections made to the Socinian position: that with grace bought at this point, why did the Son need to die? In making Adam and Eve so active in already unwinding

---

[30] See John Rogers, 'Milton and the Heretical Priesthood of Christ', in David Loewenstein and John Marshall, eds, *Heresy, Literature and Politics*, 203–20.

the consequences of the Fall, is Milton not denying the special place of Christian witness, and even more, showing little difference between Jews and Christians?

In *Paradise Lost* so much poetic energy has been directed at showing the proximity of unfallen man to God, and of giving human shape to the Son if not also to God, that we begin to feel an anthropomorphizing energy throughout the poem, as its total argument comes together in our minds. Thus, at the sentencing of man in Book XI of *Paradise Lost*, man's crime is to have become like God and the angels: 'like one of us man is become.' (XI.84) To eat the fruit of the Tree of Life would be to live forever, or, so Milton adds to Genesis, to 'dream at least to live/ For ever' (XI.95–6). This seems to repeat how things had been before the Fall, but the point here is the proximity in standing of the 'sons' of God (XI.84): the angels and mankind, and with a more distant prospect, the fallen angels, yet more 'sons', once blessed. How far are we from the story of the sons of God in the Book of Enoch, who came down from a mountain, made love to the women and bred a race of giants, or from the early commentaries on Gen. 6 that assumed fallen angels had mated with women (Milton alludes to the Scripture at XI.621–2)? Adam and Eve first appear as 'Godlike erect', meaning, one initially supposes, that they are as beautiful as the pagan gods (IV.289–90). But can that be right? Are they not made in the image of God, and has Milton not slipped to saying that they look like Him? When Adam says that in his dream he could see that Eve was less a resemblance of God than he was (VIII.543–4), is he not talking in the most literal of senses?

In his taking on of the major heresies of his age, in particular monism, mortalism and anti-trinitarianism, Milton was going to a remarkable extreme in remaking theology, including apparently, major aspects of Church government, into a new system where man begins to challenge God across the sea of angels, fallen and unfallen, and whatever the claims of Milton's 'good God'. But no one noticed for a long time, or if they did, it was in the way of private observations. Very few could see with John Toland that Milton was a proto-deist, and most happily assumed that *Paradise Lost* being in English was at last the great national epic because it re-presented the Bible in remarkable English verse.[31] Those today who have claimed theological orthodoxy for Milton see

<hr>

[31] See John Toland, *Amyntor, or, A defence of Milton's life* (London, 1699); idem, *Clito; a poem on the force of eloquence* (London, 1700). On the history of *Paradise Lost's* reception, see

him in this light. It took a very long time for the truth of Milton's here-sies to be visible. If I had more time and space, it would be possible to show the impact of innovative Protestant theologies transforming literary form, with *Paradise Lost* as a prime example. In the meantime, a reformed stage obsessed with the comedy of manners or the replaying of civil war themes of regicide in heroic tragedy, had no place for the aesthetico-theological drama of Shakespeare's theatre. Who would have wanted those debates after 1660? And thus, as Shakespeare's plays were republished after 1660, and sometimes rewritten, their 'theology' of the living image became part of what was quintessentially the language of the drama, not the vital disputes of the Church.

You might expect a study of this kind to start with a consideration of the rise of the conversion narrative, an ordinance within the gathered churches: that a believer gives a narrative of how she or he came to be saved as well as a confession of faith in order to join a church. That would be a very linear and straightforward account of literature's contribution to, and role in, the diversity of Church history in the period.[32] We could look at spiritual autobiography and its impact in structural and stylistic ways on the rise of the novel and eventually the novel's love affair in the nineteenth-century with denominational difference. But here I am trying to tell a different story. In 1662, and in England (not Scotland) when the Book of Common Prayer was reintro-duced, with it came of course a mid-sixteenth-century liturgy, so that the official language of sacramental rites was considerably out of tune with most seventeenth-century divinity. A compromise meant that theologians and scholars were ignored. I am suggesting that the debates at stake then were in fact dealt with in what has been retrieved as imag-inative literature, most of which was in a sense an important part of the body of the Church at this time. In a period in which so much was invested by all parties of all kinds in the spread of religion in various kinds of print, we might well wonder why it has taken so long to notice these precise territories and mechanisms of cultural richness.

Princeton University

Anne-Julia Zwierlein, *Majestick Milton: British Imperial Expansion and Transformations of 'Para-dise Lost', 1667–1837* (Münster, 2001).

[32] And as extensively discussed in John Stachniewski, *The Persecutory Imagination: English Puritanism and the Literature of Religious Despair* (Oxford, 1991), Pt I.

'CONTRARIE TO THE DIRECTORIE': PRESBYTERIANS AND PEOPLE IN LANCASHIRE, 1646-53

by ALEX CRAVEN

IN 1645, Parliament swept away the Anglican liturgy of the Church of England, replacing the Book of Common Prayer with a new Presbyterian alternative, the Directory.[1] The Episcopal hierarchy of the Church had already been demolished, and it was expected that the national Church would be reformed along puritan lines. The campaign to impose Presbyterian discipline in England, and the concomitant struggle for a reformation of manners, has received much attention from historians. There is little doubt that nationally these new measures failed, with John Morrill asserting that 'these ordinances were not only largely ignored but actively resisted'.[2] Presbyterian classes were successfully erected in a handful of places, however, including Lancashire. This should not surprise us, given the county's long reputation for Puritanism. Nine classes were created at Manchester, Bury, Whalley, Warrington, Walton, Leyland, Preston, Lancaster and Ulverston, and a Provincial Assembly met at Preston.[3] The full minutes of Manchester and Bury classes, and the several extant sets of churchwardens' accounts, offer a fascinating insight into the workings of this new system.[4] The popular reaction to the new order is also demonstrated;

[1] *A Directory for the Publique Worship of God Throughout the Three Kingdoms of England, Ireland and Scotland, Together with an Ordinance of Parliament for the taking away of the Book of Common Prayer and for establishing and observing this present Directory throughout the Kingdom of England and Dominion of Wales* (London, 1645) [hereafter: Directory].

[2] John Morrill, 'The Church in England 1642-9', in idem, ed., *Reactions to the English Civil War* (Basingtoke, 1982), 89-114, at 90.

[3] W. A. Shaw, *A History of the English Church during the Civil Wars and under the Commonwealth*, 2 vols (London, 1900), 2: 30.

[4] *Minutes of the Manchester Presbyterian Classis*, ed. W. A. Shaw, Chetham Society, 3 vols, ns 20, 22, 24 (1890-2); *Minutes of the Bury Presbyterian Classis*, ed. W. A. Shaw, Chetham Society, ns 36, 41 (1896 and 1898); *Cartmel Churchwardens' Accounts 1597-1659*, Cumbria (Kendal) Record Office, WPR/89/W1-2; *Childwall Churchwardens' Accounts 1571-1674*, trans. E. Saxton, Liv[erpool] R[ecord] O[ffice], H283.1ALL; *Chorley Churchwardens Accounts 1651-3*, Lanc[a]s[hire] R[ecord] O[ffice], DDHk/10/3/1; *Middleton Churchwardens' Accounts 1647-1678*, Manchester C[entral] L[ibrary], L56/2/1/1; *Padiham Churchwardens' Accounts 1623-87*, LancsRO, PR2863/2/1; *Prescot Churchwardens' Accounts 1635-1663*, ed. Thomas Steel, *Record*

people who travelled to banned services demonstrated where they stood on the liturgical divide, as did those who presented offenders for punishment. This essay, therefore, seeks to evaluate the efforts to erect Presbyterianism within a county where we might reasonably expect it could succeed. The outcome of this struggle will tell us much about the chances of a national Presbyterian Church of England's survival.

For the drive to impose discipline to succeed the support of the Lancashire clergy was essential, but the classes struggled to impose their authority. Many refused to recognize the classes, others refused to work with elders; elsewhere, men refused to take up the office of elder when elected. This reluctance became such a problem that in 1649 the Provincial Assembly pleaded with elders to 'attend constantly their classicall congregationall and provinciall meetings, and to suffer noe discouragements from anie disaffected partie to weaken their hands in that worke'.[5] The appeal fell upon deaf ears; at Manchester, it was reported, the elders 'doe fall off from their offices', whilst at Bury no meetings were possible between August 1651 and February 1651/2, 'through the defaulte of ruleing eld[e]rs'.[6] This had serious implications for the enforcement of Presbyterian discipline, much of which would have been conducted by the elders within their congregations. The most scandalous cases should have found their way before the classes, but the lack of authority wielded by the classes is striking. Between 1647 and 1653, the classes of Manchester and Bury dealt with just twelve cases of scandalous behaviour, eight of which were accusations of sexual impropriety: fornication, adultery or incest.[7] What little authority they could command dwindled during the Commonwealth; only three of these cases arose after 1649, demonstrating the failure of the Presbyterian clergy to discipline the masses under the Republic. Nor was this the result of the increased prosecution by magistrates following the introduction of harsh legislation against incest, adultery and fornication, the quarter sessions rarely dealing with these crimes.[8]

Society of Lancashire and Cheshire 137 (2002) [hereafter: RSLC]; Ribchester Select Vestry Minutes, LancsRO, PR2905/2/1; The Churchwardens' Accounts of Walton-on-the-Hill, Lancashire 1627–1667, ed. Esther Ramsey and Alison Maddock, RSLC 141 (2005); Whalley Churchwardens' Accounts 1636–1709, LancsRO, PR8; Warrington Vestry Minutes 1628–1700, Warrington Library, mf35 reel 23.

5 Manchester Classis, 126
6 Ibid., 153; Bury Classis, 127.
7 Manchester Classis, 49–50, 134, 189, 206; Bury Classis, 19–20, 23, 29.
8 Alex Craven, 'Coercion and Compromise: Lancashire Provincial Politics and the

The Directory of Worship brought ceremonies into line with Presbyterian practice and suppressed customs and items of Church
furnishing considered superstitious or idolatrous. Based upon research
in counties in the east and west of the country, Morrill estimated that
fewer than a quarter of English parishes purchased the Directory. We
might expect to find a much higher percentage of churches in possession of the Directory in a county such as Lancashire. Despite this, only
three Lancashire churches recorded purchasing a Directory: Prescot,
Didsbury and Burnley.[9] Of course, the possession of the Directory was
not proof of its use. By examining the administration of the Eucharist,
the conferment of baptism, and the observation of the new festival
calendar, we can further judge the extent to which the Directory was
adopted in Lancashire.

Anglican requirements for the Eucharist to be celebrated at
Christmas, Easter and Whitsun were banned in 1646. Instead, the
Directory recommended regular communions, interpreted by Morrill
to mean at least once per quarter, on dates not coinciding with the
traditional calendar. Morrill found that 43% of the parishes he studied
celebrated communion at least at Easter in 1650, whilst only 20% of the
remainder did so at other times in the year, as required by the Directory.[10] However, Ronald Hutton found that only 9% of a much larger
sample 'consistently recorded festival communions throughout the
Interregnum', and the only evidence for the survival of the ancient
feasts in Protestant Lancashire is from Kirkham, where Easter was celebrated in 1653.[11] At Whalley, the ancient observances of Lent, Whit
and Christmas were replaced during the Republic by services in July,
October and January, whilst they had ceased to be observed at Prescot
in 1645, if not before.[12]

The nature of the communicants was also transformed. Whereas the
Church of England had allowed all but the especially scandalous to take

---

Creation of the English Republic, 1648–53', unpublished Ph.D. thesis, University of
Manchester, 2004, 94–6.

[9] Morrill, 'The Church in England', 90, 104; *Prescot Churchwardens' Accounts*, 114; John
Booker, *A History of the Ancient Chapels of Didsbury and Chorlton*, Chetham Society, os 42
(1857), 87; *The Registers of the Parish Church of Burnley 1562–1653*, ed. William Farrer,
Lancashire Parish Register Society 2 (1899), 116.

[10] Morrill, 'Church in England', 106–7.

[11] Ronald Hutton, *The Rise and Fall of Merry England* (Oxford, 1994), 214; *The Records of
the Thirty Men of the Parish of Kirkham*, ed. R. Cunliffe Shaw and Helen Shaw (Kendal, 1930),
40.

[12] *Prescot Churchwardens' Accounts*, xxxi; LancsRO, PR8, 41–6.

communion, under Presbyterian discipline only those deemed worthy following examination by their elders were admitted.[13] Therefore, where the Directory was in use we should find 'closed communions'. The issuing of tickets for entry to communion was certainly introduced at Prestwich and Bolton. At the latter, a furious dispute between Richard Heywood and the elders split the congregation, and the practice was discarded.[14] At Altham, the pastor Thomas Jolly covenanted with a small group of his congregation to separate from 'the unworthy', denying communion to all but the 'Saints visible to the eye of rational charity'. This represented a deep division within the parish: the small 'gathered church within the Church' numbered only twenty-nine people in a community estimated to comprise 150 families.[15]

Many ministers were unconvinced by the severity of Presbyterian discipline concerning the Eucharist. John Lake, the royalist minister at Oldham and future bishop of Chichester, was accused by the Manchester classis of administering the sacrament 'in a general and promiscuous way'. They complained of his 'irregular walking herein, to the rule of the word & expresse command of the civill authority'. Lake's actions eventually led to a hearing before local JPs, where he was accused of giving communion to 'loose persons' and to 'severall cavaliers and disaffected persons that came from remote parts upon purpose', and of having exploited Presbyterian hostility to the Engagement to ensure that 'loose persons of his own nomination' were elected churchwardens. Lake had the support of his patron, the JP James Assheton of Chadderton, who had removed his predecessor for refusing the Engagement. Ultimately, the classis could chastise Lake only weakly from afar, despite the plea from his enemies that his actions 'very much discorish the harts of the godly'.[16]

The purchase of bread and wine offers further insight into sacramental practice in Lancashire. Closed communions would need much

---

13 Morrill, 'Church in England', 105–6.

14 A dispute within the congregation at Prestwich demonstrates that communion tickets had been introduced there: *Manchester Classis*, 60–1, 74. For Bolton, see J. Horsfall Turner, ed., *Rev. Oliver Heywood 1630–1702: His Autobiography, Diaries, Anecdote and Event Books*, 4 vols (Brighouse, 1882–5), 1: 27–9, 78–81; *Bury Classis*, 71, 95–7, 112–14.

15 *The Note Book of the Rev Thomas Jolly*, ed. Henry Fishwick, Chetham Society, ns 33 (1894), 121–30; Patrick Collinson, 'The English Conventicle', in W. J. Sheils and Diana Wood, eds, *Voluntary Religion*, SCH 23 (Woodbridge, 1986), 223–59, at 256.

16 *Manchester Classis*, 158, 162–4, 375–95; John Vicars, *Dagon Demolished* (London, 1660), 7–8; William Farrer and J. Brownbill, eds, *VCH Lancaster*, 8 vols (London, 1992), 6: 117.

less bread and wine, and Morrill expected them to be only a third of the cost of open communions.[17] However, the evidence shows that closed communions were a rarity in Lancashire. At Prescot, monthly closed communions had been celebrated since before the wars, but were discarded following the death of the vicar Richard Day in 1650. The first communion of his successor, John Withens, in April 1651, required three times the average amount spent previously on the sacrament, whilst communion was celebrated only twice in the following year.[18] The evidence from Whalley suggests that, if anything, the number of communicants grew under the Republic; whereas they had used four or five quarts of wine in the 1630s, they required seven quarts during the 1650s. This might be proof of Anglicans seeking out Prayer Book services; certainly the vicar readily conformed at the Restoration. However, the parish did purchase a pewter christening bowl in conformity with the Directory, although it did this only in 1651. Alternatively, the increased attendance may reflect a different pattern of services. Where the Eucharist was celebrated six times a year during the 1630s, this was halved during the 1650s. What seems clear is that open communions were practised at Whalley throughout the 1650s.[19] Kirkham was another parish where it seems unlikely that closed communions were practised, with ninety-two quarts of wine being bought in 1652 alone.[20] Ultimately, it seems that efforts to introduce tighter controls over the sacrament in Lancashire during the mid-seventeenth century largely failed.

Morrill also found that 38% of his sample suspended the Eucharist to avoid conflict, as did Ralph Josselin in his Essex parish. The phenomenon was not unknown in Lancashire. At Childwall no communions were recorded after 1647, although this may reflect the imperfection of the accounts. Their omission from the fuller accounts of Walton-on-the-Hill, however, surely indicates suspension.[21] At Warrington, the deletion of the words 'bread & wine for the monthlie Communion' from a list of items to be paid for by a church levy of 1650 may indicate a suspension; alternatively, it may be that, following the introduction of

---

[17] Morrill, 'Church in England', 106.
[18] *Prescot Churchwardens' Accounts*, xxx–xxxii, 147, 151.
[19] VCH Lancaster 6: 358; LancsRO, PR8, 39, 41, 46, 48, 51.
[20] *Thirty Men of Kirkham*, 39.
[21] LivRO, H283.1ALL, 199–200; *Churchwardens' Accounts of Walton-on-the-Hill*, esp. xxx–xxxi.

closed communions, it was no longer thought appropriate that the entire parish should bear the cost.[22]

The Directory dramatically altered the major rites of passage, stripping them of contentious medieval remnants. However, the old rituals remained popular and several ministers were presented for not conforming to the Directory. Once again, these incidents reveal the impotence of the classes. Lake baptized bastards at Oldham, the schoolmaster at Prestwich was 'baptiseinge children privately without order' and making 'clandestine marriages', and a Mr Rothwell committed similar offences in Bolton and Bury. Samuel Felgate claimed to be unfamiliar with the Directory, a situation which surely should have been ascertained by the Bury classis at his ordination in December 1649. John Odcroft caused concern by 'making clandestine wedings, baptizeinge children, and concerning his liffe and conversacon' but, despite an appeal to local justices, nothing came of it.[23]

The Directory removed the sign of the cross from the baptism service, replaced godparents with parents, and ordered the service to take place 'in the face of the congregation . . . and not in the places where fonts in the time of popery were unfitly and superstitiously placed'. Simple pewter basins replaced fonts, although no order was given for the latter's removal.[24] Didsbury, Cartmel and Padiham all purchased bowls in 1645, Whalley and Prescot in 1651, and Childwall only in 1653.[25] However, purchasing a basin was a simple and cheap way to conform to the new order: possession was not proof that it was used. Nevertheless, the new service was adopted in some parishes. At Preston, the font was abandoned as early as April 1645,[26] and there is evidence that elsewhere fonts were removed or destroyed. An order of 1647 instructing Flixton to remove its font implies that other congre-

22 Warrington Library, mf35 reel 23, 57; Morrill, 'Church in England', 107.

23 *Manchester Classis*, 98–9, 101, 109, 162, 166, 378–9; *Bury Classis*, 106–7, 121–2, 252. Rothwell was probably vicar of Leyland. An apparently spurious story suggested he was ejected in 1650 and preached in the Bolton and Bury area, but he remained at Leyland until at least 1656. That he was a beneficed minister only emphasizes the impotence of the classes when dealing with dissident clerics. VCH Lancaster 6; 8; *The Register Book of . . . Leyland, 1653–1710*, ed. W. S. White, *RSLC* 21 (1890), 25.

24 *Directory*, 19–20; David Cressy, *Birth, Marriage and Death* (Oxford, 1997), 173–7.

25 Booker, *Didsbury and Chorlton*, 87; *Cartmeltonia*, ed. William Ffolliott (London, 1854), 45; *Prescot Churchwardens' Accounts*, 146; LancsRO, PR8, 40; LancsRO, PR2863/2/1; LivRO, H283.1ALL.

26 Manchester CL, *The Registers of Preston Parish Church 1642–1657*, Unpublished Transcript.

gations in the Manchester classis had already done so.[27] Whittington, Ormskirk, Warton, Kirkham, Croston, Great Harwood and Hoole all erected new fonts following the Restoration, suggesting the destruction of the old ones.[28] Even so, the majority of Lancashire's fonts survived unscathed, suffering only neglect during their obsolescence. Two infants were baptized in 'the ould font' at Lancaster in July 1661, implying that it had stood unused until then, whilst the old font at Oldham was still lying 'indecently in the belfry in scorn and derision'.[29]

This rejection of Presbyterian baptism is also evidenced in Lancashire's parish registers. Wrigley and Schofield found a significant drop in the number of children baptized during the mid-seventeenth century. This can only partly be blamed upon the disruption caused by war, dearth and dislocation, and the rejection by separatist sects, such as the Quakers in north Lonsdale, of the formal institutions of the Church. Whereas the annual average of 10,377 baptisms between 1630 and 1644 was estimated by Wrigley and Scholfield to represent 93% of all births, the annual average of 8,192 baptisms between 1645 and 1653 constituted only 82.5% of births.[30] Christopher Durston has argued that the decline in the recording of baptisms in these years was the result of the introduction of the Directory, as parents sought covert – and so unrecorded – ceremonies according to the banned Prayer Book. This drop would have been particularly 'concentrated within the small minority of parishes which had obtained a [Directory] and were using it regularly, and that within these communities it had a striking impact.'[31]

Therefore, statistical analysis of parish registers might provide further evidence of the spread of the Directory. Parochial records are not a perfect source of information, and many registers suffered neglect, damage or destruction during the 1640s and 1650s, when

---

[27] *Manchester Classis*, 46.
[28] *The Registers of the Parish Church of Whittington 1538–1764*, ed. Fanny Wrigley and Thomas H. Winder, *LPRS* 3 (1899), 43; Nikolaus Pevsner, *North Lancashire* (London, 1969), 110, 132, 146, 184, 255; VCH Lancaster 7: 148.
[29] VCH Lancaster 5: 105; *The Registers of the Parish Church of Lancaster 1599–1690*, ed. H. Brierley, *LPRS* 32 (1908), 127.
[30] E. A. Wrigley and R. S. Schofield, *The Population History of England 1541–1871* (London, 1981), 228–36.
[31] Christopher Durston, 'Puritan Rule and the Failure of Cultural Revolution, 1645–1660', in Christopher Durston and Jacqueline Eales, eds, *The Culture of English Puritanism, 1560–1700* (Basingstoke, 1996), 210–33, at 226–7.

Lancashire experienced armed conflict, two Scottish invasions, and regular outbreaks of plague. In an effort to achieve continuity, only those registers with records between the key dates of 1642 and 1653 have been considered; these dates were thought to be essential if any impact of the Directory was to be demonstrated. To ensure that the results are not distorted, the data from chapels and churches have been collated separately. Although some chapels had larger congregations than several parishes, in other ways they had more in common with one another than with the parish churches. Whilst chapel livings remained poor, and the security of their position uncertain, vacancies were always more likely at the chapels. This no doubt accounts for the wild fluctuations in the chapel data, as revealed by Table 1. Although the chapels also experienced a general downward trend in the number of baptisms recorded, it was much less pronounced than the reduction at churches. Whilst the annual average of baptisms at Lancashire parish churches fell by 32.5% in the seven years following the introduction of the Directory, the same figure for the chapelries was just 21.9%. Because of the problems with the chapel data, this paper will focus only upon baptisms recorded at parish churches.

Table 1: Average number of baptisms in Lancashire, 1635–65

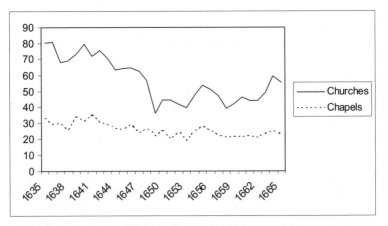

Lancashire was a county where we might expect the Directory to have been widely imposed, and analysis of the extant parish registers provides graphic evidence of this. The data strongly suggest that the introduction of the Directory in Lancashire parishes met with the great disapproval of many parishioners. Table 1 shows the average number of baptisms recorded each year at fifty-seven Lancashire churches and chapels.[32]

The registers demonstrate a sharp drop in the number of baptisms recorded in Lancashire following the introduction of the Directory. Following a gradual decline in the average number of recorded baptisms at parish churches, from a peak of 82.7 in 1640 to 63.6 in 1646, a more dramatic drop saw this figure reach just 35.5 in 1649, suggesting a violent reaction to the Directory.[33] The average annual number of baptisms recorded at parish churches between 1646 and 1653 was 48.2, less than two-thirds of the figure for the years from 1635 to 1645. The temporary change, between 1653 and 1657, to the recording of births rather than baptisms reveals that the significant decrease in the level of baptisms was not the result of a much-reduced birth rate. Following the reintroduction of the Prayer Book in 1660, baptisms returned almost to the pre-Directory level, reaching an average of 61.4 in 1664, despite the continuing national decline in fertility found by Wrigley and Schofield. That this demonstrates a continuing loyalty to Anglicanism is shown by a few examples of late baptisms in the early 1660s. At Cartmel, four children born late in the 1650s were baptized in 1662 and 1663, one aged seven; a child was baptized at Manchester in 1663 'being foure yeares and three quarters', whilst a six-year-old was baptized at Bury in 1661. Perhaps the most remarkable case was that of the sixteen-year-old baptized at Bury in 1662. Strikingly, this would have put his birth at approximately the time that the Directory should have been adopted.[34]

This can be further illustrated with specific examples. At Prescot, a parish that purchased the Directory, the average number of baptisms

[32] Parish churches: Aldingham, Aughton, Bolton, Brindle, Bury, Cartmel, Croston, Dalton, Deane, Eccles, Eccleston, Flixton, Garstang, Halton, Huyton, Kirkham, Lancaster, Leigh, Manchester, Middleton, Pennington, Prescot, Preston, Prestwich, Radcliffe, Rochdale, Sefton, Standish, Tatham, Tunstall, Urswick, Warrington, Warton, Whalley, Whittington and Wigan. Chapels: Altham, Blackrod, Bispham, Burnley, Caton, Chorley, Church, Colne, Coniston, Didsbury, Farnworth, Goosnargh, Harwood, Melling (Halsall), Newchurch-in-Culcheth, Newchurch-in-Pendle, Oldham, Padiham, and Pilling.

[33] This may have been particularly low because of plague outbreaks; R. Sharpe France, 'A History of Plague in Lancashire', *Transactions of the Historic Society of Lancashire and Cheshire* 90 (1938), 94–9; Craven, 'Coercion and Compromise', 72–82.

[34] *The Registers of the Parish Church of Cartmel 1660–1723*, ed. Robert Dickinson, LPRS 96 (1957), 4–6; *The Registers of the Cathedral Church of Manchester 1653–1665/6*, ed. J. Flitcroft and E. B. Leech, LPRS 89 (1949), 35; *The Registers of the Parish Church of Bury 1647–1698*, ed. Archibald Sparke, *LPRS* 24 (1905), 31, 34.

following its introduction fell to 69.8 a year between 1646 and 1653, from an average of 127.3 in the ten years preceding the Directory. Richard Heyricke, warden of the Collegiate Church in Manchester and a leading member of the Assembly of Divines, emphasized the town's long puritan tradition in 1646, describing it as 'a Town famous for Religion ever since the Reformation . . . a Goshen, a place of light, when most places of the Land have been places of darknesse . . .'[35] Yet, even here the level of baptisms fell by 40% after the introduction of the Directory, from an annual average of 289.2 baptisms in the period 1635–44 to just 177.1 a year in 1646–53. There was a similar pattern at other parishes with strong puritan sensibilities: at Bolton, the 'Geneva of the north', recorded baptisms were reduced by almost a half, Wigan's average was more than halved, and significant reductions were noted at many other parishes, including Bury, Leigh and Rochdale. Unsurprisingly, the number of baptisms at parishes where the Directory was probably never introduced remained fairly stable: at Flixton, for example, the annual average of 41.7 during the years 1635–45 rose slightly to 42.6 for 1646–53. However, a similar situation obtained at Burnley, a congregation where the purchase of a Directory is explicitly recorded. It is not clear why: it may be that the Directory was never in fact used, or it may mean that the congregation was already worshipping in a way that differed little from the Directory.

Extending this process to the county as a whole, we might speculate about both the extent to which the Directory was adopted, and also how effective the operation of each classis was. As Table 2 reveals, each of Lancashire's nine classes experienced a noticeable drop in the number of recorded baptisms, but the most significant reductions were experienced in the south and east of the county. Leyland classis, home to renowned Presbyterians such as Edward Gee and James Hyett, also saw a drop in the baptismal rate by over a third. Meanwhile, the west and north appear to have been largely unaffected by the Directory. The large number of Catholics in these parts probably meant that only a minority of each community attended the parish church. The exception is Ulverston classis, where the average fell by two-fifths. This might be partly explained by the arrival of the Presbyterian Phillip Bennett at Cartmel, where the annual average of baptisms was reduced by over a half, but also to the rise of the Quakers in the area.

---

[35] Richard Heyricke, *Queen Esthers Resolves* (London, 1646), 24.

Table 2: The average number of baptisms in Lancashire by classis, 1635–53

	Manc.	Bury	Whalley	Warr.	Walton
1635–45	113.17	124.71	40.45	125.71	30.36
1646–53	74.07	80.31	22.5	77.91	23.79
Decrease	35.5%	35.6%	44.4%	38%	21.6%

	Leyland	Preston	Lanc.	Ulv.
1635–45	40.72	72.09	34.61	35.8
1646–53	25.58	58.5	28.73	21.53
Decrease	37.2%	18.8%	16.9%	39.9%

The evidence of classis minutes and churchwardens' accounts overwhelmingly demonstrates that, even in those communities nationally renowned for their devotion to godliness, many parishioners rejected the discipline of the new Presbyterian classes. Lancashire is famed for its large Catholic and godly communities, and, from 1652, for the rise of Quakerism in the north of the county, but the continued loyalty to Anglicanism within the county during the 1640s and 1650s should also not be underestimated. The wider significance of Lancashire's experience is twofold. Firstly, it is clear that the Presbyterian liturgy of the Directory was introduced into a number of Lancashire parishes during the 1640s and 1650s. Whilst Morrill expected only a fifth of churches to adopt the Directory, in godly Lancashire the figure was clearly much higher. This is amply illustrated by the replacement of the traditional paraphernalia of the liturgy, the extensive rejection of baptism in a number of Lancashire parishes after 1646 and, of course, the evidence of functioning classes. However, the manifest rejection of this new order in Lancashire reveals the ultimate limitations of the 'cultural revolution' of the 1650s. If the Directory failed in so famed a godly county, it must surely fail everywhere.

Manchester Metropolitan University

'THE CLERGY WHO AFFECT TO CALL THEMSELVES ORTHODOX': THOMAS SECKER AND THE DEFENCE OF ANGLICAN ORTHODOXY, 1758–68

by ROBERT G. INGRAM

THE spectre of the seventeenth century loomed large in the eighteenth century.[1] The Anglican orthodox were particularly aghast at the radical assault on the religio-political order during the previous century and feared a reprise during theirs. In 1734, for instance, Thomas Secker (1693–1768) warned his audience at St James's, Westminster, that Charles I's execution was 'a most peculiarly instructive example of divine judgments, brought down by a sinful people on their own heads'.[2] In all his providential interventions in human affairs, God teaches 'an awful regard to himself, as moral governor of the world; and a faithful practice of true religion'. And what drew his divine wrath upon Britain during the 1650s was the abandonment of 'real religion' for 'hypocrisy, superstition, and enthusiasm'.[3] Certainly Laud and his followers might have displayed 'an over warm zeal, and very blameable stiffness and severity', Secker acknowledged. 'But there was also, in the enemies of the church, a most provoking bitterness and perverseness; with a wild eagerness for innovation, founded on ignorant prejudices, which their heated fancies raised into necessary truths; and then, looking on them, as the cause of Christ, they thought themselves bound and commissioned to overturn whatever was contrary to them.'[4]

---

[1] Blair Worden, *Roundhead Reputations: the English Civil Wars and the Passions of Posterity* (London, 2001), 65–215; J. C. D. Clark, *English Society, 1660–1832: Religion, Ideology and Politics during the Ancien Regime* (Cambridge, 2000), 43–123; J. G. A. Pocock, 'Within the Margins: the Definitions of Orthodoxy', in Roger Lund, ed., *The Margins of Orthodoxy: Heterodox Writing and Cultural Response, 1660–1750* (Cambridge, 1995), 33–53, at 38.

[2] 'Sermon preached in the parish church of St. James, Westminster, January 30, 1733–4 [Isaiah 32: 9]', in Thomas Secker, *The Works of Thomas Secker, L.L.D., late Lord Archbishop of Canterbury: to which is prefixed a review of his life and character*, 4 vols (Edinburgh, 1799) [hereafter: *Works*], 3: 423. Compare 'Sermon preached before the House of Lords, in the Abbey-Church of Westminster, on Thursday, May 29, 1739 [Psalm 106: 12–13]', in *Works*, 3: 460–71.

[3] 'Sermon preached ... [on] January 30, 1733–34', 425.

[4] Ibid., 426.

The lessons to be drawn from the seventeenth-century 'troubles' remained relevant to Secker and his contemporaries because theology and politics were so tightly and organically intertwined during the eighteenth century. Put simply, theological heterodoxy threatened the religio-political order, theological orthodoxy buttressed it, and the great unravelling of society during the mid-seventeenth century proved it.[5] At stake in eighteenth-century religious debate, then, was the survival of both Church and state, issues that had heightened importance for a nation at war. Not surprisingly, the promotion of orthodoxy and defence against heterodoxy were central to the orthodox Anglican reform effort Thomas Secker pursued when he was archbishop of Canterbury from 1758 to 1768.[6]

The eighteenth-century Church of England and its leaders faced a number of challenges, particularly during Secker's archiepiscopate.[7] Secker's vision of reform was capacious enough to encompass a wide range of concerns, from pastoral provision to the established Church's involvement in politics, education, charity, the Atlantic empire, and European affairs. But an equally – if not even more – important part of that vision, especially in an intellectual climate not overwhelmingly supportive of durable truths, was the defence of orthodox Christian doctrine (as spelled out in the ancient Church creeds) and orthodox Anglican doctrine (as spelled out in the Thirty-Nine Articles). During the mid-eighteenth century, *reform* was a sensibility that used the old to grapple with the new. It was both a call for change and a way of understanding, responding to, and managing change that looked to the past for answers to current problems. Insofar as theology was concerned, Secker believed that the durable truths espoused by the apostolic and patristic fathers required defending, not jettisoning. Reformation was restoration, and it required discipline – understood both as a firm resolve to resist corrosive innovation and punitive action itself – to deal

---

[5] Justin Champion, ' "Religion's Safe, with Priestcraft is the War": Augustan Anti-clericalism and the Legacy of the English Revolution, 1660–1720', *The European Legacy* 5: 4 (2000), 547–61; A. M. C. Waterman, 'The Nexus between Theology and Political Doctrine in Church and Dissent', in Knud Haakonssen, ed., *Enlightenment and Religion: Rational Dissent in Eighteenth-Century Britain* (Cambridge, 1996), 193–218; Clark, *English Society, 1660–1832*, 318–422.

[6] Robert G. Ingram, *Thomas Secker: Religion, Reform, and Modernity, 1700–1770* (forth-coming) will anatomize Secker's orthodox reform efforts fully.

[7] Bob Harris, *Politics and the Nation: Britain in the Mid-Eighteenth Century* (Oxford, 2002) nicely captures the turbulence of mid-eighteenth-century Britain.

with his own age's intellectual and theological diversity which, unchecked, threatened the religio-political order.

England's Enlightenment, it has been argued, was 'decidedly clerical and intellectually conservative'.[8] Yet the clerical Enlightenment was also a pugilistic Enlightenment, and the intellectual contretemps often took on the character of a back-alley brawl with few, if any holds barred. With Church courts emasculated and with the state reluctant to stand shoulder-to-shoulder with them to defend orthodoxy, orthodox clergy had to get their hands dirty in intellectual combat. One of the leaders of the orthodox counter-offensive was Thomas Secker. Many at the time believed that Secker was a vigilant and, if necessary, vengeful leader of the established Church. 'It was commonly said he had two paper books', wrote one cleric, 'one called the *black*, the other the *white* book; in which he entered down such notices as he received concerning the different characters of each, as they happened to suit the design of either book. Those whose character he found to be bad, he resolved never to promote nor did, paying no regard to any solicitations made in their behalf.'[9] Secker's concern extended beyond clerical character to clerical beliefs, and his insistent defence of orthodoxy rankled many of his contemporaries. Some whinged that Secker's doctrinal rigidity was prelatical and authoritarian.[10] In the face of determined opponents, Secker thought, the orthodox needed to offer a spirited, determined, and persistent front. This essay is about Secker's leadership of the orthodox during his archiepiscopate and about the ways he used discipline to grapple with the problem of diversity.

[8] B. W. Young, *Religion and Enlightenment in Eighteenth-Century England: Theological Debate from Locke to Burke* (Oxford, 1998), 6. See also, J. G. A. Pocock, 'Post-Puritan England and the Problem of the Enlightenment', in Perez Zagorin, ed., *Culture and Politics from Puritanism to the Enlightenment* (Berkeley and Los Angeles, CA, 1980), 91–112; idem, 'Clergy and Commerce: the Conservative Enlightenment in England', in R. Ajello, E. Contese, and V. Piano, eds, *L'età dei Lumi: Studi storici sul settecento europeo in onore di Franco Venturi*, 2 vols (Naples, 1985), 1: 523–62; idem, 'Conservative Enlightenment and Democratic Revolutions: the American and French Cases in British Perspective', *Government and Opposition* 24: 1 (1989), 81–105.

[9] John Nichols, *Literary Anecdotes of the Eighteenth Century*, 9 vols (London, 1812–15), 3: 751.

[10] Thomas Gwatkin, *Remarks upon the second and third of the Three letters against the Confessional by a country clergyman* (London, 1768), 43.

I

Secker laid much of the responsibility for the spread of heterodoxy on Anglican clerics. The problem, as Secker saw it, was that '[o]ur clergy have dwelt too much upon mere morality, and too little on the peculiar doctrines of the Gospel'.[11] Clerics' role in preventing the populace from lapsing into the 'crime of heterodoxy' was a theme he fleshed out in his episcopal charges and other published writings.[12] Since the way to the soul was through the head, not the heart, Secker repeatedly urged clergy to explain clearly the meaning of the catechism and creeds to their parishioners.[13] It also accounts for his refusal to ordain the mani- festly ignorant.[14] For this former religious nonconformist, the affective religion of the evangelical revival held little appeal and, indeed, as a manifestation of 'enthusiasm', could be positively pernicious. But teaching orthodox doctrine vigorously and vociferously from parish pulpits was only a partial solution to the problem of heterodoxy: Lambeth needed to provide the strategic vision, tactical leadership, and long-range artillery to support the clerical infantry in the parishes.

Secker understood that an important part of his job as archbishop was to cultivate orthodox scholarship, to which perhaps his most lasting contribution was to biblical studies. Though loath to support a new, more accurate Authorized Version (AV) of the Bible – 'the last thing I want is to be the patron of undertakings from which too much quarelling is likely to arise', he explained – he did support those whose work aimed to clear up mistakes in the current AV.[15] He was, for instance, chief patron of the most ambitious orthodox biblical project

---

[11] John Nichols, *Illustrations of the Literary History of the Eighteenth Century*, 8 vols (London, 1817–1858), 3: 497.

[12] See, for instance, Secker, *Oratio quam coram Synodo Provinciae Cantuariensis anno 1761 convocata habendam scripserat, sed morbo praepeditus non habuit, Archiepiscopus* [hereafter: *Oratio*], in *Works*, 4: 217–30. Quotations from the *Oratio* are taken from *The Acts of the Canterbury Convocation, 1761–1852*, ed. Gerald Bray (typescript): London, Lambeth Palace Library, shelfmark H5021.A1 [R], 357–67, at 361–2.

[13] Secker, *Eight Charges delivered to the Clergy of the Dioceses of Oxford and Canterbury* (London, 1769) ['Charge of 1741'], 48–54; idem, *Lectures on the Catechism of the Church of England; with a Discourse on Confirmation* (8th edn, London, 1799), 5–9.

[14] See, for instance, Lambeth Palace, Secker Papers 3, fol. 147: Secker to Matthew Kenrick, 26 March 1762.

[15] *Oratio*, 363. See also Scott Mandelbrote, 'The English Bible and its Readers in the Eighteenth Century', in Isabel Rivers, ed., *Books and Their Readers in Eighteenth-Century England: New Essays* (London, 2001), 35–78; N. W. Hitchin, 'The Politics of English Bible Translation in Georgian Britain', *TRHS* ser. 6, 9 (1999), 67–92.

in the eighteenth century, Benjamin Kennicott's collation of all the known manuscript editions of the Hebrew Bible.[16] Its aim was to recover the Old Testament's original text by ferreting out the errors, omissions, and additions that had accumulated across the centuries; its purpose was, ultimately, to pave the way for a new, more accurate translation in the future. It took Kennicott over a decade to complete the work, during which time Secker served as his chief advisor, fund-raiser, and connection to continental scholars. In the end, Kennicott's work earned him an international reputation and was an important step in the development of modern biblical criticism.[17] Secker also made Lambeth Palace a centre of orthodox biblical scholarship during the eighteenth century. Jeremy Gregory has noted the degree to which Georgian archbishops created a 'clerical enclave' at Lambeth, the heart of the archiepiscopal administrative machine: Secker clearly hoped to make the library there a welcome home to orthodox biblical scholars, as well.[18] During the preparation of his new translation of Isaiah, Robert Lowth consulted Secker's marginal notes in manuscript study Bibles in Lambeth Palace library.[19] Lowth particularly praised the 'candour and modesty' of Secker's notes, 'for there is hardly a proposed emendation, however ingenious and probable, to which he has not added the objections, which occurred to him, against it'. The notes would, Lowth added, 'be of infinite service, whenever that necessary work, a New Translation, or Revision of the present Translation, of the Holy Scriptures for the use of our Church, shall be undertaken'.[20] These notes were evidently thought by many to be useful, for a number of other orthodox biblical scholars, including James Merrick, William Newcome, Benjamin Blayney, Thomas Wintle, and William Hayward

---

[16] Lambeth Palace, Secker Papers 2, fols 1–88; R. W. Greaves and John Macauley, eds, *The Autobiography of Thomas Secker, Archbishop of Canterbury* (Lawrence, KS, 1988) [hereafter: *Autobiography*]; BL, Add. MS 32902, fols 104–5: Secker to Duke of Newcastle, 8 February 1769.

[17] David S. Katz, *God's Last Words: Reading the English Bible from the Reformation to Fundamentalism* (New Haven, CT, 2004), 204–9; David Ruderman, *Jewish Enlightenment in an English Key: Anglo-Jewry's Construction of Modern Jewish Thought* (Princeton, NJ, 2000), 23–56.

[18] Jeremy Gregory, *Restoration, Reformation, and Reform: Archbishops of Canterbury and their Diocese, 1660–1828* (Oxford, 2000), 33.

[19] Robert Lowth, *Isaiah: a New Translation*, 2 vols (3rd edn, London, 1795), 1: xci. Lowth repeatedly cited Secker's Lambeth biblical notes as an authority in his translation of Isaiah. Ruderman, *Jewish Enlightenment*, 57–88 and Katz, *God's Last Words*, 153–9 assess the importance of Lowth's work on the Bible as literature.

[20] Ibid., xcii.

Roberts, also made use of Secker's Hebrew notes in the library at Lambeth Palace for their own biblical translations.[21] Blayney specifically left his biblical manuscripts and notes to the library at Lambeth Palace to be used 'in the like manner and for the like purposes as the manuscripts of Archbishop Secker'.[22] This pattern of cultivating orthodox scholars extended well beyond biblical scholarship, as well. While he rejected their natural philosophy and idiosyncratic biblical interpretative method, Secker nonetheless also embraced within his orthodox scholarly circle a number of the more influential Hutchinsonians, whose staunch defence of orthodox trinitarianism he appreciated.[23] So too were vocal defenders of revealed religion drawn into his orbit.[24]

If Secker promoted orthodoxy by cultivating orthodox scholars, he also defended it through more aggressive, and at times coercive, means. His treatment of the Socinian and mortalist Peter Peckard is particularly telling.[25] The rector of Fletton near Peterborough, Peckard had been offered a lucrative crown living in 1760, and had to ask Secker for a dispensation to hold the livings in plurality. Secker used the opportunity to make Peckard jump through a series of hoops to get the dispensation. Though Peckard arrived at Lambeth with 'all the common credentials requisite for a dispensation, and in the common forms', Secker made Peckard write lengthy Latin explanations of his earlier writings on mortalism, the heresy which holds that the soul 'sleeps'

---

[21] William Declair Tattersall, *Improved psalmody* (London, 1794), 4; Benjamin Blayney, *Jeremiah and Lamentations: a new translation with notes critical, philological, and explanatory* (Oxford, 1784), vii; William Newcome, *An attempt towards an improved version, a metrical arrangement, and an explanation of the prophet Ezekiel* (Dublin, 1788); Thomas Wintle, *Daniel, an improved version attempted* (Oxford, 1792), xvii, xxvii, xli; W. H. Roberts, *Corrections of various passages of the English translation of the Old Testament* (London, 1794), 232. Even a Roman Catholic like Alexander Geddes sought out Secker's advice on questions of biblical translation: *Critical remarks on the Hebrew scriptures*, 2 vols (London, 1800), 1: 36. Compare Richard Hurd, *A discourse, by way of general preface, to the quarto edition of Bishop Warburton's works* (London, 1794), 82–3 for contemporary criticism of the quality of Secker's biblical scholarship.

[22] Lambeth Palace, MS 2577, front cover.

[23] See Herbert and Carol Schneider, eds, *Samuel Johnson: His Career and Writings*, 4 vols (New York, 1929), 4: 71: Secker to Samuel Johnson, 4 November 1760 for Secker's objections to Hutchinsonian natural philosophy.

[24] *Autobiography*, 35, 42.

[25] Peckard detailed his treatment by Secker in three letters to Francis Blackburne (dated 3 November, 5 December, and 6 December 1760): Francis Blackburne, *The Works of . . . Francis Blackburne, M.A. . . .; with some of the life and writings of the author* (Cambridge, 1804), xciv–cvii. Unless otherwise noted, the information in this paragraph is drawn from these letters.

ROBERT G. INGRAM

between death and the body's resurrection.[26] Displeased with Peckard's
initial responses, Secker's chaplain forced him to write two further
essays, on the internal and external truths of Christianity. Furthermore,
Secker made Peckard submit a new *testimonium* for dispensation in
which was inserted a clause affirming that Peckard 'had not published
anything contrary to the doctrine of the church of England'.[27] Peckard,
then, was forced to return home to get his paperwork in 'due form',
after which Secker grilled him personally. Having read through
Peckard's mortalist writings and made extensive notes on them, Secker
sat Peckard down, telling him that 'he did not send for me to dispute
the point with me, but that he did not require any answer from me.
That his present intent was to give me some advice, which he hoped by
the blessing of God, might have a good influence on me.'[28] That advice
took the form of a monologue, which Peckard was not allowed to
interrupt, on the errors of mortalism; Secker ended the lecture
requiring Peckard to have yet another interview with his domestic
chaplain. More importantly, he forced Peckard to assent to four articles,
which were an effective renunciation of mortalism. Only after all of
this did Secker grant Peckard his dispensation, and the latter never
again published in support of the mortalist heresy. Bullying could
work.

We know about Peckard's treatment at Secker's hands from a series
of letters he wrote to fellow mortalist Francis Blackburne. As Brian
Young has observed, we see in Secker and Blackburne the twin poles of
England's clerical Enlightenment. Secker, a former Dissenter, found
Blackburne's anti-dogmatism subversive, while Blackburne, a heterodox
Anglican, thought Secker's reliance on any religious authority outside
of the Bible was, at best, a betrayal of Protestantism and, at worst,
intellectually corrupt. Their enmity was real; their battles were fierce,
public, and concerned fundamental issues about the established
Church's status and privilege.

Secker led the orthodox counter-offensive against the most serious
intellectual and political challenge to the established Church during the
mid-eighteenth century, occasioned by the publication of Blackburne's

26 Ibid., xciv-ci. B. W. Young, ' "The Soul-Sleeping System": Politics and Heresy in Eighteenth-Century England', *JEH* 45 (1994), 64–81 and Thomas Ahnert, 'The Soul, Natural
Religion, and Moral Philosophy in the Scottish Enlightenment', *Eighteenth-Century Thought* 2
(2004), 233–53 provide further context.
27 Ibid., cii.
28 Ibid., ciii.

The Confessional (1766). Blackburne, who occupied what might anachronistically be called the liberal wing of the Georgian Church, believed in scriptural sufficiency and argued that clerical subscription requirements to the Thirty-Nine Articles should be abolished because the articles were man-made formulae. He first aired these views in an anonymous response to William Samuel Powell's Cambridge commencement sermon of 1757.[29] There Blackburne rejected Samuel Clarke's contention that 'every person may reasonably agree to such forms, whenever he can in any sense at all reconcile them with Scripture'.[30] Instead, he believed that this latitudinarian formula for subscription to the Anglican articles proposed by Clarke and seconded by Powell was casuitical: it was, he argued, 'a Defence conducted on such principles as manifestly tend to confound the common use of language'.[31] Blackburne also accused the Church's leaders of blocking efforts to reform subscription requirements. 'A large majority of the clergy, either really are, or affect to be persuaded, that no alterations in the constitution of our church are at all necessary', he wrote. 'At the head of these are some of the most opulent and dignified of the order. Vigorous opposition from there is certain and formidable, and sufficient to intimidate the few in comparison, who are affected with a different sense of their situation'.[32] Eight years later, Blackburne made a lengthy and systematic assault on the subscription requirements in the anonymously published *Confessional*, a work that sparked a vigorous, at times vitriolic, debate on the very nature of the established Church's status and privileges.[33]

Secker thought *The Confessional* posed a sufficient threat to the Church to co-ordinate responses to it, and worked to have a rebuttal in print as soon as possible.[34] William Jones, the Hutchinsonian rector of

[29] [Francis Blackburne], *Remarks on the Revd. Dr. Powell's sermon in defence of subscriptions, preached before the University of Cambridge on the commencement Sunday 1757* (London, 1758).

[30] Quoted in Martin Fitzpatrick, 'Latitudinarianism at the Parting of the Ways: a Suggestion', in John Walsh, Colin Haydon, and Stephen Taylor, eds, *The Church of England, c.1689–c.1833: From Toleration to Tractarianism* (Cambridge, 1993), 209–27, at 213.

[31] Blackburne, *Remarks on . . . Dr. Powell's sermon*, 70–1.

[32] Ibid., x.

[33] On the theology and politics of the subscription controversy, see Young, *Religion and Enlightenment*, 45–80; G. M. Ditchfield, 'The Subscription Issue in British Parliamentary Politics, 1772–79', *Parliamentary History* 7 (1988), 45–80; and Fitzpatrick, 'Latitudinarianism at the Parting of the Ways', 209–27.

[34] Aston, 'The Limits of Latitudinarianism', 407–33 explains why many Anglicans viewed Blackburne's assault on clerical subscription requirements as a logical follow-up to Robert Clayton's heterodox *An essay on spirit* (Dublin, 1750).

Pluckley, volunteered to draft a retort, and Secker threw himself fully into the project. George Horne explained that Secker 'addres'd a long letter to [Jones] full of seasonable directions about the turn and temper of mind to be obser'vd in a reply to such a work, and wherein He offers all the assistance in his Power towards the execution of it'.[35] Secker recalled later, 'I gave him Directions about the Manner of writing, sent him very large Remarks upon it, & furnished him with Books. He made a Beginning, which he sent me, & I returned him Many Corrections on it'.[36] Jones, however, soon became too ill to continue the project, and Secker 'engaged' Glocester Ridley, 'who had also supplied Mr. Jones with Observations', to draft the response. During the mid 1760s, Ridley had established a reputation as an orthodox writer, having published on the Eucharist, the operations of the Holy Ghost, and providential theology. He was one of Secker's favorites, and the archbishop involved himself heavily in the writing process, noting 'I wrote a great part of each of them, & furnished him all the Help that was in my power.'[37] He even took to the pages of London newspapers to defend Ridley.[38] It is suggestive that a number of others connected to Secker – including George Horne, Wiliam Jones, John Rotheram, Josiah Tucker, and Thomas Rutherforth – published defences of subscription during the ensuing controversy.

Blackburne's son also suggests that Secker tried to take a more punitive line against Blackburne. Blackburne had published the work anonymously but, it seems, Secker used his contacts to ferret out his name:

> When the book was published, it appeared from the clamour that was raised against it, that grievous offence was taken at it by that part of the clergy who affect to call themselves orthodox. The indignation of Archbishop Secker was excessive. His mask of moderation fell off at once. He employed all his emissaries to find out the author, and by the industry of Rivington, and the communicative disposition of Millar, he succeeded.[39]

---

[35] London, BL, Add. MS 39311, fol. 180: Horne to George Berkeley, Jr, 17 July 1766.

[36] *Autobiography*, 52.

[37] Ibid., 68.

[38] See, for instance, *London Chronicle* 23 (12–14 April 1768), 359 where Secker defended Ridley under the pseudonym 'Oxoniensis'. In particular, he was responding to attacks on Ridley's critique of *The Confessional* by 'Old Milton' and 'Cantabrigiensus' that had appeared in earlier editions of the same paper.

[39] Blackburne, 'Life of Francis Blackburne', xxxiii.

Edmund Keene, bishop of Chester and Blackburne's diocesan, then warned Blackburne that any hopes he held of career advancement would vanish if he did not renounce *The Confessional*: 'mentioning the resentment of the Archbishop of Canterbury ... [Keene] intimated that if the suspicion which fell upon Mr. B. was groundless, he would do well to silence the imputation, by publicly disavowing the work in print; for that every door of access to farther preferment would otherwise be shut against him'.[40] Blackburne had, however, set his mind against ever again subscribing to the Thirty-Nine Articles; he would remain archdeacon of Cleveland, a post he took up in 1750, until his death in 1787.

In addition to questioning the need for subscription requirements, Blackburne also accused the Church of England of being soft on Roman Catholicism and accused prominent orthodox clergy of harboring pro-Catholic sympathies. Here he was influenced by his close friend, Thomas Hollis, an anti-Catholic zealot, radical Whig, and former friend of Secker, who had encouraged Blackburne to publish *The Confessional* in the first place. Hollis also coordinated the stream of anti-Catholic pieces by Blackburne, Theophilus Lindsey, William Harris, and Caleb Fleming that appeared in the *London Chronicle* during the late 1760s.[41] Secker, Hollis thought, was too lenient on Catholics, and he complained to Jonathan Mayhew that Secker had forsaken the 'hard unsplendid work at home, the watching, *da vero*, against the evil morals, conduct of his own vast Flock, and the alarming growth of Popery'.[42] In *The Confessional*, Blackburne had also cast aspersions on William Wake's correspondence with Gallican Catholics during the early eighteenth century, correspondence that had been aimed at forming ecumenical ties between the Church of England and the Gallican Church. Secker had Osmund Beauvoir copy original letters between Wake and Beauvoir's father, who had been domestic chaplain to England's diplomatic representative to France during the late 1710s, and had Edward Bentham make extracts from Wake's papers at Christ

---

[40] Ibid.

[41] Colin Bonwick, 'Hollis, Thomas (1720–1774)', *ODNB*.

[42] *Proceedings of the Massachusetts Historical Society* 69 (1947–50), 171–2: Hollis to Mayhew, 24 June 1765. Secker's work to establish Anglican bishops in North America particularly enraged the Hollisites, who feared they would enable and encourage the spread of popery throughout the continent. Blackburne was a particularly fierce critic of the scheme to plant an American episcopate: Francis Blackburne, *A critical commentary on Archbishop Secker's letter to the Right Honourable Horace Walpole, concerning bishops in America* (London, 1770).

Church, Oxford, to clear the former archbishop's name. Then, Secker recalled, 'I methodized both these, & sent what I had done to Dr. [Robert] Richardson, Sir Joseph Yorkes Chaplain at the Hague to be communicated to Mr. [Archibald] Maclaine for the Foundation of his Defence of the Abp'.[43] A year later, Secker wrote a number of letters that he placed in *St. James's Chronicle* to counter Blackburne and Caleb Fleming's charges that Joseph Butler had died a Roman Catholic.[44] For all of this, Secker earned Blackburne's lasting enmity. 'The Archbishop', he wrote 'was indefatigable in tracing out the anonymous authors of what he called obnoxious books; and sometimes used means to gratify his passion which would not have passed for allowable practice among the horse-dealers in Smithfield.'[45]

II

It might not have been pretty, but Secker's way planted the seeds of a successful defence of Anglican orthodoxy in the late eighteenth century.[46] Some might accuse Secker of suffering from a failure of imagination. Without doubt, he was inherently cautious and unwilling to expose the Church to negative press: 'I am far from being against all Efforts to Amendment', he explained once, 'but I think they should be made, not only at favourable opportunities, which all are not that seem to be, but in moderate Degrees. For if we aim too much we shall get nothing, but perhaps be losers.'[47] He also tended to fight almost exclusively about the status and reputation of the established Church: in retrospect, these might look like intramural squabbles which were

[43] *Autobiography*, 57. Maclaine's defence appeared in a book-length appendix to the second edition of J. L. Mosheim, *An Ecclesiastical History*, ed. and trans. Archibald Maclaine (London, 1768), 45–137. See also, Nichols, *Literary Anecdotes*, 2: 40.

[44] *Autobiography*, 58, 61, 178. These rumours were spread by [Francis Blackburne], *The Root of Protestant Errors Examined* (London, 1752). Richard Baron's *Pillars of Priestcraft and Orthodoxy Shaken* (London, 1767) identified Blackburne as the author of the *Root of Protestant Errors*.

[45] Francis Blackburne, *Memoirs of Thomas Hollis*, 2 vols (London, 1780), 1: 406–7.

[46] Nigel Aston, 'Anglican Responses to Anticlericalism in the "Long" Eighteenth Century, c.1689–1830', in Nigel Aston and Matthew Cragoe, eds, *Anticlericalism in Britain, c.1500–1914* (Stroud, 2000), 115–37, at 122; idem, 'The Limits of Latitudinarianism: English Reactions to Bishop Clayton's *An Essay on Spirit*', *JEH* 49: 3 (1998), 407–33, at 433; idem, 'Infidelity Ancient and Modern: George Horne Reads Edward Gibbon', *Albion* 27: 4 (1995), 561–82, at 561.

[47] Lambeth Palace, Secker Papers 7, fols 150–1: Secker to Theophilus Alexander, 4 December 1762.

important to stamp out doctrinal diversity, defend the institution, and present a unified face to the world, but which did little to address the fundamental questions about the nature of religious belief itself that were arguably of a much more subversive nature. Secker thought the analogical proof of God and the historical proof of miracles were sufficient for rational men, and it is striking that while Francis Blackburne drove him to distraction, David Hume did not. Yet to accuse Secker of a failure of imagination is to miss the point, for he aimed to return the Church to a golden age, not to transform it or its beliefs into something new. He envisioned restoring the Church to its ancient glories by the methods of its first fathers: 'Others may point out shortcuts, but these lead only to rough and precipitous places', he warned. 'It was by these means that the doctors of the first centuries flourished, and the same means are entrusted to us. There is no other way to be respected, and if other ways forward exist, we would not serve the interests of men or attain to eternal life by following them.'[48]

Ohio University

---

[48] *Oratio*, 366.

DISCIPLINING DIVERSITY:
THE ROMAN INQUISITION AND
SOCIAL CONTROL IN MALTA, 1743–98

by FRANS CIAPPARA

HAVING lost northern Europe to the Protestants the Catholic Church tried to preserve control over what remained of the *respublica christiana*.[1] The attempt was twofold. First, it was political. The popes declared the entire Catholic world for their diocese. 'The government of the Christian peoples', Pius V observed, 'belongs to Us and We should see that they are governed with charity'.[2] Second, the popes admitted that the Reformation had been the result partly of the religious and spiritual shortcomings of the Church itself and tried to make the requisite internal reforms. The Council of Trent defined Catholic doctrine and anathemized whoever disagreed with it.[3] Seminaries were set up to train the clergy while the lay population was held under tight control. The Jesuits and the Office of the Holy Roman Inquisition were the main instruments of discipline.[4] In this article I will explore the ways in which the Holy Office impinged on Maltese society during the time of the last eight inquisitors. Fortunately the archive deposits of the Inquisition in Malta are nearly complete[5] and the recent opening of the Vatican archives[6] has added further to our knowledge of the Maltese Holy Office.

Technically the Roman Inquisition had been established to hunt

---

[1] See P. Prodi, *Una Storia della Giustizia: dal pluralismo dei fori al moderno dualismo tra coscienza e diritto* (Bologna, 2000), 269–324. See also C. Donati, 'La Chiesa di Roma tra antico Regime e riforme settecentesche (1675–1760)', in G. Chittolini and G. Miccoli, eds, *Storia d'Italia, annali 9: la chiesa e il potero politico dal Medioevo all'età contemporanea* (Turin, 1986), 721–66.

[2] Quoted in Massimo Carlo Giannini, 'Tra politica, fiscalità e religione: Filippo II di Spagna e la pubblicazione della bolla "In Coena Domini" (1567–1570)', *Annali dell'Istituto storico italo-germanico in Trento* 23 (1997), 83–152.

[3] H. J. Schroeder, ed., *Canons and Decrees of the Council of Trent* (Rockford, IL, 1978).

[4] H. Outram Evennett, *The Spirit of the Counter-Reformation* (Cambridge, 1968) is still valid.

[5] For a description of the Maltese Inquisition archives, see Frans Ciappara, *The Roman Inquisition in Enlightened Malta* (Malta, 2000), 1–13.

[6] For the importance of this event, Adriano Prosperi, 'Per l'apertura dell'archivio del S. Uffizio', in idem, *L'Inquisizione romana: letture e ricerche* (Rome, 2003), 297–310.

down Protestants.[7] But it also represented a serious attempt at the internal renewal of the Catholic Church.[8] The two impulses were not mutually exclusive and their leaders could be found in both camps.[9] This means that one did not have to be a follower of the Protestant reformers to fall into the inquisitors' clutches. This was especially true in the period under discussion since by the eighteenth century Protestantism had definitely established itself as the religion of the northern half of Europe. Indeed, as in Spain, those Protestants who appeared before the Maltese Tribunal did so voluntarily in order to join the Catholic Church.[10]

Simply put, the Tribunal had come a long way from the sixteenth century, its interests now lying nearer home.[11] It was concerned with people like the poor and ignorant Gaetano Schembri, who practised what the authorities considered to be a debased form of religion and was thus in need of instruction in the true faith. On 21 April 1792 this 'tall and lean fellow with moustaches, bristling hair and whitish face' was seriously admonished not to dabble in witchcraft but, as he ignored this warning, he was arrested on 22 August 1793. He was released after two months only to be taken into custody again two years later. Gaetano, whose wife was now pregnant, was imprisoned for the last time on 26 March 1797.[12]

With their missionary zeal the inquisitors aimed to activate Catholic life and replace 'popular religion' with the official religion as defined by the Church.[13] Eighteenth-century Malta certainly was not a *pays de mission*, comparable to southern Italy as described by the Jesuits.[14]

7 L. von Pastor, *Storia dei Papi v, Paolo III (1534–1549)* (Rome, 1914), 673–6.

8 See Anthony D. Wright, *The Counter-Reformation: Catholic Europe and the Non-Christian World* (Aldershot, 2005).

9 For a discussion of the subject, see H. Jedin, *Riforma Cattolica o Controriforma?* (Brescia, 1967).

10 W. Monter, *Frontiers of Heresy: the Spanish Inquisition from the Basque Lands to Sicily* (Cambridge, 1990), 250.

11 R. Martin, *Witchcraft and the Inquisition in Venice, 1550–1650* (Oxford, 1989), 216; J. Martin, *Venice's Hidden Enemies: Italian Heretics in a Renaissance City* (London, 1993), 226–7.

12 Mdina, Cathedral Museum, Archives of the Inquisition, Malta, Proceedings 137, fols 193r–324v [hereafter: AIM and Proc.].

13 W. A. Christian, Christian, Jr, *Local Religion in Sixteenth-Century Spain* (Princeton, NJ, 1981); A. Prosperi, 'La religione della Controriforma e le feste del Maggio nell'Appennino Tosco-Emiliano', *Critica Storica* 18: 2 (1981–2), 202–22. See also the essays in K. Cooper and J. Gregory, eds, *Elite and Popular Religion*, SCH 42 (Woodbridge, 2006).

14 Jennifer D. Selwyn, *A Paradise Inhabited by Devils: the Jesuits' Civilising Mission in Early Modern Naples* (Aldershot, 2004).

Table 1: Heresies brought before the Holy Office, 1744–98

Heresy	Total	%
Blasphemy	1030	33.3
Witchcraft	883	28.9
Heretical propositions	429	14.1
Apostasy	281	9.2
'Heresy' (Catholics joining Protestants)	116	3.8
Non-observation of fast days	102	3.3
Polygamy	57	1.9
Offences against sacraments	56	1.9
Illicit life	43	1.3
Freemasonry	22	0.7
Forbidden books	21	0.7
Offences against the Tribunal	6	0.2
Greek orthodoxy	3	0.1

Sources: Mdina, AIM, Proc. 120A–141

However, for all the earnestness of Church authorities, religious diversity, as Table 1 shows, was all too evident.

What needs to be examined is how this far-reaching endeavour – which has been called 'without doubt the most ambitious attempt at acculturation known in Europe before the implementation of free and compulsory education at the end of the nineteenth century' – succeeded.[15] In other words, how effective was the inquisitors' attempt to make a mark on late eighteenth-century Maltese society? And what forms of discipline were employed?

For all practical purposes, the captain was the only law enforcement officer the inquisitors had in Malta. It was he who led the accused to prison, who checked that Jews wore their distinctive mark and that Protestants did not disseminate literature ridiculing the Catholic religion. He prevented suspects from escaping, reported Christian apostates found on Turkish ships captured by the galleys of Malta, and, also,

---

[15] '. . . ce qui fut sans doute la plus grande entreprise d'acculturation que l'Europe ait connue jusqu'à l'implantation de l'école gratuite et obligatoire à la fin du XIXè siècle.' Jean-Pierre Dedieu, *L'administration de la Foi: l'Inquisition de Tolède (XVIᵉ–XVIIIᵉ Siècle)* (Madrid, 1989), 360.

made diligent searches in the houses of those accused of having forbidden books in their possession.[16]

However, the inquisitors also deployed a vast array of other weapons in the exercise of their office. They made effective use, for instance, of documentary evidence, which constituted a form of perpetual and unfailing memory. Since everything brought before them was committed to writing, these records could be used later on against the defendant. This was possible because a suspect did not have a new file opened every time he was accused but charges instead kept on accumulating until the inquisitors thought it appropriate to arrest him. Moreover, these registers were compiled in alphabetical order to make it easy to trace recidivists. It was because they held such importance that archives were kept under the watchful eye of the inquisitors, who excommunicated anyone who attempted to steal them.[17]

As has been observed for other Catholic countries,[18] in Malta the Inquisition was dependant to a very large extent upon ordinary men and women. But although the duty of tale-telling was incumbent on everyone, people were reluctant to be their brothers' keepers. Secrecy was promised to all informants but this was no foolproof shield against reprisal. In a community practising face-to-face relations it was easy to get to know your denouncer, especially if, as generally happened, some personal litigation had taken place. In view of this fear, therefore, it is no surprise that the majority of the denunciations were self-reports. Of a sample of 1467 individuals who between 1743 and 1798 appeared before the inquisitors 936 (63.8 per cent) concerned people who accused themselves.[19] One of them was Michele Saliba of Valletta, who on 26 March 1783 denounced himself for blasphemy after having been ordered to do so by his confessor.[20]

This brings us to one of the major means of discipline wielded by the Tribunal: confession.[21] In the Middle Ages absolution set a heretic free from his guilt. Now sacramental and oral confession was transformed

16 F. Ciappara, *Society and the Inquisition in Early Modern Malta* (Malta, 2001), 330.
17 James Given, 'The Inquisitors of Languedoc and the Medieval Technology of Power', *AHR* 94: 2 (1989), 347–51.
18 Sara T. Nalle, 'Inquisitors, Priests and the People during the Catholic Reformation in Spain', *Sixteenth Century Journal* 18: 4 (1987), 557–87, at 567.
19 Calculated from data in Ciappara, *Society and the Inquisition*, Table 9.1, 466.
20 Mdina, AIM, Proc. 134A, fols 171r–172v.
21 For the importance of confession in the Counter-Reformation Church, see Wietse de Boer, *La conquista dell'anima: fede, disciplina e ordine pubblico nella Milano della Controriforma* (Turin, 2004); Roberto Rusconi, *L'ordine dei peccati: la confessione tra Medioevo ed età moderna* (Bologna, 2002), 277–341.

into a written denunciation and those absolved by a confessor could still be proceeded against by the Holy Office. Put in the words of canon law, heretics were reconciled by confessors only in the court of conscience but they had to be forgiven also in the exterior court of the inquisitor. If this did entail a diminution of priestly power on the one hand, on the other the clergy also became collaborators in the work of the Inquisition.[22] As Adriano Prosperi put it in his magisterial study, confession was placed 'at the service of the Holy Office'.[23] In Malta there are no instances where, as at Modena,[24] the parish priest himself exercised the powers of the inquisitor, but, as well as its proper pastoral and sacramental function, the confessional also initiated inquisition trials.[25]

Having been refused absolution, penitents had to report themselves to the inquisitor 'for conscience's sake'. But such self-reporting was not necessarily an expression of unalloyed piety.[26] As soon as they knew that suspicions were piling up against them, penitents tried to forestall informers, hoping to be dismissed by a simple warning and prevent, as Giacinto Cassia put it, 'imprisonment and shame'.[27]

A couple of comments must be brought into consideration before we continue. There can be no argument that the stifling of thought is unacceptable and contrary to moral justice. However, it must not be imagined that defendants were at the mercy of sadistic inquisitors. The Roman Inquisition followed the rule of law;[28] and even a convinced Jew, like the famous historian Cecil Roth, could not fail to be deeply impressed by the methods, and indeed, the conscientiousness, of the inquisitorial procedure.[29]

[22] A. Del Col, *L'Inquisizione nel patriarcato e diocesi di Aquileia 1557–1559* (Trieste, 1998), lvii–lxii.
[23] Adriano Prosperi, *Tribunali della coscienza: inquisitori, confessori, missionari* (Turin, 1996), 431–64.
[24] S. Peyronel Rambaldi, 'Podestà e Inquisitori nella Montagna Modenese: riorganizzazione inquisitoriale e resistenze locali (1570–1590)', in A. Del Col and G. Paolin, eds, *Inquisizione romana in Italia nell'età moderna* (Rome, 1991), 297–328.
[25] For the vital role played by the clergy, especially parish priests in the detection and repression of heresy, see J. B. Given, *Inquisition and Medieval Society: Power, Discipline and Resistance in Languedoc* (Ithaca, NY, 1997), 198–202.
[26] P. Lopez, *Clero, eresia e magia nella Napoli del Viceregno* (Naples, 1984), 185–6.
[27] Mdina, AIM, Proc. 15, fol. 15v.
[28] F. Ciappara, 'The Roman Inquisition and the Jews in Seventeenth- and Eighteenth-Century Malta', in *Le Inquisizioni cristiane e gli ebrei*, Atti della Tavola Rotonda, Rome, 20–21 December 2001 (Rome, 2003), 449–70.
[29] C. Roth, 'The Inquisitional Archives as a Source of English History', *TRHS*, ser. 4, 18 (1935), 107–22, at 107.

The accused was brought to trial only after meticulous investigation. If he or she suspected that some minister of the Tribunal was unfavourable to his or her cause, the defendant could ask him to recuse himself. They brought their own witnesses, they had a defence counsel, and in some very rare instances, were able to confront their accuser. Suggestive questioning was considered to be 'a most grave crime' and torture was used only sparingly, twenty-four times in all between 1743 and 1798. Moreover, the right of appeal to Rome was an integral part of the procedure.[30]

Of the 1467 persons in our sample only a mere 51 (3.5 per cent) were detained. Not all those taken into custody were convicted, and another sixteen were released. Of the remaining thirty-five, one 'heretic' was condemned to hard labour while a sorceress was ordered to leave her home-town and to go and live in the countryside.[31]

Given such statistical leniency, why did Maltese people fear the Inquisition? Why, for example, was Catarina so depressed, agonized and almost in tears, claiming that she would rather be killed and exiled than appear before the Tribunal?[32] It is clear that people must have felt overwhelmed by the unfamiliar surroundings of the 'big house', as one simple woman referred to the palace of the Inquisition.[33] Some were so overpowered by the unusual setting that they entered the court-room screaming. Maria Mercieca interrupted her trial with cries and hysterical laughter; others were lost for words.[34]

The fear of being found guilty was overwhelming. 'Among all the crimes there is none which carries more shame both for the accused and his family, one contemporary observer noted, than to be convicted by the Holy Office'.[35] Having been found guilty by the Inquisition carried such a stigma that parties in lawsuits mentioned this fact to disqualify their opponents' testimony. Cesare Rossi's relatives, therefore, tried to bribe the inquisitor not to release his effigy to the secular

---

[30] For an excellent overview, see J. Tedeschi, 'The Organization and Procedure of the Roman Inquisition: a Sketch', in idem, *The Prosecution of Heresy: Collected Studies on the Inquisition in Early Modern Italy* (Binghamton, NY, 1991), 127–203.

[31] Calculated from data in Ciappara, *Society and the Inquisition*, Appendix 3, 518–38.

[32] Mdina, AIM, Proc. 123A, fol. 168r.

[33] Mdina, AIM, Proc. 130, fol. 472r. On this topic, see A. Del Col, 'I processi dell'Inquisizione come fonte: considerazioni diplomatiche e storiche', *Annuario dell'Istituto storico italiano per L'età moderna e contemporanea* 35–6 (1983–4), 31–49, at 41.

[34] Mdina, AIM, Proc. 123A, fol. 55v.

[35] Mdina, AIM, Miscellanea 2, 76.

government to have it burnt.[36] Nuns, indeed, did not allow the officials of the Holy Office to approach their convents; they denounced themselves to their confessor at night-time when the other nuns were having supper.[37]

The inquisitors made skilful use of this stigma, which marked out the accused and set them apart. It is true that by the second half of the eighteenth century 'heretics' were again eligible for public office,[38] and the penitential garment, *habitello* or *sanbenito*, was no longer worn.[39] Nor were sentences read any more from the pulpit (*auto de fe*) but in the *camera secreta* of the inquisitor's palace in the presence of the penitent and two witnesses.[40] However, if the Tribunal discarded these catechetical sessions on a grand scale,[41] it had other ways to reaffirm society's moral order and avenge the 'collective conscience'. The accused was exposed inside a church or in front of its main door during High Mass.[42] Bare-headed and on his or her knees, the accused was made to look foolish with a note displayed on the chest denoting the relevant crime while, in cases of blasphemy, a gag was put in his or her mouth.[43] Priests who had solicited their penitents in the confessional-box renounced their sinfulness in the presence of other confessors.[44] And a friar would pay for his heretical propositions by remaining on his knees in the refectory while his companions ate their meals.[45]

Flogging, with the concomitant disgrace of infamy and dishonour, was part of this process.[46] The condemned, wearing a mitre on his or her head and a placard on the chest, had to sit on an ass or a donkey with hands tied. Heralded by the secular court's trumpeter, he or she was whipped at every corner of the cities of Senglea, Cospicua, Vittoriosa and Valletta.[47]

But if punishment served as an example to other members of the

---

[36] Midna, AIM, Correspondence 3, fol. 39r, 30 August 1613 [hereafter: Corresp.].

[37] Mdina, AIM, Proc. 127A, fol. 251r.

[38] Mdina, AIM, Proc. 22, fol. 229r.

[39] Mdina, AIM, Proc. 103C, fol. 914v.

[40] Mdina, AIM, Corresp. 23, fol. 47r, 15 December 1725.

[41] M. Flynn, 'Mimesis of the Last Judgment: the Spanish *Auto de fé*', *Sixteenth Century Journal* 22: 2 (1991), 281–97.

[42] Mdina, AIM, Proc. 115A, fol. 441r.

[43] Mdina, AIM, Proc. 125A, fol. 29v.

[44] Mdina, AIM, Corresp. 14, fol. 142r, 8 July 1684.

[45] Mdina, AIM, Corresp. 10, fol. 111r, 1656.

[46] Mdina, AIM, Proc. 125B, fols 459r–527v.

[47] Mdina, AIM, Proc. 125C, fol. 1405r.

Christian community, it was mainly intended to bring the sinners themselves to a state of grace.[48] 'So that from God Our Lord you obtain mercy and pardon more easily for your sins and errors', sinners received a spiritual penance. They were to confess and receive communion on the four main feasts of the Church for the next two or four years, as well as recite the rosary every Saturday.[49] Sinners could also be made to say the seven penitential psalms with their litanies every Friday, and be told to do this on their knees;[50] and there is one case of a penitent who had to recite the creed three times every Sunday, kneeling before a holy picture.[51]

Another form of discipline was imprisonment.[52] The data from Malta completely counter the suggestion that conditions in prison were purposely bad to make the inmates bend to the inquisitor's wishes. No doubt, as one doctor testified, the place of imprisonment was damp and cold and the inmates could be bitten by flies, but at least they had candle light, slept in beds on straw mattresses, and were covered by a sheet and a blanket. They were visited by their relatives and they were able to call a doctor when in need. The poor among them, for example abandoned slaves, were supported by the Tribunal.[53]

The point to be made here is that the prisons were supposed to be as much places of reflection as of punishment. The inquisitors firmly believed in the possibility of moral rehabilitation, and earnestly tried to change the prisoners' way of life. The accused were made to realize that they had erred, a matter which would not always have been clear to them. This can be seen in the case of parents who, drawing on the popular tradition of changelings, took their sick child to an abandoned church on the outskirts of a village; laying it down on the floor they said, 'Give me my child because this is not mine'.[54] It was explained to them that such a belief tied them to a pact with the devil. Were they not imploring the malign spirit to take back the sick child and restore

---

[48] For shaming in pre-Reformation London, see Richard M. Wunderli, *London Church Courts and Society on the Eve of the Reformation* (Cambridge, MA, 1981), 50–1.

[49] Mdina, AIM, Proc. 134A, fols 209r, 488v.

[50] Mdina, AIM, Proc. 121B, fol. 736r.

[51] Mdina, AIM, Proc. 131B, fol. 593r.

[52] For the new role of prisons as places of punishment rather than detention, see N. Sarti, 'Appunti su carcere-custodia e carcere-pena nella dottrina civilistica dei secoli XII–XVI', *Rivista di storia del diritto italiano* 53–4 (1980–1), 67–110.

[53] Ciappara, *Society and the Inquisition*, 489–90.

[54] Mdina, AIM, Proc. 85A, fol. 193r.

the stolen one? If they were addressing God, why did they make it a point not to say the name of Jesus, or to mention that the church that they were in contained no images of the saints? Why did they not sign themselves with the cross, and was the child not dressed in any sacred object?[55]

Explanation and clarification was especially required in witchcraft cases. The guilty party was asked why had the sacraments and sacramentals been used in such experiments? And, taking a cue from St Thomas Aquinas's *Summa Contra Gentiles*,[56] sinners were asked why had blessed water, incense, candles, oil and the host been used for purposes other than to worship God?[57] Did they not imply, therefore, reverence towards a power other than God Himself? Were not alum, salt, money, and morsels of bread, as used in witchcraft cases, forms of remuneration to the devil? And by attributing to Satan powers that were God's alone, did they not place the devil on a par with God? Could he, for example, foresee the future, *occulta Dei*?[58] Was not divination a sacrilegious wish to take from God the mastery over time? Was not man's life solely in the hands of God, and was it not the case that witchcraft could not cause illness and death? Can the devil force the free will of men into love or hate? Is it not unworthy to ask God for such base and selfish ends as to further adultery, theft and murder? Were not such invocations, therefore, directed at Satan? And didn't 'unknown characters' represent the names of devils?[59] Further, wasn't the riding through the air on 'a big ugly animal which seemed like a cow' completely improbable?[60]

[55] J.-C. Schmitt, *Medioevo "Superstizioso"* (Rome-Bari, 1997), 132–6, at 142; K. Thomas, *Religion and the Decline of Magic: Studies in Popular Beliefs in Sixteenth- and Seventeenth-Century England* (London, 1971), 612–13.

[56] For the translation of relevant parts of this work, see A. C. Kors and E. Peters, eds, *Witchcraft in Europe, 1100–1700: a Documentary History* (Philadelphia, PA, 1991), 53–62.

[57] For the way sacramentals could become magical, see R. W. Scribner, 'The Reformation, Popular Magic, and the *Disenchantment of the World*', *Journal of Interdisciplinary History* 23: 3 (1993), 475–94, at 480. For their similarity, working on two different levels, the material and the supernatural worlds, see his other article 'Elements of Popular Belief', in T. A. Brady Jr, H. A. Oberman, and J. D. Tracy, eds, *Handbook of European History, 1400–1600: Late Middle Ages, Renaissance and Reformation, vol. 1; Structures and Assertions* (New York, 1994), 231–62.

[58] On this topic, Verbeeck-Verhelst, 'Magie et Curiosité au XVIIᵉ Siècle', *Revue d'Histoire Ecclésiastique* 83: 2 (1988), 349–68.

[59] On the condemnation of beneficent magic as originating from the devil just like *malefice* magic, see S. Clark and P. T. J. Morgan, 'Religion and Magic in Elizabethan Wales: Robert Holland's Dialogue on Witchcraft', *JEH* 27: 1 (1976), 31–46.

[60] Mdina, AIM, Corresp. 27, fols 114r–16r, 17 March 1742.

This 'pastoral' programme was conducted with sensitivity[61] with the hope that 'if it will ever be possible this soul will be gained for God'.[62] The cardinal inquisitors on 25 March 1747 directed that Mgr Passionei was to 'nourish the prisoners often with the Divine Word and spiritual advice to prepare them to receive the sacraments frequently and with great profit'.[63]

It was this kind of spiritual counselling which converted the Savoyard Jean de Grett, a sergeant in the Grand Master's regiment. On 10 October 1776, after eight hearings, he was still a Deist: 'I believe in that law that God instilled in the heart of mankind. All the other laws,' he resolutely maintained, 'including the Catholic Church's, were all made by man and I disbelieve them.'[64] The next day the Tribunal's chancellor and the two resident catechists started teaching him the articles of the Catholic faith. At first his soul had been troubled by a thousand errors, they commented, but now 'he is a totally changed man, persuaded of the truth of Catholicism and desirous of being a good and true Catholic'.[65]

The Inquisition's main aim had been vindicated, resulting not in the death of the heretic but his conversion, 'that he may turn from his way and live'.[66] Inquisitors were the Church's sentries so that, as one of the manuals put it, 'in the mistiness of the night of the present century the soul's spiritual peace remains undisturbed and all reach the clear day of eternal happiness in heaven'.[67]

* * *

This essay has revealed the various ways in which the Roman Inquisition disciplined the mental habits of the inhabitants of Malta, especially by means of confession, shame, imprisonment and spiritual counselling. But before we conclude, it is pertinent to ask how successful this endeavour had been. In addressing this question, it is salutary to remember that the second half of the eighteenth century witnessed a sustained attack against the Inquisition elsewhere in Europe. In Parma,

---

61 Mdina, AIM, Corresp. 13, fol. 143r, 29 February 1676.
62 Mdina, AIM, Corresp. 10, fol. 77r, 13 May 1656.
63 Mdina, AIM, Corresp. 29, fol. 7r.
64 Mdina, AIM, Proc. 131B, fols 549r–602v.
65 Mdina, AIM, Corresp. 96, fol. 241r, 30 December 1776.
66 (Ezek. 33: 11)
67 E. Masini, *Sacro arsenale, overo prattica dell'Officio della S. Inquisizione ampliata* (Genoa, 1625), 6.

Du Tillot abolished the Holy Office in 1769,[68] and Modena followed suit ten years later.[69] In Sicily the viceroy, Marquis Caracciolo, cried with joy when in 1782 'this terrible monster' was abolished.[70]

Did the Holy Office in Malta experience the hostility which other Tribunals were experiencing on the Continent, or did it still continue to function as an agent of discipline? Inquisitor Salviati harboured no doubts about the intentions of his enemies to deprive him of his powers. In 1771 he declined to cite one of the servants of John Dodsworth, the British consul in Malta, because he feared reprisals.[71] Likewise, Inquisitor Lante did not summon the witnesses against the cook of the admiral of the Order of St John because 'much inconvenience would result'.[72] His successor Inquisitor Zondadari in 1778 notified Rome that the soldiers of the 'New Regiment' were not being allowed by their officers to go to the Holy Office.[73] And in 1784 he was informed that Naples was trying to suppress the Tribunal in Malta.[74]

Figure 1: Denunciations by Year, 1744-1798

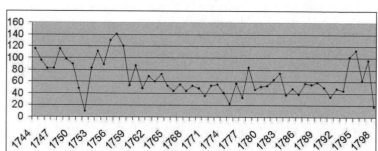

68 F. Venturi, *Settecento riformatore, vol. 2: La chiesa e la repubblica dentro i loro limiti* (Turin, 1976), 234.

69 A. Biondi, 'Lunga durata e microarticolazione nel territorio di un Ufficio dell'Inquisizione: Il Sacro Tribunale a Modena (1292–1785)', *Annali dell'Istituto Storico Italo-Germanico in Trento* 8 (1982), 73–90.

70 Quoted in F. Renda, 'Società e Politica nella Sicilia del Settecento', in *La Sicilia nel Settecento*, Attis del Convegno di Studi, 2 vols (Messina, 2–4 October 1981) (Messina, 1986), 1: 25–6.

71 Mdina, AIM, Corresp. 96, fol. 135r, 22 November 1758.

72 Mdina, AIM, Corresp. 96, fols 218r–v, 30 July 1771.

73 Mdina, AIM, Corresp. 34, fol. 56r, 13 June 1778.

74 Mdina, AIM, Corresp. 101, fol. 142v, 13 January 1784.

However, it would be an error to conclude that the Maltese Holy Office was under severe stress. Contrary to the situation in Toledo[75] and Italy, where 'the various branches of the Roman Inquisition were somnolent',[76] it remained active until its abolition in 1798 (see Figure 1), holding the conscience of the inhabitants firmly in its grip.[77]

University of Malta

[75] Dedieu, *L'Administration de la Foi*, 238–43, 351.
[76] E. W. Monter and J. Tedeschi, 'Towards a Statistical Profile of the Italian Inquisitions, Sixteenth to Eighteenth Centuries', in G. Henningsen, J. Tedeschi, and C. Amiel, eds, *The Inquisition in Early Modern Europe: Studies on Sources and Methods* (Dekalb, IL, 1976), 130–57, at 133. See also G. Romeo, *L'Inquisizione nell'Italia Moderna* (Rome-Bari, 2002), 95–119.
[77] Ciappara, Society and the Inquisition, 65–7.

CHARLES HADDON SPURGEON, THE PASTORS' COLLEGE AND THE DOWNGRADE CONTROVERSY

by IAN RANDALL

CHARLES Haddon Spurgeon (1834–92) began his pastoral ministry in a village Baptist chapel in Cambridgeshire but became a national voice in Victorian England through his ministry in London.[1] The huge crowds his preaching attracted necessitated the building of the Metropolitan Tabernacle, at the Elephant and Castle, which accommodated over 5,000 people. 'By common consent', says David Bebbington, Spurgeon was 'the greatest English-speaking preacher of the century'.[2] Spurgeon, like other nineteenth-century ecclesiastical figures, was involved in theological controversies, including the 'Downgrade Controversy', in which, in typically robust style, he attacked theological liberalism. In August 1887, he trumpeted: 'The Atonement is scouted, the inspiration of Scripture derided, the Holy Spirit degraded into an influence, the punishment of sin turned into a fiction, and the resurrection into a myth . . .'[3] The Downgrade controversy has not attracted nearly as much attention as debates provoked in the nineteenth century by *Essays and Reviews* (1860) and *Lux Mundi* (1889), perhaps because the latter affected Anglicanism rather than the Free Churches.[4] But since as many people were attending Free Churches as Anglican churches, the issues raised in the Downgrade, as the most serious nineteenth-century Free Church dispute, are of considerable significance.[5]

This study will examine one aspect of the impact of the Downgrade – the effect on pastors trained by Spurgeon. Several major enterprises were pioneered by Spurgeon, notably an orphanage and a college for

[1] For Spurgeon's life see P. S. Kruppa, *Charles Haddon Spurgeon: a Preacher's Progress* (New York, 1982).

[2] D. W. Bebbington, *The Dominance of Evangelicalism* (Leicester, 2005), 37.

[3] *The Sword and the Trowel* [hereafter: Spurgeon, *The Sword*], August 1887, 397.

[4] The typical relative coverage can be seen in G. Parsons, ed., *Religion in Victorian Britain, vol. 2: Controversies* (Manchester, 1988).

[5] K. W. Clements, *Lovers of Discord* (London, 1988), 11–16.

ministerial training, the Pastors' College (later Spurgeon's College).[6] In 1891 he gave an account of how the College had trained 845 ministerial students. Many had planted new Baptist causes and had contributed to rapid Baptist growth. The College, said Spurgeon, had 'opened a door of hope' for budding young ministers.[7] Although there has been analysis of the Downgrade and its consequences,[8] its effects on the hundreds of Baptist ministers trained at the Pastors' College have not been explored. The effects were traumatic and they offer insight into issues of discipline and diversity as played out in a nineteenth-century controversy that had the potential to rupture the evangelical community of the time. In order to understand the repercussions of Spurgeon's stance for those trained at the College I have looked at a hitherto unused archive relating to the College Conference. Students and alumni of the College were members of the Pastors' College Association, which was usually known as College Conference since an annual conference was held for a week in March or April, attracting about 400 pastors.

In October 1887 Spurgeon withdrew from the Baptist Union, denouncing the 'spectacle of professedly orthodox Christians publicly avowing their union with those who deny the faith'. It is unclear which Baptists (if any) were denying the faith, but Spurgeon decided that his own position would be one of 'independency'.[9] Following his resignation, Spurgeon commented that his 'hearty union' with ministers trained at the College would be maintained, whether or not they left the Baptist Union – and few did.[10] Soon, however, the College's fellowship was strained to breaking point. The Baptist weekly, *The Freeman*, carried a report on 10 February 1888 about a meeting of London College Conference ministers. About 100 of them met under Spurgeon's presidency – he was College and Conference President – and agreed a motion put by C. H. Spurgeon's brother that Conference members be reminded of the grounds of the College Association: '(1) the doctrines

---

[6] For the College see D. W. Bebbington, 'Spurgeon and British Evangelical Theological Education', in D. G. Hart and R. A. Mohler, Jr, eds, *Theological Education in the Evangelical Tradition* (Grand Rapids, MI, 1996), 217–34; I. M. Randall, *A School of the Prophets* (London, 2005).

[7] *Annual Paper Concerning the Lord's Work in Connection with the Pastors' College* (London, 1890–1), 3.

[8] See esp. M. Hopkins, *Nonconformity's Romantic Generation* (Carlisle, 2004), chs 5 and 7.

[9] Spurgeon, *The Sword*, November 1887, 560.

[10] Spurgeon, *The Sword*, January 1888, 44.

of grace, (2) believers' baptism, and (3) earnest endeavours to win souls to Christ'. These points were uncontroversial, although 'doctrines of grace' was a term open to interpretation, but the resolution added that if any Conference members had 'quitted the old faith' and espoused the possibility of repentance in the afterlife – 'probation after death' – or universal salvation they should resign from Conference. This motion was passed with only five dissenting (it was not clear how many abstained), and it was agreed that the resolution would be sent to Conference members. If accepted by a majority then only those agreeing to it would be members in the future.[11]

The issues at stake had to do with discipline and diversity against a background of wider theological debate. The new College Conference statement, with its clauses ruling out 'the larger hope' (as it was often termed), represented a restriction of the basis under which Conference operated. As such it provoked a fierce debate about the limits of legitimate diversity possible within such a fellowship of evangelical ministers. Events moved quickly. A voting paper was sent out to all Conference members asking them to reply within a week voting 'yes' or 'no' to the London ministers' resolution. The voting slips that were returned show that 423 of the members of Conference responded, out of 604 members engaged 'in the work of the Lord', nearly all as Baptist pastors, missionaries and evangelists.[12] Only twenty who voted ultimately voted 'no' (in one case 'No, no, no'), but others were clearly unhappy and refused to commit themselves. Some changed their initial vote to 'yes' after persuasion. The letters received from ministers across the country indicate that deep divisions had opened up within the Spurgeonic constituency over the 'Downgrade'.

About a third of those who responded were not content simply to fill in a voting slip, but wrote private letters. The responses fall into several categories. First there were those who expressed wholehearted theological support for the stricter discipline being promoted by Spurgeon. Thus Thomas Medhurst, who was Spurgeon's first student and who held several significant pastorates, hoped 'our beloved President will find that but very few of our number are infected with the heresy that is working such sad havoc among our Churches'. Medhurst wanted within Conference only those loyal to 'the faith once for all delivered to

---

11 *Freeman*, 10 February 1888, 81.
12 Spurgeon, *The Sword*, June 1888, 336.

the saints'.[13] The 'faith once delivered' featured in several letters. John Markham, an evangelist who trained a decade later than Medhurst, was combative. He claimed that his views had consistently been those of Spurgeon, of Puritans such as Elisha Coles, and of Baptists like John Gill. Markham hoped that Spurgeon would be able to 'smite harder than ever the enemies of the Lord of hosts, in the Churches (so called) of the day'.[14] Others trained in the 1870s expressed similar sentiments. A minister from Camberwell was 'amazed and grieved' that anyone trained at the College 'could so far depart from the clear, honest, common-sense understanding of the scriptures, as to believe either in future probation or the escape of the ungodly from condemnation.' His wife suggested that such people should repay the money provided for their training.[15] David Chapman, from Lincolnshire, averred that it was 'time someone spoke out against this new fangled theology'.[16]

Another group, probably the majority of Conference members, was equally supportive of Spurgeon but this support had personal loyalty to Spurgeon as its most obvious ingredient. A minister from Princes Risborough, a student in the 1870s, expressed 'deep sympathy with our beloved President'.[17] Jesse Aubrey from Aldershot dramatically compared Spurgeon to Athanasius *contra mundum*.[18] The description 'beloved President' was used by many correspondents, indicating the personal relationship which former students felt they had with Spurgeon. This sense of being personally involved was vividly portrayed by a pastor from Northampton, who hoped College Conference would be like the 300 'chosen of the Lord' to follow Gideon – in one of the Old Testament battles.[19] The process by which Gideon's 300 were chosen was one in which numbers were whittled down. The resonance with Spurgeon's disciplinary procedure was clear. In similar vein, Charles Fowler from Forest Gate, London, anticipated that Spurgeon's efforts would 'mark an epoch in the history of the College and of the Church'.[20] This belief was to prove correct, although the unfolding

---

[13] Thomas Medhurst, 11 February 1888. Responses are held: London, Spurgeon's College Heritage Room, MS B1.16.
[14] John Markham, 13 February 1888.
[15] William Sullivan, 11 February 1888.
[16] David Chapman, 11 February 1888.
[17] William Coombes, 13 February 1888.
[18] Jesse Aubrey, 13 February 1888.
[19] Henry Bradford, 13 February 1888.
[20] Charles Fowler, 14 February 1888.

story would be much more complex than many in the 'yes' camp imagined.

This complexity was evident among those who said they would back Spurgeon, but with reservations. This lack of wholehearted support surprised Spurgeon in the Downgrade. John Cole, from Bedford, a student in the 1860s, rejected 'broad theology' and argued for an evangelical basis of faith, but whereas Spurgeon was a committed Calvinist, Cole stated regarding the 'five points' of Calvinism that 'though I once accepted them, I cannot now give them my adhesion'.[21] Walter Hackney, who trained in the 1870s and was a minister in Birmingham, wrote making similar points. He asked: 'How do you define that term "The Doctrines of Grace"? Does it include views about election, and particular redemption taught by Coles – or even Hodge? If so I think it very unfortunate to ask any such acceptance as the price of our adhesion to the Conference.' Hackney did not want to be excluded, and indeed a decade later he became a tutor at the College.[22] It is clear that a significant number of ministers changed their views during their ministry – while remaining avowedly evangelical. Although there is no pattern linking length of time in ministry and theological position, a minister from Diss, Norfolk, did claim that students who were Calvinists in College later 'frequently become free-willers' – Arminians.[23] Many within Spurgeon's circle supported him while affirming greater evangelical diversity.

Among those affirming diversity were those who wrote rejecting the changes proposed to Conference rules. Some used explicitly theological arguments. Jabez Dodwell, near Banbury, who trained in the 1860s, argued that it was wrong to regard differences over future punishment as a disqualification for fellowship.[24] A student from the same era, ministering in Peckham, similarly refused to sign the new statement; it made him 'sick at heart'.[25] R. P. Javan, from New Basford, Nottingham, a student in the 1870s, expressed thanks for the College and emphasized that he was not a believer in the 'New Theology', but on the issue of what happened after death he refused to pronounce on probation or eternal torment.[26] Clearly he could not remain as a Conference

21 John Cole, 11 February 1888.
22 Walter Hackney, 14 February 1888.
23 George Pope, 13 February 1888.
24 Jabez Dodwell, 22 February 1888.
25 T. Harley, 11 February 1888.
26 R. P. Javan, 13 February 1888.

member. A contemporary of Javan's, G. W. Tooley, argued that Spurgeon's own theological approach had changed. Previously those with a 'larger hope' had been 'rash' or 'too broad', and were dealt with in a loving way. Tooley accepted that in his stance he was not representative of the majority, but added defiantly: 'Nor was Christ on Calvary'.[27] This group of dissenters affirmed theological development. Arthur Wood from Mutley Baptist Church, Plymouth, alleged that even in College many students doubted the Calvinistic doctrines 'taught in their extreme form by Hodge and Coles', and that doctrinal modification continued.[28]

Others who objected did so on the grounds that Nonconformist tradition allowed freedom of conscience. Writing from Warwick, a minister who originally had a Methodist background considered that the discipline introduced was 'contrary to the root principle of all Nonconformity': the right of each person to find and hold the truth.[29] A recent student, Thomas Judd, stated bluntly: 'I am against coercion in any form'. He added that he had refused to sign a teetotal pledge at College and that he would 'never cease to be [a] free man' – as encouraged to be by the College tutors.[30] Walter Richards from Fraserburgh, Scotland, recalled 'the differences manifested in our discussions by our tutors' as to what was included in the doctrines of grace.[31] This variety was tolerated. Indeed one tutor, F. G. Marchant, in agreeing to the new Conference basis, commented 'with the modifications in which I have always been known to hold some of the Doctrines of Grace'. Later the issue of Marchant's beliefs – he did not accept the view that Christ died only for the elect – became a matter for public debate in College and the College trustees decided he should no longer deliver theological lectures.[32] Spurgeon's limitation of diversity continued to have effects.

Finally, there were those who wrote to object specifically to Spurgeon's procedures over Conference membership. Clarence Chambers, a student in the 1860s, whose son Oswald became a well-known devotional speaker, voted in favour of the doctrinal basis but against excluding anyone. He quoted the hymn, 'Lead Kindly Light', by John

27 G. W. Tooley, undated letter.
28 Arthur Wood, 15 February 1888.
29 J. Hutchison, 13 February 1888.
30 T. A. Judd, 11 February 1888.
31 Walter Richards, 15 February 1888.
32 Minutes of a Special Meeting of Pastors' College Trustees, 30 July 1896.

Henry Newman.[33] William Elliott from Pollockshields, Scotland, made similar objections to the exclusions, and a year later Elliott joined the Church of England.[34] For some the procedure was likely to be pastorally disastrous. A pastor from Chester had been struggling in areas of his faith and had received help from College Conference. 'Don't thumbscrew others into false professions', he pleaded, 'or drive them away from our helpful circle.'[35] For Henry Dyer from Rickmansworth what was deeply unsatisfactory was that previously any discipline taken was only for unworthy conduct or withdrawal from Baptist life. Conference for him had been a friendly gathering for fellowship, with Spurgeon the 'genial and generous Host', and he praised Spurgeon's 'kindness, wisdom and faithfulness, both in College and since'.[36]

As these letters were received it became evident that Spurgeon had miscalculated the degree of opposition to the attempt to enforce his new stance. Some ministers embarked on a public debate. C. A. Davis, formerly pastor of Sion, Bradford, a leading Yorkshire Baptist church, and now at the historic King's Road Baptist Church, Reading, contacted Conference members to organize a petition. As he did so, Davis – like many others – expressed his sorrow about developments: 'The spirit of brotherhood which has prevailed until now', he said, 'has made our Conference one of the happiest and most united associations in the world.' Within a week over 100 ministers had signed a protest.[37] Another leading opponent was E. G. Gange, at the famous Broadmead Baptist Church, Bristol, a distinguished Conference member and speaker. Gange wrote on 14 February 1888 emphasizing that he held to evangelical doctrine, but continuing: 'At the same time my detestation of dictation and bigotry is such that I have elected to go out with the heretics (if such they be) rather than remain with the bigots.' He objected to the prohibition on discussion of diversity. It was 'unworthy of a pettifogging Attorney'. Gange suggested that the expulsions could be contested in law. What if those expelled from Conference attended – would the new discipline include police removing them by force?[38]

Spurgeon's response was to write a letter in *The Baptist*, which was widely read in Spurgeonic circles, in which he attempted to restate his

33 Clarence Chambers, 14 February 1888.
34 W. H. Elliott, 11 February 1888.
35 Abraham Mills, 18 February 1888.
36 Henry Dyer, 14 February 1888. Dyer also wrote jointly with five other ministers.
37 *Freeman*, 17 February 1888, 113.
38 E. G. Gange, 14 February 1988.

position more persuasively. He explained that 'the doctrines of grace' did not mean Calvinism, but 'common evangelical truth'. He argued that there had 'always been a great breadth of thought among us within the bounds of the old orthodox faith'. This was Spurgeon's attempt to affirm evangelical diversity. Spurgeon also took responsibility for what had been done at the London meeting and appealed to Conference ministers' loyalty to him. He rejected debate at the forthcoming Conference, clearly favouring *dictat*. Finally, he insisted that he would not remain in fellowship with those holding 'post-mortem salvation' and even threatened to resign from Conference himself.[39] On the same day Gange expressed his opposite view in public. Writing in *The Freeman*, he referred to the predestinarian doctrines taught in some College text-books as 'doctrines of despair and doom' from which he had been emancipated. Also, he considered that some Conference members who believed in the 'Larger Hope' could 'declare that the Saviour was never so precious to them; His Cross their only hope; on His atoning sacrifice they implicitly rely; His glad Gospel they proclaim with growing confidence; and for His coming they watch and wait.' Gange acknowledged that Spurgeon had the right to change the Conference rules, but he pleaded for a proper discussion.[40]

Spurgeon's letter in *The Baptist* proved to be decisive and the tide began to turn Spurgeon's way. George Smith from Bexleyheath wrote on 21 February noting that often complainants had secured their pastorates with Spurgeon's help and arguing that Spurgeon had 'gone as far as it is possible for him to go in his desire to meet all reasonable objections'.[41] From 21 February onwards many letters were written in this vein. Jesse Dupee in Potters Bar, his first pastorate after leaving College, confessed that although he believed in the doctrines of grace it was 'not according to Calvin's interpretation of them, nor exactly as our beloved President puts them', describing himself as one of the 'broad' students in College. At first he had hesitated about supporting Spurgeon, but after the letter in *The Baptist* felt he could do so.[42] Robert Glendenning, from Elgin, Scotland, also in his first pastorate, had signed the appeal by C. A. Davis, but wrote on 22 February to say that

---

39 *The Baptist*, 17 February 1888, 5.
40 *Freeman*, 17 February 1888, 101.
41 George Smith, 21 February 1888.
42 Jesse Dupee, 15 February 1888; 21 February 1888.

in view of what Spurgeon had said he was supporting him.[43] Pastors who had previously voted 'no' changed their minds in the light of Spurgeon's explanation that the doctrines of grace did not equal Calvinism.[44] There had also been those unhappy about London ministers taking decisions, but when Spurgeon assumed personal responsibility this objection was removed.[45] It was widely accepted that as Spurgeon had set up the Conference he could determine issues of discipline.

There were, however, some who still struggled. William Townsend from Canterbury wrote on 22 February to say that he was 'greatly exercised' about eternal punishment and 'the doctrine of Election'. He explained: 'I am giving all the time I can spare from my work to the study of these questions, and I humbly trust God for the aid of His Spirit.' It was deeply painful to him to anticipate being cut off from Conference.[46] J. W. Ewing, in Wandsworth, who would go to the large Rye Lane Chapel, Peckham, and was later Superintendent for the Metropolitan Area, strategically refused to vote (as did others), since 'yes' would exclude those 'with us in essential truths', and 'no' would mean Spurgeon was no longer Conference President.[47] Other ministers continued to oppose Spurgeon's policy and to seek to gather support. W. B. Haynes, a student at the College in the 1870s, who was minister at The Green, Stafford, wrote in *The Freeman* about the 'obnoxious resolution' and recalled that when Spurgeon had reissued the *Baptist Confession of Faith* in 1855 he had explained that it was not a rule by which people were fettered.[48] It appeared that in the Downgrade diversity was rejected.

College Conference was now divided into two camps. A letter appeared in *The Freeman* on 24 February 1888, expressing full support for Spurgeon, from fourteen ministers. They included several who pastored London churches with congregations of 1,000 or more – A. G. Brown at the East London Tabernacle, William Cuff in Shoreditch, C. B. Sawday, at King's Cross, William Williams at Upton Chapel, Lambeth, and John Wilson in Woolwich.[49] In the same issue of *The*

43 Robert Glendenning, 2 February 1888.
44 Arthur Wood, 23 February 1888.
45 Charles Joseph, 23 February 1888.
46 William Townsend, 22 February 1888.
47 J. W. Ewing, 22 February 1888.
48 *Freeman*, 17 February 1888, 101.
49 *Freeman*, 24 February 1888, 129.

Freeman fourteen other leading ministers, while voicing great personal affection for Spurgeon, signed a statement opposing the new doctrinal tests. The signatories included C. A. Davis, J. C. Thompson, minister of Brondesbury Chapel, London, E. G. Gange, T. G. Tarn, of St Andrew's Street, Cambridge, and George Hill at South Parade, Leeds. All endorsed the original Conference basis, including: 'The inspiration and authority of Holy Scripture as the supreme and sufficient rule of our faith and practice; the Deity, the Incarnation, the Resurrection, and the Sacrificial work of our Lord; justification by faith – a faith which works by love and produces holiness; the work of the Holy Spirit in the conversion of sinners and in sanctification.'[50]

The ministers who opposed Spurgeon's policy insisted that they were true to the gospel. As the debate continued in *The Freeman*, J. C. Thompson maintained that when he entered the College he held 'the vital doctrines of the Gospel' – salvation by grace through faith in Christ – and still did. It was his trust in Christ's 'infinite sacrifice' that led him to 'have the largest possible hope for mankind'. Crucially, however, he denied 'everlasting conscious torment for any created spirit for whom Jesus died'.[51] It was generally assumed that Spurgeon opposed conditional immortality (the view that the lost cease to exist), although one minister was told that such a belief was not a bar to Conference membership.[52] Another, Thomas Greenwood, later a leading London minister, was inclined to conditionalism and recalled consulting Spurgeon who replied: 'That is all right, Tom; we want you; come in with us.'[53] For his part C. A. Davis made clear that neither he nor his fellow-signatories held post-mortem salvation.[54] The old Conference gave way to a College Evangelical Association, with new members signing what was essentially the Evangelical Alliance basis of faith. Out of 604 members of the old Conference, 432 agreed with the revised stipulations and joined the new Association.[55] Spurgeon spoke of the split as his 'sorest wound of all'.[56]

This episode illustrates the debates over discipline and theological

---

50 Ibid.
51 *Freeman*, 2 March 1888, 137.
52 J. C. Foster, 16 February 1888, 21 February 1888.
53 Minutes of the Executive Committee of Spurgeon's College Council, 28 November 1946.
54 *Freeman*, 2 March 1888, 137.
55 *Freeman*, 16 March 1888, 168.
56 Spurgeon, *The Sword*, March 1888, 148.

diversity within a significant evangelical community. The College Conference developed through the training offered by the Pastors' College and Spurgeon expected that those who entered ministry after that training would continue to promote the beliefs they had imbibed at College. At the same time he accepted that there would be some diversity. However, the students had been taught to think for themselves and when, in the light of the Downgrade controversy, Spurgeon attempted to introduce a stricter doctrinal regime there were protests. Most Conference members supported Spurgeon, but for many this support was based as much on personal loyalty as on theological grounds. The reactions within College Conference help to explain why so few of the Baptist ministers trained at the Pastors' College left the Baptist Union when Spurgeon resigned. It is clear that in general they had a wider view of evangelical Baptist identity. In the twentieth century 'echoes of the controversy' continued to be heard in evangelical circles, particularly in connection with the pan-denominational growth of Fundamentalist views. Some Fundamentalists have seen themselves as heirs of Spurgeon. As David Bebbington notes, Spurgeon's name was repeatedly invoked in the 1920s by those attacking theological liberalism.[57] By contrast with some evangelicals who have taken up Fundamentalist stances, however, other evangelicals have welcomed wider thinking.[58] Issues connected with the Downgrade contributed to recurring tensions over discipline and diversity in an evangelical context.

Spurgeon's College, London

[57] D. W. Bebbington, 'Baptists and Fundamentalism in Inter-War Britain', in K. Robbins, ed., *Protestant Evangelicalism: Britain, Ireland, Germany and America, c.1750–c.1950*, SCH.S. 7 (Oxford, 1990), 297–326, at 303.
[58] Clements, *Lovers of Discord*, 16, and chs 5 and 8; cf. I. M. Randall, *The English Baptists of the Twentieth Century* (Didcot, 2005), 99–104, 120–6, 169–75, 365–82.

DISCIPLINE AND COMPREHENSIVENESS: THE CHURCH OF ENGLAND AND PRAYER BOOK REVISION IN THE 1920s*

by JOHN G. MAIDEN

THE Prayer Book revision controversy was among the most significant events in the Church of England during the twentieth century. The proposals to revise the 1662 Book of Common Prayer provoked considerable opposition from both Evangelicals and Anglo-Catholics, and culminated with the House of Commons rejecting a revised book in 1927 and a re-revised version in 1928. This paper will argue that two issues, ecclesiastical authority and Anglican identity, were central to the controversy. It will then suggest that the aims and policy of the bishops' revision led to the failure of the book. In taking this angle, it will analyse the controversy from a new perspective, as previous studies have focused on liturgical developments, Church parties and disestablishment.[1] The controversy is bound up with the broader and ongoing problem of maintaining discipline and diversity within the Anglican Communion. The Anglo-Catholic – Evangelical tensions of the 1920s were a precursor to Liberal – Evangelical conflicts on issues such as the ordination of women and sexuality. Therefore, by examining the revision controversy from the angle of discipline and comprehensiveness, a longer perspective is given to later Anglican difficulties.[2]

The *raison d'etre* of the revision project was the re-establishment of order to parish services. Revision should be seen as the climax to the 'problem' of the rise of illegal Anglo-Catholic ritual practices in the

* I am grateful to the Anglo-Catholic History Society for providing a bursary to present this paper at the Ecclesiastical History Society Summer Meeting, 2005. The Darwell Stone Papers were consulted with permission of the Principal and Chapter of Pusey House, Oxford.

[1] For other perspectives on the revision controversy, see R. C. D. Jasper, *The Development of Anglican Liturgy* (London, 1938); M. Wellings, *Evangelicals Embattled: Responses of Evangelicals in the Church of England to Ritualism, Darwinism and Theological Liberalism, 1890–1930* (Carlisle, 2003); M. Grimley, *Citizenship, Community, and the Church of England Liberal: Anglican Theories of State between the Wars* (Oxford, 2004), ch. 4.

[2] On Anglican identity, see P. Avis, *Anglicanism and the Christian Church* (Edinburgh, 1989); Diarmaid MacCulloch, 'The Myth of the English Reformation', *Journal of British Studies* 30: 1 (1991), 1–19.

Church from the 1860s. In mid-1927 Hensley Henson, the bishop of Durham, indicated the motivation behind the proposals, saying:

> The scale and persistence of the disorder, the high character of many of the offending clergymen and the eminence of some, the growing indications of popular sympathy which they evoked, and the evident dislike of coercive legal proceedings against men of piety and devotion, raised in many minds the question whether clerical disorder might not have a deeper and worthier root, and whether that root might not be removed by deliberate and reasoned concessions.[3]

Whereas previously the bishops had attempted to prevent illegal practices through legal prosecution, most notoriously with the 1874 Public Worship Regulation Act, liturgical revision marked an official change in policy from suppression to compromise.[4] In this sense, revision was an exercise in ecclesiastical diplomacy between the bishops and the Anglo-Catholic party. The other main issue was the identity of the Church of England, for which there were three main models of conceptualization in the early twentieth century. First was the intransigent 'either-or' model, located in the extreme wings of the Church, in which any deviation from either Protestant or Catholic positions was deemed heresy. Second, was the 'via media' or 'bridge-church' model. There were many variations of understanding within this theory and it was used by broad church Anglicans and some moderates in the Evangelical and Anglo-Catholic parties. The basic premise was that the Church of England represented a unique middle-way between Catholic and Protestant belief, and reflected diversity within the boundaries of Anglican traditions and formularies. Third was a 'wholly inclusive' model, which defined the Church of England as an institution without walls in which 'extreme men', such as theological liberals and advanced Anglo-Catholics, could be tolerated. As Nigel Yates has suggested, the response to the fragmentation of Anglican unity following the rise of ritualism was the emergence of a dominant liberal Anglican movement during the Davidson era. These liberal Anglican leaders were 'self-proclaimed prophets of the Anglican via-media'.[5] The 1920s revision

---

[3] Quoted in the *Church Times*, 22 April 1927, 463.

[4] For a detailed study of the Act, see J. Bentley, *Ritualism and Politics in Victorian Britain: the Attempt to Legislate for Belief* (Oxford, 1978), 128–42.

[5] N. Yates, *Anglican Ritualism in Victorian Britain, 1830–1910* (Oxford, 1999), 8.

project saw the bishops apply this 'bridge-church' model, using the Baxterian principle of 'tolerating the tolerable' to find a middle ground between conformity and comprehensiveness in the Church.

The bishops' fundamental aim in revising the Prayer Book was to restore peace and order, or, as G. K. A. Bell, the dean of Canterbury, said in a BBC address, the intention 'was not to gratify this or that party in any of their unreasonable demands: but to do that which in our best understandings we conceived might most tend to the preservation of peace and unity in the Church'.[6] The process began with the 1906 report of the Royal Commission on Ecclesiastical Discipline on ritualism. This report recommended a revision of the Prayer Book and made two main conclusions. Firstly, that the laws of public worship in the Church needed 'greater elasticity' in order to provide for the religious needs of the generation. Secondly, that certain extreme practices, especially reservation of the sacrament under conditions leading to corporate adoration, should be made to cease.[7] Over the next twenty years the Convocations and the Church Assembly discussed the various aspects of revision before leaving the bishops to formulate a final measure.[8] The revised books of 1927–8, although differing slightly in substance, made the following main offers of compromise towards the Anglo-Catholic party. Firstly, they sanctioned a more 'Catholic' alternative Order of Holy Communion, but followed an Eastern Orthodox rather than Roman Catholic pattern of consecration in order to traverse more extreme views on the Real Presence of Christ. Secondly, the books authorized perpetual reservation of the sacraments, a long standing demand of Anglo-Catholics, but used stringent reservation rubrics to prevent extreme practices such as corporate adoration. These concessions received a mixed response from an Anglo-Catholic movement which was far from homogeneous. Many moderate and liberal priests found the offer acceptable because they contended that belief in the Real Presence did not necessitate extra-liturgical devotions.[9] Conversely, many 'advanced' or Anglo-Papist priests, for whom continental and Ultramontane practices were indispensable, viewed the revision as an anti-Catholic 'weapon of war' forged against them.[10] The bishops

---

6 *The Times*, 19 February 1927, 19.

7 Jasper, *Anglican Liturgy*, 77–8.

8 See G. K. A. Bell, *Randall Davidson: Archbishop of Canterbury* (London, 1938), 1328–38.

9 See, for example, the response of Charles Gore, *Church Times*, 1 April 1927, 375.

10 London, Lambeth Palace Library, Papers of the Confraternity of the Blessed Sacrament, MSS 2898, fol. 49.

were aware that an act of loyalty was required from 'advanced' priests. Arthur Headlam, the bishop of Gloucester, informed one Evangelical churchman:

> After all you must realise that for the Anglo-Catholics the situation created is more difficult than for any other section. Those of other sections have not had their individual freedom interfered with at all, but the Anglo-Catholics are perfectly aware that the whole aim of revision is to prevent some of the extremer ones from doing the things they wish to do.[11]

There were various factors behind the bishops' proposals. Despite Archbishop Davidson's limited involvement in the bishops' discussions, the revision reflected his style of churchmanship. His tenure in leadership was influenced by a commitment to comprehensiveness in the Church rather than a dogmatic theological agenda. In 1917 he wrote that his aim was to 'assert in practice the thoughtful and deliberate comprehensiveness of the Church of England, as contrasted with the clear-cut lines and fences of demarcation which mark the rulings of the Church of Rome, and the corresponding . . . rulings of protesting sects'.[12] The Davidson primacy also saw the ecumenical overtures of the 1920 Lambeth Appeal and the unofficial conversations with the Roman Catholic Church at Malines. Similarly, the revised Prayer Book articulated an ecumenical and inclusive ecclesiastical vision.

Revision was also a response to the changing ecclesiastical environment. The background to the process was the meteoric rise of the Anglo-Catholic party in the Church of England during the 1920s. Studies of Anglo-Catholicism have argued that the era was the 'golden age', 'triumphal period' and 'high-water mark' of the party.[13] The increasing influence of the party was affirmed as moderate forms of Catholic worship became normal practice in the Church, most noticeably with the publication of the *English Hymnal* (1906) by Percy Dearmer and Ralph Vaughan Williams.[14] In 1923, Walter Frere, an avowedly Anglo-Catholic bishop, took his place on the Episcopal bench. Significantly, during the period, Bishops Winnington-Ingram of

---

[11] Lambeth Palace Library, MS Headlam 2624, fol. 151.

[12] Bell, *Randall Davidson*, 795.

[13] See A. Hastings, *A History of English Christianity, 1920–1990* (London, 1986), 195; W. S. F. Pickering, *Anglo-Catholicism: a Study in Religious Ambiguity* (London, 1991), 48; A. Vidler, *Scenes From a Clerical Life* (London, 1977), 45.

[14] Jasper, *Anglican Liturgy*, 81.

London, Wakefield of Birmingham and Ridgeway of Chester began to sanction permanent reservation for the sick only in certain parishes. The ballooning attendances at the Anglo-Catholic Congresses emphasized the increasing strength of the party, and from 1920 to 1933 the turn-out increased from thirteen thousand to seventy thousand.[15] Anglo-Catholicism was losing its label as a 'fringe' or 'protest' movement, and developing opportunities to become a major powerbroker in the Church. The seismic shift in spirituality which accompanied the First World War added to the popularity of Anglo-Catholicism. The shadow of death and the tragedy of mass bereavement had a huge effect and many began to desire a more tangible, sacramental form of Christianity. In London, Bishop Winnington-Ingram admitted that regulations regarding extra-liturgical devotions had broken down and ritual chaos ensued.[16]

The bishops were convinced that the new liturgy should somehow reflect religious change. The determination to respond to religious change was expressed in a frank address by a vociferous Hensley Henson to a joint meeting of the Convocations in 1927. He argued that recent developments had the effect of 'forcing into the necessity of decision a great many questions which were latent a few years ago'.[17] He compared the bishop of Norwich, who had opposed the book because of its Catholic emphasis, to a Stylites pillar saint, arguing that his colleague was as aloof to change as the saint and as rigidly dogmatic as his pillar.[18] To some, the crux of the matter was that the situation regarding Anglo-Catholicism was similar to that faced by the Methodists before the schism of the eighteenth century. Davidson noted in his diary a determination not to allow Anglo-Catholics leave fellowship in the same way as the Methodists.[19] William Temple, the bishop of Manchester, argued that 'to drive out from the Church all in whom spiritual vitality leads at any time to practices ... which are outside the existing limits of variety, is the surest way to sterilize the Church'.[20]

[15] Pickering, *Anglo-Catholicism*, 56.
[16] S. C. Carpenter, *Winnington-Ingram: the Biography of Arthur Foley Winnington-Ingram, Bishop of London 1901–1939* (London, 1949), 201.
[17] *The Guardian*, 1 April 1927, 249.
[18] Ibid.
[19] Lambeth Palace, Davidson Private Papers, vol. 16, fol. 91; W. Temple, *The Prayer Book Crisis* (London, 1928), 27–8.
[20] Ibid., 28.

Thus, the revision project exemplified the developing spirit of ecumenicalism and inclusion in twentieth-century Anglicanism.

The exact character of this comprehensiveness was determined by three main guiding principles. Firstly, according to Theodore Woods, bishop of Winchester, the revised book was to express 'unity in variety'.[21] Undoubtedly, some bishops saw revision as an attempt to break out of the prison of uniformity that dominated the national Church following the Reformation and prevented tolerance and variety in worship.[22]

Secondly, this comprehensiveness was to be strictly limited, or as Cosmo Lang, the archbishop of York, summarized, 'fellowship, if it is to be real, must have its limits'.[23] The bishops affirmed that the Church of England should remain a cohesive institutional unit within the bounds of its doctrines and traditions. Sydney Dark, editor of the *Church Times*, summarized that the purpose of revision was to maintain a Church in which 'Protestants and Catholics may worship together, so long as the Protestant is not too Protestant and the Catholic is not too Catholic'.[24] In the mind of some Anglo-Catholics, revision was placing severe limitations on comprehensiveness. Many priests had benefited from the fact that the 1662 book was notoriously flexible and susceptible to being 'worked'. Some Anglo-Catholics argued that the 1662 book was not explicit in preventing perpetual reservation without a diocesan's permission[25] and that the 'Black Rubric' did not forbid the teaching of transubstantiation or outlaw the adoration of the sacrament.[26] The 1927 and 1928 revisions attempted to set a new benchmark for lawful liturgical practices. Hence, one moderate Anglo-Catholic journal argued that revision prevented real comprehensiveness and lamented an old book that was 'freely interpreted' and whose rubrics 'were not worded exactly enough to prevent an elastic interpretation'.[27] Undoubtedly, the bishops hoped that a revision accepted by the Convocations, diocesan conferences and the National Assembly would give a legitimacy and authenticity to episcopal authority and

---

[21] T. Woods, *The Prayer Book Revised* (London, 1927), 75.
[22] Ibid.
[23] *The Guardian*, 11 February 1927, 105.
[24] *Church Times*, 1 April 1927, 377.
[25] Lewis Low, *Reservation and the Book of Common Prayer: an Enquiry* (London, 1928).
[26] See address by Darwell Stone, Lambeth Palace Library, Papers of Confraternity of the Blessed Sacrament, MSS 2898, 67.
[27] *Green Quarterly*, Summer 1928, vol. 4, no. 3, 132.

that Anglo-Catholics would be loyal to the Church rather than their conscience.

Thirdly, the limits of comprehensiveness were demarcated by the theological and liturgical consensus of agreement reached by the bishops. The revisions were an expression of moderate 'bridge-church' thinking. A central theme of the book was compromise between Protestant and Catholic dogmatisms on the status of the consecrated elements. Prominent bishops, such as Theodore Woods, Arthur Headlam, William Temple and Winfred Burrows of Chichester articulated, to varying degrees, a middle-way theology of the 'Real Presence' of Christ at communion.[28] They argued that different views of the Lord's presence had traditionally been held within the Church of England. While these bishops rejected any notion of transubstantiation, they refuted a Zwinglian memorialist interpretation of communion. William Temple reminded conservative Evangelicals that Martin Luther's belief in consubstantiation led him to oppose Zwingli and that Calvin espoused a theology of a *signa exhibitiva*, or real spiritual presence. Furthermore, he argued that Nicholas Ridley, the English reformer, took a Calvinistic view on the elements, citing his words, 'he doth not lie who saith Christ to be offered'.[29] The view that there was a new meaning and power in the consecrated elements justified, for instance, the Invocation of the Holy Spirit, the Anthem 'Blessed is he that cometh in the name of the Lord' and continuous reservation of the sacrament in the revised book.

Similarly, this commitment to a 'bridge-church' theology ruled out various liturgical practices which were seen to be outside the limits of comprehension. It was agreed that extra-liturgical corporate devotions were prohibited in the revised book. The pro-revision bishops argued that there was no justification for separating the consecrated elements from the sacrament of communion, as this was contrary to the Thirty-Nine Articles and the traditions of the primitive Church and Eastern Orthodox churches.[30] It is impossible to ascertain to what extent this consensus of agreement was motivated by theological conviction or ecclesiastical pragmatism. However, the moderate bishops were open in

[28] Woods, *Prayer Book Revised*, 93; R. C. D. Jasper, *Arthur Caley Headlam* (Leighton Buzzard, 1960), 183; Temple, *Prayer Book Crisis*, 21–6; W. O. Burrows, *An Address in Explanation of the Prayer Book Measure* (London, 1927), 32.

[29] Temple discusses the views of various English reformers in *Prayer Book Crisis*, 18–25.

[30] Lambeth Palace Library, Davidson Papers, vol. 452, fols 243–4; H. Henson, *The Book and the Vote* (London, 1928), 65–6.

their view that revision enriched the liturgy and re-emphasized the breadth of Anglican doctrine.

In their promise to restore peace and order to the Church, the second aim of revision was to improve ecclesiastical discipline. In regards to Anglo-Catholicism, Theodore Woods described the lawlessness of the early-twentieth century, saying:

> Bishops have been accused (quite justly) of 'winking' at methods and practices which are not permitted by the strict letter of the law. Clergymen who have been allowed an inch have been accused (quite justly) of taking an ell; of doing things which they hoped would go unnoticed by the Bishop; of being careful *not* to ask the Bishop's permission in cases where it was in doubt.[31]

By the 1920s the Church of England was in a state of liturgical chaos. The attitudes of advanced Anglo-Catholic priests were in part responsible for this situation, both because of their 'working' of the 1662 Prayer Book and their cunning avoidance of episcopal interference. Alan Wilkinson has argued that a 'self-deception about authority' was a major flaw in Anglo-Catholicism during the period.[32] The situation was worsened by the lack of continuity and unity amongst the bishops in their reactions to ritual lawlessness. For instance, in the Diocese of London, Bishop Winnington-Ingram's affection for his Anglo-Catholic clergy prevented him from enforcing the laws of the Church with any meaningful success.[33]

The bishops intended that revision would restore order by offering both sides a 'clean slate'. It offered a framework by which the boundaries of legal practice could be clearly defined. A vital component of the revision proposal was a clear commitment by the bishops to collective authority. In October 1927, Randall Davidson wrote a widely publicized letter to Canon Storr, a liberal evangelical, saying that the book would be 'faithfully administered' and that all the bishops would 'act together' in the matter.[34] When Davidson received a deputation from Anglo-Catholic supporters in September 1927, he was careful to inform them that the bishops did 'mean business' and intend to secure

---

[31] Woods, *Prayer Book Revised*, 14.
[32] A. Wilkinson, *The Community of the Resurrection: a Centenary History* (London, 1992), 185–6.
[33] Carpenter, *Winnington-Ingram*, 199–201.
[34] *The Guardian*, 4 November 1927, 821.

obedience.[35] Thus, the official line was that the revised book represented a new regime and that the bishops would police the Church collectively.

However, significantly, neither penalties for disobedience nor the procedures for enforcing discipline were prescribed within the revision proposals. Although it was suggested that continued disobedience might result in penal action, the central purpose of the book was to restore discipline through consensus. If the proposals were approved by Convocations and the National Assembly, the bishops, in enforcing the rubrics, would authoritatively express a consensus within the Church. The bishops argued that revision would provide an irresistible 'moral appeal'[36] to loyalty, especially Anglo-Catholics, amongst whom the idea of obedience was esteemed. Davidson told the National Church Assembly in 1927 that 'the greatest churchmen have always recognised that their power of discipline ... depends most on their ability to reveal to the transgressor the inherent truth and reasonableness' of the rules.[37]

The bishops failed to convince large sections of the Church and a majority of the Houses of Parliament that revision would restore 'peace and order' in the Church. Both Anglo-Catholics and Protestants found reasons to reject the compromise. A significant number of Anglo-Catholics disagreed with the bishops' model of comprehensiveness. Significantly, no major Anglo-Catholic organization supported the revision. The English Church Union, the main clerical and lay body, was too divided to take an official stance on the 1927 revision. The Federation of Catholic Priests, which represented around 1400 priests, and the Confraternity of the Blessed Sacrament, with a membership of 1800 priests and 22,000 laity, both passed resolutions against revision.[38] In 1928, Anglo-Catholic opinion solidified against revision as the bishops added more stringent reservation rubrics to placate Protestants in Parliament. Bishop Frere, who had influenced moderate Anglo-Catholics to accept the proposals, withdrew his support on the grounds that the new restrictions were unfair.[39] Many Anglo-Catholics agreed with Viscount Halifax, the former President of the English Church

35 Lambeth Palace Library, Davidson Papers, vol. 453, 106–7.
36 A term used by the Bishops of Southwark and Winchester, see *The Guardian*, 20 May 1927, 390; Woods, *Prayer Book Revised*, 17.
37 *The Guardian*, 8 July 1927, 517.
38 Papers of the Confraternity of the Blessed Sacrament, MSS. 2898, fol. 60; Oxford, Pusey House Library, Darwell Stone Papers, Box D5.
39 *Church Union Gazette*, April 1928, 78.

Union, that the proposals were 'neither sufficient in generosity nor sufficient in understanding to bring peace'.[40] By using revision to regulate a middle-way of interpretation of the Real Presence and outlawing services of corporate devotion the bishops were cutting across an expression of advanced Anglo-Catholic worship. This policy troubled the consciences of various moderate party members. Kenneth Ingram, editor of the high-brow *Green Quarterly* magazine, wrote that 'it would have been as impossible in the Church Assembly to plead for services of adoration as to expect Mussolini to allow free speech in Italy',[41] and argued against revision because it was intolerant of so many of his brethren. The reaction of discontent priests and laymen had a critical effect on Parliament, where many MPs became convinced that the promise of 'peace and unity' was unachievable.

The bishops failed to convince many Protestants that the new book would be enforced collectively and with integrity. The Evangelical rumour-mill was rife with suggestions that some bishops were less than intent to 'act together'. Warnings given by some prominent churchmen, that there was no serious indication that all the bishops would enforce order, fuelled these concerns.[42] The rumours were probably not without substance. For instance, Edwyn Hoskins, an Anglo-Catholic fellow of Corpus Christi, Cambridge, held a secret meeting with a prominent bishop, who informed him that a large number of his colleagues were against securing rigid conformity through disciplinary action. The anonymous diocesan suggested that revision would set a standard of worship, and that under its influence, and the persuasion of bishops, lawless priests would gradually conform to it.[43] Although there is a lack of firm written evidence, it appears that some bishops had a slippery attitude towards discipline.

Thus, the book was rejected by large sections of the Church because of confusion surrounding the question of discipline. The bishops were unclear as to how exactly the book would be used to bring order to the Church. The overriding spirit of revision was to leave the days of ecclesiastical prosecutions behind and bring about order through a 'moral appeal' to loyalty to the Church and the goodwill of the parties. At the

[40] *Church Times*, 1 April 1927, 429; also C. Lindley, *Viscount Halifax*, 1885–1934, 2 vols (Glasgow, 1936), 2: 345–7.
[41] *Green Quarterly*, Spring 1928, vol. 5, no. 2, 103.
[42] B. Pollock, *Prayer Book Revision: an Alternative Policy* (London, 1927), 7.
[43] Oxford, Pusey House Library, Darwell Stone Papers, Box G12.

same time, the archbishop had promised that the bishops intended to enforce the book with strictness. The variety of statements made on the subject had the effect of creating anxiety in both wings of the Church, as the Evangelicals feared further illegalities, and Anglo-Catholics were anxious that the bishops would take an intolerant attitude towards them.

The determination of the bishops to use their book emphasized the dominance of a moderate 'via media' model of the Church in the period. This ideal was reiterated in Hensley Henson's *The Church of England* (1930), Cyril Garbett's *The Claims of the Church of England* (1947) and implied in the 1948 Report of the Committee on the Unity of the Church. Despite its lack of legal sanction, the bishops would encourage the use of the 1928 revised book until further alternative services were devised by the Liturgical Commission during the 1960s. Overall, the problematical twin aims of revision – the enlargement of comprehensiveness and restoration of discipline – created an uneasy tension in the Church. The difficulties surrounding the Church parties were too deep-seated and complex to be solved by one action. A period of gradual change and experimentation may have been more successful and less controversial. In his book *Anglicanism*, Stephen Neill admitted that since the birth of the Oxford Movement tensions had been so great in the Church of England that outsiders have often wondered how those who differed so sharply on various critical issues were able to remain in communion.[44] Alongside Tractarianism, the birth of theological liberalism has heightened this tension within the Church. The 1920s Prayer Book revision controversy gives an example of one way in which the episcopate has attempted to resolve the paradox of unity and variety and gives a longer perspective to those facing similar issues in the contemporary context.

University of Stirling

---

[44] S. Neill, *Anglicanism* (3rd edn, London, 1928), 426.

DISCIPLINE IN DISPUTE:
THE ORIGINS AND EARLY HISTORY OF THE METHODIST SACRAMENTAL FELLOWSHIP

by MARTIN WELLINGS

W HEN the annual Methodist Conference assembled in Newcastle-upon-Tyne on 14 July 1936, the retiring President appeared wearing the moderator's gown presented to the Connexion the previous summer. In his *Methodist Recorder* column, W. F. Howard wondered: 'Will the Protestant Truth Society discover some subtle Romeward predilection in this departure from our ancient wont and usage?', but reassured his readers that 'It is a simple Geneva gown, ... black enough for John Knox himself.'[1]

Howard's humour alluded to a controversy sparked by the recent formation of the Methodist Sacramental Fellowship (MSF), a devotional society representing 'catholic Methodism'. Inaugurated in 1935, the MSF provoked considerable disquiet within the Connexion and also attracted the attention of campaigners from the further reaches of the 'Protestant underworld', who saw it as another manifestation of a 'Romeward drift' among the Free Churches. The MSF was promoted by its instigators as an endeavour to strengthen waning discipline and to reinforce a strand of authentic Methodist theology and practice which they feared was in danger of eclipse. In response, others argued that the Fellowship pushed diversity in Methodism beyond the bounds of legitimacy and urged that disciplinary action should be taken against it. The controversy of 1935–8 thus tested Methodism's willingness to tolerate diversity and its ability to enforce discipline, marking a stage in the Connexion's shift from an ideal of homogeneity to an acknowledgement of pluralism.[2]

The immediate origins of the MSF coincided with the birth of the Methodist Church of Great Britain in 1932. On 22 September, about a

---

[1] *Methodist Recorder* (London), 23 July 1936, 25.

[2] John A. Vickers ed., *A Dictionary of Methodism in Great Britain and Ireland* (Peterborough, 2000), 234–5; George Thompson Brake, *Policy and Politics in British Methodism 1932–82* (London, 1984), 365–7; John Newton, *Heart Speaks to Heart* (London, 1994), 68–84; John C. Bowmer, *The Lord's Supper in Methodism 1791–1960* (London, 1961), 49–50.

dozen younger ministers met for a retreat at Sidcup 'to celebrate Holy Communion [and] to talk together about our own faith and practice as Methodist ministers, and further about the present conditions and the functions or *raison d'être* of modern Methodism as belonging to the Church Catholic.'[3] Further meetings followed and the MSF was formally launched at a conference at Penrhos College, Colwyn Bay, in August 1935. A brief account of the conference and the aims of the new movement appeared in the Methodist press, and public controversy began soon afterwards, intensifying in the wake of the second conference in April 1936, and continuing until the Methodist Conference delivered its verdict on the Fellowship in summer 1938.

In his apologia for the MSF, A. S. Gregory traced the genesis of the movement to three friends' concern for 'a more ordered devotional life, both privately and in the public worship of the Methodist people'.[4] The real driving force behind the early developments was Gregory's cousin Theo (T. S.) Gregory, and clues to the programme of the fledgling movement may be found in the 'basis of discussion' which he prepared for the Sidcup meeting and in the 'Proposed Basis of a Methodist Catholic Society' which was debated at a retreat at Epsom in May 1933. It would seem that a group of ministers, mostly younger men from the Wesleyan tradition in Methodism, felt unsettled in their own devotional practice and spiritual experience, but also deeply troubled by the theology and ethos they perceived to be increasingly influential in their Church.

Gregory's 1932 document posited 'a certain dissatisfaction and uncertainty (a) as regards our own faith and practice [and] (b) as regards the present state and future prospects of Meth[odis]m'.[5] Interestingly, the first point was left undeveloped in the paper, although early meetings of the nascent Fellowship gave considerable attention to the devotional life and to the crafting of a daily office. A morning office based on the service of prime in the 1928 Prayer Book was presented to the May 1933 Epsom retreat and the participants 'took the vow, by standing in silence, to say the office daily.'[6] A shorter office, devised

---

[3] Typed circular, December 1932, MSF archive. I am grateful to the Revd Norman Wallwork for access to the MSF papers in his stewardship. The archive is not catalogued and is only loosely organized into yearly files.

[4] A. S. Gregory, *The Methodist Sacramental Fellowship* (London, 1954), 6–7.

[5] T. S. Gregory, 'Retreat at Sidcup Sept 1932: Suggested Basis of Discussion', MSF archive.

[6] 'Retreat report, Epsom, May 1933', MSF archive.

specifically for the MSF, was adopted by the inaugural conference in 1935.[7]

The quest for a deeper devotional life was not unusual in Methodism, nor was it a monopoly of the MSF. In the 1930s Methodist spirituality was expressed in various forms and MSF members were involved in the Fellowship of the Kingdom and the Methodist School of Fellowship. Senior Methodists like Henry Lunn and A. E. Whitham had long found aspects of Catholic spirituality enriching, while liturgical order and structured devotions appealed to a growing appreciation of aesthetics and a desire for beauty in worship among Free Church people.[8] In drawing on Roman Catholic devotional material, moreover, the MSF could appeal to John Wesley or even to Samuel Chadwick,[9] although mainstream Methodists might have been perturbed to discover that several members found the crucifix 'a great aid to concentration'.[10]

Although it mentioned the devotional life in passing, Gregory's 1932 paper had much more to say about theological concerns. Methodism, he claimed, was affected by the 'Humanist' tendencies of contemporary theology, whose symptoms included 'variety of belief among ministers' and 'ambiguity' in the doctrinal standards of the united Church.[11] The early papers of the MSF were clear that Methodism was too diverse in its doctrine, tolerating modernist teaching and failing to proclaim a full-blooded Catholic Christianity.[12]

Again, these concerns were not exclusive to the MSF. Gregory identified fundamentalists and Barthians as possible allies, but feared that most Methodists were either engaged in a 'search for eighteenth-century experience' or promoting united Methodism as a 'Free Church' in opposition to the Church of England.[13] Gregory argued that the true

---

[7] *Methodist Recorder*, 19 September 1935, 12.

[8] Gordon S. Wakefield, *Methodist Spirituality* (Peterborough, 1999), part 3; Ian M. Randall, *Evangelical Experiences: a Study in the Spirituality of English Evangelicalism, 1918–39* (Carlisle, 1999), chs 4, 5, and 9; D. W. Bebbington, *Evangelicalism in Modern Britain: a History from the 1730s to the 1980s* (London, 1989), 203–7; Norman Wallwork, 'Developments in Liturgy and Worship in Twentieth-Century Nonconformity', in Alan P. F. Sell and Anthony R. Cross, eds, *Protestant Nonconformity in the Twentieth Century* (Carlisle, 2003), 102–31.

[9] A. E. Whitham, 'Friendliness in Earnest', *Methodist Recorder*, 19 November 1936, 11.

[10] 'Methods of Private Prayer', MSF archive (undated typescript, filed in 1934 folder).

[11] Gregory, 'Suggested Basis'.

[12] 'Draft Memorandum prepared at the Inception of the Movement', MSF archive (undated typescript, filed in 1934 folder).

[13] Gregory, 'Suggested Basis'.

way forward for Methodism lay in a vigorous reassertion of Catholic orthodoxy, a renewal of discipline in private prayer and Church life, a recovery of sacramental practice and a commitment 'to press urgently for our early reunion with the Church of England'.[14]

Was the formation of the MSF a direct response to Methodist Union? Certainly most of the founding members were Wesleyans and issues of doctrinal clarity, sacramental worship and Methodism's relationship with the Church of England were concerns of the Wesleyan 'Other Side' during the reunion negotiations. Wesleyanism too, however, had its militant Protestants, its modernists and its committed Free Churchmen, so the influx of a substantial body of liberal Protestants in 1932 may have exacerbated the concerns of 'right wing' Wesleyans, but it did not create them.[15]

The years between 1932 and 1935 saw the aims and approach of the MSF honed and clarified. The 'Methodist Catholic Society' became the 'Methodist Sacramental Fellowship', open to lay people. The detailed doctrinal basis proposed in 1933 was discarded in favour of a more concise formula, giving as the MSF's first object: 'reaffirmation of the FAITH that inspired the Evangelical Revival and the hymns of the Wesleys – the Faith that is formulated in the NICENE CREED.' The sacramental emphasis of the Fellowship was expressed in the second object: 'making of THE HOLY COMMUNION central in the life of the Methodist Church.' After much debate, 'early reunion with the Church of England' in the third object was softened to prayer 'for the corporate reunion of all believers'.[16] By the time this form of words was settled, Gregory had resigned from the Methodist ministry and been received into the Roman Catholic Church. The committee pressed ahead regardless, postponing the inaugural conference from April to August and recruiting A. E. Whitham as the Fellowship's first President.[17]

Stirrings of anxiety about the MSF soon followed the press reports of the Colwyn Bay conference. A flurry of letters in the autumn of 1935

14 'Draft Memorandum'.
15 Robert Currie, *Methodism Divided: a Study in the Sociology of Ecumenicalism* (London, 1968), ch. 8.
16 *In Defence of the Methodist Sacramental Fellowship at the Conference of the Methodist Church at Hull, 1938* (Southport, 1938), inside front cover (MSF Pamphlet, no. 7, reporting a speech by J. E. Rattenbury).
17 Gordon S. Wakefield, *T. S. Gregory* (Emsworth, 2000), 22–3, 30; *Methodist Times and Leader* (London) [hereafter: *Methodist Times*], 28 February 1935, 4. For Whitham, see A. E. Whitham, *The Discipline and Culture of the Spiritual Life* (London, 1938), 9–10, and *Minutes of the Methodist Conference* (London, 1938), 192.

debated the intentions of the new movement.[18] This correspondence
soon died down, but the controversy was reignited during 1936. In
April the Fellowship held its second conference, at Selly Oak, and
invited two provocative guest speakers, Edward Leach, one of the band
of Anglo-Catholic 'rebels' in public conflict with Bishop Barnes of
Birmingham,[19] and Wilbert Howard, tutor at Handsworth College.
Howard challenged the wisdom of forming a society like the MSF in
the immediate aftermath of Methodist Union.[20] Disregarding Howard's
warnings, those leading worship at Selly Oak used more ceremonial
than was customary in Methodism, donning cassock and surplice,
placing lighted candles on the Communion table and adopting the
eastward position. Unfortunately for the MSF, the conference had been
infiltrated by an agent of the Protestant Truth Society (PTS), and his
surreptitious notes of the proceedings were published in the *Churchman's Magazine* in June 1936 under the heading '"Orchardism" in the
Methodist Church'.[21] The PTS and its indefatigable secretary J. A.
Kensit drew on nearly half a century of campaigning, principally
against Anglo-Catholicism in the Church of England but latterly also
against alleged ritualism in the Free Churches, and their talent for
exploiting Protestant fears was formidable. A stream of articles, speedily
converted into cheap pamphlets, warned that Methodism was facing a
Romeward drift. For the next two years the PTS used its publications
and its network of itinerant Wickliffe Preachers to foster anxiety about
the MSF.[22] At the outset of his attack, Kensit instigated an inflamma-
tory article in *Joyful News*, the weekly paper associated with Cliff
College and the conservative evangelical constituency in Methodism,
suggesting that Methodist theological colleges were nurturing
Romanism among student ministers.[23] This drew a blistering riposte

[18] *Methodist Times*, 26 September 1935, 19; 3 October 1935, 18; 10 October 1935, 20;
Methodist Recorder, 31 October 1935, 21; 7 November 1935, 23; 14 November 1935, 13; 21
November 1935, 23; 28 November 1935, 26; 5 December 1935, 37.
[19] Alec Vidler, *Scenes from a Clerical Life* (London, 1977), 57–74; John Barnes, *Ahead of His
Age: Bishop Barnes of Birmingham* (London, 1979), chs 5 and 6.
[20] Compare *Methodist Times*, 30 April 1935, 6, with Howard's own account in a letter to
A. S. Gregory, 27 November 1936, MSF archive.
[21] '"Orchardism" in the Methodist Church', *Churchman's Magazine* (London) [hereafter:
Churchman's], June 1936, 146–50. The agent, A. W. Martin, was detected at, and evicted
from, the 1937 conference: *Churchman's*, June 1937, 163; *Methodist Times*, 1 July 1937, 8
[22] Nine articles appeared in the *Churchman's* between June and December 1936, six in
1937 and five in 1938.
[23] 'Metholay' [J. Crowlesmith], 'Roman Catholicism in the Methodist Church: "The
Methodist Sacramental Fellowship"', *Joyful News* (London), 11 June 1936, 2.

from Howard,[24] but awareness and suspicion of the MSF grew from the summer of 1936. Besides critical letters in the press, steps were taken to ask the Methodist Conference to investigate or suppress the Fellowship. The MSF committee defended itself in a manifesto in September 1936, thus adding fuel to the controversy.[25] Before the official investigation began in 1937, therefore, the principal charges against the MSF had already been thoroughly rehearsed and debated.

The accusation of deliberate Romanizing was promoted by the PTS. Kensit sought to link the MSF to W. E. Orchard, the flamboyant Presbyterian minister who seceded to Rome in 1932.[26] T. S. Gregory's secession inevitably encouraged the comparison, and the transition from Gregory, 'a Romanist in Methodism', to the MSF as 'a Romeward movement' was quickly made in the autumn of 1935.[27] Responding to the critics, A. W. Barr claimed that the MSF was 'an attempt to call Methodism back to the very things for lack of which some are leaving us for Rome'.[28] Tom Sykes, from the Primitive Methodist tradition, rejected the Fellowship's manifesto appeal to John Wesley as a smokescreen, alleging that 'the base of operations is Rome.' Ben Drewery dismissed this as 'pernicious misrepresentation', but the accusations continued.[29]

Was this charge pure Kensitite propaganda? The MSF, particularly in its early days, gave shelter to several eccentrics and extremists, whose behaviour lent colour to Protestant fears.[30] Behind the warning shot published in *Joyful News* in June 1936 stood two men who were well-placed to understand the concerns of ordinary Methodists: the columnist 'Metholay' (John Crowlesmith), whose minister son attended the 1933 Epsom retreat,[31] and W. H. Heap, Chairman of the East Anglia District. Heap's editorial postbag brought evidence of the anxieties

---

[24] *Methodist Recorder*, 18 June 1936, 23; *Methodist Times*, 18 June 1936, 18; *Joyful News*, 25 June 1936, 2.

[25] *Methodist Recorder*, 3 September 1936, 18; *Methodist Times*, 3 September 1936, 18; *Joyful News*, 3 September 1936, 3.

[26] Elaine Kaye and Ross Mackenzie, *W. E. Orchard: a Study in Christian Exploration* (Oxford, 1990), 96–100.

[27] *Methodist Times*, 2 May 1935, 20; 26 September 1935, 19.

[28] Ibid., 3 October 1935, 18.

[29] Ibid., 10 September 1936, 20; 17 September 1936, 18.

[30] In print, Howard called them 'sentimentalists' and 'cranks': *Joyful News*, 25 June 1936, 2; in his letter of 27 November 1936 to A. S. Gregory he described one prominent MSF eccentric, E. J. B. Kirtlan, as 'that uncertified lunatic': MSF archive.

[31] *Who's Who in Methodism 1933* (London, 1933), 296; *Methodist Recorder*, 6 June 1935, 17.

stirred up by the alleged behaviour of MSF members, and he told an interviewer in April 1937 of a retreat for younger ministers where some had complained because he did not turn east for Communion.[32] Although he indignantly rebutted the allegations in *Joyful News* in public, in private Howard wrote frankly to A. S. Gregory about the 'notoriously foolish fellows' who were 'conspicuous' in the Fellowship and suggested that his cousin had 'infected some of the more impressionable youngsters in the colleges' before his secession.[33]

Those who did not accept the PTS conspiracy theory were concerned nonetheless about the MSF's stated aim of making Communion 'central' in the life of the Methodist Church. This drew criticism from correspondents who argued that evangelism, prayer, preaching or the class meeting ought to occupy that place. In each case the MSF was accused of moving away from authentic Methodism. George Jackson feared the spread of 'churchy' habits among younger Methodist ministers.[34] James Nightingale, a supernumerary minister, reported from Sunderland that former Wesleyan, Primitive and United Methodists agreed that the Church needed militancy, not millinery.[35] Challenging the claim that more formal worship would stem the haemorrhage of members, Heap argued that Methodism's natural constituency was drawn by 'a warm-hearted evangelical religion', not by stately buildings, prayers read from books, and more frequent Communions.[36] Critics of the MSF argued that the genius of Methodism was evangelical and experiential, not sacramental. In response, the MSF asserted that the sacramental and evangelical emphases in Methodism were properly two sides of the same coin. As the bicentenary of 1738 approached, contemporary controversies inflamed debates about the interpretation of the 'evangelical conversion' of the Wesleys.[37]

The final charge levelled at the MSF was that it was divisive. Here the context of Methodist Union was significant: the surge of optimism

---

[32] *Methodist Times*, 1 April 1937, 1.
[33] Howard to Gregory, 27 November 1936.
[34] *Methodist Recorder*, 3 October 1935, 11.
[35] *Methodist Times*, 22 October 1936, 18.
[36] *Joyful News*, 8 July 1937, 1.
[37] The principal protagonists in this debate were Rattenbury, Jackson and Henry Bett: see, for example, Bett, *The Spirit of Methodism* (London, 1937), 64–99, with critical review by Rattenbury in *Methodist Times*, 29 July 1937, 9, with debate picked up by Jackson in *Methodist Recorder*, 3 March 1938, 11 and 31 March 1938, 13, with response by Rattenbury, ibid., 7 April 1938, 23.

felt in 1932 was accompanied by an awareness of the delicacy of the task facing the 'new Methodism' after years of denominational rivalry. James Nightingale observed that the protracted press correspondence about the MSF 'is not helping to make Methodist union more vital and more real',[38] and his concerns were shared by senior officers of the Connexion. Robert Bond, Secretary of the Conference, wrote to Whitham after meeting the MSF leaders expressing his fear that the Fellowship would damage unity by fostering the maintenance of 'sectional loyalties'. 'For the sake of the whole Church', Bond hoped to persuade the leaders 'to cease the Organised Fellowship'.[39] At a more instinctive level, many Methodists deplored the creation of a sectional organization and were dismayed that it could adopt the name 'Methodist' without Conference approval. This reaction expressed an assumption, deep-rooted in the Methodist psyche, that the Church was a single organism – one 'Connexion'. Although the protracted negotiations for union had forced Methodists to recognize differences of belief and emphasis among themselves, the experience of a shared discipline, the commitment to 'our doctrines', the reiterated emphasis on 'fellowship' as a distinctive feature of Methodist identity and the appeal to shared religious experience made it hard to accept organized diversity. Almost regardless of the particular aims of the MSF, there were Methodists who believed that the very existence of such an organization was improper and disloyal.[40]

Methodist discipline was a matter for the annual Conference, a body of some nine hundred ministerial and lay representatives. Circuit meetings could register concerns by sending memorials to the Conference, and the first memorial on the MSF was submitted by the Hereford Circuit in 1936. The Conference avoided the issue, accepting an explanation that the memorial was factually inaccurate.[41] In 1937, however, one District Synod (Chester and Warrington) and fourteen circuits asked for an investigation, and a committee of enquiry was established. The anxious circuits were all in the Midlands and north of England; ten

---

[38] *Methodist Times*, 22 October 1936, 18.

[39] Robert Bond to A. E. Whitham, 25 May 1937, MSF archive.

[40] The language of 'fellowship' and 'experience' was all-pervasive in Methodist publications of the 1930s. See, for instance, Bett, *Spirit of Methodism*, 131–47. 'Metholay' missed 'the Methodist fellowship' when he attended a cathedral service: *Joyful News*, 8 October 1936, 2.

[41] *Agenda of Conference 1936* (London, 1936), 5; *Methodist Recorder*, 23 July 1936, 14. Heap attributed the Hereford memorial to a Local Preacher in a London circuit: *Joyful News*, 3 September 1936, 3.

were ex-Primitive Methodist circuits served exclusively by ex-Primitive ministers; the others were amalgamated circuits with a mixture of ministers. The wording of the memorials was similar enough to suggest co-ordination.[42]

It seems that Whitham and Heap agreed on a broad-based member-ship for the committee of enquiry, but their plan was overruled, producing a body unsympathetic to the MSF.[43] Whitham, the only MSF representative, died suddenly in January 1938 and was not replaced. The committee declined an invitation to attend the MSF conference at Easter 1938, but asked Rattenbury, Whitham's successor as President of the Fellowship, to present the case for the MSF at its meeting on 2 June. Rattenbury read a statement which anticipated his speech to the Hull Conference a month later. The statement placed the emphases of the MSF firmly in an unbroken tradition from the Wesleys, claiming that it sought 'to restore a lost balance' in Meth-odism. A robust defence of the MSF's Protestant loyalties was inter-spersed with pointed thrusts at some members of the committee. Rattenbury argued that the MSF could not disband voluntarily without conceding the truth of the false allegations of Romanizing, and he made a shrewd appeal to fair play against the work of external agitators. He concluded with a pledge that 'so long as I am President of this society it shall do nothing inconsistent either with the principles of the Protestant Reformation or with the Standards or Constitution of the Methodist Church.'[44]

The committee's report to the Conference comprised a rebuke to the MSF. It disagreed with the Fellowship that there was evidence of widespread unfaithfulness to Methodist doctrine. It challenged the use of the word 'central' with regard to Holy Communion, suggesting that the MSF had 'given to this Sacrament a position which is not in harmony with the teaching and practice of the Methodist Church'. It asserted that the MSF had not helped the cause of reunion, particularly among the Free Churches, and suggested that nothing sought by the Fellowship 'cannot be found in the usual ministrations and teaching of

[42] *Agenda of Conference 1937* (London, 1937), 1–9. The circuits and their ministers may be identified from the *Minutes of Conference 1936* (London, 1936).

[43] *Methodist Recorder*, 21 July 1938, 28.

[44] 'Methodist Conference Committee of Enquiry: Copy of Statement made by the Revd Dr Rattenbury ... 2 June 1938', MSF archive. One of Rattenbury's targets was Richard Pyke, who published an article on 'The Lord's Supper: Its Significance as a Memorial', *Methodist Recorder*, 20 January 1938, 9.

our Church'. The committee stopped short of recommending the disbanding of the Fellowship, although that hope might be read between the lines of its report. The committee concluded, however, that 'it is in accordance with our traditions to allow freedom of thought to men who may not appear to preserve a sense of proportion, but who are impelled by a burning sincerity to preach the truth as they see it'.[45]

The report was presented for adoption by the Conference in speeches of studied moderation. Ensor Walters, who chaired the committee and wrote the report, paid tribute to Whitham and Ratten-bury, suggested that 'the unrest of two years ago was passing away' and asked that the report be accepted without discussion. Rattenbury, however, wished to speak, and made, in Howard's estimation, 'one of the most impressive speeches of his life'. By emphasizing the MSF's roots in the tradition of the Wesleys, by exposing the absurdity of 'no popery' sentiment, by pinning the blame for the agitation firmly on the PTS and by promising to curb any 'individual extravagances' of MSF members, Rattenbury won the sympathy and support of the Confer-ence and ensured that the report was merely received and then put aside. In Howard's judgement, 'Agitation on both sides ought now to cease', and it did. The PTS continued to denounce the MSF and to detect Jesuit conspiracies in Methodism, but the campaign was a shadow of its former self and it found no support within the Connexion.[46]

Howard's analysis of the 1938 debate ascribed the agitation entirely to the 'foolish indiscretions' of some MSF members and the interfer-ence of the PTS. This account, although persuasive up to a point, was that of a connexional insider, keen to emphasize unity, and it needs to be nuanced by some other observations. There were real tensions in Methodism in 1932, predating but also exacerbated by union. The MSF began as the 'new Methodism' was exploring its identity, and both the shaping of the Fellowship and reactions to it were affected by this. The events of 1937-8 helped the Fellowship, because the investigation by an obviously unsympathetic committee demonstrated even to the most suspicious that the MSF could claim a legitimate place within the family of Methodist traditions. The death of some of the Fellowship's

---

[45] *Agenda of Conference 1938* (London, 1938), 493-5.
[46] *Methodist Recorder*, 21 July 1938, 19-20, 28; *Joyful News*, 28 July 1938, 4; *Churchman's*, September 1938, 231-3. The MSF published Rattenbury's speech as a pamphlet, *In Defence of the Methodist Sacramental Fellowship* (see n. 16 above).

more controversial members and Rattenbury's accession to the presidency may also have helped.[47] The PTS gadfly initially provoked a response but soon became a general irritant whose presence was almost universally resented.[48]

When T. S. Gregory and his colleagues launched their vision of a 'Methodist Catholic Society' in 1932 they were troubled by diversity and anxious to re-impose a stricter discipline on their Church. By 1938, the MSF was appealing to a tradition of toleration to justify its own right to exist as one strand within the spectrum of Methodist belief and practice. By repudiating the vision and allowing the appeal, arguably the Methodist Church signalled a victory for diversity and a defeat for discipline. In so doing it took a further step towards the practice and acknowledgement of pluralism, which has become characteristic of Methodism and of all the mainstream Free Churches during the twentieth century.

Kidlington, Oxfordshire

[47] Kirtlan died in January 1937: *Methodist Times*, 14 January 1937, 3. Gordon Wakefield's judgement that 'no one could accuse [Rattenbury] of being an encassocked romanizer' (*Methodist Spirituality*, 74) underestimates the PTS, but holds good for Methodism.

[48] Heap gave favourable notices to PTS publications in *Joyful News*, but noted as early as 1936 that Conference was 'in no mood to brook outside interference': *Joyful News*, 6 August 1936, 2.

'A CHURCH WITHOUT DISCIPLINE IS NO CHURCH AT ALL': DISCIPLINE AND DIVERSITY IN NINETEENTH- AND TWENTIETH-CENTURY ANGLICANISM

by FRANCES KNIGHT

I N the early years of the twenty-first century, ecclesiastical discipline in an Anglican context has been very much a hot topic. Internationally, there has been intense debate over the decision by the Episcopal Church in the United States of America to ordain Gene Robinson, a continent yet avowedly homosexual priest, as one of its bishops, and over the decision of the diocese of New Westminster in Canada to authorize liturgical services of blessing for same-sex couples. The Windsor Report of 2004 was commissioned in order to formulate a Communion-wide response to these developments,[1] and although 'discipline' is a word which is very seldom in its pages, it is, in effect, a study of the disciplinary framework which its authors believe necessary in order for the Anglican Communion to hold together. At a local level, the Church of England's clerical discipline procedures are being thoroughly overhauled, following the General Synod of the Church of England's 1996 report on clergy discipline and the ecclesiastical courts.[2] This paper seeks to explore the themes of discipline and diversity in both an international and an English context. It attempts to shed a little more light on how the Anglican Communion, particularly in the former British Empire, got itself into its current position, as a loosely-federated assembly of provincial synods, without a central framework for handling disciplinary matters. Secondly, it examines how the Church of England has handled discipline in relation to its clergy since the mid-nineteenth century.

When the primates of the Anglican Communion emerged from their meeting in Newry in February 2005, it was clear that the Anglican Communion was in real and serious difficulty. Not only were the

---

[1] The Lambeth Commission on Communion, *The Windsor Report 2004* (London, 2004).
[2] General Synod of the Church of England, *Under Authority: the Report of the General Synod Working Party reviewing Clergy Discipline and the working of the Ecclesiastical Courts* (London, 1996).

Americans and the Canadians to be excluded from one of the four instruments of Anglican unity, the Anglican Consultative Council, up until the time of the Lambeth Conference in 2008,[3] the Communion itself was preparing to redefine itself as a 'Covenant' of more loosely connected Churches, something which had emerged as one of the 'big ideas' in the Windsor Report.[4] The Anglican Communion was clearly testing the limits of its diversity in a way which perhaps surprised even those who had grown used to the idea that diversity is part of the essence of Anglicanism.[5] The archbishops' refusal to share in the Eucharist together, the logical consequence of the impaired communion which they had declared in 2004, was certainly the most potent symbol to emerge from the primates' meeting in Newry. By the summer of 2005, the skies were darkening further. The English House of Bishops had responded to the impending change in the law, which from December 2005 would permit the registration of civil partnerships for same-sex couples throughout the United Kingdom, by declaring that it would be permissible for clergy to register a civil partnership as long as they pledged celibacy. This announcement was seized upon by some African Church leaders as tantamount to the Church of England endorsing gay clerical marriage. In September 2005, the Church of Nigeria announced a reworded constitution which removed all references to communion with the see of Canterbury.[6]

The Anglican Communion built itself a time bomb with a very long fuse when, at some point in the nineteenth century, it adopted the probably unconscious assumption that its overseas bishops would always be 'people like us', in other words Oxbridge-educated Britons, or (mainly) Ivy League-educated Americans. The bishops, it was assumed, would all be bound together by an intricate network of personal relationships, and by a deep sense of respect, loyalty and affection for the office of the Archbishop of Canterbury. It was also expected that the bishops would continue to be shaped chiefly by their identity

[3] The other three instruments of unity are the Lambeth Conference, the Primates' Meeting and the Archbishop of Canterbury.

[4] *Windsor Report*, Appendix Two.

[5] 'Diversity is a great strength; without care, however, it can also be a source of great tension and division'. Ibid., paragraph 71.

[6] At the point when this paper received its final revision, in January 2006, it remained unclear what the implications of this would be, although it appeared that support for Peter Akinola, the Archbishop of Nigeria, was less strong amongst some other leaders of the Anglican Churches of the Global South than it had been a few months earlier.

as bishops, as 'successors of the apostles', and not by any strong sense of being representative of their clergy or laity, or of the cultural values of the part of the world in which their sees were located. Indeed, the practice of exporting British men to the colonial bishoprics, which lasted well into the mid-twentieth century, generally had the effect of suppressing until very recent times the sense of bishops as *representative* of the values of their people.[7] The full implications of this recent shift were most clearly seen in Newry in February 2005, when it became publicly clear that the archbishops, rather than simply fulfilling their traditional role of disciplining their clergy, wanted to discipline each other. There were, of course, a number of historical precedents for this, the most famous of which is Bishop Gray of Cape Town's attempts to discipline Bishop Colenso of Natal in the 1860s.[8] The Anglican Communion as we know it, with its Lambeth Conference, the once-a-decade meeting of bishops from the Anglican Communion worldwide, would certainly not have come into existence in the way that it did had it not been for the need to handle the fall-out from the spat between Gray and Colenso. Interestingly, the way in which the Colenso issue was manoeuvred on to the agenda by pressure from participating bishops found resonances with the authors of the *Windsor Report*, as 'a foretaste of what would follow in international gatherings of Anglicans, when contentious topics arise'.[9] But, whatever interesting ironies this state of affairs appears to present to contemporary observers, Gray versus Colenso was an archbishop taking action against one of his diocesans, with the whole of the rest of the episcopate, even the liberal broad churchmen, agreeing that Colenso's theological position was misguided, and that Gray was right to take action against him, even if they disagreed about how it should be done.[10] To this extent, the

---

[7] There are of course some notable exceptions, for example Archbishop Trevor Huddleston (1913–98), best known for his work in South Africa from 1943 to 1956, and then Bishop of Masasi, Tanzania, from 1960 to 1968, and finally Archbishop of the Indian Ocean, from 1978 to 1983. For more on the representative nature of Anglican bishops, see Michael Nazir-Ali in *Working with the Spirit: Choosing Diocesan Bishops* (London, 2001), 107. He argues that a bishop represents the local church to the wider world, but also the other way round. The bishop represents Christ to the people, but also the people and their prayers to God.

[8] A less famous example is that of Bishop Benjamin T. Onderdonk of New York, a noted high churchman who was convicted of sexual impropriety in 1844. The Episcopal Church's General Convention permitted a re-election to Onderdonk's semi-vacant see in 1852. George E. De Mille, *The Catholic Movement in the American Episcopal Church* (Philadelphia, PA, 1950), 63–5.

[9] *Windsor Report*, paragraph 100.

[10] Alan M. G. Stephenson, *The First Lambeth Conference 1867* (London, 1967), 136.

Colenso case could be understood as essentially a local matter, albeit one which, like a bad smell, hung around the whole of the first Lambeth Conference in September 1867. Charles Thomas Longley, the archbishop of Canterbury who was responsible for initiating the Lambeth Conference, would not, in his wildest dreams, have ever imagined that archbishops could become as diverse in their opinions as Peter Akinola, the Primate of All Nigeria, or Frank Griswold, the Presiding Bishop of the Episcopal Church in the United States of America. If he had, he might have placed less emphasis on supporting the development of emerging forms of self-government in the colonial churches, and more on the authoritative position of Canterbury. Nevertheless, had he attempted that strategy he would almost certainly have encountered stiff opposition from the American bishops. As citizens of the United States, they had a particular political problem with accepting the authority of a foreigner, particularly one who was a senior member of the establishment in a former colonial power. For these reasons there had been some doubt in 1867, and again at the time of the second Lambeth Conference in 1878, as to whether the Americans would feel able to accept the Archbishop of Canterbury's invitation.

* * *

Although Archbishop Longley was broadly supportive of self-determination for the colonial Churches, other senior figures at the first Lambeth Conference, most notably A. C. Tait of London, who would, in just over a year, succeed Longley at Canterbury, were far more cautious. The broad church Tait remained committed to the royal supremacy. His position was that large sums of money had been given for the endowment of the colonial churches, on the under-standing that the doctrinal and disciplinary system of the English Church should, as far as possible, be observed. He knew that ultimately, the loosening of ties between the colonial churches and the English Church would be necessary, but he believed it to be expedient for this to be postponed for as long as possible, 'in order that these young Churches might have time to settle themselves firmly upon the lines of English law before they should be called upon to stand alone'.[11] There was real tension between Tait, his allies Thirlwall of St David's and

---

[11] R. T. Davidson and W. Benham, *Life of Archibald Campbell Tait, Archbishop of Canterbury*, 2 vols (London, 1891), 2: 397.

Sumner of Winchester, and some of the most prominent colonial bishops, particularly Gray of Cape Town, Selwyn of New Zealand and Williams of Quebec. The colonials had come to Lambeth in the hope of transforming the Conference into a pan-Anglican synod, which could function as the final court of appeal in spiritual matters, either for the whole Anglican Communion, or for the home and colonial churches. On the final day of the Conference, Selwyn made a speech on this theme which was described by the normally-sympathetic Samuel Wilberforce as 'grand but over-strong'.[12] Selwyn was shot down by Tait, and after a somewhat acrimonious debate, Wilberforce suggested that the matter should be referred to a committee, which would deliberate after the Conference had concluded.[13] This committee met two months later in November 1867, under the chairmanship of Selwyn, and was also responsible for setting out the blueprint for diocesan and provincial synods, which, as we shall see, were already coming into existence in some parts of the Anglican world. The idea of a higher synod which would act as a single court of appeal for Anglicanism worldwide was, however, swiftly abandoned. The committee concluded that the established status of several provinces would make impossible the creation of any assembly that would be competent to enact canons or frame definitions that would be binding on all parts of the Anglican world. The pan-Anglican synod was killed off by those who a few weeks earlier had championed it, and with it died the notion that one single disciplinary framework would ever be established within Anglicanism.[14]

The deliberations of the first Lambeth Conference were heavily influenced by two judgements which had emerged a few years earlier from the Judicial Committee of the Privy Council. This court, as the supreme appellate tribunal for the British Empire, held sway over the life, liberties and property of more than a quarter of the world's population.[15] The judgements in question were on the appeal of William Long versus the bishop of Cape Town, and the judgement on

---

[12] A. R. Ashwell and R. G. Wilberforce, *Life of the Right Reverend Samuel Wilberforce DD*, 3 vols (London, 1883), 3: 231.

[13] Stephenson, *First Lambeth Conference*, 279–81.

[14] Ibid., 306–8.

[15] See P. A. Howell, *The Judicial Committee of the Privy Council 1833–1876: Its Origins, Structure and Development* (Cambridge, 1979) and S. M. Waddams, *Law, Politics and the Church of England: the Career of Stephen Lushington* (Cambridge, 1992).

the petition of Colenso.[16] The Judicial Committee of the Privy Council
had been set up in 1833, and, from 1850, all sorts of appeals relating to
matters of Anglican doctrine and liturgical practice came before it. It is
usually presented as having been an entirely secular body, consisting of
senior judges. Its habit, in the second half of the nineteenth century, of
overturning the verdicts of lower courts, and particularly the ecclesiastical Court of Arches, was widely regarded then, and since, as a disgrace;
the ultimate in Erastian sell-outs. Indeed, it had been Selwyn's dislike of
the Judicial Committee which had been at the root of his proposal for
creating a pan-Anglican synod as a final court of appeal. This churchly
disapproval is still retained in the fact that ecclesiastical courts today are
not bound by any precedents set by the Judicial Committee of the Privy
Council in the period from 1833 to 1965. In fact, although the Judicial
Committee was obviously secular in constitution, it did contain episcopal representation and, during the period 1833 to 1876, the bishops
and archbishops C. J. Blomfield, Thomas Musgrave, J. B. Sumner, A. C.
Tait, C. T. Longley, William Thomson and John Jackson were all
involved with it, in their capacity as privy councillors.[17] But to return to
the Privy Council's judgements on Long and Colenso. In the wake of
these judgements, Anglicanism worldwide had to recognize that it had
lost the powers which it thought it had possessed to discipline clergy
and bishops.[18] This was a crisis, but it was a crisis which brought about
the very rapid creation of clear-cut new structures for the administration of ecclesiastical discipline (and indeed for authentic, locally-rooted
self-government within the Anglican Communion). Without Long and
Colenso, it is much less certain that the Anglican Communion would
have developed in the way that it is today – a loosely associated family

16   The full titles are: *Judgment of the Lords of the Judicial Committee of the Privy Council on the
Appeal of the Rev William Long v. the Right Rev Robert Gray, D.D., Bishop of Cape Town, from the
Supreme Court of the Cape of Good Hope; delivered June 24, 1863* and *Judgment of the Lords of the
Judicial Committee of the Privy Council upon the Petition of the Lord Bishop of Natal, referred to the
Judicial Committee of Her Majesty's Order in Council of the 10th June, 1864; delivered 20th March
1865*. Both are reproduced in full in Charles Gray, *Life of Robert Gray, Bishop of Cape Town and
Metropolitan of Africa*, 2 vols (London, 1876), 2: 577–91 and 641–50.
17   Howell, *Judicial Committee*, 234–7. Technically, the archbishops and bishops who were
members were only there for the purposes of appeals brought under the Church Discipline
Act, 1840. However, it is evident that there was episcopal representation during the Gorham
Judgment. See Owen Chadwick, *The Victorian Church*, Pt I (3rd edn, London, 1971), 258–9.
18   In reality, these powers had always been somewhat limited and difficult to exercise, as
is shown in the discussion which follows of the situation both before and after the passing of
the 1840 Church Discipline Act.

of self-governing churches, in which the archbishop of Canterbury is treated more as a respected senior relative, offering symbolic unity (and de facto more distantly related to some members of his family than to others), than as an authoritative holy father.[19]

In the medium term, the Colenso case led to futile attempts to depose Colenso from his see and to the setting up of a rival bishop at Pietermaritzburg. It is, however, in the earlier case of Gray versus Long, the final outcome of which, in 1863, overlapped with the beginning of the Colenso case, that some of the most fundamental issues surrounding the rights and limitations of Anglican bishops in a colonial setting were articulated. William Long was one of a handful of Anglican clergy in Cape Town, and he objected to being instructed to attend Gray's diocesan synod, on the basis that his attendance would be tantamount to secession from the Church of England because, in his view, the Church of South Africa did not legally exist.[20] He believed that he and his fellow Anglicans on the Cape were simply English people abroad; they were not members of a newly-emerging Church of South Africa, and they were wary of any attempts to impose new structures which weakened their direct link to the Church of England 'at home'. Gray, on the other hand, clearly saw himself as the principal bishop in the Church of Africa; he had been captivated by the romance of taking the Anglican form of Christianity to a new continent, and wanted to free it as far as possible from the disabilities which he saw as inherent in its connection with the English state.[21]

To these conflicting ecclesiologies were added a number of legal irregularities, the most serious of which was a defect in Gray's letters patent, which effectively reduced his powers of autonomous action. All the earliest consecrations of bishops for the colonies had been accompanied by letters patent, which were bestowed by the crown and issued from the Colonial Office, outlining the bishop's powers and jurisdiction. At the beginning of the colonial period, it was considered that the royal supremacy existed in the colonies in exactly the same way that it did in Britain, and the first generation of colonial bishops believed that it was the validity of their letters patent that gave them the authority to

---

[19] It is a major theme of the *Windsor Report* to try to pull Anglicanism back from its current position, by giving greater authority to the Archbishop of Canterbury, and the other instruments of unity.

[20] W. M. Jacob, *The Making of the Anglican Church Worldwide* (London, 1997), 147.

[21] Peter Hinchliff, *John William Colenso: Bishop of Natal* (London, 1964), 127–9.

discipline their clergy. In fact, the document also served to limit the powers of bishops, as when Thomas Middleton, the first bishop of Calcutta, was permitted to create three archdeaconries in his new diocese, but no more, because his letters patent had stipulated three only. As independent legislatures began to be introduced into the colonies, the status of the bishops' letters patent became unclear. The independent legislatures obviously had no desire to preserve the privileges of the Church of England. But it took the London Colonial Office some time to come to terms with this situation, and there are examples of bishops being granted letters patent as they went off to minister within newly-independent legislatures, or being issued with new ones with slightly amended powers.[22] Gray himself fell into this category. He had been granted his original letters patent for Cape Town in 1847, when all legislative authority in the colony was still vested in the crown. By the time his diocese was reorganized and divided in 1853, the crown had granted South Africa a constitution, and a colonial legislature and representative institutions had been established. Although Gray was given a fresh letters patent for his new metropolitical see of South Africa, it was later found that the powers conveyed by the document had been considerably curtailed as a result of the changing constitutional arrangements within which he was now operating.[23]

Gray was not the first colonial bishop to establish a diocesan synod as the key instrument for oversight and discipline. The diocesan synod in its nineteenth-century form had originated with Bishop Selwyn of New Zealand, who had summoned his clergy at Waimate in 1844. In 1850, Selwyn took part in the Sydney conference, an embryo provincial synod summoned by Bishop Broughton of Australia. Among other things, this conference established the principle that discipline over the clergy was to be exercised by the diocesan bishop concerned, and over a bishop by the other bishops of his province.[24] Diocesan synods had also existed in Canada since 1853. In summoning a synod, Gray knew that he was operating without reference to the existing South African legal structures, but he had taken the advice of the attorney general of South

22 Stephenson, *First Lambeth Conference*, 59, 64–5. See Jacob, *Making of the Anglican Church* for more on the introduction, use and abandonment of letters patent, esp. 74, 93–4, 103, 123–4, 126, 137, 146, 150–1, 154–5.
23 Gray, *Life of Gray*, 1: 474–5.
24 Stephenson, *First Lambeth Conference*, 66–8. The point was reinforced in the deliberations of the Committee on Synodical Government which Selwyn chaired, and which met in the November after the 1867 Lambeth Conference. Ibid., 307.

Africa, who had advised him that there was no English law to prohibit the assembly of a synod in the colony.[25]

In 1860, Gray decided the time was ripe to take disciplinary action against Long; he was clearly not yet aware of the limitations of his new letters patent. On any reckoning, this was an extreme reaction, which is illustrative of the tiny scale of the colonial churches, of the more authoritarian tendencies of the colonial bishops, and of their very different way of doing things. In London, one cleric missing from a diocesan synod would hardly have been noticed, and no bishop of London would have contemplated disciplinary action in such circumstances. For Gray, it became a *cause célèbre*, and he decided to refer Long to his own diocesan court, a body comprising himself and five of his senior clergy, which he had established at the first diocesan synod in 1856. Naturally, Long failed to recognize the legality of the court, because he failed to recognize the legality of the synod which had set it up.[26] Nevertheless, he appeared before it on 4 February 1861, and was sentenced to three months suspension from duties. In recognition that he had a wife and children, he was spared any financial loss during his suspension, a fact which reflects the gentlemanly spirit in which Anglican discipline was pursued in the colonies. Long ignored the ban, and continued to officiate as before. Gray served a second citation upon him and, when this was ignored, he deprived him for contumacy and appointed another clergyman to his parish. Long responded by applying to the Supreme Court of South Africa for an interdict to prevent the bishop disturbing him in his church. The Court granted this for one Sunday, and then called upon the bishop of Cape Town to explain why the interdict should not be made absolute.[27] Thus the newly-established South African judiciary, who were mainly Dutchmen together with a few Scots, found themselves confronting an English colonial bishop in a Cape Town court house. On the basis that nobody else in Cape Town understood ecclesiastical law as well as he did, Gray conducted his own defence. It also saved him £100 in legal fees, for like all nineteenth-century bishops, Gray was always concerned about the great expense involved in bringing disciplinary action against the clergy.

It was Gray's contention that a Church without its own internal

---

[25] Jacob, *Making of the Anglican Church*, 145.
[26] Ibid., 147.
[27] Gray, *Life of Gray*, 1: 474.

disciplinary mechanisms was 'no Church at all'.[28] His claim to jurisdiction over Long was based on his contention that first, he and Long were bound by the laws of the 'particular religious association' to which they both belonged; secondly, by the Queen's letters patent (although he agreed that it was muddled, he was not yet prepared to admit that it was invalid; a conclusion to which he came later); and thirdly, by the personal contract into which he and Long had entered. As we shall see, the first of these arguments, that regulations should be binding upon those who were willing to be bound by them by virtue of their membership of a voluntary religious association, was the one on which the greatest weight would be placed in establishing the future basis for disciplinary arrangements in the colonial churches. Long denied that he had entered into a contract with Gray, because he said that he had not consented to one. The chief justice of the South African Supreme Court rejected this argument, on the grounds that Long must have been consenting when he accepted a licence from the bishop, and that he had also entered into a consensual contract when he had been ordained priest by him. Thus the court ruled that Bishop Gray did indeed have jurisdiction over Long. Long announced that he would appeal to the Privy Council in London. Initially, Gray was unperturbed by this, writing to a friend that 'No judges in England would upset the judgement of the Supreme Court here, that religious bodies are to govern their own internal affairs by their own laws, without interference from secular Courts, provided they do nothing against the law of the land.'[29] Gray had not reckoned on the Judicial Committee of the Privy Council, and he could not have been more wrong.[30]

In 1863, the Judicial Committee of the Privy Council reversed the decision of the South African Supreme Court. They concluded that Gray's second letters patent, of 1853, was ineffectual for creating any ecclesiastical or civil jurisdiction, and that his first letters patent, of 1847, was no longer valid. Whereas Long had clearly voluntarily submitted himself to the authority of the bishop, and had thus indicated that he was indeed in a contractual relationship with him, he had

---

28 Ibid., 1: 490.
29 Ibid., 1: 509.
30 As late as September 1867, Selwyn continued to believe that if a pan-Anglican final court of appeal were brought into existence, both the Judicial Committee of the Privy Council, and the Supreme Court in the United States would have to take note of it, even if it could have no direct influence on them. Stephenson, *First Lambeth Conference*, 279. As we have seen, he changed his view by the following November.

nevertheless been illegally deprived of his benefice, because he had refused to recognize a diocesan synod which had itself been illegally summoned. Whereas diocesan synods might be lawfully held in England without the license of the Crown, it was determined that this did not extend to the colonies. The Judicial Committee seemed unclear about the extent to which the 1840 Church Discipline Act was enforceable in the colonies, but concluded that Gray would have been better advised to follow the precepts laid down in that legislation, than to have attempted to devise his own disciplinary mechanism for dealing with Long. The most significant part of the judgement was that:

> The Church of England, in places where there is no church established by law, is in the same situation with any other religious body, in no better, but in no worse position, and the members may adopt, as the members of any other communion may adopt, rules for enforcing discipline within their body, which will be binding on those who expressly or by implication have assented to them.[31]

This ruling from the Judicial Committee of the Privy Council appeared to throw the colonial churches into chaos, but, in the longer term, it gave them a powerful weapon: allowing them to determine their own laws without reference to England. Gray had, unwisely, commenced disciplinary action against Colenso in May 1863, a month before the Judicial Committee had delivered its verdict in the Long case. As a high churchman who failed to recognize the right of the Judicial Committee to intervene in spiritual matters, Gray ploughed on, and in December 1863 he found Colenso guilty on nine charges of heresy. After giving him a four-month period to recant, he announced that he had deposed him from his see of Natal. Colenso, failing to recognize Gray's jurisdiction even to the extent of appealing against it, applied directly to the Privy Council. On 20 March 1865, they ruled that Gray had no jurisdiction over Colenso because of the defect in his second letters patent. Colenso continued to maintain that he was bishop of Natal, and went on to sue the Colonial Bishoprics Fund successfully for loss of stipend. In a further case, he won control over all Church property in his diocese.[32]

In a Canute-like gesture, Gray excommunicated Colenso in January

---

[31] Gray, *Life of Gray*, 1: 514. The entire judgment is reproduced as Appendix One in ibid., 2: 577–91.
[32] Jacob, *Making of the Anglican Church*, 150–1.

1866, but his immediate reaction to the news of the judgement shows that he was not, in fact, unduly perturbed. He wrote:

> I never felt more sure of my ground than I now do. The judgment has endorsed all my views about our relation to the Mother Church: our proper title, our being wholly without law save as framed by ourselves; the worthlessness of letters patent. The only regret I have is that I was made to appear and plead before those crafty and designing lawyers! . . . I hope now to have a Provincial Synod, on the Bishop of Graham's Town's return, with the Clergy and Laity. Really the upshot of all this is that the Bishops must stand up and say, Here are we, the Bishops of the Church of S. Africa; we are a voluntary religious association; these are our terms; who likes to join us? The Provincial Synod must lay down, as it has already in part done, the laws and regulations of our particular religious association. What can the rest do but accept them or quit the association? Of course I will never have anything to do with Parliaments. God be thanked that we have escaped almost entirely (and soon shall escape altogether) these fetters forged by states for the bondage of the Church of God . . . We shall never rest until we have flung them altogether from us.[33]

Over the next five years, this was indeed what transpired. In 1869, the South African bishops met and formally adopted the principles set out at the Lambeth Conference two years earlier on the government of independent provinces, and invited representatives of their diocesan clergy and laity to meet with them as a provincial synod. At its first session, which lasted for six weeks in January and February 1870, the provincial synod brought itself into being as a voluntary association, recognizing and accepting the jurisdiction of the bishops, and explicitly declaring that it was not bound by any legal tribunal other than its own courts. The canons passed at the South African provincial synod were modelled on those which had already been adopted by the provincial synods in Canada and New Zealand.[34] The South Africa synod of 1870 was very significant for future developments, and it seems to have been exhausting for all concerned. 'We have fairly worn out our laity, and

[33] Gray, *Life of Gray*, 2: 200–1. Letter to Edward Gray, 9 May 1865. Gray had had to wait on tenterhooks for seven weeks for news of the judgment to reach him in Cape Town.
[34] Jacob, *Making of the Anglican Church*, 179.

not a few take occasional naps' the bishop wrote. He himself collapsed with nervous exhaustion when the synod was over.[35]

It was to be the synodical, associational model of Church that would determine the future pattern of Church governance within worldwide Anglicanism, setting the provinces on different paths that would lead to Uganda and Nigeria in one direction, and to New Hampshire and New Westminster in another.[36] As Professor Sykes points out in his contribution to this volume, the principle became further articulated by the Chicago-Lambeth Quadrilateral of 1888, which asserted the significance of 'The Historic Episcopate, *locally adapted* in the methods of its administration to the varying needs of the nations and peoples called of God into the Unity of His Church' (my italics).[37] Nineteenth-century colonial bishops were naturally attracted to local adaptation, which usually meant that they felt empowered to exert a much stronger discipline than would have been the case had they been in England. They approved of synodical government, because they could imagine it as the method operative in the early Church, and it was also operative in America.

Alan Hayes has argued that in Canada, bishops at first looked to synodical government specifically to give them the coercive authority that they thought they needed to discipline recalcitrant clergy. When synodical government began to be spoken of in Canada in 1851, all six bishops were typical of the colonial episcopate, in that they were die-hard autocrats who were accustomed to governing imperiously. He notes that in Quebec City, fears that synods would lead to episcopal rule, and to the loss of effective rights of appeal to governors and colonial secretaries, led on one occasion to a riot that required police intervention.[38] How then did these bishops in Canada accommodate the paradox that synodical government, in its modern Anglican form, meant representation for the clergy and the laity? Hayes suggests that

---

35 Gray, *Life of Gray*, 2: 485–90.
36 Alan Hayes has argued that in Canada, the synodical model of government remained extremely forceful until the 1930s, when it began to be replaced by what he terms the bureaucratic model, which weakened the powers of synods and strengthened those of bishops. He argues that since the 1970s, there has been a complete refusal in some dioceses to acknowledge the powers which Victorian Anglicans in Canada gave to synods, as key canons have been redrafted in order to give the impression that current levels of episcopal power have always existed. Alan L. Hayes, *Anglicans in Canada: Controversies and Identity in Historical Perspective* (Urbana and Chicago, IL, 2004), 101–11.
37 See Stephen Sykes, 'The Anglican Experience of Authority', 419–27, in this volume.
38 Hayes, *Anglicans in Canada*, 87, 89.

they simply could not imagine anything as wildly democratic as the system which finally emerged; a system in which synods could pass resolutions on practically anything they pleased, including doctrine, and could initiate Church legislation and set constitutional limits on the prerogative of bishops. What the bishops had envisaged was a system in which bishops led, clergy supported, and lay people followed. They imagined that the laity would be chiefly useful for raising funds, and for engaging in political advocacy with secular leaders.[39] At Fredericton, evangelical clergy and laity resisted the synodical desires of the high church bishop John Medley until 1866. In that year, Medley used a speech to frighten the diocese with the lack of disciplinary mechanisms at his disposal, in the wake of the Long and Colenso judgements. As a bishop stripped of all powers of discipline, he argued, he could not even stop a cleric who chose to offer public prayers to a statue of the Virgin Mary. On hearing this, the meeting unanimously resolved that a synod should be formed.[40]

In reality, once created, the Canadian synods took on a life of their own, and they had already become powerful entities well before the first Lambeth conference in 1867. Canadian synods began to do three things. First, they began to elect bishops; secondly, they sought legal incorporation, meaning that they, rather than the bishop, now owned a diocese's property, and managed its finances; thirdly, they began to create canon law. An Act of 1856 in the Province of Canada empowered the synod to 'make regulations for enforcing discipline in the Church'. By 1858, the diocese of Toronto had completed a thorough investigation of English canon law, and determined that very little of it was applicable in Canada. They proceeded to draft a new code of canon law, which the synod accepted. In future years, Canadian civil courts would hold bishops accountable to the terms of the canons, not because they were really 'law' in a civil sense, but because they represented a form of contract among members of a voluntary association.[41] In a

---

[39] Ibid., 88.

[40] *An Address of the Lord Bishop of Fredericton, at a Meeting of the Clergy and Lay Delegates, Convened by the Unanimous Desire of the Clergy Present at the Late Visitation of the Diocese, 5 July 1866* (n.p., n.d.). For more on the setting up of synodical government in the diocese of Fredericton, see Barry Craig, 'Bishop John Medley: Missionary and Reformer', unpublished Ph.D. thesis, University of Wales, Lampeter, 2001, 235–57.

[41] Hayes, *Anglicans in Canada*, 91. This practice has also been noticed in the disestablished Church in Wales. For more on the current relationship between the Church of England and English law, together with helpful comparisons with the Roman Catholic

number of court cases, the rights of synods were upheld against the rights of bishops, and it became an enshrined principle that once a bishop had given up any authority to his synod, he could not reclaim it.[42]

* * *

Whilst the Anglican Churches in the British Empire began to develop synodical government very rapidly from the mid-nineteenth century, in England synodical government was not formally adopted until 1970. The roots of the change, however, clearly date from the mid-nineteenth century, with the introduction of diocesan conferences and the revival of the two ancient provincial assemblies of the English clergy, the Convocation of Canterbury, revived in 1852, and the Convocation of York, revived in 1861, together with the addition of a House of Laymen, in 1885. In 1920, a further structure, the Church Assembly, was formed. This was the immediate ancestor of the General Synod, and effectively functioned as a national synod for the two provinces of Canterbury and York.[43]

Whereas, as we have seen, colonial synods quickly took it upon themselves to deal with disciplinary matters,[44] the established status of the Church of England meant that, at least until it was given more independent powers under the terms of the Enabling Act of 1919, it had to rely on Acts of Parliament to define the necessary procedures. The three major pieces of legislation were the Church Discipline Act of 1840, the Public Worship Regulation Act of 1874 and the Clergy Discipline Act of 1892. The two earlier Acts have been discussed at some length by Arthur Burns and Nigel Yates. Burns focussed on the 1840 Church Discipline Act, the circumstances that resulted in its drafting, and the events which followed. Yates also discussed the 1840 Act but

position, see Norman Doe, *The Legal Framework of the Church of England: a Critical Study in a Comparative Context* (Oxford, 1996).

[42] Hayes, *Anglicans in Canada*, 91.

[43] The revival of the Canterbury and York Convocations left the Irish clergy without a voice, until the Church of Ireland was disestablished in 1871. The Welsh Church was disestablished in 1920, and developed its own form of synodical government – the Governing Body – at that point. For a discussion, see P. M. H. Bell, *Disestablishment in Ireland and Wales* (London, 1969).

[44] The first Lambeth Conference, in 1867, further accelerated this state of affairs when it recommended that wherever a Church was not established by law, provincial synods ought to establish rules and procedures for disciplining clergy. Jacob, *Making of the Anglican Church*, 167.

his main focus was on the Public Worship Regulation Act, which attempted to curb ritual excesses.[45]

The Anglican Canons of 1603, which survived until 1969 and were not revised at all until 1865, had dealt very extensively with traditional disciplinary concerns within the ministry.[46] Nevertheless, it was the Church Discipline Act of 1840 that was the first legislative measure to be devoted to clergy discipline since before the Reformation. This long-awaited measure was intended to replace the extremely expensive and slow procedures of the diocesan consistory courts, and to establish the diocesan bishop, rather than the courts, as the source of jurisdiction. Stung by such notorious cases as that involving the Revd Dr Edward Drax Free, which had dragged on in the Court of Arches from 1826 to 1830, at an estimated cost of £1500, bishops had all but given up initiating formal proceedings.[47] Instead, they relied on the easier, much cheaper but nevertheless sometimes remarkably effective method of delivering a stern rebuke to the offending clergyman, and exhorting him to resign, or at least to become non-resident and employ a curate.[48] The 1840 Church Discipline Act gave more power to bishops, and also empowered them to make use of the newly-emerging 'middle management' of the rural deans and the archdeacons who were supposed to conduct preliminary enquiries *in situ*. Although this seemed a sensible innovation, in reality the process remained extremely slow, expensive and lacking in clarity, and it is rightly judged as an almost total failure.[49] Meanwhile, in the increasingly polarized world of the Church of England in the later 1840s, the extent to which bishops should be given more power was in itself becoming a source of controversy. This was true particularly amongst Evangelicals, and lay people. Various attempts to revise the legislation in the second half of the 1840s floundered as increasingly polarized groups of churchmen failed to agree on

[45] Arthur Burns, in his chapter 'Disciplining the Delinquent: Prelate, Peers or Professionals?', in *The Diocesan Revival in the Church of England c. 1800–1870* (Oxford, 1999), 162–91; Nigel Yates, particularly in his chapter 'The Attempt to Control Anglican Ritualism', in *Anglican Ritualism in Victorian Britain 1830–1910* (Oxford, 1999), 213–76.

[46] For the Anglican Canons, see Gerald Bray, ed., *The Anglican Canons 1529–1947*, Church of England Record Society 6 (Woodbridge, 1998).

[47] Burns, *Diocesan Revival*, 164. Burns suggests that between 1827 and 1832 only 2.57% of the ecclesiastical courts' business was taken up with discipline cases.

[48] Frances Knight, 'Ministering to the Ministers: the Discipline of Recalcitrant Clergy in the Diocese of Lincoln 1830–1845', in W. J. Sheils and Diana Wood eds, *The Ministry: Clerical and Lay*, SCH 26 (Oxford, 1989), 359–63.

[49] Burns, *Diocesan Revival*, 173–81.

the extent to which (if at all) episcopal rights under the Act should be enhanced.[50]

A particular problem was that the framers of the legislation had supposed that breaches of clerical discipline would involve the traditional misdemeanours; neglect of the parish, immorality, habitual drunkenness or similar. In fact what happened was that the Act had to be used to prosecute an increasing number of offenders whose offences were purely theological. It was used as a means of disciplining Anglo-Catholics with deeply cherished doctrinal beliefs, rather than, as had been intended, a relatively straightforward means of removing adulterers and habitual drunks from the ranks of the Church's ministry. The case of Ditcher versus Denison, which was brought under the 1840 Act, ran for four and a half years in the mid-1850s and centred on the orthodoxy of George Anthony Denison's beliefs about the real presence in the Eucharist.[51] It became imperative that doctrinal views should be separated from moral failure in dealing with delinquent clergy. Eventually, following the rise of ritualism and a change in the political complexion of the government, separate legislation, focused on ritual offences only was introduced in the form of the Public Worship Regulation Act of 1874, but this too is judged a failure by most historians.[52] Certainly, most bishops were extremely reluctant to implement it, and, if anything, it enhanced the reputations of the relatively few clergy who were prosecuted under it – becoming a sort of Anglo-Catholic equivalent to the modern day Anti-Social Behaviour Order.

The Public Worship Regulation Act had very little effect on its professed aim, that of checking the spread of ritualism, which was emerging as a tendency that would not be arrested either by parliamentary or by ecclesiastical legislation. The latter was contemplated following the revival of the Convocations of Canterbury and York, when a very comprehensive attempt to produce a thoroughly revised version of the Anglican canons (known as the deposited canons of 1874 and 1879), was drafted and discussed, only to sink without trace. This was because both bishops and clergy knew that any attempts to define the limits of acceptable ritualist behaviour would simply result in a plethora of court cases, and that a new set of canons would be widely ignored and there-

---

[50] Ibid., 176–7.

[51] Owen Chadwick, *The Victorian Church*, pt 1 (3rd edn, London, 1971), 491–5.

[52] See, for example, Nigel Yates, *Anglican Ritualism in Victorian Britain 1830–1910* (Oxford, 1999), 237–78.

fore discredited, almost as soon as they were promulgated.[53] The content of the deposited canons reveals, however, that, to a remarkable extent, the canons of 1603 were still seen as being relevant to the late-nineteenth century Church. In order to bring the 1603 canons in line with parliamentary changes, between 1892 and 1961 canons 142, 143 and 144 were simply tacked on. The new canons dealt with such matters as vacancies in benefices arising under the 1892 Clergy Discipline Act, and the setting up of provincial courts under the Incumbents (Discipline) Measure of 1947.[54]

In 1892, Parliament passed a new Clergy Discipline Act, aimed at rooting out clergy who had fallen short of the expected standards.[55] The Act was explicit about what its drafters had in mind: treason or felony, or anything resulting in a sentence of imprisonment; also bastardy, divorce or adultery, or being the subject of a separation order under the Matrimonial Causes Act of 1878. The Act was also explicit about what was not included: offences against doctrine or ritual were inadmissible; 'Nothing in this Act shall render a clergyman liable to be tried or sentenced under this Act in respect of any question of doctrine or ritual'.[56] Thus the distinction between reserved cases (doctrine and ritual) and conduct cases (moral failings) was established at this point. Further refinements came with the Incumbents (Discipline) Measure of 1947. In addition to the offences that had been listed in 1892, two new ones were added, 'conduct unbecoming the character of a clerk in Holy Orders' and 'serious, persistent or continuous neglect of duty'. No allegations could be brought 'in respect of any question of doctrine, ritual or ceremonial, or of the social or political opinions of the incumbent'.[57] This latter addition is significant, and appears to have been intended to prevent right-wing parishioners attempting to bring cases against the much more highly-politicized and leftward leaning clergy

---

[53] Bray, *Anglican Canons*, lxxviii–lxxxiii. Bray makes the important point that the drafting and consultation which took place over the deposited canons of 1874–79 was the first time in the history of the Church of England that its laws were discussed and to some extent framed by the Church as a whole, rather than by a few lawyers and bishops in committee. He suggests that the suggestions submitted for these canons give a clearer picture of the overall state of the Church at this period than the ritualist controversies which have tended to occupy historians.

[54] Ibid., 447–51.

[55] *An Act for better enforcing Discipline in the Case of Crimes and other Offences against Morality committed by Clergymen 55 & 56 Vict c. 32* (June 1892).

[56] Ibid., 13 (I) a.

[57] *Incumbents (Discipline) Measure 10 & 11 Geo. 6. No. 1 1947*, Paragraph 2.

of the mid-twentieth century. The wording was strengthened in the Ecclesiastical Jurisdiction Measure of 1963, which protected clergy from disciplinary proceedings on account of their political opinions or activities. It is worth noting that this concession was significantly modified in the Church of England's most recent, 1996, report on clergy discipline, which, whilst continuing to extend protection to a cleric for his or her political opinions, refused to grant the same immunity for his or her political activities. Any political activities which led to a cleric neglecting the duties of office could lead to disciplinary action, a proviso which seems to have been aimed at clergy with particularly strong and time-consuming commitments to, for example, Third World or environmental causes.[58]

* * *

In recent years, the Church of England has, in certain respects, departed from the course on which it set itself in 1840, and has advocated a return to some of the pre-1840 methods of dealing with clerical discipline. This is seen most clearly in the recommendation in 1996 that discipline cases should no longer be handled locally, but at a national or provincial level by a clergy discipline tribunal made up of those unconnected to the diocese in which the complaint had arisen.[59] Although some attention was paid to the ecclesiological importance of bishops within the disciplinary process, a greater recognition was given to the arbitrariness of decisions arising from the fact that one bishop's idea of a minor misdemeanour may be another's idea of a resignation-inducing crime.[60] In other respects, however, the Church's policy has remained consistent over several centuries, and has been focussed particularly on the desire that clerical discipline should be relatively straightforward and cheap to administer. The Church has, however, consistently failed to achieve either objective, even in the years since 1919, when the Enabling Act disentangled it from day-to-day dependence on parliamentary legislation. In the period between 1963 and 1995, only three cases ever reached the stage of trial before the consistory court, and the total cost of these three cases, all heard under the 1963 Ecclesiastical

[58] General Synod, *Under Authority*, 45, 85. Paragraph 5.36 also includes political activity that breaks the law, although this would seem to be covered by the recommendation that any conduct that results in a cleric being convicted in a secular court is in itself an ecclesiastical offence.
[59] Ibid., 57–60.
[60] Ibid., 30–3.

Jurisdiction Measure, was a little over £438,000.[61] This did not indicate a system which was either easy to administer, or offered value for money, particularly bearing in mind the money values of the period.[62]

In the nineteenth century, the Church of England's disciplinary procedures were largely at the mercy of the outcomes of court cases brought under the relevant Acts of Parliament, and upon the judgements of the Judicial Committee of the Privy Council. It is hardly surprising, therefore, that Anglican discipline emerged in a somewhat haphazard and unpredictable way, forged as it was by the verdicts and precedents of the English courts. The judgement on the appeal of Long versus Gray, in 1863, was undoubtedly the most significant legal moment in the history of Anglican discipline. In response to losing the powers which they had thought they possessed to discipline clerics and bishops, and having abandoned the notion of creating a pan-Anglican synod that could act as a final court of appeal, Anglican provinces all over the world began to redouble their efforts to create their own, locally-operated, synodically-based disciplinary systems. The irony is that the development of this synodical process has led, in many places, to such a sturdy form of self-government, autonomy and inculturation, that the Anglican Communion today is having to devise a new disciplinary framework, in an attempt to hold together the warring members of its worldwide family.[63]

University of Wales, Lampeter

---

[61] Ibid., 107.

[62] The cases took place in 1969–70, 1991–92, and 1995. General Synod, *Under Authority*, 106–8.

[63] I am very grateful for the comments of all those who either read or heard earlier versions of this paper, and particularly for the observations made by Bill Jacob and David Thompson.

THE ANGLICAN EXPERIENCE OF AUTHORITY

by STEPHEN SYKES

I

SEVERAL years ago, I had a conversation with an American Roman Catholic Archbishop with a substantial theological background, in the course of which I asked him to be frank about his impression of the American Episcopal Church. His reply was memorable: 'They appear not to want to say no to anything.' This encapsulates the inherent difficulty in the idea of 'inclusiveness', or in the much-claimed virtue of 'comprehensiveness' which Anglicans and Episcopalians are wont to make. Two problems immediately present themselves. The first is that, without difficulty one can suggest views or actions of which it would be impossible for a church to be inclusive, at least with any semblance of loyalty to the New Testament. Then, secondly, the inclusion of disputed actions, such as the ordination of gay persons, presents a different order of difficulty from inclusiveness in relation to disputed beliefs. Churches characteristically have rules about who may, or may not be ordained into a representative ministry. Ordinands are 'tried and examined'. But tolerance of diversity of belief is one thing: tolerance of diversity of practice another, as the churches of the Anglican Communion discovered when they simultaneously ordained women to the priesthood, but extended tolerance to the beliefs of those who asserted that the priesthood was reserved to males. The illogicality of that position is exposed by the discovery that those being received into the Church of England from the Roman Catholic Church were publicly required to state that they accepted the ministry of the Church of England – a higher requirement than was imposed on newly ordained Anglican clergy.[1] On the other hand, it was argued at the time, and the argument has force, that an acknowledged state of incoherence was preferable to overt schism.

The question needs to be pressed, however, how it comes about that, to a not unsympathetic observer, Anglicans seem to have lost the

---

[1] In 1998, this was emended to a general acceptance of 'teaching, discipline and authority of the Church of England'. See *Initiation Services* (London, 1998), 110.

capacity or desire to exercise discipline. In this contribution I propose to explore the suggestion that contemporary attitudes towards the existence of boundaries and the necessity of guarding them are the consequence of the peculiar character of the European reformations. In this matter Anglicans would appear to share much in common with European protestant denominations; it has to do, in short, with the uncertainty and instability of the particular way in which the churches of the reformation attempted to define and police the boundaries of their respective institutions.

The establishment of legitimate authority within the growing and expanding Christian movement of the early centuries was a complex process, involving both a written authority, an 'old' followed by a 'new' sacred text, and the living authority of designated teachers. Both processes embody what Max Weber termed 'the routinization of charisma',[2] a movement already under way within the communities portrayed in the pages of the New Testament, as the disputes about, and arrangements for, the handing on of leadership clearly evidence. Embodied within these processes seems to be a dialectic between, on the one hand, an instinct for unification, extraordinary claims for the unity of all things in Christ, and a contrasting movement of separation in pursuit of holiness, or a life in fellowship with God. David Martin speaks of this as a 'double structure', and identifies it as lying within the central conception of redemption, the achievement of unity and 'at-one-ment'. Because those who seek a universal truth must be distinguished from the 'world' as it is at present, 'unity breeds disunity and the universal embrace creates antagonism'. 'When men seek to make all brothers they begin a process of estrangement.' There is, he argues, a complementary paradox; a new idea can only maintain itself by lodging itself as a tradition. 'Change requires inertia, the dynamic must have recourse to the static.'[3] This is how the Christian myth is constituted of warring alternatives, operating as a kind of inner logic. It expresses itself in the capacity which Christianity has, on the one hand, for adaptiveness within an overarching framework, followed by episodes of revolt

---

[2] It was Weber's view that after the death or departure of an exceptional (or charismatic) teacher a movement would experience a reversion to a different form or forms of authority, better adapted to conditions of everyday existence. See 'The Nature of Charismatic Domination', in W. G. Runciman, ed., *Weber: Selections in Translation* (Cambridge, 1978), 226–50 from Max Weber, *Wirtschaft und Gesellschaft*, 2 vols (4th edn, Tübingen, 1956), 2: 662–79.

[3] David Martin, *The Breaking of the Image* (Oxford, 1980), 171.

and separation. Characteristically the former finds itself at home with the living authority of an authorized leadership, while the latter looks, as did the European reformers, to the written authority of the sacred text; but the distinction is not fixed or invariable, since the movement of unification has its sources within the text, and the text itself needs authorized expositors.

Within European Christianity, it is the instinct for adaptiveness which has led to the modern large-scale abandonment of fundamentalism, a feat which, for the most part, the Roman Catholic Church has carried out without extensive damage to its overarching framework. This instinct characteristically expresses itself in the willingness to submit the sacred writings to the same literary and historical scrutiny given to other ancient texts, and in a confidence in the unitary character of the wisdom by which those texts ought to be interpreted. Of course, opinions vary on a host of critical matters, on which there tends to be a relatively conservative Vatican line.[4] Nonetheless the new methods have been embraced. Although this was not achieved without considerable battles, as the anti-modernist controversies of the later nineteenth and early twentieth centuries demonstrate, it is notable that the stability provided by the institution has enabled the Catholic Church to negotiate the transition from the fundamentalism of past centuries.

The same might well have been true for the Anglican Communion. Indeed, in the midst of the anti-modernist crisis in the Catholic Church, the encyclical letter of the Lambeth Conference, devoting itself to the heated question of biblical criticism, asserted:

> We pass on to the consideration of the standards of all our teaching, the Bible and the Book of Common Prayer. The critical study of the Bible by competent scholars is essential to the maintenance in the Church of a healthy faith. That faith is already in serious danger which refuses to face questions that may be raised either on the authority or the genuineness of any part of the Scriptures that have come down to us. Such refusal creates painful suspicion in the minds of many whom we have to teach, and will weaken the strength of our own conviction of the truth that God has revealed to us. A faith which is always or often attended by a

---

[4] See 'The Document of the Pontifical Biblical Commission', *The Interpretation of the Bible in the Church* (Sherbrooke, Que., 1994), 188–9, with a cautious preface by Cardinal Joseph Ratzinger.

secret fear that we dare not inquire lest inquiry should lead us to
results inconsistent with what we believe, is already infected with a
disease which may soon destroy it.[5]

But these were days when the Communion could well adopt, as Frances
Knight has aptly put it, 'the probably unconscious assumption that its
overseas bishops would always be "people like us".'[6] But in the modern
Anglican Communion, lacking any central monitoring of theological
education, fundamentalism has again become the default position for
theological education in many parts of the world, and calls for separation from 'worldly' standards and wisdom, in the pursuit of holiness,
have become intense and attractive. In this respect recent Anglican experience is close to that of many Protestant churches.

II

Though other Protestant churches face similar challenges, the Anglican
case is complicated by a denominationally specific legacy reaching back
to the sixteenth century. The Tudor attempt at settling the relationship
of sacred text and living leadership is embodied in theory in the
Thirty-Nine Articles issued under Elizabeth in 1559. Article 20, 'Of the
authoritie of the Church', reads as follows.

> The Church hath power to decree Rites or Ceremonies, and
> authoritie in controversies of fayth: And yet it is not lawfull for the
> Church to ordayne any thyng that is contrarie to God's worde
> written, neyther may it so expounde one place of scripture, that it
> be repugnant to another. Wherefore, although the Churche be a
> witnesse and keeper of holy writ: yet, as it ought not to decree any
> thing agaynst the same, so besides the same, ought it not to enforce
> any thing to be beleved for necessitie of salvation.[7]

What is plainly insisted on here is a limit to the Church's power 'to
decree Rites and Ceremonies'; yet the uncertainty of the distinction is
mirrored in a later Article (36) asserting that the ordinal issued in the

[5] The Most Revd Randall T. Davidson, ed., *The Five Lambeth Conferences* (London, 1920),
188–9.
[6] See Frances Knight, 'A Church without discipline is no Church at all': Discipline and
Diversity in Nineteenth- and Twentieth-Century Anglicanism', 399–418, in this volume.
[7] Text in E. C. S. Gibson, *The Thirty-Nine Articles of the Church of England* (London,
1896), 511.

second year of King Edward was a proper exercise of that power, containing nothing superstitious or ungodly, an assertion made, of course, in the face of expressions of the opposite view.

The problem for the establishing of legitimate authority in the sixteenth century can be posed with the help of Weber's distinction of types. By challenging the structures of the medieval Church, the English reformers had undermined the 'legal-rational' authority of the pope and bishops. Their point was, precisely, that that authority had ordained many things 'contrarie to God's word written'; their appeal was, principally, to a form of 'charismatic authority', the charisma of a teacher or interpreter of scripture, the very Word of God. But not of any self-appointed teacher. As Article 23 went on to explain with care:

> And those we ought to iudge lawfully called and sent, whiche be chosen and called to this worke by men who have publique authoritie geuen unto them in the congregation, to call and sende ministers into the Lordes vineyarde.[8]

These, of course, were the bishops, the new bishops expected (as a Collect in the new Ordinal reminded them) 'diligently [to] preach Thy word, and duly administer the godly Discipline thereof'. But because controversies were rife and because the Church had 'authoritie in controversies of fayth', it was also implied that the bishops in particular had responsibility for maintaining the stability and integrity of the faith. Of them, after all, at their consecration it had been asked:

> Will you then faithfully exercise yourselfe in the sayed holy scriptures, and call upon god by prayer, for the true understanding of the same, so as ye maye be able by them to teache and exhorte with wholesome doctryne, and to withstande and conuince the gainsaiers.[9]

The recognition in the Ordinal of the activity of 'gainsaiers' is a further sign of the difficulty which the new settlement incorporated, that of the possibility of challenge from other 'charismatic' leaders, not bishops, but persons with the requisite educational and rhetorical gifts, interpreting the same written authority, but in a different sense.

---

[8] Gibson, *Thirty-Nine Articles*, 573.

[9] Text in *The Two Liturgies, A.D. 1549, and A.D. 1552: with other documents set forth by Authorities in the reign of King Edward VI*, ed. Joseph Ketley, Parker Society 29 (Cambridge, 1844), 352.

Cranmer understood perfectly well that the very retention of the three orders of ministry, of bishops, priests and deacons, was itself challenged; hence the defiant statement, in the Preface to the Ordinal, that:

> It is euident unto all men diligently readinge holy scripture, and auncient auuthours, that from the Apostles tyme there hath bene these ordres of Ministers in Christ's Church: Bishopes, Priestes, and Deacones.[10]

The coupling of 'holye Scripture' and 'auncient auuthours' suggests a recognition that the reading merely of holy scripture might not carry full evidential weight. Oliver O'Donovan argues that because Cranmer made no attempt to show that the orders are required by scripture, the retention of the episcopate 'belongs within the sphere of legitimate freedom exercised by the church in its context'.[11] And he points, rightly, to Richard Hooker's subtle defence of St Jerome's opinion that the office rests on tradition rather than any specific instruction of Christ.

But, as is well known, in the face of a confident Reformed counter-assertion to the effect that monepiscopacy was precisely not an institution in conformity to apostolic practice, the Anglican defence of episcopacy hardened. What had begun as an appeal to the charisma of an authorized teacher (and we note the importance in this regard of the ceremony in which the new priests and bishops are handed a copy of the Bible), was given a more legal-rational form, closer in character to the episcopacy it had replaced.

One possible piece of evidence in favour of this way of construing the evidence may be the long-standing ambivalence of Anglicans in the Protestant or more recent, Evangelical tradition towards bishops. If, as I have suggested, there is a dialectic in Christianity between adaptiveness and revolt, and if the former is more inclined to appeal to the living authority of an authorized leadership, while the latter orientates itself to the sacred text, it is intelligible why Anglican Evangelicals may well prefer the authority of any 'charismatic' biblical interpreter to their own bishop, or indeed to look for 'alternative episcopal oversight' from a reliable, like-minded Evangelical bishop.

So far I have not attempted to give any account of Anglican experi-

[10] Ibid., 331.
[11] O. O'Donovan, *On the Thirty-Nine Articles: a Conversation with Tudor Christianity* (Exeter, 1986), 109.

ence of the third of Weber's categories of legitimate authority, the traditional; and to fail to do so would be disastrous, not least in an assembly of Church historians. Traditional authority rests on an established belief in the sanctity of tradition and the acceptance of those chosen to rule in accordance with the customs and practices within this tradition. To continue the title and the office of bishop, with the express intention that they continue to be 'reverently used and esteemed' (as the Preface to the Ordinal insisted), is precisely to invoke the legitimacy of this traditional authority. In Book 7 of his *Ecclesiastical Polity* Richard Hooker is at pains to defend both the 'great authority' and the 'great honour' accorded to bishops; and among the arguments assembled to demonstrate 'what good doth publickly grow from the Prelacy' is the astonishing (to us) consideration that it benefits a Kingdom when bishops are reckoned to match the leading men of the commonwealth, in an equal yoke, 'as with a courteous bridle, a mean to keep them lovingly in aw that are exorbitant, and to correct such excesses in them, as whereunto their courage, state and dignity make them over prone'.[12] As for the honour paid to bishops, it 'is for decency, order, and quietness' sake so needful, that both Imperial Laws and Canons Ecclesiastical have made their special provisions for it', nor may 'our Saviour's invective against the vain affectation of Superiority' stand in the way of 'these seemly differences usual in giving and taking honour'.[13] From such argument it is absolutely apparent that Hooker intends the authority of bishops to benefit from the order of society as a whole, and that it should be an element within it. Behind this lies, of course, the Tudor conception of a society in which the life of the Church falls under the jurisdiction of the monarch, subject to the authority of the Word of God, which, as Article 37 asserted, the monarch was not entitled to expound.

The picture which is emerging of the Anglican understanding of authority is thus complex. It validated the overthrow of the legal, rational authority of the medieval episcopate; substituting the charismatic authority of the true (and lawfully called and sent) expositor of the Word of God. But by retaining the office and title of bishop, it made possible the investing of such persons with very substantial traditional authority. It was this complex office, at once charismatic and

12 Richard Hooker, *Of the Laws of Ecclesiastical Polity*, 7.18.10 (ed. P. G. Stanwood, 3 vols [Cambridge, MA, 1981], 3: 261).
13 Ibid., 7.20.2 (Stanwood, 3: 267).

traditional, which was routinized in the early seventeenth century, with a more thorough-going legal-rational emphasis, bolstered by the insistence that bishops constituted a separate, third Order in the Church, not a division of honour within the office of priesthood as had been earlier maintained. But despite a profound instinct for adaptiveness Anglicanism incorporates the memory of that revolutionary movement when the old order was challenged.

III

So far we have only considered aspects of the history of the Church of England; the question naturally arises whether the development of the Anglican Communion carries any signs of the same tendencies. In her fascinating study of the implications of the Colenso affair, Dr Knight has shown that the 1865 ruling of the Judicial Committee of the Privy Council, though it appeared to throw the colonial churches into chaos, in the long run provided them with a powerful weapon, enabling them to determine their own laws without reference to England. In effect, it has given the (eventually) autonomous provinces permission to adapt their form of Church government to local cultural conditions. It is precisely this feature of episcopacy to which the 1888 Chicago-Lambeth Quadrilateral refers in its formulation of its fourth article.

> The Historic Episcopate, locally adapted in the methods of its administration to the varying needs of the nations and peoples called of God into the Unity of His Church.[14]

This particular text, we should note, quotes in its entirety the resolution of the bishops of the Episcopal Church in the United States, adopted in Chicago, 1886. Its origins, further, lie in the determination of William Reed Huntingdon, Episcopal priest and author of *The Church-Idea: an Essay Towards Unity* (1870), to separate the principles of Anglicanism from the 'cloud of non-essentials' in which the English State-Church had muffled it.[15] It is particularly striking that it is the episcopate which is thought to lend itself to local contextual adaptiveness, suggesting that

---

[14] Resolutions formally adopted by the Lambeth Conference of 1888 in Davidson, ed., *Five Lambeth Conferences*, 122.

[15] See J. Robert Wright, 'Heritage and Vision: the Chicago–Lambeth Quadrilateral', in idem. ed., *Quadrilateral at One Hundred* (London, 1988), 8–46, at 10.

'the needs of the nations' were capable of incorporation into the mission of the Church.

One may hazard the observation that, just as the choice of Episcopal bishops in the United States is by the 'locally adapted' method of democratic election, the local politics of equality and 'inclusiveness' would produce an openly homosexual candidate. It is intelligible that that particular development should take place in the authorized leadership of the Church, just as one can readily understand why the opposition to it appeals, in particular, to the authority of the sacred text.

At the beginning of this paper I spoke of 'the uncertainty and instability of the particular way in which the churches of the reformation attempted to define and police the boundaries of their respective institutions'. Although the episcopal office was intended to be a source of stability and continuity, within Anglicanism it has functioned as a way in which this confession had adapted itself to local conditions – and it is precisely this adaptiveness which gives rise to movements of revolt and separation. The trick, of course, is to find ways of keeping such movements within reach.

St John's College, Durham University